THE UNITED STATES AIR FORCE
IN SOUTHEAST ASIA

The Advisory Years To 1965

by

ROBERT F. FUTRELL

With the assistance of
MARTIN BLUMENSON

OFFICE OF AIR FORCE HISTORY
UNITED STATES AIR FORCE
WASHINGTON, D.C., 1981

Foreword

This publication is the first of a series titled *The United States Air Force in Southeast Asia*. It tells the story of the Air Force's involvement in the region from the end of the second World War until the major infusion of American troops into Vietnam in 1965. During these years, and most noticeably after 1961, the Air Force's principal role in Southeast Asia was to advise the Vietnamese Air Force in its struggle against insurgents seeking the collapse of the Saigon government.

This story includes some issues of universal applicability to the Air Force: the role of air power in an insurgency, the most effective way to advise a foreign ally, and how to coordinate with other American agencies (both military and civilian) which are doing the same thing. It also deals with issues unique to the Vietnamese conflict: how to coordinate a centralized, technological modern air force with a feudal, decentralized, indigenous one without overwhelming it, and how best to adapt fighter, reconnaissance, airlift, and liaison planes to a jungle environment.

Additional volumes in this series will tell the story of the Air Force in South Vietnam, in Laos, and over North Vietnam until the cessation of the Air Force's direct role in 1973.

JOHN W. HUSTON
Major General, USAF
Chief, Office of Air Force History

Preface

Robert Frank Futrell's works on Air Force history span the decades from the second World War to Vietnam. For the former conflict he contributed sections to *The Army Air Forces in World War II*, edited by Craven and Cate. His volume *The United States Air Force in Korea, 1950-1953* is the official history of the Air Force in that action. His *Ideas, Concepts, Doctrine* book is a fundamental primer of basic thinking about air power among American military services from 1907 through 1964. Before his retirement in 1974, Dr. Futrell wrote a detailed manuscript on the early years of the USAF involvement in the Vietnamese war. I consider it an honor to have been called upon to prepare this manuscript for publication.

I wish to thank Major General John W. Huston, Chief, Office of Air Force History, for a hospitable environment; Dr. Stanley L. Falk, Chief Historian, for invaluable counsel and support; Mr. Max Rosenberg, Deputy Chief Historian, Mr. Carl Berger, Chief, Histories Division, Colonel John Schlight, Chief, Special Histories Branch, and Mr. Jacob Van Staaveren, historian, for helpful comments; Dr. George M. Watson for responses to my requests for information; and all the members of the Office of Air Force History for making me feel at home.

I am responsible for any omissions or distortions in this narrative.

Martin Blumenson

Contents

	Page
Foreword	iii
Preface	v

Part One: The Truman Years

I.	Origins of the American Commitment to Vietnam	3

Part Two: The Eisenhower Years

II.	Dien Bien Phu	15
III.	The Geneva Agreements and French Withdrawal	29
IV.	U.S. Command Problems in the Pacific: Emphasis on Southeast Asia	41
V.	Strained Civil-Military Relations in South Vietnam, 1957-1960	49

Part Three: The Kennedy Years

VI.	Initial Challenges and Actions	63
VII.	Opening Farm Gate	79
VIII.	The Taylor Mission	85
IX.	U.S. Command Arrangements: 2d ADVON and MACV	93
X.	Tactical Air Control, Mule Train, and Ranch Hand	103
XI.	Air Policy: Too Cautious?	119
XII.	Farm Gate and the Vietnamese Air Force	127
XIII.	Air Operations, 1962: Interdiction, Strikes, and Reconnaissance	135
XIV.	Ap Bac and Related Matters	151
XV.	Air Operations, 1963	167
XVI.	Collapse of the Diem Government	185

Part Four: The Johnson Years

XVII.	Objectives Confirmed, Methods Expanded	195
XVIII.	The War in Vietnam, 1964	207
XIX.	The Gulf of Tonkin Incident	227
XX.	Diffusion of Air Assets	236
XXI.	End of the Advisory Phase	253

Appendices

1. Growth of Major United States Air Force and Vietnamese Air Force Units to February 1965 271

	Page
2. Development of a Viet Cong Antiaircraft Capability, 1962-1965	283
Notes	287
Glossary	325
Bibliographic Note	347
Index	357

Photographs

	Page
F-8F Bearcats ferried to Vietnam; C-47 and C-119s with French markings	8
B-26 bombers; Morane-500 Crickets; F-8F Bearcats at Dien Bien Phu	9
USAF C-124 at Ceylon airlifting French soldiers to Vietnam; French paratroop drop; French Foreign Legion	20
President Eisenhower, Gen. Paul Ely, and Adm. Arthur W. Radford; supplies unloaded in Indochina under the Military Defense Assistance Program	21
Refugees fleeing from North Vietnam when the country was divided at the 17th parallel	32
Richard M. Nixon, Pierre Mendes-France, and John Foster Dulles; Operation Wounded Warrior: USAF evacuation of French Foreign Legionnaires after Dien Bien Phu	33
Gen. Nathan F. Twining; Gen. J. Lawton Collins and Premier Ngo Dinh Diem; MAAG Headquarters in Saigon	38
Gen. Laurence S. Kuter; Gen. Thomas D. White	45
L-19s of the Vietnamese Air Force; Sikorsky H-19 helicopter at Tan Son Nhut	51
W. Averell Harriman, President Kennedy, and Dean Rusk; Robert S. McNamara and Gen. Lyman L. Lemnitzer; members of the Vietnamese Self Defense Corps from Buon Enao; female members of the Civil Defense Guard at Hao Cain	66
T-28 fighter-bombers; Lt. Richard A. Mathison and A1C Tri Pham Minh, VNAF, stand with a collection of Farm Gate aircraft; T-28 in foreground, B-26 in left background, A-1E in right background, and C-47 in distance; RF-101 Voodoo	77
Gen. Maxwell D. Taylor, Gen. Emmett O'Donnell, Jr., Adm. J. H. Sides, and Lt. Gen. C. A. Roberts, in Hawaii; Gen. Paul D. Harkins, Adm. Harry D. Felt, and Ambassador Frederick E. Nolting at Tan Son Nhut Airport; Gen. Curtis E. LeMay	87

  Page

Brig. Gen. Rollen Anthis and Air Force Secretary Eugene Zuckert on
    tour in the Pacific 99

Viet Cong prisoners unload rice from a C-123 at Quang Ngai during a
    Mule Train resupply mission; supplies pushed from a C-123 for an
    outpost at Binh Hung; C-123s at Da Nang; aerial view of a
    government outpost 109

C-123s on a defoliation mission; brass sprayers in the rear of a C-123;
    C-123K aircraft at Hickam AFB, Hawaii, enroute to Vietnam for
    defoliation activities 114

C-123B on defoliation mission near Saigon; view from inside a C-123
    as it sprays foliage; USNS *Core* in Saigon harbor with a cargo of
    Ranch Hand spray and equipment 115

Vietnamese officers and American advisers plan an airlift of Vietnamese
    paratroopers at Tan Son Nhut; 1st Lt. Wilfred G. Narr demonstrates
    aircraft maneuvers to Vietnamese students at Moody AFB, Ga.; AIC
    H. R. Wilson and AIC R. L. Fleury install rockets into a B-26
    bomber at Bien Hoa; F-102 Delta Daggers 130

Maj. Ivan L. Slavich briefs Gen. Earle G. Wheeler and Gen. Paul D.
    Harkins on a rocket mount of the UH-1B helicopter; ARVN para-
    trooper prepares for a jump over Cu Chi; TSgt William W. Cameron
    instructs Vietnamese airmen in the operation of the gunsight on a
    T-28; Vietnamese tanks move toward the burning presidential palace
    after its bombing 164

ARVN paratroopers leap from USAF C-123; O-1E Bird Dog FAC;
    Capt. B. D. Lassman and Capt. D. F. Schell with Vietnamese
    observer 180

Vietnamese troops outside the presidential palace in Saigon 192

Pres. Johnson, W. Averell Harriman; Adm. U.S. Grant Sharp, Jr.;
    Maj. Gen. Joseph H. Moore, Gen. Jacob E. Smart, with Maj. Xuan
    Vinh, VNAF 209

Air Commodore Nguyen Cao Ky and Col. William E. Bethea;
    Gen. William Westmoreland; A1E aircraft; VNAF CH-34
    helicopter 222

Outposts or hamlets of South Vietnam 223

USS *Ticonderoga* 231

Canberra bomber; rocket pod on F-100; Australian Caribou aircraft at
   Tan Son Nhut 238

A1C Leonard A. Rowe; SSgt Harold Inman; AC-47 at Tan Son Nhut;
   7.62 minigun mounted in AC-47 242

Loudspeakers installed in C-47; leaflets dropped from a C-47 249

B-57 destroyed by Viet Cong mortar attack; Brink BOQ area, following
   terrorist attack 262

Maps, Charts, and Graphs

	Page
Southeast Asia	facing p. 1
Organizational Chart — Far East Air Forces	11
Principal USAF/VNAF Airfields in South Vietnam, to February 1965	51
South Vietnam's Provinces	57
U.S. Command Arrangements — Vietnam, July 1962	99
Air Operations — 1962	137
ARVN Corps Areas (Until November 1962)	154
ARVN Corps Tactical Zones (After November 1962)	155
Air Operations — 1963	176
Air Operations in South Vietnam, 1964 to February 1965	200
USAF Support Bases Outside Vietnam	231
Barrell Roll Campaign in Laos — December 1964 - January 1965	258
Diagram of "L" or Triangular Defense System	284
RVN Countrywide Totals — VC Antiaircraft Incidents	285

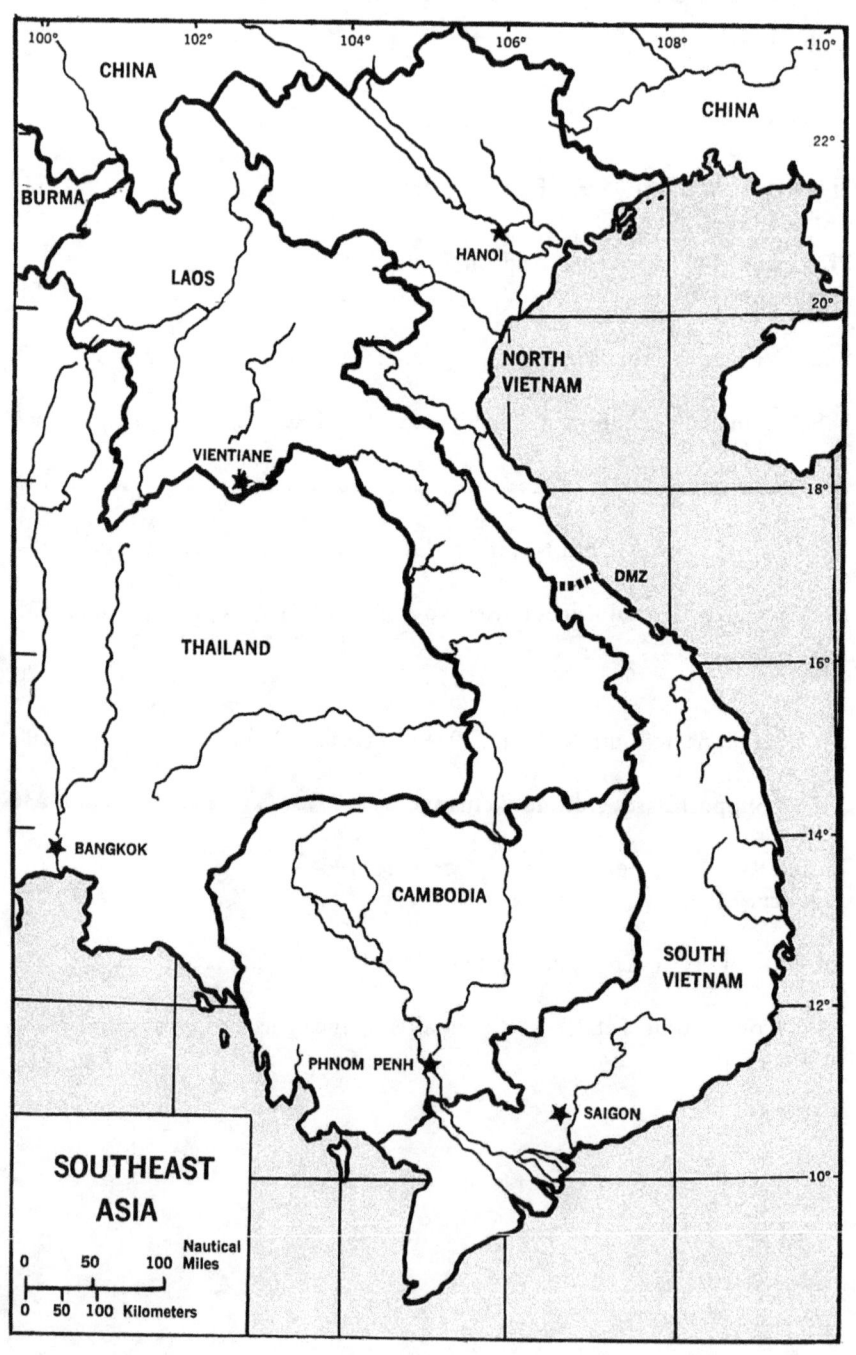

Part One:

The Truman Years

I. Origins of The American Commitment to Vietnam

About 700 miles west of the Philippine Islands, across the China Sea, lies the great Indochinese peninsula. China is to the north, Burma to the west, and Malaysia to the south. The western part of the peninsula holds Thailand (ancient Siam) while the eastern portion contains Laos, Cambodia, and Vietnam (formerly elements of French Indochina). This area of Southeast Asia (SEA) attracted little American interest and attention until the closing months of World War II.

American policymakers who shared President Franklin D. Roosevelt's anticolonial sentiments expected Indochina to be freed from French hegemony. Yet France reestablished control over Laos, Cambodia, and Vietnam, which had been part of the French Empire since the 19th century. To some extent this occurred because the British government wished to resuscitate France as a European power to help Britain balance somewhat the growing strength of the Soviet Union. The United States acquiesced in this aim, and increasingly so as the confrontation of the postwar superpowers evolved into the cold war. It was the cold war that drew the United States into this region.[1]

Japan had virtually occupied Laos, Cambodia, and Vietnam after the fall of France in 1940. While allowing the French to maintain a presence and a measure of control, the Japanese incorporated the Indochinese economic resources into their system. In March 1945, with Metropolitan France liberated and a full-fledged member of the Allied coalition, the Japanese interned French civilian and military officials and removed the pretense of a combined occupation.[2]

French police agencies and other offices of internal control having been eliminated, indigenous groups seeking Vietnamese independence began to expand their activities. The most vigorous organization was the Viet Minh. Dominated by the Indochinese communist party and directed by Ho Chi Minh, the Viet Minh launched guerrilla operations against the Japanese and soon claimed to control much of northern Vietnam, the Tonkin provinces. To help harass the Japanese and also to gather intelligence, the U.S. Office of Strategic Services sent several small teams to Vietnam.

By the time of the Japanese surrender in August 1945, the Viet Minh had emerged as the leading nationalist group in Vietnam. Viet Minh soldiers on August 19 arrived in Hanoi, capital of Tonkin, and assumed de facto control. In Hue, capital of Annam, the central provinces, Emperor Bao Dai, last of the Vietnamese royal family and a puppet of both France and Japan, abdicated. In Saigon, capital of Cochin China in the south, a committee took power while recognizing the overall authority of the Hanoi regime. On December 2 in Hanoi, Ho Chi Minh proclaimed the independence of the Democratic Republic of Vietnam.

Meanwhile, the war in Europe had closed and in July 1945 the Potsdam Conference convened. The American, British, and Russian representatives agreed to include French military forces in operations being planned in Asia, chiefly to liberate Indochina. The conferees also acted to regularize operational boundaries. The China Theater under Generalissimo Chiang Kai-shek was extended southward to the 16th parallel, just below Tourane (Da Nang). The territory south of that line came under the Southeast Asia Command headed by Admiral Lord Louis Mountbatten. This division determined who was to exercise control after the Japanese capitulation.[3]

In August 1945, Chinese nationalist troops moved into Tonkin and part of Annam, while British troops occupied the rest of Annam and all of Cochin China. The British restored French authority in the south, and the French brought military forces into the country and ruthlessly suppressed Vietnamese aspirations for independence. Despite some continuing guerrilla activity, the French had regained their former colonial status and were well established in Saigon by the end of the year.

In the north the Chinese refused to intervene in a contest between the well-organized Viet Minh and the small numbers of French. Concerned by the threat of the Chinese communists under Mao Tse-tung, the Chinese nationalists were reluctant to see the triumph of Ho Chi Minh in Vietnam. They preferred the return of the French if France would abandon territorial and economic rights formerly granted as concessions in China. This generally neutral stance fueled the struggle for power between the Viet Minh and the French. A guerrilla war of low intensity soon developed.

When the French agreed to renounce their concessions early in 1946, Nationalist China recognized French sovereignty in Indochina and moved Chinese troops out of Vietnam. By the end of March, they were being replaced by French military forces.

Ho Chi Minh had been negotiating with the French authorities for recognition of his new government and ultimate independence. The exchanges were futile and incidents of violence multiplied. The climax came in November 1946 after a French patrol boat in Haiphong harbor clashed with Vietnamese militia. The French responded by brutally bombarding the city and killing an estimated 6,000 civilians, whereupon Ho broke off the talks. In December he moved his government into the mountains of Tonkin and opened full-scale guerrilla war by attacking the French in Hanoi.

American policymakers had conflicting feelings. Their sympathy for the Vietnamese nationalists left them reluctant to see France restore control by force—they wanted French authority to enjoy the support of the Vietnamese people. On the other hand, Americans were uneasy because Vietnamese independence might produce a communist state.[4]

THE ORIGINS OF AMERICAN COMMITMENT

Hoping that the Vietnamese were more nationalistic than communistic, U.S. government officials urged the French to end the guerrilla warfare and to find a political solution acceptable to both parties. If France made a bona fide accommodation to ultimate Vietnamese sovereignty, Ho's strength might collapse. Continually advocating an equitable solution to the problem of conflicting claims to power, the United States prohibited the export of war materials to the French in Vietnam, although munitions sent to Metropolitan France could, of course, be reshipped to Southeast Asia.[5]

While combating Ho's guerrilla activities, France entered into negotiations with anti-Ho Vietnamese parties. To give these elements a native leader, the French in the spring of 1949 installed Bao Dai, the former emperor, as the chief of state of an entity formed by the union of Tonkin, Annam, and Cochin China. But this was hardly more than a show of sovereignty, for the French retained control of Vietnamese foreign and military affairs.[6]

Troubled American officials began to accept this arrangement as the cold war intensified everywhere. The Greek civil war, the Berlin blockade, the coup d'etat in Czechoslovakia, as well as the successes of the Chinese communists against the nationalists, led to a heightened concern with worldwide communism that appeared to be monolithic. Surely, Ho Chi Minh's communist affiliation was part of a growing global menace. To cope with this and to rehabilitate Western Europe as a force against communist encroachment, the United States early in 1949 helped to form and joined the North Atlantic Treaty Organization (NATO) for mutual defense.

The final triumph of the Chinese communists in October 1949 seemed to confirm the worst American fears. It spurred the Congress to pass the Mutual Defense Assistance Act designed to deal with the cold war. The President was empowered to dispense funds to various nations, including "the general area of China" which was extended to cover Southeast Asia and specifically Vietnam.[7]

The ongoing guerrilla war in Vietnam that weakened French support of NATO and the defense of Western Europe, the arrival of Chinese communist troops at the northern frontier of Vietnam at the beginning of 1950, the formal recognition of Ho Chi Minh's Democratic Republic of Vietnam by Communist China and the Soviet Union in January 1950—all persuaded the United States government to adopt the Bao Dai solution. On February 7, 1950, the United States extended diplomatic recognition to the State of Vietnam as well as to the Kingdoms of Cambodia and Laos.

Nine days later, France requested American economic and military assistance for prosecution of the war in Indochina. Unable to bear the burden without American aid, France was thinking of withdrawing from the region if Ho Chi Minh received increasing resources from China and the Soviet Union.[8]

What the French needed immediately were ammunition, napalm, and barbed wire to help defend perimeters around Hanoi and Haiphong against Viet Minh attacks. Their air units in the Far East possessed only obsolete and miscellaneous aircraft.* Few fully trained military maintenance technicians were on hand because of a general shortage in Metropolitan France, where the French Air Force depended in large part on contract aircraft maintenance.⁹

President Harry S. Truman regarded the emergence of Communist China as an extension of Soviet power and saw the growth of communist influence over Asia as a threat to American interests. He instructed the National Security Council to formulate a policy for strengthening non-communist Asian nations. The result was a resolve to block communist expansion by collective and bilateral security treaties. Since the Joint Chiefs of Staff (JCS) had already recommended spending funds to support anti-communist forces in Indochina, $75 million allocated in the Mutual Defense Assistance Act for "the general area of China" was appropriately at hand.

The French wanted a substantial and long-term American commitment. And in the spring of 1950, American decisionmakers all opposed what was called losing Southeast Asia to communism. Consequently, the United States Government during fiscal year 1951 decided to provide $164 million in military aid to France for use in Indochina.¹⁰

Whatever doubts some American officials may have had that French military success, predicated on American military assistance, would necessarily lead to a strengthened non-communist government in Vietnam vanished in the face of two events. The first was intelligence confirmation of increasing aid to the Viet Minh by the People's Republic of China. The second was the invasion of the Republic of Korea on June 25, 1950, by the communist forces of the Democratic People's Republic of Korea.

Now the struggle seemed absolutely clear. As President Truman told Americans on June 27, the communists had "passed beyond the use of subversion to conquer independent nations and will now use armed invasion and war." The United States, he promised, would resist aggression in Korea and at the same time accelerate military assistance to France and the Associated States in Indochina (Vietnam, Laos, and Cambodia).¹¹ Even as he spoke, eight C-47 transports were being prepared for delivery to Metropolitan France. Because the situation was critical in Southeast Asia, American pilots flew these planes direct to Saigon and turned them over even before formal U.S. agencies were in the country to coordinate shipments of assistance materials. These eight aircraft were the first aviation aid furnished by the United States to the French in Vietnam.

As American forces entered the war in Korea and as the French resisted Viet Minh attacks in Tonkin, Donald R. Heath became the U.S. Minister to the Associated States on July 6, 1950. The initial elements of the U.S. Military

---

*French Air Force Indochina consisted of two squadrons totaling forty-six British MK-IX Spitfires, three squadrons of sixty-three American F-63 Kingcobras, two squadrons of thirty-five German JU-52 transports, and one squadron of twenty American C-47s, plus some light liaison planes. The French Navy had a patrol squadron of eight American PBY-5A Catalinas and a reconnaissance squadron of nine British Supermarine-1 Sea Otters. A lack of specialized aircraft required the use of fighters for reconnaissance, strafing, and bombing missions. In general, however, bombardment was conducted by PBY patrol planes and by JU-52 transports under contract.

THE ORIGINS OF AMERICAN COMMITMENT

Assistance Advisory Group (MAAG) entered Saigon on August 3. Brig. Gen. Francis G. Brink, USA, assumed command on October 10, and Lt. Col. Edmund F. Freeman, the Air Attaché in Saigon, handled air assistance duties until the Air Force Section of MAAG-Indochina came into being on November 8 under Col. Joseph B. Wells.[12]

Mr. Heath was the Chief of Mission and the senior U.S. representative in Saigon. General Brink, the MAAG chief, was his military advisor. MAAG received and reviewed requests for American aid to the ground, naval, and air forces, established requirements and, after coordinating with Heath, submitted them to the Department of Defense (DOD).[13]

Although Americans hoped to work directly with the Vietnamese as well as with the French, the French termed the Bao Dai government and its military forces incapable of dealing with assistance matters. French troops were carrying the burden of the war, and the few Vietnamese units in existence had limited capacities except as auxiliaries.

As a consequence, MAAG received requests from the French, transferred title of military assistance program materials to them, and tried to insure the proper use of the items supplied. On December 23, 1950, the United States, France, Vietnam, Cambodia, and Laos signed the Mutual Defense Assistance Agreement. A provision stipulated that American goods destined for Indochina would pass through French hands.[14]

The military assistance effort had three priorities. The first was responding to emergency requests to enable French forces to meet immediate threats. The second was improving French military capabilities. The third and least important was developing indigenous Vietnamese armed forces.

With respect to aviation requirements, not until October 1950, when forty U.S. Navy F-6F Hellcats arrived in Saigon aboard a French carrier, could the United States make available fighter aircraft to replace the old MK-IX Spitfires.

While the French requested F-63 Kingcobras primarily because of their 37-mm cannon, the United States Air Force (USAF)* had no spare parts or ammunition for these obsolete aircraft and instead furnished ninety F-8F Bearcat fighters, which were ferried to Vietnam in February and March 1951. Delays in installing ground equipment postponed the arrival in Vietnam of five RB-26 reconnaissance planes until July. Twenty-four B-26 bombers were renovated and transported to Hawaii by carrier in December, then flown to Tourane. Nine others flew from Sacramento to Hawaii and on to Vietnam at the of the year.

These deliveries completed the initial aviation schedules under the Mutual Defense Assistance Program. The planes enabled the French to expand sortie rates from an average of 450 a week in the summer of 1950 to 930 in the spring of 1951.[15]

---

*Hereafter in this work, the terms "Air Force," "Army," "Navy," and "Marine Corps" will mean "U.S. Air Force," "U.S. Army," "U.S. Navy," and "U.S. Marine Corps." Military forces of other nations will be specifically designated, for example, "French Air Force."

THE ADVISORY YEARS

(Bottom) F-8F Bearcats ferried to Vietnam. (Upper left) C-47 with French markings. (Upper right) USAF C-119s with French markings leave Haiphong to drop supplies at Dien Bien Phu.

P. 9: (Top) B-26s. (Center) Morane-500 Crickets. (Bottom) F-8F Bearcats on Dien Bien Phu Airfield.

Courtesy: French E.C.P. Armées

Courtesy: French E.C.P. Armées

THE ORIGINS OF AMERICAN COMMITMENT

Courtesy: French E.C.P. Armées

THE ADVISORY YEARS

Despite higher American priorities in Korea, U.S. materiel dispatched to Vietnam helped the campaigning. High Commissioner and Commander in Chief Gen. Jean de Lattre de Tassigny said in January 1951 that U.S. air resources, "especially napalm bombs, arrived in the nick of time." Mr. Heath believed that "French superiority in aviation and artillery was responsible for turning back a Viet Minh offensive. In particular, the use of napalm . . . was a decisive factor in the French holding operations."[16]

Further French victories in May 1951 compelled the Viet Minh to abandon battles of confrontation and to retreat to lower-key guerrilla operations of harassment and ambush. The war assumed the characteristics of a stalemate.[17]

For a variety of reasons—to gain the initiative, to respond to American urging for a greater Vietnamese stake in the struggle, to allow France to contribute more to the NATO defenses in Europe—the French acceded to a request from Bao Dai and projected an expansion of Vietnamese military forces. They opened an air training center at Nha Trang Airfield in June 1951 and a Vietnamese Air Force office in Saigon during July. Furnishing for training several Morane-500 Cricket liaison aircraft (French-built version of the German Fieseler Storch), the French established the Vietnamese 312th Special Mission Squadron at Tan Son Nhut Airfield near Saigon. Though the first Vietnamese flyers received their training in Metropolitan France, French instructors at Nha Trang started in March 1952 to train small numbers of pilots, observers, and maintenance men.

These efforts permitted the activation in 1953 of two Vietnamese Cricket observation squadrons and in 1954 of a light combat assault liaison squadron equipped with French Dassault M.D.-315 Flamants. The three squadrons were reorganized on July 1, 1954, into the Vietnamese 1st Liaison Group. Although the air training program had significance for the future, it yielded only a token number of Vietnamese liaison pilots and observers who had begun to fly combat missions under French control toward the end of 1952.[18]

By then the new MAAG chief, Brig. Gen. Thomas J. H. Trapnell, USA, and Col. Arvid E. Olson, chief of the MAAG Air Force Section, were concerned over the effectiveness of French Air Force Indochina. It was limited to a personnel ceiling of 10,000 men and still suffered from a scarcity of technicians. Aircraft maintenance and supply were consequently marginal. Plagued by poor consumption records, the French found it difficult to project future materiel requirements. At the same time, the Korean War imposed its own needs. American deliveries to Vietnam decreased, and F-8Fs and B-26s scheduled to meet increasing attrition remained unsent during 1952. Yet ten C-47s arriving in March and April 1952, and ten more in September and October bolstered the French.[19]

The French flew the C-47s to their limits to meet stepped-up action by the Viet Minh in October. The planes performed so well that Gen. Raoul Salan, who had replaced de Lattre, asked General Trapnell for additional ones. Trapnell passed the request to Washington and, toward the end of the year, Far East Air Forces (FEAF) headquarters in Tokyo received instructions to fill the order.

THE ORIGINS OF AMERICAN COMMITMENT

FEAF hurriedly dispatched twenty-one C-47s to Clark Air Base in the Philippines. There, the 24th Air Depot Wing removed USAF insignia, added paradrop equipment, and delivered the planes to the French at Nha Trang. To provide technicians for better maintenance and supply, the wing sent a temporary duty force to Nha Trang on January 4, 1953. This was the first USAF contingent, exclusive of the MAAG, to deploy to Vietnam. They remained in the country until French troops relieved them on August 14.[20]

While the United States was funding approximately one-third of the costs of military operations, the French, despite limited success in northwest Tonkin, became increasingly disheartened by their own casualties and expenditures. Appropriations from Bao Dai's government and from the French National Assembly for continuing military operations were difficult to obtain.[21] As Secretary of State Dean Acheson informed President-elect Dwight D. Eisenhower in November 1952, the French, in Paris as well as in Vietnam, were wavering in their support for the war. They wanted international backing and additional assistance for their efforts.[22]

Dealing with this problem would be one of President Eisenhower's concerns.

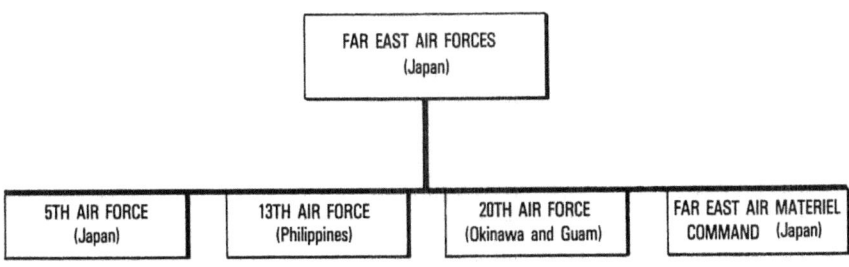

JUNE 1950

Part Two:

The Eisenhower Years

II. Dien Bien Phu

Early in his administration, President Eisenhower decided that three actions were necessary for French success in Indochina. France had to give "greater reality" to Vietnamese nationalistic aspirations and thereby deny the Viet Minh their claim of struggling for independence. With the Vietnamese people thus allowed a greater stake in their destiny, the French had to place more reliance on indigenous military forces, requiring better equipment and training facilities. Finally, the free world had to furnish more assistance to France, which alone was carrying on what appeared to be an international struggle.[1]

In March 1953 Secretary of State John Foster Dulles advised French authorities that the United States would enlarge its fiscal support if France framed an acceptable plan for resolving the war.[2] Before the French government could make a detailed response, the Viet Minh launched another offensive in western Tonkin in April 1953, moved into Laos, and threatened Thailand.[3]

A NATO foreign ministers conference was in progress in Paris and French officials asked Dulles for the loan of C-119 transports to lift tanks and other heavy equipment into Laos. Although Eisenhower was unwilling to employ USAF crews on these combat missions, he agreed to lend the planes if Civil Air Transport contract crews from Taiwan flew them. These arrangements made, FEAF received the order to provide the aircraft. In May USAF crews flew six C-119s to Nha Trang where contract pilots took them to Cat Bi Airfield near Haiphong. The 24th Air Depot Wing sent a supporting maintenance and supply detachment to Cat Bi, and then to Gia Lam Airfield near Hanoi. The aircraft and detachment withdrew from Vietnam late in July after satisfying the requirement.[4]

General Henri Eugene Navarre, a new commander in chief, arrived in Vietnam in May 1953, with instructions to defeat the Viet Minh and bring the war to a close in conformance with American provisos. Navarre drew a plan to use mobile strike forces against main enemy units. He hoped to expand support, heighten cooperation among ground, naval, and air forces, secure fresh reinforcements from France, and improve Vietnamese forces. He proposed to lure the Viet Minh into open battle, break up their main forces by 1955, and reduce them to a low level of guerrilla warfare that for the most part indigenous troops could contain.[5]

To help Navarre and incidentally to observe the local conditions, an American joint military mission headed by Army Lt. Gen. John W. O'Daniel and including Maj. Gen. Chester E. McCarty, commander of FEAF's 315th Air Division (Combat Cargo), reached Saigon on June 20. O'Daniel was favorably impressed with Navarre's plan. So was McCarty. Because of the personnel shortages in French Air Force Indochina, McCarty noted, deliveries of more U.S. aircraft without air and maintenance crews made little sense. Navarre wanted extra paratroop lift capacity, and McCarty proposed to lend the French C-119s. The planes could be dispatched to Cat Bi a day before a planned operation, flown in combat by French crews, and returned to Clark Air Base for maintenance.[6]

The commander of French Air Force Indochina rejected the C-119s. Instead, he requested MAAG in August 1953 to supply twenty-five C-47s plus necessary equipment by October 1. Pulled out of units in the United States, these aircraft were delivered to Vietnam in December.[7]

The armistice in Korea, signed on July 27, 1953, raised the possibility of greater support not only by the United States for the French but by Communist China for the Viet Minh as well. American officials nevertheless believed in the efficacy of Navarre's plan. When the French government in September agreed to the eventual independence of Vietnam, the United States promised to make available—in addition to the assistance funds already committed to the French and the Associated States of Vietnam, Cambodia, and Laos—$305 million by the end of 1954. In March 1954 the United States would offer to boost the amount and to reimburse France up to $785 million for expenditures in Indochina during calendar year 1954.[8]

In Vietnam, Navarre said he would keep General Trapnell and MAAG informed of operational plans and not limit their function simply to handling materiel requests. Expecting MAAG to play a larger role in assisting the French, Secretary of Defense Charles E. Wilson in January 1954 augmented the Air Force Section from seven officers and eight airmen to thirty officers and thirty-five airmen. Yet, despite public announcements in Washington of all-out American support, MAAG continued to have little influence on French activities. MAAG complained (as other bodies with similar missions elsewhere normally noted) that the French were reluctant to accept advice. They generally expected the United States to deliver everything requested, regardless of their ability to use or to maintain it.[9]

Starting his operations in the fall of 1953, General Navarre focused on the plain of Dien Bien Phu. Located in northwest Tonkin and near the border of Laos, it controlled the main road between the two regions. A strongly fortified air and ground base at Dien Bien Phu would reestablish French authority in the area and block Viet Minh incursions into the neighboring kingdom.[10]

Paratroopers jumped onto an airstrip at Dien Bien Phu on November 20, and began to fortify the area. They needed heavy equipment, including large quantities of barbed wire. On December 5 FEAF started to ferry 315th Air Division C-119s to Cat Bi Airfield for further flight by French military or by civilian contract crews. At Cat Bi a detachment of the 483d Troop Carrier Wing, the 8081st Aerial Resupply Unit, and a provisional maintenance squadron of the Far East Air Logistics Force supported from twelve to twenty-two C-119s at any given time.[11]

As Navarre developed an enclave in northwestern Tonkin, he had to weaken the French defenses of Hanoi and Haiphong. In December 1953 and in January 1954, Viet Minh attacks threatened French security in those cities. Even more serious was a growing Viet Minh concentration around Dien Bien Phu.[12]

DIEN BIEN PHU

The American government noted the dangers, and Assistant Secretary of Defense for International Security Affairs Frank C. Nash directed the military services to give the highest priority to the Mutual Assistance Program without regard to funding. On January 16, 1954, President Eisenhower instructed Defense Secretary Wilson to report to him all that could be done to help the French without actually committing U.S. forces to combat. To permit the French to counter Viet Minh incursions into Laos, six long-range B-26s arrived in Indochina in January. When the French then requested twenty-two more, ten to offset attrition and twelve to augment bombing capabilities, Assistant Secretary Nash on January 29 resolved to provide them even if they had to come from operational USAF squadrons in the Far East. Notified of the decision, FEAF ferried sixteen of its planes from Japan to Clark Air Base where French markings were painted on, then delivered them to Tourane in mid-February. These aircraft remained on loan until sixteen B-26s and three RB-26s, funded by the Mutual Defense Assistance Program, could reach Indochina later in February and March.[13]

Despite talk of getting additional aviation personnel from France and of using Vietnamese to augment French service troops, the French air units remained approximately one-fourth undermanned. FEAF received instructions on January 31 to organize for duty in Vietnam several provisional C-47 and B-26 maintenance and supply units, with a composite strength of some three hundred men. Brig. Gen. Albert G. Hewitt, commander of Far East Air Logistics Force, arrived in Saigon on February 2, 1954, and established a B-26 detachment at Tourane and a C-47 detachment at Do Son Airfield near Haiphong. Three days later, the members of this highly classified undertaking began to be airlifted in. President Eisenhower informed the American public that "some airplane mechanics . . . who would not get touched by combat" had been sent to Vietnam.[14]

Support of the French bothered Gen. Otto P. Weyland, FEAF commanding general. Because furnishing USAF personnel hampered his own combat readiness, he preferred the French to receive American funds for contract maintenance. Traveling to Vietnam early in February, General Weyland gained the impression that the French problems were "primarily political and psychological." The Vietnamese disliked the French and served poorly under them. More serious, the Vietnamese laborers who worked at the Hanoi airfields by day might well be joining the Viet Minh at night.[15]

As growing communist forces gathered around Dien Bien Phu and cut the surface routes to the garrison, General Navarre airlifted new French and Vietnamese troops into the airhead. By mid-January 1954, air supply required twenty C-119 and fifty C-47 sorties each day. The security of this airlift seemed threatened when radio intercepts reported Viet Minh stockpiling of 37-mm rapid-fire, Soviet-made antiaircraft (AA) artillery ammunition nearby. At the request of the Army attaché in Saigon, two FEAF experts in antiaircraft warfare, Captains Robert M. Lloyd and Robert W. Hicks, visited Vietnam between January 16 and February 5. They warned that 37-mm guns sited along the limited air approaches to Dien Bien Phu would have "considerable success" against low-flying transports. But after studying aerial photographs, the officers concluded that the French had exaggerated the threat—there were no enemy 37-mm guns in the area.[16]

President Eisenhower was apprehensive that the Viet Minh would overrun the troops besieged in the isolated fortress at Dien Bien Phu, but Navarre remained optimistic. The position was attracting a large part of the Viet Minh military forces and if they attacked, the French would inflict heavy casualties on them. The report of the American antiaircraft artillery experts was reassuring. French Minister of Defense Rene Pleven and Armed Forces Chief of Staff Lt. Gen. Paul H. R. Ely visited the site in February and were impressed with the strength of the defenses. General O'Daniel enthusiastically reported the land garrison able to withstand any attack that the Viet Minh could launch "at present." The USAF directorate of intelligence decided in March 1954 that Ho Chi Minh would be "stupid" to attack and take heavy losses when "hit and run" tactics were so much more effective.[17]

In talks completed on February 18, 1954, France, the United States, Great Britain, and the Soviet Union agreed to discuss political solutions for Korea and Indochina at a conference to be held in Geneva on April 26. Secretary of State Dulles had opposed setting a specific date for further international negotiations, arguing that a fixed time would tempt Ho Chi Minh into a spectacular operation.[18]

His concern was prophetic—Ho sought an all-out victory at Dien Bien Phu. Chinese advisors had trained and equipped Viet Minh artillery and antiaircraft units. Disassembled weapons, brought in on the backs of human carriers, had been reassembled and placed in positions concealed under heavy vegetation in the hills surrounding the French garrison. Artillery pieces included 75- and 105-mm howitzers, the latter of American manufacture that had been captured in Korea. Among the antiaircraft arms were Soviet-made 37-mm automatic weapons and 12.7-mm heavy machineguns. A 100-mile road was opened to a major depot on the Chinese border, and a fleet of 1,000 trucks arriving from China assured sufficient shells for a high rate of fire.[19]

Before the Viet Minh launched their attack against Dien Bien Phu, guerrillas struck the Gia Lam and Cat Bi airfields inside the Hanoi-Haiphong perimeter. On the night of March 3, infiltrators used plastic explosives to damage or destroy ten civil transport aircraft at Gia Lam. Three nights later at Cat Bi, guerrillas destroyed one B-26 and six Morane-500 Crickets and damaged three parked B-26s.[20]

The attack against Dien Bien Phu began on March 10 with shelling of the two airstrips. At nightfall on the 13th the Viet Minh mounted massed assaults against outposts. Although the French dropped two paratroop battalions into Dien Bien Phu on March 14 and 16, the Viet Minh clung to the surrounding hills and sent artillery fire plunging down upon the garrison and airstrips. Ground support came from all available air units of French Air Force Indochina, the French aircraft carrier *Arromanches*, and from some naval patrol airmen flying

PB4Y-2 Privateers out of Cat Bi. Sorties during the week of March 11-17 averaged forty-three per day.

On the 14th communist gunners closed the principal airstrip at Dien Bien Phu, then destroyed seven F-8Fs, two C-47s, one C-119, four Crickets, and two H-19B helicopters on the ground. A B-26 hit by antiaircraft fire crashed upon landing at Cat Bi. Enemy fire the next day downed one F-6F and one F-8F. That same week, flak damaged three F-8Fs and one C-119. C-47s and smaller planes sneaked into the airstrip at night for two weeks to evacuate casualties. These missions ceased after an air ambulance was destroyed by artillery on March 28.[21]

French fighters and light bombers giving direct and close air support to the ground troops had to operate from higher altitudes because of the accurate antiaircraft fire. The crews therefore found it harder to locate and hit dug-in and carefully camouflaged positions. Since napalm dropped by C-47s seemed particularly potent, the French on March 18 asked to use FEAF C-119s for larger napalm drops on moonlit nights. While General Weyland thought the C-119s rather vulnerable for such work, he agreed to furnish them. One plane carrying 4,000 gallons of drummed napalm crashed during takeoff from Cat Bi on March 23. Nevertheless, the French flew some C-119 drops with satisfactory results. But napalm, effective in the rice paddies of the Red River Delta, was less suitable to the canopied and rain-soaked forest around Dien Bien Phu.[22]

With the major airstrip at Dien Bien Phu closed, the 170 tons of ammunition and 32 of food required each day to sustain the garrison had to be dropped into ever-shrinking zones. All military air transports, including American C-119s, were committed to this resupply, even though high-altitude drops from 8,000 to 10,000 feet dispersed much cargo into Viet Minh territory. Drops from 3,000 to 4,000 feet were impossible because of the 37-mm antiaircraft fire. Supplies in lieu of aircraft and crews were sacrificed, and one-half to two-thirds of the items fell into enemy hands.[23]

President Eisenhower seriously considered a direct U.S. military intervention. But judging adequate ground forces to be already engaged, he was reluctant to commit American ground troops in Southeast Asia or to employ air units squarely in support of the French. He was unwilling to authorize stronger U.S. measures unless a coalition of powers, including Britain in particular, gave moral meaning to such an undertaking.[24]

Talk of using American air and naval forces to support the French prompted Vice Chief of Staff Gen. Thomas D. White to direct a study on how best to employ the Air Force in Indochina. Army Chief of Staff Gen. Matthew B. Ridgway dispatched a team of officers under Maj. Gen. James M. Gavin to Vietnam to gather facts on a possible ground force commitment. President Eisenhower, noting that General Trapnell was due for rotation, directed that General O'Daniel, an experienced combat commander who still visited Indochina periodically, be assigned as Chief of MAAG.[25]

In Washington on March 20, French General Ely met with President Eisenhower, Secretary of State Dulles, and Chairman of the Joint Chiefs of Staff Admiral Arthur W. Radford, USN, who were gravely and sympathetically

THE ADVISORY YEARS

Courtesy: USIA

DIEN BIEN PHU

P. 20: (Top) USAF C-124 at Ceylon airlifting French soldiers to Vietnam. (Center) French paratroopers. (Bottom) French Foreign Legion.

P. 21: (Top) President Eisenhower with Gen Paul Ely and Adm. Arthur W. Radford. (Below) Supplies unloaded in Indochina under the Military Defense Assistance Program.

concerned about the situation. Eisenhower directed Radford to give the French whatever materials they requested. He was speaking of logistic assistance, but Ely had the impression that much more was involved in the offer. Dulles reiterated the position that overt U.S. participation in the war would depend on French willingness to expand the training of indigenous forces and to give ultimate independence to the Associated States. Radford was more encouraging. He spoke of direct U.S. intervention by sixty B-29 bombers escorted by 150 carrier aircraft of the Seventh Fleet against the Viet Minh at Dien Bien Phu.

In Paris, Ely reported Radford's personal assurance of naval air support if the situation required it. The French government on March 29 then sent Col. Raymond Brohon to Vietnam to see if American intervention was needed to save Dien Bien Phu.[26]

In Hanoi, Brohon told General Navarre of possible American air strikes. At first feeling that they might trigger overt Chinese intervention, Navarre informed General Ely on the night of April 3 that direct American action might "have a decisive effect particularly if it comes before the [next] Viet-Minh assault." The Viet Minh had already launched a massed attack on the evening of March 30, and were about to mount another on the night of April 4. They seemed to be taking heavy casualties.[27]

On the 3d of April in Paris, the French government asked the United States to fly two battalions of French paratroopers and some naval personnel from France to Vietnam. The Americans agreed and set the first airlift for the 15th.[28] Alerted on April 3 to assume the mission, the United States Air Forces in Europe planned to use C-119s of the 322d Air Division (Combat Cargo). On the 6th, however, Prime Minister Jawaharlal Nehru refused to permit flights over India, even though the troops transported would be unarmed and dressed in civilian clothes. Air Force headquarters accordingly directed the 62d Troop Carrier Wing to deploy C-124s from Larson Air Force Base, Washington. On April 20, six C-124s picked up 514 passengers in Paris and Tunis and traveled to Vietnam, with intermediate refueling stops in Libya, Egypt, Saudi Arabia, Pakistan, Ceylon, and Thailand. The planes unloaded at Tourane on the 23d. A second lift of five C-124s departed Marseilles with 452 passengers on May 5, followed much the same route, and arrived at Tourane on the 8th.[29]

Meanwhile, at midnight on April 4, Premier Joseph Laniel asked Ambassador C. Douglas Dillon for strikes by Navy carrier pilots against Viet Minh artillery around the besieged French forces. As an alternative, he requested the immediate loan of ten to twenty B-29s, these to be maintained by USAF personnel and flown by French crews.[30]

Secretary Dulles had earlier spoken of the determination of the United States to resist Chinese aggression. In a speech to the Overseas Press Club in Washington on March 29, he expressed strong opposition by "whatever means" against the extension of communist power into Southeast Asia.[31]

British Foreign Secretary Anthony Eden wanted to be sure exactly what Dulles meant, for Eden thought it useless to encourage the French in an adventure that would succeed only with more than limited military assistance.

Accordingly, the British Ambassador Roger M. Makins informed Dulles that his government believed the French situation in Indochina to be beyond salvage. It was therefore important, he said, to refrain from jeopardizing the negotiations to be held in Geneva.[32]

Secretary Dulles, Admiral Radford, and Deputy Secretary of Defense Roger M. Kyes on April 3 briefed a select group of congressional leaders. The latter made it clear that the Congress would support no unilateral U.S. intervention in Indochina unless three conditions were met: unified action by the non-communist nations in Southeast Asia and by the United Kingdom, complete independence to be granted to the Associated States, and continuation by the French of their military effort on the same scale after other nations entered the conflict.[33]

Because congressional support for U.S. air and naval assistance to France depended on a British alignment, President Eisenhower wrote Prime Minister Winston Churchill a personal letter on April 4. Churchill's response three days later indicated little enthusiasm for involvement.[34]

On April 5 Dulles had revealed in testimony before the House foreign affairs committee that the Chinese were "coming awfully close" to overt military intervention. This, he said, Eisenhower would not countenance. Yet, given the British position, the United States on the 6th informed France that other circumstances were necessary for a direct American role in Vietnam.[35]

On the same day, Gen. Nathan F. Twining, Air Force Chief of Staff, recommended against lending B-29 aircraft for two reasons. The French had little ability to operate the planes and none to support them. Suitable targets for the large bombers were absent.[36]

General Navarre informed Paris on April 7 that he lacked French flight crews to man borrowed B-29s. Furthermore, without fighter escorts, the B-29s might be shot down if the Chinese sent in MIG jets.[37]

Convinced of Indochina's major importance to the free world, President Eisenhower on the 7th explained to the press why he thought so. The surrender of any free people to communism, he said, was inimical to freedom everywhere. The loss of Vietnam would expose other nations in Southeast Asia to communist aggression. "You have a row of dominoes set up, you knock over the first one, and what will happen to the last one is the certainty it will go over very quickly."[38]

American military studies were far from optimistic about the prospect of employing U.S. combat forces to support the French. A FEAF staff paper stressed the point that the French still followed an "arrogant" colonial policy and had so alienated native loyalties as to make a military solution probably impossible. Besides, rigid ceilings on French military manpower and a reluctance to develop native forces had dashed what hope there might have been to deal with the Viet Minh militarily. More specifically, the French had failed to exploit their planes fully, for they had neither interdicted enemy supply routes nor properly used air strikes against the hostile concentrations ringing the fortress.[39]

A USAF staff study concluded that air power would contribute to the efforts of land forces, but several factors would seriously inhibit air effectiveness.

Cited were the character of the ground operations, the terrain, the weather, the absence among the indigenous population of a will to fight, the general scarcity of good air targets, and the want of target information.[40]

The Army fact-finding team headed by General Gavin reported that eight U.S. divisions plus thirty-five engineer battalions would have to fight in the Hanoi Delta and possibly seize Hainan Island. Because Southeast Asia had no good ports, airfields, and land communications, support requirements were tremendous. "We finally decided when we were all through," Gavin said later, "that what we were talking about doing was going to war with Red China under conditions that were appallingly disadvantageous." Ridgway sent the report to President Eisenhower who was struck by the enormity of the requirements posited.[41]

Yet U.S. military commanders in the Far East tried to furnish all-out logistic support to the French, even drawing equipment from American units. Gen. Earle E. Partridge, who assumed command of Far East Air Forces on March 26, 1954, directed "full, prompt, and effective" action. Thus, when the French High Commissioner asked Ambassador Heath early in April for eighteen C-47s to replace losses, the planes were flown from Japan to Tourane on April 9 and placed on loan. When the French wanted twenty-five B-26B aircraft, these too were provided. Other expedited deliveries included H-19 helicopters taken from Marine Corps units in the Far East, L-20 liaison aircraft from the Air Force, and twelve F-8F replacement aircraft diverted from Thailand commitments. The carrier *Saipan* brought twenty-five F-4U Corsair fighters to Tourane to augment the F-6Fs aboard the *Arromanches*. While FEAF sent large air shipments of munitions, paraflares, and white-phosphorus bombs, larger deliveries of heavier ordnance came by surface vessels loaded in Korea and Okinawa.[42]

Maj. Gen. Jacob E. Smart, FEAF deputy for operations, offered the French on April 7 the Hail (Lazy Dog) munitions stored in Japan. These small finned bullets had been manufactured for antipersonnel missions during the Korean War but had never been used in combat. With 11,200 of the missiles packed in a cluster adapter about the size and weight of a 500-pound bomb, the tactic was to drop the clusters from 15,000 feet and burst them at 5,000 feet. This allowed the finned bullets to gain lethal velocity as they approached the ground.[43]

Five million of these small missiles and 500 cluster adapters arrived at Haiphong on April 16, but the ship was delayed on berthing and did not unload until the 23d. When the shipment was unpacked, about half the missiles were corroded and many had damaged fins that affected their ballistic flight. Two FEAF technical experts, Lt. Col. William B. Sanders and Maj. Robert V. Prouty, urged the French to employ the finned bullets in a fairly large strike against enemy personnel. The French, however, preferred to use them against antiaircraft artillery emplacements. Four PB4Y-2 aircraft, each carrying 12 cluster units, opened the attack and through May 2 dropped 227 units; B-26s dropped 132.

Though Sanders and Prouty were unable to obtain concrete evaluations of results, the French appeared to be happy with circumstantial evidence. On April

30 and May 1 the missile bombs were extensively employed in conjunction with air resupply missions, and on these dates C-119 crews reported less antiaircraft fire than usual. Perhaps more indicative, the Viet Minh dispersed their antiaircraft batteries. To Sanders it seemed that "the finned bullet attacks were successful but only due to volume rather than good delivery tactics."[44]

When Generals Partridge and Smart visited Vietnam during April 14-18, General Navarre asked whether B-29 operations were feasible. On his way home, Partridge radioed Brig. Gen. Joseph D. C. Caldara, commander of the FEAF Bomber Command (Provisional), to meet him at Haneda airport in Tokyo. There Partridge told Caldara of Navarre's request. According to Navarre, B-29 operations had been cleared through diplomatic channels. Partridge had received no such directive. In any case, Caldara was to go to Vietnam and see whether B-29s would be effective. If so and B-29 flights were authorized, Caldara would have complete operational control. Partridge wanted him to employ his force as a total unit under mass-strike conditions.[45]

Leaving Japan on the following day, Caldara flew to Saigon. After conferring with Robert McClintock, Chargé d'Affaires at the American Embassy, and with French officials, Caldara received an intelligence briefing. He then flew over Dien Bien Phu. He concluded that there were "no true B-29 targets." But if B-29s were "the only aircraft that can put the required tonnage on the roads and supply areas, we can do the job if directed." The monsoon weather had set in, limiting visual bombing. Hence bombing by shoran radar or by airborne radar would be essential.

Believing that B-29 operations could best be mounted from Clark Air Base in the Philippines, General Caldara planned to fly a maximum effort strike with 1/10-second-delay-fused, 500-pound general purpose bombs. Navy fighters operating from carriers would escort the bombers. "The bombing raid," Caldara later reminisced, "could have effectively destroyed the entire enemy force surrounding Dien Bien Phu."

This may have been wishful thinking. Although General Navarre repeatedly sought information on the ability of the B-29s to destroy antiaircraft facilities, he felt that the absence of ground-based radar guidance made a mass strike so close to the camp impossible. He preferred an American air strike against the major Viet Minh supply base at Tuan Giao, a road-junction town about fifty miles northeast of Dien Bien Phu. Caldara made a personal aerial reconnaissance of the enemy supply lines from Dien Bien Phu to the Chinese border and presented target information to the French. In Hanoi he discovered the French possessed more fighter-bombers and light bombers than they could use on any given day because of personnel and maintenance restrictions. Finally, Caldara judged a mass bombing by B-29s to be impractical under the conditions. He also informed Partridge, who directed him to return to Japan.[46]

Arriving in Paris on April 19, Secretary Dulles learned that the situation at Dien Bien Phu was "virtually hopeless." It could be saved only through U.S. air intervention. Dulles suggested to the French government that Generals Navarre and O'Daniel hold an emergency consultation. But on the 23d when Navarre asked for an American B-29 air strike, Dulles told Foreign Minister Georges Bidault that direct U.S. intervention required a prior political basis.

Dulles conferred with Admiral Radford when the latter reached Paris on the evening of April 24, and they concluded that it was too late for United States action. In Geneva the following evening, Foreign Secretary Anthony Eden made it quite clear that the United Kingdom opposed direct American air involvement. Discussions next turned toward a new policy on the basis of a French defeat in northwest Tonkin.[47]

With direct American intervention ruled out, the sole hope for continued French resistance at Dien Bien Phu rested on reinforcing the garrison. Paratroopers flown from France to Vietnam in USAF aircraft offered the prospect of releasing experienced paratrooper battalions in reserve at Hanoi. Nevertheless, the dispatch of relief was meaningful only if air transport supply was available.

Navarre dropped small numbers of paratroopers into Dien Bien Phu on the nights of May 3, 4, and 5, but canceled another planned drop because of scarce airlift. Through April and early May, French combat aircraft and transports operated under the most severe restrictions of adverse weather and terrain as well as of hostile ground fire.[48]

As the defensive perimeter at Dien Bien Phu contracted, the drop zone diminished to a diameter of about 2,000 yards. Antiaircraft weapons sited on high ridges alongside the drop zone caught aircraft flying through the slot in a murderous crossfire. To escape flak, French C-47s dropped parabundles from 10,000 feet and had to make several passes over the target before they could kick out their complete loads. In deference to the ground fire, C-119s raised their drop altitude to 5,000 feet, and dumped their loads quickly in a single pass. Hardly safe from flak at that height, Civil Air Transport pilots complained that the C-47s dropped parabundles through their flights and that escorting flak-suppression aircraft were dropping bombs through flight formations. These were hazardous conditions for civilian crews whose contracts made no mention of flying in active combat areas.

To increase drop accuracy at 8,000 to 10,000 feet, French airborne technicians devised an ingenious procedure. They used a refueling line to hobble a cargo parachute until it neared the ground. Then an explosive time-delay fuze cut the line and allowed the parachute to deploy. The device appeared to work, and a detachment of the U.S. Army 8081st Quartermaster Airborne Supply and Packaging Company, which loaded C-119s at Cat Bi, adopted the parachute delay apparatus and used it on all C-119 drops during the last two weeks of the Dien Bien Phu campaign.[49]

Fragments of a 37-mm shell severely injured Civil Air Transport pilot Paul Holden on April 24. His fellow civilians refused to fly to Dien Bien Phu again without adequate combat air support, so French military pilots manned the C-119s. On the 26th, antiaircraft fire downed one F-6F and two B-26s. Flak-suppression missions (including a heavy concentration of Hail missiles), flown at the expense of close air support strikes and supply line interdiction, improved the situation. The civilian pilots returned to their planes on the 30th. Breaking a short period of silence, 37-mm guns on May 6 scored hits on one C-119 and shot down another flown by civilian pilot James B. McGovern.*[50]

On the 6th planes delivered 196 tons of supplies to the garrison. What was to be the final Viet Minh assault started that evening. At noon of the 7th, soldiers broke into the heart of the French defenses, and the battle ended several hours later. Ho Chi Minh had scored a decisive victory that coincided with the negotiations in Geneva. There, delegates had failed to reach political agreement on Korea and were about to take up the problem of restoring peace to Indochina.[51]

---

*A legendary figure in Asia, McGovern had come to be known as "Earthquake McGoon" in deference to his huge size and black beard. He was a Fourteenth Air Force pilot in World War II and remained in the Far East with the Civil Air Transport Company. He died in the C-119 crash.

III. The Geneva Agreements and French Withdrawal

Victory at Dien Bien Phu allowed the Viet Minh to move troops and weapons toward the Hanoi-Haiphong perimeter. During the night of May 12, 500 Vietnamese regulars at Hanoi deserted with their arms. Grave doubts about holding the Red River Delta arose among the French. Deciding that the safety of the Expeditionary Corps in Vietnam had become the prime consideration, the government directed the French commander to withdraw. He could retire as far as the 18th parallel to safeguard the southern part of Vietnam.[1]

Although President Eisenhower believed overt Chinese intervention in Indochina hardly likely, he permitted the military services to plan for the contingency. Identifying the options open to the United States may have benefited French morale. At the time, Adm. Felix B. Stump, USN, was Commander in Chief, Pacific Command (CINCPAC), the unified commander responsible for U.S. military operations in Asia south of the 30th parallel. He conceived that an American commander of a Southeast Asia Defense Command ought to move into Vietnam with U.S. naval and air forces, perhaps eight Army divisions, and probably exercise operational control over the French forces.[2]

General Partridge, FEAF commander, promptly protested Admiral Stump's concept because it would divide the unity of air command in the Pacific and base air units on hazardous airfields. Less than enthusiastic about B-29s with conventional weapons, Partridge favored using carriers. Believing the struggle to be basically a civil war in which long-term pacification and unification rather than destruction were the prime objectives, he thought that conventionally armed B-29s might produce favorable short-term psychological effects but no lasting results. Indecisive and devastating air attacks would be counterproductive because the real task was to build indigenous military, economic, political, and psychological leadership.[3]

Toward the end of May, the Joint Chiefs of Staff were reluctant to place large numbers of American forces in Vietnam. They wished to avoid a defensive Korea-type response and preferred an offensive against mainland China, including attacks against the Chinese war-making capability and "employing atomic weapons, whenever necessary."[4]

President Eisenhower sent General Trapnell, MAAG-Indochina chief, to Paris at the end of May to discuss cooperative planning with General Ely, who was preparing to go to Vietnam as Commander in Chief and High Commissioner. When Ely failed to receive positive assurance of U.S. intervention even in the event of an overt Chinese attack, he was unwilling to accept an overall American commander and was averse to having American ground troops, except for one or two divisions as a show of good faith.[5]

After that, the prospects of American intervention diminished. Discussions in Geneva on Indochina commenced May 8 between delegates from the United States, the United Kingdom, the Union of Soviet Socialist Republics, France, the People's Republic of China, the Kingdoms of Laos and Cambodia, the State of Vietnam, and the Democratic Republic of Vietnam. The question was how to end the war between France (and its adherents) and the Viet Minh, the former supported by the United States and the latter by Communist China and the Soviet Union. The Viet Minh delegate was hardly anxious to compromise. He felt that the French colonials had been defeated and that all of Vietnam lay within Ho Chi Minh's grasp.

Seeing little chance of holding an enclave in Tonkin, the French in June were agreeable to a partitioning of Vietnam that would leave the southern part to them. By then, the Viet Minh were establishing control over the central highlands. On the 24th, in Mang Yang Pass, they cut off and virtually destroyed 3,600 men of French Mobile Group 100 that was withdrawing toward Pleiku along Route 19.

The Viet Minh continued their military successes and the Geneva negotiations dragged on. Between June 25-28 in Washington, President Eisenhower and Prime Minister Churchill drew up a paper and offered it to the French as the basis for an armistice. Pledging to press for a collective defense of Southeast Asia, they warned that the international situation would be "seriously aggravated" if the French government refused to accept an agreement.[6]

The Soviet Union seemed more interested in Europe than in Southeast Asia. Informed speculation indicated that Foreign Minister Vyacheslav M. Molotov proffered Premier Pierre Mendes-France a somewhat favorable settlement in Indochina if the French abstained from participating in a European Defense Community. At the same time, Chinese Foreign Minister Chou En-lai, apparently impressed with the atomic might of the United States, hoped to demilitarize Indochina to deny the Americans bases there.[7]

On July 8 in Geneva, serious discussions centered around the place where a dividing line could be drawn across Vietnam. The French insisted on the 18th parallel, while the North Vietnamese argued for the 14th. After a private discussion between Mendes-France and Chou En-lai in Bern, the Viet Minh accepted the 17th parallel as the demarcation, and the negotiations moved rapidly to a conclusion on July 21.[8]

Signing an agreement on Vietnam, French and Viet Minh military representatives established two states separated at the 17th parallel, a demilitarized zone on each side of the line, and the withdrawal of French troops from the North and of Viet Minh from the South. They prohibited introducing fresh troops, arms, and munitions, as well as building new military bases in Vietnam. International Control Commission teams from Canada, India, and Poland were to supervise the implementation of the armistice and to report violations that might lead to resumed hostilities. Finally, there were to be, by July 1956, elections throughout Vietnam to unify the country. Consultations between representatives of the two

GENEVA AGREEMENTS AND FRENCH WITHDRAWAL

parts, North and South, were to start no later than July 20, 1955, to prepare for the vote.[9]

The Soviet Union wished all parties to accept the Geneva accords formally, but the United States preferred to keep them a matter between the two principals. Nevertheless the American delegate, Under Secretary of State Walter B. Smith, gave assurance that the United States would "refrain from the threat or the use of force to disturb" the agreements and would "view any renewal of the aggression in violation of the . . . agreements with grave concern and as seriously threatening international peace and security." The delegate from South Vietnam solemnly protested that his country was not bound by agreements. He objected that the French High Command had arrogated to itself the right to fix a date for a future election, a political rather than a military decision.[10]

The Geneva accords led to the removal of USAF logistic support detachments, and General Partridge had started the withdrawal as early as May 13. But when the French need for support to hold the Red River Delta slowed the evacuation, Partridge directed the detachments to take necessary measures for their own safety and security.[11]

The C-47 detachment at Do Son Airfield departed on June 29. The C-119 detachment at Cat Bi moved on May 23 to Tourane and joined the B-26 support group.[12]

On July 13 Defense Secretary Wilson ordered immediate suspension of all materiel shipments to Indochina. The Air Force stopped all deliveries, started to recover the B-26 and C-119 aircraft on loan, and arranged to evacuate its personnel. Much materiel already en route to Indochina in French-controlled ships could not be diverted, and eventually ended up in French dumps and depots. The B-26 and C-119 logistic support detachments remained at Tourane on aircraft recovery missions until the last of the loaned planes returned to Clark Air Base on September 6.[13]

The USAF units had little trouble evacuating their own people from Vietnam, but were hard-pressed to fulfill other personnel movements. The French requested assistance to repatriate wounded men from North Vietnam, and five C-124s moved 504 individuals. The 315th Air Division and 6481st Medical Air Evacuation Group handled these patients from Saigon hospitals via Clark Air Base to Tachikawa Air Base, Japan, where Military Air Transport Service (MATS) craft flew them to the United States and finally to France and North Africa. The Navy hospital ship *Haven* moved 725 men from Vietnam to Oran, Algeria, and to Marseilles.[14]

Air Force transports flew U.S. nationals from the Hanoi-Haiphong area; the Philippine Air Lines evacuated Filipino residents; Civil Air Transport planes took out Chinese; U.S. Navy Amphibious Group One and the Military Sea Transport Service lifted supplies and thousands of Vietnamese refugees to safety.

The largest of these movements by far took place between July 10, 1954, and July 30, 1955. Before the Viet Minh stopped the migration, about 880,000 Vietnamese fled from the North to the South.[15]

THE ADVISORY YEARS

Refugees fleeing from North Vietnam when the country was divided at the 17th parallel.

Courtesy: USIA

GENEVA AGREEMENTS AND FRENCH WITHDRAWAL

(Right) Richard M. Nixon, Pierre Mendes-France, and John Foster Dulles.

(Below) Operation Wounded Warrior: USAF evacuation of French Foreign Legionnaires after Dien Bien Phu.

Courtesy: John Schlight

Few efforts were made to evaluate the air operations of the Indochina War, quite possibly because of a general feeling that it was pointless to draw lessons from a conflict that was doomed from the start. The French had been unable to win the support of the people where the war was fought.

Even so, at General Twining's direction, General Hewitt visited the region and prepared a detailed report. His main conclusion was that the manpower strength of the French Air Force had been hopelessly inadequate to support 182,000 ground troops dispersed in many garrisons. Air operations were largely responses to urgent ground force requests. In consequence the French had tried to do too much, in far too many places, with much too little.[16]

Summarizing the reasons for this lackluster performance, FEAF noted the personnel shortages and the poor organization. Often more aircraft than pilots were available, and too few maintenance men were on hand to keep planes serviceable. Furthermore, tactical air planners had been unable to develop targets in the "monsoon mountain mass" of North Vietnam, and interdiction missions had been relatively ineffective against enemy supply lines, particularly against the flow of goods from China.[17] Both General Hewitt's and FEAF's assessment implied that the existing problems were correctable. But neither echoed an earlier estimate by Gen. G. J. M. Chassin, French air commander, who suggested that the Viet Minh tactics of concealment, dispersal, surprise, and psychological warfare were extremely difficult to counter with fast-flying military planes.[18]

President Eisenhower welcomed the end of bloodshed in Indochina. American assistance, he said, had been unable to cure an "unsound relationship between the Asiatics and the French" and had therefore been "of only limited value."[19]

Two Vietnams emerged. In both, most people lived in two great river deltas, the Red in the north and the Mekong in the south, as well as in the lowlands between the sea and the mountains.

North Vietnam, under Ho Chi Minh at Hanoi, had about 16 million people including a communist political elite and battle-hardened military forces. Brutal collectivization programs in 1954 and 1955 decreased the popularity of the revolutionaries. The migration of nearly a million inhabitants south during the year after the Geneva accords was a protest against the regime and the conditions of life. But the communists confidently expected the national reunification plebiscite in 1956 to deliver the other Vietnam peacefully to them.

In South Vietnam, with 14 million people, failure of the French to develop indigenous leaders hampered the anti-communist nationalists. During the absence of Bao Dai in France, control of the state devolved upon Ngo Dinh Diem, a member of the Catholic minority. He became head of the cabinet in Saigon on June 18, 1954, and a few weeks later was invested as President of the Council of Ministers. Not widely known in the country and somewhat aloof, Diem depended heavily for advice on his immediate family, especially on his brother and political counselor, Ngo Dinh Nhu.[20]

GENEVA AGREEMENTS AND FRENCH WITHDRAWAL

Ho Chi Minh made no secret of his determination to extend his control over all of Vietnam. Immediately after the Geneva agreements, he called for a "long and arduous struggle" to win the south, which he described as "territories of ours."[21] He soon sent cadres across the 17th parallel, and they became known as Viet Cong. They expanded the communist apparatus in the south, prepared for future infiltration of men from the north, and worked for eventual unification under Hanoi through subversion as well as open conflict.

President Eisenhower retained the U.S. Embassy in Saigon, and worked to strengthen the indigenous government in conjunction with the French, who had agreed to stay in Indochina until national forces could emerge. To compensate for and bolster the weak government, Secretary Dulles actively concerned himself with stimulating strong native military forces.[22]

According to a National Security Council (NSC) paper in August 1954, the Viet Minh victory in Tonkin had enhanced communist military and political prestige in Asia. Now the Viet Minh were certain to try to extend their influence beyond North Vietnam by military and non-military pressures, that is, by overt aggression and by exploiting internal political instabilities and economic weaknesses in neighboring free countries.

To counter this estimated course of action, the United States decided to pursue three principal policies: negotiate a Southeast Asia security treaty pledging members to act promptly against armed aggression; swiftly support legitimate governments requesting and requiring assistance to defeat local subversion and rebellion; and, more specifically, support France in assisting the South Vietnamese to gain and maintain the military forces and the economic conditions needed to meet foreign aggression and insure internal security.[23]

Moving speedily, the United States, Great Britain, France, Australia, New Zealand, Pakistan, Thailand, and the Philippines signed the Southeast Asia Defense Treaty in Manila on September 8, 1954. The major threats triggering the agreement were subversion from within and aggression from outside a country. Although an individual nation had primary responsibility for countersubversive activities, the Southeast Asia Treaty Organization (SEATO) would act as a clearing house to exchange information among the members and to discuss common policies. It was external armed aggression against any member that was recognized as the main common danger, and this the members pledged to meet collectively. Because the Geneva agreements prevented Vietnam, Laos, and Cambodia from joining the organization, SEATO spread its protection to them. In the case of Vietnam, the United States would work through the French to maintain the military forces "necessary for internal security." For all members, the United States would discharge its treaty obligations by deploying mobile forces rapidly into the area rather than by stationing units in the region. The treaty became effective in February 1955.[24]

Since SEATO was to be a shield against external aggression, Secretary Dulles felt that South Vietnam needed military forces for internal security only. The Joint Chiefs of Staff were hesitant to spend scarce funds in Vietnam until a stable government existed. They believed, however, that U.S. military assistance to Vietnam should afford both internal security and limited defense against external attack.[25]

Much of the American problem stemmed from the kind of government in South Vietnam. The Saigon government had yet to consolidate its power, and there were conspiracies to unseat Diem. The Joint Chiefs wanted a reasonably strong civil government in control before the United States undertook a military training mission. Secretary Dulles understood this concern, but he thought that well-trained armed forces would strengthen the Vietnamese government. Under pressure from Dulles, the Joint Chiefs conceded that five indigenous divisions would permit Vietnam to maintain internal security and present a limited response to external attack. But it would take two or three years to train that force. If the United States decided to do the training, it should be assigned low priority so as not to impair more promising programs elsewhere.[26]

Between 1945-1954 the French had built up the Vietnamese regular and paramilitary forces to varying degrees of effectiveness. The Vietnamese Air Force consisted of the 1st Liaison Group with two squadrons of Morane-500 Cricket liaison planes and one squadron of Dassault M.D.-315 light combat assault aircraft, and a training center at Nha Trang. Few Vietnamese had held high rank. Most were inexperienced. Enlisted desertions were frequent and damaging.[27]

The French had declined the offer of American help in training the Vietnamese, but they changed their minds about the time of the Geneva accords. Generals O'Daniel and Ely in Saigon agreed that the United States should assume some responsibility. The Geneva agreements fixed the maximum strength of the MAAG at 342 U.S. officers and men, the number in the country when the accords were signed. Since this group was too small to do a great deal, the French retained management of the programs.

In October the Joint Chiefs ruled that the MAAG in Saigon could execute a training mission if this became a political necessity and if the French refrained from interfering. After a National Security Council meeting, the President ordered Ambassador Heath and General O'Daniel to "collaborate in setting in motion a crash program designed to bring about an improvement in the loyalty and effectiveness of the Free Vietnamese forces." He instructed the Joint Chiefs to prepare a long-range program to reorganize and train the minimum number of Vietnamese forces necessary to preserve internal security.[28]

The President also wrote to Diem to ask for Vietnamese-American cooperation on developing a strong and stable state capable of resisting subversion and aggression. In return for U.S. assistance, Eisenhower expected Diem to reform his government, make it responsive to the nationalist aspirations of the Vietnamese people, and shape it into a representative and democratic regime.[29]

American policy statements stressed internal security considerations, but public announcements indicated the intention to strengthen the nation to repel aggression as well as subversion. The military forces projected were modeled on the U.S. tri-service pattern. They were more suitable for conventional military operations than for internal security and counterinsurgency activities.[30]

To dramatize interest in Vietnam and to evaluate the situation, President

Eisenhower sent General J. Lawton Collins, USA, to Saigon as a special U.S. representative on November 3, 1954. Among other missions, Collins was to look into the question of insuring the loyalty of the army to the government. Shortly after Collins arrived, a Vietnamese general officer who had challenged Diem's control departed for France. This resolved a struggle for the direction of the government in favor of Diem. Stability seemed enhanced.[31]

Working within strength figures stipulated by the Joint Chiefs of Staff, Collins at first negotiated solely with the French. After January 1, 1955, when the union of the Associated States with France terminated, Collins conferred directly with Diem's government. He secured agreement for American support of a Vietnamese army numbering 94,000 men, enough for a mobile battle corps of three field divisions and one regimental combat team. MAAG was to assume full responsibility for assisting the Vietnamese government to organize and train this armed force. Due to the personnel ceiling on MAAG, the French would help. On February 12, 1955, the United States formally took over all Vietnamese military training.[32]

Initial Vietnamese ground operations against the Viet Cong were encouraging. To destroy communist domination in certain areas, a Vietnamese brigade conducted a pacification operation in the Mekong Delta in February and March. In April and May larger forces pacified the Quang Ngai and Binh Dinh Provinces on the coast of the South China Sea. The soldiers broke up armed bands, destroyed arms caches, provided local security, and resettled refugees from North Vietnam on vacant lands.[33]

During March, Diem's troops also put down a rebellion by the Binh Xuyen politico-religious sect, a revolt that spread to the Cao Dai and Hoa Hao sects. Driving the dissidents out of the city, the Vietnamese army crushed their armed forces in a final campaign in the Rung Sat swamps southwest of Saigon in September and October. Occupation of the Tay Ninh Province broke the Cao Dai insurgency.

The army performed well and the air force afforded moderate aid in the form of Cricket liaison flights that conducted surveillance, directed artillery, and dropped psychological warfare leaflets. These successes gave confidence to Diem and optimism to the Americans, who hoped that continued support would enable the government to "pull through."[34]

Further encouragement came when Diem formed two new local defense organizations. He recruited men for the Civil Guard and assigned them to work with provincial chiefs as a rural police. He created the Self Defense Corps whose members used obsolete weapons to protect their homes, villages, and hamlets under the district chiefs.[35]

Air Force studies suggested that the most immediate danger to Southeast Asia was subversion. But this was out of context with proposals to equip national air forces with conventional aircraft. In addition, there was need to develop indigenous equipment and techniques in line with U.S. doctrine, so American jet aircraft could function in the event of a U.S. deployment to meet a SEATO emergency. On May 5, 1955, General Twining approved an Air Force Council

THE ADVISORY YEARS

(Left) Gen. Nathan F. Twining.

(Center) Gen. J. Lawton Collins and Premier Ngo Dinh Diem.

(Below) MAAG Headquarters in Saigon.

Courtesy: USIA

policy that the national air forces in the Pacific-Far East should be shaped to cope with internal aggression, to defend to a limited degree against external aggression, and to furnish air base complexes suitable for USAF use if necessary.[36] Whether the three were compatible remained to be seen.

In September 1955 a program to forge indigenous countersubversive military forces seemed to demand highly mobile ground commando troops operating closely with tactical air; slow-flying conventional strike aircraft carrying diversified weapons and loitering over target areas for extended periods, plus visual and photo-reconnaissance planes, light transports, and helicopters; and a strong militia to overcome communist infiltration at local levels.[37]

The Joint Chiefs of Staff believed that a U.S. effort to defend South Vietnam against external aggression under SEATO procedures would be substantial, costly, and difficult to manage, especially without atomic weapons. To defeat a North Vietnamese invasion would call for two to four Army divisions besides the South Vietnamese ground forces. To invade and occupy North Vietnam would take eight U.S. divisions. Moreover, quite a few Air Force tactical fighter wings would have to be committed, and this depended on proper air facilities. To prepare to meet a North Vietnamese invasion in the near future, the Joint Chiefs suggested increasing the efficiency of the South Vietnamese forces and improving the air bases in the country and in neighboring states.[38]

When Ho Chi Minh called upon Diem to open negotiations for a national plebiscite, not only Diem but Dulles protested publicly. An honest election would be impossible, they said, because the totalitarian regime in Hanoi would direct the vote of the people it controlled in the more populous North. Diem on August 9 positively rejected elections as long as the communist regime refused to grant democratic freedoms and fundamental rights to the people of North Vietnam. An October vote in South Vietnam gave Diem a mandate to set up a republic under his presidency. On October 26, 1955, the Republic of Vietnam came into being, and on the same day the United States extended recognition and established diplomatic relations.[39]

Because Ho Chi Minh was building a powerful army in North Vietnam, an invasion of South Vietnam would overwhelm Diem's forces that were organized and equipped chiefly for internal security.[40] MAAG had therefore suggested that the Vietnamese army concentrate on repelling outside attack and that the United States concentrate on training the Civil Guard and Self Defense Corps. Approving, the Joint Chiefs recommended that General Collins' ceiling of 94,000 men for the Vietnamese military forces be raised to 150,000. This would be enough for 4 field divisions, 6 light divisions, 13 territorial regiments; and about 4,000 air, 4,000 navy, and 5,000 civilian employees.[41]

Lt. Gen. Samuel T. Williams, USA, was appointed the new MAAG chief in Saigon. Arriving on November 15, 1955, he had to deal at once with an impending withdrawal of French forces to meet the revolt in Algeria.[42] Under arrangements made by General O'Daniel, French advisors were serving with American personnel in a Training Relations and Instructions Mission. The French departure required a larger American complement. While the International Control Commission was unwilling to approve a bigger MAAG, it allowed the United States to sent 350 men to Vietnam as a Temporary Equipment Recovery Mission to inventory and remove surplus equipment. Stretching the authority granted, MAAG employed these personnel as logistical advisors to replace the French working with Vietnamese army units. They became the Combat Arms Training and Organization Division of MAAG. On April 23, 1956, the last French commander in chief in Indochina closed his headquarters and left for France.[43]

According to General Williams, pacification duty left the Vietnamese army little time for division combat training. Scattered miscellaneous units were hard to organize into a cohesive field force. President Diem described the light divisions as relics of the French colonial belief that the Vietnamese made poor soldiers and therefore had to work in small units. Increasingly, Diem wished his army to be organized and trained for field operations in conjunction with the SEATO nations. When British and Canadian authorities insisted that this would violate the Geneva accords and provoke particular disaffection in India, the United States refrained.[44]

South Vietnam's refusal to conduct elections to reunify the two Vietnams in accordance with the Geneva agreement led American officials during the winter of 1955-56 to expect a North Vietnamese invasion sometime after July 1956, the date when the elections would have taken place. Nothing happened, and two months later President Eisenhower decided to help South Vietnam build armed forces for internal security and also for limited initial resistance to North Vietnamese attack. The United States encouraged the South Vietnamese to align their military growth to U.S. military doctrine.[45]

As the United States prepared the Vietnamese to combat subversion and to repel invasion as well, it seemed unable to decide which was the greater threat. The objectives for expanded national and regional defenses — even the distinction between the two — were vague, confused, and at times conflicting. This aggravated the problem American advisors faced in adapting U.S. materiel and procedures to a strange environment.

IV. U.S. Command Problems in the Pacific: Emphasis on Southeast Asia

Authorities in Washington had closely managed the assistance to France during the Indochina War, but U.S. commanders in the Pacific exercised increasing influence afterward. They looked to American military interests on a divided basis. The Far East and United Nations Commands existed on the one hand and the Pacific Command on the other. Because of budgetary constraints, the latter had no Air Force theater headquarters or tactical units. All USAF resources were assigned to Far East Air Forces, headquartered in Tokyo. Under FEAF were Fifth Air Force and 315th Air Division (Combat Cargo) in Japan, and Thirteenth Air Force in the Philippines.[1]

After March 26, 1954, Admiral Stump, Commander in Chief, Pacific Command, became responsible for reviewing all military assistance programs in this area, which took in Southeast Asia. Since Stump found it hard to manage without an air headquarters, the Joint Chiefs on March 31 directed General Twining to create a command at Hickam AFB, Hawaii. Hence Pacific Air Force (PAF) came into being under Maj. Gen. Sory Smith on the 1st of July. While Smith reported directly to Admiral Stump, he likewise answered to General Partridge, FEAF commander. This reflected an understanding that all USAF tactical air units in the Pacific and Far East would be assigned to FEAF in the interest of command unity throughout both theaters. Stump, who was described as "exceedingly if not unduly sensitive on the subject of command prerogatives," found it vexing, and understandably so, that FEAF should have a say in CINCPAC's area of responsibility. Yet General Partridge considered that a common USAF policy for the Pacific and Far East areas required him to be abreast of events in both places. He directed the Far East Air Logistics Force to have the 6410th Materiel Group support all air components in Southeast Asia.[2]

In February 1955, when General Partridge held a conference of air attachés and MAAG-Air representatives from all nations in Southeast Asia to discuss problems and programs, Admiral Stump reminded him of CINCPAC's primary responsibility for that area. Stump wanted General Smith to help promote projects consistent with U.S. military and political objectives in the Pacific Command. Placing Thirteenth Air Force under PAF on June 1 facilitated his wish.[3]

Under revised directives issued by Defense Secretary Wilson in July, Admiral Stump gained more authority in carrying out the Mutual Defense Assistance Program. Unified commanders like him were to be in the direct line of command over the MAAGs in their areas. Thus Army, Navy, and Air Force personnel assigned to MAAGs were no longer "allocated to CINCPAC" but rather placed under his direct command. Stump therefore integrated the control of assistance programs in his headquarters. Only on technical matters did he allow MAAG chiefs to communicate directly with their military departments, their component commanders, and other service agencies. As for Stump's component Army, Navy, and Air Force commanders, they were limited to advising CINCPAC.[4]

The Air Force's centralization of global logistics under the Air Materiel Command further diluted FEAF influence over assistance concerns. General Partridge insisted on controlling his logistics, but Gen. Laurence S. Kuter who replaced him on June 4, 1955, accepted the new concept in the interest of economy and efficiency. Transferred to Air Materiel Command on October 1, 1955, Far East Air Logistics Force was redesignated Air Materiel Force Pacific Area. Under this organization the Northern Air Material Area Pacific handled support and technical assistance for Japan and Korea. The Southern Air Materiel Area Pacific at Clark Air Base similarly served Okinawa, Taiwan, the Philippines, Laos, Thailand, Cambodia, Guam, and Vietnam.[5]

MAAG-Air personnel now went straight to these materiel commands with their logistic problems, without need to go through the theater air command. In November 1955 Far East Air Force headquarters invited MAAG-Air representatives to a conference in Tokyo. Again CINCPAC objected that FEAF had no right to indoctrinate air sections with its philosophy and concepts.[6]

The inspection team dispatched by General Smith to Southeast Asia in November-December 1955 reported that the Army appeared to be dominating the MAAGs. To some extent, no doubt, this was in response to the desire of the individual countries. Still most MAAG chiefs, deputy chiefs, and chiefs of staff were Army officers. In Vietnam the MAAG-Air Section people were described as being "relegated to a minor role and treated as junior partners," without access to current war plans and unable to coordinate or consult with MAAG-Air sections in neighboring countries. There was a "deplorable lack of definite relationship" between the indigenous air forces supported by mutual defense assistance programs and the overall strategic objectives of the United States.[7]

After remarking on the close association between the Japanese and Korean Air Forces and Fifth Air Force, General Kuter urged Thirteenth Air Force (now under PAF) to foster similar rapport with indigenous air forces in Southeast Asia. On February 17, 1956, Smith charged Thirteenth Air Force with monitoring and reviewing assistance programs in SEA so that national air forces were developed in line with U.S. strategic aims.[8]

Austerely manned, Thirteenth Air Force headquarters needed twenty-eight more manpower spaces to perform the additional task. These slots were not to be had because the entire Air Force was trying to build to an authorized 137 wings without increasing personnel. Kuter and Smith conferred in April 1956 on how to improve the review and monitoring of assistance activities. In May and November, Air Materiel Force Pacific Area sponsored conferences of MAAG-Air representatives to the same end.[9]

Air commanders were disturbed by Admiral Stump's reliance on subordinate command organizations for local operations. As a matter of principle,

USAF leaders advocated centralized direction and control of air operations in the Pacific and Far East areas. Local control of tactical air units would restrict their operations to arbitrary and often meaningless geographic boundaries. Furthermore, air units would go under operational control of a commander who had little or no experience in training, equipping, and operating them.[10]

General Smith therefore protested the assignment of tactical air units to a subordinate unified command. It would, he said, partition air power to defend local pieces of scattered real estate. Smith, as Stump's theater air commander, should manage all air operations in Pacific Command in order to use the available units most effectively regardless of their locations. Stump pointed out that his area was too vast for overall direction of local operations from Hawaii. The division of command responsibilities between component commanders, he said, had led to disaster at Pearl Harbor in 1941, and he preferred a single commander responsible in each operational area for all military operations there. Kuter called the potential commitment of USAF squadrons to local defenses in Vietnam and elsewhere in Southeast Asia a "further emasculation of air power."[11]

When President Eisenhower, the National Security Council, and the Joint Chiefs directed CINCPAC in July 1956 to prepare a contingency plan for defending South Vietnam against overt external attack, Admiral Stump thought in terms of setting up a U.S.-Vietnam Defense Command. The commander was to receive from Fifth Air Force the operational control of earmarked air defense and supporting forces, and from PAF a senior Air Force officer as the air component commander, plus staff personnel. The Joint Chiefs accepted this proposal.[12]

While the prospective proliferation of subordinate unified commands threatened the unity of air power, other developments changed the picture. The consolidation of the United Nations, Far East, and Pacific Commands had come under study in the spring of 1955, after Secretary of Defense Wilson objected to the worldwide command structure that he deemed too large, unwieldy, and expensive. He wanted the system simplified and reduced, and the Joint Chiefs asked commanders for comments. General Kuter recommended a single U.S. unified command in the Pacific. The Joint Chiefs agreed early in 1956, and Secretary Wilson approved discontinuing the Far East Command (FEC) in favor of the Pacific Command, which was to be the single unified command in the Pacific and Far East areas. Headquarters Pacific Air Force then became PACAF/FEAF(Rear) on July 1, which foreshadowed another change, and the headquarters in Japan moved to Hawaii.[13]

General Kuter suggested in August that the Pacific Command have three principal component commands, namely U.S. Army Pacific, U.S. Navy Pacific, and U.S. Air Force Pacific, and four subordinate joint commands — Hawaiian, Southern Pacific, Northern Pacific, and Marianas-Bonin. All forces allocated to CINCPAC, Kuter thought, should be assigned to the principal component commanders for operational control in peace and in war. The subordinate joint commands should have no combat responsibilities but rather should support ambassadors and MAAGs, coordinate administrative and logistic activities, and perform other non-combat obligations in their areas. In a local war, a CINCPAC-designated task force commander selected from the military service predominantly involved would assume operational control of joint task forces. During local engagements, the Commander in Chief, Air Force Pacific, should have complete responsibility for air defense throughout the entire Pacific.[14]

In October Admiral Stump and Army Gen. Lyman L. Lemnitzer, FEC commander in chief, recommended three component commands — Pacific Fleet, Pacific Air Forces, and Army, Pacific, each to administer, train, support, and operate allocated forces. Stump and Lemnitzer wished to retain existing subordinate unified commands and to establish two additional commands in the northwest Pacific. The plan failed to meet Secretary Wilson's demand for economy. It was reworked in Washington and resubmitted to the Secretary in December.[15]

Reorganization as approved early in 1957 made the Pacific Command the single unified command directly responsible to the Joint Chiefs of Staff, with the Navy serving as executive agent. Under CINCPAC were three major component commands: United States Army, Pacific (USARPAC), United States Pacific Fleet (PACFLT), and Pacific Air Forces (PACAF), each headed by a commander in chief. According to CINCPAC instructions, PACFLT and PACAF were to perform air tasks on a mutually supporting basis. Only three subordinate unified commands remained. The Commander, Fifth Air Force, assumed responsibility as Commander, United States Forces, Japan, and received a joint staff but had no unified operational responsibilities. The Commanding General, Eighth Army, headed United States Forces in Korea and also served as Commander in Chief, United Nations Command. The Taiwan Defense Command continued unchanged. In the Philippines, Ryukyus, and Marianas-Bonin, CINCPAC representatives coordinated matters. In countries where no U.S. operating forces were located, the MAAG chief was the CINCPAC representative. All MAAGs were directly responsible to CINCPAC.[16]

On the 1st of June, General Kuter opened his Headquarters Pacific Air Forces at Hickam AFB, consolidating for the first time USAF tactical forces in the Pacific and Far East areas under a single commander. Unity of command of all theater air power was nonetheless missing. Not only did PACAF and PACFLT have to cooperate on air tasks, but Admiral Stump — not Kuter — had the responsibility to develop indigenous air forces. Kuter could just advise Stump whether assistance programs squared with U.S. policies and objectives. In Kuter's view, indigenous air forces in Southeast Asia were hardly being helped to grow in harmony with USAF objectives. That is, the forces were not prepared to cope with internal subversion, to give limited defense against overt external aggression, and — perhaps most important — to offer suitable bases for U.S. air units that might be committed operationally. National air forces were being equipped with slow, conventional aircraft for combating insurgency. Air facilities that USAF jet aircraft could use in time of emergency were generally lacking.[17]

U.S. COMMAND PROBLEMS IN THE PACIFIC

(Left) Gen. Laurence S. Kuter
(Above) Gen. Thomas D. White

Kuter instructed the commanders of the Fifth and Thirteenth Air Forces in August 1957 to act as "rallying points" for informal discussion with indigenous air leaders. In November he invited air attachés and MAAG-Air representatives to a conference in Hawaii, and urged them to work together to create a common purpose in the "packets of democratic air power" forming in Southeast Asia. Improving air facilities ranked high on his agenda.[18]

Planning for the possible deployment of U.S. forces during the early months of 1958, the Commander in Chief, Pacific Air Forces, conceived of the mobile strike force. It would depart its home base within 24 hours after receiving an execution order, and engage in 15 days of self-supporting combat in Southeast Asia.[19] Since General Kuter wanted Thirteenth Air Force to have a dominant role in SEA air activities, he charged Maj. Gen. Thomas S. Moorman (who became Thirteenth's commander on March 4) to take command of the PACAF Mobile Strike Force when it deployed through Clark Air Base. The force included three troop carrier squadrons and one combat airlift support unit from the 315th Air Division (Combat Cargo); a fighter squadron, a bomber squadron, a reconnaissance task unit with photo processing cell, and half of an air refueling squadron from Fifth Air Force; one fighter squadron from Thirteenth Air Force; and a search and rescue detachment from the 31st Air Rescue Squadron of Air Rescue Service (Pacific). Clark Air Base was to furnish logistic support, and Thirteenth Air Force was empowered to draw on PACAF resources to establish detachments at forward air bases.[20]

Because commitment of this mobile strike force would reduce the general war deterrent elsewhere, Tactical Air Command (TAC) began to alert in the United States a composite air strike force for rapid global deployment, mainly to back up an immediate response by PACAF to aggression.[21]

During April 1958 the PACAF mobile strike force concept was tested in a SEATO exercise in Thailand against a simulated land aggressor force. For the first time in a SEATO exercise, nuclear weapons were inserted into the scenario. One observer, Lt. Gen. Frederic H. Smith, Jr., Fifth Air Force commander, believed it vital to interdict an enemy land force by air. Upon returning to Japan, he directed a staff study on the use of nuclear weapons if the Chinese invaded Southeast Asia.[22] In contrast, CINCPAC regarded forward defense in the Pacific as resting upon the twin pillars of strong mobile U.S. forces and of allied ones strengthened by American military assistance programs.[23]

The Department of Defense Reorganization Act of 1958 markedly broadened CINCPAC's authority as a unified commander. Army, Navy, and Air Force units previously allocated to him were now under his "full operational command." The roles of the military departments and of the component commanders were confined to the administration and support of Army, Navy, or Air Force units assigned to the unified commanders. A new CINCPAC, Adm. Harry D. Felt — an experienced naval aviator whose exceptionally long tenure was to last from July 31, 1958, through June 1964 — would exercise operational command through his component commanders or through the commanders of subordinate unified commands.[24]

Responsible for the immense area of the Pacific and its islands — excluding the Aleutians and the Bering Sea, but including Japan, Korea, Southeast Asia, and the eastern part of the Indian Ocean — Admiral Felt as CINCPAC was comparable to a theater commander in World War II. All the U.S. armed forces in that region were under him, and Vietnam was one of his obligations. Headquartered at Pearl Harbor, he also had at Hawaii the major subordinate commands of USARPAC, PACFLT, and PACAF, each headed by a component commander. Logistic and support forces, subordinate unified or triservice commanders, area representatives, and military assistance advisory groups like the one in Vietnam were also under him. His mission was to defend the United States against attack and "to support and advance United States policy and interests in the Pacific Command area."[25]

An advocate of the twin-pillar strategy, Admiral Felt perceived the separation between U.S. strategic planning and military assistance programs. The remedy involved, on the one hand, completing a CINCPAC contingency concept for Southeast Asia as a whole and, on the other hand, relating each country program to the entire strategy. A joint U.S. task force, he believed, should respond to aggression in Southeast Asia. He accordingly arranged for Marine forces on Okinawa to become the nucleus of a permanent CINCPAC Joint Task Force (JTF) 116. Since Marines would be airlifted to meet an emergency, the initial commander of this force was to be a Marine officer. When Army reinforcements arrived by air and sea, command was to pass to an Army officer.

PACAF designated the Thirteenth Air Force commander to head the air component of JTF 116 in order to establish his authority over affairs in Southeast Asia.[26]

During the autumn of 1958, Admiral Felt began to show the MAAGs how to relate their programs to regional as well as to country needs.[27] PACAF's major task was to build air facilities and an air operating environment in Southeast Asia. General Kuter and Lt. Gen. William F. McKee, vice commander of Air Materiel Command, felt that aviation projects of the Military Assistance Program (MAP) and of the International Cooperation Administration, Central Intelligence Agency (CIA), were oriented to individual countries. They saw no reason why these projects could not be loosely connected to regional defense as a whole. Better relations between PACAF and MAAG-Air personnel, they believed, would ensure that petroleum, oil, and lubricants (POL), ammunition, ground-to-air communications, fire trucks, refueling vehicles, and other essentials would be in place. Maintained by indigenous air forces, these services would be available for USAF use if necessary.[28] In June 1959 the MAAGs received from CINCPAC the first of a series of lists setting forth the priorities for accomplishing projects of this nature.[29]

But coordination between CINCPAC contingency planning against an overt aggression and individual country assistance programs continued to be inadequate. For example, the latter were not designed or funded to build facilities that could be used by USAF units. These projects were the responsibility of the Department of Defense. The Office of the Assistant Secretary of Defense for International Security Affairs, which reviewed assistance programs, was often compelled to delete projects for indigenous military forces in Southeast Asia that could not be justified according to the law. The MAAGs also hesitated to recommend projects warranted only by U.S. interest. In Laos, for instance, it was "extremely difficult to explain why you need an 8,000-foot heavy duty runway, flat concrete, and sweepers to go with it in a country that uses Gooney Birds."[30]

Another set of programs sprang from the Army orientation of the MAAGs. For example, aviation equipment obtainable through military assistance programs was relatively high-priced and competed with projects desired by the Army. After visiting Pacific areas in 1959, Maj. Gen. Donald R. Hutchinson, USAF assistant for mutual security, found that Army officers held 15 of 23 worldwide MAAG chief positions. This, he suggested, resulted in unbalanced recommendations from the field. The Air Force sought a more equitable manning ratio, but it would take several years to bring about changes.[31]

Despite these difficulties, General White (who had replaced General Twining as Chief of Staff) wished PACAF to exert a strong influence on air matters throughout the Pacific, to include assistance programs. Soon after Gen. Emmett O'Donnell became Commander in Chief, PACAF, on August 1, 1959, MAAG-Air representatives were allowed to deal directly with the Air Materiel Force Pacific Area. Amendments to USAF manuals in September and November 1959 permitted PACAF to administer contracted technical services for the military assistance program. In February 1960 a change in a USAF regulation directed all communications on air logistic matters to be routed through PACAF, and a revision of a DOD directive on military assistance instructed unified commanders to draw upon the advice of component commanders. What this meant, White reminded O'Donnell on March 25, was O'Donnell's growing role in the air aspects of military assistance. "To an increasing degree," White wrote, "the capability of MAP air forces must be oriented toward complementing the USAF war effort, and your active participation in MAP planning toward that end is urged."[32]

By spring of 1960, General O'Donnell had gained some informal influence in military assistance matters, but no more than advisory authority. His advice was not regularly sought after nor was it always accepted when volunteered. Essentially, PACAF could have little impact on military assistance programs because it had no official part in starting, programming, and carrying out country projects. Through communications to the MAAG-Air sections, which were authorized to give technical support, PACAF views could be inserted into assistance deliberations. All proposals, however, required MAAG chief approval before submission to CINCPAC. The PACAF commander in chief as advisor could submit assistance proposals direct to CINCPAC, but these were invariably referred to the MAAG chief for comment. Though Air Force headquarters looked to O'Donnell for information on military assistance programs, he was outside the relevant command channel. A case in point was the construction programs handled for CINCPAC by the Navy's Bureau of Pacific Docks. Responsible Air Force officers in the field found it hard to get specific facts about the exact status of these projects.[33]

As matters stood in 1960, the Southeast Asia Mutual Defense Assistance Program activities in progress since 1954 had failed to fulfill emerging requirements for internal country defense or for cooperative regional defense. On the whole, little stress had been given to developing indigenous air capabilities despite the rather large allocation of efforts, funds, and manpower to indigenous ground forces. The country air forces in Southeast Asia remained small and lacked sufficient personnel with basic skills to achieve rapid expansion. None had well-organized systems for operations and training, supply and maintenance, intelligence and communications-electronics, or civil engineering.[34] But organizational arrangements were in process of change.

V. Strained Civil-Military Relations in South Vietnam 1957-1960

President Diem visited Washington in May 1957. Among other matters, he wished American support for an army of 170,000 men and ten divisions. Although Elbridge Durbrow, Ambassador to Vietnam, believed that a military establishment this large would be a drain on the Vietnamese economy, President Eisenhower seemed to give tacit approval when he and Diem issued a joint communiqué. The two countries would continue to work for a peaceful unification of Vietnam, and the United States would support South Vietnam against communist encroachment.

By 1958 the Army of the Republic of Vietnam was a force of 150,000 men organized into seven infantry divisions, one small brigade, and five territorial regiments. Diem had released the army from internal security duties to permit intensive field training. General Williams, the MAAG chief, was confident that these troops could deter North Vietnam from orthodox military attack. They could delay an invasion for fifteen days before falling back to Da Nang, where they could hold out for thirty days more. Presumably, outside assistance would have arrived by then to launch a counteroffensive or to defend the Saigon-Mekong Delta area.[1]

But whether the Vietnamese ground forces could eliminate subversion and insurgency had yet to be seen.

While extraordinary priority was given to developing the army, only passing attention was accorded the Vietnamese Air Force, for it was regarded as incapable of playing a substantial role in larger SEATO operations. Instead, it was to deal with minor operations, mainly to give tactical support to ground activity in the country through airlift, paradrops, visual and photo reconnaissance, and medical evacuation.[2]

Planning for the Vietnamese Air Force had begun in January 1955, when General Collins, focusing chiefly on the Vietnamese army, explained that South Vietnam would rely for the most part on SEATO air support. The Vietnamese Air Force was to have an initial strength of 3,000 men organized in two liaison squadrons and one air transport squadron — "a small Air Force that will be used for liaison purposes, observation, and adjustment of fire, that kind of thing." Later, another transport squadron and a fighter squadron were to be added.[3]

Few MAAG spaces were allocated to USAF advisors, for the French were to organize and train the Vietnamese Air Force. U.S. aircraft deliveries to Vietnam in August 1955 under the Mutual Defense Assistance Program equipped the Vietnamese Air Force with aircraft and materiel released by the French —twenty-eight F-8F fighter-bombers, thirty-five C-47 transports, and sixty L-19 planes. When the French returned excess H-19 helicopters to American custody, they were transferred to Vietnam for airlift and air rescue missions.[4]

Because French officers had commanded Vietnamese air units, Vietnamese pilots gained little command experience. Vietnamese army officers were therefore permitted to transfer to high-level air force posts. Despite difficulties in securing sufficient qualified personnel, VNAF units were created. The 1st Air Transport Squadron came into being at Tan Son Nhut on July 1, 1955, with C-47s. It was organized a year later as the 1st Air Transport Group consisting of the 1st and 2nd Air Transport Squadrons and thirty-two C-47s. The Vietnamese took over the Nha Trang training center on July 7, 1955, and using L-19s formed the 1st and 2nd Liaison Squadrons. The French conducted an F-8F transition course at Cap Saint Jacques (Vung Tau) Airfield, and on June 1, 1956, the 1st Fighter Squadron was born at Bien Hoa and assigned twenty-five F-8Fs. Apart from these aircraft afforded by military assistance funds, the Vietnamese Air Force operated a special air mission squadron at Tan Son Nhut having one L-26 Aero Commander light transport, three C-47s, and three Beechcraft C-45s. Created without helicopters at Tan Son Nhut on June 1, 1957, the 1st Helicopter Squadron flew with the French unit that served the International Control Commission. When the French left in April 1958, they gave their ten excess H-19s to the Vietnamese.[5]

While the French presence officially ended in April 1956, the Vietnamese government continued to contract with France for Air Force training. This arrangement left the USAF officers assigned to MAAG with few duties. They advised when requested to do so, tried to stay abreast of programs, and underwent some special training in the United States. When the French turned over the depot at Bien Hoa to the Vietnamese and suddenly withdrew their supply advisors, Air Force personnel informally filled the vacuum. In November 1956 the French agreed to relinquish their training functions to USAF advisors, and after 1957 Diem refrained from renewing training contracts with France. On June 1, 1957, complete responsibility for Vietnamese aviation assistance passed to the United States.[6]

American advisors discovered that Vietnamese air officers were fairly good pilots, yet young and relatively inexperienced. Very few appeared to have mastered basic concepts of how to employ aircraft against any enemy. Consequently the Vietnamese army dominated the Joint General Staff and frequently President Diem himself directed air missions. Diem preferred airborne operations over air strikes, for the latter often endangered innocent people. Above all, he favored ground operations.[7]

Weak in command and staff experience, the Vietnamese Air Force suffered especially in logistic support. Teams from the Southern Air Materiel Area Pacific, based in the Philippines during 1957-58, converted French systems to USAF procedures. Still the F-8Fs, — old Navy fighters worn out when the French transferred them — presented insoluble problems. The Vietnamese possessed limited maintenance skills, and spare parts were in short supply. In October 1958, when word came that armed T-28 trainers would replace the

STRAINED CIVIL-MILITARY RELATIONS IN SOUTH VIETNAM, 1957-1960

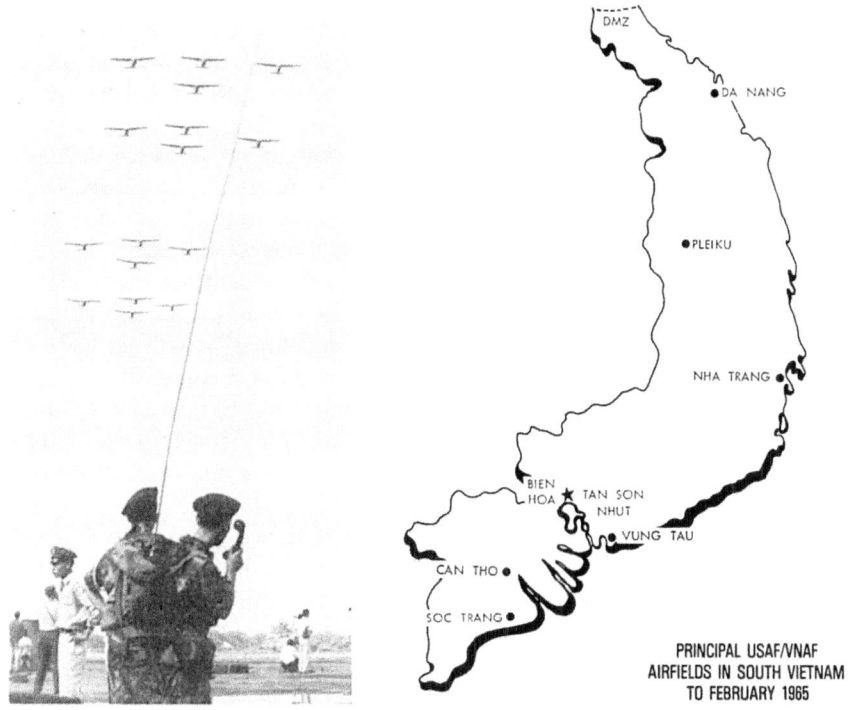

PRINCIPAL USAF/VNAF
AIRFIELDS IN SOUTH VIETNAM
TO FEBRUARY 1965

L-19s of the
Vietnamese Air Force.

A USAF Sikorsky H-19 helicopter
at Tan Son Nhut Air Base.

THE ADVISORY YEARS

F-8Fs, the Vietnamese were disappointed. They wanted jet aircraft because the Thais, Filipinos, and Chinese Nationalists had them. But the Geneva accords prohibited the introduction of jets and, on the ground of maintenance alone, MAAG felt that the Vietnamese establishment was not sophisticated enough to handle them.[8]

By mid-1956 American aid built a 7,200-foot runway at Tan Son Nhut, South Vietnam's international airport. The U.S. International Cooperation Administration next started work on another concrete runway, this one 10,000 feet long. Though the French in 1953-54 had laid a NATO-standard 7,800-foot asphalt runway at Da Nang, there were no runway lights or maintenance buildings. The depot at Bien Hoa featured permanent warehouses and hangars, but its pierced-steel runways could not be greatly expanded. The French had also operated a 5,900-foot pierced-steel runway at Cap Saint Jacques. Even so, the airfield was stripped of necessary facilities at the time F-8F transition training ended. At all of these airfields, the Vietnamese Air Force looked to the Vietnamese army for air base maintenance, ordnance, quartermaster, signal, and other specialized support.[9]

Yet all seemed to be going smoothly enough. Secretary of State Dulles could say in 1958 that the communist process "of trying to pick up one country after another has been pretty well brought to a stop by our collective defense treaties around the world which give notice that the Soviets cannot attack one without everybody coming to its defense." In other words, the American threat of massive retaliation and the collective free world defensive alliances were preserving the peace in Southeast Asia.[10]

In South Vietnam there was incipient trouble. Certain conditions enhanced enemy efforts to disrupt life. The abolition of elected village councils in June 1956, the use of a compulsory labor as a tax in kind, experiments in forced resettlement, maladroit attempts to turn peasants into landholders, and other measures promoted discontent in the countryside. The absence of police in many rural areas, a scarcity of civil servants on local levels, and the inability of new and hastily organized paramilitary forces to substitute for an effective constabulary badly handicapped the Saigon government in dealing with guerrillas who exploited dissatisfactions of one sort or another. By 1958 many persons wedded to the unification of Vietnam under control of the North were ready "to launch immediately an armed struggle" to sustain the communist movement and to secure its forces in the south.[11]

In September 1958 North Vietnam proposed to South Vietnam an understanding on peaceful relations. The Diem government declined the offer because communist guerrillas in South Vietnam had kidnapped 236 persons and assassinated 193 that year. Political killings in the south would continue to mount, and the local communists or Viet Cong would step up attacks on South Vietnamese armed forces.[12]

The Central Committee of the Lao Dong Party in North Vietnam convened in May 1959. It decided "to continue the national democratic revolution in South Vietnam" and "to use force to overthrow the feudalist imperialist regime in order to establish a revolutionary democratic situation and create the conditions for the peaceful reunification of the Fatherland."[13]

This signaled the beginning of warfare in South Vietnam and the resumption of warfare in Laos, both of which coincided with Chinese probes across the border of India.[14] The People's Army of Vietnam, commonly referred to as the North Vietnamese army, sent several combat units to drive the Laotian military from the border between Laos and South Vietnam. In their wake came transportation units to set up relay stations for a buildup and infiltration into the two countries.[15]

The Viet Cong opened guerrilla war in September 1959, when they ambushed two Vietnamese army companies in the marshy Plain of Reeds southwest of Saigon. In October they attacked a small force in Kien Phong Province. In Viet Cong words, "the armed struggle was launched."[16] Hanoi's policy directives, the growth of North Vietnamese army activities, and a marked increase in confirmed infiltrations into South Vietnam made clear Hanoi's declaration of war on the Republic of Vietnam and the commitment of its political and military apparatus to that end.[17]

To American authorities in Saigon, optimistic assessments obscured the full dimension of the threat. While his government was apparently stimulating economic growth and internal stability, President Diem closely controlled its intelligence activities, often for his own political purposes. He had little knowledge of Viet Cong leadership, tactics, organization, logistics, and plans.[18] As a result, U.S. assistance programs in 1959 and 1960 were oriented less toward internal threat in South Vietnam than toward the overt threat presented by communist activities in Laos and particularly in the sparsely populated central highlands of Vietnam adjacent to the Laotian border.

Diem had been interested in the latter area since 1957, when he conceived a program for building "agrovilles" or "new communities" around Pleiku, Kontum, and Ban Me Thuot. Without American assistance funds, Diem settled farmers there on new agricultural lands so as to strengthen security. By February 1959 he had established twenty-eight outposts, and on July 7 he announced an expanded program to create more "prosperity and density centers" in exposed rural areas.[19]

In February 1960 the Government of Vietnam wanted trailwatchers and commandos along the border to protect these new settlements.

Accordingly, the Vietnamese ranger training center was organized at Da Nang. At this time the Viet Cong were thought to number 3,000-5,000 full-time elite and regular troops, plus intelligence agents, recruiters, terrorists, service troops, and part-time guerrillas. Because the authority to keep in South Vietnam personnel of the Temporary Equipment Recovery Mission who augmented the MAAG was expiring, the United States decided in May to double the MAAG component to 685 men. This was done in spite of North Vietnam's protest to the International Control Commission. Several U.S. Army Special Forces teams arrived during the month, and Diem formed a Vietnamese ranger force with a projected strength of 10,000 men.[20]

THE ADVISORY YEARS

By then the Joint Chiefs of Staff had directed the senior American officials in Saigon and CINCPAC to draw up a broad counterinsurgency plan as a guide to the Diem government and to the small MAAG in South Vietnam. CINCPAC's plan contained among its key provisions a Vietnamese command and control system to integrate military and civil counterinsurgency operations. A bona fide military field command might end President Diem's meddling in operational affairs. Also needed was first-rate, centrally controlled intelligence and counterintelligence within the Vietnamese government. Ambassador Durbrow believed these to be all-important. The problem was to persuade Diem to approve and implement them.[21]

Other proposed measures included better use of the Vietnamese forces to fight guerrillas without lessening their ability to meet an overt attack; improved governmental financial procedures; border and coastal patrols to stop infiltration and outside support of the anti-government guerrillas; better communications nets; more attention to civil affairs and psychological warfare; closer planning for economic growth and political stability; and moving the Vietnamese Civil Guard from the Ministry of Interior to the Ministry of Defense.

Army Lt. Gen. Lionel C. McGarr became the MAAG chief on August 31, 1960. He and Ambassador Durbrow elaborated the broad plan and worked with Vietnamese officials during the autumn and winter of 1960. In October General McGarr recommended and Admiral Felt concurred in enlarging the Vietnamese army from 150,000 to 170,000 men. Durbrow objected. A bigger army, he thought, would bring economic hardship to the country. He also desired to use the prospect of a greater military force as pressure on Diem for political reforms.

To ease counterinsurgency operations, Diem transferred the Civil Guard to the Ministry of Defense in November, and in the following month MAAG took responsibility for training and equipping it. Shortages in military assistance funds limited support to 32,000 instead of the planned 68,000 Civil Guard members.[22]

To USAF officers the measures for Vietnamese stability were, as Maj. Gen. Theodore R. Milton, Thirteenth Air Force commander said, "entirely dominated by classic ground-force thinking."[23] The Vietnamese Air Force had obsolescent aircraft and lacked trained pilots and technically qualified support personnel. Diem had worsened the tight personnel situation in August 1959 by terminating contracts with French air crews and service technicians who operated the Air Vietnam commercial airline. He replaced them with military flight crews and mechanics.[24]

After a mysterious crash in August, President Diem grounded all the obsolete F-8Fs of the 1st Fighter Squadron, then in September asked for jets to replace them. He pointed to the U.S. jets given to Thailand and the Philippines. Sympathetic, Admiral Felt had two T-33 trainers and four RT-33 photo-recon aircraft added in the military assistance program funding for fiscal year (FY) 1961. These would be the beginning of a jet as well as a reconnaissance force. But the planes, while remaining pledged, were not delivered because the Geneva accords prohibited introducing jets into the country. To replace the F-8Fs, the first notion was to make AD-4s available from Navy stocks. The Navy, however, could not forecast continued supplies for these obsolete planes. Thus, the program was amended early in 1960 to include AD-6 aircraft still operational in the U.S. Fleet. The first six arrived in Vietnam in September 1960, and twenty-five more were delivered in May 1961.[25]

When in late 1960 some Vietnamese army rangers were ready for field operations, the H-19B helicopters handed down by the French to the 1st Helicopter Squadron were worn out. MAAG secured approval for a hurried shipment of eleven H-34Cs from the Army. They were airlifted to Saigon without renovation, four in December and the others soon afterward.[26]

The AD-6s and H-34s had no immediate impact on operations. The high aircraft out-of-commission rates stemmed from poor maintenance and supply at Bien Hoa. Also to blame was the long pipeline time for processing spare parts requisitions through USAF logistic channels to Army and Navy sources. Yet between August and October 1960, the 1st Fighter Squadron flew twenty combat sorties, the L-19 liaison planes logged 917 combat hours, the helicopters accumulated 166 hours on operational missions, and C-47s of the 1st Air Transport Group flew thirty-two sorties.[27]

Only five airfields were usable for AD-6 operations; no communications network served dispersed airfields; and President Diem believed that air units could not operate effectively from dispersed locations distant from depot supplies. The Vietnamese Air Force was oriented to the support of the Vietnamese army operations, but the ground troops gave little attention to spotting targets suitable for air strikes. About ninety percent of the ground targets were located by Vietnamese Air Force observers who flew in L-19s, based at the same fields as the fighters.

Approval for aircraft to strike ground targets was required from province chief, regional commander, the Joint General Staff, and sometimes Diem himself. As a final guaranty against bombing mistakes that might hurt the government's image, politically cleared and technically competent observers had to mark approved targets before air strikes could be launched against them — a rule of engagement reportedly directed by Diem.

A USAF team visiting South Vietnam reported, "The high level approval required for on-call fighter strikes, along with poor communications and/or procedures for requesting strikes, builds in excessive delays for efficient use of tactical air effort. This is particularly true in view of the hit-and-run guerrilla tactics of the Viet Cong."[28]

Internal subversion in Southeast Asia still seemed minor in 1960. In comparison, China appeared to be threatening stability and peace. To counter this, the United States continued to rely on the presence of SEATO and on the credibility of its own treaty commitments in the area to discourage Chinese adventurism.[29]

While the Chinese cited Nikolai Lenin to prove that war was useful for extending communism, Premier Nikita Khrushchev spoke to the United Nations General Assembly in September on "the grave danger of colonial wars growing into a new world war." Sino-Soviet doctrinal divergencies came under debate in November 1960 in Moscow. The apparent outcome was a compromise announced on January 6, 1961, when Khrushchev noted that "world wars" and "local wars that would grow into a world thermonuclear war" were to be avoided while "national liberation wars" through which colonial peoples could attain independence were "not only admissible but inevitable" and merited full communist support.[30]

Meanwhile, the Lao Dong Party in Hanoi had announced on September 10, 1960, the formation in South Vietnam of "a broad national united front" of workers, peasants, and soldiers dedicated to overthrowing the Diem government. Thereafter, the tempo of Viet Cong infiltration and insurgency quickened. Viet Cong units of 100-300 men began to mount raids around Saigon. Even more serious, Diem charged in October that attacks in the Kontum-Pleiku area involved regular North Vietnamese military units operating out of Laos. This was aggression in the formal sense.[31]

The inability of the Diem government to deal with the Viet Cong sparked dissatisfaction within the Vietnamese army and led to an attempted coup on November 11. A paratroop force seized government centers in Saigon, prepared to attack the presidential palace, and called for Diem's resignation on the grounds of his autocratic rule, his nepotism, and his ineffective fight against communism. The chief of staff of the Joint General Staff led loyal troops into the capital and subdued the rebels on the following day.[32]

Although Diem's brother and political adviser, Ngo Dinh Nhu, announced the introduction of some reforms, Diem remained reluctant to decentralize his authoritarian controls. Instead of delegating authority to military commanders as Admiral Felt and General McGarr had recommended, Diem sought to enhance his position by fragmenting and dividing the military hierarchy. Diem made army regional commanders (later corps tactical zone commanders) independent of one another but each responsible to him. Since he appointed and removed province chiefs, many of whom were military officers, Diem frequently gave them command over army units operating within their provinces. Hence the field commanders looked to two superiors, their next higher military commander in the chain of command and the politico-military province chief. These tangled lines checked the quick movement and close control of units and reserves, including the employment of Vietnamese Air Force units. But Diem insisted on tight control of operations, chiefly those of the air force, because he feared a revolt or a coup against his government.

There was also evidence that the Viet Cong benefited from security leaks at high levels. At times Viet Cong fed false information into the intelligence system to prompt bombardment of innocent targets. Now and then a province chief requested air strikes for his own private purpose, for example, in another province whose chief he disliked. Within this climate of suspicion, local officials had to go on record as approving air strikes flown in their areas of authority. All this spawned complexities, hesitations, and delays.[33]

STRAINED CIVIL-MILITARY RELATIONS IN SOUTH VIETNAM, 1957-1960

THE ADVISORY YEARS

Apparently viewing the November coup attempt as proof of massive discontent within the Republic of Vietnam Armed Forces, Hanoi swiftly set up a shadow government in the south. The National Front for Liberation of South Vietnam (NFLSVN) was formally established on December 20, 1960. Even though it embraced a broad range of non-communist and nationalist opposition to President Diem, the Lao Dong Party in North Vietnam ordered its operations.[34]

In Saigon, Diem and Nhu felt that American officials had favored the November coup, and relations with Ambassador Durbrow grew more and more strained. There was also persistent discontent in the Vietnamese armed forces, for Diem's promise to liberalize the government had built up hope among officers. His refusal to do so produced deep disappointment.[35]

By this time, warfare had erupted within neighboring Laos. On December 14, 1960, CINCPAC declared an alert for all units to comprise Joint Task Force 116 if the United States decided to intervene. Thailand was willing to transfer ten T-6 aircraft to Laos in exchange for more modern T-37 jets from the United States. President Eisenhower favored a SEATO reaction in Laos and Admiral Felt suggested offensive air action, but the SEATO allies were less than enthusiastic. Upon direction from Washington, Felt declared a higher alert for JTF 116 on December 31, and he requested a C-130 transportation squadron from the United States. With the arrival of the 773d Troop Carrier Squadron at Clark on the 2d of January, the task force was fully prepared to assist the Laotian government.[36]

Three days later, President Charles De Gaulle made clear France's refusal to take part in a SEATO intervention. As instructed from Washington, CINCPAC reduced the alert on January 6. The State Department said on the 7th that the United States would work with other free nations to pursue "whatever measures seem most promising."[37]

Dispatches from Southeast Asia in 1959 and 1960 competed for attention with louder signals from regions traditionally more vital to the United States. In January 1959 Fidel Castro and his guerrillas became the Government of Cuba. As the months passed, Castro's orientation and outlook grew ever more Marxist, a development that evoked the whole complex of policies and emotions arising out of the Monroe Doctrine. At the same time, Premier Khrushchev repeatedly drew attention to the precarious status of West Berlin, a small island in the sea of Soviet-dominated Eastern Europe.

In Southeast Asia, along the northwestern frontier of the Republic of Vietnam and along the entire western frontier of North Vietnam was the Kingdom of Laos. This geographically vulnerable, largely unadministered, politically fragile country was an obvious avenue of approach for infiltrators from North Vietnam to the northern provinces and central highlands of South Vietnam. Given the difficulties of the Laotian government in making its will effective, a neutral Laos seemed to many U.S. officials only somewhat less a danger to Diem's government than did a communist Laos.

STRAINED CIVIL-MILITARY RELATIONS IN SOUTH VIETNAM, 1957-1960

All of these problems were weighed by officials who were very much aware that President Eisenhower's tenure would end in January 1961. As President Eisenhower later explained, he wanted to make no major commitment in the closing weeks of his administration that would obligate his successor to a predetermined course of action. Briefing President-elect John F. Kennedy on the 19th of January, Eisenhower emphasized that Laos as the key to all of Southeast Asia must be defended. If the allies failed to do so, he said, "our unilateral intervention would be our last desperate hope."[38] What happened in Laos, of course, had meaning for Vietnam.

Part Three:

The Kennedy Years

VI. Initial Challenges and Actions

President Kennedy took office two weeks after Premier Khrushchev announced Soviet support for what he termed "wars of national liberation." These were neither the nuclear exchanges that had preoccupied American military thinkers nor limited wars like Korea. Rather, a war of national liberation consisted of subversion and guerrilla actions at a level far below that likely to trigger nuclear retaliation. Such a war could nevertheless erode the will and power of the target state until it was helpless.

The President tried to determine the real import of the Khrushchev doctrine and the exact nature of the communist threat to Southeast Asia. Realizing that the United States had few troops specially trained and equipped for counterinsurgency warfare, he directed Secretary of Defense Robert S. McNamara on February 1, 1961, to increase them. On March 28 Kennedy asked the Congress to give him the means to deal with "small externally supported bands of men." Pointing to nonnuclear, limited, guerrilla warfare as the most constant threat to free world security since 1945, the President wanted to be able to respond to this kind of aggression with nonnuclear weapons and to "help train local forces to be equally effective" against their enemies. The main burden of defense against overt attack, subversion, and guerrilla warfare had to rest on local populations and their military forces. Still, the United States needed strong and highly mobile units ready to combat the so-called lesser forms of conflict.[1]

Pursuing this aim in June, President Kennedy specified that the Joint Chiefs' "responsibility for the defense of the nation in the cold war [was] similar to that which they have in conventional hostilities." Air Force officials assumed that the new technique was to rank in importance with "preparation for conventional warfare." This belief seemed justified in July when the President transferred from the Central Intelligence Agency to the Department of Defense the responsibility for preparing and mounting large paramilitary operations, wholly or partially covert, requiring many militarily trained personnel and the type of equipment or military experience peculiar to the armed forces.[2]

Spurring these actions was the worsening situation in Laos. Fighting there between the government forces and the pro-communist Pathet Lao intensified. Both sides had outside support, alternating victories and defeats, and several coups d'etat had taken place. American concern centered not only on Laos but on the possible adverse consequences in Vietnam. During the first two months of his administration, President Kennedy "probably spent more time on Laos than on anything else."[3]

Events in Cuba, climaxing at the Bay of Pigs in April, shaped the President's thinking. Urged to at least commit U.S. air power in Laos, Kennedy replied, "I just don't think we ought to be involved in Laos, particularly where we might find ourselves fighting millions of Chinese troops in the jungles. In any event, I don't see how we can make any move in Laos, which is 5,000 miles away, if we don't make a move in Cuba, which is only 90 miles away."[4]

The Soviets had called on April 4 for a cease-fire in Laos and an international conference to resolve the problems. The Joint Chiefs were troubled. Diplomatic negotiations would probably result in a neutralized Laos, perhaps eventually a communist Laos, because SEATO had failed to curb the obvious aggression there. Laos behind the Iron Curtain would expose Thailand and South Vietnam to further communist infiltration. Most of the 12,000 Viet Cong guerrillas in South Vietnam had come through the Laotian panhandle or the thinly populated northeastern corner of Cambodia.[5]

So serious did affairs appear that Kennedy on April 20 changed the advisory military body in Laos to a Military Assistance Advisory Group. He ordered the MAAG members to put on their uniforms and work closely with the demoralized Laotian troops. At Camp Courtney, Okinawa, Joint Task Force 116 (it and its air component redesignated SEATO Field Forces) readied for action. Open U.S. commitment in Laos looked imminent until Great Britain joined the Soviet Union on the 24th in appealing for a cease-fire and an international conference in Geneva.[6]

The conference opened at Geneva in May, a time when retired General of the Army Douglas MacArthur advised President Kennedy against putting American ground forces on the mainland of Asia. If the United States intervened in Southeast Asia, he said, it must be ready to use nuclear weapons to meet a Chinese entry into the conflict. The Joint Chiefs of Staff categorically informed Defense Secretary McNamara that

> any intervention with United States forces in Laos, either unilaterally or under SEATO auspices, should be taken only after firm U.S. governmental decision to the effect that the United States is thereby prepared and committed to succeed in its military intervention regardless of the extent of possible consequent Communist escalation; this is an unequivocal position which is fundamental to United States military actions.[7]

To Secretary McNamara it seemed clear that the United States must soon decide whether or not to stand up and fight. Yet according to Army Chief of Staff Gen. George H. Decker, the United States could hardly hope to win a conventional war in Southeast Asia. General Decker suggested moving American troops into Thailand and South Vietnam to see if that would produce a cease-fire in Laos. But if the United States went into Laos, "we should go in to win, and that means Hanoi, China, and maybe even using nuclear bombs." Lacking enthusiasm for a ground war in Laos, Decker said later that

> this is the last place in the world I would like to see ... [U.S. forces] committed unless absolutely necessary.... If it were only the Pathet Lao that was involved, there would be no problem. But undoubtedly North Vietnamese would come in and probably the Chinese Communists and when they do, it is hard to predict where our commitment would stop.[8]

General Curtis E. LeMay, Air Force Chief of Staff, was dubious of U.S. policy on Laos, but he believed a cease-fire impossible without American military action. That meant nuclear weapons if the Chinese entered the conflict. General O'Donnell at PACAF estimated that his air forces could prosecute a "small war" in Laos with conventional weapons. He envisioned an enlarged conflict including North Vietnam or China as requiring a "truly massive increase" in U.S. ground and air forces.[9]

President Kennedy deferred sending U.S. troops into Laos, tried to salvage as much as possible from a cease-fire, and offered reassurances to Thailand and South Vietnam. The Geneva negotiations produced no solution, but at a summit meeting in Vienna on June 4, Khrushchev agreed with Kennedy's proposal —"we all get out of Laos" and have "a neutral and independent Laos under a government chosen by the Laotians." But as late as April 1962, the State Department would find it "very hard to prophesy what is going to happen in Laos."[10]

Part of the difficulties in dealing with a possible use of force, General LeMay believed, was due to President Kennedy's procedural habits and tendencies. The President seemed to depend on ad hoc committees in lieu of the Joint Chiefs, leading to vetoes, stalling, lengthy discussions, and too many people "in the act and making decisions in areas where they weren't competent." This approach to policy, LeMay believed, failed to recognize that "going to war is a very serious business and once you make that decision that you're going to do that, then you ought to be prepared to do just that."[11]

General LeMay's uneasiness with President Kennedy's methods came at a time when other international crises clamored for attention. The Soviets were again threatening allied rights of access to West Berlin, so Kennedy requested and the Congress authorized the call to active duty of more than 147,700 Army, Navy, Marine Corps, and Air Force personnel. Included were thirty-six squadrons and 26,575 members of the Air National Guard and the Air Force Reserve. On September 1 the Soviet Union broke the nuclear test moratorium of several years by exploding megatonic nuclear bombs in the atmosphere. The President instructed Defense Secretary McNamara to resume American nuclear tests.[12]

Though Laos overshadowed South Vietnam in SEA affairs during the first months of President Kennedy's administration, the fates of the two countries were intertwined. Soon after taking office the President considered plans to combat the insurgency in Vietnam. He agreed to enlarge the Republic of Vietnam Armed Forces by 20,000 men and to expand military training for the Civil Guard. In February he directed Ambassador Durbrow to secure President Diem's cooperation on these and other matters.[13]

In November 1960 President Eisenhower had strengthened the role of American Ambassadors in all countries. Each had "affirmative responsibility" for all U.S. activities, including military assistance. The Ambassador was to be informed on all that took place and to report "promptly to the President" whenever necessary. In May 1961 President Kennedy reiterated this instruction. However, he exempted American military forces in the field from the Ambassador's direct authority — they were responsible through military channels. In Southeast Asia CINCPAC, an area commander, reported to the Joint Chiefs of Staff, the Secretary of Defense, and the President. While the Ambassador was

THE ADVISORY YEARS

Courtesy: John F. Kennedy Library

Courtesy: U.S. Navy

(Upper left) W. Averell Harriman, Pres. Kennedy, and Dean Rusk.

(Above) Robert S. McNamara and Gen. Lyman L. Lemnitzer.

(Left) Members of the Vietnamese Self Defense Corps from Buon Enao

(Below) Female members of the Civil Defense Guard at Hao Cain.

outside this line, he was the Chief of Mission. He worked hand in glove with the military commander in the mutual exchange of information, the coordination of programs, and the formulation of policy.[14]

In early 1961, six Vietnamese Air Force squadrons were combat-ready —one AD-6 fighter, two C-47 transport, two L-19 liaison, and one H-19 helicopter. The fighter unit by March had upped its monthly sortie rate 200 percent, from 40 to 120.[15]

The Army of the Republic of Vietnam comprised seven infantry divisions, one airborne group, and nineteen separate battalions. Their limited combat readiness reflected "inexperienced leadership above the battalion level, inadequate logistical and technical service development, and other deficiencies of an organizational nature." The enduring need to divert troops to internal security missions interrupted training.[16]

Complementing the army were several paramilitary forces. The 68,000 men of the Civil Guard (later called Regional Forces) had been organized in 1955 and were controlled by the province chiefs. Since October 1960 under the Ministry of Defense, the Civil Guard could neither arrest nor investigate. Members had the mission of patrolling. The Self Defense Force of 40,000 men constituted a full-time home guard defending its members' villages, and it was under the district chiefs. The United States moved quickly in 1961 to arm and train these two forces so as to free the army from static defense missions.[17]

Against these forces and the general population, the Viet Cong had redoubled their campaign of terror during the first part of 1961, perhaps to disrupt presidential elections scheduled for April 9. The number of Viet Cong in South Vietnam swelled to around 14,000. By March the North Vietnamese army units in southern Laos seemed strong enough to push across the border and set up a "popular" government in the central highlands. If this took place, the Sino-Soviet bloc might pursue the technique used in Laos — recognize the shadow regime as the legitimate government of South Vietnam and furnish assistance. But what impressed President Kennedy above all were the assassinations. Sustained by North Vietnam, well-disciplined Viet Cong guerrillas in 1960 had killed over 4,000 civil officers, 2,000 state employees, and 2,000 police in South Vietnam.[18]

The elections in April were reasonably orderly, and President Diem received an overwhelming vote. With Diem's position as head of state thereby confirmed and apparently secure, President Kennedy sent Chairman of the Joint Chiefs of Staff General Lemnitzer and Under Secretary of State W. Averell Harriman to Saigon to support Ambassador Durbrow who was pressing Diem to make certain reforms. Calling on Diem, they urged him in particular to form a military field command and a central intelligence organization. Inasmuch as these creations might nurture potential political rivals, Diem found the decision hard to make. He did agree to try to upgrade the paramilitary forces, get better intelligence, start a junk navy to stop enemy infiltration by sea, establish internal security councils, decentralize his government, and undertake fiscal reforms.[19]

Afterwards Diem reactivated the National Internal Security Council, founded a National Intelligence Agency, and appointed a commander of the Army Field Forces who was to work closely with General McGarr, the MAAG chief, on counterinsurgency. Abolishing the military regional headquarters, Diem divided the country into three tactical zones and a special tactical zone for Saigon, the capital. The commanders were responsible to the Army Field Forces commander, and they were to conduct all antiguerrilla military operations. The tactical zones could be further segmented into subzones coinciding for the most part with provincial boundaries. In them the military chief might also be a provincial chief and therefore would be in both civil and military chains of command.[20]

On April 20, 1961, in Washington — one day after the Bay of Pigs invasion of Cuba collapsed — President Kennedy asked Deputy Secretary of Defense Roswell L. Gilpatric to draw up a comprehensive program. It was to cover military, social, and political actions, and be tailored to prevent a communist takeover in South Vietnam. The deputy Defense secretary swiftly organized an interagency committee and wrote a first-draft plan in about a week. His preface set the tone of the paper, "Come what may, the U.S. intends to *win* this battle." Gilpatric's military recommendations apparently aimed to hearten national policy after the Bay of Pigs and to affirm explicitly American resolve to pay the cost of commitments in Southeast Asia. The recommendations included the installation of radar surveillance in South Vietnam, which would involve the U.S. Air Force; increasing the MAAG so it could train and support 20,000 more Vietnamese soldiers, thus building the army to 170,000; supplying arms and training to the paramilitary forces; and furnishing equipment for a small naval force.

At a National Security Council meeting on the 29th, Kennedy approved several measures: establishing a combat development and test center in Vietnam, expanding civic action and economic development programs, augmenting the 685-man MAAG by approximately 100 advisors, and adding to the Military Assistance Program for FY 1961 a heavy radar facility to be sited near Da Nang to observe and report Soviet flights across the Laotian border.[21]

Meeting on May 4 with Senator J. William Fulbright, chairman of the foreign relations committee, Kennedy discussed the possibility of sending U.S. combat forces into South Vietnam. Probably as a result of this talk, the President told newsmen the next day that U.S. intervention would be inappropriate without prior discussions with Vietnamese leaders. The Air Force plans division informed General LeMay that the President's statement was "the first example of the type of over-all plan that the Air Force has advocated for some time." The division advised strong support. By May 10, however, the plans division was opposing premature commitment of U.S. forces to South Vietnam because it might "reduce pressure on Vietnam for initiative and forceful action," provoke the Chinese communists into intervening, and have a bad effect on American allies.[22]

INITIAL CHALLENGES AND ACTIONS

In contrast, JCS Chairman General Lemnitzer felt a sense of urgency. He frequently spoke of the possible "loss of Vietnam," termed the military threat extremely serious, and deplored the tendency of the U.S. government to waste time in quibbling over policy.[23]

At Secretary McNamara's request to consider the commitment of American forces, the Joint Chiefs on May 10 favored an immediate deployment to provide a visible and "significant" deterrent to North Vietnamese and Chinese intervention. They believed it would release Vietnamese armed forces from static missions and enable active counterinsurgency operations, help train Vietnamese forces, be a nucleus for a U.S. buildup in the case of allied SEATO operations, and show the firm intent of American policy in Southeast Asia. The JCS leaned toward dispatching two reinforced infantry battalions to the central highlands to set up and operate two division training centers for the Vietnamese army. Having U.S. combat forces in the country was bound to bolster Vietnamese morale.

Asked to estimate U.S. force requirements, Admiral Felt, CINCPAC, discussed the matter with his component commanders on May 11. To General O'Donnell, South Vietnam was so deficient in airfields and ground facilities that only a few turnaround B-57s and F-102s could operate from Tan Son Nhut for short periods.

Admiral Felt recommended the dispatch to Vietnam of one Army infantry division with supporting troops; eight B-57s for border surveillance, close support, and anti-Viet Cong operations; four F-102s for air defense; and possibly two or three jet reconnaissance aircraft. If American forces were committed, Felt suggested that the MAAG chief be designated Commander, United States Forces, Vietnam, and be charged with control, under CINCPAC direction, of all U.S. forces there.[24]

By then President Kennedy had decided against an open and substantial commitment of conventional U.S. combat troops. On May 11 he directed the Office of the Secretary of Defense (OSD) and the Joint Chiefs to continue studying potential U.S. task force structures for Vietnam and to assess the value and the cost of increasing the Vietnamese armed forces from 170,000 to 200,000 men. These actions were to signify "an intensified endeavor to win the struggle against communism and to further the social and economic advance of Vietnam" in cooperation with President Diem. The rationale, provided by the National Security Council, was "to prevent Communist domination in South Vietnam; to create in that country a viable and increasingly democratic society, and to initiate, on an accelerated basis, a series of mutually supporting actions of a military, political, economic, psychological and covert character designed to achieve this objective."[25]

On the same day, the President committed an Army Special Forces group of 400 men to Vietnam. Its task was to organize the Tribal Area Development Program to clear and hold certain Viet Cong-controlled areas, mainly along the land border. This was the beginning of the Civilian Irregular Defense Group, initially supervised by the Central Intelligence Agency. Raising, training, leading, and supporting irregular forces would hardly be possible without airlift, medical evacuation, and close air support. The Air Force would soon be involved.[26]

Also on May 11, the President sent Vice President Lyndon B. Johnson to Saigon to demonstrate continuing U.S. support for Diem. Johnson's visit was designed to strengthen Diem's position at home, to make him feel safe enough to delegate power to subordinates (chiefly to a functioning field force command), to encourage accelerated Vietnamese and American actions, and to give Diem confidence in the United States. Johnson carried a letter from Kennedy promising more U.S. assistance if Diem promoted the economic and political development of his country.[27]

Johnson and Diem discussed the question of committing U.S. forces to South Vietnam, and Johnson had the impression that "Asian leaders — at this time— do not want American troops involved in Southeast Asia other than on training missions." The Embassy confirmed this point of view. Diem would welcome American combat forces solely in the case of overt aggression.[28]

When Johnson asked Diem what he thought his country's military needs were, Diem said he would give a detailed answer later. He observed dryly that the Vietnamese were not "accustomed to being asked for our own views on our needs."[29] A communiqué issued on May 13 at the conclusion of their talks made no mention of committing U.S. forces.

Upon his return to Washington, the Vice President said he saw no need for American troops in Vietnam except to help the Vietnamese train their forces. The nations of Southeast Asia had to make decided efforts, with stronger American support, to develop their economic and political systems and to provide for their own defense. He passed on Diem's concern that the communists would employ the same strategy they had used in Laos — infiltration, aerial resupply, and establishment of a recognizable government. "Any help," Johnson said, "economic as well as military, we give less developed nations to secure and maintain their freedom must be part of a mutual effort. These nations cannot be saved by the United States alone. To the extent the southeast Asian nations are prepared to take the necessary measures to make our assistance effective, we can be — and must be — unstinting in our assistance."[30]

Deputy Defense Secretary Gilpatric's Committee on Vietnam consisted of members of the State and Defense Departments. On May 19 it proposed these objectives for American forces that might be deployed to Vietnam: deter the North Vietnamese and Chinese, release Vietnamese forces for fuller use in operations, train local troops, form a nucleus for future U.S. buildup, and demonstrate American firmness. The committee favored the founding of two training centers, each to be run by a reinforced U.S. infantry battalion, and the sending of minimal air and naval forces to stop infiltration and act against the insurgents. The Army urged deploying an infantry division plus special forces. The Air Force was reluctant to place combat units in a country where the major threat appeared to be insurgency and where the Vietnamese Air Force could afford the limited air support required by that threat.[31]

INITIAL CHALLENGES AND ACTIONS

Hoping to help the people of South Vietnam help themselves, President Kennedy sent to Admiral Felt and to Ambassador Frederick E. Nolting, Jr. (who had replaced Durbrow) thirty separate actions he wished carried out. The program encompassed: political activities to buttress Diem's confidence in the United States, to heighten his popular support at home, and to improve Vietnam's relations with its neighbors, chiefly Cambodia; economic measures to let Vietnam support larger military forces; and military proposals including the installation of a radar surveillance system, a 20,000-man expansion of the Vietnamese armed forces, more support for the Civil Guard and Self Defense Corps, and an augmented MAAG. The President also desired a stop to infiltration into South Vietnam and a facility to test new techniques against insurgency.[32]

Diem issued decrees to carry out the counterinsurgency measures proposed by the Americans, but the extent of his implementation was far from clear. He went on using command and intelligence agencies for political ends, mostly to maintain a balance among several local Vietnamese factions and their senior officers of the armed forces competing for favor and power.[33]

It soon became evident to Americans that the threat to Vietnam was more severe than had been suspected. At the summit in Vienna early in June 1961, Kennedy found Khrushchev willing to accept a neutralization of Laos but not of Vietnam. Reflecting upon this refusal, Secretary of State Dean Rusk later suggested that the United States should have said quite simply, "You can't have South Vietnam." Perhaps that would have prevented misunderstanding within the communist world of the American position on Southeast Asia.[34]

Although the Joint Chiefs and CINCPAC advocated deploying U.S. forces for combat in South Vietnam to counter the Viet Cong, the President put faith in his program of helping the Vietnamese. Yet there were warnings in June 1961 that "the prospects for stability and progress are not too bright," due to intensified communist warfare and "a lack of real popular support for Diem's government."[35]

In that month President Diem asked the United States to support a Vietnamese army of 270,000 (one airborne and fourteen infantry divisions). An expanded MAAG to operate training centers, he said, "would serve the dual purpose of providing an expression of the United States' determination to halt the tide of Communist aggression and of preparing our forces in the minimum of time."[36]

In response the Joint Chiefs on June 21 recommended building the Vietnamese armed forces to 200,000 men and adding "two division equivalents, including necessary Navy and Air Force augmentation." Gilpatric counseled deferral of this action until the earlier 20,000-man increase had been assimilated.[37]

To see if the South Vietnamese economy could sustain enlarged military forces, Kennedy sent a financial survey group headed by Dr. Eugene Staley to Saigon. Reporting in July, Staley favored further aid for Vietnam but warned against expecting military operations to achieve lasting results without economic progress. A free society and a self-sustaining economy in Vietnam gave the best basis of hope for the future.[38]

Military planners in Washington came to the same conclusion in July and August 1961. Adding to the Vietnamese armed forces or deploying two reinforced American battalions would hardly solve the problems. Preventing the communist domination of South Vietnam had to come through a series of mutually supporting political, military, economic, psychological, and covert actions.[39]

Cool to Diem's request for more soldiers, the Joint Chiefs of Staff on August 3 decided that a nine-division force of 200,000 Vietnamese was sufficient. They thought priority should go to training the 20,000-man increase, the Civil Guard, and the Self Defense Corps, as well as to retraining existing forces. On August 11 President Kennedy approved U.S. support for a Vietnamese military establishment of 200,000 men. As Secretary of Defense McNamara told his principal subordinates a week later, internal security was the first priority, although military operations would give no lasting results without "continued and accelerated" economic and social progress.[40] But in September the Viet Cong intensified the conflict, occupying towns, cutting roads, slowing the flow of rice to market, and impeding other commercial traffic. They also assassinated about 1,000 people each month, mainly intermediate government officials. Although the Vietnamese army had mauled several large guerrilla units in the Mekong Delta during June, it was able to do so because the foe stood and fought in the open. This was an ominous sign, since Viet Cong strength in combat units was now an estimated 13,000-15,000 men. The evaluation division of the Air Staff in Washington felt that "the communists are making a determined bid to take over that nation, and perhaps all of Southeast Asia, in the very near future."[41]

Infiltrators in 1959 and 1960 had been chiefly administrators, propagandists, and logisticians. In 1961 combat soldiers—mostly trained veterans of the war against France and many of them born in South Vietnam—arrived and formed main force battalions and combat support companies. They had pushed south along two routes. The primary one was a corridor along the border. The other, 100 kilometers to the east, was called Ho Chi Minh Trail by the Americans, a name they later gave the whole system.

These small determined men moved beneath the forest canopy, brushed away their tracks when necessary, preserved rigid march discipline, and kept their movements secret. They traveled in groups of several hundred, an estimated 6,200 in 1961, 13,000 in 1962. Their presence was mirrored in the rise of incidents involving the assassination of officials, the destruction of government outposts, and the eagerness of guerrillas to fight in the open.[42]

There were 41 reported battles in the country during August 1961 but 450 in September. A telling action took place on the 18th of September. Around 1,500 guerrillas overran Phuoc Vinh, the capital of Phuoc Thanh Province. They publicly beheaded the province chief, held the town most of the day, and left before the Vietnamese troops arrived. President Diem was alarmed by the

INITIAL CHALLENGES AND ACTIONS

infiltrators streaming from North Vietnam through Laos and by the Viet Cong's ability to assemble large units, to operate in battalions, to use extensive radio command nets, and to raid key provincial cities. On September 29 Diem asked Ambassador Nolting for a bilateral defense treaty with the United States. He pressed Admiral Felt, CINCPAC, for a "large increase in advisors of all types" and for American tactical air squadrons to help break up big communist units massing for attack. Diem's apprehension colored his address before the National Assembly on October 2: "It is no longer a guerrilla war. It is a war waged by an enemy who attacks us with regular units fully and heavily equipped and who seeks a strategic decision in Southeast Asia in conformity with the order of the Communist International."[43]

Controlling infiltration into the country was virtually impossible. South Vietnam's land border stretched 900 miles along neighboring Cambodia, Laos, and North Vietnam. Three-quarters of this distance consisted of rugged mountains, the rest of swamps and jungles. Portions of the frontier had never been precisely delineated. MAAG suggested using helicopters to patrol the border, but maintenance facilities were in short supply or entirely lacking. Surveillance by high-performance aircraft was hardly enough. Requesting SEATO forces to exercise border control would only place these units in a vulnerable position, grossly complicate communications and logistical support, and reduce but certainly not stop Viet Cong crossings.

The best technique came into being about the time of the Laotian crisis in May. The Vietnamese set up patrol bases and primitive airfields along the border. Manned by regular army troops, rangers, Civil Guard companies, and Montagnard scouts, these facilities were home for the roving patrols that located, harassed, and ambushed infiltrators. The landing strips made air resupply by C-47s possible. The ranger training center, which had been moved from Da Nang to Nha Trang, recruited and instructed Montagnard scouts. But the core of the system was the group of 400 Special Forces troops committed by President Kennedy. They brought direction and substance to the border-control program.[44]

To fulfill President Kennedy's desire for developing counterinsurgency methods, Defense Secretary McNamara directed the Defense Department's Advanced Research Projects Agency (ARPA) to create a Combat Development and Test Center in Vietnam. When its functions appeared to overlap and conflict with the MAAG's, Vietnamese and American officials agreed on June 29 to locate a small center within the Vietnamese armed forces headquarters in Saigon, to work with the Joint General Staff. With direct channels to ARPA and CINCPAC, the center served as a focal point for technical contract analysts dispatched to the country by ARPA and by the director of Defense research and engineering. By the 5th of August, the center was searching for a chemical agent to kill the tapioca plant (a food source for guerrillas), probing the use of patrol dogs, and considering the employment of chemical defoliants to deprive the Viet Cong of assembly and ambush areas.[45]

THE ADVISORY YEARS

Installing surveillance radar to record Soviet overflights in clandestine supply and intelligence missions—as President Kennedy wished—was not easy. The Vietnamese armed forces were without aircraft control and warning. At Tan Son Nhut their 1st Radar Squadron owned two light TPS-1D search radars and two TPS-10D height finders. This equipment was stored from 1954 to 1958, then the Vietnamese Air Force utilized it merely for training. The 1st Squadron had never actually controlled aircraft, and many of its U.S.-trained technicians were assigned elsewhere, often in unrelated jobs.[46]

Military Assistance Program funds covered the installation of two heavy combination FPS-20/-6 radars at Tan Son Nhut and Da Nang, but delivery was impossible before September 1962. To fill the gap and to speed refresher training of Vietnamese technicians, Admiral Felt requested and Air Force headquarters directed on September 11, 1961, the deployment of a mobile combat reporting post to Vietnam. It came from the 507th Tactical Control Group at Shaw Air Force Base, South Carolina.

The combat reporting post comprised 67 men plus MPS-11 search and MPS-16 height-finder radars. This secret movement (all identification markings on boxed equipment were painted out) was airlifted to Vietnam during September 26-October 3. The installation started operating at Tan Son Nhut on the 5th of October and eventually received 314 more USAF personnel. A center was organized to control and report flights, and training of Vietnamese technicians commenced.

As the first USAF unit to arrive in Vietnam on a permanent duty status, the combat reporting post formed the nucleus of a tactical air control system. The personnel supervised construction of a tent city, met incoming aircraft, and in general eased the arrival of other officers and airmen ordered to Vietnam. They began "a radar capability to support interceptor and other combat activities in the event that U.S. or other allied forces must at some point be deployed to the country in an emergency."[47]

Other USAF resources soon arrived to bolster photo reconnaissance. A single RT-33 had reconnoitered Laos until May 1961, but the United States suspended the mission to respect the cease-fire and the Geneva conference on Laos. The flights resumed on October 4. Shortly after the Saigon government asked for more photo reconnaissance to assist intelligence gathering, Fifth Air Force was ordered to move a detachment of its 15th Tactical Reconnaissance Squadron from Okinawa to Saigon. The detachment got to Tan Son Nhut on the morning of October 18, just after the Mekong River had overflowed its banks. The severe flooding spread to the greater part of three delta provinces, left 320,000 people homeless, and destroyed 1,000 kilometers of roads and 10 million acres of crops.

The four RF-101 aircraft, six flight crews, a photo processing unit, and support personnel were all known as Pipe Stem. Flights got under way on October 20, photographing the Mekong floods as well as areas controlled by the Viet Cong. During a month of operations, Pipe Stem flew sixty-seven photo sorties within the country, along the border, and to the Tchepone area of Laos.

INITIAL CHALLENGES AND ACTIONS

Another detachment of four Fifth Air Force RF-101s, flight crews, photo processing unit, and support personnel reached Don Muang, Thailand, on November 6. Nicknamed Able Mable, it took over the reconnaissance missions on the 10th, leaving the RT-33 to transport film to a processing center at Tan Son Nhut or Clark. Filling the needs of the MAAGs in Laos and Vietnam, the first flights were mostly over Laos. But before long the pilots were flying seventy-five percent of their sorties over South Vietnam.[48]

Despite the buildup of American assistance, signs in Vietnam were mixed. President Diem had formed a Central Intelligence Organization, was improving the Civil Guard, was adding 20,000 men to the army, and had created a ranger force. American advisors were working down to company level, and small, helicopter-borne, quick-reaction units were being organized. Yet Diem's National Internal Security Council did a poor job of supervising the execution of military, political, and economic measures. Military units had scant time for rest and retraining. Province chiefs paid slight attention to the chain of command. Vietnamese forces diverted aircraft from troop lift to administrative purposes. Perhaps most disheartening, several Vietnamese military leaders asked U.S. officials what American reaction might be to a coup d'etat against President Diem.

Inefficiency abounded. A typical example took place in autumn 1961. Several Vietnamese AD-6s got orders to strike Viet Cong troops gathered on the Bien Hoa side of a river dividing that province from Phuoc Thanh. By the time the fighters came, the guerrillas had crossed the river. While the planes orbited for three hours, the Phuoc Thanh Province chief could not be found to approve the strike.[49]

The Vietnamese Air Force was rated combat ready. Plans to expand it gained Military Assistance Program backing for second fighter and helicopter squadrons, one photo reconnaissance unit, and a third L-19 liaison squadron. Even though the Geneva accords forbade introducing jet aircraft into the country, there was some talk in American circles during 1961 of giving the Vietnamese surplus F-86 jets. This, it was said, would merely match the many communist violations since 1954.[50]

The Joint Chiefs of Staff frankly suggested that T-/RT-33 jets be delivered to the Vietnamese for reconnaissance. Even a few jet planes would impel the Vietnamese to expand and upgrade ground facilities—extremely valuable actions in light of possible future commitment of U.S. air units. Admiral Felt, CINCPAC, favored turning over several photo jets to the Vietnamese. The USAF planners in Washington warned, "immediate and serious degradation in the military effectiveness of the Vietnamese could result" from the absence of jets. The State Department stood solidly against the idea and in October Ambassador Nolting stopped trying to equip the Vietnamese with jet planes. Secretary McNamara told the Navy to send thirty piston-engine T-28 fighters to Saigon. The Air Force handled the transportation of these aircraft from the west coast to Vietnam. The first fifteen were in place by mid-December.[51]

THE ADVISORY YEARS

All this was—in retrospect at least—a prelude to two decisions made by President Kennedy on October 11, 1961. The President perused Diem's address of October 2 to the National Assembly that termed hostilities in Vietnam as changed and extremely serious. He also noted the stream of threat and vituperation flowing from Hanoi. Then Kennedy on the morning of the 11th ordered a USAF combat detachment to Vietnam. In the afternoon he sent his military adviser, Gen. Maxwell D. Taylor, to Saigon to find out how best to help the Diem government.

INITIAL CHALLENGES AND ACTIONS

(Left) T-28 fighter-bombers.

(Center) Lt. Richard A. Mathison and A1C Tri Pham Minh, VNAF, stand with a collection of Farm Gate aircraft: T-28 in foreground, a B-26 in left background, A-1E in right background and a C-47 in distance.

(Bottom) RF-101 Voodoo.

VII. Opening Farm Gate

The USAF combat detachment that President Kennedy ordered to Vietnam on October 11, 1961, had its roots in a small, secret organization created in the late 1950s when General LeMay was Vice Chief of Staff. In March 1961 LeMay responded to the President's instructions for the armed services to examine how each could best contribute to counterinsurgency. When there was no doubt about communist aggression, LeMay personally favored a direct and open American response with the necessary strength. He defined "necessary" as "*more* than is actually necessary to do the job," hitting "with overwhelming weight" to avoid "stretching things out over a period of time." LeMay, soon to be Chief of Staff, was very much aware that the military services had to abide by different rules. Tactical Air Command was therefore directed to form a small, elite, volunteer unit around the organization. Its mission would be air operations in support of ground forces to be flown in older conventional aircraft.

The 4400th Combat Crew Training Squadron (nicknamed Jungle Jim) came into being at Eglin Air Force Base, Florida, on April 14, 1961. Commanded by Col. Benjamin H. King, the unit had 124 officers and 228 airmen, sixteen C-47s, eight B-26s, and eight T-28s. Equal numbers of the same types of aircraft were in temporary storage. The squadron's mission of training indigenous air forces in counterinsurgency would combine with a mission of air operations.[1]

Officers and airmen of the 4400th—at times called air commandos—were volunteers, above average in physique, hardiness, and sense of adventure. Each was closely interviewed and approved by Colonel King. Next came psychiatric screening at Lackland Air Force Base, Texas, and survival indoctrination at Stead Air Force Base, Nevada. Those completing the program were certified to be emotionally mature, highly motivated, and stable. Unfortunately, not all were mentally attuned to teaching members of other cultures or in fact to perform a training mission—they were combat-oriented. Later, several men would prove unable to work with Asian officers. As volunteers dwindled, the rigorous standards were eventually lowered. The picturesque air commando uniform, personally picked by General LeMay, featured an Australian-type bush hat (with turned-up brim), fatigues, and combat boots.[2]

Two of the three types of Jungle Jim aircraft were extensively modified. The T-28 received armorplate and carried about 1,500 pounds of bombs and rockets, plus two .50-caliber machineguns with 350 rounds per gun. Loaded, the aircraft could speed at 160 knots to a target 200 miles distant then return to base. The C-47 (redesignated SC-47 after modification) boasted twice the normal fuel load, a stronger landing gear suited to dirt strips, and jet-assisted takeoff (JATO) racks for operations from short fields. The B-26 twin-engine attack bomber needed no modification, carrying 6,000 pounds of bombs and rockets, plus machineguns.

When fully loaded, it had a combat radius of 400 miles at a normal speed of 200 knots and could loiter 30 to 45 minutes. The B-26 was designed for a glide bomb-delivery pattern, not for dive-bombing with rolling pullouts nor for landing with external ordnance in place after an aborted mission.[3]

To halt communist infiltration into South Vietnam, the Joint Chiefs on August 24 suggested to Secretary McNamara air interdiction of the inland trails over which the Viet Cong secured supplies. If the United States had no desire to commit American forces openly, why not institute unconventional, guerrilla-type operations.[4]

The President had mentioned several times to the Secretary of Defense the benefits of testing counterinsurgency techniques in Vietnam. On September 5 McNamara informed the three service secretaries that he intended to establish an experimental command under MAAG as a laboratory for refining organizational and operational procedures. General LeMay at this point invited Secretary of the Air Force Eugene M. Zuckert's attention to the 4400th Combat Crew Training Squadron. Sending an element of the unit to Vietnam would be an ideal way to devise and evaluate special warfare methods. On September 19 Secretary Zuckert recommended this to Secretary McNamara. A detachment of the 4400th had just become operationally ready. If moved to Vietnam, it would acquire counterinsurgency experience and at the same time train the Vietnamese.[5]

McNamara liked the proposal, asked the Joint Chiefs of Staff for comment, and on October 5 had their recommendation to place a detachment of Jungle Jim with MAAG in Vietnam. The Secretary next made the idea known to the President.[6]

President Kennedy weighed the burgeoning Viet Cong strength, the more frequent reference in planning papers to U.S. covert operations, the desire of the Joint Chiefs to make a reassuring commitment of air strength to Vietnam, and President Diem's change of heart on acceptance of American combat units in his country. On the morning of October 11, 1961, the Commander in Chief authorized the deployment of the Jungle Jim squadron to Vietnam "to serve under the MAAG as a training mission and not for combat at the present time."[7]

But the 4400th was not specifically a training unit—it was "designed to fight." It had been "singled out" for deployment because its combat capacity and involvement would shore up "South Vietnamese sagging morale."[8]

The President's decision five months earlier to send an Army Special Forces group to Vietnam now enunciated a new mission statement for Jungle Jim. It was to train indigenous airmen while working with and supporting the Special Forces, rangers, and irregular forces along the border. In this light, General LeMay saw the USAF unit as a regular part of the triservice team. Essentially, however, Jungle Jim was an experiment and one of its purposes was to forge counterinsurgency tactics. It could use sod runways and operate austerely in remote areas; carry out strike, reconnaissance, and airlift missions; fly close support for ground troops; drop small forces up to company-size; deliver supplies; and perform medical evacuation.[9]

OPENING FARM GATE

Thus it was that 155 Air Force officers and airmen, volunteers to support friendly guerrillas, flying eight extemporized fighter-bombers, four light bombers of World War II vintage, and four twin-engine transports designed prior to the second World War, learned that they would go to Vietnam to support the government of President Diem. Exactly how was in some dispute.[10]

On the 13th of October, Colonel King and two of his officers visited Hawaii to coordinate Jungle Jim's movement with Admiral Felt, CINCPAC, who "enthusiastically supported the approved deployment." In Saigon the three officers briefed Ambassador Nolting who was happy to have Jungle Jim to train Vietnamese, develop tactics and techniques, and conduct other operations "as directed by the Ambassador." He asked that all aircraft arrive with Vietnamese insignia.[11]

Returning to Hawaii, King was assured by PACAF officers that no major problems existed. A tent camp would be ready for the detachment's arrival at Bien Hoa Airfield and support arrangements were underway. On October 28 Felt asked that the detachment be sent forward at once, without waiting for the Air Force to procure some L-28 Helio Super Courier light aircraft and Sidewinder air-to-air missiles for the T-28s.[12] At Eglin the task force designated for Vietnam received the formal name of Detachment 2A, 4400th Combat Crew Training Squadron, and the code name of Farm Gate.[13]

Meantime, members of the 6009th Tactical Support Group under Col. Claude G. McKinney, Jr., entered Vietnam with the utmost secrecy during late October. These officers and airmen deployed on temporary duty from Tachikawa Air Base, Japan, to Clark, then to Bien Hoa where they prepared the base facility for Farm Gate. Additional detachments came from Thirteenth Air Force and PACAF (chiefly from the 6010th Tactical Support Group) to service and support the beginnings of an expanded USAF presence in Vietnam and elsewhere in Southeast Asia. All were formed into numbered temporary duty detachments on November 15—7 and 8 at Tan Son Nhut, 9 at Bien Hoa, and 10 at Don Muang, Thailand. Detachment 7 was a headquarters staff; 8 operated the "prime set-up" for an air operations and a combat reporting center, as well as a photo processing cell; while 9 and 10 maintained and serviced aircraft.[14]

Farm Gate departed Florida on the 5th of November. Four SC-47s flew to Clark Air Base. Eight T-28s were disassembled in California and, together with 140 officers and airmen, were ferried to Clark by MATS. After reassembly, Colonel King led two flights of T-28s to Tan Son Nhut. The detachment became operationally ready on the 16th, though a week passed before the last of the SC-47s and T-28s arrived. Farm Gate accepted four B-26s previously sent to the Far East. These hardnosed, strafing-model, light bombers reached Bien Hoa near the close of December.[15]

At Bien Hoa the Farm Gate detachment found a rundown French air base with a flight surface consisting of a single pierced-steel-plank runway 5,800 by 150 feet. Tear-outs in the steel tie strips demanded constant attention of welding crews, and the 315th Air Division C-130s bringing in communications equipment for a tactical air control system further tore up the runway. About 700

Vietnamese soldiers defended the airfield, because heavy vegetation and swampy terrain nearby afforded good cover for Viet Cong troops surrounding the air base. Farm Gate at once contacted the two USAF mobile reporting posts at Tan Son Nhut, and set about to organize a tactical air control system of sorts and to establish communications and supply requirements.[16]

The members of Farm Gate thought they were to conduct combat operations while training the Vietnamese. That was how General LeMay had briefed Colonel King, and King was more than willing to make his unit combat capable and responsive to Ambassador Nolting and to American military authorities. In early familiarization flights, T-28 crews trailed Vietnamese AD-6s to targets, observed their attack procedures, and, when authorized, fired on targets. The 155 men were highly motivated and eager to fight.[17]

Nevertheless, on November 16 Admiral Felt tasked Farm Gate with conducting tactical training and pilot upgrading for the Vietnamese. President Kennedy was advised that the unit was "training Vietnamese aircrews and supporting Vietnamese operations against the Viet Cong."[18]

Uncertainties of mission and the absence of combat lowered morale from the start. The pilots expected to carry an air offensive to the Viet Cong. Instead, they trained and supplemented the Vietnamese Air Force, seeking to evolve techniques for what McNamara described to the press as "not full-scale warfare but guerrilla warfare." Without clearcut agreement at higher levels on Farm Gate's mission, the early operations tended to be improvised and experimental rather than systematic.[19]

Farm Gate's first regular employment was to reconnoiter and count the junk and sampan traffic in Vietnam coastal waters, a tedious job lasting from December 6 through 22, 1961. C-47s and pairs of T-28s flew four-hour search patterns and recorded sightings. Thirty-seven sorties turned up 6,294 vessels, but the aircrews had no way to tell how many were enemy. MAAG was equally at a loss to interpret the findings. The long uneventful flight patterns were a physical hardship for the T-28 crews. They were not allowed to crack their canopies in flight, even though weakened by the cockpit heat from the tropical sun. A second series flown during February 5-7, 1962, furnished no meaningful intelligence.[20]

Farm Gate likewise also acquired the mission of supporting the Army Special Forces and their Civilian Irregular Defense Group. The C-47s operated under an ad hoc system free of MAAG and Vietnamese army control, to keep materiel, transportation, and funds in U.S. hands. The aircraft delivered locally procured items and emergency ones flown in from the United States. (Formal supply accountability was discarded.) These operations were small, Farm Gate flying just 205 sorties in the first six months of 1962.[21]

While valuable, these missions were outside of what Farm Gate wanted to do. When Admiral Felt on December 4, 1961, directed General O'Donnell at PACAF to ready plans for operations, O'Donnell at once permitted Farm Gate to fly combat missions "with at least one South Vietnamese national aboard any aircraft so committed." Secretary McNamara, meeting with the Joint Chiefs that day, approved combat with mixed crews. On December 6 the Joint Chiefs

OPENING FARM GATE

granted formal authority for Farm Gate aircraft to fly combat if Vietnamese were aboard for training.[22]

On the 6th PACAF submitted to CINCPAC the same concept for operations. Actually, U.S. aircraft and personnel would support Vietnamese armed forces and help them deny the Viet Cong supply routes and concentration areas, fly armed patrols of South Vietnam's land and sea borders, and seek out and destroy Viet Cong headquarters as well as communist airlift into South Vietnam.[23]

Together, Vietnamese and Americans were to destroy Viet Cong lifelines and support bases. From Bien Hoa, Tan Son Nhut, and combat air bases to be developed at Da Nang and Pleiku, air operations were to stress photo reconnaissance, surveillance, interdiction, and close support of ground operations.[24]

Needed at once were a tactical air control system and a jointly manned American-Vietnamese air operations center. When Admiral Felt approved a limited tactical air control system on December 8, it appeared that operations would get under way. Thirteenth Air Force issued a draft plan on the 10th and distinguished between combat actions performed in support of the Vietnamese within South Vietnam and advisory and training actions. On the 15th, Ambassador Nolting directed that no combat mission of any description be undertaken without his consent.[25]

The next day, General Lemnitzer suggested that Farm Gate should not wait for "tailor-made jobs" but should center on training. Secretary McNamara repeated his approval of combat missions if the planes had Vietnamese aboard. However, he wanted all such flights to be confined to South Vietnam owing to the experimental nature of the program. Stressing the difference between "riding double" combat training missions and operational missions, he charged CINCPAC with the latter. He wanted Admiral Felt to use combat missions solely for "important jobs" and to monitor them closely. In other words, according to McNamara, "Jungle Jim is to be used for training and operational missions in South Vietnam with Vietnamese riding rear seats."[26]

On December 19 the Joint Chiefs sent a message "to insure no misunderstanding in the authority granted for the use of Jungle Jim aircraft." Farm Gate's principal purpose was training Vietnamese Air Force personnel. On the following day, Admiral Felt made known his conviction that Farm Gate, besides training Vietnamese, could carry out "all kinds of conventional combat and combat support flights" if a Vietnamese was on board to receive training.[27]

Admiral Felt's conviction sparked a reexamination of American policy in Washington. The National Security Council inclined toward authorizing U.S. uniformed personnel in Vietnam for "instruction in and execution of air-ground support techniques." That appeared broad enough to embrace all U.S. air actions. Yet the State Department view, later voiced by W. Averell Harriman, held that the statement hardly covered interdiction air strikes far from friendly ground troops. General Lemnitzer forwarded detailed clarifying instructions to Admiral Felt and General McGarr on December 26. He wanted Farm Gate to conduct combat missions only when the Vietnamese Air Force could not.

THE ADVISORY YEARS

Combined crews on combat missions would fulfill the purpose of training—to allow Vietnamese to fly these missions alone as soon as possible.

When General Lemnitzer's directive reached Farm Gate on the afternoon of the 26th a strike mission was in the air. Two Farm Gate T-28s were escorting two Vietnamese AD-6s to hit Viet Cong houses and rice fields about fifty miles north of Saigon. Despite recall efforts, the strike went on. But thereafter, the possibility of an independent American combat role came to an end.[28]

Determining Farm Gate's mission and its place in the organizational and command structure would be the subject of continuing discussion and controversy. Meanwhile General Maxwell Taylor had visited Vietnam and had reported his observations to the President, thereby shaping and refining the purpose and direction of national policy.

VIII. The Taylor Mission

Several hours after announcing on October 11, 1961, the dispatch of Farm Gate to Vietnam, President Kennedy disclosed that he was sending his military adviser General Taylor to Saigon. Taylor was to make an "educated military guess" of the situation in the country and to find "ways in which we can perhaps better assist the Government of Vietnam in meeting this threat to its independence." In his letter of instructions to the general, Kennedy said, "the initial responsibility for the effective maintenance of the independence of South Vietnam rests with the people and government of that country." Concerned with political, social, and economic matters in addition to military problems, the President appointed Walt W. Rostow as Taylor's deputy. Actually, Taylor was to advise the President whether to deploy U.S. combat forces for a direct role in Vietnam, or to continue U.S. training and support functions only.[1]

Public knowledge of Taylor's mission produced an immediate reaction from the communists. On October 12 Premier Chou En-lai warned that China could scarcely "be indifferent to the increasingly grave situation caused by United States imperialism in South Vietnam." Ho Chi Minh went to Peking for discussions. The Soviet Union linked the Taylor mission with flagging diplomatic discussions at Geneva and charged the United States with planning to send troops to Vietnam to bring pressure to bear on the situation in Laos. On October 14 North Vietnam protested to the International Control Commission that the Taylor mission was meant to "intensify United States intervention in South Vietnam and prepare the way for introducing United States troops."[2]

What was the exact state of affairs in South Vietnam? Increases in Viet Cong numbers, aggressiveness, and incidents constantly surprised the Vietnamese National Intelligence Agency. United States intelligence estimates placed the strength of Viet Cong main forces at 17,000 men, eighty to ninety percent of whom were recruited locally.[3] President Diem was complaining to the International Control Commission of the international threat to his government, Hanoi's determination to "liberate the south," the massive infiltration of communist agents, the ruthless strategy of terror waged against the South Vietnamese people, and the endeavors to establish "liberated territory" in the central reaches of the Republic, susceptible of gaining recognition and support from the communist powers. CINCPAC intelligence assessments identified enemy goals as consolidating control over the richer agricultural areas of the country, isolating Saigon and the Diem government from the people, and keeping the infiltration approaches into South Vietnam open.[4]

What military assistance did the South Vietnamese want? As the Vietnamese defense minister told Ambassador Nolting on October 13, Diem wished American combat units or "combat training units" to be stationed near the 17th parallel to make a show of force and also to free Vietnamese units for antiguerrilla action.[5]

THE ADVISORY YEARS

En route to Saigon, Taylor and Rostow stopped off in Hawaii for a briefing by Admiral Felt. The admiral stressed that the Vietnamese required prompt U.S. assistance. He pinpointed two serious Vietnamese weaknesses—the tendency of province chiefs to meddle in military matters, and the penchant of military commanders to stay in static defensive positions. Felt indorsed the Farm Gate commitment, but saw no present need for other American combat forces to take a direct part in the war. He recommended continuing USAF reconnaissance flights, accelerating the delivery of T-28s, and refining military communications. He wanted the primitive airstrip at Pleiku enlarged and stores of ammunition, equipment, and war consumables positioned at bases for a possible introduction of SEATO forces.[6]

The Taylor-Rostow mission arrived at Tan Son Nhut on October 18, spent six days in Vietnam, and departed for Baguio in the Philippines, where the group sent President Kennedy an interim report. By November 3 the members drew up a lengthy final report.

General Taylor defined the situation in South Vietnam as "an acute crisis of confidence" at every social level—doubt on the seriousness of the U.S. commitment, concern over Viet Cong successes, and discouragement over recent floods that burdened an "already strained state." The military crisis mirrored political weakness. Diem was "an old fashioned Asian ruler, seeking to maintain all the strings of power in his own hands, while fragmenting power beneath him." The military suffered from skimpy intelligence, scant command control, and sparse mobility. A "lack of target intelligence and a frustrating structure" hampered the "small but capable" Vietnamese Air Force. It had made no significant contribution to the struggle, because there had been little photo reconnaissance before the USAF Able Mable missions. "While the very nature of guerrilla war makes good targets hard to find," Taylor noted, "sophisticated aerial photography should find such good targets as there are." Finally, the general saw "none of the controlling structure necessary for effective tactical operations."

There were less than 800 American military personnel and even fewer civilians in the country. None worked inside Vietnamese ministries, and few were in the field, for Diem preferred Americans to remain in Saigon. Some U.S. officials apparently thought it improper to report anything critical of the Diem government. As a result, it was not easy to secure a thorough estimate of the situation. Still the unsettled Laotian situation had probably lessened Vietnamese confidence in the United States, and a more visible U.S. military presence might restore Vietnamese morale.

General Taylor's recommendations included continuing USAF reconnaissance flights in Vietnam, setting up a U.S. tactical air-ground system run partially as a training program, giving Farm Gate a liberal rather than a restrictive mission, and improving Vietnamese air facilities. He saw no reason to commit U.S. combat forces in a direct role for the moment. He envisioned success as hinging on Diem's willingness to undertake political and social reforms.[7]

With a clear impression that "a U.S. military presence of some kind" was greatly desired, General Taylor reported that he leaned toward bolstering Ameri-

THE TAYLOR MISSION

(Top) Gen. Maxwell D. Taylor, Gen. Emmett O'Donnell, Jr., Adm. J. H. Sides, and Lt. Gen. C. A. Roberts, in Hawaii;

(Center) Gen. Paul D. Harkins, Adm. Harry D. Felt, and Ambassador Frederick E. Nolting at Tan Son Nhut Airport.

(Bottom) Gen. Curtis E. LeMay.

can military aid and advisory support for a broadly conceived counterguerrilla campaign. Central to his concept was making MAAG an operational headquarters for a theater of war, with 8,000 military advisors to quicken Vietnamese training, upgrade intelligence and communications, enrich research and development, and give quick military and economic support to Vietnamese offensive operations. An alternative was to deploy perhaps 10,000 U.S. ground troops for defense, to release the Vietnamese army for active counterinsurgency.

Though Taylor and his colleagues believed American support for counterinsurgency inside Vietnam to be basic, they warned against sending more U.S. reinforcements until the nature of any final settlement in Laos and the way in which Hanoi adjusted to it were clear. If Hanoi persisted in its guerrilla infiltration, the United States would be forced "to attack the source of guerrilla aggression in North Viet-Nam and impose on the Hanoi government a price for participating in the current war which is commensurate with the damage inflicted on its neighbors to the south."[8]

The Joint Chiefs of Staff did not care for the interim and final Taylor-Rostow reports. They wanted a positive American commitment to the clear objective of preventing the fall of South Vietnam, even if that meant U.S. military forces must fight. The loss of South Vietnam would lead to communist control over neighboring nations, and the chiefs favored an immediate deployment of strong American combat forces instead of a gradual entry of combat support units. They proposed to warn Hanoi of punitive action unless Viet Cong aggression ceased. There was little chance of staving off the fall of South Vietnam without U.S. forces "on a substantial scale." The United States could persuade North Vietnam of its serious intent solely by a "clear commitment" to keep South Vietnam out of the communist camp, plus a diplomatic warning to Hanoi that its continued support of the Viet Cong would bring American retaliation. A long war and perhaps the intervention of the People's Republic of China might ensue. If it did, the United States would have to put at least 205,000 military men into the field.[9]

Secretary McNamara discussed the matter with the Joint Chiefs. On November 8 he informed President Kennedy of his and their support of the Taylor-Rostow recommendations as "first steps" toward realizing the American aim—averting the fall of South Vietnam. Defending Southeast Asia would take no more than six U.S. divisions, about 205,000 men. The United States, however, should introduce major U.S. units into Vietnam only if it was willing to make an unalterable espousal of that goal.[10]

McNamara and the Joint Chiefs were candid in saying that success would turn upon many factors "not within our control—notably the conduct of Diem himself and other leaders in the area." They were uneasy about American domestic political problems, but expected Congress to "respond better to a firm initial position than to courses of action that lead us in only gradually, and that in the meantime are sure to involve casualties." The key, of course, was the firmness of American intent. Without that, there was no point to deploy sizable units.[11]

THE TAYLOR MISSION

As chairman of the State Department Policy Planning Council, Walt Rostow argued for a contingency policy of retaliation against North Vietnam, a program graduated to match the intensity of Hanoi's support of the Viet Cong. Upon his request, PACAF furnished Rostow with two lists of aerial targets in North Vietnam.[12]

Admiral Felt clung to his earlier opinion. The United States should not send large combat forces until the lesser measures, suggested by him and substantially approved by General Taylor, were implemented.[13]

President Kennedy was loath to approve an extensive open-ended commitment. "They want a force of American troops," he told an aide, and he likened that force to the units sent to Germany earlier in the year.

> They say it's necessary in order restore confidence and maintain morale. But it will be just like Berlin. The troops will march in; the bands will play; the crowds will cheer; and in four days everyone will have forgotten. Then we will be told we have to send in more troops. It's like taking a drink. The effect wears off, and you have to take another.

According to Kennedy, the war could be won only so long as it remained Vietnam's war. Otherwise, the Americans would lose like the French.[14]

On November 8 Secretary of Defense McNamara, together with the Joint Chiefs, had been "inclined" to recommend a firm commitment to preclude the takeover of South Vietnam even if it meant direct military action. Three days later, McNamara joined with Secretary of State Rusk in proposing a more moderate stance in line with President Kennedy's thinking. The Defense secretary urged the instant dispatch of modest support units and further study before resolving to send large organized units for actual or potential combat.[15]

The National Security Council and State and Defense representatives weighed on November 11 American military options in Vietnam. On the 13th a State-Defense memorandum generally followed the Rusk-McNamara view. There was to be no swift overt commitment of U.S. combat troops to Vietnam. A unilateral employment independent of SEATO action might trigger a military escalation, provoke apathy and perhaps hostility among South Vietnamese, jeopardize the chances for a political settlement in Laos, and promote domestic political repercussions in the United States.[16]

Also on November 13 Kennedy approved the lesser measures—more airlift (helicopters, light planes, and transports) for the Diem forces, along with the USAF personnel and planes for reconnaissance and defoliation. Nine days later the President advised Diem of American willingness to expand aid, men, and equipment for a combined undertaking to speed Vietnamese training and to help fashion better communications and intelligence. In return, Diem would have to put South Vietnam on a firm war footing, mobilize his resources, give his government adequate authority, and overhaul the military establishment and command structure. Meanwhile, uniformed U.S. military personnel in the country would furnish airlift for Vietnamese forces, air reconnaissance, photography, instruction in and execution of air-ground support techniques, and special intelligence.[17]

THE ADVISORY YEARS

There was neither a statement of American national objectives nor a provision for stronger U.S. military actions should these first-phase measures prove insufficient. The Air Staff regarded this as a much "watered down" policy. It differed mainly from the Joint Chiefs' position by adding the quid pro quo approach to the Republic of Vietnam. That is, American commitments would grow solely in response to positive Vietnamese actions.[18]

At a meeting of the Joint Chiefs of Staff on December 5, General LeMay expressed his grave concern. He labeled what Rusk and McNamara had proposed and what the President had approved as inadequate. The greater U.S. assistance was still insufficient to defeat the Viet Cong. Southeast Asia was the best place for a showdown between the United States and the communists. This was not because of the local terrain or political situation. It was because "U.S. military intervention in Southeast Asia, including the use of nuclear weapons, could be followed by many layers of escalation before the ultimate confrontation would occur." In contrast, the Secretaries of State and Defense had apparently tried to "obscure, play-down, or delay the determined and decisive action required to effectively combat" the communist threat.[19]

LeMay urged the Joint Chiefs to suggest that President Kennedy deploy sizable American forces to Vietnam. He wanted them to "press for high-level accord" on a "clear statement of U.S. objectives in the area," and to tell McNamara that "timely, positive military actions are essential."[20] He desired at least a definite contingency commitment to insert U.S. forces into Vietnam for open operations when required. What the Air Force chief thought were suitable forces for the commitment would be an Army brigade task force; a Marine division and its complementary air wing; plus a tactical fighter squadron, a tactical bomber squadron, and a tactical reconnaissance task force.[21] These units would free the bulk of Diem's forces to root out the guerrillas and to secure South Vietnam's borders. They would also "bolster Diem's political position and insure his regime and tenure in office." LeMay envisaged no open engagement with the enemy but could not rule it out. "Enemy military actions," he said, "would not alter the political objective, but such actions may compel military responses which would not necessarily be confined to South Vietnam." But there was "no feasible military alternative of lesser magnitude" that would prevent the "loss of South Vietnam and ultimately of Southeast Asia."[22]

The Joint Chiefs referred LeMay's proposal to the Joint Strategic Survey Council, a group of senior officers freed from day-to-day matters so they could take a detached view of broad military and political questions. Asked to examine the rationale for deploying U.S. troops to South Vietnam, they replied on December 7. "The recently authorized measures, even when implemented," they said, "will prove to be inadequate." The council called attention to "the deteriorating military situation and the tenuous character of the South Vietnam government," which made it "imperative that the United States government take the initiative." To "reassure President Diem that the United States will support his government and will discourage and oppose any internal factions which seek to overthrow him," U.S. combat forces and those of its Asian allies should go to

THE TAYLOR MISSION

South Vietnam strong enough "to assure the South Vietnamese of our determination to support their government and to defeat communist aggression." There should be "a military command and modus operandi in South Vietnam which will assure loyalty and maximum combat effectiveness in the campaign against the communists."[23]

Secretary McNamara was not convinced. As he afterwards told the President, "I am not prepared to endorse the views of the Chiefs until we have had more experience with our present program in South Vietnam." Kennedy agreed.[24]

General LeMay clearly doubted if the administration actually had a firm and definite Vietnam policy. In his opinion, he later observed, none of the American military chiefs "really believed" that the United States was undertaking "anything except [having] some diplomatic fiddling around with a little more aid program."[25]

Part of this feeling might have flowed from LeMay's frustration over major constraints hindering the Air Force's influence in SEA—too few and too junior USAF officers in the MAAGs, PACAF's restricted voice in Vietnamese affairs, the inability of the indigenous air forces to cope with the insurgency, and "inadequate ground environment for employment of USAF air power on a large scale." Moreover, Secretary McNamara kept a tight rein on the military services. In mid-November, for example, the movement of three single-engine liaison aircraft to Vietnam required his permission. Little wonder that USAF leadership felt cramped and uncomfortable.[26]

Maybe it was no coincidence that on December 5—the day General LeMay voiced his concern to the JCS—Admiral Felt dispatched a warning to the Joint Chiefs. He reported that General McGarr, MAAG chief in Saigon, and Sir Robert G. K. Thompson,* head of a British advisory mission to Saigon, were both uneasy because the situation in South Vietnam was "more than serious. It is critical, with the peak of the crisis possible at any moment."[27]

---

*Sir Robert had figured prominently in subduing the guerrillas in Malaysia.

IX. U.S. Command Arrangements: 2d ADVON and MACV

Acceptance of the Taylor-Rostow recommendations of November 3, 1961, marked a shift in American policy "from advice to limited partnership and working collaboration" with the Vietnamese. More material assistance would accompany increased American participation in the war. American advisors, "as friends and partners," were to show the Vietnamese "how the job might be done—not tell them or do it for them."[1]

By November 13, using such expressions as "proceed urgently" and "with all possible speed," Defense Secretary McNamara had authorized a host of measures. Among them were increased airlift, including sixteen C-123s, for the Vietnamese armed forces; help with aerial reconnaissance, photography, air-ground support, and installing a tactical air control system; small naval craft with advisors and crews to cut enemy waterborne infiltration and resupply; training and equipment for the Civil Guard and Self Defense Corps to free Vietnamese army units for offensive operations; personnel and equipment to enhance military-political intelligence at all levels; more economic support to afford better military pay, food, and medicine; relief and rehabilitation in the flooded areas; "individual administrators and advisors for insertion into the governmental machinery of South Viet-Nam in types and numbers to be agreed upon by the two governments"; and surveys in all provinces to discover how best to deal with the insurgency.[2]

Assuming that Diem would formally agree later, the Defense secretary instructed the Joint Chiefs of Staff to proceed. McNamara personally monitored the aid program, requiring a progress report every Monday. He wanted men and materiel for a tactical air control system to go to Vietnam as soon as possible. He wanted thirty T-28s rushed out to give the Vietnamese a second fighter squadron. And he wanted more U.S. advisors in place. By June 30, 1962, there would be 6,419 Americans in South Vietnam.[3]

As McNamara informed Admiral Felt and General McGarr:

> Political uncertainty of Diem's position and doubt as to his willingness to take steps to make his government more effective must not prevent us from going ahead full blast (without publicity, until political discussions are completed) on all possible actions short of large scale introduction of US combat forces . . . . Fundamentally, we must adjust ourselves to a perennially unclear political framework and to a policy that for overall national reasons sets limits on military actions.[4]

Early in December, President Diem made an affirmative but hedged response to the Kennedy program. His memorandum distinguished between domestic and military matters and clearly defined the latter. For example,

American helicopter and naval units were to be under exclusive U.S. command. Diem's government would take no decisions or actions entailing combined operations "without full prior consultation with the qualified U.S. agencies." Although doubting that Diem's reply would be fully acceptable, Ambassador Nolting radioed the State Department, "I nevertheless think memorandum represents U.S. moving confidently ahead."[5]

The new Kennedy program dictated that the MAAG in Saigon be reorganized and augmented. Then it could better help subdue the subversion and insurgency, and as "an advanced party" command forces sent to Vietnam to oppose aggression in SEATO terms. In the latter case, Task Force 116 was the ready force. Admiral Felt had said in May 1961 that, if large-scale U.S. combat forces entered Vietnam, he would name the MAAG chief as the Commander, United States Forces, Vietnam. This commander would function under CINCPAC control.

Now there was talk of appointing a four-star general to command U.S. forces in Vietnam. As early as November 1, the State Department was skeptical about the necessity. Secretary Rusk said, "While attaching greatest possible importance to security in Southeast Asia, I would be reluctant to see" the United States further commit "American prestige to a losing horse." Ambassador John K. Galbraith in India pointed to Diem as "a wasting asset" who was "losing, not gaining, popularity." The United States, he thought, should refrain from putting American ground troops into Vietnam and from overcommitting.[6]

On November 22 the Joint Chiefs recommended to the Secretary of Defense a new subordinate unified command under CINCPAC. It would be designated as United States Forces, Vietnam, and organized in Saigon with Army, Navy, and Air Force component commands. The commander in Vietnam was to have four stars and be coequal with the Ambassador. He would draw together all American military activities in the country related to counterinsurgency, including intelligence, MAAG, and whatever economic assistance had military implications. A four-star commander would signal a considerable commitment of American prestige and a major endorsement of Diem's government. Consequently the Joint Chiefs wished, before altering the command structure, to have the United States clearly spell out its objectives in Vietnam and extract a pledge for a suitable military program from Diem. McNamara approved on November 27.[7]

The proposed command ran counter to CINCPAC contingency planning for a possible deployment of JTF 116. Admiral Felt nonetheless admitted that it was justified in light of an enlarged MAAG, PACAF units deployed into Vietnam, and the arrival of Army helicopter companies. Drawing up a detailed table of distribution, Felt suggested an Army general as the commander and a small joint staff with USAF officers as chief of staff, J-2 (Intelligence), and J-5 (Plans). The new command, the CINCPAC thought, might well give Diem the assurance of American support that he appeared to need before carrying out his own program.[8]

2d ADVON AND MACV

United States Army, Pacific (in Hawaii) favored a separate theater of operations for Vietnam removed from CINCPAC control, but acquiesced in "double hatting" the MAAG chief as commander of U.S. forces. On that basis, General McGarr took operational control of Farm Gate. Admiral Felt accepted this for Farm Gate's training mission, but PACAF pointed out that the detachment had a second mission of combat operations. By law MAAGs could not command operational forces. Foreseeing widespread air activities in Vietnam and other parts of Southeast Asia, PACAF wanted to establish an advanced echelon of Thirteenth Air Force in Saigon to command USAF units in SEA.[9]

Admiral Felt agreed. The MAAG chief, working with his Air Force Section chief, would handle Farm Gate's training missions, while CINCPAC through PACAF and an advanced echelon of Thirteenth Air Force, would take care of any combat operations. The MAAG Air Force Section chief and the commander of the advanced echelon could be the same officer. Assigned to MAAG, he would have dual responsibilities to MAAG and to PACAF. Above all, there was to be no appearance of a new American command moving into Vietnam.[10]

To fill the two hats, General O'Donnell of PACAF nominated Brig. Gen. Rollen H. Anthis, an outstanding officer serving as Thirteenth Air Force vice commander. Admiral Felt, CINCPAC, approved the choice. General Anthis assumed command of 2d Advanced Echelon (ADVON)[11] and, needing personnel for the organization, took control of the four small temporary duty detachments (7, 8, 9, and 10). Detachment 7 at Saigon became in effect the 2d ADVON staff.[12]

On November 20 Anthis settled 2d ADVON at the Brink Hotel in downtown Saigon, sharing space with the MAAG Air Force Section. The new commander realized after a few days that he was too far from his operating units. Whereupon, he moved 2d ADVON to Tan Son Nhut and into a building near Vietnamese Air Force headquarters. His Vietnamese neighbors were puzzled by Anthis' presence.

When Ambassador Nolting first found out about 2d ADVON on the 24th, he was not only puzzled but surprised. General Anthis told him that 2d ADVON controlled USAF operating units in Vietnam but not the training units. Nolting found it "incomprehensible" for American authorities to form a new U.S. military headquarters without consulting him and the Vietnamese government. The Ambassador instructed the 2d ADVON commander to delay further organizational activities until Nolting received clarification of the relationship of the headquarters to the Embassy. He solicited from Anthis "a precise understanding that any combat operation in Viet Nam carried out by elements of this command will be cleared in advance with me [Nolting]."

Apprised of the Ambassador's reaction, Admiral Felt advised Anthis to avoid creating a new headquarters. He was to locate in General McGarr's MAAG headquarters and "conduct his advance echelon business through Det[achment] 7 in Saigon." After fresh study, Felt termed 2d ADVON neither a command nor a headquarters. Since its purpose was to administer, control, and support units, it was simply a "facility" for coordination. Nolting might have

95

thought this a distinction without a difference, but he learned that the Diem government had no objection. He accepted 2d ADVON as needed to administer and control PACAF elements that might be deployed to Southeast Asia in coordination with MAAG.[13]

Thirteenth Air Force specified that 2d ADVON execute with the Vietnamese Air Force "sustained offensive, defense, and reconnaissance air operations aimed at the destruction or neutralization of Viet Cong forces, resources, and communications within the borders of South Vietnam." General Anthis was to "set the pattern for Vietnamese Air Force operations."[14] In short, he was to act as the commander of a tactical air force.

But the peculiarly ad hoc nature of the organization led to problems. For example, what control did unit commanders have over their logistic support? In the standard USAF command, such questions had been carefully worked out through the years, but for 2d ADVON they needed to be rethought. Furthermore, General Anthis faced a somewhat more complex chain of command. He reported to CINCPAC through PACAF on operational matters, but he went direct to Thirteenth Air Force on strictly USAF operational, logistic, and administrative issues.[15]

Colonel King, the Farm Gate commander, was also confused. When 2d ADVON's Detachment 9 at Bien Hoa tried to take operational control of his unit, King protested this as inconsistent with General LeMay's instructions. He understood that Detachment 9 was limited to furnishing base logistic support. King prevailed in this matter, but proved less successful in clarifying his own operational mission. He visited Saigon and was unable to see General Anthis. But the 2d ADVON operations officer speculated that it was highly unlikely for Farm Gate even to be cleared for daylight combat. King's officers then borrowed several aerial flares from the Vietnamese, pressed an SC-47 into service for improvised flaredrops, and under the illumination made strike passes with their T-28s. Colonel King went back to Saigon and reported that his unit could make night attacks.

As King later recalled, 2d ADVON dispatched a C-47 and some T-28s on at least two night attacks later in November. Against an enemy position in the jungle south of Da Lat, the T-28 pilots never saw an exact target under the flarelight, and merely placed their ordnance into the trees. Flying to the aid of a fort in the delta under attack, the T-28 crews found the air strike request to be several days old. When they arrived on the scene, there were no targets. Another mission in late November responded to a report of Viet Cong intention to cut the railroad between Bien Hoa and Nha Trang. Bearing flares in addition to their guns, four T-28s reconnoitered the rail line. They illuminated and inspected possible ambush sites but saw no sign of the enemy.[16]

While the Departments of State and Defense discussed organizing the American command in Vietnam, MAAG was "over its head in operations and intelligence planning to the neglect of its primary duty, the training and advisory effort."[17] Authorized a strength of 685 persons in May 1961, MAAG at the end of the year had 2,394 Military Assistance Program spaces and 5,435 others.[18]

A compromise worked out by Secretaries McNamara and Rusk in December envisioned a Military Assistance Command, Vietnam (MACV) under CINCPAC, roughly modeled on the United States Taiwan Defense Command. To highlight the "positive impact of change" in American policy, McNamara desired the MACV commander to be a four-star Army general. He suggested Lt. Gen. Paul D. Harkins to the President as "an imaginative officer, fully qualified to fill what I consider to be the most difficult job in the U.S. Army."[19]

Commander of United States Army, Pacific, and a protege of Generals George S. Patton, Jr., and Maxwell D. Taylor, Harkins was summoned to Florida in January 1962. There in a brief interview, President Kennedy said he was pleased that the general spoke French, told him to assist Diem and the South Vietnamese people, and wished him well.

With Diem's blessing, CINCPAC created the new command in Saigon on February 8, 1962. Harkins became commander with a promotion to full general. On the 10th PACAF designated General Anthis, 2d ADVON commander, to be the air component commander and to further serve as Thirteenth Air Force and PACAF air commander for all USAF matters in Southeast Asia.[20]

The Joint Chiefs of Staff had recommended status for General Harkins "co-equal" with Ambassador Nolting, but the term was absent from the MACV mission statement. Harkins nonetheless owned broader than normal authority. He was to assist and support the Government of Vietnam in its quest for security through defeating communist insurgency and resisting overt aggression. He was charged with all American military policy, operations, and aid in South Vietnam. On U.S. and Vietnamese military operations, he could go straight to President Diem and other governmental leaders. He had direct access to CINCPAC and through him to the JCS and the Secretary of Defense. He was to consult with the Ambassador on political affairs and keep him abreast of military matters. As CINCPAC's single spokesman in South Vietnam, Harkins exercised operational command of all U.S forces and military agencies assigned or attached to MACV, including the Military Assistance Advisory Group.[21]

For MACV's joint staff, Admiral Felt had recommended USAF officers as chief of staff, J-2 (Intelligence), and J-5 (Plans). Even so, General Harkins picked a Marine officer, Maj. Gen. Richard G. Weede, to be his chief of staff and advocated Air Force officers for J-3 (Operations), J-2, and J-5. Secretary McNamara wanted the Army to have the J-3 billet, but Felt believed this would unbalance the staff. He proposed upgrading J-5 to a brigadier general slot and allocating it to the Air Force, while the deputy J-3 would be a USAF colonel. General LeMay tried in vain to persuade McNamara to change his mind on the chief of staff and J-3 positions. The MACV manning authority was approved by the Defense Secretary on March 2. It gave the Air Force none of the key operational spots and only one of the five general officer billets—J-5, filled by Brig. Gen. John A. Dunning. Of the 105 officer spaces, the Army got 54 compared to 29 for the Navy and Marines and 22 for the Air Force.[22]

General Harkins shifted MAAG's operations and intelligence functions to MACV. He appointed Maj. Gen. Charles J. Timmes, USA, to be MAAG chief

(Timmes had been McGarr's deputy). The MAAG was split into Army, Navy, and Air Force Sections. Each handled military assistance, plans and programs, training and logistic advice to the Vietnamese, and administration of American field advisory detachments.[23]

Yet the separation of functions between MACV and MAAG remained fuzzy. General Harkins opposed Anthis' serving as both the MACV air component commander and chief of the MAAG Air Force Section. He suggested and Admiral Felt directed on May 12, 1962, that General Anthis be relieved as MAAG chief of Air Force Section and replaced by the USAF colonel who was the deputy.

General LeMay saw the change as a complication, for the USAF liaison officers with Vietnamese army divisions, who should have been under Anthis' command, were instead assigned to the MAAG. LeMay also protested the proposed reduction in rank of the MAAG chief of Air Force Section. General Anthis held his two jobs a while longer.

Felt and Harkins agreed in October to accept Brig. Gen. Robert R. Rowland as MAAG chief of Air Force Section. On December 1, 1962, Rowland relieved Anthis of his MAAG duty. Although Anthis and Rowland worked well together, some MAAG-Air officers wondered how far they might go in advising and training before entering into operational activities.[24]

Believing that he was "responsible for all that U.S. military do or fail to do in South Vietnam," General Harkins argued for full operational command over all American military resources in the country, to include projected covert operations. Admiral Felt thought otherwise. On April 20, 1962, he placed under MACV operational command those units having the primary mission of advising and assisting the training of Vietnamese military and paramilitary forces. Other units were to remain under CINCPAC component commanders. General Anthis deemed this interpretation important because the Air Force was meagerly represented on the MACV staff.[25]

The United States Army, Pacific—unlike the Air Force—elected to give MACV operational command over the Army helicopter companies in Vietnam. Created as the MACV component Army command, the United States Army Support Group, Vietnam, furnished administrative and logistic support to Army units in the country. General Harkins exercised direct operational command over U.S. Army helicopter companies through the MAAG senior Army advisor at each Vietnamese corps headquarters.

This arrangement appeared contrary to the principle restraining a unified commander from personally commanding a component force. Moreover, the MACV joint staff had to handle peculiarly Army matters that might have been more properly the work of an Army component command staff. The extra workload was often cited as a compelling reason for so many Army personnel on the MACV staff.[26]

Since MACV's birth on February 8, 1962, had been publicized, Lt. Gen. Thomas S. Moorman, vice commander in chief of PACAF, saw no reason why 2d ADVON should stay a paper organization. On February 20 General Moor-

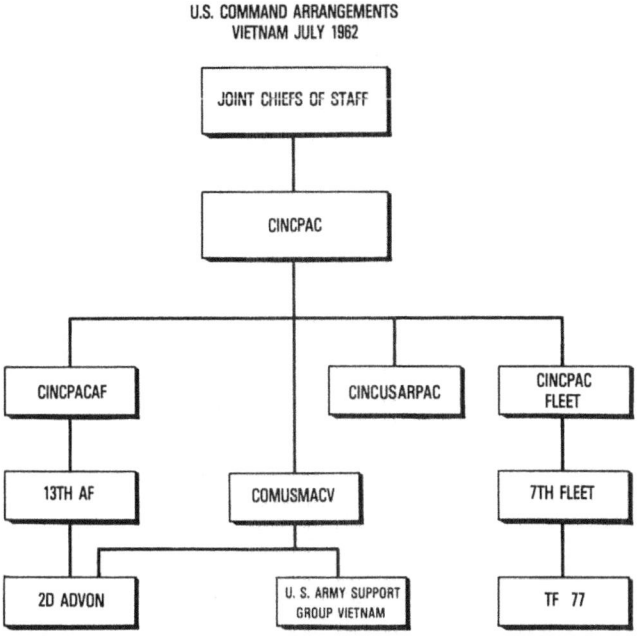

U.S. COMMAND ARRANGEMENTS
VIETNAM JULY 1962

Brig. Gen. Rollen Anthis and Air Force Secretary Eugene Zuckert on tour in the Pacific.

man asked Admiral Felt to accept a reorganization of 2d ADVON to make it a standard USAF air division. This meaningful designation would clear up the Air Force organization in Southeast Asia.[27]

Timing of the proposal was inopportune. The International Control Commission was examining MACV to see if its presence in the country violated the Geneva agreements. Under Secretary of State George W. Ball urged the United States to go along with the commission and "play the game partly their way." In response to questions from the press, President Kennedy insisted that no U.S. combat forces were in Vietnam. He did admit that training units were authorized to fire in self-protection if fired upon. Consequently, Felt and Harkins considered it impolitic to reorganize 2d ADVON into an air division at this time. Doing so could be misconstrued as the introduction of a large operational command.[28]

Visiting Vietnam in April 1962, General LeMay decided that something had to be done about 2d ADVON and its nondescript detachments. On some bases there were as many as nine separate air detachments, and no one person or organization was in charge. The Chief of Staff called for an air division to replace 2d ADVON and for an air base structure at each major operating location. Air Force headquarters prepared to replace 2d ADVON with a regularly constituted unit to which other units and personnel could be legitimately assigned.[29]

Two events hastened acceptance of this action. When American forces were deployed to Thailand on May 15, General Harkins was additionally designated commander of United States Military Assistance Command, Thailand. And on June 2 the International Control Commission labeled North Vietnamese activities as aggression and the establishment of MACV as a violation.[30]

Meanwhile the decision had been made to reveal the USAF role in Vietnam. Speaking in Los Angeles on April 27, General LeMay announced that the Farm Gate air commandos had the code name of Jungle Jim and were instructing allied crews in all phases of air operations. "This is a realistic training program," the Chief of Staff concluded. "Those people, the Vietnamese, are at war. Our instructors occasionally accompany them on combat missions. Our pilots are armed. They will protect themselves if fired upon."[31]

The *New York Times* remarked that the Air Force, besides stressing massive retaliation with nuclear weapons, was as much involved "in the guerrilla-warfare training" and in counterinsurgency as the other armed services.[32] Radio Hanoi broadcast that U.S. officers served in combat while instructing Vietnamese, adding: "American pilots are often at the controls in air strikes." Radio Peking depicted Farm Gate doings with considerable precision.[33] The reaction of the Farm Gate personnel—or air commandos, as they might now be styled—was that LeMay's speech legitimized their existence.[34]

Under Secretary of State George W. Ball spoke in Detroit on May 1, stressing that no American combat forces were in Vietnam and that the United States was neither fighting nor running the war.[35] The press reported Farm Gate's activities as follows: "None of these men are designated combat troops *per se*, but some will be fighting, just as their counterparts are today. . . . Sometimes an American instructor pilot has been at the controls in a strafing pass at jungle targets or on a bomb run."[36] Again: "Americans are also flying on bombing and strafing missions. . . . U.S. Air Force pilots fly B-26 bombers and T-28 fighter-bombers in air strikes against the Viet Cong and in support of ground troops."[37]

Still the Air Force was generally hidden behind the name Farm Gate, even though newspapers covered Army and Marine helicopter operations and the work of the Special Forces. If the air commandos and the USAF echelons above them were denied the recognition they wished, there was nevertheless a movement toward the conventional. On May 20 PACAF suggested and Air Force headquarters later approved redesignating the supporting detachments in South Vietnam. The 6220th, 6221st, 6222d, and 6223d Air Base Squadrons were formed respectively at Tan Son Nhut, Bien Hoa, Da Nang, and Nha Trang. All four units were assigned to 2d ADVON on June 7. Detachment 7 became Headquarters 2d Advanced Echelon, Thirteenth Air Force, and Detachment 10 became Headquarters 6010th Tactical Group.

Converting 2d ADVON to an air division was eased on July 19, when Ambassador Nolting no longer opposed the redesignation if it could be done without publicity. With the discontinuance of Headquarters 2d ADVON on October 8, the 2d Air Division was organized at Tan Son Nhut under General Anthis and assigned to Thirteenth Air Force.[38] This regularization of USAF unit organization indicated a movement away from counterinsurgency concepts and toward the conventional.

General Anthis served as the air component commander both in South Vietnam and Thailand, under General Harkins as commander of MACV and of Military Assistance Command, Thailand. Anthis was also responsible for U.S. air counterinsurgency in Vietnam.[39] PACAF saw that 2d Air Division, a forward echelon of Thirteenth Air Force and an operating headquarters in a forward area, could not do air planning for Southeast Asia as a whole. Since Thirteenth Air Force and PACAF afforded administrative and logistic support for air activities and plans, the MACV staff (though composed chiefly of Army officers) became the air planning agency. Although Thirteenth Air Force sent temporary duty officers to augment 2d Air Division planning, the command arrangement was awkward and hindered air actions.

Generals LeMay and O'Donnell wanted the MACV commander to have more and closer day-to-day associations with senior USAF officers. During his visit to Saigon in April 1962, LeMay had tried to persuade General Harkins to put more Air Force officers on the MACV staff. Harkins was unsympathetic but agreed to consider it if Anthis or Dunning could make a convincing case.

Upon returning to Washington, the Chief of Staff was critical of the MACV commander, believing air activities to be "depreciated in South Vietnam rather than appreciated." At a JCS meeting attended by Defense Secretary McNamara, General LeMay charged that air planning was often omitted from field operations, that General Anthis had difficulty seeing General Harkins, and that neither Harkins nor his chief of staff, General Weede, understood air operations.

Asked to comment, Anthis said he had direct access to General Harkins and had never been reluctant to give his views. Admiral Felt, CINCPAC, confirmed

Anthis' ability to speak with the MACV commander at any time. He further certified that Harkins and Weede were superior officers and fully experienced in air-ground tactics. Harkins was angered by what he described as General LeMay's "preferring charges" against him in Washington. He explained that the Air Force chief seemed to be thinking of command and control of large numbers of aircraft as in World War II, whereas there were essentially limited tactical opportunities for relatively few USAF aircraft in Vietnam.[40]

Throughout 1962 the MACV staff deficiencies were clear to Air Force officers who sought to unite air and ground power in utmost cooperation against the insurgency. But the defects were scarcely understood by those who believed that counterinsurgency was chiefly an Army mission and that USAF contributions could be but secondary. Secretary McNamara for one argued that the Army must be in the driver's seat. "If you have two or three men engaged in an operation," he explained, "one has to be primary. The Army has to be primary in land war. The Air Force is there to serve the Army in the airlift role and the close support role, and the Air Force must tailor its activities to the Army."[41]

As CINCPAC divorced PACAF from operational considerations and confined its authority to logistic support of 2d ADVON and, of late, to the 2d Air Division, General Anthis found it hard to secure a prompt hearing at MACV for his proposals. He discovered that several of his written communications were slow to reach General Harkins. The MACV commander's duties often took him from Saigon, and his staff carried on much of the business of command. Harkins followed Army practice in using his J-3 (Operations) for daily operational planning. Hence his J-5 (Plans), General Dunning, was frequently outside the routine MACV activity, especially since the J-5 division was situated in another part of Saigon away from the major MACV staff offices.[42]

X. Tactical Air Control, Mule Train, and Ranch Hand

The Viet Cong thought in November 1961 that victory was virtually in their grasp. Completing the first phase of insurgency, they had surrounded Saigon and other urban centers and blocked many highways. For the second phase, they set up subversive apparatus and were mounting overt attacks by guerrillas, many of whom had been trained in the north. During each of the first four months of 1962, an estimated 1,000 communists entered South Vietnam. Soviet aircraft stood ready to support two North Vietnamese regiments, poised in the Laotian panhandle for a possible thrust across the border. Either the North Vietnamese meant to move through the central highlands to cut South Vietnam in half, or they were forging an infantry division for attacks on Saigon. Both seemed likely alternatives.[1]

To hide its control over the insurgency, Hanoi in late 1961 renamed the southern branch of the Lao Dong Party the "People's Revolutionary Party." On December 7 the Provincial Committee of the Lao Dong Party in South Vietnam's Ba Xuyen Province declared:

> The People's Revolutionary Party has only the appearance of an independent existence; actually our party is nothing but the Lao Dong Party of Viet-Nam, unified from North to South, under the direction of the Central Executive Committee of the Party, the Chief of which is President Ho.

Securing a copy of this statement, President Diem sent it to President Kennedy with the comment, "Here at last is a public admission of what has always been clear—the Viet Cong campaign against my people is led by communists."[2]

There was nothing new in this—the point was, how to combat it? The actions of President Diem's government in November and December 1961 did nothing to reassure American observers. The apparent response to American demands for reforms appeared in a series of newspaper articles. Presumably prepared in the presidential palace, these pieces denounced the United States for imperialism. Still fearing a coup, Diem resisted forming an unbroken military command chain and giving confidence and authority to the chief of the Field Command. Diem was not alone in feeling that the United States was pushing too hard. At times several Vietnamese officers referred to counterinsurgency measures as the "American plan." They were far from convinced that U.S. ideas and methods would work in their country. In consequence Diem continued to approve every U.S. military advisor, explaining that he "didn't want to give the monopoly on nationalism to Ho Chi Minh."[3]

Having commenced resettlement projects, President Diem was drawn to the ideas of Sir Robert G. K. Thompson (former secretary of defense of the Federation of Malaya). Sir Robert arrived in Saigon during September 1961 as head of a British advisory mission. He suggested a program of strategic and defended hamlets to clear communists from the Mekong Delta. That same month, Diem started the Strategic Hamlet Program under the sponsorship of his brother, Ngo Dinh Nhu. It would take more than military activity to subdue the guerrillas, Diem judged, and permanent victory rested on restoring the faith of the people in the government. Resettlement, he felt, would help.[4]

In contrast, American officials pinned their hopes on a centralized nationwide counterinsurgency strategy to secure Saigon, other major centers, and lines of communications. It would also keep the Viet Cong off-balance with search-and-destroy operations to clear, seize, and hold what were becoming sizable Viet Cong base areas known as zones. The strategy further sought to seal off the border against infiltrators.[5]

In January and February 1962, Diem gradually conceded the need for a national concept of action, and he seemed to tilt toward a master plan by approving a series of separate projects in various places. The Vietnamese president desired that his and Farm Gate's aircraft attack Viet Cong supply routes. He appeared willing to authorize saturation air attacks against communist zones without exact targeting. Because his troops could not enter these areas, he deemed them solidly hostile.

In comparison, Generals O'Donnell and McGarr believed indiscriminate bombing might well disturb pacification efforts. Sir Robert Thompson also thought that innocent casualties would alienate potentially friendly people. At least two influential men in the State Department, W. Averell Harriman and Roger Hilsman, shared Thompson's view.[6]

American officials devised strategic guidelines for a massive counterinsurgency operation. Due to internal political reasons, Diem refused to accept an overall Vietnamese military commander. He opted for each corps tactical zone commander's having a "forward command post." More to Diem's liking was his decree of February 3 that designated an Inter-Ministry Committee for Strategic Hamlets to draw up a national plan. Besides the 784 defended hamlets completed and the 453 being built, he planned 6,066 more in 1962.

Failing to convince the Vietnamese to accept all-out military counterinsurgency, Defense Secretary McNamara acceded to a concept of smaller clear-and-hold operations. CINCPAC wished them to begin in Binh Duong Province where large communist groups threatened Saigon and Bien Hoa. But Thompson pointed out that a cleared Binh Duong would be hard to hold without pouring in thousands of troops. Diem okayed the Binh Duong mission, which got under way in March as the publicized beginning of the countrywide Strategic Hamlet Program. As he told Thompson, "It makes the Americans happy, and it does not worry either me or the Viet Cong." Decentralized clear-and-hold operations and the Strategic Hamlet Program comprised the major ventures against the Viet Cong.[7]

Having repeatedly ordered the U.S. military services to come up with special measures for countering the insurgency, President Kennedy remained dissatisfied with results. Urged by the Joint Chiefs and CIA to create a single authority in Washington to fuse all efforts, he formed on January 18, 1962, the Special Group (Counterinsurgency) chaired by General Taylor.[8] The group worked on the premise that subversive insurgency was a valid form of politico-military conflict, equal in status to conventional warfare. That perception was to be properly reflected in the organization and doctrine of all American programs. The group was to judge how well U.S. resources and actions dealt with subversion in South Vietnam, Laos, and Thailand. To coordinate with the group, the joint staff of the JCS gained a new office—the Special Assistant to the Director for Counterinsurgency and Special Activities.[9]

Indecision in autumn 1961 over American advisors engaging in combat now vanished. The special group pinpointed the particular character of counterinsurgency. Subtly but perhaps not always clearly, the group pushed for less American and more Vietnamese involvement in the war. This point of view clashed with President Kennedy's intent to have U.S. armed services use Vietnam as a laboratory for studying and testing counterinsurgency techniques and equipment. The President encouraged civil and military agencies to send senior officials on temporary duty to Vietnam for orientation and learning.

By November 1962 the Joint Chiefs of Staff mirrored the new outlook. The "scale of United States involvement and the level of force," they said, "should be limited" and merely supplement that of indigenous forces. Where guerrilla warfare flared, American military men were to give "operational assistance" to show U.S. resolve. They were to extend material aid and planning guidance, and to furnish intelligence, operational, and communications facilities that could be further expanded should the United States enter the war. American representatives were to "bring the combat conditions under control and . . . reestablish stability" by using Vietnamese forces in "well coordinated, integrated, and adequately supported operations." Yet the United States might have to act "outside the . . . host country" to deny safe havens to insurgents spilling across country borders. Somewhat contrary to the prevailing emphasis on training Vietnamese armed forces, the U.S. military services were expressly directed to refine their own doctrine, tactics, procedures, organization, and equipment.[10]

A wide assortment of schemes was tried amid a lingering uncertainty about the thrust of American policy and strategy. Nevertheless, President Kennedy's and Secretary McNamara's program of expanded American assistance sparked some noteworthy achievements.

For the United States Air Force in Vietnam, "the most pressing requirement" was a strong countrywide tactical air control system. The system would enable "effective and responsive Vietnamese Air Force tactical air operations," and squeeze the most from scarce Vietnamese and American air power. If President Diem saw how well central control worked, he might scrap the divided control of military and provincial chiefs. Since the Vietnamese could not run a control system, it would be "US manned and oriented."[11]

A tactical air control system had proved its worth in World War II and the Korean War both for air defense and close support. An air operations center

THE ADVISORY YEARS

afforded centralized planning, direction, and control of air operations in a combat theater. Supporting it was a reporting center for radar and other warning services. In each major ground command area were subordinate air support operations centers and warning posts.

PACAF and Thirteenth Air Force planned such a system for Vietnam in December 1961. Tied in with a combat operations center manned by U.S. and Vietnamese personnel for the Joint General Staff, an air operations center for overall control at Tan Son Nhut would also support the III Corps Tactical Zone headquarters. Two subordinate air support operations centers at Da Nang and Pleiku would serve the I and II Corps headquarters. Secretary McNamara rejected the idea of phasing in this system. He directed General O'Donnell to set it up at once from PACAF assets.

Transports from the 315th Air Division airlifted men and equipment into South Vietnam from January 2 to 14, 1962. The USAF 5th Tactical Control Group worked at Tan Son Nhut and Da Nang, while Vietnamese operated at Pleiku. The Air Force ran a communications center at Tan Son Nhut, and sent high-frequency radio teletype circuits to Da Nang, Bien Hoa, Pleiku, and Nha Trang.[12]

The initial system began operating on January 13, 1962. To avoid innocent targets, air strikes needed President Diem's prior personal approval. General Anthis briefed Diem and stressed how the system's instant information on enemy and friendly air activities led to quick response. Persuaded, he permitted the joint operations center to authorize air strikes.

This austere system brimmed with problems. Corps commanders reserved specific strike and transport aircraft for their own purposes, thereby taking them out of central control. Additional duties of officers at the center consumed part of their time. Vietnamese personnel were accustomed to afternoon siestas precisely during the hours when plans were readied and warning orders issued for the next day. Several Americans had no background for their jobs. Many grew impatient because work took longer when Vietnamese were involved. Quite a few of them were highly competent, but the air operations center was certainly not a Vietnamese "directed and operated facility" as eventually intended. It was rather "a USAF facility with some Vietnamese Air Force participation." Still the workers at Da Nang and Pleiku skipped siestas and performed well, due to insistence by their USAF counterparts that the Vietnamese themselves plan and monitor missions.[13]

A number of junior Vietnamese officers acted as forward air controllers and as air liaison officers with the ground forces. They were as hesitant to control strikes or to give advice as the ground commanders were to accept their services. Lacking authority and seemingly uninformed, these young officers appeared merely to transmit requests for information to their headquarters over communications nets not always secure.

Five USAF forward air controllers came to the country on February 15, 1962. They were pilots who were highly qualified to direct strike aircraft to targets by talking with them from observation planes in the area. The initial Air

Force liaison officers to advise and assist Vietnamese ground commanders got to Vietnam in April.

At first the USAF controllers were attached to Vietnamese ground forces likely to clash with the enemy. President Diem wished only rated Vietnamese observers to control strikes, so the Americans worked mainly as assistant air liaison officers. They also flew the L-19 for the Vietnamese observer-forward air controller and would help him. And they served as duty officers in the air operations center.[14]

Crippling the tactical air control system were the limited and failure-prone communications between the centers and the airfields. Through the early break-in period, numerous communications equipment failures took place. PACAF had obtained newly developed AN/TSC-15 high-frequency single-sideband radios for long-distance voice and teletype channels. The sets reached Clark on December 30, 1961, for field installation by the 1st Mobile Communications Group. Problems arose at once. Operators in the small mobile vans sweltered as temperatures often soared to 130 degrees Fahrenheit. Atmospheric conditions caused poor transmission and extensive use jammed the bands.

Mr. McNamara in January 1962 approved a JCS request for a civilian contractor to install an MRC-85 tropospheric scatter communications system. Page Communications Engineers, Inc., set about supplying many main link channels that joined Saigon, Nha Trang, Pleiku, and Da Nang. One channel linked Pleiku with Ubon, Thailand. Not until Page wound up its work in September 1962 were there rapid, positive, and dependable communications for central control over air operations.[15]

The air control system in being sufficed for a few forces, but an entirely integrated countrywide structure would enhance air power and train Vietnamese. It would in addition be a framework, under American command and control, for directing Farm Gate and USAF operational units later deployed to Vietnam.

Yet General McGarr, the MAAG chief, undermined the concept of a centralized tactical air control system by his handling of the two Army H-21 helicopter transport companies deployed to Vietnam in November 1961.[16] He assigned them to senior Army advisors of corps, then urged the Joint General Staff to reorganize the three Vietnamese L-19 liaison squadrons and the one H-34 helicopter squadron into four composite groups. He wanted three of the groups located at the three corps field headquarters and the fourth held in general support. That would give each Vietnamese army corps the helicopters and planes to conduct reconnaissance, move platoon- or company-size combat patrols, transport critical supplies, evacuate casualties, and perform staff and command liaison. When McGarr asked for Army CV-2 Caribou light transports, L-20 and L-18 liaison aircraft, and UH-1 (formerly HU-1) Iroquois helicopters for better support of the MAAG Army field advisors, he planned to place this air fleet under local rather than central control.[17]

Some Vietnamese questioned this parceling out of pilots and technicians of the Vietnamese Air Force, for it seemed to point to an "army air force." The main hope for expanding tactical fighter strength lay in upgrading L-19 and C-47 pilots. This would be impossible if the liaison squadrons passed to army control. Beyond that, maintenance and repair facilities at the corps headquarters for helicopters and liaison craft were few.[18]

Impetus for centralized airlift control came from the arrival in January 1962 of Mule Train, a temporary duty detachment designed to give logistic support to Vietnamese and American forces. Mule Train drew its aircraft and personnel from Tactical Air Command's 346th Troop Carrier Squadron (Assault) at Pope Air Force Base, North Carolina. Sixteen C-123 Providers arrived overseas in January, the first four touching down at Tan Son Nhut on the 2d. Mule Train had 243 officers and airmen and was complete with its own maintenance, air base personnel, medical detachment, and loadmasters. The commander was Lt. Col. Floyd D. Shofner.

In March permanent duty personnel from the 776th Troop Carrier Squadron started to replace the original Mule Train. The transfer was finished in June.

Of the sixteen Mule Train C-123s, four were at Clark in the Philippines, ten at Tan Son Nhut, and two at Da Nang. Operational control rested with CINCPAC through PACAF, Thirteenth Air Force, and 2d ADVON. A joint aircraft allocation board in the MAAG J-4 (Logistics) represented interested agencies and commands, set movement priorities, and designated space requirements. The airlift branch of the joint operations center, part of the tactical air control system, directed flights. Specialists on temporary duty from PACAF's 315th Air Division (Combat Cargo) joined Vietnamese Air Force officers in the airlift branch to control Mule Train. And they often helped the Vietnamese work the 1st Transport Group.[19]

In the initial seven weeks, Mule Train flew more than 500 sorties of 1,693 flying hours, moved 695 tons of cargo and over 3,600 passengers, and kept an operational readiness rate of eighty-five percent. Every C-123 was scheduled for 50 flying hours monthly, leaving time for training, testing, and flight to Clark for maintenance. The number of sorties rose steadily, from 296 in January to 1,102 in June.[20]

In February alone, Mule Train conveyed 1,035 passengers and 449 tons of cargo, dropped 174.5 tons of resupply to outposts, and transported 996 troops for airborne training. Frequently employed in long hauls with light loads, the C-123s operated at about ninety percent of capacity. They were supposed to support tactical operations, but made mostly routine cargo and passenger flights through 1962. The airlift system was not very efficient.[21]

Management of the Vietnamese C-47s was worse. The airlift branch could not consistently obtain firm priorities, and sudden shifts in daily orders stirred confusion at the operating and air terminal levels. Many times USAF personnel scheduling C-123s accepted Vietnamese requests based on sketchy C-47 mission reports. While C-47 crew shortages prevented peak operations, the 1st Transportation Group devoted about twenty-five percent of its effort to transporting very important persons (VIPs).[22]

TACTICAL AIR CONTROL, MULE TRAIN, AND RANCH HAND

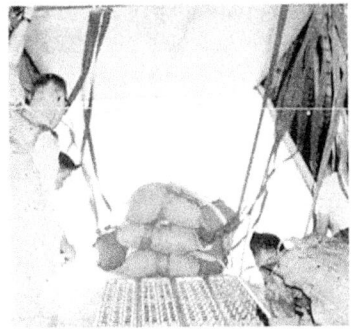

(Upper left) Viet Cong prisoners unload rice from a C-123 at Quang Ngai during a Mule Train resupply mission.

(Above) Supplies pushed from a C-123 for an outpost at Binh Hung.

(Left) C-123s at Da Nang.

(Below) Aerial view of a government outpost.

THE ADVISORY YEARS

Upgrading Vietnamese C-47 pilots to fill T-28 cockpits stripped the transport group, and Secretary McNamara authorized thirty USAF pilots to augment the unit. The pilots reached Tan Son Nhut in March and April. At once their relations with the Vietnamese pilots become prickly. Tension built until August when the commander, Lt. Col. Nguyen Cao Ky, assembled them all and asked that they work together. The meeting cleared the air, cemented close cordial relations, and boosted the sortie rate.[23]

To meet Army needs, the Air Force had developed the C-123 as an assault transport capable of carrying eight tons. In the late 1950s, however, the Army procured the CV-2 Caribou transport featuring a 2½-ton capacity and good short-takeoff-and-landing characteristics. By March 1962 Army leaders were pressuring Admiral Felt, CINCPAC, to approve a Caribou company for Vietnam. Late that month, General Harkins put in for a Caribou company and one squadron of C-123s. He intended that the Caribous concentrate on delivering supplies (chiefly food) to American advisors and isolated troops at remote spots. Of the 182 airfields in Vietnam, Harkins pointed out that 162 could accommodate CV-2s while only 115 could handle C-123s. To avoid additional overcrowding at Tan Son Nhut, he planned to base the Caribous at the unoccupied airfield of Vung Tau.[24]

To check General Harkins' evaluation of airfields, the 2d ADVON surveyed operating conditions. Aerial photographs disclosed fewer fields than listed, for some had been duplicated under French and Vietnamese names. Many small ones were unfit for either C-123s or CV-2s due to low load-bearing capacity, vegetation, or danger from the Viet Cong. At first 83 airfields seemed possible for C-123s, but another survey showed that 145 of the current 153 fields were suitable in dry weather.[25]

Admiral Felt was out of sympathy with General Harkins' desire for extra airlift. The Army's 18th Fixed Wing Aviation Company at Da Nang already owned sixteen U-1 Otters for corps support. A light utility plane, the Otter could haul one ton of small bulk cargo or seven to eight passengers. Additional aircraft, Felt believed, would overload the few facilities in South Vietnam. He favored better use of the C-123s and C-47s on hand.[26]

Like Felt, General LeMay and his party visiting Vietnam in April 1962 thought more transports, whether C-123s or CV-2s, to be unnecessary. To attain better airlift, they suggested assigning an experienced officer to establish tighter control. Col. George M. Foster, formerly PACAF director of transportation, reported to General Anthis for duty on May 1. Later in the month, Tactical Air Force Transport Squadron Provisional-1 was formed at Tan Son Nhut to bring the management of Mule Train and other C-123s under a single commander.[27]

General Harkins was still bent on securing CV-2 Caribous. He suggested using C-123 Providers to handle the main-line, long-haul airlift to thirty-nine airheads. At the same time, Caribous would take care of short-haul, feeder air transport to fifty-four locations. (The CV-2 could manage items too bulky and heavy for the U-1 Otters and UH-1 helicopters.) Once more the MACV commander requested an additional C-123 squadron and an Army CV-2 company.

TACTICAL AIR CONTROL, MULE TRAIN, AND RANCH HAND

Five of the C-123s were earmarked for Mule Train, five for airstrip alert, two for training, and four for maintenance and reserve. Two of the CV-2s were tagged for each corps to directly support advisors, four for the air transport system, two for MACV staff support, and four for maintenance and reserve.[28]

Admiral Felt acceded but told General Harkins that daily air supply to fifty-four points through thirty-nine airheads meant "many of your customers are eating too high on the hog." The Army's 1st Aviation Company of CV-2 Caribous went to Thailand with Joint Task Force 116, mainly for testing under field conditions. From Thailand the Army sent six CV-2s to Vietnam for dispersal in pairs to the corps advisors. American activities in Thailand tapered off during December, and General Harkins reassembled the whole Caribou company in Vietnam. He gave as his reasons the increased need for airlift and the desire for further field tests.[29]

When the JCS ordered Tactical Air Command to deploy a second C-123 unit to Vietnam, the 777th Troop Carrier Squadron at Pope furnished sixteen aircraft. These C-123s staged through Clark, four of them flying on to Thailand. The other twelve arrived at Da Nang on June 15, 1962, going under the Tactical Air Force Transport Squadron Provisional-2.[30]

General Moorman, PACAF vice commander in chief, had proposed that the 315th Air Division (Combat Cargo) form a lower headquarters in Vietnam to control the C-123s. General Milton, Thirteenth Air Force commander, protested the proposal. He said it would add another air headquarters in Vietnam independent of 2d ADVON, thereby tangling relations with MACV. Moorman next asked Milton to set up a combat cargo group in Vietnam under the operational control of General Anthis, the MACV air component commander. In addition to the airlift units assigned or attached to 2d ADVON, Anthis would control all USAF air terminal facilities in Southeast Asia. Moorman thought a Southeast Asia Airlift System complete with a combat cargo group to be "the damnedest exercise in overstaffing a proposal that I have ever heard of." Milton accepted the idea because it achieved professional supervision "without creating another little empire."[31]

General Moorman asked Admiral Felt to approve the plan for centralized control of regional airlift, and he requested General Harkins to establish an airlift allocations board. The board would require fifty more people in Thailand and Vietnam along with small movement control sections at Tan Son Nhut and Da Nang and in Thailand. Moorman also wanted an aerial port squadron in Vietnam. The overall concept appealed to Harkins, but he thought that the MACV J-4 could discharge the duties of the airlift allocation board. He agreed to let the system take in all Army, Navy, Marine, and Air Force airlift save helicopters. Felt then directed the MACV commander to form a joint airlift allocation board within his J-4, and told Moorman to create a combat cargo group as planned. At Tan Son Nhut PACAF organized the 6492d Combat Cargo Group (Troop Carrier) and its 6493d Aerial Port Squadron. Both provisional units were replaced in December 1962 by the 315th Troop Carrier Group (Assault) and the 8th Aerial Port Squadron.[32]

General Harkins directed the Joint Airlift Allocations Board in J-4 to approve all C-123 missions in Southeast Asia. But his chief of staff, General Weede, deviated from CINCPAC guidance. Weede neither defined General Anthis' responsibilities in the airlift system as the air component commander, nor made clear the combat cargo group's functions in running the air terminals. Nevertheless, the Southeast Asia Airlift System was broad enough to encompass Army Caribous, Marine R-4Ds, Vietnamese and Air Force C-47s, and USAF C-123s.

Airlift specialists were interested in a clean and straight-line organization. At the same time, General Anthis expected the C-123s also to fly tactical airlift generated through the air operations center of the tactical air control system. The arrival of the additional C-123s in June 1962 allowed the creation of a fire brigade, quick reaction force. Placed on a thirty-minute alert for emergency employment twenty-four hours a day, this composite force consisted of five C-123s, five (later six) C-47s, one L-19, and five hundred Vietnamese airborne troops.

The planes dropped all the paratroopers during a demonstration on June 5. Impressed, the Joint General Staff and the 2d Air Division planned to locate paratroop battalions and transport aircraft together at eight dispersed locations. The concept was never completely carried out, and despite its intrinsic merit the fire brigade idea fell into disuse. Tying down C-47s and C-123s to alert status turned out to be a waste of airlift.[33]

Between June and December 1962, the C-123s for the most part flew cargo and passenger missions instead of the tactical airlift for which they had been intended. This was due chiefly to the country's surface transportation being vulnerable to Viet Cong ambush.[34]

Along with Mule Train had come six C-123s equipped for defoliation operations and known as Ranch Hand. These planes plus sixty-nine men selected from the Special Aerial Spray Flight at Langley Air Force Base, Virginia, and the 464th Troop Carrier Wing at Pope made up the Tactical Air Force Transport Squadron Provisional-1. With Capt. Carl W. Marshall as officer-in-charge, the unit reached Clark on December 6, 1961, and there awaited policy decisions. It was assigned to PACAF and 2d ADVON but MAAG handled the planning and coordinating.[35]

The Advanced Research Projects Agency had been conducting small-scale defoliant tests in South Vietnam since August 1961. Pleased with the results, President Diem became an ardent advocate of the use of herbicides both to destroy crops and to strip away foliage concealing enemy activities. The MAAG readied a plan to try defoliant chemicals against border areas, Viet Cong crops, and Viet Cong base areas in Zone D. The JCS endorsed this plan on November 3, and Defense Secretary McNamara on the 7th ordered the Air Force to send planes, crews, and chemicals to South Vietnam. On November 30 President Kennedy approved the defoliation guidelines suggested by the Departments of State and Defense.[36]

TACTICAL AIR CONTROL, MULE TRAIN, AND RANCH HAND

The approvals were cautious. They called for carefully controlled defoliation flights along key roads and railways before undertaking food denial. There was to be no spraying in Zone D or along the border "until there are realistic possibilities of immediate military exploitation." In other words, spraying for the sake of spraying was out—it had to be linked with ground tactical operations. In theory the Vietnamese government was managing the operations and the United States was simply supplying the means and serving as a consultant.

United States planners saw the technique as an excellent measure to counter ambush, the classic guerrilla tactic mastered by the foe. Killing foliage would deny him hiding along roads and railways. The outcome of wiping out his crops was less certain.[37] But into the summer of 1962, General O'Donnell and Ambassador Nolting continued to harbor reservations on the untried chemicals. The State Department remained apprehensive that the common nontoxic herbicides would provoke communist charges of chemical warfare. In the meantime, however, Secretary McNamara was eager to continue defoliation activities.

Since the Viet Cong had already gathered their seasonal crops when the spray planes entered the country, the initial plan was to defoliate along 300 miles of strategic roads north and northeast of Saigon. President Kennedy severely pared this proposal on January 3, 1962. He authorized experimental spraying against separate targets that comprised merely 16 of the nearly 60 miles between Bien Hoa and Vung Tau on Route 15.[38]

The State Department wanted no advance notice aside from local and low-key warnings. Still, the Vietnamese government on January 10, 1962, "announced plans to conduct an experiment to rid certain key communications routes of thick tropical vegetation. U.S. assistance has been sought to aid Vietnamese personnel in this undertaking." Because the C-123 spray planes had no armorplating, General O'Donnell voiced concern that advance notice of flights would expose them to Viet Cong ground fire. The 2d ADVON consequently scheduled fighter cover from Farm Gate.[39]

According to the rules then in force, a Vietnamese needed to be aboard each spray plane. The planes were to stay clear of areas where food crops were growing. Province chiefs had to be alerted three days in advance of flights so they could explain the nontoxic spraying to their citizens.

Three C-123s, each fitted with an internal 1,000-gallon chemical tank and removable spray bars attached under the wings, departed Clark and arrived at Tan Son Nhut on January 7, 1962. After poring over aerial photos, the crews flew two familiarization sweeps along Highway 15 before embarking on their first full-scale mission on the 13th. For three days the planes sprayed a 200-meter-wide swath on both sides of selected segments of Route 15. Complete defoliation in ten days was counted on. However the leaves turned brown slowly, the vegetation remained alive, and few immediate military advantages resulted. Several tries at burning the sprayed areas fizzled.

The Viet Cong turned the spraying into a propaganda advantage. They claimed that the spray was chemical warfare and led the peasants to believe it was to blame for all dying plants. A Vietnamese government board established to

THE ADVISORY YEARS

TACTICAL AIR CONTROL, MULE TRAIN, AND RANCH HAND

P. 114: (Top) C-123 on a defoliation mission.

(Center) Brass sprayers in the rear of a C-123.

(Bottom) C-123K aircraft at Hickam AFB, Hawaii, en route to Vietnam for defoliation activities.

P. 115: (Right) C-123B on defoliation mission near Saigon.

(Center) View from inside a C-123 as it sprays foliage.

(Bottom) USNS *Core* in Saigon harbor with a cargo of Ranch Hand spray and equipment.

evaluate claims for accidental destruction angered those people whose suits were denied.

On February 2, 1962, a C-123 on a low-level training mission was lost. The cause of the crash was not clear. Enemy ground fire or sabotage was suspected, but the exact reason was never officially proved.[40] The three crewmen were the first USAF fatalities in South Vietnam.

By February several U.S. officials concluded that the spray project was badly managed. General O'Donnell termed it "a blooper from start to finish." He sought to discontinue the program, reconvert the C-123s to standard transports, and give them to Mule Train. He told Secretary McNamara that the spray operations were a waste of aircraft, and he recommended removal of the tanks and spray plumbing. General Moorman joined O'Donnell in calling the project militarily ineffective, and the State Department labeled it "too reminiscent of gas warfare." In the face of this opposition, McNamara went for continued herbicide experiments. He decided to press ARPA to make the spray work, sending a scientific team to Vietnam in April for a technical assessment. Brig. Gen. Fred J. Delmore, USA, commanding general of the Chemical Corps Research and Development Command, headed the team.[41]

General Delmore quickly discovered what had gone wrong with the Ranch Hand defoliant missions. Most of the plants had been dormant, and the herbicide was a growth-regulating chemical that worked only on actively growing plants. Furthermore, the spray system had dispensed too light a dose of chemicals. The system required readjustment and modifications.

These findings reassured President Diem. He was willing to begin herbicide operations against Viet Cong crops in the central highlands, where guerrillas were seizing food from the Montagnard tribal people. Relocating the Montagnards to strategic hamlets and destroying the crops would cause the Viet Cong to go hungry.[42]

Secretary McNamara agreed to seek approval for the use of herbicides against Viet Cong crops. Ambassador Nolting and General Harkins in July forwarded a specific proposal to allow the South Vietnamese to spray 2,500 acres in Phu Yen Province.[43]

Following the Viet Cong's killing of two Vietnamese perimeter guards near the Bien Hoa Airfield, Admiral Felt suggested spraying the areas around airstrips. Approval came in late June from Washington for defoliating the forest area north of the Bien Hoa runway. Vietnamese H-34 helicopters made these flights in July.

General Harkins next urged that Ranch Hand C-123s treat some 9,000 acres (around fourteen square miles) of mangrove forests bordering the rivers and canals of the Ca Mau Peninsula to deprive the communists of ambush cover. After approval, two C-123s started the spray operations on September 3. Another spray-equipped C-123 sent from the United States joined in later. Finished on October 11, the flights killed ninety to ninety-five percent of the vegetation along the waterway. It was estimated that the view from the air was five to seven times better than before.

This success spurred the Vietnamese armed forces on December 3 to seek widespread defoliation of around 90,000 acres alongside Vietnam's main highways. The State and Defense Departments let Harkins and Nolting approve operations to clear roadsides, powerlines, railroads, and areas adjacent to depots, airfields, and other field installations. Other targets took presidential approval. Inasmuch as the Vietnamese now wanted to spray on their own, McNamara wondered aloud why Diem did not buy weed-killing chemicals on the open market and go ahead.[44]

Viet Cong propaganda scoring defoliation handed Diem's government an unforeseen advantage. The Montagnards, who had been impressed with Ho Chi Minh's victory over the French, came to believe that the power to kill trees would bring victory to the Republic of Vietnam. Many of them left the highlands for resettlement in strategic hamlets. This migration reduced the Viet Cong's food supply, and guerrillas had to switch from fighting to farming.[45]

In Washington on September 25, 1962, the Vietnamese Deputy Minister of Defense pressed President Kennedy to authorize the use of chemicals to destroy crops. Kennedy agreed a few days later, and the State and Defense Departments authorized Harkins and Nolting to proceed with limited test crop destruction operations as long as they took precautions to prevent damage to innocent people and to feed refugees from sprayed areas. State insisted on approving every crop-destruction target, however.[46]

The rice crop in Phu Yen Province had matured by this time and appeared to be no longer a valid target. The State Department approved an alternate area in Phuoc Long Province and, on November 21 and 23, five Vietnamese H-34 helicopters treated about 775 acres of rice, potatoes, manioc, beans, and peanuts. This operation destroyed food sufficient to feed 1,000 communists for over a year. During February, May, and June 1963, Vietnamese ground troops sprayed portions of Thua Thien Province by hand.[47]

In general the Joint Chiefs of Staff favored further spraying, but President Kennedy withheld blanket authority. He did not wish it to appear that Americans were making war upon Vietnamese peasants.[48]

XI. Air Policy: Too Cautious?

During a conversation with President Kennedy in November 1961, Secretary of Defense McNamara had "volunteered to look after" the Vietnam War. To do this he set up monthly conferences in Hawaii or Saigon.[1] There, he and a Joint Chiefs of Staff member (usually the chairman) met with the Commander in Chief, Pacific Command, the Ambassador to Vietnam, and various component and unified commanders. The conferees discussed problems, courses of action, and progress. They traded views, reports, and briefings, and kept each other current on events in Southeast Asia and in Washington. Secretary McNamara often settled things on the spot, accepting or rejecting subordinates' suggestions.

A case in point was the first Secretary of Defense Conference held on December 16, 1961, in Hawaii. Mr. McNamara opened the meeting by stressing that the President did not desire to introduce American combat troops openly into Vietnam at that time. The Secretary conveyed his concern over the danger of alienating the Vietnamese people by careless bombing. The Army "has a particularly important role to play," he said. "While naval and air support operations are desirable, they won't be too effective, and we should not think they will win the war." McNamara wanted the C-123s in Vietnam used not for taxi service but for tactical airlift in support of the combat effort, to include drops of materiel and of Vietnamese troops. His one objective in Vietnam was "to win this battle."[2]

A chief order of business was the CINCPAC plan "to guide" the Vietnamese armed forces in a field campaign against the insurgents. The operations projected were in terms of task forces. Three or four battalions of infantry with supporting artillery and logistic units would attack Viet Cong bases, cut lines of communication, and clear and hold ground gained. No one knew what resources President Diem would give to this program. If Diem refused to take American advice, JCS Chairman Lemnitzer pointed out, the United States would be "in a bad fix." Mr. McNamara brushed this aside and brusquely told his followers to get on with their jobs.[3]

General O'Donnell, PACAF commander in chief, was impressed with McNamara's extremely strong statements of American determination to keep Vietnam from falling to the communists. But it soon became evident to him that strong talk did not necessarily mean strong action. The United States had chosen a prudent — perhaps too prudent — course and was accenting ground rather than air action. O'Donnell said that he personally deplored "overcontrol from the Washington level" but "as a soldier would comply with the spirit of the policy to be ultra cautious." Admiral Felt, CINCPAC, likewise believed that policies curbing air power were scarcely in the best American interest. General LeMay, Air Force chief, was also impatient with "our own military rules to handicap ourselves." He later reminisced: "If Khrushchev had been running it [the war], he couldn't have done any better, as far as handicapping us, by what we did to ourselves all through the thing from start to finish."[4]

In January 1962 USAF planners felt sure they had solved the problem of creating a "clear, realistic, jointly agreed concept for the elimination of Viet Cong influence." Their idea called for a quick reaction force of Vietnamese airborne troops, lifted and supported by U.S. or Vietnamese transport and strike aircraft. All would respond to radio calls from villages under communist attack, thus supplying the "missing ingredient of truly effective action in South Vietnam." This simple and direct reaction to overt enemy assaults on villages would entail nine Vietnamese battalions of paratroopers, ten C-123s, forty T-28s, and eighty H-34 helicopters. Split among several locations, the force would be on twenty-four-hour alert — quick to react to calls for help from communications teams in villages.[5]

Since Farm Gate was to take part in the program, precise targeting was a must. Guerrilla warfare blurred distinctions. The insurgents disguised themselves as civilians, found shelter among the populace, and depended on innocent inhabitants for food and other items. President Diem emphatically insisted that his airmen exercise utmost care to avoid angering the people by injuring innocents. Carelessness during an air strike could lead to a prison sentence.[6]

Thirteenth Air Force asked PACAF to lay down rules of engagement for Farm Gate, and the request was referred to CINCPAC for resolution. Admiral Felt stressed caution. The French Foreign Legion in Indochina had tried to work free of restraints hamstringing operations, on the basis that the native people knew that innocent and guilty would suffer alike if they harbored Viet Minh members. The French command had rejected this view, and "more temperate policies for using air power prevailed — although many tragic errors in target designation continued to be made until the end of the war." According to Felt, a realistic policy pivoted on good air-ground communications and on being "as careful as possible when shooting things up around friendly forces."[7]

Farm Gate bombs hit a Cambodian village by accident on January 21, 1962, killing several civilians. The incident raised at the "highest level" of the U.S. government the question of how to select targets without imperiling innocent people. To guide the discussion expected at the next conference attended by the Secretary of Defense, PACAF offered:

> We must exercise the greatest possible control and discretion to assure that we achieve our objectives without undue or unnecessary alienation of the civilian populace. If we are to avoid the imposition of highly limiting controls on the application of Farm Gate, we must make every effort to avoid another incident and, in addition, demonstrate the effectiveness of our control and ability to discriminate in the selection and designation of targets as well as in the conduct of air strikes.[8]

At the February conference, General Anthis depicted targeting and control of air strikes as oriented to protect the lives and property of friendly civilians. He said that all ground force requests for close air support or interdiction were carefully verified as justifiable before being met. Air Force personnel scrutinized every strike request and had recently denied two. Once a daylight strike was approved, a Vietnamese forward air controller directed it. Anthis knew of no attacks on friendly people.

Defense Secretary McNamara answered the 2d ADVON commander by spelling out guidelines. Air Force personnel were not to engage in strikes on Cambodian territory. They were to balance risk against gain. For example, a mission was probably unacceptable if eight Americans were training a single Vietnamese, or if there was a chance of killing innocent people to get a few Viet Cong.

By reason of this policy, more than half of the T-28s flying strike missions in 1962 returned to base with unused ordnance. One USAF forward air controller had seen Vietnamese troops after an engagement "put 60 artillery rounds into a village for no apparent reason and kill women and children." Yet he knew of no instance when "we indiscriminately went into any area and just for the heck of it bombed and strafed." In contrast, armed helicopters seemed almost free of the rules of engagement. These craft had no rigid target selection, no radar control for target location, and no forward air controllers to monitor their firing.[9]

During the night of March 1, 1962, the Viet Cong stormed an outpost about thirty miles north of Saigon. The call for help flashed to the air operations center thence to Farm Gate. An SC-47 flareship and two T-28s (carrying napalm, rockets, and .50-cal machineguns) scrambled, with radar at Tan Son Nhut vectoring them to the scene. Under the light of the blossoming flares, the T-28s pummeled the enemy. He broke off the assault and the outpost held. Five communist bodies were found the following day, along with evidence that more had been wounded.[10]

On March 3, II Corps asked for an immediate strike on a Viet Cong meeting near a village 105 miles northeast of Saigon. After clearance by Field Command, the air operations center sent one B-26 and two AD-6s, loaded with napalm, fragmentation bombs, rockets, .50-cal machineguns, and .20-mm cannon. The aircraft arrived to find the Viet Cong in the midst of a training exercise. The strike killed twelve.[11]

At times coordination failures hurt operations. On March 2, for example, eleven U.S. Army helicopters lifted and landed four ranger companies, a reconnaissance company, and a platoon of 105-mm howitzers in the Vinh Binh area to encircle a Viet Cong village. The Vietnamese and Farm Gate gave air cover with two T-28s and two L-19s. But the ground units were in the wrong places, and air-ground communications were absent. Although the two strike aircraft and the two liaison planes were overhead and available, they could deliver no supporting fire. The ground troops killed one Viet Cong and captured thirty-three suspects.[12]

While lapses in coordination and communications marred some operations, results in general infused mild optimism. On March 4 a Vietnamese L-19 serving with an army task force spied a company of Viet Cong (fifty to seventy men). They were situated near the bend of a river about thirty miles northeast of Tan Son Nhut. Vietnamese AD-6s scrambled within fifteen minutes, armed solely with 20-mm cannon since the planes were forbidden to carry bombs. Asked to

THE ADVISORY YEARS

assist, Farm Gate flew a series of strikes. Vietnamese reports the next day claimed fifty to sixty Viet Cong dead. A U.S. advisor put the figure at twenty-five.[13]

As MAAG told Defense Secretary McNamara on February 19, 1962: "South Vietnam had earlier been described as a country going down a steep slope to disaster. We can't say that the direction has been reversed, but for the moment the slope has leveled out a bit."[14]

For Farm Gate personnel the slope still seemed to be downhill. Their tasks were largely routine, and morale sagged. Being specially chosen, highly motivated survivors of rigorous training and selection, they expected to work with friendly guerrillas fighting behind enemy lines. But apart from a few challenging Special Forces missions, they performed close air support, airlift, medical evacuation, and psychological warfare — not at all what they had volunteered to do. The rules of engagement stymied these men — carry Vietnamese insignia and a Vietnamese airman, and do nothing that the Vietnamese Air Force can do itself.[15]

A chance to tackle something more exacting in psychological warfare had arisen in December 1961. Because certain areas controlled by the Viet Cong were open only to counterpropaganda by air, 2d ADVON turned to Farm Gate for testing loudspeaker and leaflet operations. Targets embraced the town of Ban Me Thuot, Pleiku, and Kontum, along with the villages of Polei Kleng and Polei Krong. Farm Gate planes carried out the broadcast and leaflet flights. To stave off starvation in Polei Krong, the aircraft further dropped rice and salt.[16]

Brig. Gen. Edward G. Lansdale, USAF counterinsurgency specialist, questioned the rationale of the tests. He suggested that unless technical experts knew precisely what they wished to achieve, probably nothing could be accomplished.[17]

On January 30, 1962, 2d ADVON put in for three officers, two specialists, and one clerk, all well-versed in "military-political-economic-psychological aspects" of this type of warfare. They would develop, test, and conduct operations in the "ideal environment" of South Vietnam. Missions suggested were dropping leaflets, food, and clothing. Unfortunately, no psychological warfare specialists were on hand. There had been several hundred trained officers in the early 1950s, but the Air Force had inactivated psychological warfare units in 1958.[18]

Farm Gate nonetheless flew seven missions from December 14, 1961, to February 11, 1962, dropping leaflets and making aerial broadcasts. The initial flights impressed Vietnamese villagers, but speaker quality was marginal. For the messages to be heard from the speakers in the belly of the SC-47, the run over the target needed to be at 600 feet at an airspeed of 100 knots or less. Even then, the message could not exceed sixty seconds. The speakers were later mounted on a rack in the plane's door. This let the aircraft circle an area while a crewman aimed the speakers at a specific spot. Still, the run had to be at a dangerously low 500 feet.

On February 11 an SC-47 took off in good weather for a routine leaflet mission south of Da Lat. The aircraft crashed for reasons unknown, killing eight Americans (six Air Force and two Army) plus one Vietnamese. This flight was portrayed without success as an attempt to train the lone Vietnamese aboard. Press and congressional reports characterized as "fiction" the labeling of American missions as "solely in the transportation and training of Vietnamese units."[19]

During the third Secretary of Defense Conference in Hawaii in February, Mr. McNamara said he wanted the Vietnamese to take over psychological warfare operations as soon as they could equip their C-47s with speakers.

Admiral Felt, CINCPAC, remarked that, although U.S. personnel "engaged in combat" from time to time, this was purely incidental to their training missions. He deemed these combat ventures as nothing more than support operations, and said "this should be fixed in the minds of the pilots and other U.S. personnel." McNamara then ordered action "to eliminate references to U.S. activities as combat operations; they are to be spoken of and reported as training or support activities regardless of the fact that incidental combat may be involved." To inquiries from the press, McNamara's office underscored the U.S. role as limited to advice, logistics, and training.[20]

United Press International published the essence of the Farm Gate combat story on March 9, 1962, reporting that U.S. airmen for two months had taken a direct part in attacks, and that Vietnamese had acted as copilots on these flights. According to the official explanation, the story added, this was an emergency measure until the Vietnamese Air Force could be trained. General Anthis, 2d ADVON commander, commented on the story's origin: "Due to the joint USAF-VNAF status of Farm Gate and the large number of people of both nationalities involved, it is extremely difficult to maintain strict secrecy concerning this operation."[21]

This situation bred difficulties regarding the amenities of life in the field for Americans. The first USAF arrivals had been hurried to South Vietnam to operate under wartime conditions. They and their successors over several years were bound by peacetime directives and procedures. These strictures were rendered more onerous by Secretary McNamara's centralizing decision-making at the highest Defense levels. Freshly arrived officers and airmen had their earliest brush with Vietnam at an airfield that was not a USAF base. At a military or civil Vietnamese base, the Air Force was a tenant because the U.S. government adhered to Article 18 of the Geneva agreement forbidding new military installations in South Vietnam.[22]

The physical layout of Vietnamese bases was crude. At some the main roads crossed runways, and at others the roads sliced through military areas next to the runways. Many fields wanted fences. Not until 1965 were there revetments to shelter aircraft.[23]

Tan Son Nhut, the Saigon airfield, was an international facility run by the Vietnamese Department of Civil Aviation. The Vietnamese Air Force was a tenant located in the southwest part of the field. The U.S. Air Force was supposed to approach the Department of Civil Aviation through the Vietnamese Air Force. In practice, however, the Americans made contacts with the government civilian aviation personnel who could give help and support. The Air Force borrowed one side of a hangar and an officer for the flight line. An arbitrary announcement solved flight control — any USAF aircraft operating at Tan Son Nhut would be under 2d ADVON authority and would file its flight plan with base operations. The Army and MAAG cooperated in filing flight plans and juggling parking space. Space was so scarce that the alert pad blocked the flow of planes taxiing for takeoff. But the civilian authorities were understanding and helpful.[24]

Bien Hoa was about ten miles from the outskirts of Saigon. This airfield's chief problem, aside from limited runways, was security. The field was garrisoned by a battalion of regular infantry, reinforced by a rifle company, two mortar companies, four armored cars, and two 105-mm howitzers. A company of rangers provided distant patrols, and a sixty-man Vietnamese Air Force police detachment gave interior security. Farm Gate formed twelve fifteen-man combat teams, each with at least one Browning automatic rifle, and fused them into base defense plans. The flight-line area was the final defensive position.[25]

In general USAF personnel coped with the poor facilities, but the supply picture was bleak. Paperwork was sketchy on the stocks prepositioned in South Vietnam before the Air Force buildup. Most POL came through the port of Saigon and was distributed commercially, a system vulnerable to interruption and blackmail. There were no on-hand reserves of electric generators, portable buildings, bulldozers, crash firefighting equipment, graders, or construction equipment. Due to the distance, expendable items trickled in from the United States through Clark. Large items coming by ship took sixty days.[26]

The supply problems had a number of offshoots. In late February 1962, for example, 2d ADVON requested the removal of grass and the renovation of fencing and lighting at the transmitter site. There was no action until a grass fire nearly destroyed antennas, cables, and the building itself. The grass was bulldozed the next day, but nothing was done to fix the fences and lights. Thirteenth Air Force refused a March request for six hundred dollars to shelter the TSC-15 vans, in which the daytime temperatures of the working areas rose to 130 degrees Fahrenheit. Thirteenth suggested that the workers be moved to tents.

Men departing the United States for Vietnam duty in many cases did not know their destination in advance. Unable to bring useful items with them, they often went to the nearest town and bought minor things out of their own pockets. MAAG was generous and shared its meager stocks informally. Scrounging was frequently resorted to. Short supplies, particularly of paper, affected billeting, mess, pay, and mail.[27]

In the early days, the cramped quarters were lean-to tents or quickly built Vietnamese-style hutments. Numerous rats and insects made it difficult to sleep. There was no hot water even after USAF personnel had been in the country for a year. Offices were crowded and desks, chairs, and tables often improvised.[28]

After adjusting to their quarters, the new arrivals faced hazards in the mess. Baked goods and ices were sources of infection. Unsanitary practices in local baking firms finally ended local procurement. There was too little refrigeration space under U.S. control, and ice freezers for the field were not to be had. Locally hired employees at snack bars in officers' and service clubs were poorly supervised. The outcome was a high sick rate.[29]

No wonder that General LeMay, during his Vietnam visit in April 1962, found USAF aircraft to be underutilized.[30]

Lowered vitality and loss of energy among the men grew out of chronic low-level fevers, dysentery attacks, and too few fresh fruits and vegetables. Medical detachments of the U.S. Army gave local area medical support. Hospitalization became available on April 18, 1962, when its 8th Field Hospital opened at Nha Trang.[31]

Pay was erratic. Checks regularly arrived late and at times never. Men could not meet mess bills and travel expenses. Emergency casual payments often resulted in overpayments.[32]

Mail service was primitive. Units outside of Saigon received no regular deliveries, and no arrangements existed to buy stamps, cash money orders, or dispatch classified mail. Mail came through Clark on Mondays, Wednesdays, and Fridays. The U.S. Army post office in Saigon was closed on Saturdays and Sundays. Recipients of classified or registered mail were notified informally and needed to make their own delivery arrangements.[33]

Aggravating these problems were austere maintenance procedures, 2d ADVON's unconventional organization, adherence in Washington to peacetime practices in procurement and purchase, and the general inability to forecast the number of Americans committed to South Vietnam. Ironically, USAF personnel were not in the jungle with guerrillas but were for the most part in or near metropolitan Saigon, a seaport and industrial center of almost two million people in 1962. There, the Air Force engaged in routine tasks and trained the Vietnamese Air Force, which began to expand and to fly more operational missions.

XII. Farm Gate and the Vietnamese Air Force

Farm Gate, Detachments 7 through 10, and miscellaneous units contained 838 USAF personnel by the end of 1961. Together these units made up a modest strike, photo-reconnaissance, and airlift force. But far more significant, they were the nucleus of a rapidly expanding American effort. Since the rules of engagement confined USAF planes to missions the Vietnamese were unable to perform, strengthening the Vietnamese Air Force was all-important.

The 1st Fighter Squadron at Bien Hoa owned twenty AD-6s, each capable of flying one operational sortie per day. The 2d Fighter Squadron at Nha Trang was being readied for combat. Because it was to receive thirty T-28As and fourteen T-28Bs, the pilots would require transition training in gunnery, bombing, and rocketry. The 1st, 2d, and 3d Liaison Squadrons had fifteen L-19s apiece and needed more pilots. Hence additional officers would undergo flight training in the United States.

The AD-6 pilots were proficient in daytime flight, but their former carrier aircraft lacked landing lights. This and the frequently inoperable flight instruments prevented pilots from gaining experience in night and all-weather flying. They showed slight interest in flying night combat, even though the Viet Cong operated mostly during the hours of darkness.

To secure combat missions, Colonel King had proved that T-28s and B-26s could fly night missions under flarelight furnished by SC-47s. But when saddled with training the Vietnamese, the Farm Gate commander was surprised and disappointed. He continued to discuss with General Anthis, 2d ADVON commander, whether training was the cover for combat or the primary mission. As King later frankly admitted, he "resisted" Anthis' instructions.

Grudgingly, Farm Gate commenced the training. Vietnamese AD-6 pilots served as crewmembers on B-26s and T-28s, but disliked flying in the T-28 rear seats. Yet, they could not take over the front seat on combat missions until they were qualified in every respect. At that point no need existed for a Farm Gate instructor in the rear seat. Backseat combat training was more political than practical.

The basing of Farm Gate and the Vietnamese AD-6s at Bien Hoa might have eased combined missions, but the air operations center went on issuing separate orders. Colonel King nevertheless promoted training and demonstrated that air detachments could operate from remote locations a long while. This success eventually moved the 1st Fighter Squadron to stage two AD-6s each to Pleiku and Da Nang. King also sent four T-28 pilots to Nha Trang to give Vietnamese instructors flight training.[1]

More to Farm Gate's liking was the mission of January 3, 1962. Alerted to Viet Cong sampans drawn up under camouflage south of Saigon, Colonel King and Lt. Col. Robert L. Gleason made an afternoon flight and took photographs of the exact spot. Shortly after dark, King led a bomb and rocket strike. The SC-47 flareship approached the target area with the T-28s in trail and about 2,000 feet higher. After the flares ignited, the strike aircraft swooped down and demolished the enemy boats. Photos revealed that one 500-pound bomb, dropped by Capt. William E. Dougherty, scored a perfect strike in the middle of the sampans.[2]

Such rapid reaction induced the joint operations center to place an SC-47 on strip alert, ready to join T-28s and B-26s in night action. While these tactics failed to wipe out enemy units, they forced the Viet Cong to break off attacks and fade into the jungle. Meanwhile, Vietnamese C-47 crews were sufficiently trained by February 1962 to fly night missions with Farm Gate.[3]

Farm Gate experience in the first months of 1962 dictated a change in ordnance loads. The detachment sharply cut back on general purpose bombs, and shifted from the 250-pound bomb to the M-1A2 cluster of six 20-pound bombs. By June, Farm Gate upped its use of rockets, napalm, and strafing. Sometimes more than one canister of napalm was required to burn a hole in the ground cover.

Strike aircraft inhibited the Viet Cong from firing. If the aircrews spied the source, they quickly opened up with formidable firepower. The T-28 packed two .50-caliber machineguns, the B-26 eight. Both planes carried bombs and rockets.[4]

The white smoke of the M-19 marker dissipated too swiftly, while the aircrews rarely saw the red smoke of the M-18 through the jungle canopy. Smoke bombs in general were unreliable, and the method of dropping them on poorly defined targets was "most ineffective."[5]

The first combined American-Vietnamese air operation occurred near the end of December 1961. Two U.S. Army helicopter companies whisked 360 Vietnamese troops to five landing zones in the Viet Cong-dominated Zone D, then several days later brought in additional troops. A Vietnamese L-19 forward air controller and two AD-6 bombers orbited the area but saw no targets. The troops failed in their main mission — capture of a radio transmitter — but killed two Viet Cong, wounded one, and captured forty-six suspects.

A larger operation took place on January 5, 1962, to rescue prisoners in a Viet Cong camp near Saigon. A Vietnamese forward air controller directed AD-6s, T-28s, and B-26s to fly preparatory strikes. Under this cover, thirty-one H-21 helicopters shuttled in 1,000 Vietnamese troops. These efforts went for naught — the information about the prison camp proved to be erroneous.[6]

A number of the problems in search-and-destroy operations stemmed from three factors: preliminary air reconnaissance tended to destroy surprise, plans on occasion were too complex for the fledgling Vietnamese Air Force to carry through, and coordination between ground and air units was weak.[7]

The air defense system likewise left much to be desired. Since the Soviet Union had transport aircraft at Hanoi, a key aim of the American presence was to deter this airlift from extending to Laos and from affording air support to the Viet Cong. Rumors in early 1962 told of Viet Cong in the central highlands receiving secret air resupply drops. Time and again the air warning radars at Tan Son Nhut and Da Nang together with the light radar at Pleiku picked up unidentified tracks. At times these turned out to be tricks of the atmosphere, but often were U.S. Army aircraft on flights the reporting center knew nothing of. On the other hand, the Da Nang radar could not detect planes flying at low and middle levels because the terrain to the west screened them. Furthermore, the AD-6s, T-28s, and B-26s were unsuitable for intercepting communist aircraft penetrating South Vietnamese airspace. In February 1962 General O'Donnell called for unified air action. To establish "law and order in the air," he suggested that the air operations center control and coordinate all air operations, including helicopter combat support.[8]

Two mutinous Vietnamese flyers first tested the air defense system, designed to signal communist intrusion. On the morning of February 26, 1962, the two diverted their AD-6s from a planned strike in the delta, and zeroed in on President Diem's palace. The 1st Fighter Squadron scrambled two flights of AD-6s to intercept the rebels, but the planes merely gathered hits from small-arms fire. Farm Gate aircraft took to the air to elude possible destruction on the ground. Antiaircraft fire downed one of the two attacking planes, and its pilot was captured. The other escaped to Phnom Penh, Cambodia, where he emerged unscathed from a crash landing. Interrogation of the captured flyer confirmed that the two pilots were engaged in a vendetta against Diem's brother, Ngo Dinh Nhu.

Although there appeared to be no general plot against the government, Diem grounded the Vietnamese Air Force temporarily. Later he permitted the Vietnamese strike planes to carry only 20-mm ammunition. Still later he ostensibly authorized the planes a full array of ordnance, but the Joint General Staff restricted bombloads for missions in II and III Corps. Ambassador Nolting secured permission from Washington for Farm Gate aircraft to support ground operations. To dispel the impression that the United States was taking over the fighting, AD-6s had to accompany American planes.[9]

In March 1962 a total of 1,861 incidents (attacks, acts of terrorism, sabotage, and subversion) stirred apprehension that the communists were about to step up the war.[10] Pleiku radar on the evening of the 19th showed seven unknown flight tracks over the central highlands. Farm Gate scrambled a B-26 from Bien Hoa, and when it reached the area, radar control placed the aircraft directly over one of the tracks. The crew saw nothing. The next day, reconnaissance pilots noticed some bundles in the trees. On the night of the 20th, Tan Son Nhut radar detected unknown tracks leading out of Cambodia. Two Farm Gate T-28s were scrambled but the tracks faded. Soon after these T-28s were recalled, Pleiku reported ten to fifteen low-altitude tracks emerging from Cambodia. One SC-47 and two RB-26s were dispatched from Bien Hoa. The SC-47 dispensed flares while the RB-26s searched in vain.[11]

Upset over the sharp rise in Viet Cong incidents, President Diem asked for U.S. jet interceptors to deal with enemy overflights. Ambassador Nolting quickly cleared the request with Washington. On March 22 the 405th Tactical Fighter

THE ADVISORY YEARS

(Above) Vietnamese officers and American advisors plan an airlift of Vietnamese paratroopers at Tan Son Nhut.

(Top right) 1st Lt. Wilfred G. Narr demonstrates airlift maneuvers with model of a T-28 aircraft as two Vietnamese students look on at Moody AFB, Ga.

(Right) A1C H. R. Wilson and A1C R. L. Fleury install rockets into a B-26 bomber at Bien Hoa.

(Below) F-102 Delta Daggers.

FARM GATE AND THE VIETNAMESE AIR FORCE

Wing deployed a detachment of the 509th Fighter Interceptor Squadron from Clark Air Base to Tan Son Nhut. The detachment's aircraft consisted of three single-seat F-102s and one TF-102 with side-by-side seating. The Joint Chiefs of Staff authorized Americans to engage and destroy hostile aircraft encountered over South Vietnam.[12]

The speedy arrival of the F-102s pleased the Vietnamese government.[13] Still the air defense system was far from perfect. In training exercises, the F-102s flew much too fast to intercept the slow liaison planes that acted as enemy intruders. Experience also taught that two pilots in a TF-102 had a better chance to intercept than one pilot in an F-102. Further TF-102s were therefore drawn from the Fifth and Thirteenth Air Forces. On July 21 Admiral Felt ordered three Navy AD-5Q interceptors from Cubi Point, Philippines, to relieve the F-102s. From then on, F-102s and Navy interceptors alternated six-week tours of air defense duty.[14]

As air defense and traffic control improved, the unknown radar tracks diminished. To help radar tell friendly from enemy planes, MACV on August 22 ordered every American military aircraft to emit Identification Friend or Foe impulses if equipped to do so. When months passed without enemy air activity, General Harkins said it was certain there was "no air battle in Vietnam, and there are no indications that one will develop."[15]

The sudden jump in Viet Cong incidents during March 1962 led USAF officers to raise the question of enlarging Farm Gate with four B-26s now in the Far East and with four T-28s. They reasoned that B-26s were the best tactical aircraft for counterinsurgency, T-28s were needed for detachments at smaller airfields, and Vietnamese forces were still learning how to use air power with ground operations. General Harkins and Ambassador Nolting backed the proposal. Defense Secretary McNamara, however, noted that the Vietnamese 2d Fighter Squadron was becoming operational. He asked how much longer American pilots had to fly with the Vietnamese. General Anthis replied that Farm Gate would have to serve as a demonstration force and to check the state of Vietnamese training and standardization for quite a while. McNamara okayed the request but delivery of the planes to Farm Gate was delayed due to the Vietnamese Air Force buildup.[16]

During General LeMay's Vietnam visit in April 1962, the initial expansion of Vietnamese strike aircraft neared its end. The thirty USAF C-47 pilots assigned to the 1st Transportation Group had released seasoned Vietnamese pilots to fighter cockpits. Moreoever, twenty-five T-28 pilots were combat-ready for the 2d Fighter Squadron. With thirty flying hours a month planned for T-28s and twenty-five for AD-6s, the Vietnamese could complete 140 T-28 and fifty-five AD-6 sorties each week. Since the training of T-28 pilots was drawing to a close, Farm Gate found it harder to get Vietnamese crewmen for its flights. Though LeMay noticed marked improvement among the Vietnamese, he doubted they could meet all their operational demands for some time to come. Because Farm Gate was flying less than it could, LeMay wanted the crews to log more missions. This would allow American airmen rotating through Vietnam to attain valued experience that might well be needed elsewhere. He suggested relaxing the restrictions calling for a Vietnamese crewman to be aboard Farm Gate planes and confining Farm Gate to offensive missions beyond the competence of the Vietnamese.[17]

General LeMay won little support for these proposals in Washington. Secretary McNamara sought to shave American participation in Vietnam, so as to attain an all-out Vietnamese military effort. Counterinsurgency doctrine required indigenous forces to fight their own war. McNamara was thus interested in having the Vietnamese take over the Farm Gate planes as soon as possible.[18]

Hampered by the original rules and restrictions and the scarcity of Vietnamese trainees, General Anthis secured the assignment of eleven Vietnamese aviation cadets to Farm Gate. Until they could attend flight training in the United States, the cadets served as the Vietnamese member of every Farm Gate crew.[19]

Based at Nha Trang but with a detachment of six T-28s at Da Nang, the 2d Fighter Squadron became fully operational in mid-1962. This afforded much-needed air power in the central and northern areas of Vietnam, freeing the 1st Fighter Squadron and Farm Gate for operations in the south. As a result, Vietnamese and Farm Gate sorties multiplied, mainly for interdiction and close support. Still the Vietnamese asked for too few air missions. They neglected to have aircraft cover convoys and trains, to escort helicopter assault operations, and to fly even more interdiction and close support strikes.

But augmenting the Vietnamese Air Force seemed to have been successful. Secretary McNamara was so pleased with the progress that he told General Harkins to firm up a program for phaseout of major U.S. combat, advisory, and logistic activities within three years.[20]

The Secretary was unaware of the glaring deficiencies that impeded the Vietnamese. Pilots continued in short supply and many of those flying needed more training. The two fighter squadrons had fewer than a dozen qualified flight leaders, and ground personnel were generally inefficient. The T-28s lacked ample firepower and would someday have to be replaced, calling for more pilot training. A lack of proficiency in night and all-weather flying diluted efficiency. Rather than the average of one hour or less, Vietnamese turnaround time between missions averaged between two and three hours. The fastest scramble time for a Vietnamese C-47 flareship was forty minutes, and over an hour was normal. The Vietnamese were cleared to operate with a full array of ordnance, but their strike aircraft were armed solely with napalm, rockets, small fragmentation bombs, and cannons. They were reluctant to move aircraft to advanced locations because of poor housing and messing at Da Nang and Pleiku, and the low pay for temporary duty.

General Anthis estimated that the two Vietnamese fighter squadrons, with twenty-seven T-28s and twenty-two AD-6s, should generate 1,470 operational sorties a month — seventy percent for combat and thirty percent for training and maintenance. Actually an average of seven AD-6s, eleven T-28s, eleven L-19s, and eight C-47s were available each day to the tactical air control system.

FARM GATE AND THE VIETNAMESE AIR FORCE

Since the number of Vietnamese combat sorties fell short of meeting the rising demands for air missions, Farm Gate operations reached new high levels. By August it was clear that Farm Gate had to have fresh aircraft and crews. The coming of two new U.S. Army helicopter companies in September meant even greater requirements for escort and supply sorties by strike aircraft. This clashed with Secretary McNamara's desire to phase out American units.[21]

General Anthis had foreseen that mission demands would compel Farm Gate planes to stretch beyond monthly programmed flying hours. He suggested that additional USAF units be allocated to Vietnam, chiefly to allow air strike teams to be kept permanently on station at Pleiku and Soc Trang. Thirteenth Air Force in mid-August sent Farm Gate four B-26s from Far East assets.[22]

Farm Gate continued to fly too many hours, and in September Anthis asked for ten more B-26s, five T-28s, and two C-47s. General Harkins made no reply, but PACAF recommended that the Air Staff put the proposal on the agenda of the October Secretary of Defense Conference. Gen. Walter C. Sweeney, Jr., commander of Tactical Air Command, and Brig. Gen. Gilbert L. Pritchard, Special Air Warfare Center commander, agreed that the Air Force could furnish the planes and crews. However, they cautioned Anthis to "go slow" in adding to Farm Gate until he was completely convinced that the Vietnamese were doing as much as they could. Sweeney did not want Farm Gate "to become a crutch to compromise progressive and objective development of indigenous capabilities."[23]

Allegedly to confuse the Viet Cong, the Vietnamese renumbered their squadrons in September.[24] With the new designations went an emphasis on the organizational unity of the Vietnamese Air Force. Perhaps the structure was partly inspired by the proposal of the U.S. Army Chief of Staff, Gen. George H. Decker, to transfer Vietnamese helicopter and liaison squadrons to the Vietnamese army.[25]

Securing the go-ahead from the Air Staff in October to give additional aircraft to Farm Gate, PACAF suggested this action to CINCPAC. Briefed on October 8 in Hawaii, Defense Secretary McNamara was still bent on building a wholly adequate Vietnamese Air Force. He said there should not be 130 but 300 or more Vietnamese officers taking flight training in the United States. Since no Vietnamese pilots were in training to fly B-26s, the Secretary asked Admiral Felt to explore the prospect of procuring thirty Chinese Nationalists for the Vietnamese C-47s. This would release thirty transport pilots for B-26 transitional training. As for Farm Gate expansion, McNamara said, if General Harkins needed a bigger program, he should present his case to the Joint Chiefs of Staff. He himself was "cool" to the idea, for it was contrary to the President's desire to build indigenous forces. Farm Gate ought to train Vietnamese rather than to operate.[26]

Farm Gate operations in August had soared to sixty-five percent over those in July. But in September they had to be pruned to thirty-seven percent of the July totals, owing chiefly to the one-crew-per-aircraft manning ratio — not enough to sustain the high rate of missions. The Vietnamese wanted the eleven aviation cadets returned for language training before going on to the United

States to become pilots. To furnish the crewmen required on Farm Gate planes, the Vietnamese Air Force sent fifteen noncommissioned officers to Farm Gate. This plugged the gap but was a subterfuge, because the enlisted Vietnamese were uninterested in flight training. When General Moorman, Thirteenth Air Force commander, heard of the arrangement, he urged Anthis to do his best to meet McNamara's wishes.[27]

Admiral Felt visited Vietnam in late October and talked with Anthis. He said Vietnamese opposition had scuttled the prospect of using Chinese pilots to fly Vietnamese transports. Any Farm Gate growth would have to be small and piecemeal.[28]

Acting on Anthis' suggestion to shore up Farm Gate, General Harkins in November asked for five T-28s, ten B-26s, and two C-47s. More, he said, would likely be required in the future. Admiral Felt routed the request to the Joint Chiefs, adding that he saw no other way to secure the urgently needed combat air power.[29]

The Joint Chiefs of Staff well knew that President Kennedy wished the Americans to prepare the Vietnamese to fight their own war. Hence in November and December the chiefs carefully weighed the question of bolstering Farm Gate. They likewise plumbed the oft-stated position that counterinsurgency was for the most part a ground war, with air forces accounting for maybe ten percent of the effort. Some USAF officers viewed counting Viet Cong casualties as an "unpleasant task" and "not necessarily the military objective." Even so, statistics on the number of enemy killed, wounded, and captured were important. In all known cases where ground forces entered areas struck by air, their actual body count exceeded aircrew claims. (Of the estimated number of enemy casualties in 1962, twenty-eight percent were due to Vietnamese and American air power.) Yet air operations did more. They shrunk the enemy's options, crimped his movements and attacks, flew in men and supplies to assault him, protected surface convoys and trains as well as heliborne assaults, and thwarted the foe from massing large forces in the field. Air power had proved — at least to USAF officers — that it held equal rank with ground operations in any counterinsurgency venture.[30]

This assessment was not altogether shared in Washington. Following a visit to Southeast Asia in December 1962, Roger Hilsman, Assistant Secretary of State for Far Eastern Affairs, and the President's Special Assistant for Far Eastern Affairs, Michael V. Forrestal, reported:

> On the use of air power and the danger of adverse political effects, our impression is that the controls on air strikes and the procedures for checking intelligence against all sources are excellent. In spite of this, however, it is difficult to be sure that air power is being used in a way that minimizes the adverse political effects . . . and the use of air power is going up enormously.[31]

In December the Joint Chiefs recommended expanding Farm Gate, so it could keep abreast of the burgeoning requests for air support. The Secretary of Defense concurred, the State Department agreed, and on the last day of the year the President approved the requested increase in Farm Gate aircraft.[32]

XIII. Air Operations, 1962: Interdiction, Strikes, and Reconnaissance

In World War II and the Korean conflict, interdiction had slowed the flow of enemy forces, supplies, and equipment into and within battle areas. In Vietnam, according to General Anthis, "the most lucrative targets" were Viet Cong training areas, troop concentrations, supply depots, and sampans. Admiral Felt and General O'Donnell had the same impression. Interdiction air attacks against Viet Cong base areas held a special attraction because the Vietnamese ground forces seldom penetrated to them.[1]

Yet air interdiction was very complex. The Viet Cong rarely wore distinctive uniforms, and they mingled freely with civilians. To tell them from the general populace called for timely intelligence and reliable aerial reconnaissance. Unfortunately, the Vietnamese Air Force owned but two C-47s rigged with cameras for day photography. The single air photo intelligence center and its twelve photo observers were situated in the J-2 division of the Joint General Staff. The L-19 observers could do visual reconnaissance, but the best of them were being shifted to tactical fighters.[2]

Able Mable RF-101s operated out of Don Muang Airport near Bangkok, Thailand. They sustained a daily sortie rate of 2.8 flights, and photographed high-priority areas of interest to MACV and the Vietnamese. When over South Vietnam, these planes as a rule staged through Tan Son Nhut, where they turned over their film to the small USAF photo processing cell for interpretation. Although the RF-101 was good for general reconnaissance of clearly fixed targets, it was not suited to spotting an enemy who hid under heavy foliage by day and moved at night. Furthermore, processing and interpreting the photography in Saigon, then delivering it to requesting units by U.S. Army courier plane, usually took several days. Some ground commanders complained that the interval between a request and a delivery was at times thirty to forty-five days.[3]

Intelligence from members of the enemy forces was needed, and it was scarce. Starting in December 1961, U.S. intelligence advisors did their best to teach their methods to Vietnamese. Besides the 44 specialists in MACV J-2 (Intelligence), 230 Americans worked with Vietnamese units in the field. Unproductive from the USAF point of view, MACV intelligence was oriented toward ground operations.[4]

Normally, Vietnamese interrogations of prisoners should have yielded significant information. But the law authorized the military to hold prisoners only two days before handing them over to provincial authorities for a court hearing. This was not time enough to learn about enemy activities vulnerable to air interdiction.

THE ADVISORY YEARS

Vietnamese army units in the field, provincial officials, and covert agents could request Saigon for specific strikes. If Saigon approved, Vietnamese pilots were free to attack these targets, usually marked by air observers. While USAF officers were not empowered to question an approved strike, General Anthis asked for "positive control" by radar or forward air controllers when Farm Gate aircraft took part. Targets were often described in vague terms like "groups of huts," "troop concentrations," or "VC strong points," and were frequently hidden under jungle cover.[5]

In spite of precautions air strikes were dangerous, particularly in heavily populated and poorly mapped regions. In January 1962, for example, Vietnamese officers wanted an air strike at dawn on the Viet Cong-held village of Ba Thu in the Parrot's Beak close to the Cambodian border in War Zone C. Because the Vietnamese could not handle predawn takeoffs, Farm Gate was asked to fly the mission. At first Colonel Gleason, Farm Gate commander, thought the target too close to Cambodia, but accepted the task when the Vietnamese labeled it crucial.

Radar at Tan Son Nhut monitored the flight, warning the planes as they neared the canal that supposedly was the border. The aircraft failed to receive the message, but an SC-47 that had performed weather reconnaisance was flying back and forth over the canal to mark it. From another SC-47 positioned along the border, Colonel Gleason led and an airborne coordinator directed the strike. As eight T-28s and three B-26s bombed, rocketed, napalmed, and strafed, the Minister of Defense and the III Corps commander watched from a C-47.

The Farm Gate commander felt sure no one had made a mistake. Yet a few days later, the Cambodian government charged T-28s with having crossed the frontier, killed a villager, and injured three others. The Vietnamese defense minister shrugged off the protest, saying that the whole area was a "VC hot bed." The State Department, however, wished to prevent disruption of Vietnamese-Cambodian relations. At American insistence Saigon apologized and awarded compensation. General Anthis, 2d ADVON commander, forbade Farm Gate to strike within five miles of the border during daylight and ten miles at night. Moreover a forward air controller, airborne or on the ground, had to mark the targets. These restrictions might have afforded the Viet Cong complete sanctuary along the border, but the rules did not apply to Vietnamese pilots who could operate more freely.[6]

Toward the end of January, all available Vietnamese and Farm Gate planes at Bien Hoa, Pleiku, and Da Nang simultaneously attacked fourteen carefully pinpointed targets in five areas. After-action reports revealed good results. The defense minister said the strikes were so timely and accurate that the Viet Cong suspected spies in their midst. All the same, top American officials had nagging doubts about the validity of the targets selected by the Vietnamese. They stressed to the Joint General Staff the value of intelligence, proper controls, and serious poststrike assessments.[7]

Admiral Felt, CINCPAC, knew the problems of bombing areas where friendly and hostile people intermingled. Impressed by Vietnamese officers who wanted to avoid using weapons against innocent persons, he sponsored better air-ground communications for close air support.[8]

At the Secretary of Defense Conference on February 19, 1962, General Anthis showed how air interdiction hurt the Viet Cong. Defense Secretary McNamara evinced interest in using flares for strikes to relieve outposts under night assault. He ordered CINCPAC and MACV to furnish hamlets cheap but efficient short-range VHF-FM voice radios, so they could call for help when attacked. The Secretary warned that U.S. advisors were to do nothing that the Vietnamese could do for themselves, and were to risk hazards only when inescapable.[9]

Well-managed interdiction based on hard intelligence worked remarkably well. On March 2 the II Corps commander requested an immediate strike against a group of Viet Cong holding a meeting in the village of Hung Nhon. The air operations center validated the request and dispatched two Vietnamese AD-6s and a Farm Gate B-26. They killed at least twelve.[10]

Even so, the issue of haphazard air attacks lived on. Two U.S. Army advisors informed Army Brig. Gen. Harvey J. Jablonsky, the MACV J-4 (Logistics), that the Viet Cong were exploiting strafing and bombing attacks for propaganda purposes. By removing just the killed and wounded males, they gave the villagers the idea that the women and children left behind were the targets and victims of air strikes. Jablonsky passed this information on to Ambassador Nolting, who on March 3 met with Generals Harkins, Timmes, Jablonsky, and

AIR OPERATIONS 1962

Anthis. Nolting at first thought of curtailing air activity, but Jablonsky would not cite instances of air attack. Harkins then pointed out that tighter curbs would benefit merely the Viet Cong.[11]

General Jablonsky in Hawaii repeated the charge he had made in Saigon, and the question was reexamined at the Secretary of Defense Conference of March 21. Ambassador Nolting urged close scrutiny to prevent killing innocent people, and Defense Secretary McNamara agreed to allow air operations to go on under strict controls and stringent intelligence criteria. Roger Hilsman, Assistant Secretary of State for Far Eastern Affairs, later defined this decision as the worst of two worlds — military men disturbed by air restrictions and diplomats fretting about propaganda benefits to the enemy.[12]

To assist the Vietnamese in gathering better intelligence of air force interest, Admiral Felt authorized and the Air Force sent a detachment of the 6499th Support Group to Saigon. Six officer and six enlisted intelligence specialists arrived in March, but two officers were unqualified and removed. Denied direct access to enemy prisoners, the others could ask questions only through Vietnamese interrogators.[13]

An additional obstacle was the lengthy procedure in processing a request for a preplanned interdiction strike. The 2d ADVON intelligence directorate could propose a target, and the Joint General Staff's air photo intelligence center researched and prepared data sheets and folders. One copy went to the province chief for checking, a second to the air operations center for preliminary planning. Field Command next decided if the target was susceptible to ground action, which took precedence over air. These steps could consume several days or several weeks. Actually, most intelligence rose from the ground force division and province chief levels. These authorities often suggested targets to the corps commander who routed the requests to the operations center. Yet no matter how intelligence generated strikes, the province chief was the key. He alone determined whether bombing a target would imperil his people.[14]

To pinpoint Viet Cong radio transmitters for air intelligence, the Air Force delivered a C-54 to Vietnam in March 1962. The transport featured infrared detectors, cameras, and a high-frequency direction finder.[15] About the same time, the U.S. Army Security Agency put airborne radio homing units in three Army L-20s. During their first operational flight on the 12th of April, the C-54 and L-20s came upon far more Viet Cong radio transmitters than expected. However, the direction finding equipment could not give a precise fix on the radio sites. The Viet Cong radios were short-range, low-power sets, and they operated in periodic short bursts. Though the American eqipment was not advanced enough to place the signals accurately, the C-54 flew 102 special missions in ten months. The cameras worked fine for ordinary photography, but the infrared and the direction finder did poorly.[16]

The USAF pilots could return fire against "a known source" in self-defense, but needed to be very careful for they rarely knew a source's exact location. In the daytime, Farm Gate planes could not fire unless under positive control of a Vietnamese forward air controller, and cooperation with Vietnamese L-19 controllers was frequently difficult. In addition the elaborate reconnaissance and the target marking no doubt alerted the Viet Cong to impending strikes. This impeded action against an already elusive foe.[17]

In the spring of 1962, interdiction focused on small groups of guerrillas and sampans near Vietnamese army positions. Then late in May, the Joint General Staff and MACV targeted the Do Xa War Zone headquarters area of Interzone V. With utmost care they identified, authenticated, and pinpointed nineteen targets spread over an area of 230 square miles. As a final validation, a plane flew a Viet Cong defector over the area.

Vietnamese and American aircraft — eleven B-26s, eleven AD-6s, and six T-28s — took off on May 27. Bad weather obscured five of the targets, but the planes made repeated strikes on the other fourteen. Regardless of the careful preparations, a B-26 pounded the friendly village of Dak Ket, killing four persons and demolishing a dozen buildings. The strike pilots saw no Viet Cong on any of their runs, but bomb damage assessment photography showed a command post wiped out, fourteen other structures burned and destroyed, and thirty damaged. The Vietnamese field commanders hailed the attacks as a "total success," and Ngo Dinh Nhu (President Diem's brother) reported about four hundred enemy killed. Some Viet Cong defectors later credited their change of heart to the bombings.[18]

Both PACAF and 2d ADVON were willing to accept the mission of disrupting Viet Cong security in base areas beyond the reach of ground forces. The American Embassy in Saigon nonetheless questioned the wisdom of the attacks. Some U.S. observers were positive that air power at Dak Ket had killed no more than fifty of the enemy. The commander of Interzone V had escaped. Innocents had been killed. Consequently, General Anthis ordered Farm Gate no longer to fly free-area missions without a forward air controller.[19]

As spring wore on, a more extreme belief nudged aside assertions of how air interdiction hurt pacification because it endangered guiltless people. On April 15 MACV published the first extensive Viet Cong order of battle, listing eighteeen battalions, seventy-nine companies, and 137 platoons. The overall strength was put at 16,305, less than the 25,000 estimated by the Vietnamese. But backing up the regular troops were paramilitary organizations of around 10,000 part-time guerrillas. And over the first two weeks of May, 1,000 to 1,800 more Viet Cong had stolen into Zone D from Laos to form a new battalion. After weighing this information, MACV J-2 (Intelligence) concluded that air interdiction had no military effect on the Viet Cong.[20]

What then could isolate the Viet Cong from the populace who furnished them food and other supplies? Or from their logistic routes that brought them weapons, ammunition, medical materials, and fresh troops? There was no other way than by air interdiction and ground thrusts into enemy base areas. Admiral Felt desired these missions continued. He especially wanted Vietnamese rangers and regular units to fight guerrilla-style in the Viet Cong war zones. "It is, of course, basic to our side," Felt told General Harkins, "that the initiative be denied the VC. Our concept is to harass them, push them down and extend them far

THE ADVISORY YEARS

beyond the capabilities of their logistics support, thus destroying them." On the other hand, Harkins deemed nearly all of the ground commanders too inexperienced for large-scale efforts, and the rangers lacked leaders for extended field operations.[21]

Unlike the army, the Vietnamese Air Force could carry the war into the jungle areas held by the Viet Cong. What the pilots needed was valid target intelligence. In August Col. Ralph A. Newman, air liaison officer with Vietnamese Air Force Field Command, instructed liaison officers to work closely with the ground forces at division and regimental levels. The aim was to identify targets for interdiction, chiefly for Vietnamese planes returning from sorties with unused ordnance. Most crews hesitated to land with bombs and rockets hanging outside the aircraft, and since 1958 had jettisoned them on vacant land near the airfields. Aware of this waste, General Anthis proposed assigning preplanned targets, preferably in Zone D, so at least the munitions would fall on Viet Cong territory. Anthis and the air liaison officers pressured I and II Corps to accept this proposal. They stressed that a backlog of such targets would ease scheduling, distribution, and use of aircraft, as well as keep the Viet Cong off-balance. By September 1962, however, the suggestion was still hanging fire.[22]

Admiral Felt asked General Harkins, MACV commander, whether "area denial" methods might make Zone D too hot for the Viet Cong. Felt advised:

> Entire extent of techniques and devices available for such purpose should be used. We have in mind, for example, scatter bombing with butterfly bombs, proven lethal in Korea, and other type AF mines. We also visualize use of chemical irritants and defoliants to expose targets for air strikes.... In other words we want to destroy or drive sick, starved, blistered, and blasted Viet Cong from Zone D so that we can scoop them up outside of their nest or prevent them from setting foot in the area again.[23]

Thus spurred, MACV and the Joint General Staff started to target War Zones D and X (headquarters of Viet Cong Interzone V) for an intensive air campaign. On October 3 the 5th Division submitted 129 specific targets. President Diem next ordered a five-day bombing attack in Zone D to begin on November 1, followed by a Special Forces ground penetration. He also called for the I and II Corps to cooperate in a similar bombing and to follow up penetration into War Zone X which lay in the mountains dividing the two corps. Gradually, the corps commanders and Field Command obtained many more targets through military channels. Provincial chiefs designated free areas for air attack. Vietnamese crews could strike these areas without a forward air controller, but Farm Gate had to have targets marked by a Vietnamese L-19.[24]

Review of the free areas came when Vietnam's strained relations with Cambodia worsened. Feeling threatened by both South Vietnam and Thailand, Cambodia on August 20, 1962, had appealed to President Kennedy for a neutral status like that of Laos. President Diem resented the implication that South Vietnam was an aggressor. He said there was little question that Viet Cong redoubts drew support from across the border. Vietnamese troops who carried out sporadic raids into Cambodia had captured communist weapons and ammunition destined for the Viet Cong. Undeterred, Prince Norodom Sihanouk, Cambodian Chief of State, charged on September 10 that Vietnamese amphibious craft under air cover had violated his country's soil. Any more such aggressive acts, he threatened, would lead to severed diplomatic relations, recognition of North Vietnam, and closer ties with China. Five weeks later, Vietnamese naval forces moved against the island of Phu Quoc near the Cambodian coast. They seized seventeen tons of ingredients for making explosives.[25]

Sihanouk's threat to invite Chinese assistance startled the State Department. Ambassador Nolting met with President Diem and stressed there must be no military action that might bring Chinese Communist forces onto Vietnam's flank. In compliance the Joint General Staff banned ground and air operations within ten kilometers of the Cambodian border. If a river, road, or other physical feature clearly marked the border, Vietnamese forces could pursue the enemy to within two and one-half kilometers. Otherwise the chase would cease at eight kilometers. Vietnamese pilots could open fire on a hostile aircraft ten kilometers inside South Vietnam, if certain that the plane would fall inside Vietnamese territory if shot down.[26]

Though the border restrictions did not sit well with Vietnamese officials, Secretary of State Dean Rusk and the Joint Chiefs of Staff wondered whether the restraints went far enough. "Militarily," Rusk cabled Nolting,

> there is general agreement that success lies not in drawing tight cordon sanitaire in Maginot manner along vaguely defined frontier but primarily in working outwards from rural areas won . . . and, secondarily, through strikes against VC strongholds. Usefulness of latter, when carried out near frontier, must be considered less important than political-diplomatic problem.

The Joint Chiefs suggested a new name be found for "free areas." Admiral Felt did not object, and 2d Air Division (formerly 2d ADVON) commenced to call them "approved interdiction targets."[27]

To General Anthis, sponsorship of "area denial" by Admiral Felt "smacked of indiscriminate bombing." Even in Zone D it was impossible to know positively that all victims were Viet Cong. When Felt proposed having C-123s drop ten thousand pounds of napalm on marked targets during a ground offensive into Zone D, Secretary Rusk objected. He wanted napalm confined to high-priority targets that were clearly Viet Cong installations. Moreover, the State Department retained the right to pass on all plans meaning to use napalm in large amounts.

In the end, General Harkins withheld USAF aircraft from delivering napalm in Zone D and allowed the Vietnamese to do so. Ambassador Nolting supported this decision. The curbs put on Americans made it hard to carry the war to the heart of the enemy sanctuaries. The best that General Anthis could do was to allow F-102s to fly across Zone D at night, breaking the sound barrier and causing sonic booms. "It may not destroy anything," Anthis said, "but I can say positively there has been considerable VC sleep lost in the last few weeks."[28]

Scarcely less important than interdiction was USAF support of Vietnamese ground operations. Air Force officers constantly offered air support to ground commanders through the tactical air control system. To sell this support, steps were taken to strengthen the air operations center at Tan Son Nhut and the radar facilities at Da Nang and Pleiku, procure and employ American air liaison officers and forward air controllers, and persuade locally powerful army commanders to coordinate with air forces. In general these commanders were jealous of their authority, secretive about their plans, and inexperienced in applying tactical air support. Inasmuch as the air operations center depended on day-to-day knowledge of Vietnamese ground operations, U.S. Army and Vietnamese liaison officers were assigned to the center in February 1962. The idea was to inject tactical air into operational planning at the outset.[29]

If Vietnamese ground commanders had but an inkling of how the support system was supposed to work, U.S. Army advisors had not the air experience to qualify them as air liaison officers. They refused to accept the tactical air control system outright, and from the USAF view were "quick to criticize, slow to help."[30]

Bolstering of the joint operations center was one of the benefits accruing from the April 1962 visit of General LeMay. He ordered several USAF officers assigned to the center, Lt. Col. Charles J. Bowers assuming the duties of deputy director. These officers monitored and encouraged the submission of daily requirements for air support, and allocated sorties on the basis of available aircraft.[31]

Quite a few things weakened centralized control of tactical aircraft. Inexperienced personnel and unreliable equipment bred problems. In April, for example, communications between Tan Son Nhut and Da Nang remained out for three days. Moving aircraft from rotational duty at Da Nang and Pleiku demanded special approval from Vietnamese Air Force headquarters. Consequently, the air operations center could not route these planes rapidly to areas of greater need. Also, the center was heavily committed to operations requested by Field Command and III Corps. This led I Corps at Da Nang and II Corps at Pleiku to look upon the AD-6s at these fields as theirs to use without telling the center. Likewise, the fighter squadron at Nha Trang now and then flew T-28 strikes in response to local requests without the center's knowledge. When General Anthis made staff visits to corps, division, regimental, and battalion headquarters, he found little understanding of how the tactical air control system was meant to function.[32]

Attempts to bring helicopter activities under the air operations center did not go well. General Harkins in April directed armed tactical aircraft to accompany helicopter assault missions. He was therefore certain that the center was wholly aware of all U.S. Army flight operations in the country. Yet Army ground liaison officers readily admitted that the MACV order for escort planes was observed only about ten percent of the time.[33]

The figure of ten percent was misleading, seeing that these ground operations mostly involved small forces of company or platoon size in very brief firefights. Since the air operations center was unable to coordinate all air operations, it could not wholly exploit available air support. Data on ground operations being planned was often not to be had. The commanders were sensitive to Viet Cong espionage, and personally drew up and launched actions with scant notice even to their own staffs. A few commanders went so far as to suspect the center to be a Viet Cong source of information — and with reason. The Vietnamese Air Force dispatched fragmentary operations orders from Tan Son Nhut to its squadrons in the clear. Because the teletype circuits were possibly insecure, there were inevitable leaks.[34]

U.S. Army officers disliked the tactical air control system, deeming it too rigid. Accordingly, there was no realistic policy governing the relationship between fixed-wing aircraft and helicopters. In June MACV gave General Anthis "coordinating authority" over all air operations. In July General Harkins ordered helicopter support missions to have proper air escort, unless the helicopter unit commander judged it unnecessary. In August Admiral Felt considered it essential to have every type of air operation coordinated by the air operations center, and to have air cover from fixed-wing aircraft for each helicopter operation. Not until December 1962 did the latter requirement go into force.[35]

Air strikes close to friendly troops called for close cooperation between air missions and the movement and fire of ground units. As in Korea, tactical air control parties came to be used. The Air Force supplied a seasoned fighter pilot to serve as the air liaison member of the control party. The Army furnished the vehicles and mechanics, radio gear and operators. The AN/VRC-30 ground mobile radio jeep carried the air liaison officer and Army members of the control party. The vehicle's radios linked with the forward air controller and the strike pilots above, and with ground and air units. The control party's work was thwarted whenever the jeep was slowed or stopped by cut and mired roads, ambush parties, and jungles and swamps.

A further frustration was the meager experience of Vietnamese in coordinating air-ground operations. The shortage of L-19 pilots prevented the assignment of air liaison officers to ground units. The foremost need was to secure sufficient two-man L-19 crews (pilot and observer) to place AD-6 strike aircraft on the target. So in lieu of an air liaison officer, the Vietnamese Air Force sometimes designated an L-19 crew to serve as forward air controller for a ground unit during a single operation. The pilot and observer repaired to the unit, received briefings on the planning action, and tried to become familiar with the procedures and terrain. The crew then returned home to conduct other air control and reconnaissance missions. On the day of the operation, however, the L-19 crew flew back and controlled air strikes for the ground unit.

Unable to operate at night, L-19 crews in daytime usually flew at 3,000 to 5,000 feet, far too high for good surveillance and target marking. The air observer marked targets for fighters by radio direction or hand-thrown smoke grenade, commonly by both methods. Criticism and penalty awaited an L-19 crew if ground fire damaged the plane. The observer was subject to severe punishment if he erred in marking a target and friendly casualties resulted.[36]

To communicate with regular troops, the Civil Guard, and the Self Defense Corps units, L-19s carried AN/PRC-10 Army radios lashed to their backseats. Because the plane could power only its own radios or the PRC-10, the crew could not converse with strike aircraft and ground forces at the same time. The PRC-10 lash-up was a poor makeshift, and ground units wanted man-pack radios that could mesh with existing UHF/VHF airborne sets. No such radios were obtainable in 1962. The U.S. Agency for International Development was giving large numbers of radios to provincial paramilitary forces. These sets were the commercially procured HT-1 and TR-20 with characteristics similar to those of the PRC-10. An an interim measure, MAAG refitted U.S. Army helicopters and Vietnamese and Farm Gate aircraft with the AN/ARC-44 Army radio. This set could tie in with the PRC-10, HT-1, and TR-20.

Complications of this sort paled beside the general insufficiency of the L-19s. They were often simply unavailable. In April, for example, Farm Gate pilots arrived over the target and could see a firefight on the ground. But the Vietnamese controller never showed up.[37]

Toward the end of 1962, Farm Gate received two L-28As (later known as U-10As) for forward air controller duty. They were too costly for such use. Moreover, Farm Gate still had to have Vietnamese air observers or air guides on the ground to mark targets for strikes.[38]

Three U.S. Army helicopter companies, each attached to a corps, enabled troops to move swiftly against the Viet Cong. On the way to the target areas, the chopper pilots liked to fly at 700 feet and hug the terrain. Their success led Secretary of Defense McNamara to deploy a Marine squadron of twenty-four UH-34D helicopters to Vietnam. Afterwards he moved two more Army H-21 companies to the country, plus a company of fifteen armed UH-1A and UH-1B helicopters from Okinawa and Thailand. Manned by Americans, these gunships were to deliver "suppressive fire," now deemed to be self-defense. In September 1962 the Joint Chiefs of Staff ordered all helicopter gunships bearing U.S. markings to carry a Vietnamese observer.[39]

In July 1962, strike aircraft flew 139 combat sorties in support of helicopters. Farm Gate (now commanded by Lt. Col. Eugene H. Mueller, Jr.) perfected tactics whereby two T-28s supported each helicopter flight. One T-28 swooped down to 200 feet, flew slightly ahead of the leading helicopter, and made slow turns to search for the enemy. The second T-28 stayed above the formation, set to make a firing pass on a target. As the helicopters approached in trail for landing, the strike aircraft flew on each side and strafed the flanks to suppress enemy fire.[40]

Despite Admiral Felt's belief that transport helicopters constantly required fighter escort, General Harkins authorized helicopter gunships to operate alone if need be. Bad weather now and then grounded strike aircraft but not necessarily helicopters. In addition, escorts were hard put to fly slowly enough to stay with the helicopters. Seeking to put U.S. Army air operations under the tactical air control system, General Anthis warned Harkins against fighting two distinct air wars. On the other hand, Army officers tended to see armed helicopters best used when under a ground commander's control and carrying out local operations. In August, MACV gave the tactical air control system supremacy solely over air traffic control.[41]

The Viet Cong ambushed 462 road convoys during the first seven months of 1962, most of them in III Corps north of Saigon and near Zone D. On the morning of June 16, some four to five hundred Viet Cong took up ambush positions along the road to Bien Hoa about five kilometers south of Ben Cat. Opening fire on the convoy in mid-morning, the communists killed two American advisors and twenty-three Vietnamese. The column requested air support, and three hours elapsed before the strike units at Bien Hoa got orders to take off. By that time, the enemy was withdrawing toward Zone D. Even so, a B-26 and two AD-6s under L-19 control killed fifty enemy and enabled pursuing Vietnamese troops to recover nearly all the equipment and weapons stolen from the convoy. Air Force officers pointed out to Vietnamese commanders that a single L-19 over the convoy would probably have sighted and reported the enemy, and no doubt would have prevented the ambush.[42]

On July 14 a Viet Cong battalion ambushed a convoy en route from Saigon to Phuoc Long, killing twenty-five persons (including a U.S. Army advisor) and wounding twenty-nine others. The convoy had not asked for air cover. In fact, neither III Corps nor Field Command had known that the column was on the road. The request for air support came one and one-half hours after the fighting erupted. By then the guerrillas had long been gone.[43]

General Anthis emphasized to MACV the advantages of air cover for convoys and rail movements. Not only would tactical air enhance security, it would also absorb Vietnamese and Farm Gate sorties currently unused. At General Harkins' suggestion, President Diem in August directed his army commanders to call on the Vietnamese Air Force to protect trains and convoys conveying arms, ammunition, and other critical cargo.[44]

The simple presence of the unarmed L-19 often broke up an ambush. On August 3, two L-19s spied 200 guerrillas lying in wait between Quang Ngai and Da Nang for an ammunition train headed north. When the planes appeared, the Viet Cong fled. Later that month, an L-19 stopped the first vehicle of a convoy just short of an explosive charge.[45]

In contrast to the 32 requests for convoy escort from January to July 1962, there were 506 between August and October. Doing most of the train and truck convoy escort, L-19s flew ahead of the movement and searched for signs of ambush. They radioed for ground or air reinforcement as required. Except for the compulsory combat air cover for high-priority cargoes, tactical aircraft selected to escort usually stayed on ground alert. The combination of planes devoted to this duty constituted about ten percent of the total tactical air effort. Convoys would have incurred less damage, had they kept travel to days and hours when aircraft were on hand to afford cover and protection. The technique was effective. From July on, no train or convoy escorted by air ran into ambush for several months.[46]

Helicopter assault operations proved more complex than train or convoy escort. On August 30, I Corps mounted an air-ground operation fifty-five miles south of Da Nang. Plans envisioned ten Vietnamese H-34s and twelve U.S. Army H-21s to lift two hundred rangers and two hundred Special Forces troops to the battle area. Four T-28s would fly helicopter escort while four AD-6s, four T-28s, and one B-26 readied the landing zone. A CV-2 Caribou out of Da Nang was to be the airborne command post. The I Corps air liaison officer, Lt. Col. Byron R. Kalin, pointed out in vain that the Caribou lacked the fuel capacity for orbiting during the whole operation. The plane would have to return to Da Nang for refueling.

Early on D-day, six C-123s ferried two hundred Vietnamese troops from Da Nang to Quang Ngai to join the others. The Caribou command post checked the weather in the battle area and signaled for the first heli-lift of two hundred troops. The strike planes made their prelanding attacks but, by the time the helicopters came, fog had rolled into some of the landing areas. The Caribou sent the helicopters back to Quang Ngai. When the fog lifted, the Caribou called for the mission to continue. Although the four T-28s escorting the helicopters completed another prelanding strike, the Viet Cong opened up on the choppers with sharp fire. A damaged H-21 escaped to an emergency landing area. After the crew was rescued, a T-28 destroyed the craft to avert its capture.

Subsequent to the safe landing of a second wave of helicopters, the Caribou needed to go to Da Nang for refueling. While it was away for over an hour, orbiting fighters relayed messages to the commander. But he was out of direct contact with his troops.

The fighting on the ground was inconclusive, and in mid-afternoon helicopters began extracting the forces. As the last chopper left the scene, the Viet Cong opened fire, downing another H-21. The wounded crewmen were rescued, and a T-28 shattered the copter on the ground.[47]

Why were the T-28s unable to suppress the Viet Cong fire? The Caribou's limited communications for directing fighters and ground troops were frequently interrupted for one reason or other. Target marking was poor. An American forward air controller flew an L-19 over the area for three hours at 2,000 feet. His Vietnamese observer marked just one target, the smoke bomb missing by 3,000 feet. Lastly, the delay between the prelanding strikes and the first helicopter landing had likely alerted the Viet Cong.[48]

At Da Nang on September 22, the 2d Division commander planned a heliborne attack to begin on the 24th. The six Vietnamese T-28s on station could not muster the firepower for the air support required. Delayed until fresh aircraft arrived, the operation went on September 26. By then, the Viet Cong had slipped away.[49]

The growing accuracy of Viet Cong ground fire against aircraft caused concern among USAF officers. The toll of Farm Gate planes shot down mounted — a T-28 on August 28, 1962, a U-10 on October 17, and a low-flying B-26 on November 5. Other aircraft were damaged. Following a night napalm strike, Lt. Col. Miles M. Doyle nursed his B-26 home after losing an engine to .30-caliber rounds. To silence enemy gunners, the Farm Gate commander ordered his pilots to strafe while delivering ordnance at low levels.[50]

Army pilots of armed helicopters were optimistic about the defensive abilities of the UH-1. The chopper carried two eight-tube 2.75-inch rocket pods and two .30-caliber machineguns (each mounted on a landing skid). General Anthis continued to plead for the UH-1 and other U.S. Army aircraft to go under the tactical air control system. Meanwhile, the Army used the gunships for firepower formerly furnished by artillery, explaining that the UH1s supplemented rather than replaced strike aircraft.[51]

A vital adjunct to interdiction and close support was air reconnaissance, and MAAG in April 1962 had projected a program for the Vietnamese. Its centerpiece was the transfer to them of four RT-33 photo jets. Since the State Department did not at first object to the transfer, Thirteenth Air Force made ready to train pilots for the planes. Next, MAAG formally asked for the RT-33s together with three RC-47s and fourteen RT-28s. The RC-47s would get photo coverage under way at once, and small Vietnamese photo processing cells at Pleiku and Da Nang could supplement the American facility at Tan Son Nhut.

Examining the proposal in June, CINCPAC recommended that three camera-equipped C-47s be secured, one for each corps; two Able Mable RF-101s be completely committed to missions in Vietnam; a Vietnamese photo processing cell be opened at Tan Son Nhut; and an austere USAF reconnaissance technical squadron be set up in Saigon for detailed photo interpretation and target production for all of Southeast Asia.[52]

At the Secretary of Defense Conference in Hawaii on July 23, 1962, Admiral Felt spoke out strongly for giving the Vietnamese RT-33 photo jets. Mr. McNamara was negative because of the Geneva accords, and he questioned the superiority of the RT-33 over conventional aircraft. General Harkins favored the photo jets but suggested a compromise — bring two USAF RF-101s to Vietnam and furnish the Vietnamese RC-47s and RT-28Bs. Two weeks later, Admiral Felt urged the Joint Chiefs to approve the RT-33s as superior reconnaissance planes needed for intelligence. He noted that the Army had sent some jet turbine-powered UH-1A helicopters to Vietnam. The admiral opposed RC-47s because in Laos they were vulnerable to ground fire. He thought it difficult and expensive to modify the RT-28 into a camera plane that at best would have moderate performance.[53]

The State Department now strenuously opposed jet photo planes for the Vietnamese on political grounds. And Secretary McNamara remained unconvinced that Admiral Felt had made his case. Although the RT-33s stayed in the Military Assistance Program, three camera-equipped RC-47s and eighteen RT-28s arrived to buttress reconnaissance. At Tan Son Nhut the Vietnamese activated the 716th Composite Reconnaissance Squadron. It accepted two C-45 photo aircraft, one having a six-inch and the other a twelve-inch vertical camera. While awaiting more planes, pilots of the 716th Squadron flew strike missions in T-28s. Not until mid-1964 would the Vietnamese attain a fully operational reconnaissance program. Meantime, the Air Force's 13th Reconnaisance Technical Squadron (thirteen officers and eighty-four airmen) would be formed at Tan Son Nhut.[54]

Until the Vietnamese could do their own air reconnaissance, Able Mable RF-101s were for a while deployed to Saigon. In July 1962 the Geneva agreement suspended aerial reconnaissance over Laos, and by October Able Mable was flying about eighty-eight percent of its sorties over Vietnam. This sparked the move in December of all four RF-101s to Tan Son Nhut, where they continued to fly 2.8 sorties a day. Flying from Vietnam rather than Thailand widely expanded the total photo coverage per sortie.[55]

Detecting the Viet Cong from the air demanded night and infrared photography, side-looking airborne radar, and infrared "snooper scope" techniques. Most of these methods were still in development. In April 1962 MACV had secured two RB-26C night photo aircraft for Farm Gate, the planes reaching Bien Hoa in May.[56] During the last half of 1962, they gave good service in the face of obstacles. Flash-illuminant cartridges were in short supply. Reflections from flooded rice paddies blurred night photos. A ground accident on October 20 put one RB-26C permanently out of action.[57]

The coming of the Army's 23d Special Air Warfare Detachment to Nha Trang in September 1962 reinforced reconnaissance. The detachment had six OV-1 Mohawk turboprop observation aircraft, rigged with cameras and .50-caliber machineguns. It further featured two portable laboratories to process photographs at division headquarters and at remote locations. Split into teams of two, the OV-1s assumed direct support of Vietnamese ground units. The Mohawks flew mostly visual and photo reconnaissance, but carried Vietnamese observers who could approve targets.[58]

General Anthis still felt it foolish to give aircraft to ground unit commanders. When he protested to General Harkins, the reply was, "We must all be objective." A USAF forward air controller with the 23d Division at Ban Me Thuot noted in November that the Mohawk detachment could make a nine-hour delivery on photo requests, compared to the normal USAF time of seven days. Apprised of this, Anthis could only hope that the U.S. Air Force might not lose assigned roles and missions because of a failure to provide resources to perform them. Even with RF-101s flying from Tan Son Nhut and the photo processing cell working at peak efficiency, photo delivery took from three and one-half to more than five hours. The local Mohawks could deliver emergency photo requests within two to three hours.[59]

Admiral Felt pondered the status of the OV-1s. Was their local employment an economical use of force? Or did their presence ignore the basic U.S. policy of having Americans train the Vietnamese instead of fighting their war for them? Yet General Harkins cited the excellent results chalked up by Mohawks, and on December 14 asked for four more. Like the helicopter gunships, Harkins explained, the OV-1s complemented but did not compete with USAF air power.[60]

Nevertheless, by December 1962 the Army had 199 aircraft in Vietnam, the Air Force 61; there were eight Army generals, three Air Force. As the USAF director of plans noted:

> It may be improper to say we are at war with the Army. However, we believe that if the Army efforts are successful, they may have a long term adverse effect in the U.S. military posture that could be more important than the battle presently being waged with the Viet Cong.[61]

Both Army and Vietnamese Air Force aircraft remained outside the tactical air control system. As early as May 1962, Brig. Gen. Stephen D. McElroy, Thirteenth Air Force vice commander, commented on the situation to General Anthis. Air Force T-28s flew combat while Vietnamese T-28s were on the ground. Army helicopters made combat lifts while Vietnamese H-34s were unused, unreported, or transporting passengers. In response, Anthis acknowledged this "sensitive subject." "Progress," he said, "can only be measured in small units" — meaning inches.[62]

A team from the Royal Australian Air Force noticed the same condition. The Vietnamese Air Force (along with the navy) did not perform up to its full potential. Perhaps this was due to the absence of proper representation at senior military levels. Hence there was no joint planning as practiced in more sophisticated armed services, and air force "views and requirements receive little consideration."[63]

In June 1962 the forty-nine Vietnamese strike aircraft flew but 412 of the 1,029 sorties of which they were capable. Too few flight leaders, no desire to fly combat, and scarce targets were the causes. Flying fell off markedly during weekends, siesta hours, nights, and bad weather. At any rate, the picture was not entirely dismal — the 412 sorties in June were a decided improvement over the 150 in January.[64]

The signs were mixed as 1962 closed. But it was unmistakably clear that the Republic of Vietnam, so shaky at the start of the year, had not collapsed. Even more encouraging was the attitude of the National Liberation Front, Hanoi's political structure in South Vietnam. Its press release in July 1962 called for the creation of a neutral state much like Laos. Was Hanoi thinking of abandoning the effort to unify Vietnam by force? And what was the meaning of Ho Chi Minh's quoted statement praising Diem's patriotism? In 1959 Ho had predicted the defeat of South Vietnam in a year. In September 1962 he began saying that victory might take fifteen to twenty years. Was he concerned that the Americans might bomb North Vietnam?[65]

The war against the Viet Cong, President Diem informed the National Assembly on October 9, had taken an "incontestable turn" for the better. Later that month, Admiral Felt and Ambassador Nolting bolstered Diem by assuring him that the American resolve to resist communism in Vietnam would not weaken.[66]

Obviously, then, the step-up in U.S. support for Vietnam that had started late in 1961 seemed to be working.

XIV. Ap Bac and Related Matters

American support arrested many adverse trends in Vietnam, and by May 1962 Secretary of Defense McNamara was looking ahead to the end of the counterinsurgency. As he said at his conference in Honolulu, the Military Assistance Program for Vietnam would then be somewhere between $50 million and $75 million a year.[1] McNamara was hoping to phase out the war in Vietnam and in the near future to send home major U.S. combat, advisory, and logistic activities. No doubt heartened by the signing of a new agreement on Laos, he directed General Harkins, MACV commander, to draw up a program. The plan would prepare Vietnamese armed forces to fight and win the war themselves, so that a systematic withdrawal of American forces could be geared to the headway made.

"Six months ago," said the Defense secretary, "we had practically nothing and we have made tremendous progress to date. However, we have been concentrating on short term crash-type actions and now must look ahead to a carefully conceived long-range program." He then asked how long it would take to eliminate the Viet Cong as a "disturbing force." General Harkins replied, "About one year from the time that we are able to get . . . [the Vietnamese] fully operational and really pressing the VC in all areas."

Assuming that it would take about three years to bring the Viet Cong "under control," the Secretary directed Harkins to plan on this basis. Besides training the Vietnamese to manage the war themselves, Harkins was to arrange a turnover of materiel to them. "The objective," McNamara said, "is to give SVN an adequate military capability without the need for special U.S. military assistance."[2]

The size of the American contributions was substantial. By mid-August there would be 11,412 U.S. personnel in Vietnam—2,282 Air Force, 7,946 Army, 643 Navy, and 541 Marine Corps. Of the $767 million in materiel programmed since 1956, more than $600 million had been delivered. Airfields refurbished, or set to be, included Tan Son Nhut, Bien Hoa, Pleiku, Nha Trang, Da Nang, Qui Nhon, Ban Me Thuot, Hue, and Tuy Hoa. A like upgrading of land and naval facilities was underway. The Military Assistance Program, subject to congressional approval, called for $177 million in fiscal year 1962 and $167 million the next year. Over and above these totals, the United States had given Vietnam over $1.5 billion for roads, railways, electric lines, water, communications, hospitals, and schools.[3]

U.S. advisors operated from Joint General Staff to battalion level, and some worked with province chiefs and training centers. Farm Gate had trained and certified sufficient Vietnamese crews to man a second fighter squadron that flew missions out of Nha Trang. The Air Staff had approved sending four L-28s to Farm Gate for forward air controller duty. Two more glass-nosed B-26s were on hand for reconnaissance. Mule Train was supplied a second C-123 squadron to achieve the quick reaction General LeMay desired.[4]

Ignoring these hopeful signs, LeMay remained skeptical. The Air Force chief's disagreement with the war strategy was widely known among the top U.S. leaders, and Admiral Felt alluded to it at the May Secretary of Defense Conference. General O'Donnell, PACAF commander in chief, was disappointed with the emphasis on politics and economics at the conference. So many civilians were there that he could not make his points. Instead of preparing for victory in three years, he wanted to urge actions at once—"better utilization of available air in South Vietnam, improved air lift management, and . . . [a] three-star slot for the Air Force deputy" to Harkins.[5]

General Anthis told the conferees that the basic stumbling block to expanding the Vietnamese Air Force—a precondition to removing USAF elements—was the shortage of pilots. There was no debate on this.[6]

What mattered was that McNamara had set 1965 as the planning date for ending U.S. involvement in Vietnam and Harkins needed to make it possible.

By September MACV prepared a National Campaign Plan as a guide. After briefing Mr. McNamara in October, General Harkins presented the plan to the Joint General Staff and the Vietnamese president. Diem informally approved the blueprint in principle, and on November 26 did so formally. No immediate implementation followed, but rather a discussion of when execution should begin. Not really a series of maneuvers, the plan was more an organizational and conceptual framework, a setting for the process of rooting out the guerrillas. A key provision was the restructuring of the Vietnamese armed forces. This would deprive provincial chiefs of control over paramilitary forces in their areas, and of their freedom to appeal directly to Diem. Placing the paramilitary forces squarely in the military chain of command would do away with the provincial chiefs' private armies.

CINCPAC harbored reservations as to the costs and the ability of the Vietnamese to train sufficient personnel in time, and MACV revised the plan in December 1962 and again in early 1963. The plan's intelligence annex contained merely territorial data and a map of what MACV thought were the Viet Cong tactical zones and secret bases. Missing was an enemy order of battle. The Joint Chiefs nevertheless approved the plan on March 4, 1963. They recognized that success hinged on the "parallel development of many mutual supporting" programs, meant to lead ninety percent of the native population to identify with the Diem government. The trouble was that many programs lay outside the military sphere. Civilian agencies were to work on political, economic, and social problems, and much would rest on additional deficit spending by the Vietnamese government. There were no doubts expressed on Diem's administration or the course of the war. The Air Staff, however, wondered where the government could find enough trainees to fill the pilot spaces.[7]

These seemed to be mere details. More to the point was Admiral Felt's comment that Diem had "finally delegated operational authority" to his military commanders.[8]

AP BAC AND RELATED MATTERS

The National Campaign Plan called for nine regular divisions plus other Vietnamese units—a total ground combat force of about fifty-one divisions. Operating under four autonomous corps tactical zone field commanders, these troops were to decimate local Viet Cong elements, cut off replacements, and destroy supply, communications, control, and support facilities. The communists would first be hemmed into specific areas. Next would come a general offensive to annihilate them by simultaneous "explosion" operations in the four corps zones. This explosion of effort was supposed to drive the Viet Cong out of the country within a year.

"Sounds reminiscent of Korea, of course," someone said, referring to General McArthur's famous communiqué, "out of the trenches by Christmas." General Weede, MACV chief of staff, estimated that the "military effort to at least drive VC underground should be concluded in one to two years. It would then be up to GVN [Government of Vietnam] to take over to win minds of people, improve economy, conduct civic action, etc." According to General Harkins, the plan could eliminate the Viet Cong as early as 1963. President Diem apparently believed so too, but later would feel that the strategic hamlet program first had to be completed. This could not be done before the spring of 1964.[9]

Diem reorganized the military. Inactivating the central Field Command, he divided Vietnam into four corps tactical zones, created the new IV Corps in the Mekong Delta with headquarters at Can Tho, and established the Capital Military District around Saigon. The corps tactical zone commanders would be given greater responsibilities. They were to exercise operational control not only over their ground forces but over supporting Vietnamese Air Force elements as well.[10]

Exactly what control the 2d Air Division commander was to have over air operations was unstated, but General Anthis protested placing air power in the hands of the corps commanders. He wanted as always a strong tactical air control system.[11]

A related issue was how to compute the air requirements for the "explosion" ground operations. Preliminary estimates showed a doubled strike sortie rate along with an upturn in calls for reconnaissance, target spotting and identification, and aerial resupply. How much and how fast the Vietnamese Air Force could be expanded was the central question.[12]

General Rowland, chief of the MAAG Air Force Section, outlined an ambitious program. Besides a second AD-6 fighter squadron in fiscal year 1964, he projected two more fighter squadrons in fiscal year 1966. Both would be equipped with the Northrop N-156 light jet fighter (later designated the F-5 Freedom Fighter). Rowland envisioned the replacement of the T-28s in one squadron and the A-1Hs in another with F-5s sometime between 1966 and 1968. He called for a total of nine L-19 liaison squadrons (one for each regular ground division) and four helicopter squadrons. He visualized air reconnaissance handled by a squadron of four RT-33s and eighteen RT-28s. Air transport would be performed by a single squadron of C-47s during fiscal year 1965 and by two

THE ADVISORY YEARS

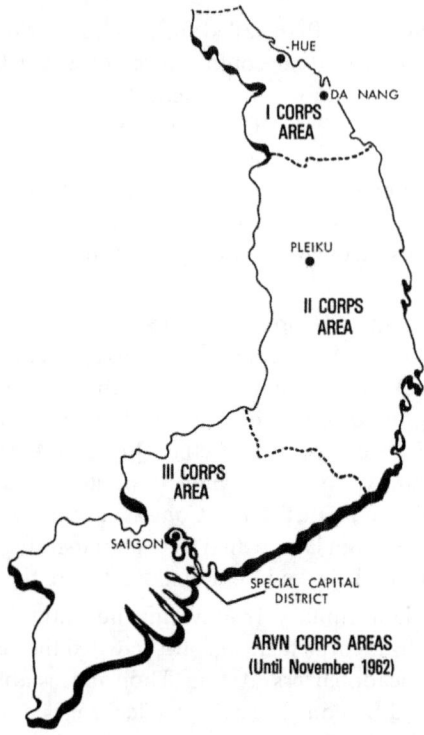

ARVN CORPS AREAS
(Until November 1962)

C-123 squadrons, one each in 1965 and 1968. This program was eventually trimmed. The nine liaison squadrons, for example, were cut to four.[13]

Rowland also pointed out the advantages of pilot training in Vietnam. In October a detachment of the Air Training Command was scheduled for movement, to open an H-19 helicopter pilot training program at Tan Son Nhut. Two months later, a second detachment was dispatched to give liaison pilot training at Nha Trang.[14]

To meet the rise in air requirements envisaged by the National Campaign Plan, General Anthis in October and November 1962 asked for these new squadrons: one T-28 (25 aircraft), one B-26 (25 planes), a third C-123 (at least), two RF-101, two RB-26, and three liaison. Anthis justified the liaison units on several grounds. General Rowland's program had been whittled down, a current shortage of forward air control craft had delayed or deferred many strike missions, and a step-up in visual reconnaissance and convoy cover could be foreseen.[15]

The MACV J-4 set forth airlift requirements in support of the National Campaign Plan. His ideas of "wholesale" and "retail" operations resembled Army thinking. He specified sealift to five port areas, then C-123 lift to various airfields where U-1 Otters, CV-2 Caribous, and helicopters working with the corps were to pick up the cargo for ultimate delivery. He estimated having to move 36,000 short tons per month by air (4.3 million ton miles of airlift). This was almost twice the capacity of the two C-123 squadrons and the CV-2 company

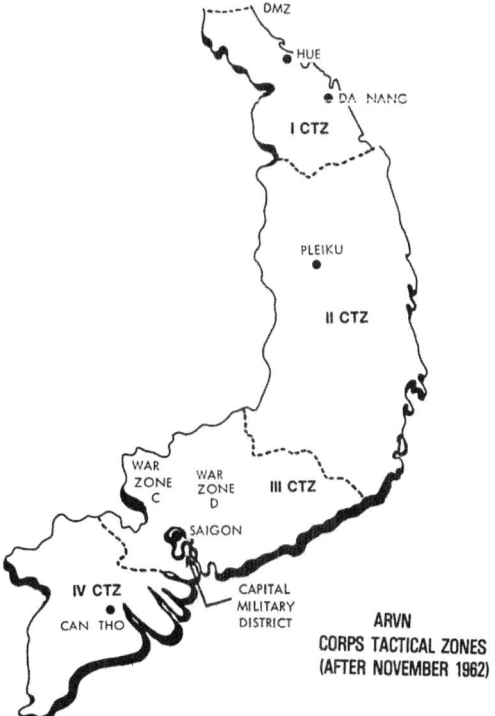

ARVN
CORPS TACTICAL ZONES
(AFTER NOVEMBER 1962)

already in Vietnam. In December General Harkins requested two more C-123 squadrons (thirty-two aircraft) and an additional CV-2 company (sixteen planes) for arrival in the first three months of 1963.[16]

At first the Civilian Irregular Defense Group program was managed out of the American Embassy by the CIA. Later the program went under MACV and the U.S. Army Special Forces (Provisional), formed at Nha Trang on September 15, 1962. Working through the tactical air control system and the air operations center, Farm Gate had serviced these units. While General Anthis wished to continue the practice, General Harkins preferred to give the Special Forces their own organic airlift and fire support—a miniature tactical air force. Harkins was thinking of setting aside four L-20s or L-28s for liaison, four CV-2 Caribous for airlift, and twelve UH-1 armed helicopters and four OV-1 Mohawks for strikes. These craft were to be controlled by the Special Forces commander at Nha Trang.

General Anthis dissented on the ground that the twenty-four aircraft would displace the Vietnamese planes at Nha Trang. He remarked that every ground unit could not have "its own separate air force." Admiral Felt ruled in favor of central control of air support. He expressly said that he would allow no assignment of air power direct to the Vietnamese irregulars or to the U.S. Special Forces. Harkins next proposed to use Air America contract airlift for this purpose. In the end, a compromise was arranged. The Mohawks and Caribous disappeared from the proposal. With Defense Secretary McNamara's approval, the Secretaries of the Army and Air Force sent twelve nonorganic helicopters and four liaison planes to Vietnam for the Special Forces, to enable team chiefs to visit remote and otherwise inaccessible posts. Harkins agreed to use the other craft within the tactical air control system. But in December and over Felt's objections, he withdrew the four Army Caribou transports from the Southeast Asia Military Airlift System and committed them to direct support of the Special Forces.[17]

Preliminary "explosion" operations got under way in late October 1962. Ranger forces gathered for a penetration into Viet Cong Zone D in Phuoc Long, Binh Long, and Phuoc Thanh Provinces (called a Special Tactical Zone). In spite of poor weather and deficient target marking, AD-6s on November 20 conducted prelanding bombardment. Five Mule Train C-123s and twelve Vietnamese C-47s dropped five hundred paratroopers at a site selected as a base camp on the eastern edge of Zone D. On December 19 troops moved into Zone D, where double tree-canopy-cover towered to eighty feet. Planes flew eight interdiction strikes and also close support missions. On the 23d a B-26 dropped napalm, and on January 1, 1963, a B-26 and two T-28s attacked with general purpose bombs. Results in this thickly forested but fairly dry terrain turned out better than expected. An Army advisor who visited four interdiction targets found proof of a hasty enemy retreat. Rockets and .50-caliber rounds had pierced the jungle canopy, and 500-pound bombs had smashed trees to scatter lethal wood fragments. There were ten fresh Viet Cong graves. In three weeks the rangers killed sixty-two Viet Cong and took ten prisoners, at a cost of twelve killed and sixty-eight wounded.[18]

When a report revealed a large Viet Cong assembly east of the city of Tay Ninh in northern Tay Ninh Province, III Corps hurriedly launched a three-day heliborne assault by the 5th Division on December 19. The size of the enemy force was overstated but the troops caught three Viet Cong. The prisoners gave the locations, functions, and staffing of twelve headquarters of the National Liberation Front. After special agents verified this information, III Corps asked the Joint General Staff to authorize a three-day strike against the headquarters. Most of the twelve lay within ten miles of the Cambodian border, too close in the opinion of Americans. The Joint General Staff disapproved the air attacks, but President Diem considered the chance too attractive. He set the operation for January 2, 1963.

The operation was planned to kick off with a heavy hour-long air attack against nine targets most distant from the border. Some delayed-action bombs would be used. Next was to be a drop of 1,250 paratroops and a helicopter landing of a ranger battalion, covered by "light strafing attacks." The fighters would fly airborne alert from daybreak to dark, with C-47s helping out through the night. President Diem wanted American pilots to keep an eye on Vietnamese troops, and prevent them from straying across the border into Cambodia. So that advance reconnaissance flights would not warn the enemy, key commanders flew over the terrain in a C-123.

AP BAC AND RELATED MATTERS

The entire force of twenty-six Vietnamese AD-6s and Farm Gate's sixteen B-26s and twenty-four T-28s at Bien Hoa engaged in the operation. Their day-long support was called "splendid." The paratroopers and rangers suffered nine casualties but killed seventy-six Viet Cong and captured individual weapons and documents. Early assessments based on prisoner of war interrogations and on an intercepted Viet Cong radio message credited the air strikes with killing about four hundred persons. Later information coming from Cambodia raised the number to between eight hundred and one thousand. American observers praised the operation as the most successful ever undertaken in III Corps, terming it an intelligent use of tactical air support.[19]

Overshadowing these encouraging successes was the failure near the village of Ap Bac in IV Corps. Ap Bac involved the 7th Division, reputed to have killed more Viet Cong in the Mekong Delta than any other division. So well had the 7th performed in the important Plain of Reeds that it appeared to have wrested control from the communists. The enemy leaders seemed on the point of pulling back their regular units to sanctuary bases.

Late in December 1962, intelligence pinpointed a Viet Cong radio in a relatively out-of-reach area near Ap Bac. The village was situated in a complex of hamlets thirty-five miles southwest of Saigon and around fifteen miles northwest of the 7th Division command post at My Tho, capital of Dinh Tuong Province. In this rice-growing delta region, canals, dikes, and dirt roads channeled movement. Villages and tree lines offered cover and concealment to defenders. Soft fertile earth made digging foxholes easy, and paddies gave good fields of fire. Nearly a company of Viet Cong troops was suspected to be in position to protect the radio, which was supposed to transmit for the Viet Cong Central Office for South Vietnam. On December 29 the newly appointed 7th Division commander decided to knock out this prize.

He selected two battalions from different regiments, a company of mechanized infantry in M-113 amphibious armored personnel carriers, a ranger company, and three battalions of artillery (two of 105-mm and one of 155-mm howitzers). A paramilitary provincial force of three battalions would help out. The division commander planned heliborne landings north and west of Ap Bac, these troops to sweep south and meet the M-113s rolling north. Lt. Col. John P. Vann, senior U.S. Army advisor, wished to start the operation at once to avert intelligence leaks. He suggested December 31 at the latest, but helicopters were not to be had before January 2, 1963.

Maj. Herbert L. Prevost, a USAF air liaison officer first learned of the operation on December 30. He readied a plan for strike aircraft support, but discovered on the 31st that all available aircraft would be supporting the operation in northern Tay Ninh Province. The U.S. Army 93d Helicopter Company nonetheless agreed to go ahead with the helicopter landings. It furnished ten transport helicopters plus one UH-1B and four HU-1A helicopter gunships (armed with rockets and machineguns) to fly cover and fire-support missions. At the final briefing on January 1 Major Prevost accented the absence of fighter support. Perhaps, he suggested, the air operations center would respond to emergency strike requests. He alerted the center to the possibility.

The provincial troops deployed at 0630 on the 2d of January, and the operation commenced shortly thereafter. Instead of meeting a Viet Cong company near Ap Bac, 7th Division ran into a battalion. Armed with heavy machineguns, automatic rifles, and 60-mm mortars, the foe was dug in under the tree lines bordering the helicopter landing zones. The first three helicopter lifts from Tan Hiep airfield landed safely, but during the landing of the fourth an H-21 was downed by enemy fire. The UH-1 gunships sought in vain to suppress the ground fire. They used up 8,400 rounds of .30-caliber and 7.62-mm machinegun ammunition along with one hundred 2.75-inch rockets. An H-21 trying to rescue the crew of the downed helicopter was shot out of the sky, and a UH-1B was disabled and it crashed. Two other damaged H-21s made it back to Tan Hiep.

At 1005 a Vietnamese L-19 over Ap Bac radioed the air operations center for help. The center diverted two AD-6s armed for strafing and they arrived at 1035. Afterwards the center kept B-26s and T-28s, also armed for strafing, continuously active in the Ap Bac area. These planes failed to quiet the enemy guns. Not until the arrival of a Farm Gate B-26 at 1540 did things look up. This aircraft's repeated runs with napalm, bombs, rockets, and guns broke the Viet Cong defensive position near the village.

By then the communists had won the battle. They pinned down the heliborne forces, and put the armored company out of action by focusing fire on the gunners of the personnel carriers. (The gunners were exposed from the waist up.)

The IV Corps commander and the senior U.S. Army advisor, Col. Daniel B. Porter, Jr., had reached Tan Hiep at noon. They suggested a paratrooper drop east of Ap Bac to block Viet Cong escape routes. The division commander and Colonel Vann agreed, and that afternoon the Joint General Staff chose three paratrooper companies from nearby Tan Son Nhut. Boarding six C-123s, 319 troops floated down close to Ap Bac at 1815. Because their drop zone placed them west rather than east of the village, they were in no position to stem the enemy retreat.

During the night separate Vietnamese units engaged in firefights with one another while the Viet Cong battalion escaped with its wounded and all but four of its dead. As regular troops moved cautiously into Ap Bac the next day, advance elements came under the fire of friendly mortars. Five men were killed and fourteen wounded.

The final reckoning was sixty-five Vietnamese and three Americans killed, one hundred Vietnamese and six U.S. advisors wounded; fourteen helicopters hit by enemy fire and five shot down. The Vietnamese captured two Viet Cong, found four bodies, and killed an estimated one hundred enemy. Afterwards the Viet Cong admitted eighteen killed, thirty-three wounded, three missing, plus twenty-nine civilians killed. Clearly the combat had been poorly managed and poorly fought. The Vietnamese and Americans lost in prestige and in reputation for power. Colonel Vann subsequently suggested that several Vietnamese officers should be relieved of command. He spoke bitterly to newsmen of wrong decisions during the battle.[20]

On General Harkin's orders, the Vietnamese Joint Operations Evaluaton Group came up with the reasons for the Ap Bac defeat. There had been no prior air-ground planning and no fighter escort for cover. When Vietnamese Air Force and Farm Gate strike aircraft were diverted to Ap Bac, the crews did not know the local situation. Communications between friendly forces had been deficient and no fire support coordination center existed. Armed H-21s had tried to rescue downed crews before Viet Cong fire was silenced. Paratroopers dropped shortly before nightfall had been improperly loaded and briefed. They had fought friendly troops. Without waiting for the formal report, Harkins asked the Vietnamese to relieve two commanders.[21]

To Admiral Felt the unescorted helicopter operation at Ap Bac was wrong. Visiting Vietnam, he spoke with Diem and senior Vietnamese and American officials. He told Harkins, "Experience has taught us that the VC are not surprised by helicopter landings and are able to ambush helicopters." Felt could "not understand" how commanders could ignore "the fundamentals of warfare" by failing to prepare the landing area. He could not conceive how they could have decided to conduct a key operation when available air support was busy elsewhere. It was time that everyone learned that armed "helicopters were no adequate substitute" for fighter support. All helicopter lifts needed strike aircraft. When Felt questioned whether MACV was downgrading air activities, General Harkins explained that there were too few tactical aircraft in Vietnam to cover every heliborne mission. As a matter of fact, he said, twenty-four operations in the preceding month had been without air cover.[22]

General Anthis proposed exact procedures to make certain that Vietnamese ground commanders and U.S. Army helicopter companies coordinated helicopter assault actions. Only the air operations center could assure that fighters preceded and protected every heliborne landing. The Vietnamese Air Force could furnish corps commanders with strafing, close air support, reconnaissance, photography, and airlift. But centralized control over all air power guaranteed fast emergency reaction.[23]

That each corps commander wielded virtually absolute control over air power within his boundaries led to peculiar situations. In January 1963, for example, air interdiction was out of the question in IV Corps. The corps commander simply refused such missions to avoid political repercussions if noncombatants were accidentally killed or wounded. On the 2d of January the I Corps commander ordered no strikes to be flown without his personal approval. Inasmuch as he was often away from his headquarters at Da Nang, it was usually impossible to fill requests from the field for immediate help. Later that year, a new I Corps commander used the Vietnamese C-47 flareships as his personal transports. He assigned helicopters and liaison planes to divisions and task forces permanently rather than in line with mission needs. The Joint General Staff required no advance notice from corps on operations being planned and executed, unless the commander wanted more aircraft from Saigon. Given these conditions, a well-coordinated countrywide air campaign against the Viet Cong was unthinkable.[24]

Also impeding well-integrated air operations was the U.S. Army practice of making aviation units an integral part of the ground forces. The bitterness of the roles-and-missions argument spilled over when General Anthis several months later pinned the failure at Ap Bac on the Army's air concepts. He dubbed the Army "a customer that is also a competitor." Seeing "the spectre of more Ap Bac's to come," he said that

> in some ways it would be better if the Army suffered a few relatively minor reverses at this time. Certainly it would be better if their concept of close air support were discredited now in a relatively inexpensive way than to wait for the ultimate catastrophe their concept must lead us to at a time and place where we will not have the elasticity we presently enjoy.[25]

Admiral Felt also believed that the air operations center and the airlift coordinating board had to be "fully exploited" for combined and joint ground and air operations. He judged this the way to make best use of limited air resources and facilities. "Until the Army air effort joins the club," General O'Donnell stated, "with the intent to cooperate wholeheartedly in the achievement of valid operational objectives, there will not be unity in the air effort."[26]

The USAF element of Strike Command, a joint readiness force in the United States, proposed a return to World War II organizational procedures. That is, the Air Force would own and man air request communications down to Army battalion level. To expand communications for air liaison officers and forward air controllers, the Air Staff furnished 2d Air Division with twenty contingency teams. Each consisted of an airman operator and a commercial KWM-2A single-sideband "suitcase" radio. Although messages were speeded to the air operations center, there were too few teams to go around. General Anthis eventually suggested setting up an air request net within the Vietnamese ground forces.[27]

General O'Donnell felt sure that the tactical air control system had proved its worth in the battle for Ap Bac. After all it had diverted planes to aid Vietnamese troops at a critical time. With an air request net, he suggested, the system would be flexible enough to support the decentralized National Campaign Plan. General Harkins disagreed. He said geography and imperfect communications ruled out direct centralized control of the total air effort. Better, he thought, to commit teams of Vietnamese and USAF strike aircraft to the corps tactical zones and under their control. Harkins said the main function of the joint operations center was to redistribute planes among the several zones according to the tempo of local operations.[28]

These and other factors induced MACV in March to form a Flight Service Center and Network at Tan Son Nhut to which every military flight would report. General Harkins sought by this action to satisfy in part Admiral Felt's wish for General Anthis, the MACV air component commander, to possess complete "coordinating authority" over air operations in Vietnam.

Seeking to settle the matter once and for all, Admiral Felt compromised. He asked Harkins to operate USAF aircraft in Vietnam under the tactical air control system. The air operations center was to assign or allocate aircraft to the control of the tactical corps for fixed periods. Felt also requested Harkins to bring U.S. Army aviation units under the control system. Placing air operations under centralized control would prevent mutual interference, facilitate flight following, simplify air defense identification problems, and upgrade combat support.[29]

General Harkins responded that the tactical air control system had not the communications for precise coordination. In July he gave the MACV J-3 Army air operations section general supervision over U.S. Marine Corps and U.S. Army aviation. He designated the Marine Corps headquarters in I Corps and the Army aviation battalion headquarters in the other corps zones to direct their air operations. General Anthis protested the arrangement, saying it would create two and perhaps five separate air control systems—and separate air wars—within Vietnam. Harkins replied, "Let's give these things a three or four month trial." He promised to change the setup if it failed to work.[30]

The controversy reflected an overall decentralization. After Michael V. Forrestal of the White House staff and Roger Hilsman of the State Department visited Vietnam in December 1962, they criticized the "elaborate, set-piece" military operations and the use of air power. Too many people, they informed President Kennedy, were managing the American effort. There was no overall direction. They recommended a single strong executive—possibly a general, preferably a civilian (an ambassador)—to dominate all departments and agencies in the country and to give a single thrust to the multiple activities.[31]

The USAF directorate of plans drafted a position paper for possible use by General LeMay at the Joint Chiefs meeting of January 7, 1963. According to the paper, the situation was of the "greatest concern," even though many U.S. programs enjoyed a long leadtime. "But when I see the Viet Cong continue to grow in strength, I can only assume that *WE ARE NOT WINNING.*" Army and Air Force doctrinal disputes ought to be taken out of Vietnam. CINCPAC's requests should receive prompt attention. Harkins was in need of the "best possible advice" through an Air Force deputy, and Anthis should manage all air operations. The major political obstacle of the war was Diem's failure to secure the real support and backing of his people. The major military obstacle was trying to erase the guerrillas in the face of a seemingly endless stream of replacements. Needed were greater U.S. air power until the Vietnamese Air Force could go it alone, in-country pilot training of Vietnamese, and destruction of Viet Cong food crops. "We should consider now the application of selected, measured sanctions against the North Vietnamese." Actions would range from infiltrating agents through air bombardment to blockade.[32]

Whatever was said at the January 7 meeting, the chiefs chose to send Gen. Earle G. Wheeler, Army Chief of Staff, and a team of senior officers from the military services to Vietnam. The group's mission was "to form a military judgment as to the prospects for a successful conclusion of the conflict within a reasonable period of time."[33]

The team spent January 14-30 in Vietnam, soon after the battle at Ap Bac. The members examined the National Campaign Plan and endorsed the concept of "many small operations with decentralized control," undertaken "at an accelerated pace by each corps, division, and sector commander in his own area." They noted with approval that the tempo of small actions was quickening to 450 per month, and they looked for an upsurge in the future. The group was pleased with what appeared to be adequate coordination of political, economic, and military matters.[34]

Paying little attention to the battle of Ap Bac, the team heard General Harkins announce satisfaction with the air organization. His staff needed no stronger Air Force representation. The OV-1 Mohawks could do more than reconnaissance. Could they be armed with rockets? Could the rule prohibiting armed helicopters from returning fire except in self-defense be changed?[35]

The Joint Chiefs of Staff swiftly authorized U.S. Army helicopters "to engage clearly identified Viet Cong elements which are considered to be a threat to the safety of the helicopters and their passengers." Admiral Felt then permitted arming the Mohawks with 2.75-inch rockets.[36]

While the Wheeler team was sympathetic toward augmenting Air Force units, the civilian leadership in Washington was more concerned with turning the conflict over to the Vietnamese. On February 2 Hanoi called upon the International Control Commission to eject from Vietnam the USAF units that were "playing a key role" and causing widespread damage. Secretary of State Rusk was disturbed. He could hardly prevent American reporters from observing and writing about U.S. operations. However, he wanted the Embassy and MACV to release no information on American combat air actions. The United States, Rusk said, ought not to hand the communists an excuse to escalate hostilities.[37]

The U.S. newspapers publicized the authorization for American helicopters to fire on the enemy. Secretary McNamara refused to comment except to say that American military personnel were under instructions to fire their weapons only when their own safety was at stake. Secretary Rusk reiterated, "Our policy remains that the American role in Vietnam be strictly limited to advisory, logistic, and training functions."[38]

General Wheeler's assessment in January 1963 rang with optimism. The situation in Vietnam, Wheeler said, had been "reoriented, in the space of a year and a half, from a circumstance of near desperation to a condition where victory is now a hopeful prospect." A heartening sign was the steep rise in American advisory strength from nine hundred at the start of 1962 to more than three thousand. At first there had been no advisors with battalions, but now there were over four hundred. In a year the number of advisors helping province chiefs had grown from two to one hundred or more. Though "we have not given Ho Chi Minh any evidence that we are prepared to call him to account for helping keep the insurgency alive," Wheeler said, "we are winning slowly in the present thrust." There was "no compelling reason to change."[39]

Air Force officers on the team did not quite agree with General Wheeler's evaluation. They believed sizable and long-lasting U.S. help a must. The war could not be won quickly, nor could it be won finally until the Vietnamese people got behind the government. This demanded military, political, and economic actions — "U.S. assistance is vitally engaged in building a country, not in defending a weak country against superior forces."[40]

MACV intelligence estimates showed that the number of full-time Viet Cong guerrillas had risen through infiltration and local recruitment to between twenty-two thousand and twenty-five thousand. Each month about five hundred stole into Vietnam by way of Laos and Cambodia. Late in January 1963 a meeting was reportedly held in the Chinese Embassy at Phnom Penh, Cambodia. Representatives of Hanoi, the National Liberation Front, and the Soviets agreed to add twelve battalions to the Viet Cong. Eight were to be transferred from Laos and four recruited in Vietnam.[41]

To the Viet Cong the battle of Ap Bac was apparently a major turning point in the war. It instilled confidence in their ability to fight American helicopters and armored vehicles. Enemy leaders took credit for a new tactic — the deliberately invited battle, described as "wipe-out-enemy-posts-and-annihilate-enemy reinforcements." They would often resort to this tactic in the Mekong Delta, almost always to good advantage.[42]

On the Vietnamese side, there was a lull in military action after Ap Bac. Admiral Felt believed the calm to have "both visible and hidden meaning." The Vietnamese seemed to be in no hurry to launch operations. General Harkins in February 1963 wrote President Diem, urging him to swiftly exploit the initiative that his forces seemed to have seized from the foe. "Time and weather," Harkins said, "are either for us or against us." The communists, he added, "must not be allowed to regroup or rest. We must attack and destroy them. We must hurt them so badly that they will be forced to apply all their remaining resources merely to survive." Otherwise the Viet Cong might "neutralize much of the gain we won at great cost and effort."[43]

But the Ap Bac engagement and American press coverage had damaged relations with the Diem government. Newspaper accounts of the battle aroused serious resentment in Vietnamese officials, particularly David Halberstam's criticism in the *New York Times* of Vietnamese performance. Newsmen spread their belief that U.S. advisors had died while trying to lead Vietnamese troops who would neither follow nor fight. Embittered Vietnamese leaders complained that correspondents were interested merely in splashing sensational news on the front pages when Americans were hurt. Madame Ngo Dinh Nhu recalled the presidential palace bombing, when she and her children were in grave danger. She said that U.S. reports revealed solely an "ill-concealed regret that the bombing had failed in its objective." The Wheeler report commented on the "mutual dislike and distrust" between the Vietnamese government and the American press. Embarrassed by the news reports of Vietnamese battlefield misconduct, President Kennedy strove to repair the eroding trust between the two governments. In his State of the Union Message to Congress on January 14, he declared that the spearhead of aggression had been blunted in Vietnam.[44]

THE ADVISORY YEARS

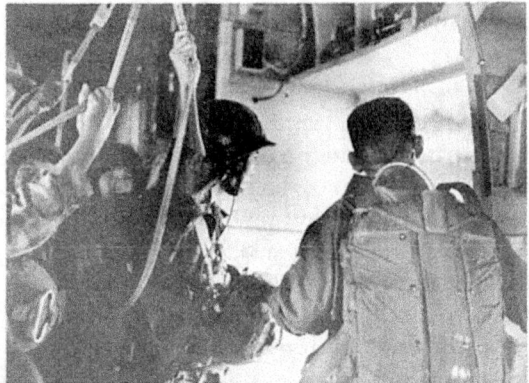

(Top left) Maj. Ivan L. Slavich briefs Gen. Earle G. Wheeler (center) and Gen. Paul D. Harkins on a rocket mount of the UH–1B helicopter.

(Top right) An ARVN paratrooper prepares for a jump over Cu Chi.

(Center) TSgt. William W. Cameron instructs Vietnamese airmen in the operation of the gunsight on a T–28.

(Below) Vietnamese tanks move toward the burning presidential palace after its bombing.

AP BAC AND RELATED MATTERS

Signs of dissension and mistrust were all too obvious. Back in November 1962, reports had reached Admiral Felt that Diem was withdrawing more into seclusion and leaving many decisions to his brother, Ngo Dinh Nhu. Both sometimes regarded the numerous American advisors as an encroachment on Vietnamese sovereignty. They feared that the cautious U.S. policy in Laos mirrored a weakening interest in Vietnam. They were upset by Senate Majority Leader Mike Mansfield's report in February 1963. It said that after seven years and four billion dollars of American aid, "the same difficulties remain, if, indeed, they have not been compounded." Vietnam was less stable and "more removed from . . . popularly responsible and responsive government." Did this foreshadow dwindling U.S. support?

The defense minister scored American allegations of hit-or-miss Vietnamese bombing as a "corrosive influence" on the military effort. American attempts to help the Government of Vietnam create an intelligence capability were probably seen by Diem as a threat to his regime. The Minister of Interior resented the involvement of Americans in the country as a danger to the republic's internal politics. President Diem labeled the Special Forces rural aid advisors and the sector advisors as "particularly irritating." Even though U.S. economic assistance financed nearly all of the counterinsurgency, Diem objected to American controls over matching counterpart funds. He called them degrading to Vietnam's independence.[45]

In a series of private and public statements during April 1963, Ngo Dinh Nhu dwelt upon U.S. "infringements" of Vietnamese sovereignty. Aid came, he said, with too many strings attached. He told CIA Chief John H. Richardson that it would help if the American presence were reduced anywhere from five hundred to three or four thousand men. Richardson got the impression that Nhu feared an emerging U.S. protectorate. Diem, Nhu said, had received many complaints from subordinates about their American counterparts. Publicly, Nhu was quoted as demanding the withdrawal of over two thousand U.S. advisors at lower unit levels. Obviously referring to Ap Bac, he said that some American casualties had occurred because the advisors were "daredevils" who exposed themselves needlessly to enemy fire. Taking this statement as a forerunner of things to come, the Vietnamese Air Force commander alerted his key personnel to the possible withdrawal of U.S. forces. He warned them to conserve reserves, prepare to go it alone, and get ready for hard days ahead.[46]

The Vietnamese government did not officially request a reduction of American personnel, but Nhu's statements induced a review of U.S. troop levels. Evidence seemed to favor a lesser commitment of forces. Sir Robert Thompson in March had reported the government as "beginning to win the shooting war against the Viet Cong," due chiefly to the American helicopters. He proposed a psychological ploy that Admiral Felt passed to the Joint Chiefs by message. "If things go right by end of 1963," Felt said, "we should take one thousand military personnel out of RVN at one time, make big proclamation out of this and publicize widely. This would show (1) RVN is winning; (2) take steam out of anti-Diemites; and (3) dramatically illustrate honesty of U.S. intentions."

THE ADVISORY YEARS

In April a U.S. National Intelligence Estimate perceived improvement in the situation, despite the absence of persuasive signs that the Viet Cong had been "grievously hurt." Ambassador Nolting in May depicted relations between Washington and Saigon as "delicate," but the political and socioeconomic conditions were promising. An excellent rice crop brightened the economic outlook. Completion of about fifty percent of the strategic hamlet program extended shelter to sixty percent of the people in defended areas. During April the Vietnamese armed forces took part in nine hundred offensive actions.[47]

These hopeful signs encouraged Secretary McNamara at his conference in Hawaii in May. He said he would remove one thousand Americans from Vietnam by the end of the year to show that things were going well. He would try to pull out units in lieu of individuals, and upon departure their equipment would be turned over the the Vietnamese. The conflict was "not a U.S. war," and the United States did not intend to fight it.[48]

Since more Americans were still arriving in Vietnam, units and individuals then en route were to continue their travel. There would be no personnel increases, however, either temporary or permanent. Each of the armed services was to take a comparable cut. To hurt operations the least, most of the returnees would come from logistic units. In November and December, 2d Air Division would lose 244 people.[49]

Maybe McNamara's action impressed the Vietnamese. In June the Joint General Staff ordered all ground forces to operate a minimum of twenty days every month, starting July 1. This was to be a "total general offensive" to attain "complete annihilation of the enemy" and "complete Vietnamese control."[50]

General Harkins was enthusiastic. The all-out campaign was soon to begin in earnest. He knew the strategy—"saturate the countryside" with small and large military actions—was correct. It would fragment and destroy the Viet Cong.[51]

Unfortunately, the Viet Cong had embarked on their own general offensive.

XV. Air Operations, 1963

Although some U.S. units were scheduled to leave Vietnam by the end of 1963, the JCS earlier that year had suggested and Secretary McNamara approved an additional C-123 Provider squadron for Da Nang. Arrival of the 777th Troop Carrier Squadron in April 1963 with sixteen C-123s augmented the airlift of the twenty-nine C-123s at Tan Son Nhut. Crew manning permitted each Provider to fly sixty hours per month. In addition eight U-1 Otters, sixteen O-1A Bird Dog observation planes, ten UH-1B Iroquois helicopters, and a second CV-2 Caribou company reached Vietnam to support the corps tactical zones and Special Forces.[1]

General Harkins, MACV commander, had agreed to place the CV-2s under the coordinated airlift system. However, Army headquarters in Hawaii urged Admiral Felt to recognize the special features of the Caribou. The Army had purchased the planes for short-takeoff-and-landing, which rendered them instantly responsive to ground commanders in combat zones. While centralized control of airlift was more efficient for cargo deliveries, swift reaction to a field commander's needs came first. In this context Harkins assigned the two Caribou companies to centralized airlift control, but one of these had the further mission of immediate support to the senior corps advisors.[2]

The Southeast Asia Airlift System managed the forty-eight Air Force C-123s, thirty-two Vietnamese C-47s, and thirty-two Army CV-2s. Though the C-123s normally made deliveries to four major depots and twenty-nine other distribution points, they actually operated at ninety-five different airfields and sixty-five drop zones. Carrying a lighter load than the C-123, the CV-2 could use shorter runways. But reversible propellers let the Provider land on wet surfaces in distances impossible for the Caribou, not yet so equipped.[3]

The 8th Aerial Port Squadron expanded in May by creating Detachments 6 and 7 at Qui Nhon and Can Tho. Temporary duty personnel served 120-day duty tours at the new sites.[4]

Much of the Southeast Asia Airlift System's work dealt with tactical operations. About thirty percent of the troop carrier flights were paradrop resupply, paratrooper drops, and assault air landings. Resolute efforts to support remote stations drew grateful praise from the ground troops. They deemed the system reliable and responsive.[5]

Uncertain surface travel, the conservative bent of logistic planners, and the use of scaled U.S. planning factors tended to inflate requirements. In October the airlift system's excess capacity prompted plans for reduction. In December MACV strength was pared by one thousand. Released were personnel of the Army's 1st Aviation Company (Caribou), the thirty USAF C-47 pilots flying with the Vietnamese Air Force, and half of the 8th Aerial Port Squadron's people. The 61st Aviation Company (Caribou) with twenty-five CV-2s stayed behind to support senior corps advisors. Some of these Caribous became spares

THE ADVISORY YEARS

to insure a certain number of operational aircraft at every corps tactical zone.[6]

The Air Force's 19th Tactical Air Support Squadron was activated at Bien Hoa in July 1963 and assigned to PACAF. The new unit's aircraft and crews trickled in. Four 0-1s and twenty-two crews were on board by July, and the remaining eighteen planes arrived on the USS *Card* in August. Since Americans were forbidden to direct air strikes, eleven seasoned Vietnamese observers were integrated into the squadron to do so. Operational in September, the unit furnished more and more forward air controllers and air liaison officers for the National Campaign Plan. Its primary mission was to train Vietnamese liaison pilots in forward air control, visual reconnaissance, combat support, and observer procedures. The aim was to replace those pilots drained off to fill fighter cockpits. The squadron was to remain in Vietnam no more than a year, then turn its 0-1s over to the Vietnamese.

Preparations to open a training center at Nha Trang were delayed because American pilots needed proficiency in the U.S Army L-19 (0-1) aircraft. General LeMay had ordered this plane sent in lieu of depleting the few L-28s in USAF stocks. As his Director of Plans, Maj. Gen. John W. Carpenter, III, said, "The Chief clearly expressed his desires toward getting on with the war against the communists in Vietnam as opposed to worrying about the source of light aircraft." After twenty-five officers and sixty-nine airmen underwent factory training in July and August, they opened the Nha Trang center in September. Trainees took one month of preflight instruction and three months of primary flight training that included eighty hours of actual flying. Vietnamese liaison pilots in reasonable numbers were ready for combat in early 1964.[7]

Twelve Air Force officers and forty-seven airmen reached Tan Son Nhut in January 1963 to train Vietnamese helicopter pilots. By June they graduated fifteen student pilots who were qualified to fly H-19s. The training went on throughout the year.[8]

Admiral Felt hoped that the Vietnamese could have the four RT-33 jets authorized by the Military Assistance Program. In February, however, Secretary of State Rusk announced that "over-riding political considerations" and "international risks" ruled out their delivery. Shortly thereafter, the Joint Chiefs approved a boost in USAF reconnaissance aircraft, including four RB-26s and two more RF-101s for Farm Gate. The RB-26s reached Tan Son Nhut in March from Fort Worth, Tex. Two of them were equipped for night photography, and the other two were experimental RB-26Ls specially outfitted with night photo and Reconofax IV infrared sensing devices. In May, Fifth Air Force's 6091st Reconnaissance Squadron flew two RB-57s to a temporary duty site at Tan Son Nhut. These jets featured advanced and improved day-and-night K-52 panoramic cameras and Reconofax VI infrared sensors.[9]

Airborne high-frequency direction finders had difficulty locating Viet Cong radio transmitters. More than two hundred enemy sets were active, but it was impossible to fix their exact sites. General Anthis and other officials thought it might be better to listen to the traffic instead of disrupting or destroying it. In any event, knowing where the radios were operating was deemed essential.[10]

Infrared devices were meant to detect thermal radiation emitted by campfires, vehicles, structures, and traffic on trails and streams. In theory the sensors could pinpoint activities hidden from normal photography. But the Reconofax IV infrared photo equipment on the RB-26Ls broke down, and the technical representative in Vietnam could not make the system (originally designed for B-58s) work. Climatic conditions, chiefly dust and dampness, fouled the sensors. Heat from the photoflare cartridge ejectors forward of the infrared system saturated the infrared detector and ruined the film.

As for the RB-57E's infrared sensors, integral components were missing. The plane's panoramic cameras provided very clear horizon-to-horizon pictures even at high speed and low altitude. Having both horizons in the shot enhanced the perspective of the photo interpreter, but he had to learn how to compensate for distortion in the wide lateral coverage.[11]

When equipment worked, the intelligence apparatus was often unable to exploit the information gathered. The zonal concept of ground operations worked against a centralized air reconnaissance network. Separating intelligence data by corps tactical zone was not easy because planes flew across corps boundaries. Moreover, there were no courier aircraft to deliver reconnaissance film rapidly throughout Vietnam before the coming of two U-3s from the United States in May. Army OV-1 Mohawks attached to Vietnamese ground divisions reacted quickly to shifting situations. However, the intelligence they collected was not fed into the national intelligence-reconnaissance setup. General Harkins still labeled the Mohawks as "complementary" rather than "competitive" to USAF and Vietnamese tactical air reconnaissance. He saw no need to coordinate them with the standard activities, saying they were "outside the specialized capabilities of other photo aircraft."[12]

Air Force planes flew nearly all the reconnaissance in 1963, yet the flights failed to glean a great deal of intelligence. By reason of weather, jungle, and forested terrain, finding and photographing the small and fleeting enemy targets was a stiff proposition.[13]

Air defense radar control centers were situated at Tan Son Nhut, Da Nang, and Pleiku. These and the radar at Ubon, Thailand, gave high-altitude surveillance. The interceptor fleet consisted of Air Force F-102 and Navy EA-1F (AD-5Q) all-weather fighters rotated to Saigon. Mountain screening cluttered radar coverage below 5,000 feet. The F-102s performed marginally in low-level interceptions, while the EA-1Fs lacked the speed to intercept aircraft intruding in areas distant from Saigon. To stretch the coverage and especially to scan much of south-central Vietnam, the Vietnamese Air Force moved a TPS-1/-10D training radar from Tan Son Nhut to Ban Me Thuot in February 1963.[14]

From February 10 to 15 an unusual number of low-level, slow-flying radar tracks appeared before midnight near Pleiku and Da Nang then disappeared before dawn. Air Force and Navy interceptors investigated, using flares and other techniques. They found nothing, the tracks vanishing from ground and air radars as the planes approached. Around Da Nang on February 14, a Navy aircraft intercepted a flight of ducks. Consequently officials concluded that migrating waterfowl had caused the unknown tracks.[15]

Convinced that no air battles would be fought in Vietnam, General Harkins nevertheless sensed the need for flight following. Since November 1961, Mule Train transport squadrons had used their network of high-frequency radios. Farm Gate crews reported their inflight positions to the nearest radar control center every thirty minutes. On January 10, 1963, an Army OV-1 was lost during an unreported flight out of Qui Nhon, and it took over two hundred fifty search sorties to find the plane. In March the Flight Service Center and Network was born at Tan Son Nhut.[16]

The reduced likelihood of communist air intrusions and the birth of the Flight Service Center and Network threw into question the need for the F-102s and EA-1Fs at Tan Son Nhut. Safety considerations alone seemed to warrant their removal, for 233 military aircraft of all sorts used the airfield, along with commercial planes. General Anthis wanted to clear the 10,000-foot runway by moving out some of the helicopters, but PACAF suggested keeping the interceptors on call in the Philippines. These planes withdrew in May. The supersonic F-102s could return to Tan Son Nhut within twelve hours, the EA-1Fs within forty-eight. There was no call for them in 1963 however.[17]

Triggered by President Kennedy's approval on December 31, 1962, to augment Farm Gate, the Air Force in 1963 acted to regularize the status of its units in Vietnam. Admiral Felt furnished the impetus when he spurned the principle hitherto held that USAF personnel sent to the country had to have prior training in counterinsurgency. Farm Gate, he said, was flying conventional missions. Airmen could accordingly be assigned on a routine permanent change of station basis. This would clear the way for doubling the number of aircrews and maintenance men, and could raise the sortie rate by twenty-five or thirty percent. Felt in addition wished to boost the number of liaison aircraft and forward air controllers by a full two squadrons, to furnish visual reconnaissance beyond anything already on hand. This, he said, would be the key to a successful National Campaign Plan.[18]

General LeMay in early February pressed for putting U.S. markings on Farm Gate aircraft. He said that "current classification restrictions on Farm Gate are considered unnecessary. Actual operation is well known through SVN and classification has become an administrative burden." The State Department queried Ambassador Nolting on a series of articles in the press on U.S. combat air activities, particularly those of American-piloted aircraft. In his reply Nolting pointed out the rather "gradual (and inevitable) uncovering of facts by U.S. journalists." That Americans flew combat aircraft was common knowledge. This was expressly true after the deaths of Capts. John P. Bartley and John F. Shaughnessy, Jr., in an RB-26 downed by Viet Cong fire on February 3, and the loss of Maj. James E. O'Neill in a crash three days later.[19] Secretary of State Rusk, however, continued to accent the American role as "strictly limited to advisory, logistic, and training functions."[20]

General LeMay in March again asked for permission to declassify Farm Gate but Ambassador Nolting said, "We are winning without such overt U.S. action."[21]

By June 1963 MACV had 16,652 people, 4,790 of them Air Force. On the 28th, Secretary of Defense McNamara froze MACV strength. To clear up the confusing array of USAF units, PACAF formed new ones without expanding manpower authorizations.[22] On July 8 Farm Gate at Bien Hoa became the 1st Air Commando Squadron (Composite), a regular PACAF organization. Although PACAF wanted the code name Farm Gate dropped, Air Force headquarters disapproved because various logistic facilities supporting Farm Gate were thoroughly familiar with the name and all it implied. As 1st Air Commando Squadron, Farm Gate contained two strike sections. The first consisted of ten B-26s with twenty-three crews (pilot and navigator) and two RB-26s. The second had thirteen T-28s with two crewmembers per plane. In addition there were two support sections, one of four psychological warfare U-10s and the other of six C-47s. The remaining eight B-26s were in detachments at Pleiku and Soc Trang.[23]

Likewise on July 8 the 33d and 34th Tactical Groups came into being. Based at Tan Son Nhut and under the 33d Tactical Group were the 33d Air Base Squadron, the 33d Consolidated Aircraft Maintenance Squadron (CAMRON), and Detachment 1 (a reconnaissance element). The 33d Group also had detachments at Can Tho and Nha Trang.

At Bien Hoa the 34th Tactical Group consisted of the 19th Tactical Air Support Squadron, the 34th Air Base Squadron, and the 34th CAMRON. Detachments of the 34th Group were at Pleiku and Soc Trang.

Directly under 2d Air Division was the 23d Air Base Group, activated at Da Nang with its 23d CAMRON. A detachment of the group at Qui Nhon was previously the 6222d Air Base Squadron.

General Anthis wanted a single control point for the packets of reconnaissance detachments called Able Mable, Black Watch, Patricia Lynn, and Sweet Sue. He therefore requested a tactical air reconnaissance squadron for his 2d Air Division, but the Air Staff could not create the unit within the authorized force structure. In consequence the commander of Detachment 1, 33d Tactical Group, exercised a loose central direction over the reconnaissance operations.

The Mule Train C-123 units became troop carrier squadrons — the 309th and 310th at Tan Son Nhut and the 311th at Da Nang. They were part of the 315th Troop Carrier Group (Assault), attached to 2d Air Division but assigned to PACAF's 315th Air Division (Combat Cargo) headquartered in Japan.

The upshot of this sweeping reorganization was to free General Anthis from dealing directly with twelve or more major subordinate units.[24]

Farm Gate gained fresh aircraft in January 1963 — five T-28s, ten B-26s, and two C-47s — and by February boasted forty-two planes and 275 men. General Anthis fashioned an air strike team of six B-26s and one C-47 at Pleiku, which had been revamped to take B-26s. He formed another of five T-28s and one C-47 at Soc Trang, where the unimproved 3,200-foot runway admitted only T-28 operations.[25]

Until General Harkins in midyear gave the Vietnamese border control troops some aircraft of their own, Farm Gate flew combat support for them. These forces embraced about five thousand Vietnamese army, rangers, and Civilian Irregular Defense Group personnel, accompanied by U.S. Special Forces advisors. They manned 103 outposts along Vietnam's 900-mile land border to cut down on Viet Cong infiltration. Varying in size from platoon to battalion, they further carried out covert penetrations across the frontier. State Department pressure prompted the Joint General Staff to forbid ground and air operations within ten kilometers of the border without prior approval. MACV termed the restriction "completely incongruous," for this strip of de facto demilitarized territory afforded the Viet Cong safe haven.[26]

Over the last days of March 1963, U.S. Special Forces mounted an operation in the Seven Mountains of southwestern Vietnam. Farm Gate bombing before the assault killed about one hundred fifty enemy and let the ground troops move into the hills. Capt. John Sercel, the 2d Air Division forward air controller assigned to the operation, went with the troops on foot and directed air strikes with a PRC-10 radio. Even though the attack brought Vietnamese territory under government control, the IV Corps commander protested the intrusion into his zone. The Joint General Staff then ruled that Special Forces teams had to request air support through Vietnamese channels.[27]

Ten days later the Joint General Staff removed earlier curbs on border operations. Vietnamese ground forces could now operate to the border wherever a geographical feature such as a river or road clearly marked it. Elsewhere they could go to within one thousand meters of the border, except along the northern part where a strip of ten thousand meters applied. Vietnamese aircraft could operate to the border where it was clearly visible, elsewhere to two thousand meters if a forward air controller was at hand, and to five thousand meters without air control. Corps headquarters rather than the Joint General Staff had to approve all actions along the frontier.[28]

The State Department ordered Ambassador Nolting to press for suspension of the new procedures since they could inflame Cambodia, North Vietnam, and China. Nolting was sympathetic to the new rules because of the considerable supplies coming across the borders to the Viet Cong. All the same, he and General Harkins talked with Vietnamese officials about how border violations seriously disturbed the common interests of Vietnam and the United States.

Admiral Felt knew border incidents could be disruptive, but thought that trimming infiltration was worth the risk. General O'Donnell proposed having U.S. aircraft survey the border to correct map errors. His proposal was shelved for fear of breaching the 1962 Geneva agreement on Laotian neutrality.[29]

At the Secretary of Defense Conference in Hawaii on May 6, the participants agreed that the troops stationed along the border must do their utmost to slow down enemy movements. But they believed putting pressure on Hanoi to be a better way to end infiltration. In April the Joint Chiefs had identified eight targets in North Vietnam that were vulnerable to attack from American carrier- and Thailand-based aircraft. Among them were the Dong Hoi and Vinh airfields, several highway bridges, POL storage, the Haiphong thermal powerplant, a rolling mill, and a chemical plant. Bombing would be a warning to Ho Chi Minh but risked bringing Chinese air assistance to North Vietnam.

Mr. McNamara now recommended to the conferees that CINCPAC embody air strikes against North Vietnam for planning options. Perhaps the State Department fetters on covert operations into North Vietnam could be loosened.[30]

Roger Hilsman of the State Department informed the group that he was optimistic about the border control exercised by the Special Forces and Montagnards. Strategic hamlets combined with Montagnard operations were making dramatic gains. He predicted, "You have circles; in the center of each circle is a Special Forces team. These circles are getting bigger. When they close up, I think you will see a noticeable choking down of the use of the infiltration groups."[31]

Admiral Felt said he also expected solid progress from the air strikes against Viet Cong war zones and bases. He scored these power centers as the "nuclei of the VC 'governmental' structure," giving "protective sanctuaries" for offensive enemy operations, and providing "little arsenals and installations." Unfortunately, all-out interdiction clashed with the individual interests of the largely independent corps commanders. While USAF liaison officers called for interdiction, air attacks not tied directly to ground operations began to decline.[32]

Vietnamese probes into Viet Cong Zone D during February and March made good use of preplanned air interdiction strikes. Rangers swept into the area later and burnt enemy headquarters and camps along the Ma Da River. They discovered deep, log-covered bunkers built by the communists to protect against air attacks. Inasmuch as fighters usually circled before striking, there was enough time for everybody to take cover.[33]

In March the Air Force and Army advisors in that area got the go-ahead for a prolonged low-priority interdiction bombing program. Planes returning to base with unused ordnance could attack targets under the direction of a Vietnamese forward air controller. Strikes got under way on April 1 and went on almost every day. It was difficult to assess results due to the jungle cover. On April 30 fighters surprised a gathering of Viet Cong and attacked. Inspecting the area the next day, the Phuoc Thanh Province chief estimated that over one hundred enemy had been killed. Viet Cong deserters confirmed that the strikes inflicted casualties, damaged morale, and kept everyone on the move, but said the attacks were no serious threat to their existence. The communists kept a firm grip on Zone D, continuing to collect road taxes and to exact tribute from plantation owners.[34]

Between April 24 and May 24 the II Corps commander spearheaded a drive into the Do Xa War Zone headquarters area of Viet Cong Interzone V, in the mountains on the borders of Quang Ngai, Kontum, and Quang Tin Provinces. His five regiments of ground troops and two battalions of Vietnamese marines totaled about ten thousand men, assisted by an air support operations center. The three days of preliminary interdiction generated thirty-six A-1H, fourteen T-28, and thirty-four B-26 sorties. Throughout the month-long operation, pilots flew 115 A-1H, 108 T-28, and seventy-four B-26 sorties. Besides killing five Viet Cong, these timely and potent air strikes destroyed 238 structures and damaged 77. The badly scattered enemy would need several months to return and reestablish Viet Cong Region 5 which, like the old Interzone V, guarded infiltration routes to base areas.[35]

Air Force and Vietnamese pilots faithfully followed the rule that air strikes had to be handled by a Vietnamese forward air controller. Although the procedure precluded armed reconnaissance aircraft from attacking targets of opportunity, it was a sound precaution against indiscriminate bombing. Crews staging to and from forward airfields were encouraged to fly low and seek out the enemy. Before they could attack, however, they needed an airborne forward air controller. Army OV-1 crews enjoyed less stringent rules of engagement. They frequently flew as low as fifty feet, enticing the Viet Cong to open fire so they could shoot back.[36]

Lt. Col. David S. Mellish, III Corps air liaison officer, secured authority in September to start an air interdiction program. Vietnamese province chiefs certified certain areas free of friendly people. The air operations center scheduled air strikes under forward air controllers into these regions. Provincial officials reviewed each target belt weekly.

This interdiction paid off in Tay Ninh and Phuoc Thanh Provinces during October, though the Viet Cong learned to disperse and take cover as soon as the L-19 dropped smoke grenades to mark targets for the strike planes. Mellish persistently urged armed reconnaissance in wholly Viet Cong sections. "Vietnamese pilots," he said, "should sweep these areas and shoot VC on sight. At present, we are ineffective because our politically inspired target-marking is the best possible air raid warning the VC could hope to have."

Col. Donald H. Ross, 2d Air Division director of operations, reminded his associates that the Vietnamese — not the Americans — were waging the war. Forward air controllers were vital to protect friendly people.[37]

Carefully targeted and controlled interdiction strikes on Viet Cong base camps, assembly areas, and logistic installations were designed to help ground troops clear and hold Vietnam. But the overriding air mission was support, preparation and cover for heliborne landings, night hamlet defense, and escort for convoys and trains.[38]

Over the first half of 1963, Vietnamese L-19s usually escorted truck convoys and trains but strike aircraft covered those transporting high-priority cargoes. Vietnamese and USAF planes flew close to one thousand sorties in these missions. The Viet Cong ambushed no surface movement having air cover, yet were quick to pounce on motor columns and trains wanting aerial escort.[39]

Developed from original Farm Gate tactics, night flare/strike missions in defense of outposts and hamlets under attack remained effective. One Vietnamese C-47 flareship stayed on night ground alert at Pleiku, a second stood similar duty at Da Nang, and a third flew airborne alert every night over III and IV Corps. Yet the commander of the 514th Fighter Squadron refused to accept orders for A-1H night-strike crews alerted at Bien Hoa and Pleiku. He argued that his pilots were not ready to fly at night, but yielded to American pressure and accepted about half of the missions requested. Fighters working with a flareship could commonly dispense with a forward air controller during strikes in defense of an installation. However, for close air support of friendly troops under attack at night, a controller was required to mark targets.

Success of flare/strike defensive missions depended upon the speed with which those under attack could report to an air support operations center. By May 1963 most villages had radios, and the time lapse between attack and report averaged about forty-eight minutes. The delay stemmed chiefly from the short ranges of the provincial radio transmitters that demanded retransmission of messages, often at district, sector, and division levels. Viet Cong attacks on hamlets and outposts from January through April were few, and an average of thirty-three C-47 sorties was flown each month. The enemy customarily broke off an attack when a flare plane came on the scene.[40]

In the far northern I Corps, the 1st and 2d Divisions controlled the coastal plain to the mountains. The Viet Cong owned the mountains aside from Special Forces camps along the Laotian border and in the A Shau Valley corridor toward Da Nang. In mid-January 1963 the U.S. Marine Corps helicopter squadron HMM-162 became operational at Da Nang, with staging areas at Hue and at a point midway between Da Nang and Quang Ngai. This unit's H-34s supported the border outposts with resupply and troop-exchange missions that normally needed no strike aircraft support. But air mobile troops assault operations took careful advance planning for fighter escort, landing-zone preparation, and air cover. In these operations the H-34s flew in three-ship elements, one minute apart, en route to the landing zone. The helicopter commanders ran the whole affair, calling for strike aircraft to neutralize enemy fire. Even though the Marine Corps helicopter commanders evaluated the Vietnamese A-1H pilots as "outstanding," they favored USAF fighters because there was no communications language problem. When a platoon of Army UH-1 helicopters at Da Nang was attainable in April, these gunships protected landing zones.

The I Corps commander had to approve all requests for air strikes. Members of 2d Air Division who visited the air operations center there had the impression that U.S. Army advisors dominated the scene. For example, the advisors funneled many air support requests to the two armed OV-1 Mohawks stationed at Da Nang.[41]

In the II Corps eight USAF B-26s joined the four Vietnamese A-1Hs at Pleiku. At once air support sorties rose, probably because Vietnamese ground officers could see the aircraft on hand. But communications with the division command posts at Qui Nhon and Quang Ngai were regularly unreliable. And bad weather in the moutains east and northeast of Pleiku repeatedly impeded flights to the coastal provinces.[42]

THE ADVISORY YEARS

AIR OPERATIONS 1963

To shake weather restrictions, MACV shifted two B-26s from Pleiku to Da Nang. Since the Vietnamese pilots were unable or unwilling to operate out of Qui Nhon and Quang Ngai, aircraft from Pleiku or Nha Trang supported the 9th and 25th Divisions.[43] The division commanders complained that they had to divulge their operational plans before they wanted to. Also for a short while, the 110th Liaison Squadron commander declined to send L-19s to Quang Ngai. He resented the time a ground force officer had "usurped the job" of a Vietnamese air observer adjusting artillery. The T-28s dispatched to Qui Nhon and Quang Tri were regularly late for planned operations, despite two days advance notice. This deprived at least one heliborne operation of air cover. "When we speak of immediate air strikes in this division," wrote Lt. Col. Henry C. Meier, 9th Division air liaison officer, "the ARVN only laugh and I can hardly blame them."[44]

Vietnamese aircrews executed well in the II Corps attack on the Do Xa headquarters area during April 24-May 24, 1963. Their performance was below par in June, when the 9th Division triggered a 800-man heliborne attack around An Khe. The L-19 chosen to work the landing zone was late, only one of the four prestrike A-1Hs properly delivered napalm, and the H-21 helicopters had to circle and wait for the air preparations. Two days later, a Vietnamese forward air controller brought prestrike A-1Hs to a landing zone ten minutes early. On five separate occasions in the course of the action, L-19 pilots and observers were

176

unable to accept strike aircraft at assigned rendezvous points. Air Force L-19s with American pilots and Vietnamese observers solved the problems.[45]

Poor performance by Vietnamese aircrews imperiled several ground operations in the II Corps. Operations nonetheless made marked gains around Saigon, disrupting a key Viet Cong base and defending strategic hamlets in Quang Ngai Province against severe communist attacks. More and more local residents came forth with information on Viet Cong movements, and the Popular Forces defending the hamlets killed 383 enemy while losing 33 of their own.[46]

In the III Corps north of Saigon, Vietnamese forces were busy. Rangers probed into Zone D, the 5th Division engaged the enemy in Zone C of Tay Ninh Province, and the 23d Division attacked Viet Cong bands and protected hamlets in the Ban Me Thuot area. Not one of these operations received enough tactical air support. The L-19s of the 112th Liaison Squadron at Tan Son Nhut worked both III and IV Corps, and thus were often unavailable to one or the other. Poor communications between III Corps headquarters and Ban Me Thuot led to authorizing the 23d Division eight T-28 sorties each day from Nha Trang. As the division pushed deeper into Tay Ninh Province and outran dependable landline communications, radio equipment troubles increasingly impeded air support. The use of U.S. Army armed helicopters for fire support came to be routine.[47]

The IV Corps employed the 7th and 21st Divisions in the generally flat and water-sodden terrain of the densely populated Mekong Delta, where transportation was mostly by canal but some by road. The ground favored the guerrillas who massed at places and times of their choosing. Skimpy landline communications made for heavy radio traffic. At Soc Trang the five USAF T-28s, together with a detachment of L-19s from the 122d Liaison Squadron at Can Tho, afforded air strikes and forward air control. Like all other airfields in the delta, Soc Trang needed development. Its unlighted 3,300-foot runway was suited solely to daytime T-28 operations. The glide slope was too steep for a T-28 to touch down safely in wet weather. Though a T-28 could take off at night or in bad weather to land after a mission it had to go to Saigon. MACV proposed constructing an airfield at Can Tho to replace Soc Trang. Even so, building a 6,000-foot runway would take nearly $4.5 million in Military Assistance Program funds and about two years to complete. The project continued under study in Hawaii.[48]

The 7th Division was distinctly less aggressive following the battle of Ap Bac. The division commander, believing that the Viet Cong were monitoring his radio, directed unit commanders to handcarry requests for air support to the division headquarters. The 21st Division engaged extensively in heliborne operations through February and March. Plans were usually too ambitious for the troops committed, and the enemy was never where he was supposed to be. Postponements and no-notice changes in plans complicated the air scheduling of escort and strike planes. After three visiting Americans were pinned down by enemy fire for an hour while strike aircraft were circling overhead and no forward air controller was to be had, three USAF pilots were assigned to the Vietnamese L-19 detachment at Can Tho.[49]

In April a daring scenario called for 21st Division troops to go to the town of Rach Gia by motor convoy and to feint away from the objective — the Viet Cong regional headquarters in western Kien Giang Province between Seven Mountains and the Cambodian border. On the following day, helicopters would land troops to storm the headquarters and to cut off probable escape routes to the mountains. Aircraft were to fly cover and support. The plan may have been compromised, for the Viet Cong withdrew from their sites several days before the assault. Then a classic demonstration of order, counterorder, and disorder took place. The division altered all helicopter radio frequencies and some participants failed to receive notice. Several strike crews orbited target areas waiting for helicopters that never appeared. The ground troops did not clash with the foe, but his fire hit two UH-1 and seven H-21 helicopters. Interdiction bombing in Seven Mountains by U.S. and Vietnamese strike pilots was said to have killed 345 fleeing Viet Cong.[50]

To prevent "whimsical uncoordinated changes in planned helicopter operations directly affecting the escort," General Anthis asked the MACV Joint Frequency Coordinating Board to set up standard radio frequencies for heliborne operations and to insist on their use. The 2d Air Division assigned one of its KWM-2A radios and an operator to the 21st Division. This gave the U.S. air liaison officer a rapid communications link to cope with sudden changes in air support needs. An Air-Ground Operations School orientation team from the United States promoted understanding among 21st Division personnel of the procedures for air support at battalion and company levels. Prestrikes, escort, and air cover were required items in 21st Division planning.[51]

On the 14th and 15th of June in Kien Giang Province, B-26 prestrikes and T-28 cover and escort helped the 21st Division kill 33 enemy (2 by air) and capture thirty. In An Xuyen Province late in June, 107 communists were killed (55 by air), seventy-two prisoners taken, and many arms and munitions captured. "Air support coordination," it was reported, "was absolutely outstanding."[51]

In contrast was the clear neglect of air support by the 7th Division early in July. The division commander aimed a heliborne thrust at a Viet Cong force in Kien Hoa Province, relying on the firepower of four UH-1 gunships. These helicopters could not knock out the guns dug in at the tree line adjacent to the landing zone. Before the afternoon was over, ground fire hit eleven helicopters and wounded three U.S. Army crewmen. Called to the scene, two B-26s, six T-28s, and two AD-6s tangled with the communists. The Viet Cong retreated at nightfall, leaving behind the twenty-four men killed by air strikes.[53]

The loss to enemy ground fire of two B-26s in February and a T-28 in June spurred a boost in air strike firepower. With two B-26s in lieu of one and four T-28s rather than two, the crews could cover each other during low-level passes. Unfortunately, bigger flights meant fewer missions. General Anthis accented the importance of good defensive flying, mutual cover, suppression of hostile fire by strafing, evasive maneuvers, and avoiding needless exposure to ground fire.[54]

Stationing Vietnamese air units at small outlying airfields closer to the ground action was well-nigh impossible. Acute shortages existed in crewchiefs, electrical specialists, armorers, and other skilled men. There was also a dearth of specialist tools, test sets, as well as bomb-handling trailers and other ground-handling equipment. In consequence the Vietnamese aircraft at forward fields were quickly out of commission.[55] Yet Col. Harvey E. Henderson, deputy commander of 2d Air Division, could say, "In my six months here, I have been amazed at the rapidity with which the VNAF have learned and improved their operations."[56]

Belying the progress was the resurgence of Viet Cong attacks. In July the communists successfully struck hamlets south of Ban Me Thuot, and ambushed the roads leading into the area. They cowed the Montagnards, who became less helpful intelligence sources. In a ten-minute attack just before midnight on July 16, twenty to thirty 60-mm mortar rounds slammed into troop housing at Can Tho Airfield and wounded seventeen Vietnamese and U.S. Special Forces troops. The guerrillas slipped away without casualties.[57]

Statistics revealed a rising trend in Viet Cong attacks and other incidents but a drop in the number of communist casualties, weapon losses, and defections. Even though General Harkins was pleased with the fifteen thousand Vietnamese operations per month in July and August, the National Campaign Plan needed a shot in the arm. Many offensive forays failed to find the foe. There were too many one-day-only operations, too few night ones. The Vietnamese did not patrol deep within Viet Cong areas, pursue enemy troops that broke contact, and capitalize on air reconnaissance.[58]

Beginning in September, the Viet Cong swept over exposed hamlets in the area south of Ban Me Thuot. In the better-defended hamlets of Quang Ngai Province, enemy "activity teams" of three to five men achieved some gains. Vietnamese intelligence identified a large-scale, well-planned communist offensive in the Mekong Delta.[59]

Visiting Vietnam during the last week of September, Secretary McNamara and General Taylor deemed the military situation good but political conditions explosive. A week later in Saigon, General Harkins told members of the House foreign affairs Far East subcommittee that the military effort was going well despite the shaky political scene. A significant JCS assessment supported this view.[60]

The faster tempo of Viet Cong attacks created new air support needs as Vietnamese and USAF air power diminished. Vietnamese Air Force units appeared to be more interested in training than in combat. The 516th Fighter Squadron commander trimmed the T-28s in his detachment at Da Nang from eight to four. He based his action on the desire to release some T-28 pilots for upgrade training to A-1Hs. In September the 514th Fighter Squadron commander gave on the average just nine of his twenty-six A-1Hs to the air operations center for daily strike missions, saying he had to divert flying hours to A-1H pilot upgrading. For reasons unclear to Americans, he regularly ignored requests for napalm strikes. This happened principally in the III and IV Corps during the rainy season, even though incendiaries worked better than explosives in the

THE ADVISORY YEARS

(Top) ARVN paratroopers leap from USAF C-123 Providers in a combat training exercise near Saigon.

(Center) O-1E Bird Dog FAC on a visual reconnaissance mission in S. Vietnam.

(Bottom) After flying convoy escort in their Bird Dog, Capt. B. D. Lassman (left) and Capt. D. F. Schell (right) confer with Vietnamese observer.

water-soaked terrain. Crews deployed for a while away from home bases seemed to be unmotivated, uneager, and unreliable.[61]

Under the rules of engagement, Farm Gate continued to fly those combat missions that the Vietnamese could not. Though given more people, Farm Gate failed to increase its sortie rate. The unit had been permitted to scale down normal maintenance because of the field operating conditions. Moreover, the planes were being overworked, and by autumn they were becoming less safe to fly. The operational readiness rate reached only fifty to sixty percent, due chiefly to spare parts shortages. Inflight mechanical failures and enemy action likewise took their toll.

A major cause of B-26 fatigue — not yet identified in the field — was the eight 750-pound bombs hung on specially designed racks under the aircraft's wings. When the B-26 was airborne, this weight did not overstress the wings. But taxiing the heavily armed plane for many months over rough runways and ramps imposed excessive "negative G-force" that brought the wings to their fatigue limit. A B-26 lost a wing in flight during a combat mission on August 16, killing two Americans and a Vietnamese. September was no better. Twenty-three aircraft suffered battle damage. Another B-26 and a T-28 crashed because of mechanical failures. On the 23d, three Viet Cong guerrillas cut through the perimeter fence at Nha Trang and with package explosives blew up two C-47s.[62]

General Anthis hoped to keep the B-26s going by having the crews fly them cautiously and use soft approach and recovery tactics. In any event, every B-26 was set for rotation through depot maintenance contracted with Air Asia in Taiwan. Anthis urged replacing the battle weary B-26s with dual-control Navy A-1E fighters or with "On Mark" B-26Ks being refurbished in the United States by the On Mark Engineering Company. In August and September the 1st Air Commando Squadron was down to an average of nine T-28s and nine to twelve B-26s. Still, Farm Gate was supposed to up its sortie rate by twenty percent to support planned Vietnamese ground offensives.[63]

Although Farm Gate owned fewer planes after October 1963, standard USAF maintenance procedures by the 34th CAMRON at Bien Hoa lifted the operationally ready rate to around seventy-eight percent. Past Farm Gate practices required thirty to forty-five minutes to refuel, rearm, and turn around a flight of two T-28s. New safety checklists made two-hour turnarounds for T-28s and three-hour ones for B-26s the norm. Too few aircraft and a cutback in flying dampened morale in the overmanned 1st Air Commando Squadron. Depressed crews waited for days to fly a strike mission.[64]

A dearth of L-19s (0-1s) and crews for forward air control also sharply curtailed combat operations. Between May and August, 431 air support requests had to be turned down. The arrival of the Army's 73d Aviation Company and the activation of the Air Force's 19th Tactical Air Support Squadron did not cure the trouble. Instead of placing the twenty-two 0-1s of the 73d Aviation Company under the tactical air control system, MACV assigned them to support Army advisors. The Vietnamese promptly withdrew their L-19s from the ground divisions because they felt that their craft were no longer needed. Army 0-1s flew the local visual reconnaissance and convoy escort previously flown by the Vietnamese liaison planes. However, removal of the L-19s deprived forward air controllers and air liaison officers of transportation, unless they could borrow O-1s from the Army advisors.

As for the 19th Tactical Air Support Squadron, it was fully operational by September 15. The unit, commanded by Lt. Col. John J. Wilfong, kept sixteen O-1s at Bien Hoa and six at Can Tho. By year's end they flew 3,862 sorties, chiefly 483 forward air control, 1,221 visual reconnaissance, and 1,518 combat support liaison. The "prompt response and can-do attitude" of the crews bred a huge demand for their services. The Americans met with slight success in trying to augment rather than supplant Vietnamese liaison operations.[65]

A few USAF pilots who flew with Vietnamese forward air controllers realized that these men had been doing a boring and fairly thankless job for many years with no end in sight. Since the average Vietnamese pilot saw the law of averages working against him, he was reluctant to fly below two thousand feet. If he directed an attack on friendly people, criminal prosecution awaited him. Nonetheless, the prevailing American view pictured Vietnamese crews as unaggressive and unreliable. By October this disapproval was being expressed by the overwhelming sentiment that "we must run things."[66]

As sorties swelled to meet Viet Cong attacks, premission briefings were seldom practical. Responding to requests, Vietnamese forward air controllers frequently flew many miles to an unfamiliar area. They radioed the ground unit to find out the locations of friendly and enemy troops, then marked targets for the strike crews. Air Force officers repeatedly urged the Vietnamese to attach air liaison officers and forward air controllers to divisions, so they could get to know the local conditions. The Vietnamese Air Force said no, citing the scarcity of qualified officers, the failure of the young ones to work well when removed from close supervision, and the discord between air and ground officers.[67]

Divisions tended to rely upon helicopter firepower. For example, in numerous small operations in Ban Me Thuot area throughout September, the 23d Division requested fighter air support only once. The lone C-47 flareship standing alert for the Saigon area could not cope with the burgeoning night attacks in the III and IV Corps. Moreover, when the Viet Cong struck the Pho Sinh outpost on the Ca Mau Peninsula during the night of August 16, the province commander's indecision delayed that C-47. In the one hour and forty-five minutes before it came, the communists overran the outpost. A few days later, the enemy sacked the Ben Tuong strategic hamlet that had been founded a year before with much fanfare. Using flareships to light the way for helicopter airlifts of company-size forces into besieged hamlets proved impractical. This was due to the great number of hamlets (some twelve hundred in the III Corps) and the slow reaction time of heliborne reinforcement units flying in the dark.[68]

The 2d Air Division wrestled with the problems. Nightly every alerted A-1H loaded strike ordnance and two flares, the latter for use if flareships were not to be had. For additional flare missions, the best bet appeared to be the C-123 which carried a spare Vietnamese navigator/communicator. However, when this crewman hand-dropped the Mark V and VI flares, they often hit the sides of the aircraft and were swept back into the open rear cargo door. To prevent this, local shops devised a flarebox that dispensed flares from the C-123's rear cargo ramp. This device let the C-123s at Tan Son Nhut join the Vietnamese C-47s, and in September 172 flare and 132 strike sorties were flown against Viet Cong night attacks. Fewer communist forays in October resulted in 60 flare and 94 strike sorties. But the pace accelerated, and up to three flareships each night were kept in the air over the IV Corps. At least one of these planes could reach any point in the delta within twenty to thirty minutes. The Viet Cong captured no outpost or hamlet after a flare/strike team arrived. Even so, the hamlet program was so overextended that in many cases the defenders could not hold off the attackers until air support got there.[69]

The vulnerable Mekong Delta induced the Viet Cong to escalate the war from simple guerrilla tactics to sustained field operations. A five-day battle erupted in the wee hours of September 10 as 81-mm mortar rounds arced onto Soc Trang Airfield. Inside of five minutes, four Farm Gate pilots scrambled two T-28s, called for flareship and more fighters, and strafed the mortar muzzle flashes. This swift air support along with Vietnamese mortar fire drove off the communists, foiling their bid to neutralize and destroy the American fighters and helicopters on the airstrip. The aggressive action of the pilots was "commendable." All the same, they had broken the rules of engagement by attacking without Vietnamese crewmen and without target assistance from a forward air controller or flareship.[70]

At about the same time, Viet Cong battalions pounded the district headquarters town of Dam Doi and Cai Nuoc near the tip of the Ca Mau Peninsula. Swarming over Cai Nuoc, they set up roadblocks and laid mines on the sole surfaced road between Bac Lieu and Ca Mau. Right after daybreak, T-28s out of Soc Trang escorted heliborne Vietnamese marines to Dam Doi and carried out prelanding strikes. Most landings went well, but that afternoon a T-28 crashed from fire received during a third pass over an enemy machinegun. A UH-1 gunship rescued the crew, and the T-28 was destroyed to keep its machinegun out of communist hands. While marines encircled Dam Doi, ten C-47s and seven C-123s flew 498 paratroopers of the 21st Division to the scene.

The battle cost the enemy 122 killed (30 by air strikes) and huge stores of munitions. Around Cai Nuoc the paratroopers killed 50 communists, captured eight, and seized weapons. The sortie rate for September 10 exceeded all past IV Corps records for a single day. Over September 10–14 the sortie total ran to seventy-two air cover, ten escort, eighteen prelanding, and twenty-two forward air control. The government troops won a victory but the Viet Cong reduced the towns to rubble and left 153 civilians killed or wounded.[71]

The most critical shortcoming was too few strike aircraft to support the bitter war in the delta. Only one B-26 could be spared to cover heliborne operations in the 2d Division area. The five USAF T-28s at Soc Trang were invaluable for quick reaction but the primitive airstrip hampered them, and their guns were too light to silence ground fire. Heavier-armed A-1Hs or B-26s at

Bien Hoa had to make a thirty-minute flight to Can Tho or a one-hour one to the deep delta. Aware of this lag, the Viet Cong usually attacked in mid-afternoon to make it difficult for aircraft to get into the area, to swing into position, and to strike during the few remaining hours of daylight.[72] In January 1964 CINCPAC approved the construction of a new airfield at Can Tho, to be ready a year later.[73]

Planning a helicopter assault into three landing zones in mid-October, the 21st Division asked for strong tactical air support. Five USAF T-28s, two A-1Hs, and one B-26 were available for cover, escort and prelanding strikes. On the morning of October 19, T-28s supported the first helicopter lift of troops which met with light ground fire at the landing zone. The Viet Cong put stiffer fire on the second heli-lift and pinned down the troops that landed. They also hit and damaged a B-26 and a T-28, forcing the planes to leave their covering stations. The third heli-lift overshot its landing zone, and enemy fire downed an H-21, injuring two of the four Americans aboard. With troops in the second and third heli-lifts nailed down, Vietnamese forward air controllers diverted all of their air cover to close air support strikes.

In response to the division commander's call for more air support, the planes returned and renewed their strikes that afternoon. Army advisors praised the aggressiveness of the support, chiefly that of the B-26. It pursued the attack with other ordnance after its guns quit, even though under fire from six to eight automatic weapons. The Viet Cong held firm in their trenches and fired doggedly at attacking aircraft. When they withdrew at nightfall under cover of rain, pursuit by flareship and fighters was out of the question because locations of government forces were uncertain. During the battle, Vietnamese flew six A-1H and eight T-28 sorties while USAF crews flew sixteen T-28 and two B-26 sorties. Ground fire struck two Vietnamese T-28s, four USAF T-28s, and two USAF B-26s. Friendly losses included forty-one killed, eighty-four wounded, (twenty-three Americans) and one H-21 shot down. Thirty-two of the enemy were killed and in addition fifty-nine freshly dug graves were found.[74]

Early on the morning of November 7, some two hundred Viet Cong attacked a pagoda and then holed up in a mud-walled fishing settlement about twenty miles from Soc Trang. In late afternoon, regular ground forces and Civil Guard troops located and surrounded them. Although no friendly people were in the village, the government troops made no assault. Instead, they let four T-28s from Soc Trang conduct repeated strikes. The next day, blood marks within the enclosure suggested that the aircraft had killed about forty Viet Cong.[75]

By the end of 1963 the government military offensive was collapsing, despite occasional and isolated successes. The Viet Cong were seizing the initiative nearly everywhere. The limited number of USAF and Vietnamese aircraft in Vietnam had nevertheless scored some tactical gains in the face of severe handicaps.[76]

XVI. Collapse of the Diem Government

At the Secretary of Defense Conference in Honolulu on May 6, 1963, the participants discussed the tensions between the American and Vietnamese governments. Ambassador Nolting labeled American-Vietnamese relations as "somewhat less than good." President Diem was intimating that the United States was infringing on Vietnamese sovereignty. Nhu, his brother and counselor, was suggesting that the American advisory effort was "appearing to tamper with Diem's political base." Both were suspicious of the strength of the American commitment and the thrust of U.S. policy. Nevertheless, Nolting said, Nhu was "efficient and continues to accumulate power." Despite causes for concern, "the Country Team is of the unanimous opinion that the current leadership is the best the U.S. can get. It is sincere, albeit not particularly adept, but it is better than most in Southeast Asia."[1]

Two days later in Saigon, demonstrators celebrating Buddha's birthday paraded with religious flags, banners, and devotional images. The procession violated the 1950 ordinance forbidding the flying of any flag in public without the national emblem beside it. A monk delivered a sermon protesting the Diem government's discrimination against Buddhists. When Civil Guard troops moved to break up the rally, an explosion killed several persons including children. In a communiqué to the press, Buddhist leaders demanded that the government admit responsibility for the loss of life, rescind the flag regulation, and give Buddhists equality with Catholics.[2]

Some eight million Vietnamese were Buddhists, as compared with one and one-half million Christians. Diem, Nhu, and their families had connections with French missionaries who represented the old order.[3]

When a Washington newspaper published an anti-American statement attributed to Ngo Dinh Nhu, Representative Otto Passman, chairman of the Subcommittee on Appropriations vented his indignation to Defense Secretary McNamara. "Certainly," Passman said, "the Diem government ought to be made to understand that the American people have no interest in propping up an unpopular regime if it is more concerned with the pursuit of personal aims than with the protection of the country from communism." An embarrassed President Kennedy told newsmen that he hoped to withdraw some Americans by the end of the year.[4]

Diem meanwhile offered no redress to a Buddhist delegation but promised to investigate the parade incident, which he believed had political rather than religious roots. Dissatisfied, Buddhists demonstrated early in June in Hue. Several deaths resulted, and disorders spread to Quang Tri and Nha Trang. While the Defense Department ordered U.S. aircraft not to transport Vietnamese troops on anti-Buddhist missions, and while General Harkins instructed

Americans to stand aloof from the controversy, Diem acknowledged various errors by his officials.

In Saigon on June 11, an aged Buddhist monk burned himself alive in public. Three days later, a New York newspaper carried a Washington correspondent's story that the United States would condemn Diem if he failed to settle the Buddhist grievances. The Vietnamese foreign minister told William C. Truehart, in charge of the Embassy during Nolting's temporary absence, that he was "deeply distressed and angry" over the news report. Truehart then asked and received permission to publicly reaffirm U.S. support of Diem. Within a few days, the government acceded to most of the Buddhist demands but refused to accept responsibility for the deaths in Hue.[5]

Buddhists demonstrated again on July 16. Crowds of monks and nuns milled in front of Nolting's residence in Saigon, calling on the United States to compel the Diem government to keep its promises. Violence erupted on the following day.

The U.S. air attaché in Saigon, Lt. Col. Robert L. F. Tyrrell, informed the Defense Intelligence Agency that the Buddhist situation was "causing continuing animosity between the government and the armed forces and is spreading to all segments of the population. It is now common to hear Vietnamese discuss the possible overthrow of the present government." At a dinner party on July 17, Maj. Gen. Duong Van Minh, Diem's military adviser, stated that "the present government cannot continue." There was speculation that Minh or Maj. Gen. Tran Van Don, chief of staff of the Joint General Staff, might head a coup. "We cannot determine if a coup is imminent," Tyrrell concluded, "[but] all of the elements are present and it appears to us to be only a matter of timing."[6]

A radio address by Diem on July 19 seemed cold to American observers, and Madame Nhu was said to have termed the Buddhist suicide a "barbeque." Admiral Felt, CINCPAC, estimated, "In view of the widespread distrust and hatred of the Nhus, man and wife, far overshadowing the popular consensus to Diem himself, it seems most likely that the Nhus would be a primary target for any serious coup group." The government's "failure or unwillingness to handle properly" the Buddhist demonstrations made a coup "more likely if the Diem government fails to accomplish reasonable and acceptable concessions to the Buddhists or if the Buddhist contagion, fanned by political opportunists and the VC, spreads into the countryside to the extent that it adversely affects the progress of the war."[7]

President Kennedy had meanwhile announced on June 27 that Henry Cabot Lodge, a major political figure, would succeed Ambassador Nolting, a career civil servant. Preparing for his new post, Lodge had a long talk in Washington with a "distinguished Vietnamese" who said that "unless they left the country, no power on earth could prevent the assassination of Mr. Diem, his brother Mr. Nhu, and Mr. Nhu's wife . . . their deaths were inevitable."[8]

Over August 14-16 several more immolations took place as expressions of discontent. Madam Nhu favored ignoring the burnings and charged the U.S. Embassy with pressuring the Diem government to silence her.[9]

COLLAPSE OF THE DIEM GOVERNMENT

To General Anthis, 2d Air Division commander, Diem was "fairly well liked" by his people, even though he had not developed all the reforms they desired and the United States wished. In contrast, Anthis deemed the Nhus "not too popular."[10]

Informed people in Saigon expected sweeping changes from Ambassador Lodge, who appeared to be proconsul for President Kennedy. Perhaps to clear the decks before Lodge's arrival, Diem held an emergency meeting with the Joint General Staff on August 20. He appointed Tran Van Don the armed forces chief of staff, and Nhu invited the senior generals to sign a paper calling upon the government to seize and silence the Buddhist leaders. At midnight Diem declared martial law and a state of siege. Under nominal army authority the Vietnamese Special Forces and police stormed Buddhist pagodas in Saigon and Hue before dawn. They rounded up monks, nuns, and students, but the Buddhist leaders escaped and took refuge in the U.S. Embassy. The pagoda raids strengthened those officials in Washington who had always questioned the fitness of Diem and his family to govern. On August 21 Under Secretary of State George W. Ball released an official statement that the United Stated deplored the repressive actions against the Buddhists.[11]

Ambassador Lodge reached Saigon on August 22. He found Embassy officials thinking that the Vietnamese generals could depose Diem, but General Don told General Harkins that they were too weak to do so. The generals wanted to end martial law quickly, to have the United States support Diem while forcing him to clean house and showing him how to delegate authority, and possibly to create an interim cabinet of officers and civilians.[12]

On August 24 Ball, Harriman, Hilsman, and Forrestal drafted and cleared with the President by phone a message of instructions to Lodge. The United States could no longer tolerate the systematic suppression of the Buddhists or Nhu's domination of the government. "We wish to give Diem reasonable opportunity to remove Nhus, but if he remains obdurate, then we are prepared to accept the obvious implication that we can no longer support Diem." Lodge was to tell the Vietnamese generals that the United States would renounce Diem unless he righted the Buddhist wrongs and formed a more responsive and representative government. The United States would take no part in any ouster, but would recognize an interim anti-communist military regime as the successor to the Diem government.[13]

On the 26th a Voice of America broadcast in Vietnamese said that high American officials blamed Nhu for the pagoda attacks and the mass arrests of monks and students. The United States, it continued, might sharply curtail aid unless President Diem rid himelf of certain associates. The Joint General Staff refuted the broadcast on the following day. Responsible military commanders, the press communique announced, had unanimously proposed martial law and related measures to Diem.[14]

Ambassador Lodge became convinced during his first week in Saigon that the Diem government was dying, the abuse of police power having caused deep resentments among the Vietnamese. The Buddhist immolations had also turned the American people and government against Diem, Secretary of State Rusk told Nolting when he returned to Washington. "We can't stand any more burning," Rusk said.[15]

At a National Security Council discussion, Nolting made the point that refusal to support Diem and Nhu would renege on past commitments. Ball argued that continued support for them risked losing the war against the Viet Cong; moreover, Diem and Nhu had massively violated their promises. Harriman felt that Nolting had been profoundly wrong for quite some time.[16]

Replying to the cabled instructions, Ambassador Lodge suggested telling the generals hostile to Diem that the United States had grave reservations about the Nhus. The State Department approved on August 28 and commented that the Nhus would have to go and "a coup will be needed." Lodge responded on the 29th, "We are launched on a course from which there is no respectable turning back: the overthrow of the Diem government." President Kennedy weighed this appraisal then ordered Lodge and Harkins to support a coup if it had a good chance of success but to avoid any direct American involvement. He authorized them to suspend U.S. air support to the Diem government whenever they wished.

Also on the 29th, Secretary of State Rusk permitted Lodge to explore Harkins' suggestion that a threat to withdraw U.S. assistance might well force Diem to drop the Nhus. This seemed to Lodge to cancel the earlier instrumentations to "make detailed plans as to how we might bring about Diem's replacement." He now understood the President to want him "not to thwart" a coup, not to help plan a coup, but rather to keep in close touch with plotters so he could let Kennedy know of developments that might need American decisions. Looking for the imminent overthrow of the government, Lodge stopped seeing Diem and Nhu.[17]

By August 29 CINCPAC alerted two Marine Corps battalions for possible commitment, and moved naval task forces and air transports to within supporting distance. Plans were set for the air evacuation from Saigon of 1,574 U.S. dependents, 1,103 civilian employees, 981 U.S.-sponsored aliens, twenty-five tourists, and seventeen alien dependents, and from Hue another 157 persons.[18]

Cambodia broke diplomatic relations with Vietnam on August 27, citing border violations and ill-treatment of Buddhists. Two days later, Charles de Gaulle offered his good offices to restore peace and harmony in Indochina by reunifying North and South Vietnam in "independence and neutrality." At the request of Asian and African members, U Thant, United Nations Secretary General, wrote on August 31 to ask Diem to insure "the exercise of fundamental human rights to all sections of the population." On that day Chiang Kai-shek talked at length with Gen. Jacob E. Smart, PACAF commander. Chiang said it was essential to win the war because Asian states were closely watching the United States in Vietnam. In Thailand influential figures told Smart that some officials doubted if the United States could be depended upon in a crisis.[19]

In a national television address on September 2, Kennedy said that the Government of Vietnam could win the war only if it had popular support. In his opinion the government was out of touch with the people. The Buddhist repres-

COLLAPSE OF THE DIEM GOVERNMENT

sions had been unwise. Could the government regain the affection of the people? "With changes in policy and perhaps with personnel," the President said, "I think it can. If it doesn't make those changes, I would think that the chances of winning would not be very good."[20]

De Gaulle's scheme to unify and neutralize Vietnam led Ngo Dinh Nhu to admit having contacted Viet Cong leaders of the National Liberation Front of South Vietnam. Apparently he was also in touch with Hanoi. On September 2 he told Lodge of his talk with the Polish member of the International Control Commission. The Pole had sought Nhu's reaction to De Gaulle's proposal, so that he could forward it to the North Vietnamese foreign minister.[21] Many top-level Vietnamese officers were convinced that Nhu would make a deal with Hanoi if he felt it to be in his best interest.[22]

Diem answered U Thant's letter on September 5. He stressed his government's actions to free the Buddhist hierarchy from political agitation and propaganda, which benefited foreign interests and harmed the Buddhist religion and the Vietnamese state. He invited U Thant to send a fact-finding mission to Vietnam. When a United Nations group visited, it reached no conclusions. Nevertheless, the Costa Rican member said that he personally had found no religious discrimination or persecution. He believed that the troubles were political and involved but a small part of the Buddhist community.[23]

On 8 September General Smart radioed General LeMay:

> My own feeling is that if we intend to remain committed in Viet Nam — and I believe that it is strongly in the national interest that we do so — then we must support Diem. Whether we like him or his family is not germane.... My conclusion is that we must stick with Diem and that we must quickly demonstrate this by positive action even though we may have to pay some price in terms of embarrassment.... We are probably going to have to swallow the fact that Diem will not exile his brother...and from my discussions I am not at all convinced that this should be our objective. I get distinct impression from Vietnamese that he is valuable and important to Diem, just as Diem is important to the nation.[24]

Unlike Nolting who had used the country team to secure policy consensus, Lodge was ordered by Kennedy to guard closely the cables they exchanged. Keeping even Harkins in the dark, he thus appeared to be running the U.S. Mission as "a one-man operation, conducted in total secrecy." General Smart noted, "The American team ... left me with the impression of a divided house and divergent directions." Opinions about Diem, as observed by Smart, ranged from the view held by John H. Richardson, CIA station chief, that Diem could be supported and Nhu was useful, to the view that the Diem government must go no matter what took its place.[25] Reports to Washington from the Embassy, MACV, and the air attaché differed markedly. Joseph A. Mendenhall of the State Department and Maj. Gen. Victor H. Krulak of the Marine Corps visited the country together to determine Vietnamese attitudes toward Diem's government. After hearing their disparate findings, President Kennedy asked whether they had visited the same country.[26]

Suspending U.S. aid to pressure Diem, as Lodge now suggested, seemed to Secretaries Rusk and McNamara to threaten the war effort. President Kennedy inclined to agree. On September 21 he again sent McNamara and General Taylor (JCS Chairman since October 1962) to gather information and to encourage Diem to solve his problems. Lodge in his briefing was pessimistic about the survival of the Diem regime. But other observations led McNamara and Taylor to conclude that the Diem government was consolidating its control throughout the country, and that the military effort still had momentum. Some military men were hostile toward the government but they were more hostile toward the Viet Cong. Reluctant to cut off economic aid, McNamara wanted more potent military action against the insurgents. More dangerous than the political ferment in Vietnam was the rising dissent among Americans at home. A need existed to build a case to be put to the people and Congress, to cement their confidence in the Kennedy administration and its handling of the war. Consequently, McNamara emphasized to Diem that he must conduct his military and political affairs in a way that would win the support of the American people. Finally, McNamara and Taylor were convinced that the war could be favorably ended in 1965, with the insurgency then shrinking to sporadic banditry in outlying areas. They accordingly announced that as scheduled there would be one thousand fewer U.S. military advisors by the close of 1963.[27]

On October 2, subsequent to a National Security Council discussion of the McNamara-Taylor report and Lodge's recommendations, President Kennedy approved the following policy statement: Since the military program in Vietnam was sound in principle and progressing, the United States would go on working with the Vietnamese people and their government. The goal would be to deny the country to communism and to suppress the externally stimulated and supported Viet Cong insurgency. Furthermore, the "United States had made clear its continued opposition to any repressive actions in South Viet-Nam. While such actions have not yet significantly affected the military effort, they could do so in the future."[28]

Events in Saigon were far from reassuring. On October 3 Vietnamese plainclothesmen assaulted American newsmen, and Lodge protested. The next day a Buddhist monk burned himself, the sixth and most publicized case. On October 16 the Senate foreign relations committee approved an amendment to the foreign aid authorization bill. It empowered the President to extend to Vietnam assistance designed purely "to further the objectives of victory in the war against communism and the return to their homeland of Americans involved in the struggle." Nhu on the 17th declared to the press that he failed to understand why the United States had "initiated a process of disintegration in Vietnam." He accused the CIA of inciting a coup against the government. Five days later, the United States announced the end of support to the Vietnamese forces unless they were shifted from police duties to field operations or related training programs.[29]

At this point, a major plot against Diem was hatching under the leadership of Generals Duong Van Minh, Tran Van Don, and Le Van Kim. They represented a coalition of older men who wanted a neutralist solution to the war, and of younger men who sought a military victory and felt sure they could secure it. With the promise of cooperation from the I, II, and III Corps commanders, the

COLLAPSE OF THE DIEM GOVERNMENT

coalition resolved to remove the IV Corps commander who was also military governor of Saigon and loyal to Diem.

Although American officials took care to avoid any part in the coup, some U.S. military circles received persistent reports that a conspiracy was afoot. On October 28 the Joint Chiefs directed CINCPAC to sail a naval task force to positions off Vietnam, and that same day three USAF F-102 jet interceptors flew to Tan Son Nhut. General Harkins was taken aback when told of these moves. He had no idea that Diem's overthrow was near.[30]

On the morning of November 1 the conspirators gathered in the Joint General Staff compound, and began to bring troops into Saigon. General Don announced that a coup had begun, and in the afternoon American CIA personnel were informed. Troops with red neckerchiefs poured into Saigon from the north. By midafternoon they captured and imprisoned all Vietnamese Special Forces in the city who were loyal to Nhu.

The rebellion ran with precision. Troops took over key installations and surrounded Diem and Nhu in the palace. Four A-1Hs and two T-28s made gun and rocket strikes against the presidential compound. Efforts of the IV Corps commander to march troops to the capital fizzled. That evening Diem and Nhu escaped from the palace through an underground passage. On the following day they surrendered. They were assassinated while being taken to the Joint General Staff complex.[31]

As the fighting in Saigon ceased on November 2, a Military Revolutionary Council of twenty-four generals and colonels under Generals Duong Van Minh and Tran Van Don became the provisional government. Besides dissolving the National Assembly, it suspended the 1956 constitution and decreed an interim one. The United States recognized the new government on November 8.[32]

Judging that the council was united and set on stepping up the war, Ambassador Lodge proposed that the United States not press for instant political reforms. The generals had agreed to pursue the strategic hamlet program (now called "fortified hamlets") and to consolidate and upgrade their defenses. They spoke of massing all military, paramilitary, and civil forces for an all-out campaign against the communist threat. In addition they recognized the Joint General Staff.

Despite their designs, major tasks remained stalled. Wholesale purges and transfers sowed concern. There was little military movement.[33]

North Vietnam exploited at once the confusion created by the coup. Viet Cong attacks rose. Because the Vietnamese Air Force was temporarily on "coup" duty, USAF crews shouldered the bulk of the operational load. On the night of November 1, for example, the mere appearance of flareships caused the Viet Cong to break off attacks on eight outposts. Over the following week the guerrillas assaulted seventy-one outposts and hamlets. Enemy pressure prompted a total of 284 flare and 298 strike sorties in November. The insurgents nevertheless inflicted about twenty-eight hundred casualties that month, demoralizing the Civil Guard and Self Defense Corps. Though Viet Cong losses were

THE ADVISORY YEARS

put at twenty-nine hundred for the period, government forces lost nearly three weapons for every one they captured.[34]

President Kennedy on November 14 announced that Rusk and McNamara were going to Honolulu for a meeting on the 20th. Its purpose was to size up the situation and to find out how to intensify the struggle and to end the American involvement. "Now," the President said, "this is our objective, to bring Americans home, permit the South Vietnamese to maintain themselves as a free and independent country, and permit democratic forces within the country to operate."[35]

Among the impressive group at the meeting in Honolulu were Secretaries Rusk and McNamara, Ambassador Lodge, presidential aide McGeorge Bundy, CIA Director John A. McCone, JCS Chairman Taylor, Admiral Felt, and Generals Smart, Harkins, and Anthis. Secretary McNamara remarked that "a certain euphoria" had set in since the coup, but actually "the Generals head a very fragile government." Rusk asked whether "an increase in dollars would make a difference in shortening the war." Lodge said he thought the Vietnamese had enough dollars; what they needed was "greater motivation." McNamara argued that more funds would help.

Despite continuing difficulties the conferees resolved to adhere to present plans. The United States would hurry the growth of Vietnamese military power and pare U.S. personnel in Vietnam. The much publicized withdrawal of one thousand Americans would therefore proceed as scheduled. The first three hundred departed on December 3, the rest ten days later.[36]

But the assassination of President Kennedy in November 1963 signaled the end of an era, and the accession of Lyndon B. Johnson to the presidency marked the beginning of another.

Vietnamese troops outside the presidential palace in Saigon.

Part Four:

The Johnson Years

XVII. Objectives Confirmed, Methods Expanded

Four days after taking office, President Johnson reaffirmed past American objectives in Vietnam. The United States was to help the republic win the war against the externally directed and sustained communist conspiracy, assist the government in developing public support, and keep U.S. military and economic aid at the same level. "This is a Vietnamese war," the President said, "and the country and the war must in the end be run solely by the Vietnamese." He reiterated the October 1963 pledge to withdraw some Americans from the country. Yet at the same time he instructed the State Department to prepare a white paper, documenting Hanoi's control of the Viet Cong and its supply of them through Laos. He further solicited JCS plans for stepped-up clandestine warfare on North Vietnam and for cross-border incursions into Laos to check infiltration.[1]

Informing General Taylor on December 2, 1963, that Vietnam was the "most critical military area" for the United States, President Johnson asked the chairman to have the Joint Chiefs assign the best available officers to Harkins —"blue-ribbon men" at every level. He also sent Secretary McNamara to visit Vietnam again.[2]

During December 19-20 in Vietnam, the Defense secretary found General Minh's government "fragile" and "indecisive and drifting." Unless current trends were reversed in the next two or three months, they would lead "to neutralization at best and more likely to a Communist-controlled state." The dilemma for American policymakers was that pouring in personnel and other resources to prosecute the war would hinder rather than help the Vietnamese stand on their own feet.

Unable to resolve the basic problem, the secretary listened to CINCPAC plans for covert actions against North Vietnam. Vietnamese troops were to carry out a wide variety of sabotage and psychological operations to pressure the insurgents with minimum risk. As for extensive forays envisioned along the Laotian border, McNamara doubted if they would be politically acceptable or militarily effective. But he approved having U-2 high-altitude photo planes in Vietnam to obtain better information on enemy infiltration routes.[3]

At McNamara's suggestion, the President on December 31 assured Minh of lasting American support. He gave final approval to clandestine actions against North Vietnam and to the U-2 flights. The movement of Strategic Air Command's U-2s to Bien Hoa proceeded so swiftly that PACAF first knew of it when the planes entered the traffic pattern at Hickam. The high-level photography later revealed extensive logistic networks in North Vietnam and Laos, supply routes capable of infiltrating large numbers of trucks, men, and material into South Vietnam.[4]

THE ADVISORY YEARS

General Harkins felt hopeful that the Viet Cong attacks had peaked immediately after the coup. His optimism was short-lived. Government ground actions that had decreased after Diem's downfall sprang back to between five hundred and six hundred a day by November 20, but they were blunted by mismanagement and defeat. A new commander spurred the lethargic 7th Division south of Saigon, but he was relieved before the month was up. Neither of two battalions conducting clearing operations in Long An Province knew that the other was there, and they fired on each other. The clash killed two men and wounded twenty, exerting a "demoralizing effect on both units."[5]

Before dawn on November 24, the aggressive 21st Division fell victim to a carefully planned and executed ambush in An Xuyen Province. After the Viet Cong struck the Cha La outpost and a strategic hamlet near the tip of the Ca Mau Peninsula, the division hurried four heli-lifts of troops into two landing zones, with tactical aircraft flying prestrike, escort, and air cover. Enemy fire downed an H-21 and damaged ten H-21s and UH-1s. While the ground troops took cover, USAF and Vietnamese A-1Hs, B-26s, and T-28s made repeated attacks in which valor at times outweighed discretion. C-47s and C-123s paradropped a battalion to pinch off the foe's withdrawal route. The guerrillas escaped because the C-123s put most of the troops on the far side of the Cai Nuoc River. Three bodies were discovered and there were signs that at least one hundred fifty insurgents had been carried away in sampans.

Brig. Gen. Robert H. York, USA, who saw the entire operation, commended the fine work of tactical air. The operation was nevertheless costly to the aircrews, most damage coming from .50-caliber fire. Aircraft losses included an H-21, a B-26 shot down with loss of the crew, and the crash landings after battle damages of two Vietnamese A-1Hs and one T-28. Ground fire hit twenty-five planes. The helicopter force had consisted of twelve H-21s and thirteen UH-1s. Its support came from four T-28s for prestrike missions, two B-26s for escort, and three B-26s, eight A-1Hs, and twelve T-28s for cover. It was the largest one-day close air support operation to date.[6]

In an otherwise cheerless month Capt. Richard W. Von Hake, air liaison officer, engineered one small air victory against the guerrillas along the Dong Nai River. The Viet Cong habitually fired at aircraft but slipped through a sweep of the area by a government battalion. On December 8 Von Hake persuaded the province chief to join him on an L-19 flight over that ground. Since the battalion had just finished its sweep, the chief felt sure he was wasting time. To his great surprise, he saw more than fifty people as the L-19 drew brisk fire.

Von Hake drafted an air strike plan and on the 9th and 12th dropped leaflets to warn that persons working with the Viet Cong were in danger. Because the area was bordered by strategic hamlets, the hamlet chiefs blocked egress from dawn to noon on December 14. On that morning Von Hake and a Vietnamese observer flew into the area, discreetly trailed by three T-28s and two B-26s. When the L-19 was fired upon, the observer marked the target and the strike planes swept in. Twenty-three enemy were killed and others wounded.[7] This modest victory showed that armed reconnaisance could succeed in Vietnam.

OBJECTIVES CONFIRMED, METHODS EXPANDED

Twice in December, guerrillas in Zone D ambushed little convoys lacking air escort. The Viet Cong waylaid one in Binh Long Province on the 23d, resulting in fourteen men killed, seven wounded, and five missing.[8]

Vietnamese and U.S. Air Force planes flew seventy-three helicopter escort sorties in November and eighty-three in December, a decrease from earlier in the year. In part the decline mirrored the slowing of Vietnamese ground operations. It also stemmed from the growing practice of letting U.S. Army helicopter gunships take the place of strike aircraft — this despite MACV directives requiring the use of Vietnamese aircraft before bringing in American planes.[9]

In III Corps the 5th Division's penchant for helicopter gunships contributed to a major defeat on the afternoon of December 31. A ranger battalion ran into about two battalions of Viet Cong ten miles west of Ben Cat and eight miles southeast of Dau Tieng. The outnumbered rangers formed a defensive perimeter and fought bravely, but they needed help. The 5th Division had several battalions at Ben Cat and Dau Tieng, close enough to the scene of action and sufficiently strong to smash the insurgents. An L-19 forward air controller and at least two A-1Hs were constantly on station over the encircled rangers. Besides the twelve 100-pound bombs and eight hundred rounds of 20-mm ammunition carried by each A-1H, more strike aircraft were available at Bien Hoa and Tan Son Nhut.

Capt. Ken C. Spears, Jr., air liaison officer, time and again asked that the A-1Hs be allowed to strike what were clearly enemy positions. But his calls fell on deaf ears. The orbiting relays of A-1Hs returned to Bien Hoa without firing a shot. The sole air strikes came from three flights of armed UH-1s and failed to uproot the guerrillas. Rescue battalions arrived at noon on January 1, 1964, long after the rangers had scattered. Ranger losses totaled six killed, twelve wounded, and thirty-one missing. An engagement that might have been a victory ended in another disheartening defeat.

Col. Harvey E. Henderson, acting 2d Air Division commander, considered the failure to capitalize on strike aircraft firepower "to border on being criminal." Ambassador Lodge cabled the same conclusion to Washington, citing "Vietnamese failures to take advantage of superiority of firepower which can be obtained by rapid reaction to VC troop concentrations." Admiral Felt bluntly told General Harkins that A-1H firepower was quite superior to that of the UH-1. "It appears to me," Felt said, "that [our] education program on the use of air power is unsatisfactory."[10]

The Vietnamese A-1H and T-28 squadrons boosted their strike sorties in November and December 1963. Still, they could not compensate for the fewer serviceable USAF B-26s and T-28s that were further diminished by battle damage. Moreover, the work of the Vietnamese forward air controllers left a lot to be desired. On December 6, for example, an L-19 and two T-28s responded to a request for an immediate strike on a Viet Cong battalion. When just ten minutes from the target, the controller pleaded the need to refuel his half-full tanks. He and the fighter pilots touched down at Tay Ninh airport, lunched during the refueling, and went on their way. By then the enemy battalion had vanished.[11]

Assessments of the political and military conditions in Vietnam at the close of 1963 were decidedly pessimistic. Severing relations with South Vietnam and the United States, Cambodia sought closer relations with China. Although communist support of the Viet Cong stealing into the delta through Cambodia had already proved "very worrisome," prospects swiftly worsened. The general situation in Vietnam had also eroded since the assassination of Diem, and would continue to be bad in 1964.[12]

During January-May 1964 Hanoi sent an estimated forty-seven hundred troops into South Vietnam. Formerly most of the infiltrators were ethnic southerners. Now there were growing numbers of native northerners, many of them drafted into the North Vietnamese Army. The Viet Cong had earlier relied on French and American weapons, chiefly from stockpiles captured before 1954 in Indochina and Korea. Currently most of the weapons were Chinese, brought by land and sea from North Vietnam.[13]

On January 22, 1964, the Joint Chiefs of Staff responded to President Johnson's November 1963 request by presenting a ten-point program of "bolder actions to arrest SVN's military/political decline." This proposed a virtual takeover of the war from the Saigon government by overt and covert bombing of North Vietnam, large-scale commando raids, mining the sea approaches, ground operations into Laos, and extended reconnaissance over both Laos and Cambodia. The plan also called for committing more U.S. forces to support combat in Vietnam and against North Vietnam.[14]

At Da Nang, where he commanded the I Corps, thirty-seven-year-old Maj. Gen. Nguyen Khanh kept close watch on the new government. He believed that some members of General Minh's 12-man Executive Committee were plotting to arrest Minh and other officers, including him, and declare for Vietnamese neutralism. After notifying General Harkins of his intentions, Khanh flew to Saigon and on January 30 headed a coalition of younger generals who managed a relatively bloodless coup. He told Harkins the next day that the coup was pro-American, pro-Western, and anti-neutralist. The new government would step up the war at once. Harkins termed Khanh the "strongest military character in the country" even though he lacked political appeal and complete control over the armed forces. Ambassador Lodge thought the United States was "beginning to make real progress" with the Minh government, but Khanh's one-man rule might be more effective. President Johnson then sent Khanh a personal note of support.[15]

A few days later, JCS Chairman Taylor readied a plan to revitalize the counterinsurgency. The key points embraced improved intelligence; a stabilized Khanh government through reforms of land tenure; liquidation of land debts, and other measures; the prospect of no more coups; a quickened campaign tempo; bolder actions against North Vietnam, maybe by Vietnamese bombing; and U.S. warnings to Hanoi to stop its aid to the Viet Cong.[16] The CIA warned that the government and armed forces of South Vietnam must show definite improvement. If not, there was an even chance at best that Khanh's administration would not survive during the following few months.[17]

OBJECTIVES CONFIRMED, METHODS EXPANDED

The new government could not immediately turn the tide. About twelve miles south of Tay Ninh City lay the village of Ben Cau, a cluster of six strategic hamlets housing some six thousand people. Before dawn on February 6, nearly one thousand guerrillas drove the Vietnamese militia out of Ben Cau. While waiting for the government forces to appear, the Viet Cong forced the villagers to dig firing positions and shelters. Although USAF officers thought that precise air attacks would dislodge the insurgents with least danger to civilians, the III Corps commander authorized firing into the village by artillery, strike aircraft, and helicopter gunships. Pairs of A-1Hs, B-26s, and T-28s struck as directed by Vietnamese forward air controllers.

The insurgents fled after dark, leaving eleven of their dead behind. Civilian casualties numbered forty-six killed, sixty wounded, and 670 burned in varying degrees. The bombardment demolished 670 houses and damaged two hundred others, depriving two thousand people of shelter. Though American relief supplies soon came, the survivors were more grateful to the enemy who made them dig for cover. Vietnamese officers said there would be no complaint about the civilian casualties. Yet the USAF counterinsurgency expert, Maj. Gen. Edward G. Lansdale, pointed out that the government forces had violated a cardinal rule by not protecting people under Viet Cong attack.[18]

Cambodia posed a prickly problem to the Khanh regime. Prince Sihanouk charged on February 11 that two Vietnamese aircraft had attacked a Cambodian village and killed five people. He held the United States partly to blame because it had "overarmed" Vietnam and "torpedoed" plans for an international conference to establish Cambodia's neutrality. Later border incidents impelled Sihanouk to accept arms from China and the Soviet Union. During Vietnamese border actions on March 19, Cambodian T-28s shot down a USAF O-1. The American pilot, Capt. Uwe-Thorsten Scobel, and the Vietnamese observer were killed.[19]

In the interim, intelligence estimates in Washington highlighted Hanoi's intent to expand support for the Viet Cong. South Vietnam's situation was seen as extremely serious. On February 20 President Johnson ordered Secretary McNamara to have the Joint Chiefs study the question of how to decrease Hanoi's activities. McNamara sent the President's directive to JCS Chairman Taylor on the 21st, adding that among alternatives being considered was "a carefully planned program designed to exert increasing military pressures" on North Vietnam.[20]

Johnson said publicly on February 21 that those directing and supplying the Viet Cong were playing "a deeply dangerous game." He also formed the Vietnam Coordinating Committee to run the Washington side of the war. The chairman was Mr. William H. Sullivan, a Foreign Service officer and the United Nations adviser to the State Department's Bureau of Far Eastern Affairs. Members represented the Department of Defense, the Agency for International Development, the Central Intelligence Agency, and the White House. The President told Sullivan to find a way to speed operations against North Vietnam and to examine how to make Hanoi desist from its hostile actions.[21]

THE ADVISORY YEARS

AIR OPERATIONS IN SOUTH VIETNAM
1964 TO FEBRUARY 1965

As the war seemed about to enter a new phase, there was talk in Washington, Hawaii, and Saigon of voluntary repatriation of U.S. dependents from Vietnam. But the hope of keeping Khanh in power led to the decision not to move dependents out of the country.[22]

General Khanh on February 22 published the National Pacification Plan that MACV had desired since Diem's overthrow. The concept called for local "spreading oil stain" or "oil spot" operations. These were military clear-and-hold actions starting in safe areas and rolling back the Viet Cong. Within pacified regions a new "life development program" would enhance the civilian standard of living. These pacification measures were to be completed in I and II Corps by January 1, 1965, and in III and IV Corps a year later.[23]

Corps commanders were to write their own plans for pursuing the overall goal. In the III Corps, for example, a program commencing in June was expected to push outward in concentric circles until the adjacent provinces of Gia Dinh, Bien Hoa, Binh Duong, Hau Nghia, Long An, and Phuoc Tuy were firmly under government control.[24]

General Harkins concluded that the offensive would work "if there are no more coups and Khanh stays alive."[25] And the Joint Chiefs accepted the oil spot idea as part of "an integrated political, socio-economic, and psychological offensive to support more fully the military effort." The chiefs endorsed giving jet aircraft to the Vietnamese Air Force and to the Farm Gate 1st Air Commando

Squadron. They likewise urged studies of how to escalate operations against North Vietnam.[26]

To PACAF, the papers and studies flowing out of Washington and Hawaii mirrored "the uneasiness with which U.S. authorities view the possibility of engaging U.S. ground forces with Communist forces anywhere." There was another way, however. Strictly USAF operations "with initial non-nuclear strikes" would hand the Air Force strong arguments for building its tactical forces. At the same time the United States would be able to react rapidly to threats, to control operations carefully, and to pull out at once if need be.[27]

General LeMay as usual had little confidence in the "very limited" actions and studies recommended by the Joint Chiefs of Staff. "We are swatting flies," he said, "when we ought to be going after the manure pile." He wanted "more positive and bolder actions" to include bombing targets in North Vietnam "*now.*" The Air Force Chief favored expanded interdiction, crop destruction, attacks on guerrillas in Laos, destroying dams and dikes in Northern Vietnam to flood croplands, disrupting power sources, bombing North Vietnamese military centers, and mining ports. He advocated sending more aircraft including jets to enlarge airdropped and airlanded operations, greater bombing of targets beyond the reach of ground forces, and heavier escort and cover. He wished to relax the barriers to cross-border actions. To keep the United States from getting bogged down in a ground war on the Asian mainland, the only hope was massive air operations.

Prodded by General LeMay and pursuing the President's expressed views, the Joint Chiefs in early March proposed overt military actions against North Vietnam. The initial phase would witness low-level reconnaissance over Laos and North Vietnam. Air strikes, amphibious raids, sabotage, and harassment of shipping were to follow. Then would come destruction of highway bridges, airfields, POL dumps, and other supply targets. The climax would be full-scale air and naval air operations against North Vietnam.

Walt W. Rostow, chairman of the Policy Planning Council at the Department of State, thought North Vietnam vulnerable to bombing. After all, Ho Chi Minh was no longer a guerrilla with nothing to lose—he had an industrial complex to protect. W. Averell Harriman and Roger Hilsman of the State Department opposed escalated measures against North Vietnam, since the Laotian infiltration routes seemed to be used but little.[28]

On March 6 Khanh fired three corps commanders and five of the nine division commanders. Soon a wholesale removal of twenty-three province chiefs ensued. The disruption of leadership shook the confidence of the armed forces and of the people. Military desertions soared. Meanwhile the prestige of the Viet Cong rose.[29]

Weakness at Saigon and decentralized military command let the corps commanders store up power. Rancor between ground commanders and province and district chiefs bred confusion and disagreement. Air Force officers sensed that uncoordinated air strikes might permit some party to make the Americans a scapegoat for a tragic incident.[30]

Before making up his mind on the options at hand, President Johnson sent Secretary McNamara and General Taylor to Vietnam. During March 8-10 they accompanied General Khanh on his speechmaking visits to Can Tho, Bac Lieu, the Hoa Hao area, Hue, and Saigon. On the platform, McNamara and Taylor stood on either side of Khanh and lifted his hands in the air as a visible sign of U.S. support.[31]

In private talks, McNamara and Taylor gained the impression that the military situation had gone downhill. Nearly forty percent of the countryside was under Viet Cong influence and control, including the critical provinces around Saigon. In eight of the forty-three provinces the insurgents held seventy-five to ninety percent of the land. Khanh was sure that his government troops could clear the country but doubted if they could keep it. He preferred covert actions against North Vietnam until "rear-area security" was set up. No one was optimistic about limited covert operations although clandestine activities could be expanded by easing curbs on bombardment. "Men, money, and materiel were no object," McNamara said. The United States had to press on. After discussing the aerial mining of North Vietnamese waters, the Defense secretary directed that mine-laying training for Vietnamese pilots begin at once.

Ambassador Lodge objected to "massive destruction" before trying a "carrot and stick" approach. The United States could offer North Vietnam advantages for ceasing aggression, while at the same time confronting Hanoi with covert actions such as unacknowledged air strikes. Photos by RF-101 reconnaissance planes revealed active Viet Cong bases right across the border in Cambodia. But hot pursuit across the frontier was ruled out, in light of American negotiations to keep Cambodia from giving up neutrality and winding up in the Hanoi and Peking camp. The political damage would far outweigh any military worth.[32]

Secretary McNamara asked if it was better to shore up the Vietnamese Air Force or to send more USAF aircraft. He learned that Americans had to "fill in the gaps caused by lack of motivation" on the part of the Vietnamese Air Force, "its inability to produce fast reaction strikes, and its reluctance to fly at night and on weekends."[33]

After a round of talks in Hawaii, McNamara and Taylor flew back to Washington. The Defense secretary proposed twelve steps to President Johnson for changing the course of the war. Though stressing actions within the country, the secretary suggested that plans be laid for border-control actions inside Laos and Cambodia on seventy-two hours notice. These would be "tit-for-tat" bomb strikes and commando raids by Vietnamese forces on such North Vietnamese targets as communications centers, training camps, and infiltration routes. For the present, McNamara resisted border-control or graduated military pressure operations. He nevertheless thought there ought to be standby plans for gradually tightening the screws on North Vietnam. The plans would be triggered on thirty days notice and involve air attacks on military and possibly industrial targets.[34]

OBJECTIVES CONFIRMED, METHODS EXPANDED

The Joint Chiefs judged the Defense secretary's program to be too sparse unless quick decisive action against North Vietnam was added. John A. McCone, CIA director, labeled McNamara's proposals "too little, too late." He urged swift operations in the south to match intensive air and naval moves on the north. General LeMay spoke to the point. He did not think that the "military tools and concepts" were "generally sound and adequate." He deplored the shackling of sound military activities with artificial political bonds that events had long made obsolete.

The National Security Council concurred in the Secretary of Defense's recommendations but warned, "The United States should commit itself to the clear objective of preventing the fall of South Viet-nam to Communism." Otherwise the result would "destroy SEATO." President Johnson harbored doubts but approved the proposals, preferring the secretary's approach to that of the Joint Chiefs of Staff. The political and military base in South Vietnam seemed too fragile to invite expanded enemy hostilities. Furthermore, striking North Vietnam might bring the Chinese and Soviets into the war. The President asked all agencies to support energetically the actions called for.[35]

Shortly afterwards the Joint Chiefs answered a question put by Johnson on March 4: Had all possible support been given American and Vietnamese units since he had become President? The chiefs said they had hoped for stronger U.S. action to encompass air reconnaissance in Laos and Cambodia, clandestine intelligence operations in Cambodia, hot pursuit by ground troops, inspection of Cambodian shipping in the Mekong Delta, and jet fighters for South Vietnam. But all had been turned down due to national policy.[36]

In a major address on March 26, 1964, Secretary of Defense McNamara explained the four options open to the President. The United States could withdraw from Vietnam but this was completely untenable. Vietnam could be neutralized, risking an eventual communist takeover. Military actions could be spread into North Vietnam, a choice being carefully studied. Or the United States could focus on helping the Vietnamese win, the option already approved by Johnson. Even if fighting beyond South Vietnam was needed, it would supplement rather than substitute for general progress and stability in the country.

The decision to center on the battle inside Vietnam underscored the demand to relax the rules of engagement for air operations. On March 27 MACV authorized strike aircraft to operate to the border if it was a river or road. Elsewhere they could fly as close as two thousand meters when directed by a forward air controller, five thousand meters when not. Aircraft were forbidden to fire across or violate the frontier without diplomatic clearance.

The State Department sympathized with the JCS stand for hot pursuit into Cambodia under certain conditions but contested any easing of the curbs. This position governed in 1964 and was reiterated firmly by MACV in October and November after aircraft flew over the border by accident.[37]

Following a SEATO Council meeting in Manila on April 15, Secretary Rusk and General Wheeler went to Saigon. With Ambassador Lodge they weighed the chances of squeezing North Vietnam by Vietnamese covert operations, by covert U.S. support for Vietnamese aerial mining and strikes, and lastly by covert American-Vietnamese naval displays, bombardments, and air attacks. Rusk felt that the limited resources given Vietnam inhibited U.S. officials from daring new efforts. He wondered whether enough Americans were aiding civil administrative services in cleared areas that had to be held. On April 28 the President therefore suggested to Lodge that "two or three hundred" troops be replaced by civilian advisors to shift the emphasis toward "the art of peace."[38]

Hanoi meanwhile became more belligerent. On April 13 Ho Chi Minh declared that if the United States carried the war to North Vietnam, he had "powerful friends ready to help" him. In the Laotian panhandle, North Vietnamese construction crews, signalmen, and truckdrivers improved infiltration routes. Also in April a North Vietnamese regiment was recalled from Laos and given special military and political training for operations in Vietnam. Hanoi began to form new regiments for dispatch southward.[39]

Having probed Laotian government forces since November 1963, Pathet Lao and North Vietnamese troops on April 27 launched heavy attacks on the Plain of Jars.[40] After boasting that they could take any district headquarters in the Mekong Delta, the Viet Cong on the night of April 12 overran the district capital of Kien Long on the Ca Mau Peninsula. In the ensuing air-ground battle, the enemy lost at least fifty-five men killed including the commander. Yet 283 Vietnamese and 9 Americans were casualties, the capital was in ruins, and some two hundred civilians were killed or wounded. On May 2 a Viet Cong underwater demolition team sank the U.S. aircraft ferry *Card* while it was berthed in the Saigon River and delivering helicopters.

Stung by these successes, General Khanh told Lodge on May 4 that he wanted to declare war on North Vietnam. He wished to have ten thousand Special Forces troops "to cover the whole Cambodian-Laotian border. Would the United States start bombing beyond the confines of South Vietnam?"[41]

On this question there was a serious split between American policymakers and even within the Joint Chiefs of Staff. General LeMay and Gen. Wallace M. Greene, Jr., USMC, had urged low-level reconnaissance and air strikes against the north by U.S. aircraft. In a shift of opinion the other JCS members— Chairman Taylor, Gen. Harold K. Johnson, USA, and Adm. David L. McDonald, USN—believed that heavy pressure was not warranted, at least for the present.

In its study of how to tighten the screws on North Vietnam, Sullivan's Vietnam Coordinating Committee noted that North Vietnam's economy was chiefly agrarian. There were relatively few industrial targets that if wiped out would have an immediate military impact. Still a steady stepup in air power, from psychological applications to selective strikes, could hurt Hanoi and slow its support to the Viet Cong.[42] CINCPAC meantime firmed up plans for the United States to take part in military operations in Laos, Cambodia, and North Vietnam if the authorities in Washington so ordered.[43]

Communist activites in the Laotian panhandle prompted the Joint Chiefs to plan with the Government of Vietnam for airlifting Vietnamese intelligence teams into the area around Tchepone. When Secretary McNamara and General Taylor visited Saigon during May 12-13, McNamara let Khanh know that bombing North Vietnam would be no substitute for clearing the Viet Cong out of South Vietnam. The two found Harkins optimistic, Westmoreland less so, and Lodge satisfied with the size and composition of U.S. efforts. "Further large scale contributions," he said, "are not warranted."[44]

The collapse of government defenses on the Plain of Jars on May 17 demanded rapid reaction within Laos and a second look at the merits of exerting pressure on North Vietnam. A National Security Council working group, chaired by Assistant Secretary of State William P. Bundy, prepared a thirty-day scenario of political actions leading to air strikes against North Vietnamese targets and a call for an international conference on Vietnam. The Joint Chiefs J-3 (Operations) listed targets in these categories of ascending importance: to convince Hanoi that it was too risky to back the Viet Cong and Pathet Lao, to deter Hanoi from escalating the conflict, and to destroy the North Vietnamese industrial base.[45]

In meetings on May 24 and 25, the executive committee of the National Security Council put forward selected portions of the scenario. President Johnson then enjoined his senior advisers to hold a major strategy conference in Hawaii on June 1 and 2.[46]

The Soviet Union early in 1964 had advocated new meetings of the Geneva powers on Vietnam and Cambodia, and on May 27 a Polish diplomatic initiative called for a conference on Laos. After hearing charges of border violations, the United Nations Security Council suggested that observers be placed along the Cambodian frontier to ease tensions. The United States and South Vietnam welcomed the proposal, but the Viet Cong and Cambodia spurned it.[47]

As acting chairman, LeMay advised the Joint Chiefs on May 28 that the United States was "losing Southeast Asia fast." The chiefs, he argued, ought to present at the upcoming Honolulu military conference a clear record on how to "start winning." He said the only way to end Hanoi's support of the insurgency in Vietnam and Laos would be to destroy its means to do so. Air attacks should be made on infiltration points at Dien Bien Phu and Vinh to show the sharp change in American outlook and resolve. On the 30th the Joint Chiefs accepted LeMay's views and passed them to McNamara. Upon his return, Chairman Taylor disagreed with these views and sent his own to the Defense secretary, initially proposing more limited actions against targets less risky than Vinh and Dien Bien Phu. The purpose, he stated, would be to impress upon Hanoi U.S. readiness to take more drastic action should North Vietnam enlarge its support for the Viet Cong.[48]

Present at the Secretary of Defense Conference on June 1 and 2 were Secretary Rusk, Ambassador Lodge, General Taylor, Admiral Felt, and Mr. Sullivan of the President's Vietnam Coordinating Committee. General Harkins, whose relations with Lodge had soured, did not attend. The atmosphere was gloomy. The talk focused on getting congressional approval for wider action in Southeast Asia. Envisioned were commitment of American divisions, a partial

U.S. mobilization, and air attacks on North Vietnam. Lodge favored a careful bombing campaign. He believed it would bolster the shaky Khanh government and impart a feeling of unity to the war-weary South Vietnamese. At the end the consensus was to wait and see what developed.[49]

Mr. James B. Seaborn, the Canadian member of the International Control Commission, visited North Vietnam and apprised the government of American thoughts on a negotiated peace based on concessions by both sides. If Hanoi would stop sending men and arms south, Washington would respond with economic aid. Denying any attempt to threaten, the United States was well aware of Hanoi's strings on the Viet Cong. If the war heated up, the greatest devastation would be loosed upon North Vietnam. Seaborn stressed President Johnson's desire for a settlement based on Hanoi's promise to abide by the Geneva agreements of 1954 and 1962. North Vietnamese officials were unimpressed. They wanted the United States to withdraw totally from Vietnam. This would be followed by a "neutral" regime in Saigon, with the National Liberation Front charting the future of the country. Seaborn during a second trip in August conveyed the warning that American patience was wearing thin. Hanoi's reply was hardly encouraging for peace.[50]

Secretary McNamara and General Taylor had asked the JCS and CINCPAC to forge a three-phase air strike plan against North Vietnam. If set in motion it would signal American readiness to attack all major military targets in the country. On July 11 the planners settled on ninety-four air strike objectives in North Vietnam—eighty-two targets and twelve armed reconnaissance routes. They next set about drafting detailed plans for this massive air action.[51]

CINCPAC rather than MACV was to have overall direction of operations against North Vietnam, through the PACAF and PACFLT commanders. But the principal thrust of American policy continued to be countering the insurgency within the borders of South Vietnam. To that end the MACV commander was to devote his full attention.[52]

XVIII. The War in Vietnam, 1964

Once asked why the United States should not have command over the Vietnamese armed forces, General Harkins replied that this would be contrary to U.S. national policy. More to the point, the Vietnamese government would not agree to the arrangement, since it jealously guarded its sovereign right to accept or reject American advice.[1] Although this question and this position were never officially challenged, certain other command problems continued to vex the carrying out of the counterinsurgency. Among them were the tie-in of MACV and MAAG; the role and influence of the U.S. Air Force in directing policy in the country, chiefly in the controversy over the single management of aircraft; and the organization of the Vietnamese Air Force. These received attention in 1964.

In the USAF view, the principal command problem in Vietnam since 1962 was the absence of experienced high-ranking air officers on the MACV joint staff to explain what air power could and could not do. The MACV staff was dominated by Army officers rather than really jointly manned. No component Army and Navy units existed under MACV with the equivalent status of the 2d Air Division.

Admiral Felt was sympathetic to having a senior USAF officer in the mainstream of MACV current operations. In September 1963 he had proposed filling the MACV chief of staff slot with a USAF officer when it became vacant in mid-1964. The Joint Chiefs of Staff approved but the Secretary of Defense did not. After talking with Harkins during his December 1963 visit to Saigon, the Defense secretary was set on making changes along lines suggested by the Army. Early in 1964 he created the new position of Deputy Commander, MACV, and named Army Lt. Gen. William C. Westmoreland to it. He placed Brig. Gen. Ben Sternberg, USA, in the J-1 (Personnel) niche. He downgraded the USAF colonel serving as J-2 (Intelligence) to Deputy J-2 and put a Marine Corps brigadier general over him. He directed Harkins to reorganize MACV and the subsequent alterations shrunk the USAF allocation of J-staff jobs to the post of J-5 (Plans) held by Maj. Gen. Milton B. Adams. McNamara nevertheless believed the Air Force to be well-represented. He pointed to the 2d Air Division commander and the MAAG Air Force Section chief who were both general officers and present in Saigon.[2]

Admiral Felt and Gen. Jacob E. Smart, PACAF commander, questioned the wisdom of revamping MACV while the Vietnamese government was trying to recover from the shock of two coups. They had not concurred in a Joint Chiefs suggestion on February 15 to merge MAAG and MACV. But a study by General Sternberg addressed the broader question. The existence of the two headquarters had surely led to duplication of effort, occasional lapses in coordination, and a needlessly complicated advisory program. If the functions were fused under

THE ADVISORY YEARS

MACV, Sternberg favored MACV as a "specified army command" in lieu of a "subordinate joint command."[3]

That would enhance the Army's role at the expense of the Navy and Air Force. While General Smart assented to the need for a large Army share in the advisory assistance effort, he failed to understand the logic of Army predominance. When McNamara and Taylor came to Hawaii in March, Smart argued for placing senior USAF officers in decisionmaking positions in the reorganized headquarters so that air power could be best employed. The secretary said he knew of no operation that had suffered from want of air support. Taylor had heard of such instances but blamed poor communications instead of faulty organization or unsound policy. Admiral Felt asserted that at times Army advisors neglected to pass along air support requests, because they wanted to use Army aircraft to further Army doctrinal concepts. McNamara refused to change his outlook.[4]

General Westmoreland, former commander of the XVIII Airborne Corps, became the deputy commander of MACV on January 27, 1964. Maj. Gen. Joseph H. Moore—a close friend of Westmoreland since boyhood—replaced General Anthis as 2d Air Division commander on the 31st. Air Force officials hoped that Moore's close ties with Westmoreland would help brighten the image, expand the influence, and enlarge the number of senior staff personnel of the Air Force, as well as clear up air problems. General Wheeler, Army Chief of Staff, ordered Westmoreland "to get the air missions straightened out." He said he would not tolerate a fight for "hide bound doctrinal concepts." If Army doctrine got in the way of the war effort, Wheeler could and would change doctrine with a stroke of his pen.[5]

Besides 104 aircraft, the 2d Air Division had about forty-six hundred people in January 1964—nearly sixty on the MACV staff, four hundred in MAAG, and more than four thousand in USAF units.[6] Yet hope for a bigger Air Force part in counterinsurgency soon vanished. The MACV J-3 complained that his USAF deputy, who was highly regarded by the 2d Air Division, was unable to "look at J-3 matters except through USAF-tinted glasses," knew nothing about ground operations, and was of little use. The deputy was succeeded by an Army officer.[7] General Moore pressed for the assignment of a USAF officer as MACV chief of staff when General Weede of the Marine Corps wound up his tour in May. Instead, Maj. Gen. Richard G. Stilwell moved from J-3 to chief of staff and another Army officer, Brig. Gen. William E. DePuy, took over the J-3 job.[8]

Perhaps foreshadowing the end of the advisory era, MAAG was closed out on May 15, 1964. Its functions went to an expanded MACV headquarters, and the Army corps advisory groups fell directly under MACV. The MAAG Air Force Section became the Air Force Advisory Group, assigned to MACV but with operational control vested in General Moore as the USAF component commander. Moore also came to be the senior advisor to the Vietnamese Air Force. General Rowland, chief of the Air Force Advisory Group, acted as Moore's deputy for the Vietnamese Air Force military assistance program.[9]

THE WAR IN VIETNAM, 1964

(Top left) President Johnson and W. Averell Harriman.

(Top right) Adm. Ulysses S. Grant Sharp, Jr.

(Bottom) Maj. Gen. Joseph H. Moore and Gen. Jacob E. Smart discuss air tactics with Maj. Xuan Vinh, commander of the 23d Air Support Group, VNAF.

Courtesy: U.S. Park Service

Courtesy: U.S. Navy

THE ADVISORY YEARS

To General Smart the new setup did little to extend air knowledge and experience at MACV. Rather than trimming the headquarters, the change triggered a request to raise staff spaces by 310 (283 U.S. Army, 24 Navy/Marine Corps, and 3 USAF). Smart recommended at least 38 more USAF officers as directorate and branch chiefs.[10] Disregarding his desires, MACV in September asked for 71 new USAF spaces mostly for field advisory work.[11]

General Westmoreland rose to MACV commander when General Harkins reached retirement age on June 20. Ambassador Lodge resigned on the 23d to join in the national elections at home, and President Johnson selected General Taylor for the post. On July 15 Admiral Felt retired and Adm. Ulysses S. Grant Sharp, Jr., became CINCPAC. A whole new leadership emerged.

Should an Air Force officer be named as Westmoreland's deputy? Westmoreland had said in early June that he needed no deputy. But General LeMay argued in JCS discussions that a deputy from another service was a must to preserve the unified nature of MACV. Because of broadening air operations he thought the deputy should be a USAF general. The Navy and Marine Corps thought so too. General Wheeler, Army chief, suggested that the 2d Air Division commander be designated Deputy Commander for Air as an additional duty if air operations grew. Chairman Taylor was for giving the deputy position to an officer who could afford across-the-board assistance to Westmoreland. Owing to the nature of operations, he wished to see a two- or three-star Army general in the job. Taylor queried Westmoreland who then said he wanted an Army general. After McNamara's approval on June 18, Lt. Gen. John L. Throckmorton was assigned.

General LeMay reiterated the need for USAF expertise on the MACV staff. In September Westmoreland proposed to give the 2d Air Division commander the second hat of Deputy Commander for Air Operations, MACV. The Air Staff and PACAF opposed this action because it offered the MACV staff no real additional help. Westmoreland nonetheless went ahead with the proposal. On November 12 CINCPAC bowed to the "political climate" and put it forward to the Joint Chiefs.[12] Not until seven months later was the new title approved.

Still the reshuffling of May 15 bestowed some benefits. Tucking the Air Force Advisory Group under 2d Air Division was long overdue and fostered unity and control.[13] The harmony between Westmoreland and Moore nurtured better working relations between MACV and 2d Air Division.[14]

Yet General Westmoreland continued to command U.S. Army components, violating the principle that commanders of unified activities must be divorced from service operations. In effect the MACV air component commander answered to the Army component commander.

Moreover, the sparse service expertise on the MACV staff made it hard to pursue joint matters properly. A case in point was the MACV airlift allocation board run by one overworked USAF officer in J-4.[15] Army officers so ruled the MACV Joint Research and Test Activity that the Air Force hesitated to test combined concepts for combinations of equipment.[16] Just eight of the forty-five authorized officer spaces in J-3 were Air Force. Only one was a colonel's slot, the newly created Deputy Assistant Chief of Staff J-3 for Air.[17]

J-3 for the most part entrusted air matters to the 2d Air Division staff, but more and more assumed control of day-to-day air operations. This was done at first through an American MACV staff element in the Vietnamese armed forces joint operations center. Later an Army air operations section was formed with J-3 personnel, to allocate Army aircraft to the corps and to control other Army aviation resources. To coordinate Army and Air Force infrared reconnaissance, the MACV Target Research and Analysis Center was founded in December 1964. This J-2 function took care of centralized targeting.[18]

The tactical air control system survived and outwardly appeared to meet doctrinal needs. Still it was soon evident that the status of the tactical air commander was severely eroded—the 2d Air Division commander had no command authority, no direct operating duties, and no staff support. Senior USAF officers perceived that the local situation in Vietnam dictated several deviations from proven tactical air doctrine. But they cautioned against adopting the MACV air control system as a model for worldwide air command and control procedures.[19]

The performance of the Vietnamese Air Force also stirred concern. Central to the Vietnamese military concept was the parceling out of resources among the four corps commanders who governed all ground, air, naval, and paramilitary forces within their areas. Air Force officers, notably General Smart, protested splintering the meager Vietnamese air power. Even so, many Army officers believed this grouping was required in what they saw as largely a ground struggle.[20]

Col. Nguyen Cao Ky had won command of the Vietnamese Air Force for his part in the Minh coup, and polished his prestige by supporting the Khanh coup. He assured Generals Moore and Rowland that he did not intend to relinquish centralized control over air power. New wings, Ky said, were to be assigned to geographical corps areas rather than to corps commanders. On March 15, Vietnamese tactical wing headquarters were transferred to the corps areas and located at Da Nang, Pleiku, and Bien Hoa. Another was projected for Can Tho when the new airfield was finished. A composite airlift and reconnaissance wing continued to operate under the air operations center.[21] The proposal to place liaison and helicopter squadrons under the corps came up in April. Ky dissented and MACV sided with him. The transfer was not carried out.[22]

General Moore worked to keep the tactical air control system intact, including the air support operations centers. Since the Vietnamese wing commanders at Da Nang and Pleiku advised and planned with corps commanders, the role of the I and II Corps air support operations centers declined. The sub-operations center at Nha Trang was shut down.[23] On the whole, Moore considered the Vietnamese Air Force organization a deviation but close enough to classical air concepts to be acceptable. Maj. Gen. Sam Maddux, Jr., Thirteenth Air Force commander, decided not to dwell on the defects.[24]

THE ADVISORY YEARS

By retaining the integrity of his command, Ky could deploy his units as a national counter-coup force. Yet American influence over Vietnamese air operations diminished. For example, the 41st Tactical Wing and I Corps staffs planned for March 30 a night medium-level bombing raid against a Viet Cong training center. Army and Air Force advisors first learned of the attack when planning was well underway and white-phosphorus bombs were requested from American stocks. Twelve T-28s and four A-1Hs participated. Colonel Ky, who rode in one of the T-28s, depicted the strike as a highly successful demonstration of a "new night bombing capability." Vietnamese army photo interpreters gave a glowing account of damages to the Viet Cong, but U.S. Army interpreters failed to find the same results.[25]

"The word for the Air Force in Vietnam," General Anthis had written in November 1963, "is austerity," having both American and Vietnamese components in mind. War-weary air commando aircraft, a fledgling Vietnamese Air Force, and a slow air request net made it difficult to seize combat opportunities.[26]

The USAF 34th Tactical Group was scheduled to phase out of Vietnam. Withdrawal would begin in mid-1964 with the departure of the 19th Tactical Air Support Squadron which furnished forward air controllers. The 1st Air Commando Squadron, due to receive in June 1964 the first two of eighteen rebuilt On Mark B-26Ks, was to leave in mid-1965. Farm Gate's B-26s were nearly worn out but the 2d Air Division expected them to survive with careful flying, if the Viet Cong introduced no heavy weapons with antiaircraft sighting devices. The new Vietnamese 518th Fighter Squadron was to get A-1Hs in March 1964. Also that month the 716th Composite Reconnaissance Squadron was programmed to have its eighteen RT-28s and three RC-47s. During the second quarter of 1964, USAF T-28s were to be replaced on a one-for-one basis with dual-piloted A-1Hs.[27]

By 1964 Vietnamese and American aircraft were furnishing but one-half of the support asked for. The reasons lay in air request net troubles and the rising damage to planes from Viet Cong ground defenses.

On February 11, after the wing of a B-26 at Eglin Air Force Base broke off in flight, all B-26s in Vietnam were taken out of combat. They could fly only straight and level with the lightest of ordnance loads.[28]

The uncertain combat worthiness of the old B-26s led PACAF to suggest deploying a squadron of the 3d Bombardment Wing's light jet B-57s from Japan to Bien Hoa. These planes were being withdrawn from the wing, but they were admirable for the war. Their jet speed spelled swift response to air support requests.[29]

The MACV commander and CINCPAC voiced grave concern over the loss of the B-26s, which General Westmoreland called his "Sunday punch." Both headquarters proposed a squadron of B-57s with Vietnamese markings and mixed crews to operate out of Bien Hoa under Farm Gate rules. On March 2 the Joint Chiefs made the same suggestion to Defense Secretary McNamara.[30]

At March conferences in Saigon, McNamara questioned General Moore regarding Vietnamese Air Force needs. The secretary judged it cheaper to give

THE WAR IN VIETNAM, 1964

the Vietnamese further aircraft than to bring in fresh USAF planes. He settled on equipping all Vietnamese fighter units with A-1Hs, twenty-five tagged for the 514th Fighter Squadron in the III Corps area to replace the T-28s. In addition he earmarked thirty for the 1st Air Command Squadron to take over from the wornout B-26s and T-28s.[31]

General Smart told McNamara in Hawaii that tactical air chalked up more than thirty percent of the enemy casualties in South Vietnam—14,944 out of 49,100 in 1962 and 1963. If a few obsolete aircraft could do this damage, think of what new and better planes could achieve. McNamara replied that he appreciated why B-57s were desired. First, however, the United States should exploit the easier method of sending in more nonjet planes to help win the war. What interested him was the possible use of B-57s in covert operations against North Vietnam. The Defense secretary's recommendations, approved by President Johnson, embodied equipping the Vietnamese with twenty-five A-1Hs in exchange for T-28s. At the close of March, forty-eight B-57s and crews flew from Yokota Air Base in Japan to Clark Air Base in the Philippines.[32]

Col. Benjamin S. Preston, Jr., commander of the 34th Tactical Group at Bien Hoa, went all out to keep his B-26s in the air. But clearly they could not be saved—every plane had cracked stress plates and loose rivets throughout its wings. On April 8 the last of the B-26s and RB-26s were to be ferried to Clark Air Base for salvage.[33]

So long as the T-28s faced no heavy ground fire, they did the job despite their fairly slow speed and small armament load. As Viet Cong firing heated up, however, they became vulnerable. On February 18 a T-28 took a hit while flying interdiction, but the crew fortunately escaped serious injury in the crash-landing. The next day a second T-28 was shot down while strafing in support of a ground operation, and the crewmen were killed. Three Vietnamese A-1Hs shared a like fate in February.[34]

Since the T-28s had outlived their safe employment in Vietnam, replacement A-1 Skyraiders came in. On March 18 the newly formed Vietnamese 518th Fighter Squadron, with ten of twenty-five authorized A-1Hs, began to fly combat from Bien Hoa.[35]

Col. George I. Ruddell, deputy to the MACV J-3, surveyed the ground-fire threat. He thought that a return to the Air Force's standard four-aircraft fighter flights was in order, with each echelon of two protecting the other during low-level passes. This called for more planes, so Ruddell recommended that the 34th Tactical Group get two squadrons each of twenty-five A-1Es in lieu of a single squadron of thirty. Harkins, Smart, and Felt approved and passed the proposal to the Joint Chiefs of Staff.[36]

Compelled to stand down the combat-worn B-26s, Colonel Preston wondered how he could keep the 1st Air Commando Squadron going. On March 24 a T-28B lost a wing and crashed while on a bomb run near Soc Trang, killing the pilot, Capt. Edwin G. Shank, Jr., and the Vietnamese crewman. All T-28s had been closely inspected and aircraft maintenance was excellent. Even so, the loss of the T-28 so soon after the B-26 wing failures impaired pilot morale. By April 1 the 2d Air Division was "practically flat out of business."

On April 9 a T-28 crew was completing a third strafing pass over a well-defended target when the wing snapped off and the plane crashed. Two specialists from the North American Aviation, Inc., flew to Bien Hoa and ran inspections. They said that the T-28 could not take the "slam-bang type flying" because it was a trainer—not a properly stressed fighter-bomber. At their suggestion, Colonel Preston retired the five remaining Farm Gate T-28s that had been in combat since November 1961. He borrowed nine newer T-28s from the Vietnamese, bringing the 1st Air Commando Squadron's combat-ready aircraft to fifteen. He warned pilots about G-limits, cautioned them not to land if carrying external ordnance, and placed limits on loading the wing stations of B-model T-28s. To cut damages from small-arms fire, Preston set a minimum altitude of 1,000 feet for attack runs. The T-28s stayed in operation until A-1Es took their place.[37]

At least 1,546 air strike requests were received in the first three months of 1964. Of the 424 not honored, 230 were due to a shortage of planes. These figures did not present a true picture, for ground commanders and forward air controllers disliked to file new requests after being turned down.[38]

Air-ground operations yielded slight results. Between January 16 and 19 the 21st Division in An Xuyen Province was supported by the most tactical air sorties yet flown in the division area—forty-four on the first day. However, the heliborne troops came to grips with no sizable enemy forces on the ground.[39] During January 17-28 the 7th Division mounted a massive search-and-clear heliborne and water invasion into the Thanh Phu District of Kien Hoa Province. Artillery fire and prelanding strikes by B-26s and T-28s supported the operation. Still, the enemy poured withering ground fire into the first waves of helicopters, peppering all thirty-two craft and downing one, a UH-1 gunship. On the 18th another armed UH-1 was hit and plunged into the water. Only the copilot and a crewman were rescued. Even with constant air cover, friendly losses totaled twenty dead, twenty-five wounded, and two UH-1s destroyed. The Viet Cong lost forty-six killed and ninety-seven captured.[40]

The main problem probably lay in the lack of directives on aerial coordination and command over a heliborne landing area. The sole person actually allowed to tell tactical air what to do was the Vietnamese forward air controller. And he had neither the rank nor the experience to be an air commander.[41]

Problems also pervaded the smaller air operations for provincial forces. In the 5th Division area of III Corps, for example, the USAF liaison officer pointed out that the Viet Cong kindled cooking fires at dusk. They could take this risk because Vietnamese strike pilots were not routinely ready to fly at night. An exception occurred on January 16 when a Vietnamese C-47 flareship and four A-1Hs struck an assembly point in Tay Ninh Province. Most night air requests were not honored. As for day pinpoint strikes, just fourteen of sixty-seven requested interdiction targets were attacked in February. Pilots of the 514th

THE WAR IN VIETNAM, 1964

Fighter Squadron said they were "sick and tired of expending their ordnance on nothing but empty fields, trees and jungles."[42]

This frustration stemmed from the drawn-out air request handling required by the 5th Division commander—all immediate sightings of the enemy vanished before being targeted. There were, however, some good results from strikes against enemy-held areas that provincial troops could not enter. These were the "remote locations" in the east coast provinces of III Corps. The Phuoc Tuy forward air controller had good rapport with the province chief, who knew the enemy's movements and could and would approve targets for air action. Elsewhere, air strikes were hindered by controllers unfamiliar with the area, and by Popular Forces commanders who feared close fire support by artillery, armed helicopters, or fighters.[43]

In light of the lag in strike aircraft response, Army advisors in III and IV Corps accented the importance of helicopter assaults. The Vietnamese as a rule needed thirty minutes to scramble fighters, while processing a request commonly consumed one hour. Colonel Mellish, air liaison officer of III Corps, urged the forward staging of aircraft to shave this delay. Three T-28s were sent on ground alert to Phan Thiet, where Viet Cong attacks were foreseen. When the foe failed to appear, the little-used T-28s remained exposed to the hazards of a primitive airstrip.[44]

The number of tactical air sorties available to the III Corps on a busy day was around 30. This contrasted sharply with the average of 275 sorties a day flown by U.S. Army planes in support of III Corps. The Army aviation assigned to the corps was sizable—seventeen utility UH-1s, eleven UH-1 gunships, two CV-2 transports, four U-1 utility transports, two OV-1 armed reconnaissance planes, and eight L-19 liaison aircraft.[45]

Lesser operations in the difficult IV Corps entailed up to four or five heliborne missions every day in the 7th and 21st Division areas. Five USAF T-28s at Soc Trang could react swiftly, but it took 1½ hours to get ground alert aircraft from Bien Hoa. Though the Vietnamese 112th Liaison Squadron kept a detachment of five O-1s at Can Tho, the planes were confined to forward air control and target-marking duty. The USAF liaison officers hitched rides on Army liaison aircraft when they could. Most of the time, however, they were grounded at the division command post. Hence their sole knowledge of the air situation at a target area came from an Army liaison communication-relay plane that flew cover over heliborne landing zones.[46]

During March barely 71 of 126 air support requests from the 7th Division could be satisfied in the IV Corps, and in April merely 84 of 148 requests were approved. The air liaison officer and forward air controller spent a lot of their time in keeping ground officers from becoming discouraged with the sparse air support. According to Lt. Col. Clarence R. Osborne, Jr., instant air support from armed UH-1 helicopters often "saved the day."[47]

On April 12 the Viet Cong destroyed the district town of Kien Long in Chuong Thien Province. The Vietnamese Air Force turned in a splendid performance, featuring an A-1H hit on a 105-mm howitzer before dawn and a

THE ADVISORY YEARS

steady stream of air support strikes throughout the day. The tactical air support system squeezed thirty to forty-five sorties out of the aircraft at Bien Hoa, but this was not enough to stave off a serious government defeat.[48]

Meanwhile, the Joint Chiefs asked if two separate air control systems operated in Vietnam and if Vietnamese commanders were getting conflicting advice from U.S. Army and USAF advisors. MACV replied that one system directed Air Force aircraft, while the other was a separate aviation headquarters that managed Army and Marine Corps air units. Since these units afforded special assistance and had "no role in the development of the Vietnamese air structure, I have been free to employ them as I see fit to [the] maximum support of the ground effort."[49]

The U.S. Army senior advisor at III Corps, a colonel, was an extreme partisan of Army aviation who slighted tactical air support. He never invited the corps USAF liaison officer to planning conferences, and as a matter of fact was not on speaking terms with him. The senior advisor prepared pacification plans that made no mention of tactical air support. When General Moore offered help, he was turned down. Moore told General Westmoreland of this, and MACV directed that province pacification plans contain an air operations annex drawn by USAF advisors. From then on, the colonel called the air liaison officer to all briefings and planning conferences.[50]

Air advisors were few among the ground units. The 2d Air Division had authority for seventeen lieutenant colonels as air liaison officers with corps and divisions, and Army advisors outranked them. There were thirty-two captains and lieutenants as air-advisor forward air controllers with regiments. In comparison Army advisors numbered up to five hundred in a corps, with assignments going down to company level. General Moore had kept the rank of air advisors low to avoid dwarfing relatively junior Vietnamese counterparts. General Maddux, Thirteenth Air Force commander, wanted a senior USAF colonel to be assigned to the Joint General Staff. He further wished corps air liaison officers to be colonels, thus giving them equal prestige with Army senior corps advisors.[51]

General Westmoreland was dead-set against raising the corps air liaison officers to the rank of colonel. He regarded the Army senior advisors as MACV senior advisors, responsible for all military matters to include the use of air power. Corps air liaison officers were supposed to advise the senior advisors, and Westmoreland assured General Moore that they would be listened to. When Moore learned that Vietnamese wing commanders would be the chief air advisors to the corps commanders, he acceded to the MACV commander's point of view.[52]

Indeed, the 2d Air Division commander felt that conflict between the two distinct control systems was overdrawn. Confident of cooperation he said, "The Army is just as strongly opposed to Air Force control of its aircraft as we are for the Army to control ours."[53] Even so, Moore desired to enlarge the tactical air control system by adding an air request communications net, manned and operated by the Air Force. It would resemble the U.S. Strike Command-Tactical Air Command system worked out during maneuvers in the United States. He hoped to do away with the long delays in passing air requests up through channels over Vietnamese army communications.[54]

General Moore's proposed net for handling Vietnamese air requests would enhance USAF advice at lower ground echelons. An Air Force pilot (forward air controller) and two radio operators were to man tactical air control parties at all levels down to battalion. They would process air support requests, provide advice, and direct close air support strikes. To man this countrywide setup, the 2d Air Division was to draw pilots from the USAF 19th Tactical Air Support Squadron. Moore envisioned a continuing need for Vietnamese controllers to mark remote and hard-to-find interdiction targets. However he saw no reason why Air Force controllers, Army liaison pilots, and Army and Vietnamese forward air guides could not mesh their efforts to designate targets for air strikes.[55]

Moore counted on speeding up the reaction of the Vietnamese Air Force by training and assigning Vietnamese down to battalion level, first as counterparts and eventually to replace USAF personnel. He also wanted an Air Force liaison officer appointed to the Joint General Staff and more Vietnamese working in its operations center. General Westmoreland added a USAF colonel as advisor to the Joint General Staff, and he authorized Moore to use PACAF resources to establish the air request net in the III Corps area. In Washington, JCS Chairman Wheeler secured McNamara's assent for the air request net. The Defense secretary let the Air Force deploy combat-ready tactical air control parties from the Tactical Air Command. They were to serve on temporary duty in Vietnam pending the procurement of personnel and equipment for the 2d Air Division.[56]

With plans for the new air request net nearing fruition, with the B-26s already retired, with the T-28s in stress trouble, with McNamara against having a B-57 squadron in South Vietnam, General Moore wrote to General LeMay in April asking for an expansion from two to three A-1E squadrons of twenty-five planes each. Two of these units at Bien Hoa would permit standard four-ship fighter formations and provide for the predicted upturn in air strikes created by the air request system. The third squadron was to be based at the new Can Tho airfield being built in the Mekong Delta and slated for completion in early 1965. Without disparaging Vietnamese progress, Moore stressed that a third USAF A-1E squadron would enable planes to respond quickly to oncall air support missions. This would set a proper example for Vietnamese airmen, whose morale tended to be low.[57]

Richard T. Sandborn, 2d Air Division operations analyst, showed that fifty A-1Es and seventy-five A-1Hs would generate 3,038 sorties per month, with ten percent for training. Considering the rise in air support requests and the demand for larger aircraft flights, Sandborn computed combat sorties at 4,476 by August 1964. He foresaw further rises in the future.[58]

General Maddux, Thirteenth Air Force commander, pointed out that a third A-1E squadron might end retention of the B-57s at Clark. But he saw no reason for making an issue of the new unit so soon, since it could not be accommodated at Can Tho until 1965. However Gen. William H. Blanchard, Air

Force Vice Chief of Staff, stated that the Air Force was planning for the third squadron to be fully equipped at Can Tho by March 1965. General Wheeler justified the A-1E expansion because of low Vietnamese performance. Nevertheless, the additional USAF planes would delay Vietnamese self-sufficiency and undermine the principle that Americans were to help rather than to fight.[59]

Two events revealed that the rule restricting USAF advisors from engaging in battle was being strained if not entirely broken. The first took place on March 8 when Col. Thomas M. Hergert, deputy chief of the MAAG Air Force Section, was killed. He was flying an A-1H as wingman to a Vietnamese flight leader on an interdiction mission. Both had made a dozen passes to deliver ordnance when Hergert's plane crashed. Smoke was seen billowing from the right-wing root just before the right wing exploded.[60]

Investigation disclosed that eighty-nine USAF pilots were flying Vietnamese aircraft. But no advisor could lead a flight, be the first to expend ordnance, or continue a mission if the Vietnamese flight leader aborted. Colonel Hergert was the twenty-eighth USAF combat fatality in Vietnam since January 1962.[61]

The second event concerned Captain Shank who had died in a T-28 crash on March 24. On April 21 U.S. Congressmen and the press were furnished several letters Shank had written home. He had criticized the airworthiness of U.S. aircraft and told of 1st Air Commando pilots flying combat missions with Vietnamese basic airmen, popularly called "sandbags." The airmen went along as the required Vietnamese crewmen, for to obtain qualified crewmembers meant diverting fifty to seventy-five Vietnamese pilots from their own planes. Seeing that these pilots were assigned on the basis of 1.5 for each cockpit, this would severely hamper Vietnamese air power. If legitimate Vietnamese observers flew with Americans, the liaison and forward air controller programs would be bankrupt. Consequently, General Moore suggested that the arbitrary requirement for a Vietnamese aboard a U.S. strike aircraft be lifted. Nonrated airmen scarcely contributed to the missions normally flown to augment Vietnamese planes.[62]

On April 29 the Joint Chiefs of Staff proposed that the number of USAF A-1Es in Vietnam be upped at once to fifty (two squadrons) and to a third squadron later. Secretary of Defense McNamara consented to the immediate increase to two squadrons, which was in line with Admiral Felt's hope for a third squadron in 1965. McNamara also accepted General Smart's suggestion to hold the B-57s at Clark as an "ace in the hole" for a contingency.[63]

Visiting Saigon in May, Secretary McNamara and General Taylor were cool toward a third A-1E squadron. Taylor said it would not sell in Washington. McNamara reiterated that U.S. forces were not to take part in combat. The secretary directed General Moore to get the Vietnamese trained so that they could do everything themselves. He ordered the Vietnamese pilot ratio raised from 1.5 to 2 per plane and the Vietnamese 716th Composite Reconnaissance Squadron fitted out with twenty-five A-1Hs by October 1 and converted to a fourth fighter squadron. This would take the place of a third U.S. A-1E squadron.[64]

Upon return to Washington, the Defense secretary in a news interview emphasized that USAF personnel were in Vietnam to train the Vietnamese to fight an "anti-guerrilla war." Within the Defense establishment he made known his intention to phase down the strike operations of the 1st Air Commando Squadron and his goal to have that unit out of Vietnam in 120 days.[65]

A few days later, Taylor reaffirmed the policy that U.S. military personnel were not to join in combat. Farm Gate aircraft could only "fly bona fide operational training missions against hostile targets to prepare the participating VNAF personnel for eventual replacement of U.S. pilots." U.S. helicopter missions would keep on introducing Americans into combat situations, but "helicopters are for use as transport." Their weapons were for self-protection. "Armed helicopters will not be used as a substitute for close air support strikes."

On June 3 Smart asked Felt and Westmoreland to clarify the JCS directive[66] that forbade Farm Gate from entering into combat but let Americans fly operational training missions against hostile targets. They replied that Farm Gate was to fly combat but to be more circumspect. Farm Gate was to further insure that Vietnamese personnel aboard American aircraft were pilot aspirants or undergoing flight training. Westmoreland thought that MACV could live with the directive and keep Farm Gate fighting. Its effect, he said, would "not be appreciable" on the 2d Air Division and on U.S. helicopters.

Toward the close of April, seventeen Vietnamese A-1Hs were combat-loaded and deployed from Bien Hoa to Da Nang. The unannounced mission turned out to be the start of a seven-battalion search-and-clear heliborne sweep in the II Corps. During April 27-May 31 the sorties flown by the Vietnamese Air Force totaled 266 L-19 and L-20, 420 A-1H and T-28, and 102 H-34. The helicopters did psychological warfare, medical evacuation, resupply, and crop destruction. A daily average of ten A-1Hs were on tap at Da Nang, and the 516th Fighter Squadron kept five T-28s at the Quang Ngai airfield for immediate air support.

The operation apparently caught the Viet Cong by surprise. Not only were many automatic weapons captured and destroyed, but enemy installations were broken up. Yet when the fighting was over, it was impossible to leave three irregular companies behind as planned because the foe had been scattered but not wiped out. Nonetheless, this example of well-coordinated combat aviation gave Smart confidence that Vietnamese air power was clearly on the upswing.[67]

Despite this burnishing of Vietnamese Air Force prestige, the month-long operation consumed almost one-half of all Vietnamese combat sorties in May. Besides, Vietnamese and USAF aircraft conversions were cutting into Vietnamese aircraft. The 1st Air Commando Squadron had borrowed fifteen T-28s from the 516th Fighter Squadron, which sent pilots to Bien Hoa for A-1 transition training given by the U.S. Pacific Fleet's Naval Air Squadron VA-152. The A-1H was bigger than the T-28 and twisted about more from the propeller torque. It had a tailwheel rather than the tricycle landing gear that the pilots were used to. Hence several A-1Hs suffered damage in ground accidents. When ten A-1Hs arrived in May, they sat on the ramps at Da Nang. Since the Vietnamese 41st CAMRON was unfamiliar with the aircraft, the in-commission rate averaged merely four or five a day and at times dipped to three.[68]

At Bien Hoa the 1st Air Commando Squadron stayed operational with the borrowed T-28s. One was lost in a takeoff accident and six were transferred on May 20 to combat in Laos. This left only eight.[69]

Due chiefly to fewer T-28s, combat sorties dwindled in May even as requests for air support climbed. In mid-month USAF personnel followed McNamara's guidance to the letter. They worked to lift the Vietnamese fighter pilot ratio to two per plane. They pushed the enlargement of the fighter force to four A-1H squadrons so that the 1st Air Commando Squadron could be withdrawn. The Defense secretary wanted the tactical reconnaissance squadron converted to the fourth fighter squadron by October. And he authorized air transport and other Vietnamese pilots to fly fighters.

As the crash plan for the secretary's program neared completion, the JCS directive banning U.S planes from combat without giving bona fide training to Vietnamese crewmembers foreshadowed a decline in USAF combat sorties. This came at the time when there were too few aircraft to meet requirements and the Vietnamese were building two new A-1H squadrons. Recognizing the emergency, MACV ruled that the 1st Air Commando Squadron could continue to fly its eight T-28s carrying Vietnamese crewmen who were not potential pilots. As soon as A-1Es replaced T-28s, however, A-1E combat operations would be held strictly to genuine training.[70]

On May 28 MACV decided to equip the present three Vietnamese fighter squadrons to attain two pilots per plane by October 1. It likewise intended to form three more fighter squadrons as soon as aircraft became available, by February 15, 1965, if all went well. Only Vietnamese pilots were to attend the intensive A-1H pilot training program. The 34th Tactical Group would present the initial two-week indoctrination, Naval Air Squadron VA-152 was to furnish the five-week transition course, and the 34th would administer the final training.[71]

Meeting with the Joint Chiefs on June 8, Secretary McNamara directed that the first four Vietnamese fighter squadrons receive primary attention, the two others secondary. On June 17 Admiral Felt accepted a PACAF evaluation and reported to the chiefs that MACV was trying to do too much too fast. He suggested that the 516th Fighter Squadron be brought to full strength in September and that the 520th Fighter Squadron be made operational at Can Tho by the end of the year. He judged that the Vietnamese could man four fighter squadrons without inactivating their two C-47 transport units. On July 24 the JCS agreed to the four-squadron projection.[72]

On May 30 Lt. Col. John M. Porter, commander of the 1st Air Commando Squadron, had led the original flight of six A-1Es from the Philippines to Bien Hoa. Colonel Preston noted that his 34th Tactical Group had "moved up into the big league . . . with a first-line aircraft." On the 31st the A-1Es flew their maiden strike sorties. Col. William E. Bethea, who assumed command of the 34th Group in June, was impressed by the plane's large and varied ordnance, takeoff from a 4,000-foot runway fully loaded, extremely long range, and good loitering. Still the A-1E's normal cruising speed of 155 knots retarded rapid response to air support requests, chiefly in the far reaches of the Mekong Delta. And the aircraft could barely defend itself in aerial combat. With twelve A-1Es on site by June 30, the T-28s were retired. The 34th Tactical Group set about giving transition training to Vietnamese pilots.[73]

Air support requests totaled 1,546 during January-March 1964 and 2,040 from April through June. Lack of aircraft accounted for 68 of the 807 requests that could not be honored in the second quarter.[74]

Generally, USAF communications were deemed better than those of the U.S. Army. General Westmoreland therefore ordered the Army aviation battalion control center, situated in the joint operations center of the Joint General Staff, to relocate within the USAF-Vietnamese air operations center. General Moore expected the move, which commenced on May 18, to enhance coordination among Army, Air Force, and Vietnamese air activities. This did not occur.[75] The single-sideband PRC-47 and KWM-2A radios were the backbone of the Vietnamese air request net. But the sets did not always work properly due to the tropical climate and inexperienced operators.[76] In addition ground commanders were unwilling to allow the air request system to function as designed. The Joint General Staff issued no directive and the ground commanders refused to be bypassed on strike firepower. In consequence the air request net served merely to provide information. All official requests continued to travel the tortuous route over the old Vietnamese army air request net.[77]

Nor did the Joint General Staff relax its ban on strike aircraft releasing ordnance close to ground forces except at the direction of a Vietnamese forward air controller. On April 23, USAF T-28s were over Vietnamese rangers who were trapped near Trung Lap. Although the planes had voice communications with a U.S. Army L-19 and with wounded American advisors on the ground, they were not permitted to attack. Armed Army helicopters arrived, were fired upon, and returned the fire. But the T-28s jettisoned their unused ordnance and returned to base.[78]

There were other problems. Unless Vietnamese pilots could speak English, USAF controllers were unable to communicate with them. Air liaison officer and forward air controller duties were clearly unpopular among Vietnamese. And the manning ratio of two pilots to each fighter aircraft sharply curtailed the number and caliber of Vietnamese pilots who could be spared for such duties. Finally, the human and natural environment worked against ground tactical air control parties. Their heavy bulky radio gear was hard to lug through the jungle. Sometimes it was out of the question to direct an air strike safely from the ground, because of the presence of civilians who could be seen solely from the air. Mountains and heavy vegetation hampered the ground view and the flat ground of the delta offered no elevations to help determine range. Numerous tree lines and canal ridges also obstructed the view.[79]

THE ADVISORY YEARS

THE WAR IN VIETNAM, 1964

P. 222: (Top left) Air Commodore Nguyen Cao Ky and Col. William E. Bethea.

(Top right) Gen. William Westmoreland.

(Center) A1E aircraft.

(Bottom) A VNAF Sikorsky CH-34 helicopter at Tan Son Nhut.

P. 223: Outposts or hamlets of S. Vietnam.

THE ADVISORY YEARS

In mid-1964 it was generally agreed that ground tactical air control parties could not take the place of airborne control. Yet potent air support demanded something better than the plodding Vietnamese L-19s and their often indifferent observers. Strong pleas to prevent the demise of the 19th Tactical Air Support Squadron proved futile. The unit remained under orders to transfer its aircraft to the Vietnamese.[80]

Like the building of the Vietnamese air strike force, the Vietnamese air strike system held promise for the future. However, neither Vietnamese air power nor control procedures were able to withstand Viet Cong attacks. Over the earlier months of 1964, C-47 and C-123 flare support for outposts and villages more than doubled and night sorties grew.[81] But on the night of July 6, when the Viet Cong assaulted the Nam Dong Special Forces camp near the demilitarized zone, a flareship orbited overhead and dropped flares till dawn. Not until first light did two A-1Hs and an O-1 forward air controller arrive over the target. Then they were unable to strike because the controller could not make radio contact with the besieged forces to verify the target. The insurgents partially overran the camp, killed fifty-five South Vietnamese, two U.S. Special Forces soldiers, and an Australian advisor. The delay in A-1H reaction stemmed from the 516th Fighter Squadron pilots being unable to fly at night. A further factor was the operating rule that barred the O-1 from making a target close to friendly forces without positive identification.[82]

A more grievous failure ensued on July 21 in Chuong Thien Province. Viet Cong stormed the Xang Cut outpost before dawn and set ambush positions along the road to be taken by relief forces. Within the one hour needed to get a Vietnamese controller to the scene, the ambush decimated the friendly troops —killing forty-one and wounding fifty-six. Two Vietnamese A-1Hs on ground alert came one and one-half hours after the air support mission was requested.[83]

On the morning of July 28, the Viet Cong hit two hamlets and a post immediately north of Ben Cat in Binh Duong Province. A battalion responded, lost a lead tank to 57-mm recoilless rifle fire, and broke apart under assault. In an initial air support strike, four USAF A-1Es accepted targets from a U.S. Army O-1 pilot. But the Vietnamese A-1H pilots next on station refused to act without a Vietnamese air controller, even though the Army liaison pilot and Vietnamese ground observer marked enemy positions with smoke rockets. By the time a Vietnamese controller got there, the guerrillas had faded into the jungle.[84]

The policy of defining counterinsurgency as something distinctly different from other states of armed conflict resulted in not developing enough air firepower to defeat the Viet Cong. Occasional two-plane air strikes on well-known enemy base areas did little more than harass. One proposed solution was to ask the civilians to leave Viet Cong havens. Then large-scale bombing of these havens could be carried out by USAF tactical aircraft from bases in Thailand, Okinawa, and the Philippines. With inflight refueling, the planes need not ever land in South Vietnam.[85]

In mid-1964 General Westmoreland was "deeply concerned" with the surge in successful Viet Cong hamlet and outpost attacks and ambushes of troop units

THE WAR IN VIETNAM, 1964

and convoys. His basic approach lay in sending more U.S. forces into the provinces at the district level. Their presence spurred Vietnamese paramilitary and lower-level units to speed up pacification.[86] Concluding that the air reaction time to night attacks was too slow, Westmoreland directed Army advisors to keep armed helicopters (some flare-equipped) on night alert at provincial headquarters.[87] He requested more Army Special Forces troops. And he asked for one helicopter company in direct support of each Vietnamese division, plus additional armed helicopter companies and platoons.[88]

In addition the MACV commander instructed General Moore and Brig. Gen. Delk M. Oden, commander of the United States Army Support Command, Vietnam, to shore up all American air support of troop movements, convoys, and reaction forces. Moore and Oden issued a formal agreement that Westmoreland placed in a MACV directive dated September 7. To refine coordination, Army and Marine Corps aviation was to be collocated as would Air Force and Vietnamese control agencies. Ground reaction forces would not normally move without air support. In many cases, armed helicopters would engage and pinpoint the enemy until more heavily armed fighters arrived. If too few fighters were to be had, extra armed helicopters would be used.[89]

The Moore-Oden agreement was perhaps useful as an interim measure required by conditions in South Vietnam. Still it differed in important respects from proven tactical air doctrine. The agreement perpetuated two separate air control systems (Air Force and Army-Marine Corps), which made it possible for a ground commander to receive conflicting advice. Time and again General LeMay protested the presence of armed helicopters in Vietnam, because tactical fighters performed better. Even so, the Moore-Oden agreement recognized complementary needs for both types of aircraft.[90]

Some USAF officers believed that the 2d Air Division was being "hoodwinked" in the roles and missions agreement, but theory had to give way to practicality. With the absence of enemy air power, armed helicopters proved useful. Their instant reply to ground fire offset their inaccurate and rather light firepower. But the Viet Cong's introduction of more .50-cal and 40-mm weapons trimmed the helicopters' advantages.

The Air Force concept of centralized control of all air resources remained "fundamental and sound" in the words of Col. Allison C. Brooks, General Moore's deputy. However, since the fairly slow A-1 aircraft in Vietnam could not be moved rapidly from one base to another, Brooks agreed they should be dispersed into the areas where the battles occurred. So long as there was no deviation from the principle of centralized control, the planes could be shifted as required without fragmenting the effort.[91]

XIX. The Gulf of Tonkin Incident

President Johnson had intimated shortly after taking office that he was inclining toward expanded covert operations against North Vietnam. With the least risk he wanted to put pressure on Hanoi, to force lessened support for the Viet Cong. The President early in January 1964 approved additional resources for covert actions, including beach landings and airdrops of Vietnamese intelligence and commando teams. Closely managing this work were the Office of the Special Assistant for Counterinsurgency and Special Activities of the Joint Chiefs of Staff (headed by General Anthis, now in Washington) and the MACV Special Operations Group in Saigon.[1]

As in other international waters, U.S. Navy patrols were routinely operating in the Gulf of Tonkin to monitor various North Vietnamese activities by visual and electronic sightings. In February U-2 aircraft from Strategic Air Command resumed their reconnaissance missions. Averaging one or two sorties a day, they photographed the border areas of Laos, Cambodia, and North Vietnam.[2] In March more naval patrolling was deemed necessary. Done by air as well as by sea, it focused on naval movements.[3] By April the sum of this intelligence suggested that Hanoi was readying forces to invade South Vietnam through Laos. So General LeMay's repeated announcements to the Joint Chiefs seemed to be sound — there could be no satisfactory solution to the situations in Laos and South Vietnam without military action against North Vietnam.[4]

At the end of June the President selected General Taylor to succeed Henry Cabot Lodge as Ambassador to Vietnam. In recognition of Taylor's prior role as one of the major architects of the war, Johnson entrusted the entire military effort to his hands. He authorized the new ambassador to wield whatever command control he thought proper. If Taylor acted independently of CINC-PAC, he would infringe on the command prerogatives of Admiral Sharp, the newly installed commander in chief. He might also split the unity of air power into three packages — operations in Vietnam and in Laos plus those planned against North Vietnam. Gen. Hunter Harris, Jr., picked to head PACAF on August 1, would find that possibility frustrating. After talking with Admiral Sharp in Hawaii, Ambassador Taylor reached Saigon on July 7. He told General Westmoreland that he would not interfere with MACV's "day to day business."[5]

To Taylor the Khanh government seemed weak. As he later wrote, "We lived dangerously in this period, never sure from night to night when a new coup might overthrow another feeble government or when we might lose some important town to a surprise attack or a military base to mortar fire."[6]

The weakness of the Saigon government, heavy deliveries of modern weapons by North Vietnam to the Viet Cong, and infiltration of North Vietnamese Army units into the south called for greater American effort. Since January the

JCS had been advocating a shift from advisory assistance to more direct aid. Now in May they proposed assigning U.S. Special Forces teams to provinces and districts as advisors to Regional and Popular Forces. General Westmoreland opposed flooding the country with American servicemen. He believed the key to success was honing the cutting edge of the small fighting units. Hence on June 25 and again on July 16, he recommended that U.S. military strength in Vietnam be expanded by about forty-two hundred men to work as advisors at the district level. Admiral Sharp agreed.[7]

On July 18 General Khanh delivered an emotional address at a rally to mark Vietnam's "day of shame," the anniversary of the country's division in 1954. He asserted that his government was unwilling to remain indifferent in the face of the firm determination of the people who wanted a "push northward" as "an appropriate means to fulfill our national history." The next day a government statement declared, "If Communist China and Communist Vietnam obstinately continue their way of aggression, the government and entire people of Vietnam will step up the war with determination until total victory liberates the whole of our national territory."[8]

One week earlier a detachment of C-130s from the USAF 6091st Reconnaissance Squadron, recently moved from Japan to Don Muang near Bangkok, had begun flying communication intercept missions off the North Vietnamese coast. On the 28th a Navy DeSoto patrol, consisting solely of the destroyer *Maddox*, also commenced sailing close to the coast to collect radar and communications intelligence and to make a "show of force."[9]

Hanoi broadcasts revealed that the North Vietnamese knew of the burgeoning covert activity. In a talk with newsmen in July, Air Commodore Nguyen Cao Ky admitted that troops were being parachuted into North Vietnam. He said training was in progress for bigger special missions, entailing ground attacks and airborne operations beyond the confines of South Vietnam.[10]

Conferring with Ambassador Taylor on July 23, General Khanh insisted that the war had entered a new phase — South Vietnam needed to be on the offensive. But the next day he asked Taylor whether he should resign. In a cable to the State Department, the Ambassador said that if the United States opposed a march to the north, the Vietnamese might break with American policy. A single "maverick pilot taking off for Hanoi with a load of bombs" could touch off an unwarranted extension of hostilities. This would cloud the chances for internal pacification in Vietnam. The chief need, Taylor felt, was a stable Vietnamese government and that required time. To gain this time, he suggested that the Vietnamese military make contingency plans for heightened actions against North Vietnam.[11]

But the Vietnamese chafed for action. Four of their patrol boats, operating under U.S. guidance, left Da Nang on July 30 and sailed north. That night they shelled a radar station on Hon Me Island and a radio transmitter on Hon Ngu Island. Both installations were off the North Vietnamese coast near Vinh, and both were deeply involved in Hanoi's sea infiltration.[12]

THE GULF OF TONKIN INCIDENT

During late afternoon on August 2, three high-speed North Vietnamese Swatow patrol boats fired on the destroyer *Maddox*, which was in international waters twenty-eight miles off the enemy's coast. The *Maddox* and planes from the carrier *Ticonderoga* returned the fire.

At first Defense Secretary McNamara thought that the attack was either a miscalculation by the government or an impulsive act of a local commander. In any event, President Johnson immediately dispatched a note of protest to Hanoi. He made public his orders that the Navy continue patrols in the Gulf of Tonkin and add a second destroyer. On August 3 the *Maddox*, now accompanied by the *C. Turner Joy*, reentered the gulf. Air patrols from the *Ticonderoga* covered both destroyers by day. That night, South Vietnamese forces raided a radar station on Cape Vinh Son and a security station near Cua Ron. After dark and in bad weather on the 4th, the *Maddox* reported that it was being fired upon.[13]

Admiral Sharp, CINCPAC, asked the JCS for a new rule of engagement allowing U.S. aircraft to pursue planes into hostile airspace instead of stopping at a three-mile line off the North Vietnamese coast. He also sought authority to launch instant punitive air strikes on North Vietnam as retaliation for the attacks on the *Maddox*.[14]

President Johnson shared this reaction — the United States had to show it meant business. He stressed in a radio and television address to the American people that the U.S. response to the hostile action would be "limited and fitting." Even so, he directed the Pacific Fleet on August 5 to make a single all-out assault on the North Vietnamese Swatow boat bases and their supporting POL storage at Vinh.

Together with the reprisal attack, the President approved and the JCS ordered emergency actions to move additional forces to the Pacific, especially into Southeast Asia. Saigon had previously agreed to positioning more USAF units in the country, and on August 5 planes began to arrive.

Six F-102 jet interceptors of the 509th Fighter Squadron flew from Clark Air Base to Da Nang. Six others from the 16th Fighter Squadron at Naha Air Base, Okinawa, touched down at Tan Son Nhut. Eight F-100s of the 615th Tactical Fighter Squadron, still on rotational deployment at Clark, went to Da Nang. On the evening of August 5, thirty-six B-57s of the 8th and 13th Bomber Squadrons had trouble getting into Bien Hoa. The rain obscured the pilots' view and made the runway slick. One plane during approach crashed in Viet Cong territory, and two suffered damage upon landing. Six RF-101s out of Kadena and Misawa Air Base, Japan, augmented the Able Mable reconnaissance planes at Tan Son Nhut. The 405th Tactical Wing sent ten F-100s from Clark to Takhli, Thailand. Eight KB-50s from PACAF's 421st Air Refueling Squadron moved from Yokota to Tan Son Nhut and Takhli. Eight F-105 jet fighters of the 36th Tactical Fighter Squadron flew from Yokota to Clark, then to Korat in Thailand on August 9.

Under JCS direction the Commander in Chief, United States Strike Command, deployed a TAC composite air strike force. F-100s of the 522d and 614th Tactical Fighter Squadrons landed at Clark on August 8-9. Six RF-101s of the

THE ADVISORY YEARS

363d Composite Reconnaissance Unit reached Kadena on the 13th. Forty-eight C-130 transports from the 314th, 463d, and 516th Troop Carrier Wings arrived at Clark and Kadena between the 9th and 21st of August. For inflight refueling the Strategic Air Command furnished forty-eight KC-135 jet tankers that operated mainly from Hickam Air Force Base in Hawaii and Andersen Air Force Base on Guam. SAC further formed a task force of eight KC-135s at Clark.[15]

General Moore on August 6 created a 2d Air Division command post at Tan Son Nhut, separate from the combined Vietnamese-USAF air operations center. Using just the U.S. side of the tactical air control system, he began to tie together all the USAF units in the area.[16]

On August 5 General Westmoreland had met with General Khanh and Vietnamese commanders to outline the purpose for the retaliatory strike on the Swatow boat bases and oil storage sites. Westmoreland advised and Khanh agreed to place the Vietnamese on maximum alert against Viet Cong reprisals. The MACV commander added that if the North Vietnamese or Chinese attacked South Vietnam, he would loose air strikes on targets of his choice without requiring "a green light from Washington." Ambassador Taylor afterwards called on Khanh. He handed him a letter from President Johnson underlining the need for the closest bilateral consultation. Khanh asured Taylor that he fully understood and accepted this requirement.[17]

The U.S. retaliatory attack on August 6 involved sixty-four aircraft, launched in two waves from the carriers *Ticonderoga* and *Constellation*. The strikes on five boat bases and the Vinh oil storage destroyed eight boats and damaged twenty-one, put the oil reservoirs ninety percent out of commission, and lost two planes to antiaircraft fire.

Shortly thereafter, at the request of the United States, the Canadian member of the International Control Commission visited the North Vietnamese premier in Hanoi. The Canadian said that the United States viewed Hanoi's role in Laos and South Vietnam as critical and threatening. He warned that if North Vietnam persisted in its aggression, it would expect to suffer the consequences. The premier was "utterly unintimidated" and "calmly resolved" to pursue his course.

His indifference might have reflected a recent increase in air strength. North Vietnamese aircraft had included thirty trainers, fifty transports, and four light helicopters. But on August 7, aerial photos of Phuc Yen airfield near Hanoi showed thirty-nine MIG-15/-17 jet fighters apparently just flown in from China. More of these jets were on Hainan Island and South China bases.[18]

General Harris, PACAF commander, saw that the MIGs on Phuc Yen posed a direct threat to his forces in Southeast Asia. He proposed to Admiral Sharp that destroying the communist jet aircraft would be a "sharp lesson" to China, and would deter any fresh enemy plans for attack. The USAF F-105s at Korat could conduct the operation, but the F-100s on alert at Da Nang were closer to the target. With cluster bomb unit (CBU-2A) munitions, the planes could prosecute a low-level, high-speed, surprise attack on the parked aircraft. Then using AGM-12B missiles as well as rockets, flak-suppression missions and

THE GULF OF TONKIN INCIDENT

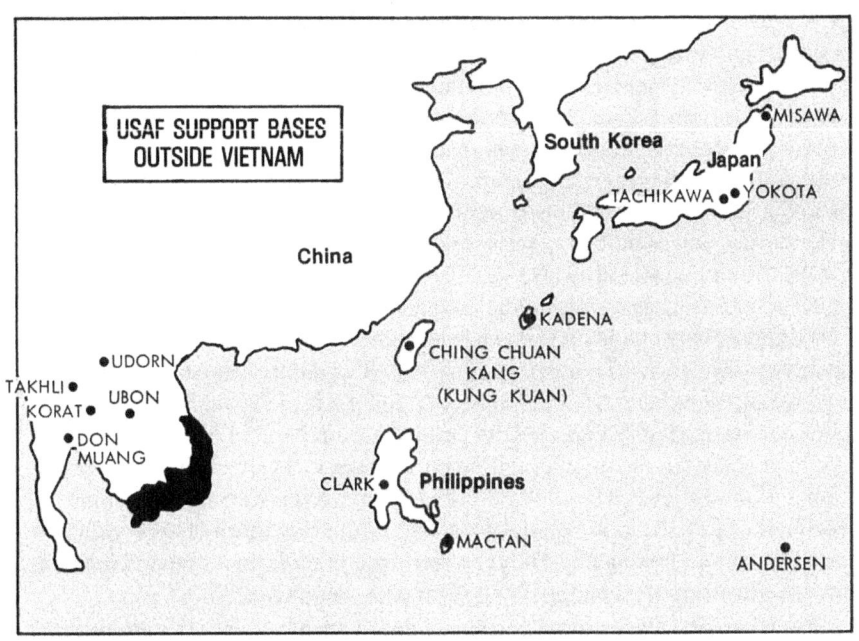

USS *Ticonderoga* Courtesy: U.S. Navy

strikes against individual surviving aircraft could be carried out.[19] But Sharp needed the go-ahead from higher authority, and it was not given.

On August 7 General Westmoreland suggested that MACV and the Vietnamese government make General Moore the combined air commander. With a Vietnamese deputy, Moore could exercise operational control over U.S.-Vietnamese air power for all missions. These would encompass air strikes into North Vietnam and Laos, defensive actions in South Vietnam, and air support of mobile ground forces in the northern provinces of South Vietnam. Assisted by MACV, the Vietnamese armed forces were to have the primary task of controlling the counterinsurgency inside the country.

Admiral Sharp made it clear that he as CINCPAC would manage the air activities against North Vietnam through PACAF and the Pacific Fleet. PACAF would work through Thirteenth Air Force and 2d Air Division. Since the latter reported to both MACV and PACAF, coordination would be easy. As for the MACV commander, he was to center on purging the Viet Cong and pacifying the country. Although events in Laos disturbed policymakers during the summer of 1964, intelligence officers looked for the most serious escalation of the conflict to occur in Vietnam. Peking and Hanoi evidently felt there was a better chance to gain power by dint of a collapse of the Saigon government.[20]

Ambassador Taylor estimated the chance of such a collapse at about fifty percent. The Khanh government had been unable to rebuild the political control structure between Saigon and the hamlets, which had disappeared following the overthrow and death of Diem in November 1963. Morale had plummeted, assisted in its drop by the constant threat of assassination or another coup. To Taylor the most valid and realistic objectives were to bolster Saigon, press the campaign against the Viet Cong, and be prepared to act against North Vietnam by January 1, 1965.[21]

At President Johnson's request, the Senate and House on August 10 enacted a joint resolution giving him authority to prosecute military operations as he saw fit. Tied to the North Vietnamese attacks on the destroyer *Maddox* in the Gulf of Tonkin, the resolution read in part:

> Consonant with the Constitution of the United States and the Charter of the United Nations and in accordance with its obligations under the Southeast Asia Collective Defense Treaty, the United States is . . . prepared, as the President determines, to take all necessary steps, including the use of armed force, to assist any member or protocol state . . . requesting assistance in defense of its freedom.

Yet there was a nagging doubt as to whether the *Maddox* had actually been attacked on the night of August 4. High-speed naval operations at night made precise observation and rapid and accurate reporting difficult. In September Hanoi would publish a lengthy white paper to justify the August 2 attack as proper defense against a covert operation. But it declared that none of its naval craft was in the area two nights later.[22]

William P. Bundy, Assistant Secretary of State for Far Eastern Affairs, was impressed by Ambassador Taylor's assessment of the Khanh government's weakness. He therefore drafted a policy memorandum for the National Security

Council entitled "Next Courses of Actions in Southeast Asia." There was to be an initial short "holding phase" for the remainder of August to avoid actions that might intensify the war. Then would come a "limited pressure" phase lasting through the rest of the year, to maintain the morale of the Khanh government without risking escalation. This phase would witness covert operations against North Vietnam, training of Vietnamese pilots to fly jet aircraft, moves across the border into the Laotian panhandle, reinstatement of naval patrols in the Gulf of Tonkin, and "tit for tat" reprisals. Finally, more serious pressures were to start on January 1, 1965. For example, initial measures to destroy enemy infiltration routes and facilities would progress to the bombardment of military targets in North Vietnam.[23]

Exactly how unstable the Khanh government was became clear on the 16th of August. The Military Revolutionary Council elected Khanh president and made Gen. Duong Van Minh supreme adviser. Student and Buddhist demonstrations instantly erupted.

In Hawaii, far from the turmoil in Saigon, Admiral Sharp thought that the United States could not afford to lose the momentum that the Tonkin Gulf response had created. He wanted to exert more pressure against the communists in Laos, both on the Plain of Jars and in the panhandle. He also wanted to expand and continue covert operations and naval patrols. Because the USAF units at Da Nang, Bien Hoa, and Tan Son Nhut were vulnerable to Viet Cong attack, he suggested that U.S. ground troops be brought to Vietnam to defend the bases. He further advocated that the United States set up a major base at Da Nang, to show that Americans meant to stay in Southeast Asia until American aims were attained.[24]

In the midst of the rioting in Saigon, Ambassador Taylor recommended that the United States try to gain time for the Khanh government. He opposed getting deeply involved with North Vietnam and possibly China. Like Bundy, he thought that Hanoi should be checked in its infiltration by limited pressure until January 1, 1965. Then such measures as covert operations, extensive patrolling, U-2 flights over North Vietnam, air and ground strikes in Laos, and bombing of the north should be stepped up.[25]

On August 24 Ambassador Taylor chaired a long session of the mission council he had formed to include General Westmoreland. The members discussed alternative options in Vietnam, but found it difficult to define an incident that warranted American reprisal.[26]

On the same day the Joint Chiefs of Staff were reviewing a list of ninety-four possible bombing targets in North Vietnam, compiled in June and July. The targets fell into five categories — airfields, lines of communication, military installations, industrial facilities, and armed reconnaissance routes.[27]

President Khanh resigned on the 25th of August. Two days later, the Military Revolutionary Council named a triumvirate of provincial leaders as an interim ruling body.[28]

Undeterred by these developments, the JCS sent the list of bombing targets to CINCPAC and directed that strike plans be devised for four patterns of attack in an ascending order of severity. The Joint Chiefs informed Secretary McNamara of their disagreement with Ambassador Taylor's position. They considered much stronger military pressures on North Vietnam to be needed, in particular to provide a psychological boost to the Saigon government. The chiefs urged bombing the listed targets in North Vietnam at once.[29]

Secretary McNamara on August 31 asked the Joint Chiefs to answer three questions about the ninety-four targets. After a full-scale assault on the targets, would enough ordnance and POL be left to defend Southeast Asia from Chinese attack? What would be the effects of each of the four patterns of attack on the North Vietnamese economy, on its capacity to support the Pathet Lao and the Viet Cong, and on its ability to enlarge North Vietnamese military forces in South Vietnam and Laos? And finally, if the destruction of the ninety-four targets failed to stifle Hanoi's will to wage war, what course of action was feasible? These were tough questions indeed.[30]

In Saigon on September 3 a fifteen-man leadership committee replaced the ruling triumvirate and picked Khanh as acting premier and Minh as chairman.

A short time later, Ambassador Taylor, Secretary of State Rusk, Secretary of Defense McNamara, and JCS Chairman Wheeler gathered to weigh courses of action for the United States. The group sharply revised Bundy's prior outline of graduated pressures. The members agreed that the Saigon government would be too weak for two or three months for the United States to take any major and deliberate action risking escalation. The communists were not likely to provoke the United States. But Saigon should be assisted to show that the United States was serious in its aims, while keeping risks low and under control. American naval patrols in the Gulf of Tonkin, suspended after the *Maddox* affair, could be resumed. The patrols ought to stay outside the twelve-mile limit and be clearly divorced from the South Vietnamese covert operations, which should concentrate on maritime raids. South Vietnamese air and ground operations, linked to air strikes by Laotian pilots in the panhandle, should begin. Lastly, the United States should be alert to answer an attack upon American personnel or a special enemy action against Vietnam. Yet it should not deliberately provoke an incident to justify a retaliation.[31]

These proposals went to the President and to the Joint Chiefs of Staff. On September 8 General LeMay told the chiefs that the courses of action did not convey a clear and positive signal to Hanoi of U.S. resolution. Gen. Wallace M. Greene, Jr., Marine Corps Commandant, sided with LeMay for he also thought that the ninety-four targets should be bombed. The next day, McNamara and Wheeler talked about the Joint Chiefs' feelings. They saw the danger to be drastic American action triggering a strong reaction that the Saigon regime could not meet.[32]

President Johnson accepted the more cautious course on September 10. He ordered U.S. naval patrols to be resumed, covert operations to be reviewed, and talks with the Laotian government to be opened on limited air and ground operations in the panhandle. But the first order of business was shoring up the Saigon government.[33]

THE GULF OF TONKIN INCIDENT

American attempts to do so met with slight success. On September 13 the IV Corps commander started a coup. Proclaiming that Khanh had capitulated to Buddhist and student demands, he led armored elements into Saigon, occupied public buildings, and disarmed the national police. The Vietnamese Air Force stayed loyal to Khanh and made a show of force against the coup. The U.S. State Department announced firm support for Khanh. The rebellious forces then withdrew. Khanh carried out sweeping changes among his military commanders, and appointed a High National Council of seventeen civilians to draft a constitution and designate a civil chief of state. Outwardly, this seemed a step toward stabilizing the government. By October 1, however, American intelligence estimated scant improvement. Meanwhile, pacification efforts virtually collapsed because the paralyzed military staff in Saigon could not reach decisions.[34]

As President Johnson desired, U.S. destroyers *Morton* and *Edwards* entered the Gulf of Tonkin on patrol. During the night of September 17, however, the ships reported and fired on radar contacts. At Joint Chief's direction, CINCPAC called for sizable reprisal air attacks on North Vietnam. Targets and weapons were changed several times, and the 2d Air Division command post was swamped with orders and counterorders. In the end, the air attacks were canceled because the Navy could not be absolutely sure that North Vietnamese action had actually occurred. The Joint Chiefs next enjoined CINCPAC to be ready to execute immediate air strikes against preselected targets when naval patrols were in the gulf. CINCPAC dictated that U.S. jets at Da Nang and Bien Hoa be alerted for attacking Phuc Yen airfield. When a SAC RB-47 was committed to weekly electronic intelligence flights over the Gulf of Tonkin, the naval patrols were abandoned.[35]

It began to appear that unless the United States assumed a more direct role in the struggle, the situation would go out of control.

XX. Diffusion of Air Assets

General Moore, the 2d Air Division commander, counted General Westmoreland as the biggest "booster" of tactical air support in Vietnam.[1] But Westmoreland's requests for more air resources in mid-1964 hewed to Army aviation doctrine. He asked for a fourth C-123 squadron (sixteen planes) to take care of "wholesale" supply under the Southeast Asia Military Airlift System, a second Army CV-2 Caribou company to handle "retail" deliveries within the corps areas, two new Army helicopter companies numbering seventy UH-1Bs (some for command use, others for gunships), and two additional airmobile platoons with twenty UH-1Bs. Among the forty-eight hundred personnel in the package were forty air liaison officer and forward air controller teams.

PACAF understood and agreed to the need for the C-123 squadron, in light of Viet Cong success in attacking surface transportation. But an extra Caribou company seemed unnecessary, if the CV-2s already in Vietnam were put under central control of the airlift system for common use. General LeMay disliked the Moore-Oden position of "complementary" needs for armed helicopters and tactical air. He objected strongly to helicopter gunships. Despite the Air Force chief's contention that strike aircraft gave more firepower, Secretary of Defense McNamara on August 7, 1964, approved Westmoreland's list of requirements.[2]

Three days later, a Royal Australian Air Force detachment of six Caribous arrived at Tan Son Nhut and went under control of the airlift system. But the new Army Caribou company reaching Vietnam in September remained outside systematic control. The Air Force Reserve furnished the fresh squadron of C-123s, the planes flown to Tan Son Nhut in mid-September by rotating replacement crews. In early October the 19th Air Commando Squadron (Troop Carrier) was formed and assigned to the 315th Troop Carrier Group.[3]

In August the Joint Chiefs of Staff had forwarded General LeMay's question on the comparative merits of tactical air and armed helicopters. General Westmoreland, MACV commander, responded and asserted that the latter had numerous advantages over strike aircraft support. General Moore took exception and argued that many of the alleged benefits were invalid. Continuing discussions consumed a lot of staff energy that might better have gone to the combat situation.[4]

Westmoreland did not neglect tactical aviation, even though he heartily endorsed armed helicopters. For the first time, MACV critiques of Vietnamese ground operations pointed out missed opportunities for tactical air support. For example, in Phu Yen Province on August 19, three battalions attacked about five hundred Viet Cong without once calling for strike aircraft. This, MACV commented, was "the major fault" of the operation.[5]

Past counterinsurgency experts had viewed air strikes as impeding pacification. Then Leon Goure, an analyst with The RAND Corporation, interviewed Viet Cong prisoners and concluded that the adverse effects were far less than assumed. He further found that since the Viet Cong were on the lookout for strike aircraft, they feared even liaison planes.[6]

Yet MACV desired more helicopters because strike aircraft and liaison planes were too few, a shortage seen by General Moore as the most important limiting factor in the USAF effort.[7] Due to training demands, only eight of the twenty-nine A-1Es of the 1st Air Commando Squadron were on hand for twelve combat sorties a day. An average of just thirty Vietnamese A-1Hs were available for thirty-five to forty-five combat sorties.[8] Eight aircraft of the 1st Air Commando Squadron crashed, at least two due to enemy ground fire. These A-1Es were shot down on the night of September 23, when silhouetted by flares while making a low-level napalm pass.[9]

General Moore had proposed in August that the Vietnamese be given a fifth and a sixth A-1H squadron, and he asked that the B-57 and F-100 jets at Bien Hoa and Da Nang be used within the country. MACV and the JCS concurred. When the Joint Chiefs took up in September the matter of lagging tactical air support, they suggested using jets but President Johnson was unwilling to do so. To up USAF sorties, Ambassador Taylor advocated deleting the need for a bona fide Vietnamese trainee pilot aboard an A-1E during a combat mission. Perhaps, the Joint Chiefs said, USAF A-1Es could fly combat while carrying a Vietnamese observer if a pilot was not on hand. Although at first "entirely negative," Secretary McNamara on September 25 agreed to permit A-1E combat operations with a Vietnamese observer or student pilot aboard.

The JCS tried again to allow USAF crews to respond to immediate and emergency air requests. But Ambassador Taylor still resisted opening the door to wider use of American crews, and McNamara agreed. In mid-October the Joint Chiefs authorized A-1Es to engage in combat with a Vietnamese pilot or observer aboard. For the Vietnamese Air Force they recommended a fifth A-1H squadron in May 1965 and a sixth in October 1965. Until then, two USAF A-1E units were required in the country.[10]

During October-December 1964 the 34th Tactical Group and the Vietnamese Air Force slightly expanded their strike aircraft. Organized under the 34th Group on October 12, the USAF 602d Fighter Commando Squadron began to build in both personnel and planes. The 520th or fourth Vietnamese fighter squadron, formed at Bien Hoa in October, prepared to move to the new Can Tho airfield.

In December the 34th Group flew about fifty A-1 sorties a day, seventeen of them available for combat. The planes performed admirably on strike missions but proved hard to maintain, chiefly due to inflight engine failures. The Americans nonetheless kept eighty percent of the aircraft operational. In contrast, the Vietnamese could muster only fifty-eight percent. For example, the 516th Fighter Squadron at Da Nang had fifteen aircraft but its sortie rate was about six per day.

The 520th Fighter Squadron flew a few missions in December, but construction lagged at Can Tho (later called Binh Thuy) and the field was insecure at night. Beginning December 20 the squadron daily deployed a detachment of five

THE ADVISORY YEARS

(Top) B-57 Canberra bomber.

(Center) A rocket pod attached to the wing pylon of an F-100 Super Sabre at Da Nang.

(Bottom) Australian Caribou aircraft at Tan Son Nhut, on hand to aid in aircraft support missions, August 10, 1964.

A-1Hs to Binh Thuy. The pilots were on call for missions until they returned to Bien Hoa just before nightfall.

The expansion of the Vietnamese Air Force was supported by adequate aircraft delivery and aircrew training. It suffered from troubles in training maintenance men, owing in part to shortages of ground support and handling equipment. The Vietnamese borrowed a few dollies, loading hoists, and other equipment from the 34th Tactical Group. Only main bases like Bien Hoa owned these items, which hardly helped the situation at forward bases.[11]

On August 8, at the height of the Tonkin Gulf crisis, PACAF issued orders inactivating the 19th Tactical Air Support Squadron as had earlier been planned.[12] General Westmoreland expressed surprise to Admiral Sharp and asked to retain the unit. In lieu of giving the O-1 liaison planes to the Vietnamese 116th Liaison Squadron as contemplated, Westmoreland proposed the purchase of U-17A aircraft to equip that unit. On September 25 Defense Secretary McNamara approved.[13]

The 19th Tactical Air Support Squadron was reactivated at Bien Hoa on October 31. MACV recommended thirty more planes for it and each of the four Vietnamese liaison units as well.[14]

The reversal of the earlier phaseout decision left the squadron in limbo. Until pipeline support could be restored, the 34th Tactical Group possessed twenty-four O-1s and twelve liaison pilots, three of whom were about to complete their tours. A detachment of O-1Fs stayed at Bien Hoa to train newly graduated Vietnamese pilots arriving from Nha Trang. Ten O-1Fs, with liaison officers and forward controllers, went under the air support operations centers.[15]

The USAF controller with the 14th Regiment at Tra Vinh was Capt. Lloyd E. Lewis. When he received an O-1 and a Vietnamese observer in September, he began to fly day-long surveillance missions coordinated with the Vinh Binh province commander. The result was an appreciable decline in Viet Cong activity. Friendly ground action became more productive as did interdiction targeting and air strikes.[16]

In September William B. Graham and Aaron H. Katz of RAND studied the use of USAF liaison officers and forward air controllers on constant visual reconnaissance and strike control. The two analysts gathered data for a new concept they called the "Single Integrated Attack Team." The idea was presented in Saigon, Hawaii, and Washington in October and next in a RAND report. The theory favored small and closely coordinated air and ground strike forces as the best counterinsurgency weapon. O-1 crews were to carry out continuous and extensive airborne surveillance and strike control. They would work with Special Forces ground teams of about eighty men, who were to hold the Viet Cong groups long enough for strike aircraft to sweep in. Unfortunately, the concept was better-suited to an insurgency in its initial stages than to the field warfare the Viet Cong were starting to wage.[17]

Meanwhile, General Khanh had embarked on a general shakeup following the abortive coup against him in September. His sweeping personnel changes in the Joint General Staff and among the field commanders produced officers unfamiliar with the air request system. To explain the system's features, a team from the USAF Air-Ground Operations School completed a countrywide circuit in October and November. But all attempts to persuade the Vietnamese to assign sufficient workers to the request net, to disperse 0-1As to forward locations, and to let others besides Vietnamese air observers mark targets were fruitless. The field commanders refused to be bypassed in requests for air strikes. Neither the Vietnamese Air Force nor ground commanders were willing to assume responsibility under civil law for mistakes that the other might make in marking targets. Strike pilots refrained from accepting targets unless a Vietnamese air observer designated them. And deploying 0-1As to forward and remote airstrips meant danger from guerrillas, logistic difficulties, and loss of command control.[18]

Despite these drawbacks, Secretary McNamara in November approved a fifth and sixth fighter squadron for the Vietnamese Air Force. He authorized building the Vietnamese liaison squadrons to thirty aircraft each, by deliveries of sixty-eight 0-1As and U-17As from March through May 1965. He said he would probably go along with General Westmoreland's request to give the 19th Tactical Air Support Squadron thirty 0-1Fs. However, he wanted to postpone his decision until the political climate in Saigon improved.[19]

The continuous surveillance concept could not be properly set in motion during the winter of 1964-65, due to the dearth of USAF and Vietnamese aircraft and forward air controllers. By December the 19th Tactical Air Support Squadron was down to seven airmen and nine pilots, when it received eight single-engine pilots who needed to be checked out in 0-1s. The Vietnamese liaison squadrons owned only sixty of 120 authorized 0-1As and U-17As. In the II Corps there were just four 0-1 controllers on hand.[20]

In compensation USAF research and development had turned out some new weapons that TAC's Special Air Warfare Center had tested. A munitions survey team visiting Vietnam thought that these weapons and new techniques ought to replace older munitions and methods.[21]

The hazards of Viet Cong ground fire to low-flying aircraft, particularly those on napalm runs, demanded a different approach to hamlet defense. Fragmentation clusters replaced napalm on night flare-assisted missions. Fighters delivered the clusters from a dive to shave the time they were silhouetted by flarelight.[22]

The 1st Combat Application Group at Eglin Air Force base had devised and tested a three-gun side-firing installation in a C-47. The Air Staff called for operational testing of these rapid-fire 7.62-mm Gatling guns (miniguns), either affixed to the racks of an A-1 or mounted and fired from the side cargo doors of an orbiting C-47. In September Mk-44 Lazy Dog free-falling finned bullets were approved for use in Vietnam. The Lazy Dog worked well at first but not in terrain covered with heavy growth. The fins of the small projectiles easily bent out of shape when loaded into the dispensers from which they were dropped. This caused the missiles to tumble and lose their impact. Moreover, the size and shape of the pattern of the falling projectiles were erratic. Clearly, Lazy Dog was no substitute for napalm when enemy and friendly troops were fairly close to each other.[23] Other new weapons also proved not entirely reliable.[24]

Tests by the 1st Combat Application Group verified that it was desirable to modify the C-47 with lateral-firing miniguns. Still PACAF and TAC were reluctant to employ the minigun-equipped plane in combat. They deemed it obsolete, vulnerable to ground fire, and unable to perform as well as strike aircraft.

To Gen. John P. McConnell, Air Force Vice Chief of Staff (who would succeed General LeMay as Chief on February 1, 1965) an armed C-47 was a highly specialized weapon for use solely in areas of light ground fire. The aircraft could fly long night alert missions and react swiftly to surprise attacks. Circling above small-arms range, it could pin down the enemy until fighters got there. The armed C-47 would help offset the shortage of strike aircraft and the inefficiency of night fighter airborne alerts.

Following a November 2 briefing on the armed C-47, General LeMay ordered a combat evaluation that got under way in early December. A test team led by Maj. Ronald W. Terry fitted two C-47s of the 34th Tactical Group with miniguns. These aircraft were an instant success against enemy troops in the open. Using an improvised gunsight and putting the plane's wing down in a "plyon 8" turn, the pilot could direct fire from the three miniguns mounted in the left-hand cargo door. When fired together, they spewed 18,000 rounds-per-minute into a space about the size of a football field. An aerial gunner cleared jams and reloaded the weapons in flight. While the small-caliber bullets were easily deflected in wooded stretches, the AC-47 gunships were outstanding for night fort and hamlet defense. Awed by the stream of tracers, the Viet Cong spoke of the new "ray gun" turned upon them.[25]

Integrated air reconnaissance fully responsive to users' needs did not develop in 1964. And the absence of a coordinated reconnaissance-intelligence-target system was a serious defect. The main stumbling block was the splintering of air reconnaissance in and out of the country. Many elements were involved, but the stateside USAF Tactical Air Reconnaissance Center placed most of the blame on the shortage of keen and influential senior Air Force officers in Vietnam.[26]

By early 1964 the reconnaissance assets of 2d Air Division had consisted of six Able Mable RF-101s, two experimental infrared RB-57s, two experimental infrared FB-26s, and two night photo RB-26Cs, plus the 13th Reconnaissance Technical Squadron (formerly a photo processing cell). All operated under Detachment 1, 33d Tactical Group, but supported the 2d Air Division director of intelligence.[27]

Time and again Col. Harvey E. Henderson, 2d Air Division deputy commander, had suggested that all these resources be brought into a tactical reconnaissance squadron. To do so, however, would have exceeded the Air Force's authorized unit force levels. Mirroring the talk of phasing out the American forces from Vietnam, planners programmed a decline in U.S. reconnaissance. Furthermore the Vietnamese 716th Composite Reconnaissance Squadron —

THE ADVISORY YEARS

(Upper right) A1C Leonard A. Rowe boresights a .50-caliber nose gun on a B-26.

(Lower right) SSgt. Harold Inman inspects the links on .50-caliber ammunition belt for a B-26.

(Center) An AC-47 aircraft at Tan Son Nhut.

(Bottom) A 7.62 minigun mounted in an AC-47.

with three RC-47s and eighteen RT-28s, together with photo processing cells in the corps tactical zones — was becoming operational. Except for problems in camera installation, this squadron was making solid progress. As the 716th reached its projected goal in early 1964 of 374 sorties a month, the Able Mable RF-101s were to depart along with six Army Mohawk armed photo-reconnaissance planes.[28]

Unforeseen events buffeted the projections. The U-2 aircraft from Bien Hoa flew very high altitude photo missions over Southeast Asia. Film from these flights swamped the 13th Reconnaissance Technical Squadron, which had to call upon other PACAF, SAC, and Navy facilities in the Philippines and Japan. Unfortunately the U-2 photography, needed for national strategic planning, had slight value for tactical users.[29] Moreover, the wing-stress weakness of the B-26 led to the removal of the RB-26s from Vietnam at the close of March 1964, diminishing night photo coverage. At the same time, the Vietnamese reconnaissance program ran into technical snags. The improved RC-47 infrared photo systems were operational in April and could locate the enemy by heat-source imagery. But MACV intelligence could not use this information because procedures had not been worked out to exploit the infrared photography.[30]

Two things were to alter sharply the whole reconnaissance program — the U.S. decision in May to begin air reconnaissance over Laos, and Secretary McNamara's orders to retrain Vietnamese RT-28 pilots for a fourth A-1H squadron. Six more USAF RF-101s arrived to augment the six Able Mable aircraft.[31] All RT-28s were removed from the Vietnamese 716th Squadron, and three RC-47s were assigned to the Vietnamese 43d Transport Group.[32] After a few transport missions, the RC-47s were restored to photo duty in the III and IV Corps.[33]

In midyear the RF-101s commenced flying out of Tan Son Nhut over Laos. Yet authorized occasional night photography and infrared reconnaissance were out of the question. The two RC-47s for this work had no self-contained navigation systems (chiefly terrain clearance radar), and mountains and uncertain weather made the flights too hazardous. The Air Force set up delivery of two more RC-47s with doppler navigation and inflight readout infrared sensors. These planes could not be modified and in place until December 1964.[34]

General Harris, PACAF commander, pressed for low-level reconnaissance to secure more detailed coverage for tactical air operations. Admiral Sharp had no hope of obtaining blanket approval for these flights, due to their danger to low-flying planes. CINCPAC needed to justify each mission to officials in Washington on a case-by-case basis.[35]

As the photo-reconnaissance workload grew in South Vietnam, PACAF sent six more RF-101s to Tan Son Nhut. Another six RF-101s that had been dispatched to Kadena in the wake of the Tonkin Gulf crisis also assisted. The Vietnamese RC-47s continued their coverage in the III and IV Corps, two Vietnamese aircrews being permanently assigned to reconnaissance. Requests for photography forwarded straight to air support operations centers markedly increased.[36]

Since photo reconnaissance could not capture rapidly shifting guerrilla operations, interest in other air reconnaissance techniques quickened. Airborne radio direction finding held promise, and the Army's 3d Radio Research Unit operated three assorted aircraft. These planes furnished important intelligence of the Viet Cong order of battle, but they could not make precise-enough fixes of enemy radio transmitters to permit air targeting.

In the United States the Air Force tested a C-47 (later an EC-47) that could plot the location of a ten-watt radio transmitter within one degree at a range of twenty-five nautical miles. In January 1964 PACAF requested seven C-47s fitted with more sensitive and accurate radio direction finders. However, the Air Force delayed approval until the experimental plane could be tested in Vietnam. Conducted during February-June 1964, the tests showed the tactical advantage of equipment that gave lines of position to an enemy transmitter regardless of the aircraft's heading. The plane could fly past a transmitter without revealing interest in it, whereas Army gear required a series of head bearings on the transmitter. Yet as the testing bore out, the C-47 direction finder was not sufficiently sensitive to plot the very low-power, short-range radios used by the insurgents.[37]

A better way to pinpoint enemy actions seemed to be infrared reconnaissance sensors. In mid-1964, while two USAF RB-57s waited for tactical work, MACV requested two Army infrared-equipped OV-1Cs to help carry out visual and photographic night surveillance. General Moore asked why the Mohawks were needed when the RB-57s were there. MACV was surprised that an infrared capability was already on hand, but proceeded to justify a requirement for four OV-1Cs. These were to feature side-looking airborne radar and infrared sensors that could be "read out" in flight. The two RB-57s had older infrared sets, requiring film to be developed and interpreted on the ground after the mission. In December the Air Force provided two extra RB-57s with inflight infrared readout. The older RB-57s were retrofitted with newer equipment and returned to service.

Word of the Mohawks authorized to MACV reached General LeMay. He wanted them put under the operational control of the 2d Air Division as part of a joint counterinsurgency reconnaissance task force. General Moore hoped to get authority to coordinate all infrared reconnaissance for MACV, but General Westmoreland favored a quite different control arrangement.[38]

In mid-1964 USAF air liaison officers and forward air controllers easily observed Viet Cong activity. Their liaison planes flew over enemy-held areas during the day and even more at night, when the guerrillas kindled fires to cook their food. The infrared sensor aircraft had the mission of collecting heat-radiating intelligence. Experimental night flights of the RB-57s produced infrared photos with "hot spots." These, when correlated with ground intelligence, confirmed the positions of Viet Cong camps in Zones C and D. The infrared section of the 13th Reconnaissance Technical Squadron processed the results of each night's infrared mission. From October 1964 on, enemy locations (usually the coordinates of the cooking-fire sites) were phoned at once to the

DIFFUSION OF AIR ASSETS

corps tactical operations center. After collation with other intelligence, infrared material was useful for artillery and air strikes.[39]

While the RB-57s were in test during July, 29 infrared targets were requested and 21 were completed. With one more RB-57 in use in December, there were 261 requests for infrared and 228 executed. Most infrared coverage was in the III Corps. To exploit both visual and infrared sightings, the 2d Air Division proposed target centers for the other corps.[40]

These centers were to funnel information and needs to the air operations center, which would coordinate strike aircraft. On December 20, 1964, however, MACV formed the Central Target Analysis and Research Center at Tan Son Nhut as a unit of MACV J-2 (Intelligence). Its main mission was to coordinate Army and Air Force infrared reconnaissance. The center set up units at the corps headquarters, and they were responsive to MACV J-2. Flights by RB-57s and OV-1Cs proved invaluable. By January 1965 the new setup was absorbing the entire infrared capability in Vietnam. In February there were so many requests for RF-101 coverage that the 13th Reconnaissance Technical Squadron was again unable to handle the processing load. Chiefly through correlation of infrared sensor indications with other intelligence, the center identified 250 possible enemy targets in two months. Included were Viet Cong battalion camps in Phuoc Tuy Province that would eventually be struck by B-57 jet bombers.[41]

Although the Air Force supported the MACV program to improve intelligence, the system removed control of infrared sorties and much of the RF-101 effort from the air operations center.[42] MACV enjoyed several intelligence sources that by law could not be disclosed to Vietnamese agencies. Consequently, the Vietnamese delayed and in some cases refused to allow strikes against targets so generated. The Central Target Analysis and Research Center worked at cross-purposes with the 2d Air Division's desire to develop close relations with province chiefs for intelligence and quick air targeting.[43]

Had the MACV system been staffed with more USAF targeting, interpretation, and reconnaissance officers, they might have produced more air strikes. But General Westmoreland regarded all air operations as support for ground troops and of necessity responsive to ground commanders. He even included interdiction, a normal USAF responsibility. Hence the MACV J-2 had the principal say on how air reconnaissance and surveillance resources were to be used. This left the 2d Air Division commander, working through the air operations center, with only nominal operational control over reconnaissance forces. These, like the aircraft flying close support and interdiction in South Vietnam, became chiefly geared to ground needs.[44]

So too the airlift. Although General LeMay preferred to have C-123 assault transports used in tactical operations rather than as logistic carriers, the insecure rail and road net imposed great stress on air. At times U.S. commanders joked that the Vietnamese army refused to travel on the ground and to keep roads and rails open because the Air Force moved everything for them. The adding of air escort for trains and convoys did little to restrain requests for air movements.[45]

THE ADVISORY YEARS

The 315th Troop Carrier Group at Tan Son Nhut operated the Southeast Asia Airlift System. Its transport control office in the air operations center managed common-use airlift in South Vietnam and Thailand. Assigned to the 315th Air Division at Tachikawa Air Base, Japan, the group came under MACV operational control exercised by the 2d Air Division.

American and Vietnamese forces projected monthly airlift requirements and sent them to the Joint Airlift Allocation Board in MACV J-4 (Logistics). The board in fact consisted of one officer in the J-4 movements branch. He screened and processed the requests, set priorities, and with the Joint General Staff levied the requirements on the airlift units by monthly increments.

The 315th Group commander also served as director of air transportation for the Southeast Asia Airlift System. In theory he could call upon the forty-eight USAF C-123s of his three squadrons, three C-47s of the 1st Air Commando Squadron, two of sixteen U.S. Army CV-2B Caribou transports, several Vietnamese C-47s, and two Bristol Type 170 transports of the Royal New Zealand Air Force operating in Thailand. Actually, three C-123s and three air commando C-47s were kept on station at Nha Trang to support U.S. Army Special Forces at remote spots. A "Fire Brigade" of three C-123s at Tan Son Nhut and one at Da Nang stood alert, ready to respond on fifteen-minute notice to the need for a paratroop drop or equivalent emergency. Besides, two C-123s were regularly allocated for service in Thailand. And the Vietnamese C-47s were usually flying other missions.[46]

Col. David T. Fleming, commander of the 315th Troop Carrier Group, depicted the airlift system as a hodgepodge of badly tacked-together elements, saturated with requirements. The sole officer on the Joint Airlift Allocation Board could not possibly screen requests for validity. Cargo that should have gone by surface transportation was airlifted, and cargo for airlift was often late or absent at air terminals. Communications for keeping track of transport flights were unreliable. Aircraft frequently left bases empty or partially loaded.[47]

The great demands constantly pushed the C-123s above their programmed sixty hours of flying time a month per aircraft. They were wearing out, stressed by landings and takeoffs on rough fields. By May 1964 skin wrinkles appeared on the top sides of two planes. Further inspection at Tan Son Nhut disclosed visible damage on all thirty-seven C-123s that had been in Vietnam for nearly three years. Eleven required extensive repairs. Those at Da Nang in the theater for a year had minor damage. Airlift further declined when three C-123s went to Thailand in July to join the two on station there. That same month, two U.S. Army Caribous were lost in crashes.

The debut in August of six CV-2B Caribous of the Royal Australian Air Force helped redress the balance. They contributed six hundred tons of short-range airlift a month, proving that all the Caribous could be scheduled and used within a centralized system.[48]

The system did well despite its shortcomings. Over the first half of 1964, the C-123s bore the bulk of the airlift load. They airdropped 1,270 tons of supplies, moved 1,252 paratroopers and 115 tons of materiel in assault missions, and flew

239 night flare sorties (dispensing flares 119 times). The air commando C-47s airdropped 405 tons of cargo and flew 1,338 airlanded resupply missions (2,010 passengers and 1,246 tons of supplies). As a rule the two U.S. Army Caribous made short hauls. They flew 7,939 airlanded sorties (4,731 passengers and 3,322 tons of cargo).[49]

The three USAF C-123s and the three air commando C-47s at Nha Trang delivered about 1,500 tons a month throughout 1964 to the scattered fortified outposts at remote sites held by Army Special Forces. Cargo loads varied from neatly packed bundles to bulky and unwieldy rolls of concertina wire, sandbags, and steel stakes — frequently a mixture of all. Landing strips at the forward locations were rough and drop zones hard to find, especially in marginal weather. Enemy ground fire made low-altitude approaches dangerous. During 1964 more C-123s were hit by ground fire than any other type of fixed-wing aircraft. Lt. Col. Victor N. Curtis, USAF air liaison officer at Nha Trang, spoke of the C-47 and C-123 crews as "some of the most professional and dedicated people" he had ever known. The Special Forces likewise appreciated the air supply. They lent a hand in rigging AN/PRC-10 radios aboard the transports for communications with the camps. But the aircraft commanders commonly relied on smoke signals to direct landings and drops. The crews manhandled their airdrop cargo in a manner reminiscent of World War II.[50]

Through the autumn of 1964, the C-123s and C-47s supporting the Special Forces ran serious risks. A C-123 on October 24 tried to resupply an outpost in western Quang Duc Province but could not make radio contact. The plane wandered over the Cambodian border and was shot down with the loss of all eight crewmen. In December half of the 310th Troop Carrier Squadron and seven of its C-123s went to Nha Trang to replace the C-47s, which were withdrawn. The seven C-123s, an Australian CV-2, and three Army CV-2s supported the Special Forces.[51]

The 4,200 new U.S. field advisors that General Westmoreland had asked for in June and July would need an average of 1,200 tons of airlift each month. Colonel Fleming therefore requested a C-123 squadron to bring his total to four. Until that unit arrived, PACAF committed eleven C-130s from the 315th Air Division to the airlift in South Vietnam. These planes worked off the backlog of air cargo at the major terminals. The Gulf of Tonkin crisis in August had triggered a hurried deployment of USAF units into South Vietnam and Thailand. The 315th Division, aided by three TAC C-130 squadrons of the Composite Air Strike Force, handled these movements. The division's Detachment 3 at Clark Air Base functioned as the movement control center.[52]

In 1962 Ranch Hand C-123s had flown a series of defoliation missions in South Vietnam. (See Chapter X.) The results led the Joint Chiefs to conclude in April 1963 that aerial spraying of herbicides had military value to kill the foliage concealing the enemy and to destroy his crops. The Kennedy administration granted joint authority to the U.S. Ambassador and MACV to order defoliation spraying. But it cleared no U.S. crews and aircraft for spray missions against Viet Cong crops. Specific approval for each crop-destruction target had to come from

Washington. The chemicals worked best in the wet season when the vegetation was actively growing. Ranch Hand therefore waited until June and July 1963 before clearing growth from the Saigon to Da Lat powerline and canals in the Ca Mau Peninsula. This and other spraying over the year improved the view and reduced cover for hostile ambush operations. There were eighty-seven square kilometers defoliated throughout 1963, compared to twenty in 1962.[53]

In January 1964 the U.S. Army division advisors were allowed to make wider use of aerial spray around depots, airfields, and outposts. They could also approve hand-spray operations against enemy crops. Warnings had to go out to the civilian population before spraying. In consequence the Ranch Hand C-123s, flying at 150 feet, were exposed to enemy ground fire. In 1962 and 1963 the average number of hits on each spray plane per mission was four small-arms bullets. The risk rose in 1964 as spray flights treated areas totally dominated by the Viet Cong. On April 30 a Ranch Hand aircraft ran into .50-caliber fire that wounded the copilot and tore forty holes in the plane. Fighters regularly escorted spray missions and struck the areas from which the C-123s took ground fire.

The Ranch Hand C-123s staged to Da Nang in May and June 1964. They set about spraying the elephant grass and other vegetation that sheltered the enemy along the roads in the A Shau-A Luoi valley and other areas near the Laotian border. Completed quickly before the Viet Cong could fully react, these flights sustained just four hits in the course of twenty-six sorties. On five spray missions in III Corps during May, C-123s were struck fifteen times by ground fire. On two occasions MACV suspended operations where heavy firing persisted.[54]

Ranch Hand functioned on temporary duty until July 1964, supported by the Tactical Air Command. Then the three spray C-123 s and their specialized crews became Detachment 1 of the 315th Troop Carrier Group, permanently assigned to PACAF. Though Vietnamese helicopters and ground troops had sprayed crops in 1962 and 1963, no American aircraft or personnel had been permitted to take part in crop destruction prior to 1964.

On July 29, 1964, Ambassador Taylor received the authority to approve crop-destruction operations without first referring them to Washington. In May VNAF helicopters had resumed crop destruction but were unable to spray crops in certain areas. Taylor therefore directed Ranch Hand to spray some crop targets, beginning on October 30. The Ranch Hand planes had to operate under the Farm Gate concept when spraying crops. That is, they carried temporary South Vietnamese markings and were under the ostensible control of a South Vietnamese "aircraft commander" who was also on board. To cut exposure to ground fire, the three Ranch Hand aircraft in August were given modified spray systems. Now they could dispense herbicides at the rate of three gallons per acre (double the old rate), and finish a mission in a single pass. Their first nineteen crop-spraying sorties lasted ten days in October, directed against rice, corn, manioc, bananas, and pineapples near War Zone D. While fighters escorted all flights, enemy ground fire scored forty hits on the C-123s.

DIFFUSION OF AIR ASSETS

(Top) Loudspeakers installed in a C–47.

(Bottom) Leaflets dropped from a C–47 Skytrain.

Broadcasts and leaflet drops over Viet Cong-held areas of South Vietnam were part of the "Open Arms" program to persuade insurgents to surrender.

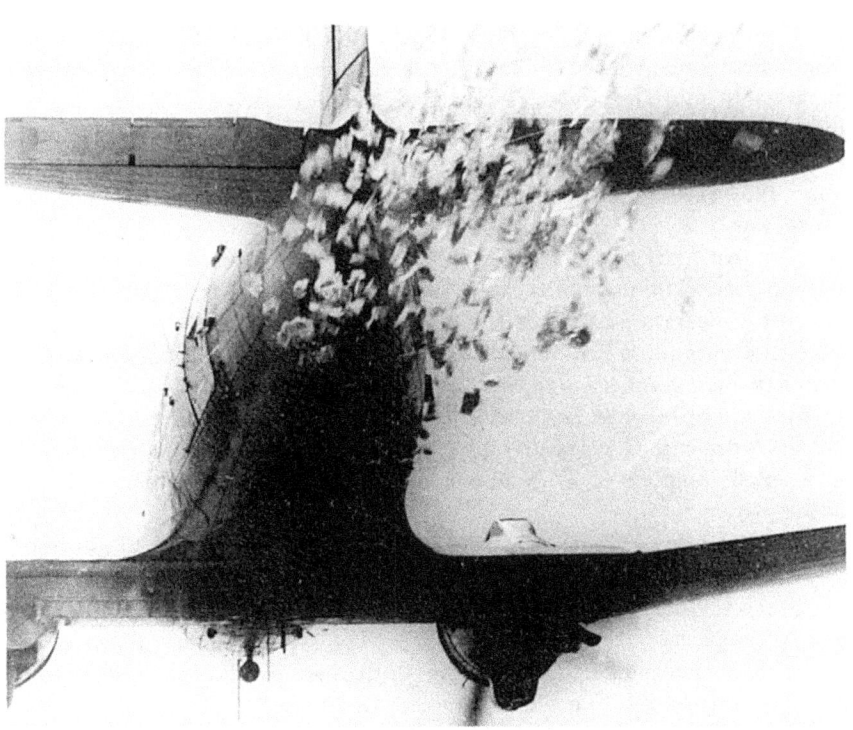

THE ADVISORY YEARS

In November and December Ranch hand sprayed enemy rice near War Zone D. An intelligence source quoted the Viet Cong Phuoc Thanh provincial committee as reporting that the destroyed rice would have fed their troops in the area for two years. During these flights ground fire shot out an engine on a C-123, and the plane barely made it back to Bien Hoa. A fourth C-123 was added in December. By the end of the year the detachment had flown seventy-two survey flights and 363 spray sorties, defoliated 353 square kilometers of vegetation, and destroyed 7,620 acres of Viet Cong crops. This contrasted with the 750 acres of crops sprayed by the Vietnamese in 1962 and the 197 acres in 1963.[55]

Concern of Washington officials over strengthening the Khanh government focused fresh attention on psychological operations during the spring of 1964. Psychological warfare had been conducted since 1961 but with uneven results. In November 1961 Farm Gate had first used four SC-47s for leaflet drops and loudspeaker broadcasts. The SC-47, however, was not well-suited to remote-area work. Farm Gate wanted a plane that could land at a forward site, pick up local officials or Viet Cong defectors, and let them speak from the air to people who would recognize their voices. To do this the L-28 Helio Super Courier (later designated U-10) seemed ideal. The aircraft, specially configured for the CIA, featured short-takeoff-and-landing and other admirable characteristics. Farm Gate requested eight L-28s and authority to create a psychological warfare branch of three qualified officers and two technicians, to forge "a sophisticated psychological warfare effort."[56]

These efforts were abruptly dampened. On February 11, 1962, a low-flying SC-47 dropping leaflets near Da Lat crashed and killed eight Americans and one Vietnamese. Embarrassed by the loss of so many Americans on a flight that was supposed to train Vietnamese, Secretary McNamara ordered leaflet and speaker missions turned over to the Vietnamese. The Joint Chiefs directed that U.S. aircraft refrain from such operations "except in unusual circumstances."[57] In June 1962 the Vietnamese equipped a C-47 with speakers for airborne broadcasts.[58]

The Air Staff and PACAF wanted Farm Gate to train Vietnamese Air Force personnel for psychological warfare. But by April 1963 the 2d Air Division director of operations, Col. Winston P. Anderson, judged the Vietnamese to have little recognition of its importance. From June 1962 through January 1963, the Vietnamese speaker-equipped C-47 had made a total of twenty-two flights—fourteen loudspeaker and eight psychological warfare. Now and then the standard C-47s dispensed leaflets, and the L-19s of the liaison squadrons participated in a small program of civic action, troop information, and enemy leaflet dissemination.[59]

In September 1962 Farm Gate received two of four authorized U-10 Helio Super Couriers, one being rigged with speakers. Between December 14, 1962, and May 13, 1963, Farm Gate made a number of flights in the U-10 to evaluate it as a psychological warfare aircraft.[60] And in May, Mr. McNamara approved the use of American planes to supplement Vietnamese psychological operations, provided minimum U.S. personnel were aboard.[61]

The mission was then divided between the Vietnamese Air Force and the 2d Air Division, with neither of them given authority to coordinate the overall psychological warfare program.[62] The 2d Air Division favored the Helio Super Courier. While the C-47 carried a navigator and was better for night flights, the U-10 was more maneuverable, not as noisy, and less susceptible to ground fire since it was smaller. The weight of the U-10's laminated fiberglass armor diminished aircraft performance, but protected the crew against light-caliber fire.

After speakers and other equipment were installed in two more U-10s, the 2d Air Division had three planes for speaker and leaflet missions. Their flights stepped up after May 1963. By October 22, 2d Air Division aircraft had flown 386 psychological warfare sorties.[63]

In the spring of 1964, aerial psychological operations were often the sole swift means of communication between the government and remote rural peoples. Since part of President Khanh's weakness stemmed from loss of contact with the hinterland, it was proposed to expand the training of Vietnamese in psychological operations. While visiting Saigon, Carl T. Rowan, director of the U.S. Information Agency, was impressed with the potential of these activities. He supported the proposal to enlarge them, which President Johnson approved on April 28.[64]

To support the Vietnamese armed forces in "political warfare," the Vietnamese Air Force set up a general political warfare directorate with headquarters at Tan Son Nhut and officers at each wing. Ten single-engine utility aircraft (six U-6As and four U-17As) were delivered to the Vietnamese Air Force for modification to psychological warfare duty.

Also over the summer of 1964, the 2d Air Division worked with the United States Army Support Command, Saigon, to test a public address system. It consisted of eight 125-watt speakers installed in a Vietnamese H-34 helicopter. Messages could be heard on the ground as the chopper flew at a fairly safe altitude of three thousand feet, but the rotor blades distorted the sound. The 2d Air Division abandoned the project, while the Army continued to maintain seven UH-1B copters fitted with the public address system.[65]

American and Vietnamese aircraft in August 1964 reached a new high of 132 psychological warfare sorties. The Vietnamese were nevertheless more concerned with internal "personnel services" to the soldiers and airmen. Caught up in the conversion to fighter aircraft, the Vietnamese paid scant attention to psychological warfare. Four U-17s were used in and around Saigon, yet only one U-6 was modified due to the complications in installing speakers.[66]

The U-10 section of the 1st Air Commando Squadron was authorized four aircraft and six pilots. An accident claimed one plane in September, and the absence of a planned flow of replacement pilots proved even more serious. In November the U-10 section was down to two pilots, each averaging more than one hundred flying hours during the month.

Psychological warfare sorties by USAF and Vietnamese aircraft totaled 106 in September, 109 in October, 69 in November, and 102 in December 1964. Although four USAF replacement pilots finally joined the U-10 section, the impression was current that "we are piddling with" psychological operations "and not getting anywhere."[67]

That impression applied also to the broader canvas of events in Vietnam.

XXI. End of The Advisory Phase

Viet Cong night outpost and hamlet attacks doubled in intensity during the last half of 1964. They were especially severe in the III and IV Corps Tactical Zones. In October the enemy scored marked successes in the II Corps, which had been almost pacified a few months earlier.[1]

General Moore thought it just a matter of time before the Viet Cong tried to spring a psychologically damaging surprise raid or a mortar bombardment on a major air base. Although the Vietnamese were responsible for interior security and perimeter defense, the 2d Air Division had its own force of one officer and 280 airmen as additional guards.

Proper aircraft dispersal was virtually impossible at the overloaded airfields, thus inviting sabotage or attack. This prompted PACAF to ask CINCPAC in August 1964 to allow one of the two B-57 squadrons to move from Bien Hoa to Takhli. Action was put off until October, when General Harris spoke personally with Admiral Sharp. The latter then permitted half of each squadron to return to Clark Air Base for training. This trimmed the number of B-57s on alert at Bien Hoa to eighteen, but the field remained overcrowded and poorly defended.

How insecure Bien Hoa was became clear on the night of November 1, when a Viet Cong mortar squadron penetrated the Vietnamese perimeter defenses. The ensuing thirty-minute barrage killed four and wounded seventy-two, destroyed five B-57s and one H-43 helicopter, and damaged thirteen B-57s and three H-43s. Vietnamese losses totaled two killed, five wounded, three A-1Hs destroyed, and three A-1Hs and two C-47s damaged. Some houses, a mess hall, vehicles, and fuel tanks were also destroyed or damaged.[2]

The attack provoked discussions on countermeasures at the highest levels of government in Washington. The Joint Chiefs of Staff had previously agreed on positive action against North Vietnam, but differed on the severity, timing, and location of that action. The major point of indecision stemmed from the stand of Ambassador Taylor. He held that the United States could start no strong move against North Vietnam until a stable government existed in Saigon. Consequently, planning for an air campaign had continued on a contingency basis. At the end of his first year in office, President Johnson remarked that his principal advisers had made no unanimous recommendation for air activity against North Vietnam.

As noted earlier, Secretary of Defense McNamara put hard questions to the Joint Chiefs regarding the effects of bombing the ninety-four strategic air targets identified in North Vietnam. In their reply the chiefs accepted CINCPAC assurances. The targets could be attacked without depleting fuel and ordnance needed to meet a Chinese intervention. CINCPAC had already prepared a plan to attack all the targets in twenty days. Since there was no doubt that Hanoi was administering and sustaining the war, General LeMay pushed for Air Force and Navy air strikes on North Vietnam's source of supply. He felt that interdiction would be far more expensive and much less efficient than closing North Vietnam's ports and destroying the supplies by strategic bombing before they started south.

General Greene, the Marine Corps Commandant, had backed LeMay but the other chiefs supported Ambassador Taylor's view. LeMay countered that there could be no sound Saigon government without morale-building offensive operations. The Vietnamese military establishment was the sole stabilizing force. If that collapsed, the United States might well have to fight to get its military advisors and their dependents out of the country.

Now, the Bien Hoa attack spurred the Joint Chiefs toward a strong reprisal. On November 1 they verbally recommended to Secretary McNamara immediate U.S. air strikes against infiltration targets in the Laotian panhandle; airlifting U.S. Army and Marine Corps units to defend Da Nang, Tan Son Nhut, and Bien Hoa; and assembling USAF units within sixty to seventy-two hours for air operations against North Vietnam. The air campaign would consist of an initial B-52 night strike flown from Guam against Phuc Yen airfield, first-light naval air strikes on other airfields and the Hanoi-Haiphong oil storage areas, and rapidly progressing attacks against the entire ninety-four targets listed.

Angered by the Bien Hoa affair, Ambassador Taylor favored limited retaliation against selected North Vietnamese targets by American and Vietnamese aircraft, coupled with a policy statement warning of a similar U.S. response to future incidents. President Johnson's civilian advisers, chiefly Secretaries Rusk and McNamara, counseled patience. The President listened. He was concerned about the upcoming election and about possible Viet Cong action against American dependents in Saigon.

Ruling out an instant response, the President ordered quick replacement of the destroyed and seriously damaged B-57s at Bien Hoa. He further directed a National Security Council working group, chaired by William P. Bundy, to outline political and military options available against North Vietnam. In its early deliberations the Bundy group leaned toward restrained action. In contrast, the Joint Chiefs on December 18 recommended, first, a hard-hitting, fast, "full-squeeze" air campaign against North Vietnam completed in twenty days. Secondly, as a fall-back position, they proposed tightly controlled and gradually increasing air pressure over a two-month period.[3]

Meanwhile on the night of November 6, Air Vice Marshal Nguyen Cao Ky led thirty-two Vietnamese A-1Hs against a Viet Cong camp in Zone D. The mission was a widely announced reprisal for the Bien Hoa incident. According to South Vietnamese intelligence reports, the attack caused five hundred enemy casualties.

On the 16th the Viet Cong troops in Zone D forayed out and battled Vietnamese forces for six hours near Ben Cat. General Khanh personally directed a massive operation in response. One hundred fifteen U.S. Army and

END OF THE ADVISORY PHASE

Vietnamese helicopters lifted twelve battalions of ground troops to the fringe of Zone D near Ben Suc. They killed 163 guerrillas (83 by air) and captured 68.[4]

These and other sizable Vietnamese assaults did not deter the insurgents surrounding Saigon. Severe floods from typhoons in November, together with resurgent communist activity, virtually collapsed governmental authority in the ten central provinces. As the floods receded, the Viet Cong moved in to take almost complete control of the countryside in the populous Quang Ngai and Binh Dinh Provinces. The enemy confined the government's presence to district towns and provincial capital cities.

Vietnamese ground forces could open a road briefly by committing four to six battalions of troops. But as soon as they withdrew, the guerrillas moved in. Constant Viet Cong actions kept the army units off-balance and cost them dearly in men, equipment, and morale. The enemy seemed to easily recruit replacements for his losses. And the National Liberation Front stood ready as a shadow government to seize power when the Saigon regime crumbled.[5]

During a press interview in Saigon on November 21, Ambassador Taylor depicted the principal problem in Vietnam as the dual inability to form a solid national government and to stop Viet Cong reinforcement. The Ambassador realized the military value of air strikes against Laotian infiltration routes and North Vietnamese infiltrator-training areas. He suggested a few selective bombings, but clung to the belief that a sound government in Saigon was the first priority. On the other hand, the Joint Chiefs more and more accepted the USAF position. Stopping Hanoi's support of the insurgency was a prerequisite for a stable Saigon regime.[6]

William Bundy's National Security Council working group outlined three possible courses of action for the United States. One envisioned reprisal attacks, intensified covert operations, resumption of offshore naval patrols, and stepped-up Laotian T-28 attacks. Another called for the "fast/full squeeze" bombing of North Vietnam favored by the Joint Chiefs, which Bundy termed "almost reckless," an invitation to Chinese intervention. The last specified a "slow squeeze" of air attacks on infiltration targets in North Vietnam. All three would give an impression of steady and deliberate pressure-building while permitting the United States to halt at any time. Bundy and Assistant Secretary of Defense John T. McNaughton liked the last option.[7]

Ambassador Taylor arrived in Washington on November 26 to join conferences on strategy. He advocated U.S. actions to restore adequate government in Saigon, refine the counterinsurgency campaign, and convince or compel Hanoi to cease helping the Viet Cong. Taylor set out a three-phase program. The first phase was to consist of heightened covert actions, anti-infiltration attacks in Laos, and reprisal bombing—all to stiffen South Vietnamese morale. The second would afford more air attacks on infiltration objectives in North Vietnam. The third was to ultimately destroy all important fixed targets in North Vietnam. He thought (much like Bundy) that the first phase should start at once.

The Ambassador believed that U.S. aircraft ought to take part in the air operations over Laos (the initial phase of the stepped-up action). This would demonstrate American willingness to share in the risks of acting against North Vietnam. Armed reconnaissance strikes on infiltration routes in the Laotian panhandle would signal a deeper U.S. involvement in the conflict and a resolve to back the governments of both South Vietnam and Laos.

Briefed on December 1, President Johnson accepted the premise that a stable South Vietnamese government was the first essential to end the insurgency. On the 2d he approved the first-phase military actions. He said that subsequent ones would project progressive air bombardment to the north rather than by functional target systems. At first the heavier Laotian T-28 and USAF strikes along Laotian infiltration routes, as well as special covert maritime operations, would be psychological warnings to Hanoi. After an unspecified transitional period, air attacks on North Vietnam would begin against infiltration objectives just beyond the demilitarized zone. Then moving northward to the 19th parallel, the strikes were to eventually hit the Hanoi airfields and POL storage, while naval forces mined and blockaded North Vietnam's ports.[8]

Upon his return to Saigon on December 7, Ambassador Taylor stressed to Vietnamese leaders that Washington wanted political stability above all.[9]

In line with the President's decision, a joint State-Defense message on December 8 instructed the U.S. Ambassador in Vientiane to seek approval for American air strikes on hostile communications in Laos. The go-ahead was given on the 10th and Secretary of Defense McNamara authorized two missions a week, each consisting of four aircraft. This very restricted bombing was nicknamed Barrel Roll.

Weekly, a National Security Council committee was to designate two segments of the line of communications for armed reconnaissance as well as a fixed target for ordnance remaining at the end of the route sweep. Both USAF and USN planes were to play a part, with MACV acting as the local coordinating authority. Publicity was forbidden as were attacks on the Laotian people. Targets of opportunity had to be "unmistakingly military activity of a transient or mobile nature." Fixed installations could be hit only during attacks on clearly identified military convoys and personnel, or as secondary targets. No mission could be launched from Thai bases or carry napalm. Secretary McNamara's explicit and detailed orders left little room for combat commanders to specify tactics, ordnance, routing, and like matters.[10]

Admiral Sharp, CINCPAC, was impressed with the high-level national interest in the armed reconnaissance program. He gave the maiden mission to the F-105 Thunderchiefs of PACAF's 80th Tactical Squadron at Korat, Thailand. Sharp selected a section of Route 8 for the armed sweep and the Nape road bridge as the target for unused ordnance. The fifteen-plane force took off from Da Nang on December 14. Three RF-101s served as pathfinders and damage-assessment craft. Eight F-100s flew combat air patrol to guard against MIG interference. Four F-105s carried 750-pound bombs, 2.75-inch rockets, and 20-mm ammunition. The mission achieved slim results because the heavy ordnance load led to miscalculation of time and distance. Short of fuel, the F-105s made a hurried attack on the bridge and missed it.

Navy planes flew on December 17. Four A-1Hs escorted by eight F-4Bs conducted armed reconnaissance of Routes 121 and 12, with the Ban Boung Bau road bridge as the fixed alternative. The aircraft failed to damage the bridge but destroyed eight buildings at one end.

The next mission sent four F-100s of the 428th Tactical Fighter Squadron along Route 8 on December 21. Lightly armed with CBU-2As and 2.75-inch rockets, the fighters became disoriented after receiving heavy flak, ran low on fuel, and found no secondary target.

Reports on the first two USAF missions disturbed General LeMay. He sent word to General Moore that he expected higher professionalism, even though he recognized that the tight curbs complicated air operations.

To prepare for the fourth mission, PACAF's 44th Tactical Fighter Squadron deployed six F-105s from Okinawa to Da Nang. Four of them reconnoitered Route 23 on December 25, with a strike against the military barracks at Tchepone. The operation went well, though the dive-bombing at Tchepone was inaccurate. During the fifth mission on December 30, four Navy A-1Hs struck the military camp.[11]

Planners for a mission on January 13 chose the Ban Ken bridge, the most important potential checkpoint on Route 7. Aerial photos showed thirty-four antiaircraft guns (37-mm and 57-mm) in place, with up to seventy more firing positions built but not occupied. The planners scheduled an RF-101 as pathfinder and another for bomb damage assessment, eight F-100s carrying CBU-2As for flak suppression, and sixteen F-105s from the 44th and 67th Tactical Fighter Squadrons as strike aircraft. The two flights of F-100s were to fly low-level and abreast across the gunsites to knock them out with cluster bombs. Immediately thereafter the F-105s would attack the bridge. Each of the first eight F-105s were to drop eight 750-pound bombs. This would be followed by eight F-105s loaded with six bombs and two AGM-12B Bullpup air-to-ground missiles. An Air America C-123 was to serve as airborne control for rescue helicopters.

The F-100s pummeled the gun positions but some firing continued. The first wave of F-105s cut the bridge with their sixty-four bombs. The F-100s and the second wave of F-105s made multiple runs on the gunsites, the mixed ordnance of the F-105s requiring at least three passes to expend. Moreover, the Thunderchiefs had to descend into flak range to control their missiles, and one plane was downed. An F-100 on its fifth pass was also shot down. Four other aircraft were damaged.

General Moore said that poor judgment was displayed in the attack. To escape the losses, the planes should have broken off the engagement after knocking out the bridge.[12]

While it seemed impossible for ground transportation to bypass the Ban Ken bridge, the communists within three days converted the top of a dam just upriver into a traffic route. Press reports of the two lost aircraft prompted Senator Wayne L. Morse to charge that the air operation violated the 1962 Geneva agreements on Laos.[13]

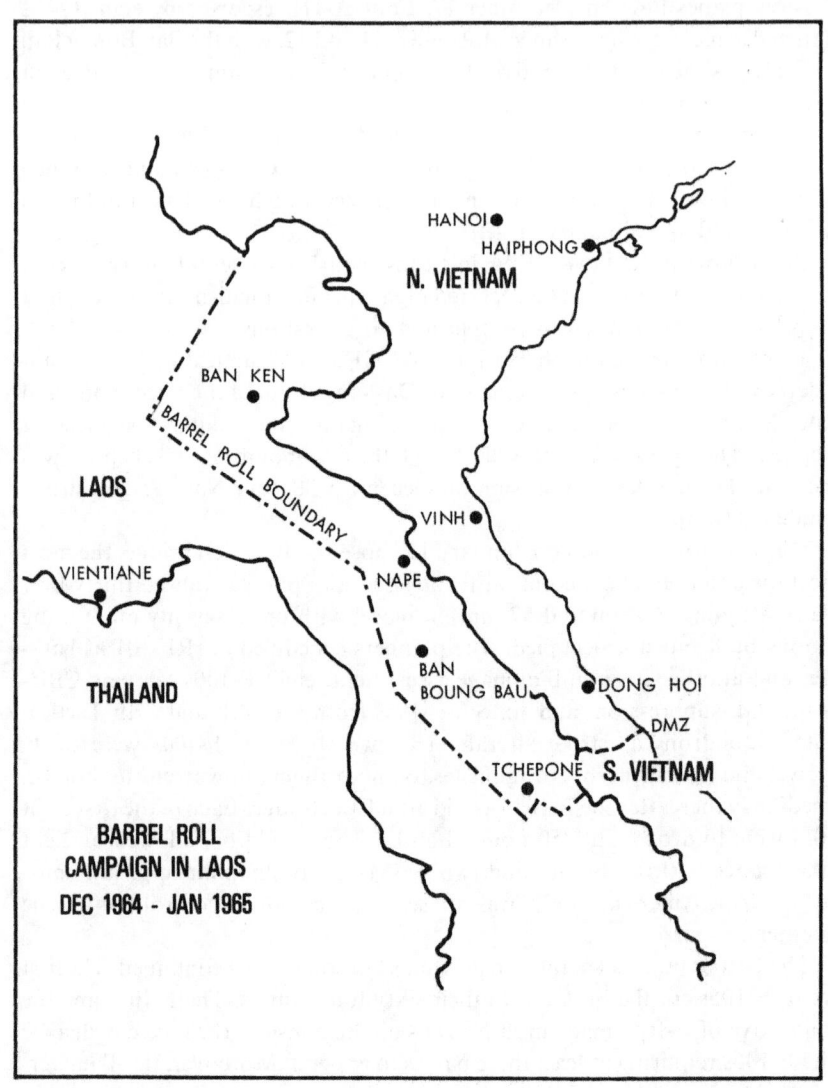

END OF THE ADVISORY PHASE

Armed reconnaissance sweeps by Seventh Fleet aircraft on January 2 and 10, 1965, detected no enemy. On the 15th, as six A-1Hs reconnoitered Route 23 at night, the flight leader became separated from the flare plane and wandered west of the road. He sighted and attacked moving trucks and also adjacent buildings that turned out to be the friendly village of Ban Tang Vai. No further secondary targets were assigned for night missions.[14]

Admiral Sharp near the end of January took a close look at this relatively small interdiction campaign, conducted at least risk and under tight control from Washington. He concluded that the program could be better managed from Laos. He insisted that militarily effective interdiction had to be constantly and completely responsive to the tactical situation. General Harris, the PACAF commander, agreed that the missions were too few to sway Hanoi. Still, they may have imparted political strength to the Laotian government at a critical juncture. In late January and early February, an armed coup was defeated.[15]

Meanwhile in South Vietnam, General Khanh and several associates had seized power from the provisional civil government on December 20, 1964. Ambassador Taylor strongly protested and after that the relations between him and Khanh were strained. Taylor was apparently concerned that the feeble Saigon government might yield to elements clamoring for a cease-fire and coalition with the National Liberation Front. He may therefore have hinted that U.S. advisors were about to take command of the Vietnamese armed forces. In any event, the unstable conditions in the country encouraged the Viet Cong. They increasingly turned from hit-and-run guerrilla tactics to more conventional mobile warfare by regular units. This pushed the United States into stronger support of the counterinsurgency.[16]

Secretary of Defense McNamara had already made clear that the conflict was chiefly a ground war in which aviation could make only secondary contributions. While this strategy precluded the full use of tactical air power,[17] the rather small Vietnamese and U.S. air operations were central to saving the Vietnamese ground forces from piecemeal defeat. On December 9, for example, A-1Hs from the Vietnamese 516th Fighter Squadron struck a Viet Cong force and left thirty-three enemy dead. The force on December 7 had attacked the An Lao district headquarters in Binh Dinh Province and ambushed government relief troops. In the three-day battle the foe inflicted battle losses of twenty-eight killed, fifty wounded, and twenty-two missing.

Also on December 9 a Viet Cong battalion assaulted and overran a government battalion command post and 105-mm howitzer platoon near Tam Ky in Quang Tin Province. A USAF captain joined the eighteen strike sorties flown by the 516th Fighter Squadron against the hill position. All the strikes were directed by an O-1A pilot and Vietnamese observer who were in the air for ten hours. Direct hits on the artillery site exploded ammunition and killed enemy gunners. The last flight of four A-1Hs landed at Da Nang after sunset when the ceiling was under five hundred feet and visibility less than a mile. Government troops retook the ground and confirmed 162 Viet Cong killed (85 by air). Friendly losses totaled 26 killed and thirty-three wounded.[18]

During the night of December 10, two Viet Cong battalions struck outposts at Long My in Chuong Thien Province and ambushed relief forces. A U.S. Army L-19 and a USAF O-1F located the ambush and put four covering A-1Es on the camouflaged foxholes. U.S. Army helicopters from Soc Trang held the enemy until Vietnamese in A-1Hs arrived and delivered ordnance in the face of intense ground fire. One A-1H was downed, three A-1Hs and five helicopters damaged. By fine teamwork the A-1Hs and armed helicopters killed about four hundred of the fifteen hundred enemy troops, and probably saved a government battalion and a regional force company from being overwhelmed.[19]

Viet Cong night attacks on hamlets and outposts soared to a new high. A total of ninety-six incidents took place over the last ten days of December, drawing flare and strike aircraft. The planes forced the foe to break off the assault in ninety-four of the cases. Still under test, AC-47 gunships joined the air alerts and performed well. On the night of December 24, for example, an AC-47 used its miniguns to blast guerrillas off the wall of a fort under siege.[20]

At night on December 27, two North Vietnamese regiments raided the hamlet of Binh Gia. The next morning a reinforced ranger battalion, aided by three armed helicopters, tried without success to relieve the hamlet. That evening the Viet Cong hit the rangers at the nearby town of Ngai Giao but were driven off. On the 29th, twenty-four U.S. Army UH-1Bs, protected by fifteen armed UH-1Bs, lifted two other ranger companies to a landing area near Binh Gia. Small-arms and machinegun fire claimed three of the helicopters. One ranger company fought its way out, the second was overrun.

The defeat seemed to have stemmed from the absence of preplanned coordination of tactical air support for the heliborne operation. Another factor was the late request for fighters, made only after the loss of the three helicopters. Eight A-1E sorties covered the downed UH-1Bs. Four Vietnamese H-34 helicopters carried ammunition into the area and evacuated wounded. A C-47 flareship lighted the scene through the night.

Escorted by fifteen armed UH-1Bs, twenty-six UH-1Bs lifted the 2d and 4th Marine Battalions into the zone. Eight helicopters were hit and one exploded, killing the crew. Finally on the afternoon of December 30, four A-1Es and five A-1Hs responded to requests. The strike aircraft blasted two spots in the rubber forests around Binh Gia that reportedly sheltered two Viet Cong battalions. At the same time, H-34s evacuated thirty-four killed and forty-nine wounded men. A C-47, four A-1Es, and one AC-47 furnished night illumination and fire support.[21]

The 4th Marine Battalion battled its way into the rubber forest on December 31, and was soon surrounded by the enemy (identified from captured documents as the 48th Main Force Viet Cong Regiment). The Marine commander radioed the USAF forward air controller overhead for air support. Four A-1Es responded and hit enemy positions with napalm and general purpose bombs. In the afternoon, eight A-1Es were scrambled and sent to the scene. But the senior ground commander ordered them returned to Bien Hoa, because air support had not been requested through Vietnamese army channels.

END OF THE ADVISORY PHASE

Armed helicopters tried to launch strikes later that day. However, they learned from U.S. Marine Corps advisors with the surrounded battalion that the thick branches of the rubber trees absorbed the rockets and machinegun fire from the air. Attacking at dusk and using massed automatic weapons, the Viet Cong overpowered the 4th Marine Battalion. All through the night of the 31st, three C-47s, two C-123s, one AC-47, and four A-1Hs supplied flare/fire support. Even so, just 232 of the 532 men of the 4th Marine Battalion managed to straggle back to Binh Gia.[22]

General Khanh took personal charge of a large operation set afoot in Phuoc Tuy Province on January 1, 1965. C-123s flew the 1st and 3d Airborne Battalions from Tan Son Nhut to Vung Tau, then helicopters whisked them to the battle area. On January 2 helicopters transported the 7th Airborne Battalion directly from Bien Hoa. Tactical fighters supported continuing operations with cover and escort, landing-zone preparations, and strikes on enemy positions.

On the 5th of January, eight A-1Es were each loaded with one Lazy Dog XM-44 cannister and normal high-explosive ordnance. The aircraft employed the Lazy Dog missiles against Viet Cong troops firing at U.S. Army helicopter observers. Government troops kept clear of the Lazy Dog zones, but U.S. Army air observers reported that after the drops they no longer received ground fire. An intelligence report stated that the Viet Cong carried away from the strike areas fifteen oxcart loads of dead and wounded.[23]

At General Khanh's order, government battalions with tanks and armored vehicles continued to swing through the safer areas of Phuoc Tuy Province. From January 10 through February 15, a small air support operations center managed the flights aiding the massive sweeps. The operations achieved little, for the Viet Cong evaded ground contact.[24]

Analysis of the Binh Gia defeat revealed a failure to use available fixed-wing air support properly. Armed helicopters were unable to provide the needed firepower. As the MACV J-3 reported, "the armed UH-1B did not possess heavy enough ordnance to destroy the VC in prepared positions or deter their assault, since they were concealed under a dense canopy of trees."[25]

Meanwhile, an incident in downtown Saigon brought the United States to the verge of direct all-out action. On Christmas Eve 1964 a 300-pound charge exploded in the Brink Hotel (bachelor officers' quarters for U.S. advisors), killing two Americans while injuring sixty-four Americans and forty-three Vietnamese. Admiral Sharp and the Joint Chiefs recommended an immediate reprisal. On December 29 President Johnson ruled against it.

The Brink Hotel explosion, a direct attack against and an open challenge to the United States, was ominous, but the battle at Binh Gia was potentially disastrous. To U.S. officials in Saigon it was a "highly visible" defeat of serious proportions. On December 31 Ambassador Taylor reversed his thinking. Bolstered by Deputy Ambassador U. Alexis Johnson and General Westmoreland, he sent a joint message to Washington. It advocated American air action against North Vietnam despite the persistent weakness of the Saigon government.[26]

THE ADVISORY YEARS

(Top) Remains of a B-57 destroyed by Viet Cong mortar attack on Bien Hoa on Nov. 1, 1964.

(Center and bottom) Brink BOQ area, following the terrorist attack on December 24, 1964.

Courtesy: U.S. Army

Courtesy: U.S. Army

Attention then turned to the air strike aircraft on hand. Attack planes in Vietnam numbered forty-eight USAF A-1Es and ninety-two A-1Hs of the Vietnamese Air Force. This combined force could fly about sixty combat and thirty training sorties a day. Air Vice Marshal Ky's need to have an elite "Palace Guard" flight of standby A-1Hs at Tan Son Nhut constrained Vietnamese combat sorties. These planes were piloted by highly trained, screened, and politically dependable personnel who routinely flew strike missions in the III and IV Corps areas. However, assignments to thwart coups and to control dissidence often diverted them from action against the Viet Cong.

Although individual Vietnamese strike crews performed valiantly, the growing independence of unit commanders diluted the control of the air operations centers. Typically, fifty percent of the aircraft were held on five-hour ground alert. A squadron deciding to fly would call for a target about an hour before the end of its ground alert and receive a set of coordinates for attack, usually in a "free-strike" zone. Hence it was difficult to scramble or to redirect aircraft to meet emergencies.

Early in January 1965 the Vietnamese 62d Tactical Wing and a detachment of the 516th Fighter Squadron's A-1Hs deployed from Pleiku to Nha Trang, where work was to start on a new runway in February. The move stationed these strike aircraft too far away to properly support the critical highland provinces, including Pleiku and Kontum.[27]

Ambassador Taylor now wanted to use the USAF B-57s at Bien Hoa in combat. He also wished to put off indefinitely the plan to form a fifth and sixth Vietnamese fighter squadron, so that the Vietnamese could focus on operations in lieu of training.[28] PACAF on January 12, 1965, suggested that heavier air demands argued for greater air assets. It asked for thirteen tactical strike squadrons in Vietnam (seven to be USAF jet units), extra USAF air liaison officers and tactical air control parties to extend direct air support nets to province and sector levels, and at least 175 USAF and Vietnamese O-1s—more if continuous air reconnaissance was authorized.[29]

Defending the role of U.S. Army helicopter gunships, General Westmoreland said that they had "performed magnificently" at Binh Gia. At a briefing on January 13, he asked if stepping up air firepower made sense in Vietnam. In other words, were there significant and vulnerable targets in Viet Cong sanctuary areas and how could they be brought under attack? General DePuy, the MACV J-3, addressed the question in a paper that was largely the work of USAF Col. Alan C. Edmunds, Deputy Assistant Chief of Staff J-3 for Air.

Targets were available, the study said, and lifting the curbs on using USAF aircraft in the country would expand air power. This could best be done by drawing on Guam-based B-52 bombers as well as USN carrier aircraft on South Vietnamese offshore stations, for air facilities in Vietnam were scarce and overcrowded. The Vietnamese ground forces were apparently unable to give a high degree of security against Viet Cong attack of air bases. And it was hard to haul ordnance and aviation fuel to Vietnamese airfields.[30]

THE ADVISORY YEARS

Air Staff analysts agreed with part of the study. Calling on aircraft outside the country would indeed alleviate the airfield security problem. As early as December 9, 1964, General LeMay had suggested sending U.S. ground combat units into Vietnam for air base defense. The Navy and Marine Corps had demurred, saying that it was contrary to national policy. The Army had objected on the ground that four divisions would be needed to defend eighteen operating sites. As for the supply system, there was no doubt that conveying POL and ordnance was cumbersome, slow, and risky. This was especially true when done by barges, lighters, and trucks requiring security guards.

On the other side of the coin, using aircraft located outside the country could hamper attempts to improve air base security and Vietnamese air facilities. Both were long overdue. Although the B-52 bombers were unmatched in all-weather, heavy saturation attacks, the long flights from Guam would be expensive. Furthermore, using these strategic bombers would reduce SAC's worldwide deterrent posture. While the interest of General Westmoreland in tactical air was encouraging, he failed to understand 2d Air Division and PACAF hopes for building a well-rounded air command, coordination, and control structure in Vietnam.[31]

On January 24, 1965, General Moore advised General Westmoreland that the fastest way to bolster air power was to make full use of the USAF resources now in the country. Moore believed that the most compelling needs were to let USAF jets fly missions in South Vietnam, do away with the requirement to carry a Vietnamese observer or trainee on operational missions, and remove helicopters from air bases to allow an expansion of facilities.[32]

Some optimistic signs emerged from the lingering debate on air demands. A measure of political stability in Saigon seemed to give the Vietnamese armed forces confidence and initiative. A MACV press release told of air attacks killing about twenty-five hundred Viet Cong in November and December 1964. Given these indications, were more strike planes really required?[33]

Vietnamese and USAF A-1s flew 2,339 combat sorties in January 1965, filling every request for close air support. The combined air forces flew a total of 4,550 sorties, yet could not meet fifty percent of the requests for all types of air activity. Estimates showed that all of them could have been met, had there been no operational restrictions.[34]

In a saturation test during January 19-21, Vietnamese and USAF A-1s dropped eight hundred tons of bombs on preplanned targets in the Boi Loi woods of Zone D. Ranch Hand C-123s then began a massive defoliation program in Boi Loi to cover forty-eight square miles of dense forest hiding a key Viet Cong base. The operation tied up many of the combined strike aircraft. On January 26 in a separate action, two government battalions surrounded an enemy battalion near Ap Bac. Helicopter gunship and A-1 strikes accounted for half of the estimated four hundred fifty insurgents killed that day.[35]

Late in January the Joint Chiefs secured approval for using USAF jet aircraft in a strike role within South Vietnam—if Ambassador Taylor agreed in advance to each mission, and if these strikes could not be carried out by

END OF THE ADVISORY PHASE

Vietnamese A-1s. According to this formula, Taylor could authorize jet air strikes solely to save American lives or to spoil huge Viet Cong attacks like the one at Binh Gia. He could do this only if the air support operations center certified that conventional aircraft were unavailable, and if a corps tactical zone commander, the Vietnamese Joint General Staff, and MACV all thought the action necessary.[36]

As for air strikes on North Vietnam, President Johnson rejected them in January 1965 despite his growing conviction that the feeble Saigon government needed help of some sort to survive.[37] Trials and tribulations, including militant Buddhist opposition, prompted CIA Director McCone to expect Khanh to fall from power and a serious political crisis to follow.[38]

On January 23, in a speech interpreted by some observers as a bid for negotiations, William P. Bundy suggested a diplomatic meeting similar to the 1954 Geneva accords as "the answer" for a secure and independent South Vietnam. Five days later, Presidential Assistant McGeorge Bundy informed President Johnson that he and Secretary McNamara were "pretty well convinced that our current policy can lead only to disastrous defeat." The preferred alternatives were to "use our military power in the Far East and to force a change of Communist policy," or to "deploy all our resources" along "a track of negotiation, aimed at salvaging what little can be preserved with no major addition to our present military risks." Secretary of State Rusk opposed both options. "The consequences of both escalation and withdrawal are so bad," he said, "that we simply must find a way of making our present policy work."

Not sure whether to support Saigon more vigorously or to disengage from a losing proposition, the President on February 4 sent a fact-finding party headed by McGeorge Bundy to Saigon. The party's arrival coincided with a visit to Hanoi by Soviet Premier Aleksei N. Kosygin. Since Khrushchev's departure from power in October 1964, Kosygin had tried to restore closer Russian ties with Hanoi. He and a sizable Moscow delegation that included top Soviet air force officials reached Hanoi on February 6.

According to the Chinese, Kosygin hoped to persuade Hanoi to halt military aid to the Viet Cong as a precondition to negotiations (as William Bundy seemed to have suggested). But in McCone's opinion, Kosygin sensed an imminent Viet Cong victory and wanted the Soviet Union to share in it. Kosygin would probably offer more economic and military aid and encourage stepped-up warfare in South Vietnam. Consequently, McCone proposed that the United States start air attacks on targets in North Vietnam. These would commence at the 17th parallel and work progressively northward.[39]

Conflicting signals stopped on Sunday morning, February 7, 1965. Viet Cong mortar squads and demolition teams attacked the small U.S. advisory detachment in II Corps, four and one-half miles north of Pleiku. In addition they struck Camp Holloway, headquarters of the U.S. Army 52d Aviation Battalion, also near Pleiku. The joint assaults killed eight Americans and wounded 104, destroyed five Army UH-1B helicopters and two CV-2 transports, three USAF

O-1Fs, and one Vietnamese O-1F. Moreover the teams damaged the main building of the advisory detachment.[40]

Bundy, Westmoreland, and Taylor jointly sent from Saigon their recommendation for a reprisal strike and President Johnson ordered an instant air response. That afternoon USN aircraft, and on the 8th Vietnamese and USAF planes, hit enemy military barracks near Dong Hoi in an operation called Flaming Dart. At the same time, PACAF air transports commenced to lift U.S. Marine Corps light antiaircraft missile units from Okinawa to Da Nang and to evacuate U.S. dependents from South Vietnam.[41]

The Viet Cong struck on the 10th near Qui Nhon, taking twenty-three American and seven South Vietnamese lives. On the following day, USAF, USN, and VNAF aircraft (in Flaming Dart II) pounded troop barracks in the North Vietnamese panhandle. The Joint Chiefs quickly ordered the deployment to South Vietnam and Thailand of four and one-half USAF tactical squadrons from bases in Japan, Okinawa, and the Philippines, and the movement of thirty B-52s to Guam.[42]

South Vietnamese control deteriorated in all of the corps tactical zones as Viet Cong action exploded. On February 8 a major enemy force crossed Route 19 between Pleiku and Qui Nhon. The crossing occurred, even though four A-1Es dropped Lazy Dogs and killed about one hundred of the enemy. The attackers then enveloped and damaged two battalions of the 40th Regiment and a troop of M-115 armored personnel carriers in Vinh Binh Province. That night an AC-47 poured 20,500 7.62-mm rounds into the area, killing around 250 enemy soldiers.

To shore up the II Corps defense, General Moore ordered eight A-1Es to Qui Nhon where conditions were "unsafe in every respect." Staying close to the scene of action, each pilot flew at least three strike sorties a day and significantly helped to blunt the enemy offensive.[43]

On February 13 President Johnson gave the green light to measured and limited air attacks on North Vietnam. Called Rolling Thunder and planned for swift execution, the strikes were delayed for two weeks by political and military turmoil in Saigon and by bad weather.

The capital was directly and immediately threatened by the Viet Cong 9th Division, which had no less than two well-armed regiments under forest cover in Phuoc Tuy Province. The mystery of how these troops were getting modern weapons was solved on February 16. A U.S. Army helicopter pilot discovered, and Vietnamese A-1Hs sank, a steel-hulled vessel at Vung Ro Bay. An investigation turned up one hundred tons of arms and ammunition in a nearby cove at Cap Varella. The U.S. Seventh Fleet at once started naval patrols to stop these deliveries.

General Westmoreland wanted to send B-57 light bombers against the Viet Cong 9th Division base camps in Phuoc Tuy Province, which had been pinpointed by infrared reconnaissance. Securing emergency authority on February 17, he planned to launch the planes on the 19th.

END OF THE ADVISORY PHASE

On that day, dissident military leaders revolted against General Khanh. Their troops seized Saigon, and took part of Tan Son Nhut to ground Ky's anticoup air force. But Ky got his planes in the air, as C-47s brought loyal troops from the I Corps to clear Saigon of the rebels. The Armed Forces Council then removed Khanh and exiled him.

At the height of the coup crisis in Saigon on the afternoon of February 19, four B-57s from Bien Hoa flew the first open USAF mission in South Vietnam as they bombed Viet Cong base camps in Phuoc Tuv. The aircraft struck again during February 21-24, while Ky kept most of the VNAF A-1Hs on countercoup alert and out of combat.[44]

Judging on February 21 that the United States was not "fully committed to winning the war in Vietnam," General Westmoreland was ready to change the nature of the American involvement. He would make more use of jet aircraft within South Vietnam, restore U.S. markings to American-manned A-1Es, and abolish the requirement for Vietnamese observers in American planes.

Enemy action on February 24 involved the elite communist battalion that had apparently just arrived in the central highlands. The battalion surrounded a ranger company and a Civilian Irregular Defense Group company on Route 19 in the An Khe valley near the Mang Yang pass (where the Viet Minh had wiped out a French mobile group in 1954). General Westmoreland used his emergency authority to commit USAF jet aircraft in an all-American relief effort. F-100s, B-57s, and A-1Es covered and supported U.S. Army UH-1Bs that rescued the surrounding men. The covering attacks by the 613th Tactical Fighter Squadron F-100s, 405th Tactical Wing B-57s, and 602d Fighter Commando Squadron A-1Es cost the enemy 150 men killed. They also allowed the helicopters to land three times in the area without a single casualty. The copters evacuated the 220 officers and men who, according to Col. Theodore C. Mataxis, U.S. Army II Corps advisor, would otherwise have been lost.[45]

The employment of B-57 and F-100 jets marked the end of the long U.S. combat advisory phase and the beginning of direct and open American action in the Vietnam War. On March 1 the new commander in chief of the Vietnamese armed forces, Maj. Gen. Tran Van Minh, established the Vietnamese Air Force air request net as the primary means to obtain immediate air support for all regular and paramilitary operations. He further removed the restriction that only a Vietnamese forward air controller could mark targets for air strikes.[46]

After approval by higher headquarters, the Joint Chiefs of Staff on March 9 directed that U.S. aircraft could be used for combat operations in South Vietnam. No strikes were permitted from Thai airfields, and American aircraft were not to accept missions that the Vietnamese Air Force could carry out. But the planes now boldly displayed U.S. insignia, and a Vietnamese airman was no longer required to be aboard in combat.[47]

The United States Air Force advisory effort spanned the decade between 1955 and early 1965, from the time the United States formally took over the training of the Vietnamese from the French until American aircraft first openly engaged in combat. During this interval the Vietnamese Air Force expanded

THE ADVISORY YEARS

from a few hundred to over ten thousand men. Its five squadrons of obsolete French and American planes at two air bases swelled to fourteen squadrons and almost three hundred more modern aircraft at five major air bases. In addition the Vietnamese Air Force forged a chain of command mirroring that of its American advisors. Most of these changes took place through the final three years of the period when the threat from the north grew ever more serious.

The U.S. Air Force experienced parallel growth in Southeast Asia during the decade. In the late 1950s there were 68 airmen stationed in Vietnam and 44 in Thailand. From 1961 on, these numbers gradually rose and on the eve of Americanization of the war stood at 6,604 and 2,943 respectively. By February 1965 the Air Force had 222 planes in South Vietnam and 83 in Thailand. Seventy percent of those in South Vietnam were clustered around the Saigon area, operating from Tan Son Nhut or Bien Hoa Air Base. The remainder were up north, primarily at Da Nang. One-third of all these aircraft were C-123 transports, operating for the most part out of Tan Son Nhut. Reconnaissance missions also originated from Tan Son Nhut, flown by RF-101s and RB-57s on temporary assignment. This Saigon base further housed a handful of F-102s for air defense. The attack fleet of forty-eight A-1Es for in-country strikes was positioned at nearby Bien Hoa, also the headquarters for the forward air control mission performed by twenty-two 0-1Fs. From Da Nang the Air Force operated one transport squadron and one temporary duty squadron of F-100s for missions in Laos. A sprinkling of support aircraft rounded out the total.

The USAF presence in Thailand was still small at the start of 1965. Air defense of the country was provided by four F-102s from Don Muang Airport outside Bangkok. Farther up-country, a squadron of F-105s at Udorn Royal Thai Air Force Base (RTAFB) and another at Takhli RTAFB flew against the infiltration routes in the Laotian panhandle. At Udorn RTAFB, just south of the Laotian capital, twenty T-28s worked to stem the Pathet Lao tide in northern Laos. These were supported by eight air rescue helicopters from the same base. None of these aircraft took part in operations in Vietnam.

Despite this sizable swelling of personnel and aircraft between 1955 and 1965, the U.S. advisory mission failed to end Hanoi's support of the insurgency in South Vietnam and Laos. The decision early in 1965 to replace advisors with combat troops recognized two facts that had come clear in late 1964: infiltration from north into South Vietnam was growing rather than tapering off, and the government of South Vietnam (still unstable since the assassination of Diem) could not cope with the situation. U.S. policymakers saw the confluence of these two factors spelling defeat for the South unless a new approach was taken. Thus the purely advisory function was abandoned in favor of direct U.S. air and ground participation in the conflict. The USAF units in place early in 1965 would form the nucleus for the coming buildup.

Appendices

Appendix 1

Growth of Major United States Air Force and
Vietnamese Air Force Units to February 1965

I. VIETNAM

	USAF	VNAF
Bien Hoa Air Base		
1955 June		Air Force Depot transferred here from Hanoi.
1956 June		1st Fighter Squadron organized, consisting of twenty-five F-8F Bearcats.
1961 November	Farm Gate arrives. Designated Detachment 2A, 4400th Combat Crew Training Squadron. Made up of four SC-47s, four RB-26s, eight T-28s, and 155 men on temporary duty.	
	Detachment 9, 13th Air Force, established to support USAF units here.	
1962 April	Farm Gate renamed Detachment 2A, 1st Commando Group (TAC).	
May	Two RB-26s of Project Blackwatch join Farm Gate.	
June	Detachment 9, 13th Air Force, replaced by 6221st Air Base Squadron.	
1963 January	Farm Gate increased to nineteen B-26s, thirteen T-28s, six C/HC-47s, and four U-10s, plus 275 men. Some aircraft deployed to Pleiku and Soc Trang.	514th Fighter Squadron (A-1Hs) replaces 1st Fighter Squadron
July	34th Tactical Group organized. 6221st Air Base Squadron renamed 34th Air Base Squadron and placed under 34th Tactical Group.	
July	19th Tactical Air Support Squadron activated under 34th Tactical Group. By August has twenty-two O-1s. Six of these go to Can Tho.	

THE ADVISORY YEARS

	USAF	VNAF
	Farm Gate renamed 1st Air Commando Squadron and assigned to 34th Tactical Group.	
October		518th Fighter Squadron (A-1Hs) activated.
1964 May-June	Farm Gate T-28s and B-26s replaced with A-1Es.	
June		23d Tactical Wing formed. Incorporates 514th, 518th, 520th (newly formed) Fighter Squadrons, and the 112th Liaison Squadron.
August	Thirty-six B-57s arrive from Clark Air Base. Eighteen return to Clark in October.	
October	A second Farm Gate squadron (602d Fighter Commando Squadron) organized and assigned to the 34th Tactical Group. Same type of aircraft (A-1Es) and missions as the 1st Air Commando Squadron.	520th Fighter Squadron activated.
	Detachment 4, Pacific Air Rescue Service, established with three H-43Fs.	

Can Tho Airfield

	USAF	VNAF
1962 June	Detachment 3, 6220th Air Base Squadron, established.	
1963 July	Detachment 2, 33d Tactical Group, replaces Detachment 3, 6220th Air Base Squadron.	
1964 January	$2.5 million approved for new airfield.	
April	Detachment 3, 619th Tactical Control Squadron (5th Tactical Control Group) organized.	74th Tactical Wing organized.
December		520th Fighter Squadron flies five A-1Hs from here during the day, and returns to Bien Hoa at night.

Da Nang Air Base

	USAF	VNAF
1955 November		1st Liaison Squadron moves here from Hue.
1957 November		Air Force Support Base 4 activated.

272

	USAF	VNAF
1961 October		2d Helicopter Squadron activated.
December		3d Liaison Squadron activated.
1962 January	1 Air Suport Operations Center formed. A Combat Reporting Post radar installed (Detachment 3, 5th Tactical Control Squadron).	
	Detachment 11, 13th Air Force, organized.	
	Two Mule Train C-123s detached here from Tan Son Nhut.	
June	Second Mule Train squadron (777th) established here with sixteen C-123s under Tactical Air Force Transport Squadron Provisional-2 (Tan Son Nhut). Twelve aircraft remain here, and four go to Don Muang, Thailand.	
	Detachment 11, 13th Air Force, renamed 6222d Air Base Squadron.	
December	Detachment 2, 8th Aerial Squadron organized.	
1963 January		213th Helicopter Squadron replaces 2d Helicopter Squadron.
		110th Liaison Squadron replaces 1st Liaison Squadron.
		114th Liaison Squadron replaces 3d Liaison Squadron (moves to Pleiku later in this year).
		Air Base 41 replaces Air Force Support Base 4 to support VNAF units.
July	6222d Air Base Squadron becomes the 23d Air Base Group (2d Air Division).	
	777th Troop Carrier Squadron redesignated as 311th Troop Carrier Squadron with permanent station here.	

THE ADVISORY YEARS

	USAF	VNAF
1964 January		41st Tactical wing established, incorporating all VNAF squadrons here.
February		516th Fighter Squadron moves here from Nha Trang.
April	Detachment 1, 619th Tactical Control Squadron, organized.	
May		217th Helicopter Squadron established. Moves to Tan San Nhut in July 1964 and to Binh Tuy in December 1965.
June	F-102s on 10-day deployment for air defense.	
July	HU-16s on temporary assignment from Clark Air Base.	
August	Six F-102s here from Clark Air Base for air defense.	
August-December .	F-100s from the 27th Tactical Fighter Wing (Cannon Air Force Base) and the 401st and 405th Tactical Fighter Wings (England Air Force Base) rotate in and out in response to the Gulf of Tonkin incident.	
December	Six F-105s arrive from Okinawa. Detachment 2, 18th Tactical Fighter Wing, established.	
1965 February	Twelve F-100s of the 3d Tactical Fighter Wing fly from here in attacks on Chap Le Barracks and in Flaming Dart.	

Nha Trang Air Base

	USAF	VNAF
1951 June		Air Training Center established.
1955 July		2d Liaison Squadron transferred from French to Vietnamese.
1959 October		2d Liaison Squadron moves to Tan Son Nhut.
1961 December		2d Fighter Squadron (T-28s) activated.
1962 February	Detachment 12, 13th Air Force, organized.	

	USAF	VNAF
June	Detachment 12, 13th Air Force, becomes 6223d Air Base Squadron.	
September		12th Air Base Squadron organized.
December	Detachment 4, 8th Aerial Port Squadron, organized.	
1963 January		2d Fighter Squadron renamed 516th Fighter Squadron.
July	37th Air Base Squadron (33d Tactical Group) replaces 6223d Air Base Squadron.	
1964 February	Three C-123s and three C-47s here to support Army Special Forces.	516th Fighter Squadron moves to Da Nang.
June		116th Liaison Squadron activated (O-1s).
1965 January		62d Tactical Wing moves here from Pleiku.

Pleiku Air Base

	USAF	VNAF
1962 March	II Air Support Operations Center fully operational.	
June	Detachment 1, 6220th Air Base Squadron, formed.	
December	Detachment 3, 8th Aerial Port Squadron, activated.	Air Base 62 activated.
1964 March		Air Base 62 becomes 62d Tactical Wing.
1965 January		62d Tactical Wing moves to Nha Trang.

Tan Son Nhut Air Base

	USAF	VNAF
1955 July		1st Transportation Squadron (C-47s) organized.
September		Air Force Communications Section formed.
1956 February		Air Traffic and Weather Section formed.
June		2d Transportation Squadron (C-47s) organized.

THE ADVISORY YEARS

	USAF	VNAF
		Headquarters Viëtnamese Air Force opens here.
1957 June		1st Helicopter Squadron (H-19s) organized.
1959 October		2d Liaison Squadron (L-19s) moves here from Nha Trang.
1961 October	Detachment 2, 507th Tactical Control Group, establishes a mobile Control and Reporting Post to train Vietnamese in the Tactical Air Control System.	
	Pipe Stem reconnaissance operations start with four RF-101s and a Photo Processing Cell.	
November	Detachments 7 and 8, 13th Air Force, organized to support USAF units.	
1962 January	Mule Train arrives. Twelve C-123s and 243 people on temporary duty to provide airlift. Two aircraft sent to Da Nang. Unit becomes permanent in June as the 776th Troop Carrier Squadron.	
	Ranch Hand arrives. Three C-123s for defoliation.	
	Joint Operations Center set up consisting of a permanent Combat Reporting Center to monitor air traffic and deploy fighters. Subordinate Air Support Operations Centers established at Da Nang and Pleiku.	
	Pipe Stem F-101s depart, leaving Photo Processing Cell (now designated as Detachment 1, 15th Technical Reconnaissance Squadron).	
February		Air Force Communications Section renamed Air Force Communications Squadron.
March	Hilo Hattie arrives, a C-54 fitted with infrared equipment for reconnaissance. Remains here until February 1963.	

276

	USAF	VNAF
	Four F-102s deployed here for air defense. Later, F-102s alternate with Navy AD-5Qs in 6-week tours of air defense duty. Operation moved to Clark Air Base in May 1963.	
April	Detachment 3, Pacific Air Rescue Center, established.	
May	Mule Train and Ranch Hand C-123s consolidated under Tactical Air Force Transport Squadron Provisional-2.	
	Two RB-57s on temporary duty from Japan.	
June	Detachment 7, 13th Air Force, renamed Headquarters 2d Advanced Echelon.	
September	Headquarters 6492d Combat Cargo Group (Troop Carrier) organized and attached to the 315th Air Division (Japan).	
October	2d Air Division replaces 2d Advanced Echelon.	
December	Headquarters 315th Troop Carrier Group (Assault) replaces 6492d Combat Cargo Group. Able Mable Reconnaissance Task Force moves its four RF-101s here from Don Muang, Thailand.	293d Helicopter Squadron activated.
1963 January		413th Air Transport Squadron replaces 1st Transport Squadron.
		415th Air Transport Squadron replaces 2d Transport Squadron.
		211th Helicopter Squadron (H-34s) replaces 1st Helicopter Squadron.
		112th Liaison Squadron (L-19s) replaces 2d Liaison Squadron. Moves to Bien Hoa in June 1964.
February	Brave Bull C-97 replaces C-54 for reconnaissance.	
March	Two RF-101s added to Able Mable.	

THE ADVISORY YEARS

	USAF	VNAF
April	13th Reconnaissance Technical Squadron activated.	
July	33d Tactical Group organized. Detachment 1 consolidates all reconnaissance units under its control.	
	309th and 310th (old 776th Troop Carrier Squadron) Troop Carrier Squadrons activated under the 315th Troop Carrier Group. Tactical Air Force Transport Squadron Provisional-2 discontinued.	
December		716th Composite Reconnaissance Squadron formed. T-28s and C-47s assigned.
1964 January		33d Tactical Wing formed. Incorporates all of the above squadrons.
April	Able Mable contingent increased to ten RF-101s.	
	619th Tactical Control Squadron organized.	
June	Detachment 2, 421st Air Refueling Squadron, arrives from Yokota for Yankee Team operations.	716th Reconnaissance Squadron inactivated. Pilots retrain for new 520th Fighter Squadron (Bien Hoa). Mission assumed by 2d Air Division.
August	2d Air Division Command Post established.	293d Helicopter Squadron inactivated.
	Six F-102s deploy here from Okinawa.	
	Six RF-101s added to Able Mable.	
October	19th Air Commando Squadron (Troop Carrier) activated under the 315th Troop Carrier Group. Assigned C-123s.	
December	FC-47 gunship used in combat for the first time.	

II. THAILAND

Don Muang Airport
(Thailand)

1961 April . . . . Control and Reporting Center and a Control and Reporting Post set up.

Bell Tone Detachment (four F-102s) of the 509th Fighter Interceptor Squadron moved here for indefinite duration.

November . . . . . Able Mable Reconnaissance Task Force formed, consisting of four RF-101s and a Photo Processing Cell.

Detachment 10, 13th Air Force, established to support USAF units.

Detachment 1, 5th Tactical Control Group, organized.

1962 June . . . . Four C-123s arrive here from Da Nang's 777th Troop Carrier Squadron.

Air Force Component Command of Joint Task Force 116 deploys here.

July . . . . Detachment 10, 13th Air Force, replaced by 6010th Tactical Group (13th Air Force).

November . . . . . Able Mable discontinues Laos flights. Continues coverage in South Vietnam.

December . . . . . . Joint Task Force 116 inactivated. Detachment 1, 8th Aerial Port Squadron, organized.

Able Mable moves to Tan Son Nhut.

1963 July . . . . 6010th Tactical Group redesignated 35th Tactical Group.

Bell Tone Detachment redesignated Detachment 4, 405th Fighter Wing.

35th Air Base Squadron (35th Tactical Group) organized.

THE ADVISORY YEARS

1964 July . . . . Detachment of 6091st Reconnaissance Squadron (C-130s) arrives.

1965 January . . . . 35th Tactical Group relieved of responsibility for air defense. It goes to Udorn Royal Thai Air Force Base.

Korat Royal Thai Air Force Base

1963 July . . . . Detachment 1, 6010th Tactical Group (Don Muang) organized.

1964 August . . . . F-105s from McConnell Air Force Base begin rotational temporary duty here.

October . . . . F-100s deployed here temporarily.

Takhli Royal Thai Air Force Base

1962 May . . . . F-100s from Cannon and England Air Force Bases begin rotational temporary duty here.

July . . . . 6011th Air Base Squadron organized.

1963 July . . . . 331st Air Base Squadron (35th Tactical Group) replaces 6011th Air Base Squadron.

1964 August . . . . Detachment 1, 421st Air Refueling Squadron, organized.

Udorn Royal Thai Air Force Base

1964 April . . . . . . Detachment 6, 1st Air Commando Wing, established with four T-28s to train the Royal Laotian Air Force.

June . . . . . . Detachment 2, 35th Tactical Group (Don Muang), organized.

July . . . . A Control and Reporting Post and an Air Support Operations Center established.

August . . . . . Deputy Commander, 2d Air Divi-

	sion, assumes control of all USAF operations in Thailand and Laos.
October	Detachment 2, 35th Tactical Group, becomes 333d Air Base Squadron.
1965 January	Deputy Commander, 2d Air Division, assumes responsibility for Thai air defense from Don Muang.

Appendix 2

Development of a Viet Cong Antiaircraft Capability
1962-1965*

By *Ronald H. Cole*

During the first three years of the war, the Viet Cong grew accustomed to their reputation for superior mobility over Saigon's forces. In the fall of 1962, however, the Vietnamese Air Force introduced heliborne and close air support operations that temporarily jarred Viet Cong complacency. The effectiveness of the South Vietnemese air strikes resulted in the Viet Cong's sagging morale, rising fear, and suspicion of spies in their midst. Defections occurred and the Viet Cong had to recruit arduously among the peasants to maintain their forces. Steps to counter the air threat intensified at once. As a stopgap, the Viet Cong instructed their soldiers to shoot directly at the fuselage of the enemy aircraft with any gun at hand or hurl a "flying bomb."†

Among the Viet Cong, only those regroupees and North Vietnamese Army cadres who had infiltrated south after 1960 had any semblance of antiaircraft training. Thus, the visceral reaction of Viet Cong officers and noncommissioned officers to South Vietnamese air operations in September 1962 was to order their men "to shoot aircraft flying straight" and to fire "liberally and with all available means." The training of gunners and the drafting of field manuals took time. Nonetheless, during the winter of 1962-63 Hanoi worked feverishly to develop antiaircraft tactics for infantry weapons that could be instantly used by men in the field. Programs to train inexperienced soldiers in the basics of antiaircraft warfare were also begun. Still, it was not until the end of 1963 that the Viet Cong had an effective antiaircraft capability.

In October 1962 Viet Cong provincial committees distributed to district and village troops the first detailed antiaircraft directive. The document depicted the vulnerable points on South Vietnamese fighters, reconnaissance aircraft, and helicopters. It further outlined procedures for organizing antiaircraft personnel and firing commands, and methods of shooting at aircraft with infantry weapons.

In a section entitled "Nature of an Objective in the Air," the directive explained how to gauge the target size of an aircraft by its shape and angle of approach. For example, "At 15° we only see the aircraft nose. Target size ¼. At 30° we can see the wing and the fuselage, equal in size. Target size ½. At 50° the wings seem longer than the fuselage. Target size ¾. At 90° we see the entire aircraft, or target size 4/4." The directive described the average fighter plane used

---

*Ronald H. Cole, "People's Army — Phase II," manuscript, September 1973, Chapter 10, Office of Air Force History files, based primarily on USAF intelligence materials.

†A "flying bomb" was a modified shell of a U.S. aircraft rocket, filled with napalm and hurled at enemy planes by means of a slingshot utilizing two bamboo trees.

by the South Vietnamese in late 1962 as about 13 meters long, and flying at 200 kilometers-per-hour at an altitude of 150 to 200 meters. Since the aircraft was therefore vulnerable to rifle and machinegun fire, a formula was devised for computing a firing lead.

The Viet Cong taught their trainees both "passive" and "active" antiaircraft tactics. Passive tactics consisted of camouflage, spiked landing zones, and "sentinel chambers." For camouflage the Viet Cong used dirty brown netting, natural cover, and concealment. To spike a possible landing zone they planted pointed bamboo shafts, 2 to 4 inches in diameter and 6 to 15 feet high, very close together in areas as large as 100 by 800 meters. The Viet Cong dug conical holes 5 feet into the ground with their walls slanted down at 50° for sentinel chambers. These echo chambers permitted a sentinel to hear an aircraft approaching from a great distance and to determine its direction of approach.

Active antiaircraft tactics included mortar assaults on landing zones, infantry charges against unloading helicopters, and the "three-man cell tecniques." In the latter method riflemen formed three 3-man cells arrayed in an L-shaped configuration with three machinegun teams. The machinegunners positioned themselves at the two ends and at the junction of the "L." (See Chart.) The riflemen and machinegunners practiced synchronized firing in this formation, which was specially designed to down fixed-wing aircraft. By December 1964 U.S. and South Vietnamese pilots had not yet assessed the success of this formidable-looking technique, since the number of Viet Cong antiaircraft attacks fluctuated monthly from 20 to 100.

DIAGRAM OF "L" OR TRIANGULAR DEFENSE SYSTEM

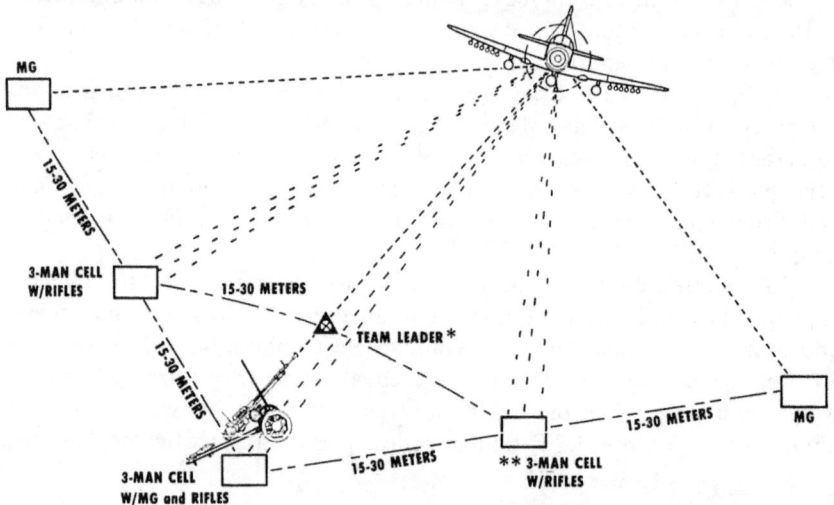

* FIRES ARE COORDINATED ON COMMAND OF TEAM LEADER.

** ONE CELL MAY BE DESIGNATED AS DECOY TO DRAW AIRCRAFT FIRE AND ALLOW AA GUN CREW TO DISENGAGE.

THE ADVISORY YEARS

The Viet Cong constructed their first antiaircraft weapons training center in Quang Ngai Province. Aerial reconnaissance revealed that this site probably offered instruction in aircraft recognition, techniques of fire, calculation of firing leads, preparation of antiaircraft sites, drills in the use of these sites, and basic tactical formations for use against South Vietnamese heliborne operations. One major difficulty persisted — the scarcity of antiaircraft weaponry.

The Viet Cong began to receive more sophisticated antiaircraft weapons from Hanoi in the fall of 1963. Infiltrators brought with them 12.7-mm (Soviet DSHK) and .50-caliber machineguns. In addition reports reached Military Assistance Command, Vietnam, of 20-mm cannon and 13.2-mm machineguns in War Zone D, and of a 35-mm antiaircraft gun in Kien Phong Province. Moreover, in April 1964 MACV J-2 (Intelligence) anticipated the early arrival of two new antiaircraft weapons from Hanoi, the 37-mm gun weighing 4,600 pounds and the 40-mm gun weighing 10,000. Within months the impact of this influx in weapons was felt.

Records of antiaircraft attacks commenced in January 1963. Monthly incidents remained low throughout 1963, rose to about 100 in January 1964, and tapered off to only 50 in March 1964. The number then climbed to more than 180 for April 1964, and the average over the next six months was at least 180 — the greatest number for any one month being nearly 400 in September 1964. After April 1964 the correlation of increased antiaircraft attacks and the quantity of antiaircraft weapons available to Viet Cong gunners is obvious. (See Graph.)

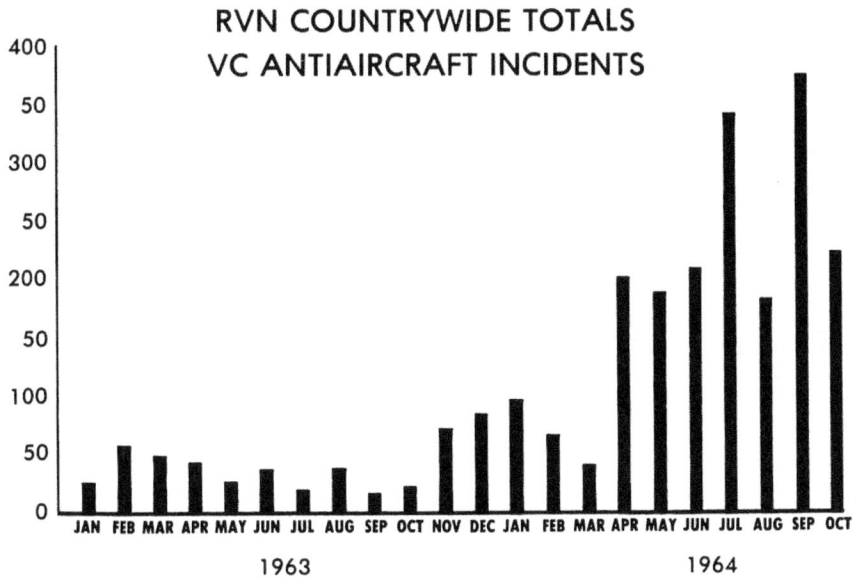

RVN COUNTRYWIDE TOTALS
VC ANTIAIRCRAFT INCIDENTS

Notes

Chapter I

Origins of the American Commitment to Vietnam

1. Grateful acknowledgement is made of the help furnished by Mr. Charles B. MacDonald of the Army's Center of Military History on the background of the American involvement in Vietnam. The literature on the roots of the American commitment to Southeast Asia is extensive, but see especially Cordell Hull, *The Memoirs of Cordell Hull* (New York, 1948), II, 1596-77; *The Public Papers and Addresses of Franklin D. Roosevelt: Victory and the Threshold of Peace* (New York, 1950), pp 562-63; Hearings before the Committee on Armed Services and the Committee on Foreign Relations, US Senate, *Military Situation in the Far East*, 82d Cong, 1st sess (Washington, 1951), pt 4, pp 1890-92; US Dept of State, *The Conference at Malta and Yalta* (Washington, 1955), p 770. See also John L. Gaddis, *The United States and the Origins of the Cold War, 1941-45* (New York, 1972).

2. Ellen Hammer, *The Struggle for Indochina* (Stanford, 1954), and Joseph Buttinger, *Vietnam: A Dragon Embattled* (New York, 1967), are especially helpful on the events in Southeast Asia during World War II and after.

3. Hull, *Memoirs*, II, 1598; Terminal Conf Papers and Minutes of Meetings, July 1945, pp 217-26, 252-53, and 305; Marcel Vigneras, *Rearming the French U.S. Army in World War II* (Washington, 1957), pp 396-99; Supreme Allied Commander Southeast Asia, *Dispatch*, pt IV-A, pp 520-28; Charles de Gaulle, *The War Memoirs of Charles de Gaulle* (New York, 1960), III, 242-43.

4. See msg, Dean Acheson to chargé in China, October 5, 1947, in *Department of Defense (The Pentagon Papers), United States-Vietnam Relations, 1945-1967* (Washington, 1971), Bk 8:49 [hereafter cited as *DOD Pentagon Papers*].

5. *Ibid.*, pp 144-49; William C. Bullitt, "The Saddest War," *Life*, Dec 29, 1947, pp 64-69; Allan B. Cole, ed, *Conflict in Indo-China and International Repercussions: A Documentary History, 1945-1955* (Ithaca, 1956), pp 83-84.

6. Military Assistance Command Vietnam Historical Monograph, *Military Assistance to the Republic of South Vietnam, 1960-1963*, p 2.

7. 63 Statutes 714, Oct 6, 1949; Hearings Held in Executive Session before the Committee on Foreign Relations, US Senate, *Economic Assistance to China and Korea: 1949-50* (Washington, 1974), p 194.

8. US Dept of State, *American Foreign Policy, 1950-1955* (Washington, 1957), pp 2364-65; *DOD Pentagon Papers*, Bk 1: II, A-17, A-35, A-36; see also Dean Acheson, *Present at the Creation: My Years in the State Department* (New York, 1967), pp 671-78.

9. HQ USAF, Air Order of Battle, Apr 1, 1950; *USAF Air Intelligence Digest*, Apr 52, p 4.

10. Memo, Gen. Omar N. Bradley to SECDEF, Apr 10, 1950; msg, Acheson to AmEmb London, May 3, 1950; Dept of State Press Release 485, Aid to Southeast Asia, May 11, 1950; all in *DOD Pentagon Papers*, Bk 8: 308-13, 321, and 327.

11. *Public Papers of the Presidents: Harry S Truman, 1950* (Washington, 1965), p 492.

12. Hearings before the Committee on Foreign Relations and the Committee on Armed Services, US Senate, *Mutual Security Act of 1951*, 82d Cong, 1st sess (Washington, 1951), pp 563-64; Edgar O'Ballance, *The Indochina War, 1945-1954: A Study in Guerrilla Warfare* (London, 1964), p 114; hist, 1020th USAF Special Activities Wg, Apr-Jun 52.

13. Study Submitted by the Subcommittee on National Security Staffing and Operations, *The Ambassador and the Problem of Coordination*, 88th Cong, 1st sess (Senate Document 36) (Washington, 1963), pp 12, 14-15, and 53-58.

14. U.S. Dept of State, *U.S. Treaties and Other International Agreements* (Washington, 1952), III, pt 2, 2756-99.

15. *USAF Air Intelligence Digest*, Apr 52, pp 6-7, Maurer Maurer, *History of USAF Activities in Support of the Mutual Defense Assistance Program* (Wright-Patterson AFB: AMC Hist Office, 1951), pt 1, pp 52-53, pt 2, pp 64-65, 80-81, and pt 3, pp 138-39.

16. *Ibid.*, pt 3, p 261; US Senate, *Mutual Security Act of 1951*, 82d Cong, 1st sess, p 564.

17. *Public Papers of the Presidents: Harry S Truman, 1951* (Washington, 1965), p 267.

18. *USAF Air Intelligence Digest*, Jun 54, pp 14-17; Presentation of Lt Col R. E. Edwards, Chief Materiel Branch, MAAG Vietnam, in Rprt *Asian-MAP Logistic Conference*, Dec 58, pp 154-60; Capt Mack D. Secord, "The Viet Nam Air Force," *Air University Review*, Nov-Dec 63, pp 60-61; Maj Oakah L. Jones, Jr., *Organization, Mission and Growth of the Vietnamese Air Force, 1949-68* (HQ PACAF, Proj CHECO, Oct 8, 1968), pp 1-3.

19. Ltr, Brig Gen T. J. H. Trapnell, Chief, MAAG-Indochina, to Gen J. Lawton Collins, CSA, Dec 20, 1952, in *DOD Pentagon Papers*,

Bk 9: 2-3, hists, 24th Air Depot Wg, Sep-Dec 52, p 50, and Jan-Jun 53, App 7; *USAF Statistical Digest*, FY 1953, p 311.
20. Hists, 24th Air Depot Wg, Sept-Dec 52, p 50, and Jan-Jun 53, App 7.
21. GHQ UNC and FEC, Intel Sum, Nov 14, 1952.
22. Harry S Truman, *Memoirs: Years of Trial and Hope* (Garden City, 1956), p 519.

Chapter II

Dien Bien Phu

1. Dwight D. Eisenhower, *The White House Years: Mandate for Change, 1953-1956* (Garden City, 1963), pp 337-38; U.S. Dept of State, *American Foreign Policy, 1950-1955*, p 2386.
2. Report of Senator Mike Mansfield on a Study Mission to the Associated States of Indochina, Oct 27, 1953, *Indochina*, 83d Cong, 1st sess (Washington, 1943), p 4; msg, Dulles to AmEmb Paris, Mar 26, 1953, in *DOD Pentagon Papers*, Bk 9: 17-18.
3. *USAF Air Intelligence Digest*, Jun 53, pp 30-34.
4. MR by Douglas MacArthur II, Apr 27, 1953, in *DOD Pentagon Papers*, Bk 9: 38; US Dept of State, *American Foreign Policy, 1950-1955*, pp 2369-70; hist, 24th Air Depot Wg, Jan-Jun 53, pp 56-67, and App 8: *History of Project Swivel Chair*. In response to a request made by the Thai Ambassador to Dulles in May, emergency air shipments of ammunition and other urgently needed items were rushed to Bangkok. U.S. Dept of State, *American Foreign Policy, 1950-1955*, p 2370.
5. Henri Navarre, *L'Agonie de l'Indochine, 1953-54* (Paris, 1956), pp 62-88.
6. Hist, Dir/Plans, USAF, Jul-Dec 53, pp 117-19; rprt, Lt Gen John W. O'Daniel to JCS (thru CINCPAC), Jul 14, 1953, in *DOD Pentagon papers*, Bk 9: 69-96; hist, 315th Air Div (Combat Cargo), Jan-Jun 54, pp 6-7.
7. Hist, Asst for Mutual Security, USAF, Jul-Dec 53, pp 45-46; USAF Statistical Summary FY 1954, p 187.
8. Dept of State, *American Foreign Policy 1950-55*, pp 2370-72; Hearings before the Committee on Foreign Affairs, House of Representatives, *The Mutual Security Act of 1954*, 83d Cong, 2d sess (Washington, 1954), pp 6-7; Hearings before the Committee on Appropriations, US Senate, *Mutual Security Appropriations for 1957*, 84th Cong, 2d sess (Washington, 1956), p 67; Eisenhower, *Mandate for Change*, p 338; memo, Bradley for SECDEF, Aug 11, 1953, in *DOD Pentagon Papers*, Bk 9: 134-37.
9. Rprt, O'Daniel to JCS, Jul 14, 1953; hist, Asst for Mutual Security, USAF, Jul-Dec 53, p 158, and Jan-Jun 54, pp 149-50; rprt, Brig Gen Albert G. Hewitt, Vice Comdr Far East Air Logistics Force, to SECDEF thru CSAF, Apr 6, 1954.
10. Navarre, *L'Agonie de l'Indochine*, pp 188-200.
11. 315th Air Div. French Indo-China Participation, 1953-1954; hist, Dir/Plans, USAF, Jan-Jun 54, pp 93-96.
12. FEAF Intel Roundup, Apr-May 54.
13. Hist, Asst for Mutual Security, USAF, Jan-Jun 54, pp 25-26; note by the Executive Secretary to the National Security Council, Jan 16, 1954, and memo by Brig Gen C. H. Bonesteel, III, CASD-ISA, Jan 29-30, 1954, in *DOD Pentagon Papers*, Bk 9: 217-18 and 240-44; ltrs, FEAF to Comdr 5AF, Apr 10, 1954; Col Robert L. Liles to Hist Ofc FEALOGFOR, Jul 15, 1954; FEAF Staff Section Monthly Hist Rprts, Dir/Ops, Feb 54.
14. U.S. Air Forces in Europe established an accelerated training program for French B-26 crews and mechanics in France, and in June, the French would allocate an additional 450 technicians to Vietnam. Rprt, Hewitt to SECDEF, Apr 6, 1954; hist, Dir/Plans, USAF, Jan-Jun 54, pp 93-96; hist, Asst for Mutual Security, USAF, Jan-Jun 54, p 145; ltr, Liles to Hist Ofc FEALOGFOR, Jul 15, 1954; HQ 6424th Air Depot Wg, Support to the French Air Force, Feb 2-Jul 17, 1954; *Public Papers of the Presidents; Dwight D. Eisenhower, 1954* (Washington, 1960), p 247.
15. "Interview with Gen Otto P. Weyland... Can Air Power Win 'Little Wars'?", *U.S. News & World Report*, Jul 23, 1954, pp 54-61; flight intvw with Weyland by Ken Leish, Jun 60.
16. Rprt, Capt Robert W. Hickey and Robert M. Floyd to Dep/Intel, FEAF, Mar 9, 1954.
17. Eisenhower, *Mandate for Change*, p 339; Navarre, *L'Agonie de l'Indochine*, pp 214, 216, and 217; rprt, O'Daniel to JCS, Feb 5, 1954, in *DOD Pentagon papers*, Bk 9: 248; *USAF Air Intelligence Digest*, Mar 54, p 11.
18. John Robinson Beal, *John Foster Dulles, 1888-1959* (New York, 1959), pp 204-06; U.S. Dept of State, *American Foreign policy, 1950-*

1955, pp 2372-73. See also *Khrushchev Remembers* (Boston, 1970), pp 481-82, for an assessment that Ho was acting in desperation early in 1954 because China was too weak to help him.

19. Navarre, *L'Agonie de l'Indochine*, p 218; Dep/Intel, 13th AF, IR-29-54, Jul 19, 1954; Air Attache Saigon, IR-142-54, Jul 9, 1954; Hearings before the Committee on Foreign Affairs, House of Representatives, *The Mutual Security Act of 1954*, 83d Cong, 2d sess (Washington, 1954), pp 9, 15, 18, 20.

20. Hist, 483d TC Wg, Jan-Jun 54, p 36; see also FEAF Intel Roundup, Jun 54, p 40.

21. Air Attaché Saigon, IR-56-54, Mar 23, 1954; Bernard B. Fall, *Street Without Joy: Insurgency in Indochina, 1946-1963*, 3d rev ed (Harrisburg, 1963), p 317.

22. Rprt, Lt Col William B. Sanders, Combat Ops Div, FEAF, to Dep Ops, FEAF, Jun 14, 1954; msg, Chief MAAG Saigon to Comdr FEAF, MG-650-D-1, Mar 18, 1954; msg, Comdr FEAF to Chief MAAG Saigon, n.d.; 315th Air Div (Combat Cargo), French Indo-China Participation, pp 17-18.

23. Hist, 315th Air Div (Combat Cargo), Jan-Jun 54, pp 26-27; Dep/Intel, 13th AF, IR-29-54, Jul 19, 1954. The expenditure of parachutes and other drop equipment nearly depleted USAF stocks in Japan, and emergency shipments had to come from the United States.

24. Eisenhower, *Mandate for Change*, p 341.

25. *Ibid.*; Jules Roy, *The Battle of Dienbienphu* (New York, 1965), p 155; hist, Dir/Plans, USAF, Jan-Jun 54, pp 90-92; Gen M. B. Ridgway, *Soldier* (New York, 1956), p 276.

26. Roy, *Battle of Dienbienphu*, pp 194-95, and 198, Eisenhower, *Mandate for Change*, p 345.

27. Roy, *Battle of Dienbienphu*, pp 214-15; Navarre, *L'Agonie de l'Indochine*, p 244; Fall, *Hell in a Very Small Place: The Siege of Dien Bien Phu* (Philadelphia, 1967), p 299; FEAF Intel Roundup, Apr-May 54, pp 22 and 24.

28. Msg, Air Dep SHAPE to CINCUSAFE, RL-1172, Apr 3, 1954; msg, CINCUSAFE to Comdr 17 AF, *et al.*, ECINC-1616-C, Apr 3, 1954.

29. Hist, USAFE, Jan-Jun 54, III, App VIIB; hist, 62d TC Wg, Jan-Jun 54; hist, Asst for Mutual Security, USAF, Jan-Jun 54, p 148.

30. Fall, *Hell in a Very Small Place*, p 302; Roy, *Battle of Dienbienphu*, pp 221-22.

31. Dept of State, *Vital Speeches of the Day*, Apr 15, 1954, p 387.

32. Anthony Eden, *The Memoirs of Anthony Eden: Full Circle* (Boston, 1960), pp 102-03.

33. Eisenhower, *Mandate for Change*, p 347; Beal, *John Foster Dulles*, pp 206-08.

34. Eisenhower, *Mandate for Change*, p 347.

35. House of Representatives, *The Mutual Security Act of 1954*, 83d Cong, 2d sess, pp 9, 15, 18, and 20; Roy, *Battle of Dienbienphu*, p 224.

36. Hist, Dir/Ops, USAF, Jan-Jun 54, pp 44-45.

37. Fall, *Hell in a Very Small Place*, pp 303-04.

38. Eisenhower, *Mandate for Change*, p 347; *Public Papers of the Presidents: Dwight D. Eisenhower, 1954* (Washington, 1960) pp 382-83.

39. Stf study, FEAF, To Recommend a Feasible Military Course of Action to Achieve U.S. Objectives in Indo-China, Apr 13, 1954.

40. Study, Apr 19, 1954, in Hist, Dir/Plans, USAF, Jan-Jun 54, pp 90-92.

41. Ridgway, *Soldier*, pp 176-277; Gavin, "Letter to Editors," *Harpers Magazine*, Feb 66, pp 16-21; Hearings before the Committee on Foreign Relations, US Senate, *Supplemental Foreign Assistance Fiscal Year 1966 — Vietnam*, 89th Cong, 2d sess (Washington, 1966), pt 1, pp 226, 234-35.

42. Hist, Asst for Mutual Security, Jan-Jun 54, pp 142-43, and 146; ltr, Liles for Historian FEALOGFOR, Jul 15, 1954; ltr, Vice Adm Edwin B. Hooper, USN (Ret), Dir/Naval Hist, to Brig Gen B. S. Gunderson, Ch/Af Hist, Dec 20, 1972; Hist, Summary, Armament Div. Dep for Materiel, FEAF, Apr 54.

43. Hist, Dir/Rqmts, FEAF, Apr 54, Tab C: Standard Operational Procedures for Use of Lazy Dog.

44. Msg, FEAF to Chief MAAG Saigon, ADO-RQMTS-3551, Apr 7, 1954; msg, FEAF to Chief MAAG Saigon, ADO-CO&T-3768, Apr 15, 1954; rprt, Sanders to Dep/Ops, FEAF, Jun 14, 1954. Survivors of the campaign later reported that their Viet Minh captors had questioned them closely about the missiles, and one repatriated French officer stated that the "cigar shaped pellets" had been very effective. Dep/Intel, 13AF, IR-29-54, Jul 19, 1954.

45. Caldara had available for combat thirty-two B-29s of the 98th Bombardment Wing at Yokota Air Base, Japan, and sixty-seven B-26s of the 307th Bombardment Wing at Kadena Air Base Okinawa.

46. Ltr, Partridge to Navarre, Apr 19, 1954; MR by Maj Gen Joseph D. Caldara (USAF-Ret), Mar 8, 1966; Caldara to Gen Curtis E. LeMay, Apr 30 and May 3, 1954; Navarre, *L'Agonie de l'Indochine*, p 244.

47. Eisenhower, *Mandate for Change*, pp 349-50; Eden, *Memoirs*, p 116; msg, Geneva (Dulles) to State, DULTE-5, Apr 25, 1954, in *DOD Pentagon Papers*, Bk 9: 388-89.

48. Early in May, the American detachment of the 483d Troop Carrier Wing that maintained the C-119s at Cat Bi secured a Ground Control Approach radar, but it was not installed, and operations in the Hanoi area continued to be hazardous. Rprt, Sanders to Dep/Ops, FEAF, Jun 14, 1954.

49. Rprt, Hewitt to SECDEF, Apr 6, 1954;

FEAF Intel Roundup, Aug 54, p 8; L. S. Waddell, "Phase Out for Charlie-One-One-Nine," *Pegasus*, Oct 55, p 4; ltr, Maj Edward S. Ash, *et al*, to Comdr 315th Air Div, subj: High Altitude Delayed Parabundle Drops, n.d. C-119 crews claimed they could put cargo pallets into a 330-yard square from 10,000 feet, but on April 27 only one-third of the dropped supplies could be retrieved. French and American cargo-dropping aircrews agreed that escorting flak suppression flights operated too high to be effective and were frequently absent when needed. In April the 483d Troop Carrier Wing had flak damage to nineteen C-119s while flying 477 sorties to deliver supplies to Dien Bien Phu. Hist, 483d TC Wg, Jan-Jun 54, pp 41, 54-55.

50. *Ibid.*, p 55; Fall, *Hell in a Very Small Place*, pp 328, 336-37, 373-74; Corey Ford, "The Flying Tigers Carry On," *Saturday Evening Post*, Feb 5, 1955, pp 24 ff, and Feb 12, 1955, pp 30 ff.

51. Fall, *Hell in a Very Small Place*, pp 374-411, 431-32, 487.

CHAPTER III

The Geneva Agreements and French Withdrawal

1. Navarre, *L'Agonie de l'Indochine*, pp 268-69; Jean Lacouture and Philippe Devillers, La Fin d'une Guerre, Indochine 1954 (Paris, 1960), pp 162-63; msg, Comdr FEAF to Comdr FEALOGFOR, *ca.* May 13, 1954, quoting msg from USAIRA Saigon, May 13, 1954.

2. Msg, CINCPAC to COMSEADEFCOM, Apr 28, 1954; CINCPAC OPlan 56-54, Apr 29, 1954.

3. Msgs, Comdr FEAF to CSAF, May 4, 1954, May 20, 1954, and Jun 7, 1954.

4. Memos, Radford for SECDEF, May 20, May 21, and May 26, 1954, in *DOD Pentagon Papers*, Bk 10: 477-82 and 487-93.

5. Eisenhower, *Mandate for Change*, p 361.

6. Fall, *Street Without Joy*, pp 169-230; Eisenhower, *Mandate for Change*, p 368; Eden *Memoirs*, p 149; *Public Papers of the Presidents: Dwight D. Eisenhower, 1954*, pp 599-600.

7. Lacouture and Devillers, *La Fin d'Une Guerre*, pp 252-68; Amry Vandenbosch and Richard A. Butwell, *Southeast Asia among the World Powers* (Lexington, 1957), pp 295-97; Chester L. Cooper, *The Lost Crusade: America in Vietnam* (New York, 1970), pp 90-91. See also Robert P. Randle, *Geneva 1954: The Settlement of the Indochinese War* (Princeton, 1969), pp 371-85.

8. Lacouture and Devillers, *La Fin d'Une Guerre*, pp 252-68; Hearings before the Subcommittee on the Far East and the Pacific of the Committee on Foreign Affairs, House of Representatives, *United States Policy Toward Asia*, 89th Cong, 2d sess (Washington, 1966), pt 2, pp 398-99. In its final form, the Geneva agreements comprised separate military accords for Vietnam, Laos, and Cambodia, an unsigned final declaration of the nations represented at Geneva, and several unilateral national declarations.

9. Peter V. Curl, ed, *Documents on American Foreign Relations, 1954* (New York, 1955), pp 283-310; Lacouture and Devillers, *La Fin d'Une Guerre*, pp 276-82.

10. Eisenhower, *Mandate for Change*, pp 370-71; Curl, *Documents*, pp 315-17.

11. Msg, Comdr FEAF to Comdr FEALOGFOR, *et al*, V-DOO-238, *ca.* May 13, 1954.

12. Dir/Hist Services, FEAF, Far East Air Forces Support of French Indo-China Operations, Jul 1, 1952-Sep 30, 1954, pp 162-71, 294-302. Guerrillas on June 14 captured five enlisted men who were illicitly beyond the airfield perimeter and held them prisoner until August 31.

13. *Ibid.*, pp 117-19; hist, Asst for Mutual Security, USAF, Jul-Dec 54, pp 23-24; FEAF Staff Section Monthly Hist Rprts, Dep/Ops, Jul-Dec 54; hist, Curr Ops Div, Aug and Sep 54; hist, 315th Air Div (Combat Cargo), Jul-Dec 54, pp 32-47.

14. Far East Forces Support of French Indo-China Operations, pp 239-48; ltr, Hooper to Gunderson, Dec 20, 1972.

15. Far East Air Forces Support of French Indo-China Operations, pp 248-51, 270-74; US Dept of State, *American Foreign Policy, 1950-1955*, p 2399.

16. Rprt, Hewitt to SECDEF, Apr 6, 1954.

17. FEAF Intel Roundup, Aug 54, pp 5-11.

18. Gen G. J. M. Chassin, "Lessons of the War in Indochina," *Interavia*, VII (1952), 670-75.

19. Eisenhower, *Mandate for Change*, pp 372-73; *Public Papers of the Presidents; Eisenhower, 1954*, p 168.

20. Lacoutre and Devillers, *La Fin d'Une Guerre*, pp 298-99; *USAF Air Intelligence Digest*, Feb 55, pp 36-37; David Halberstam, *The Making of a Quagmire* (New York, 1965), pp 38-39.

21. Ho, "Appeal Made," Jul 22, 1954, quoted in Bernard B. Fall, ed, *Ho Chi Minh on Revolution* (New York, 1967), p 272.

22. *Public Papers of the Presidents: Eisenhower, 1954*, p 168; Dept of State, *American Foreign Policy, 1950-1955*, pp 2400-01.

23. Statement of Policy by the National Security Council on Review of U.S. Policy in the Far East, Aug 20, 1954, in *DOD Pentagon Papers*, Bk 10: 731-41.

24. Curl, *Documents, 1954*, pp 319-23; Dept of State, *American Foreign Policy, 1950-1955*, pp 2334-37; FEAF Intel Roundup, Jan 66, pp 12-13, and Apr 55, p 25; hists, Dir/Plans, USAF, Jul-Dec 54, pp 57-59, and Jul-Dec 56, pp 138-39; Dep/Ops, Pacific AF, A Pacific Air Force Staff Study, Sep 55, in hist PAF, Jul-Dec 55, pt II, Doc 21; Statement of Policy by the National Security Council on Review of U.S. Policy in the Far East, Aug 20, 1954.

25. Ltrs, Dulles to Charles E. Wilson, SECDEF, Aug 18 and Oct 11, 1954; memos, Twining for SECDEF, Aug 4, 1954, and Radford for SECDEF, Sep 22, 1954, and Oct 19, 1954, in *DOD Pentagon Papers*, Bk 10: 701-02, 728-30, 756-58, 768-89, and 771-74.

26. MACV, *Military Assistance*, pp 2-5; hist, Dir/Plans, USAF, Jul-Dec 54, pp 62-65; memo, Radford for SECDEF, Sep 22, 1954, in *DOD Pentagon Papers*, Bk 10: 756-58.

27. Ltr, Dulles to Wilson, Aug 18, 1954, in *DOD Pentagon Papers*, Bk 10: 728-30; MACV, *Military Assistance to the Republic of South Vietnam*, pp 2-5; Hearings before the Subcommittee on State Department Organization and Public Affairs of the Committee on Foreign Relations, US Senate, *Situation in Vietnam*, 86th Cong, 1st sess (Washington, 1959), pt I, p 49; Robert Scigliano, *South Vietnam: Nation under Stress* (Boston, 1964), pp 162-67.

28. Hist, Dir/Plans, USAF, Jul-Dec 54, pp 62-25; memo, Radford for SECDEF, Oct 19, 1954, in *DOD Pentagon Papers*, Bk 10: 768-74; see also *DOD Pentagon Papers*, Bk 1: IV.A.4., 3-6.

29. *Public Papers of the Presidents: Eisenhower, 1954*, pp 948-49; R. Frank Futrell, "Chronology of Significant Airpower Events in Southeast Asia, 1954-1967," Aerospace Studies Institute, Air University; *Journal of Military Assistance, 1954*.

30. Statement of Policy by the National Security Council on Current U.S. Policy in the Far East, Dec 22, 1954, in *DOD Pentagon Papers*, Bk 10: 835-52; *Public Papers of the Presidents: Eisenhower, 1954*, pp 948-49; Dept of State, *American Foreign Policy, 1950-1955*, p 2403; hists, FEAF Dep/Intel, Jan 55, w/incl, and Feb 55, w/incl.

31. Curl, *Documents, 1954*, pp 237-38; "Interview with Gen J. Lawton Collins: What We're Doing in Indo-China," *U.S. News & World Report*, Mar 4, 1955, pp 82-88; *USAF Air Intelligence Digest*, Feb 55, p 38.

32. Hist, Asst for Mutual Security, USAF, Jan-Jun 55, pp 146-50; MACV, *Military Assistance*, pp 2-5; *DOD Pentagon Papers*, Bk 2: IV.A.4., 6.

33. Memo, Col Edward G. Lansdale for SEA Subcommittee of the Draper Committee, Mar 13, 1959; US Air Force Academy Oral History Program, intvw with Maj Gen Edward Lansdale, Apr 25, 1971; Edward G. Lansdale, *In the Midst of Wars: An American's Mission to Southeast Asia* (New York, 1972).

34. IR-163-55, AIRA Saigon, Oct 21, 1955; US Dept of State, *American Foreign Policy, Current Documents, 1956* (Washington, 1959), pp 859-63; Hearings before the Committee on Foreign Affairs, House of Representatives, *Mutual Security Act of 1955*, 84th Cong, 1st sess (Washington, 1955), pp 190-91.

35. HQ CINCPAC, Record, Second SECDEF Conference, Jan 15, 1962, Item 5; *DOD Pentagon Papers*, Bk 2: IV.A.4., 22-23.

36. Dep/Ops, PAF, *A Pacific Air Force Staff Study on MDAP Air Force Objectives for Title III Countries in the Pacific Command*, Sep 55.

37. *Ibid.*

38. Memo, Twining for SECDEF, Sep 9, 1955, in *DOD Pentagon Papers*, Bk 10: 1002-15.

39. Dept of State, *American Foreign Policy, 1950-1955*, p 2404; Cole, *Conflict in Indo-China*, pp 226-27.

40. Hist, Dir/Plans, USAF, Jul-Dec 55, pp 81-84.

41. *Ibid.*; *DOD Pentagon Papers*, Bk 2: IV.A.4., 20.

42. Hist, Dir/Plans, USAF, Jul-Dec 55, pp 81-84; "Why the US is Losing in Vietnam—An Inside Story, Interview with Former Chief US Military Advisor, Lt Gen Samuel T. Williams (Ret)," *U.S. News & World Report*, Nov 9, 1964, pp 62-63.

43. *Ibid.*; Hearings before a Subcommittee of the Committee on Government Operations, House of Representatives, *Foreign Aid Construction Projects*, 85th Cong. 2d sess (Washington, 1958), pp 872-73.

44. *U.S. News & World Report*, Nov 9, 1964, pp 63-64; memo, Capt B. A. Robbins, Jr., USN, May 10, 1957, in *DOD Pentagon Papers*, Bk 10: 1106-07; *USAF Journal of Mutual Security*, X (Jul 1, 1957), 128, and XI (Nov 1, 1957), 117.

45. Memo, SECDEF for SA, *et al*, Jul 16, 1956, and Statement of Policy on U.S. Policy in Mainland Southeast Asia, Sep 5, 1956, in *DOD Pentagon Papers*, Bk 10: 1064, 1082-95.

Chapter IV

U.S. Command Problems in the Pacific: Emphasis on Southeast Asia

1. Gen. L. S. Kuter, "Command and Control in Asia-Pacific Area," Lecture to Air War College, Mar 6, 1956.
2. Hist, Dir/Plans, USAF, Jan-Jun 54, p 13, and Jul-Dec 53, pp 32-33; hist, PAF, Jul-Dec 54, pp 1-9; msg, COMPAF to COMFEAF, Nov 30, 1955, in hist, PAF, Jul-Dec 55, pt 1, Doc 10; ltr, Kuter to CINCFE, Jul 11, 1955.
3. Hist, FEAF, Jan-Jun 55, III, Hist Rprt, Dir/Plans and Policy, Feb 55; hist, PAF, Jan-Jun 55, and Mar-Jul 55.
4. AMFPA—Area III MAP Logistics Conf, Nov 14-19, 1956, pp 44-48.
5. Hist, AMC, Jul-Dec 55, I, chap 1; hist, AMFPA, Oct 1, 1956-Jun 30, 1957, pp 13-28.
6. Msg, COMPAF to COMFEAF, Nov 30, 1955.
7. Hist, PAF, Jul-Dec 55, II, 72-99.
8. *Ibid.*, Jan-Jun 56, I, Doc 25; hist rprt, Dir/Intel, Doc 6, Feb 17, 1956.
9. Hist, PAF, Jan-Jun 56, I, 35; hist, PACAF/FEAF Rear, Jul-Dec 56, III, Doc 10; AMFPA Title MDAP Logistic Conf, Tachikawa, Jan 7-May 10, 1956, and Baguio, P.I., Nov 14-19, 1956.
10. Kuter, "Command and Control in Asia-Pacific Area."
11. *Ibid.*; hist, PACAF/FEAF Rear, Jul-Dec 56, II, 96-97; hist, Dir/Plans, USAF, Jan-Jun 56, pp 20-21.
12. Hists, Dir/Plans, USAF, Jul-Dec 56, pp 90-91, and 141-42, and Jan-Jun 57, p 110; hist, PACAF/FEAF Rear, Jul-Dec 56, II, 106-07.
13. Kuter, "Command and Control in the Asia-Pacific Area"; ltr, Kuter to CINCFE, Jul 11, 1955, in Hist, FEAF, Jan-Jun 55, I, pt II, Chap 3, Docs 3 and 4; hist, Dir/Plans, USAF, Jan-Jun 56, pp 54 and 56; hist, PACAF/FEAF (Rear), Jan-Jun 57, I, I.
14. FEAF Study (*ca.* Aug 6, 1956) in PAF File, Theater Reorganization, Component Commanders' Recommendations.
15. Hists, PACAF/FEAF (Rear), Jul-Dec 56, II, 102-03, and Dir/Plans, USAF, Jul-Dec 56, pp 87-89.
16. CINCPAC Instr 03020.2, Jun 20, 1957; PAF Final Rprt (Air Attache Div), Air Attache-MAAG Conf, Nov 4-8, 1957, pp I-C-6 and III-B-1. Slightly different from the others and later introduced into Vietnam was the model in Taiwan. On March 15, 1958, the headquarters of the Taiwan Defense Command and of the MAAG were consolidated, and on April 1, Maj. Gen. Fred M. Dean took command of Air Task Force 13. He also became Chief, Air Force Section, Taiwan Defense Command and Military Advisory Group. Thus the advisory functions of the Air Force Section and the operational functions of Air Task Force 13 came under a single authority even though separate command channels were preserved for the two functions. Jacob Van Staaveren, *Air Operations in the Taiwan Crisis of 1958*, USAF Historical Division Liaison Office, Nov 62, pp 11-12; hists, ATF-13(P), Jan-Jun 58, pp 3-14, and Jul-Dec 58, p 17, and 13th AF, Jul-Dec. pp 55-56.
17. Hist, PACAF/FEAF (Rear), Jan-Jun 57, I, I; Kuter "The Pacific Air Forces," *Air Force* (Oct 57), p 63; hist, Dir/Plans, USAF, Jan-Jun 58, p 100; ltr, Kuter to CINCFE, Jul 11, 1955; hist, PAF, Jan-Jun 56, III, 522-27; ltr, Smith to CINCPAC, Nov 27, 1956. The SEATO Air Link Exercise held at Bangkok in May 1957 demonstrated failures of systems to meet requirements, and the exercise went poorly. Memo, Lt Col. D. A. Clark, Rprt of Staff Visit, Dec 6, 1957 in Hist, 5th AF, Jan-Jun 58, III, App 99; hist, 315th Air Div (Combat Cargo), Jan-Jun 57; NAMAP, Asian-MAP Logistic Conf, Dec 58, p 455.
18. Command Relations Concepts of CINCPACAF, Aug 21, 1957, in Hist, PACAF, Jul-Dec 57, II; PAF Final Rprt Air Attache-MAAG Conf, Nov 4-8, 1957, Introduction.
19. Hist, Dir/Plans, USAF, Jul-Dec 56, pp 138-39.
20. PACAF Ltr 55-1, Jul 25, 1958.
21. Robert F. Futrell, *Ideas, Concepts, Doctrine: A History of Basic Thinking in the United States Air Force, 1907-1964* (Air University: Aerospace Studies Institute, 1971), I, 406-08.
22. Hist, Fifth AF, Jan-Jun 58, I, 90-100; Remarks of Lt Gen Frederic H. Smith, Jr., May 28, 1958, in *ibid.*, IV, App 101A; see also *ibid.*, Jul-Dec 58, I, 146-51; Fifth AF, Atomic Weapons in Limited Wars in Southeast Asia, Jul 22, 1958; Smith, "Nuclear Weapons and Limited War," *Air University Quarterly Review*, XII (Spring 1960), 3-27.
23. Hearings before the Subcommittee of the Committee on Appropriations, House of Representatives, *Mutual Security Appropriations for 1961 (and Related Agencies)*, 86th Cong, 2d sess, (Washington, 1960), pt 2, p 2486.
24. DOD, Annual Report of the Secretary of Defense, Jul 1, 1958, to Jun 30, 1959 (Washing-

Notes to Pages 46-53

ton, 1960), pp 35-46; hist, PACAF, Jul-Dec 58, I, pt 1, 172-75.
25. CINCPAC hist, 1964, pp 1 and 3.
26. Msg, PACAF to CSAF, PFCCS-61-7-3, Jul 12, 1961; hist, 315th Air Div (Combat Cargo), Jan-Jun 62, pp 53-54; George F. Lemmer, *The Laos Crisis of 1959* (Office of Air Force History, 1961), pp 39-49.
27. US Senate, *Mutual Security Act of 1959*, 86th Cong, 1st sess, pt 1, pp 5, 10-11, and 19-20.
28. NAMAP, Asian-MAP Logistics Conf, Dec 58, pp 451-53.
29. NAMAP, 5th Asian-MAP Logistics Conf, Nov 59, pp 67-71.
30. *Ibid*., pp 69-71; NAMAP Asian-MAP Logistic Conf, Dec 58, pp 456-58; Lemmer, *The Laos Crisis of 1959*, pp 39-49; rprt, Air Vice Marshal Kamol Thejatunga, RTAF, and Maj Gen Thomas S. Moorman, USAF, to Ch/ SEATO Mil Plng Ofc, Mar 23, 1959, p 2.

31. NAMAP, rprt of 5th Asian-MAP, Logistic Conf, Nov 59, p 353; hist, Asst for Mutual Security, USAF, Jan-Jun 60, n.p., and Jan-Jun 62, pp 35-36.
32. Hist, AMFPA, Jul 1, 1959-Mar 31, 1960, II, App 18, Dec 9, 1959; hist, PACAF, Jan-Jun 60, III; PFMLP hists, Apr 60, w/atch, Apr 17, 1960, and May 60, w/atch; Lt Col William G. Beno, "How to Improve the USAF Portion of the Military Assistance Program in Southeast Asia," (Thesis, USAWC, Apr 60).
33. PACAF Ref Bk for Jan 62 SECDEF Conf, Tab 15F: Country Force Imbalance; NAMAP, rprt of 5th Asian-MAP Logistic Conf, Nov 59, pp 53-58 and 61-62.
34. PACAF Ref Bk for Jan 62 SECDEF Conf, Tab 15F: Country Force Imbalance; NAMAP, rprt of 5th Asian-MAP Logistic Conf, Nov 59, p 353.

CHAPTER V

Strained Civil-Military Relations in South Vietnam, 1957-1960

1. *DOD Pentagon Papers*, Bk 2: IV.A.4., 24-31; *U.S. News & World Report*, Nov 9, 1964, p 63; OASD-ISA, MAP, FY 1962-66, Sep 1, 1960.
2. NAMAP, Asian-MAP Logistic Conf, Dec 58, pp 154-60.
3. Hist, Dir/Plans, USAF, Jul-Dec 55, pp 62-65; hist, Asst for Mutual Security, USAF, Jan-Jun 55, pp 146-50; MACV, *Military Assistance*, pp 2-5; rprt, Collins for SECSTATE, Jan 20, 1955, in *DOD Pentagon Papers*, Bk 10: 865-84; *U.S. News & World Report*, Mar 4, 1955, pp 82-88.
4. Hists, Asst for Mutual Security, USAF, Jan-Jun 55, p 146, Jul-Dec 55, pp 33-34, Jan-Jun 58, n.p.; *DOD Pentagon Papers*, Bk 3: IV.B.3., 125; AMFPA, Title III MDAP Logistic Conf, May 7-10, 1956, p 303; hist, PAF, Jan-Jun 56, III, 527.
5. IR-223-54, AIRA Saigon, Dec 15, 1954; IR-149-55, AIRA Saigon, Sep 15, 1955; VNAF, Welcome to Vietnam, pp 5-8; Secord, "The Viet-Nam Air Force, pp 60-61; FEAF Intel Roundup, Apr 55, pp 21-24; AMFPA Area III MAP Logistic Conf May 7-10, 1956, p 303, and Nov 14-19, 1956, p 314; rprt of Dep/Ops R&R Team to Comdr PAF, Jan 3, 1956; hist, Asst for Mutual Security, USAF, Jan-Jun 58, n.p.
6. AMFPA, Area III MAP, Logistic Conf, Nov 14-19, 1956, p 312; NAMAP, Asian-MAP Logistic Conf, Dec 58, p 154; ltr, Maj Gen Sory

Smith, Comdr PAF, to CINCPAC, Nov 27, 1956; Robbins memo, May 15, 1957; hist, PACAF/FEAF Rear, Jan-Jun 57, II; Hist Sum, Dir/Plans and Policy, Apr 57; hist Asst for Mutual Security, USAF, Jan-Jun 57, App; *USAF Journal of Mutual Security*, X (Jul 1, 1957), 106, and (Aug 1, 1957), 131.
7. Background Paper on Vietnam, prepared by Maj William L. Nicholson, III, HQ PACAF, ca. Jan 62; Robbins memo, May 15, 1957.
8. *USAF Journal of Mutual Security*, XI (Nov 1, 1957), 131; NAMAP, Asian-MAP Logsitic Conf, Dec 58, pp 154-60; hist, Asst for Mutual Security, USAF, Jul-Dec 58, n.p.; PACAF Curr Intel Sum, Oct 23, 1959, p 9.
9. USAF Summary of MDAP and Progress, No. 42, Dec 31, 1955, p 99; PACAF Base Development Plan, Jul 15, 1964, App 2, Tab G; rprt of Dep/Ops P&R Team to Comdr PAF, Jan 2, 1956; *USAF Journal of Mutual Security*, VIII (Sep 1, 1956), 137, and IX (Dec 1, 1956), 104 and 126.
10. See Dept of State, *American Foreign Policy, Current Documents, 1958*, pp 120-121.
11. *Cong Rec*, May 9, 1968, pp 12615-16.
12. Futrell "Chron"; rad, CINCPAC to DIA, Mar 63; *DOD Pentagon Papers*, Bk 2: 24,43.
13. *Ibid*., pp 68-70.
14. Lemmer, *The Laos Crisis of 1959*, p 40; memo, JCS for Dep Asst SECDEF for NSC Affairs and Plans, Jul 14, 1959, in *DOD*

293

Pentagon Papers, Bk 10: 1215; Hearings before the Committee on Appropriations, US Senate, *Mutual Security Appropriations for 1960 (and Related Agencies),* 86th Cong, 1st sess (Washington, 1959), p 511.

15. HQ MACV, "Infiltration Study," Folder Vietnam, Nov 1-30, 1965, 69A-3853, box 34.

16. Halberstam, *Making of a Quagmire,* pp 63-64; msg, AmEmb Saigon to DA, 278, Mar 7, 1960, in *DOD Pentagon Papers,* Bk 10: 1260; *Cong Rec,* May 9, 1968, p 12616.

17. Ibid.

18. HQ MACV, Sum of Highlights, Feb 8, 1962-Feb 7, 1963, p 21.

19. Memo, Lansdale for Draper Committee, Mar 13, 1959; Robert Scigliano, *South Vietnam: Nation Under Stress* (Boston, 1964), p 179; Williams "Interview"; CINCPAC Rcrd, Second SECDEF Conf, Jan 15, 1962, item 5A.

20. MACV hist monograph, *Military Assistance to the Republic of South Vietnam,* pp 6-7, 9-11; MACV, Sum of Highlights, Feb 8, 1962-Feb 7, 1963, pp 46-49; *DOD Pentagon Papers,* Bk 3: IV.B.3., 125.

21. Msg, Lemnitzer to JCS, May 8, 1961; *Journal of Mutual Assistance,* Jun 61.

22. PACAF Ref Bk for Jan 62 SECDEF Conf, Tab 6A; CINCPAC Comd Hist, 1961, pp 172 and 174-75; Scigliano, *South Vietnam,* pp 164-65; *USAF Journal of Mutual Security,* XIII (Dec 60), 149. See also msg, AmEmb Saigon to SECSTATE, 276, Jan 4, 1961, in *DOD Pentagon Papers,* Bk 10: 1357-59.

23. Maj Gen Theodore R. Milton, "Air Power: Equalizer in Southeast Asia," *Air University Review,* Nov-Dec 63, p 4.

24. *USAF Journal of Mutual Security,* XII (Sep 59), 164-55.

25. PACAF Curr Intel Sum, Oct 23, 1959, pp 9-10; hist, Asst for Mutual Security, USAF, Jan-Jun 60, n.p.; hist, PACAF, Jul-Dec 60, III; Wkly Activities Rprts, PFMLP, May 22-26 and Oct 10-14, 1960; msg, CINCPAC to DIA, Mar 13, 1963; PACAF Reference Book for Oct 8, 1962, SECDEF Conf, Vietnam Sec, Tab 4.

26. Hist, Asst for Mutual Security, USAF, Jul-Dec 60, n.p.; hist, PACAF, Jan-Jun 61, III, Wkly Activities Rprt, PFMLP, Feb 27-Mar 3, 1961.

27. Rprt of USAF Asian MAP Logistics Confs, Nov 1-3, 1960, pp 254-55, hist, PACAF, Jul-Dec 61, III; Wkly Activities Rprts, PFMLP, Jul 24-28 and Sep 18-22, 1961; rprt, Col Edwin A. Schneider, Asst for MAP, PACAF, to CINCPACAF, Oct 25, 1961.

28. *Ibid.*; intvw w/ Capt Donald V. MacKellar by J. W. Grainger, Aug 29, 1963; msg, 2d ADVON to PACAF, Jan 13, 1962; telephone conversation, Futrell and Col Harvey Brown, USAF (Ret), Sep 28, 1972.

29. US Senate, *Mutual Security Appropriations for 1960,* 86th Cong, 1st sess, p 516; see also Operations Coordinating Board, Rprt on Southeast Asia, Aug 12, 1959, and SNIE 68-2-59, The Situation in Laos, Sep 18, 1959, in *DOD Pentagon Papers,* Bk 10: 1238-39, 1242-47.

30. "Declaration on Granting Independence to Colonial Countries and Peoples," *Khrushchev in New York* (New York, 1961), p 90; Hearing before the Subcommittee to Investigate the Administration of the Internal Security Act and Internal Security Laws of the Committee on the Judiciary, US Senate, *Analysis of the Khrushchev Speech of January 6, 1961,* 87th Cong, 1st sess (Washington, 1961), pp 64-65, 77-78.

31. *Cong Rec,* May 9, 1968, p 12617; MACV hist monograph, *Military Assistance to the Republic of South Vietnam,* pp 9-11; Douglas Pike, *Viet Cong: The Organization and Techniques of National Liberation Front of South Vietnam* (Cambridge, Mass., 1966), p 79.

32. *USAF Journal of Mutual Assistance,* XIII (Dec 60), 149; Buttinger, *Vietnam,* II, 990.

33. Arthur F. Schlesinger, Jr., *A Thousand Days* (Boston, 1965), p 450; Robert Shaplen, *The Lost Revolution* (New York, 1965), p 149; Maj William L. Nicholson, III, Background Paper on Vietnam, *ca.* Jan 62; Schneider rprt; Presentation by Gen Moorman before Congressional Committee, I, 1-11; hist, 13th AF, Jul-Dec 61, I, 107-09; Intelligence Estimate, SVN, *ca.* Oct 1, 1961, in Hist, 2d ADVON, Nov 61-Oct 62, I, Doc 15.

34. *Cong Rec,* May 9, 1968, pp 12617-18; Pike, *Viet Cong, passim;* Douglas Pike, *War, Peace, and the Viet Cong* (Cambridge, Mass., 1969), pp 1-18.

35. Presentation by Gen Moorman before Cong Committee, I, 1-11; Maj William L. Nicholson, III, Background Paper on Vietnam, *ca.* Jan 62; Schneider rprt.

36. Arthur L. Dommen, *Conflict in Laos: The Politics of Neutralization* (New York, 1964), p 175; Fifth AF Wkly Intel Brief, Jan 11, 1961.

37. Dwight D. Eisenhower, *The White House Years: Waging Peace, 1956-1961* (Garden City, 1965), p 612; Lyndon B. Johnson, *The Vantage Point* (New York, 1971), p 51; Schlesinger, *Thousand Days,* pp 163-64.

38. Memo, Clark Clifford for the President, subj: Conf on Jan 19, 1961, dated Sep 29, 1967, in DOD Pentagon Papers, Bk 10: 1360-64.

Chapter VI

Initial Challenges and Actions

1. Special Message to the Congress on the Defense Budget, Mar 28, 1961, in *Public Papers of the Presidents: John F. Kennedy, 1961*, (Washington, 1962), pp 229-40.

2. AFXOPJ Book of Actions in SEA, 1961-64, No. 6-4995-52; Charles H. Hildreth, *USAF Counterinsurgency Doctrines and Capabilities, 1961-1962* (USAF Hist Div Liaison Ofc, Feb 64), pp 1-3; Presentation to the USAF Scientific Advisory Board on the Subject of Counterinsurgency by Brig Gen Adriel N. Williams, Apr 24, 1962; US Dept of State *Bulletin* 57, 280-81.

3. Maxwell D. Taylor, *Swords and Plowshares* (New York, 1972), pp 197 and 220; Futrell, "Chron."

4. Richard M. Nixon, "Cuba, Castro and John F. Kennedy," *Reader's Digest*, Nov 64, pp 290-92.

5. Dommen, *Conflict in Laos*, pp 192-95; hist, Dir/Plans, USAF, Jan-Jun 61, pp 78-81; Hearings before the Committee on Foreign Relations, US Senate, *International Development and Security*, 87th Cong, 1st sess (Washington, 1961), pt 2, p 682; 5th AF Intel Brief, May 16 and 23, 1961.

6. Hist, PACAF, Jan-Jun 61, III, Hist Rprt A-2, Apr 61; hist, 315th Air Div (Combat Cargo), Jan-Jun 61, App 0; CINCPAC Comd Hist, 1961, pt 2, pp 89-90; Schlesinger, *Thousand Days*, p 336; Richard P. Stebbins, ed. *Documents on American Foreign Relations, 1961* (New York, 1962), pp 306-10; Dommen, *Conflict in Laos*, pp 192-95.

7. US Senate, *International Development and Security*, 87th Cong, 1st sess, pt 2, p 649; Schlesinger, *Thousand Days*, pp 337-39; CINCPAC Comd Hist, 1961, pt 2, p 93; hist, Dir/Plans, USAF, Jan-Jun 61, pp 78-81.

8. Dept of State, Memo of Conversation on Laos, Apr 29, 1961, in *DOD Pentagon Papers*, Bk 11: 62-66; Hearings before the Subcommittee of the Committee on Appropriations, House of Representatives, *Department of Defense Appropriations for 1963*, 87th Cong, 2d sess, (Washington, 1962), pt 2, pp 354-56.

9. Dept of State, Memo of Conversation on Laos, cited above; ltr, O'Donnell to LeMay, May 22, 1961, in hist, PACAF, Jan-Jun 61, I, pt 2, 13-15.

10. Theodore C. Sorenson, *Kennedy* (New York, 1965), pp 644-45; Schlesinger, *Thousand Days*, pp 337-39; *DOD Pentagon Papers*, Bk 2: IV.B.1., 6-7, Taylor, pp 197, 220; Futrell, "Chron"; *Public Papers of the Presidents: Kennedy, 1961*, pp 438, 444; Hearings before the Committee on Appropriations, US Senate, *Foreign Assistance and Related Agencies Appropriations for 1962*, 87th Cong, 1st sess (Washington, 1961), pp 112-13 and 135-37; Henry F. Graff, "Teach-In on Vietnam," *New York Times Magazine*, Mar 20, 1966, pp 130-31; CQ Background, *China and U.S. Far East Policy, 1945-67*, p 104; Stebbins, *Documents*, pp 311-18; Dommen, *Conflict in Laos*, p 188; hist, PACAF, Jul-Dec 61, I, pt 2, 13-18; hist, Dir/Plans, USAF, Jul-Dec 61, pp 184-88; 5th AF Intel Brief, Apr 5, 1961; Hearings before the Committee on Foreign Relations, US Senate, *Foreign Assistance Act of 1962*, 87th Cong, 2d sess (Washington, 1962), pp 349-50 and 370.

11. Hist, Dir/Plans, USAF, Jul-Dec 61, pp 184-88; Belden Intvw with LeMay, Jul 1972.

12. *Public Papers of the Presidents: Kennedy, 1961*, pp 533, 580, and 656; Annual Report of the Dept of Defense, Fiscal Year 1962, p 56.

13. Jacob Van Staaveren, *USAF Plans and Policies in South Vietnam, 1961-1963* (USAF Hist Div Liaison Ofc, Jun 65), p 6; CINCPAC Comd Hist, 1961, pp 174-74; memo, Pres Kennedy for SECSTATE and SECDEF, Jan 30, 1961, and msg State-Defense-ISA to Saigon, 1054, Feb 3, 1961, in *DOD Pentagon Papers*, Bk 11: 13-16; rad, CINCPAC to DIA, Feb 5, 1961.

14. *Federal Register*, Nov 10, 1960, pp 10731-3; Dept of State *Bulletin* 45, 993-94.

15. *USAF Journal of Mutual Security*, Mar 61. If Vietnamese pilots were sometimes less than enthusiastic about flying or fighting, it was because they lacked the protection of insurance, death benefits, and disability pensions. They might hope that their families or clans would protect their survivors if they were killed or injured, but even so, a loss of life or a crippling injury had consequences beyond those an American might imagine on the basis of his own situation. Vietnamese pilots and aircrews flying in combat exposed their families to hazards of a most sobering variety. Kenneth Sams, *History of the Second Air Division, Jul-Dec 64*, III, 42.

16. *USAF Journal of Mutual Security*, Mar 61.

17. *DOD Pentagon Papers*, Bk 2: 30; National Intelligence Estimate, May 59; Research Analysis Corp., "U.S. Army Special Forces Operations under the Civilian Irregular Defense Groups Program in Vietnam, 1961-64" (McLean, Va., 1966), p 26; JCS History, pp 201-03. The police consisted of approximately seventy-five hundred Bureau of Investigation and ten thousand five hundred municipal police-

men who were in the cities and not available to deal with insurrection in rural areas. A CIA survey in December 1961 reported that the security forces in the fourteen provinces needed training in professional fundamentals. The following January, the Bureau of Investigation and the police were combined. JCS History, 1954-59, p 96; *DOD Pentagon Papers*, Bk 2: 23; R W. Komer, "The Malayan Emergency in Retrospect," The RAND Corp, 1972, p 38; Status Rprt on Covert Actions in Vietnam, Dec 28, 1961; Status Rprt on Instructions to Nolting, Jan 11, 1962.

18. MACV hist monograph, *Military Assistance to the Republic of South Vietnam*, pp 9-11; Fifth AF Wkly Intel Brief, Mar 22, 1961; *Public Papers of the Presidents: Kennedy, 1961*, pp 311, 340.

19. A Program of Action, Apr 26, 1961.

20. CINCPAC Comd Hist, 1961, pp 169-70; 5th AF Wkly Brief, May 11, 1961; PACAF Ref Bk for Dec 61 SECDEF Conf, Tab B-7-B; rad, UK 70272, May 8, 1961; *USAF Journal of Military Security*, Jun 61.

21. Schlesinger, *Thousand Days*, p 541; CINCPAC Comd Hist, 1961, p 175; hist, Asst for Mutual Security, USAF, Jan-Jun 61, n.p.; Van Staaveren, *USAF Plans and Policies in South Vietnam, 1961-1963*, p 7.

22. Talking Paper on Program of Action for Vietnam, Folder "Policy-Vietnam," RL (61) 38-9, (Jan 1-May 31, 1961), Sec 1, 64-A-2436; memo, AFXOD-PY to CSAF, May 10, 1961, *ibid*.

23. See rad, UK 70272, May 8, 1961.

24. Scigliano, *South Vietnam*, p 160; *Public Papers of the Presidents: Kennedy, 1961*, p. 356; AFXOPJ Book of Actions in SEA, 1961-64, Item IV-A; CINCPAC Comd Hist, 1961, pp 184-75; ltr, O'Donnell to Felt, May 17, 1961; Johnson, *Vantage Point*, p 53.

25. *DOD Pentagon Papers*, Bk 2: 19-45.

26. Kennedy Program and Commitments, 1961, pp 44-45; RAC-T-477, p 26.

27. Folder, "Policy-Vietnam, RL (61) 38-9 (Jan 1-May 31, 1961), Sec 1."

28. *DOD Pentagon Papers*, Bk 2: 55; Rprt, J-3 2434/41 to the JCS, Aug 5, 1961, quoting AmEmb Saigon 1743, May 15, 1961.

29. The Kennedy Commitments and Programs, 1961, pp 58-61.

30. Van Staaveren, *USAF Plans and Policies in South Vietnam, 1961-1963*, p 8; Dept of State Bulletin 45, 956-57; Schlesinger, *Thousand Days*, p 543; *Public Papers of the Presidents: Lyndon B. Johnson, 1965* (Washington, 1966), I, 404; NSAM 52, May 11, 1961; rprt, Lyndon B. Johnson to the President, May 23, 1961, in *DOD Pentagon Papers*, Bk 11: 136-37, 159-66.

31. Col R. M. Levy, USAF, JCS representative, Memo for the Record, May 22, 1961, incl to JCS 1992/994; msg, AFXOD to PACAF, May 19, 1961.

32. CINCPAC Comd Hist, 1961, pp 172-74.

33. *DOD Pentagon Papers*, Bk 2: 16.

34. Graff, "Teach-In on Vietnam," p 131. Rusk had recommended on May 5, 1961, that the United States refrain from placing combat forces in South Vietnam. See Levy Memo for Record, May 5, 1961, in *DOD Pentagon Papers*, Bk 11: 67-68.

35. Status Rprt on Covert Actions in Vietnam, Jun 61, p 158.

36. The Kennedy Commitments and Program, 1961, pp 58-61.

37. Hist, Dir/Plans, USAF, Jan-Jun 61, pp 44, 169-70.

38. Joint Action Program by the Viet Nam-United States Special Financial Group, in *DOD Pentagon Papers*, Bk 11: 182-226.

39. Note by Secys to JCS on Presidential Program, 2343/12, Aug 15, 1961, p 42, Folder "Policy-Vietnam," Sec 3 64A2436, #25. Covert actions are "small military type actions taken in the national interest that, if detected by friendly or unfriendly powers, can be plausibly denied by the U.S. Government. Equipment and/or personnel used in these operations are selected and prepared so as to offer the highest probability that they cannot legally be traced to the U.S. Government." Clandestine operations, in contrast, are those in which emphasis is placed on concealing the fact of the operation. Ltr, Lt Gen John K. Gerhard, USAF, DCS/Plans and Programs, to the Asst to SECDEF, Mar 28, 1962.

40. Folder, "Policy-Vietnam," RL (61) 38-9 (Jun 1-Aug 1961); Van Staaveren, *USAF Plans and Policies in South Vietnam*, pp 8-9; msg, CINCPAC to DIA, Mar 13, 1963; memo, SECDEF to Service Secys, CJCS, ASD/ISA, Aug 18, 1961.

41. *Journal of Military Assistance*, Sept 61, pp 152-53.

42. MACV J-2, Infiltration Study, Folder Vietnam 1-30, Nov 64; RAND Corp Study, *Infiltration of Personnel from North Vietnam, 1959-67*, Oct 68.

43. Hist, 5th AF, Jul-Dec 61, I, 107-09; PACAF Ref Book for Dec 61 SECDEF Conf, Tab B-2; *The Pentagon Papers as Published by the New York Times*, ed N. Sheehan, et al (New York, 1971), pp 95-96.

44. CINCPAC Comd Hist, 1961, pp 182-83; MACV, Sum of Highlights, Feb 8, 1962-Feb 7, 1963, p 41; AFXOPJ Book on Actions in SEA, 1961-64, Item IV-C; hist, Dir/Plans, USAF, Jul-Dec 61, pp 44-45; CINCPAC Rcrd of 2d SECDEF Conf, Jan 15, 1962, Item 13.

45. CINCPAC Comd Hist, 1961, p 183; hist, Asst for Mutual Security, USAF, Jan-Jun 61,

n.p.; Rprt of CSAF Visit to SVN, Apr 62.
  46. SVN Radar Environment Survey, Jul 61, in hist, 5th Tac Contr Gp, Jul-Dec 61, App XXV.
  47. Memo, Phillip F. Hilbert for Dir/Plans, Jun 8, 1961; CINCPAC Comd Hist, 1961, pp 33-34; hist, PACAF, Jul-Dec 61, III, Hist Rprt of C-E Opns, Elec Systems Div, Aug 61; hist, PFOCO, Dec 61; ltr, Brig Gen R. M. Anthis to 13th AF, n.d.; Schneider rprt; Joseph W. Grainger and TSgt George P. Day, Hist of the 2d ADVON, Nov 15, 1961-Oct 8, 1962; ltr, Lt Gen Earle E. Wheeler, Dir Jt Stf, to CJCS, Nov 14, 1961.
  48. Kennedy Program and Commitments, 1961; Futrell, "Chron"; hist, 13th AF, Jul-Dec 61, pp 69-70; hist, 2d ADVON, Nov 61-Oct 62, p 5; hist, PACAF, Jul-Dec 61, I, pt 2, 18-32, III, A-2 Monthly Hist Rprt, Oct 61; msg, CINCPAC to JCS, Nov 11, 1961; Rprt on Able Mable, *ca*. Feb 1, 1962, in hist, 2d ADVON, Nov 15, 1961-Oct 8, 1962, Doc 72; *DOD Pentagon Papers*, Bk 2: IV.B.1., 91; hist, 19th TFW, Jul-Dec 61, p 62; hist, PACAF, Jul-Dec 61, III, A-2 Monthly Hist Rprt, Oct 61; hist, PACAF, Jul-Dec 61, I, pt 2, 20-21; Daily Hist Log, Pipe Stem Det, Oct 18-21, 1961.
  49. *Journal of Military Assistance*, Sep 61, p 153; Schlesinger, *Thousand Days*, p 450; Shaplen, *Lost Revolution*, p 149; Maj William L. Nicholson, III, Background Paper on Vietnam, *ca*. Jan 62; Schneider rprt; Presentation by Gen Moorman before Congressional Committee, I, 1-11; hist 13th AF, Jul-Dec 61, I, 107-09; Intel Est, *ca*.Oct 1, 1961, in hist, 2d ADVON, Nov 61-Oct 62, I, Doc 15.
  50. Hist, Asst for Mutual Security, USAF, Jan-Jun 61, n.p., and Jul-Dec 61, pp 28-29.
  51. JCSM-700-61, Jet Aircraft for SVN, Oct 7, 1961; hist, Dir/Plans, USAF, Jul-Dec 61, p 262; AFXOPJ Book of Actions in SEA, 1961-64, Item VII-A; CINCPAC Comd Hist, 1961, p 186; HQ USAF Memo (OPS 50-61), Sep 20, 1961; hist, Asst for Mutual Security, Jul-Dec 61, n.p.; hist, PACAF, Jul-Dec 61, III, Wkly Activities Rprt, PFMLP, Dec 11-15, 1961.

Chapter VII

Opening Farm Gate

  1. Ltr, Col Robert L. Gleason to Col Ray Bowers, Ofc/AF Hist, Dec 30, 1971; Book of Actions in SEA, p 6; SO G-4, TAC, Langley AFB, Va., Apr 10, 1961; memo, Dir/Ops, USAF, Apr 27, 1961, incl 7, Vol 2; TSgt Robert J. O'Neill, History of Special Air Warfare Center, Apr-Dec 62, Air Archives; intvw with Lt Col M. M. Doyle, Bien Hoa, Feb 16, 1963; hist, 2d ADVON, Nov 61-Oct 62.
  2. Ltr, Gleason to Bowers; Doyle intvw, Feb 16, 1963.
  3. Hist, 2d ADVON, Nov 61-Oct-62, p 8; hist, 2d Air Division, Jan-Jun 64, p 4; John W. R. Taylor, ed, *Combat Aircraft of the World* (New York 1961), pp 491-92; Tactical Air Support Handbook, Oct 62, Sec IX; MR, Details on Modification and IRAN's Perf on T-28 and B-26 Acft, n.d., Binder COIN Ops 774-64, box 12, 68A-4994.
  4. AFXOPJ Book of Actions in SEA, 1961-64, Item IV-B.
  5. *Ibid.*, Item III-B, pp 21-22.
  6. CINCPAC Comd Hist, 1961, p 187.
  7. Kennedy Program and Commitments, 1961, p 84.
  8. Hist, Dir/Plans, USAF, Jul 1-Dec 31, 1961, Vol 22, 78.
  9. Book of Actions in SEA, p 2 and Item II; hist, SAWC, Apr 27-Dec 31, 1962, pp 1-10; intvw with Lt Col Charles E. Trumbo, Jr., by J. W. Grainger, Jul 13, 1963; LeMay comments, intvw by Thomas G. Belden, Mar 29, 1972; see also Proj Corona Harvest Oral Hist intvw with Brig Gen Benjamin H. King, Sep 4, 1962, pp 1-5.
  10. Rcrd, Second SECDEF Conf, Jan 15, 1962, p III-2; intvw, J. Grainger with Lt Col M. M. Doyle, Feb 16, 1963, in App D, Hist, 2d ADVON, Nov 61-Oct 62.
  11. MR, Dir/Plans, USAF, subj: CINCPAC Briefing on Jungle Jim, Oct 16, 1961.
  12. Msg, US Amb Saigon to State, Oct 13, 1961, in *New York Times, Pentagon Papers*, pp 140-41; see also Taylor, *Swords and Plowshares*, pp 227-28; CINCPAC Comd Hist, 1961, pp 187-91, Proj Corona Harvest Oral Hist intvw with Col King, pp 15-21.
  13. Detachment 1 was spending several weeks in Mali, the Republic of West Africa, training paratroopers.
  14. Progress Rprt, 6009th TSG, *ca*. Dec 5, 1961, in Hist, 2d ADVON, Nov 61-Oct 62, and Doc 6; hist, 5th AF, Jul-Dec 61, I, 53-56; msg, PACAF to 13th AF, Nov 17, 1961.
  15. Hist, SAWC, Apr-Dec 62, pp 12-13.
  16. Msg, Det 9, 2d ADVON to PACAF, Nov 21, 1961; Intel Rprt, Debriefing of the Commander and Intelligence Officer, Det 2, 4400th CCTG (Nov 61-Feb 62), Apr 1, 1962; Briefing by

Capt M. K. Palmer, Jan 16, 1962, in Hist, 5th. AF, Jan-Jun 62, II, Doc 144.

17. Hist, 2d ADVON, pp 8-9; 4400th CCTG Intel Rprt, Apr 1, 1962; msg, CSAF to CINCPAC, Nov 9, 1961; msg, CINCPAC to JCS, Nov 15, 1961; CINCPAC Rcrd, SECDEF Conf, Dec 16, 1961, msg, Item 8A; AFCHO Oral Hist Intvw with LeMay, Jun 8, 1972; telephone conversation, Futrell with Col Robert L. Gleason, Lt Col John Pattee, and Lt Col William E. Doughterty, Jul 72; Victor B. Anthony, *The Air Force in Southeast Asia: Tactics and Techniques of Night Operations, 1961-1970*, (Ofc/ AF Hist, Mar 73).

18. Msg, CINCPAC to Chief MAAG VN, Nov 16, 1961; rprt, SAF to Pres, Feb 6, 1962, Binder Vietnam 11-62.

19. Msg, CINCPAC to DIA, Mar 13, 1963; *New York Times*, Feb 20, 1962, p 3; PACAF Ref Bk for Mar 62 SECDEF Conf, Item 5.

20. PACAF Ref Bk for Jan 62 SECDEF Conf, Tab 3B, Mar 62 SECDEF Conf, Item 5; Futrell's conversation with Gleason, Jul 72.

21. Paul S. Ella, Richard P. Joyce, Robert H. Williams, and William Woodworth, *U.S. Army Special Forces and Similar Internal Defense Advisory Operations in Mainland Southeast Asia, 1962-67* (Research Analysis Corp, Jun 69), p 117.

22. Msg, JCS to CINCPAC, Dec 6, 1961; CINCPAC Comd Hist, 1961, pp 190-91; AFXOPJ Book of Actions in SEA, 1961-64, Item VII-B.

23. Msg, PACAF to CINCPAC, Dec 6, 1961; PACAF Ref Bk for Dec 61 SECDEF Conf, Action Tab H.

24. CINCPAC Comd Hist, 1961, p 171; msg, CINCPAC to Chief MAAG VN, Dec 6, 1961; CINCPAC Rcrd, SECDEF Conf, Dec 16, 1961, Item 4.

25. Msgs, PACAF to CINCPAC, Dec 8, 1961, 13th AF to PACAF, Dec 10, 1961; AFXOPJ Book of Actions in SEA, 1961-64, Item III-C; CINCPAC Comd Hist, 1961, p 188.

26. CINCPAC Rcrd, SECDEF Conf, Dec 16, 1961, Item 8A; msg, PACAF to CSAF, Dec 17, 1961.

27. Msg, CINCPAC to PACAF, Dec 20, 1961.

28. Intvw with Anthis by Gausche and Grainger, Aug 30, 1963; msgs, 13th AF to PACAF, Dec 28, 1961, CSAF to PACAF, Mar 23, 1963, JCS to CINCPAC, Dec 26, 1961; PACAF Ref Bk for Feb 62 SECDEF Conf.

Chapter VIII

The Taylor Mission

1. The President also asked the State Department to solicit comments on this question from allied nations. AFXOPJ Book of Actions in SEA, Item III-B; Van Staaveren, *USAF Plans and Policies in South Vietnam, 1961-1963*; MR, Roswell Gilpatric, Oct 11, 1961, and NSAM 104, Oct 13, 1961, in *DOD Pentagon Papers*, Bk 11: 322-38; *Public Papers of the Presidents: Kennedy, 1961*, pp 656, 660; Taylor, *Swords and Plowshares*, pp 225-26.

2. CQ Background, *China and U.S. Far East Policy, 1945-1967*, p 108; see also Cooper, *Lost Crusade*, pp 193-94.

3. MACV hist monograph, *Military Assistance to the Republic of South Vietnam, 1960-1963*, p 11; ltr, Diem to Kennedy, n.d., in *Public Papers of the Presidents: Kennedy, 1961*, pp 801-02; PACAF Reference Book for Dec 61 SECDEF Conf, Tab B-1; Intel Estimate SVN, ca. Oct 1, 1961, in Hist, 2d ADVON, I, Doc 15.

4. PACAF Reference Book for Dec 61 SECDEF Conf.

5. Msg, USAmb Saigon to State, Oct 13, 1961, in *New York Times, Pentagon Papers*, pp 140-41.

6. CINCPAC Comd Hist, 1961, pp 187-91.

7. Ltr, Taylor to the President (Taylor Rprt), Nov 3, 1961; Kennedy Program and Commitments, pp 98-99.

8. Taylor, *Swords and Plowshares*, pp 241-44; *New York Times, Pentagon Papers*, pp 141-48; *DOD Pentagon Papers*, Bk 2: IV.B.1., 100-08; Van Staveren, *USAF Plans and Policies in South Vietnam, 1961-1963*, pp 10-11; Schlesinger, *Thousand Days*, pp 546-47; Roger Hilsman, *To Move a Nation: The Politics of Foreign Policy in the Administration of John F. Kennedy* (Garden City, 1967), pp 422-23; George W. Ball, *The Discipline of Power: Essentials of a Modern World Structure* (Boston, 1968), p 334; Dept of State *Bulletin* 56, 514.

9. Covering note, sgd William P. Bundy with draft memo, SECDEF for President, Nov 6, 1961; Background Paper on CINCPAC OPlan 32-59; Kennedy Program and Commitments, 1961, pp 122-23; SM-1212-61, Recommended Change to the Proposed Memo for the Pres, Nov 6, 1961; hist, Dir/Plans, USAF, Jul-Dec 61, pp 176-78.

10. Van Staaveren, *USAF Plans and Policies*

in South Vietnam, 1961-1963, p 11; memo, McNamara for the Pres, Nov 8, 1961, in *DOD Pentagon papers*, Bk 11: 343-44.

11. Kennedy Program and Commitments, 1961, pp 122-23; Taylor, *Swords and Plowshares*, pp 245-46.

12. Schlesinger, *Thousand Days*, p 547; hist, PACAF, Jul-Dec 61, III, Monthly Hist Rprt A-2, Nov 61.

13. Msgs, CINCPAC to JCS, Oct 20, 1961, and Nov 15, 1961; *DOD Pentagon Papers*, Bk 2: IV.B.1., 88-90.

14. Schlesinger, *Thousand Days*, p 547.

15. *Ibid.*; memo, McNamara for the Pres, Nov 11, 1961, in *DOD Pentagon Papers*, Bk 11: 359-66; Taylor, *Swords and Plowshares*, pp 246-47.

16. Hist, Dir/Plans, USAF, Jul-Dec 61, pp 45-46, 176-77; Van Staaveren, *USAF Plans and Policies in South Vietnam, 1961-1963*, p 12; *DOD Pentagon Papers*, Bk 2: IV.B.1., 125-37.

17. NSAM 111, First Phase of Viet-Nam Program, Nov 22, 1961.

18. Memo, Burchinal to CSAF (sgd Col Frank R. Pancake), n.d.

19. Talking Paper on Determination of Effective U.S. Policy toward South Vietnam, Nov 13, 1961.

20. CSAFM 430-61, for the JCS on SVN, Dec 5, 1961; AFXOPJ Book on Actions in SEA, 1961-64, Item IV-D; JCSM 33-62, Jan 13, 1962, In *DOD Pentagon Papers*, Bk 12: 448-54.

21. Background Paper on CINCPAC OPlan.

22. Incl to CSAFM 430-61, Dec 5, 1961, draft memo for SECDEF. LeMay's thinking was consistent with that of the Army at least. On November 14 the Army had embarked a brigade task force in the Pacific Command, plus some thirty-five thousand combat and logistical support units from the United States, for deployment. Memo with incls, Lt Gen Earl G. Wheeler, Dir Jt Stf, to CJCS, Nov 14, 1961.

23. JCS 2343/65, Dec 7, 1961.

24. Memo, SECDEF to Pres, Jan 27, 1962, incl to JCS 2343/70.

25. LeMay intvw with Belden, Mar 29, 1972.

26. See Summary Sheet, Dir/Plans, USAF, Nov 24, 1961; memo with incls, in Jt Stf to CJCS, Nov 14, 1961.

27. Ltr, CINCPAC to JCS, Dec 5, 1961.

Chapter IX

U.S. Command Arrangements: 2d ADVON and MACV

1. *DOD Pentagon Papers*, Bk 2: IV.B.1., 90-108; PACAF Ref Bk for Dec 61 SECDEF Conf, Tab B-4.

2. The Kennedy Program and Commitments, 1961, pp 129-30; memo, SECDEF to CJCS, Nov 13, 1961.

3. Note to Control Div, Nov 28, 1961; JCS 2343/61, Note by the Secys to the JCS, Nov 30, 1961; ltr, Rear Adm R. J. Bouin to SECDEF, Dec 4, 1961.

4. Msg, McNamara to Felt and McGarr, Nov 28, 1961.

5. Msg, AmEmb Saigon to SECSTATE, Dec 4, 1961.

6. *DOD Pentagon Papers*, Bk 2: IV.B.1., 118; Hearings before the Committee on Foreign Relations, US Senate, *Foreign Assistance, 1966*, 89th Cong, 2d sess (Washington, 1966), pp 243-44, 263; msg, AmEmb New Dehli to Pres, Nov 21, 1961, in *DOD Pentagon Papers*, Bk 11: 410-18.

7. Msgs, JCS to SECDEF, Nov 22, 1961, and to CINCPAC, Nov 23 and 28, 1961; Van Staaveren, *USAF Plans and Policies in South Vietnam, 1961-1963*, pp 14-15.

8. Msg, CINCPAC to JCS, Nov 29, 1961; PACAF Ref Bk for Dec 61 SECDEF Conf, Tab B-4.

9. *Ibid.*

10. AFXOPJ Book of Actions in SEA, 1961-64, Item IIIA-L; msg, CINCPAC to PACAF and Chief MAAG, Nov 2, 1961.

11. F-100s and a control and reporting center of the Thirteenth Air Force had been at Don Muang, Thailand, since April 13, 1961, under a command element known as Thirteenth Air Force ADVON (abbreviation for Advanced Echelon). This was the first ADVON, that in Vietnam became the second.

12. Msgs, CINCPACAF to CSAF, Nov 11, 1961, PACAF to 2d ADVON, Feb 20, 1962, to 2d AD, Aug 4, 1962, to 13th AF, Nov 17, 1961; SO G-85, PACAF, Nov 15, 1963; hist, 5th AF, Jul-Dec 61, I, 53-56.

13. Msgs, Nolting to State, Nov 25, 1961, CINCPAC to JCS, Nov 25 and 29, 1961; msgs, USAIRA Saigon to CSAF, Nov 28, 1961, CINCPAC to Chief MAAG VN, Nov 25, 1961, and Nov 29, 1961; ltr, O'Donnell to CINCPAC, Dec 12, 1961; intvw with Anthis by Gausche and Grainger, Aug 30, 1963.

14. Msg, 13th AF to PACAF, Dec 10, 1961.

15. Hist, 2d ADVON, Nov 61-Oct 62, p 46.

16. This technique was evaluated as being less satisfactory than cooperative C-47 flareship/strike aircraft operations mainly because of the limited number of flares that a T-28 could load on its wing stations and the consequent reduction of ordnance that it could carry. Msg, PACAF to CSAF, Dec 17, 1961; Project Corona Harvest Oral Hist intvw with King, pp 51-56.

17. See msg, MACV to CINCPAC, Sep 17, 1962.

18. Of the former, 2,066 were allocated to the Army, 6 to the Marine Corps, 135 to the Navy, and 187 (68 officers and 119 men) to the Air Force. CINCPAC Comd Hists, 1961, p 175, and 1962, p 155; hist, PACAF, Jul-Dec 61, III; PFMLP Wkly Activities Rprt, Dec 22-29, 1961; PACAF Ref Bk for Dec 61 SECDEF Conf, Action Tab F.

19. Memo, SECDEF to Pres, Dec 22, 1961; Van Staaveren, *USAF Plans and Policies in South Vietnam, 1961-1963*, p 15.

20. Msg, PACAF to 13th AF and 2d ADVON, Feb 20, 1962.

21. AFCHO Oral Hist Intvw 522, with Gen Paul D. Harkins, Feb 23, 1972; mg, CINCPAC to DEPCINCUSARPAC, Feb 8, 1962.

22. Msgs, JCS to CINCPAC, Jan 31 and Mar 2, 1962, to MACV, Apr 7, 1962, CSAF to PACAF, Feb 21, 1962; Martin and Clever, IV, 38-39; Van Staaveren, *USAF Plans and Policies in South Vietnam, 1961-1963*, pp 16-17. Later, Brig Gen Milton B. Adams was Assistant Chief of Staff J-5 (Plans).

23. Msg, MACV to CINCPAC, Sep 17, 1962; ltr, Anthis to Eugene C. Zuckert, SAF, Jan 9, 1963; Brig Gen Frank A. Osmanski, MACV J-4, Rprt on Vietnam, Sep 26, 1963, pp 10-11.

24. Msgs, MACV to CINCPAC, Mar 1, 1962, 2d ADVON to PACAF, May 7, 1962, CINCPAC to MACV, May 12, 1962, 2d ADVON to 13th AF, May 16, 1962, CSAF to Chief MAAG, Jun 21, 1962, and CINCPAC to CSAF, Oct 31, 1962; DAF SO AA-2164, Nov 9, 1962; ltr, Anthis to Zuckert, Jan 9, 1963.

25. Msgs, CINCPAC to MACV, Feb 25, 1962, MACV to CINCPAC, Mar 1, 1962, Apr 6, 1962, Apr 7, 1962, May 6, 1962, PACAF to 13th AF and 2d ADVON, Apr 27, 1962, 2d ADVON to PACAF, May 5, 1962, PACAF to CSAF, May 12, 1962, CINCPAC to MACV, Sep 30, 1963.

26. Osmanski Rprt, pp 10-11; ltr, Anthis to Zuckert, Jan 9, 1963; msg, CNO/CSA/CSAF to CINCPACFLT, et al, May 22, 1962. Felt believed that no requirement existed for a MACV Navy component command. Yet on July 1, 1962, Headquarters Support Activity Saigon, a naval organization, came into being to provide common administrative and logistic support, including construction, commissary, exchange, and housekeeping services, to MAAG and MACV units.

27. Msg, PACAF to 13th AF and 2d ADVON, Feb 20, 1962.

28. Martin and Clever, II, 17-18; *The Public Papers of the Presidents: John F. Kennedy, 1962* (Washington, 1963), p 137; msgs, PACAF to 13th AF and 2d ADVON, Feb 20, 1962, CINCPAC to MACV, Feb 25, 1962, MACV to CINCPAC, Mar 1, 1962, and 2d ADVON to 13th AF, Mar 9, 1962.

29. Hetherington Rprt, Apr 25, 1972; msg, PACAF to 13th AF, May 24, 1962.

30. Dept of State, *American Foreign Policy: Current Documents, 1962* (Washington, 1966), pp 1103-06.

31. *NY Herald Tribune*, Apr 28, 1962.

32. *Ibid.*

33. Brig Gen Thomas R. Phillips, USA (Ret), in *St. Louis Post-Dispatch*, May 6, 1962.

34. Intvw, Grainger with Lt Col M. M. Doyle, Feb 16, 1963; Martin and Clever, App 2, COIN Intvws, Tab M.

35. *New York Times*, May 1, 1962.

36. *Chicago Tribune*, May 6, 1962.

37. A. Rose, "Our Undeclared War in Vietnam," *Reporter*, May 10, 1962.

38. Msg, PACAF to 13th AF, May 24, 1962; hist, 2d ADVON, Nov 61-Oct 62, pp 21-31, 34; msgs, CINCPAC to MACV, Jul 7 and 28, 1962, MACV to CINCPAC, Jul 19, 1962; PACAF SO G-87, Sep 24, 1962; hist, 13th AF, Jan-Jun 63, p 20.

39. Hist, 2d ADVON, Nov 61-Oct 62, p 42; msg, PACAF to 13th AF, Nov 10, 1962.

40. Msgs, 2d ADVON to 13th AF, Apr 21 and 25, 1962; Van Staaveren, *USAF Plans and Policies in South Vietnam, 1961-1963*, pp 46-47; AFCHO Oral Hist intvw with Harkins, Feb 23, 1972.

41. Hearings before the Committee on Armed Services, House of Representatives, *Military Posture*, 89th Cong, 2d sess (Washington, 1966), pp 7609-10.

42. Van Staaveren, *USAF Plans and Policies in South Vietnam, 1961-1963*, p 47; memo, Col Winston P. Anderson, Dir/Ops, 2d AD, for Anthis, Feb 23, 1963; msgs, 2d AD to PACAF, Jan 27, 1963, and Sep 29, 1963.

Chapter X

Tactical Air Control, Mule Train, and Ranch Hand

1. Wilfred G. Burchett, *Vietnam: Inside Story of the Guerrilla War* (New York, 1965), pp 88-89; PACAF Ref Bk for Jul 22-24, 1962, SECDEF Conf, Item B; MACV hist monograph, *Military Assistance to the Republic of South Vietnam, 1960-63*, pp 11-12.

2. Cong Rec, May 9, 1968, pp 12617-18; Pike, *Viet Cong*, passim, and *War, Peace, and the Viet Cong*, pp 1-18.

3. Msg, USAIRA Saigon to CSAF, Nov 28, 1961; PACAF Reference Book for Jan 1962, SECDEF Conf, Tab 13; CINCPAC Rcrd, Second SECDEF Conf, Jan 15, 1962, Item 13, and Dec 16, 1961, Item 2.

4. CINCPAC Rcrd, Second SECDEF Conf, Jan 15, 1962, Item 5A; HQ MACV, Summary of Highlights, Feb 8, 1962-Feb 7, 1963, p 97; ltr, R. K. G. Thompson to Diem, Nov 11, 1961, in *DOD Pentagon Papers*, Bk 11: 345-58.

5. CINCPAC Rcrd, Third SECDEF Conf, Feb 19, 1962, Items 2 and 4.

6. Msg, MACV to CINCPAC, Apr 14, 1962; CINCPAC Rcrd, SECDEF Conf, Dec 16, 1961, Item 2, and 3d SECDEF Conf, Feb 19, 1962, Items 3 and 5; memo, Moorman to PFDAL and PFDOP, Feb 23, 1962; Hilsman, *To Move a Nation*, pp 441-44.

7. CINCPAC Rcrd, 2d SECDEF Conf, Jan 15, 1962, Items 5, 5A, and 14, and 3d SECDEF Conf, Feb 19, 1962, Item 4; Sir Robert Thompson, *Defeating Communist Insurgency: The Lessons of Malaya and Vietnam* (New York, 1966), pp 129-39.

8. The members were Robert Kennedy, U. Alexis Johnson, Roswell L. Gilpatric, General Lemnitzer, John A. McCone, McGeorge Bundy, Edward R. Murrow, and Fowler Hamilton.

9. Taylor, *Swords and Plowshares*, pp 201-3; NSAM 124, Jan 18, 1962, in *DOD Pentagon Papers*, Bk 12: 442-44; Hearings before a Subcommittee of the Committee on Appropriations, House of Representatives, *Department of Defense Appropriations for 1965*, 88th Cong, 2d sess (Washington, 1964), pt 2, p 612.

10. Taylor, *Swords and Plowshares*, pp 201-03; NSAM 162, Jun 19, 1962, and NSAM 182, Aug 24, 1962, in *DOD Pentagon Papers*, Bk 12: 481-86; US Overseas Internal Defense Policy, Aug 1, 1962; JCSM, Nov 20, 1962.

11. AFXOPJ Book of Actions in SEA, 1961-64, p 23.

12. Hists, 13th AF, Jul-Dec 61, I, 73-74, and 1962, I, 72-74; 13th AF OPlan 226-61, Dec 30, 1961; hist, PACAF, Jul-Dec 61, III; AFXOPJ Book of Actions in SEA, 1961-64, Item III-C; hist, 315th AD, Jan-Jun 62, pp 44-45; CINCPAC Rcrd, 2d SECDEF Conf, Item 3.

13. Hist, 2d ADVON, pp XVII-XX; Chief, AF Sec, MAAGV, Agenda Book for Feb 62 SECDEF Conf, Item 3 (a)A; rprt, Brig Gen Travis M. Hetherington, DCS/Plans and Ops, PACAF, Apr 25, 1962; rprt, Lt Col Charles D. Easley, ca. Aug 5, 1962; ltr, Easley to 2 ODC, ca. Jul 1, 1962; Proj Corona Harvest Oral Hist intvw w/Anthis, pp 64-68; PACAF Ref Bk for Jan 62 SECDEF Conf, Tab 3; MACV Summary of Highlights, Feb 8, 1962-Feb 7, 1963, p 135; msg, USAIRA Saigon to CSAF, Mar 21, 1962.

14. Ralph A. Rowley, *USAF FAC Operations in Southeast Asia, 1961-65* (Ofc/AF Hist, Jan 1972), pp 15, 18, 24-25; hist, 2d ADVON, p 97; Draft presentation, Anthis for Mar 62 SECDEF Conf, Hist, 2d ADVON; rad, USAIRA Bangkok to PACAF, Jan 31, 1962.

15. PACAF Ref Bk for Dec 61 SECDEF Conf, Action Tab 1, for Jan 62 SECDEF Conf, Tab 9, for Feb 62 SECDEF Conf, Item 9; CINCPAC Rcrd, SECDEF Conf, Dec 16, 1961, Item 8-1; Rprt of CSAF's Visit to South Vietnam, Item 11; Hetherington rprt, Apr 25, 1962; Easley End of Tour Rprt, ca. Aug 5, 1962.

16. The 8th and 57th Transport Helicopter Companies arrived as identifiable units at Saigon aboard an aircraft carrier on December 11, 1962, and were so reported in the *New York Times*. The International Control Commission promptly recorded this violation of the Geneva accords. The companies were based at Tan Son Nhut and Qui Nhon under the U.S. Army senior advisors to the II and III Corps. On January 26, 1962, the U.S. Army's 93d Helicopter Company arrived at Da Nang and was placed under the U.S. Army senior advisor to the I Corps. The companies flew combat support missions and trained the Vietnamese army in air mobility tactics. U.S. Army's 18th Fixed Wing Aviation Company, with sixteen U-1 Otter aircraft, reached Nha Trang on February 7, 1962, and these liaison aircraft (able to transport two thousand pounds of cargo or eight passengers) supported the U.S. Army field advisors. The 339th Transportation Company (Maintenance) arrived on February 11, 1962. Chief, AF Sec, MAAGV, Agenda Bk for Feb 62, SECDEF Conf, Item 3 (3); CINCPAC Rcrd, 2d SECDEF Conf, Jan 16, 1962, Item 3; CINCPAC Comd Hist, 1961, p 194.

17. CINCPAC Comd Hist, 1961, p 189; msg,

USAIRA Saigon to CSAF, Nov 28, 1961; CINCPAC Rcrd, SECDEF Conf, Dec 19, 1961, Item 7; Martin and Clever, IV, 31-34.

18. Ltr, O'Donnell to CINCPAC, Dec 12, 1961; msg, USAIRA Saigon to CSAF, Nov 28, 1961; PACAF Ref Bk for Dec 61 SECDEF Conf, Tab B-1.

19. Hist, 315th TC Gp (Assault), 1962, p 16; intvw with Lt Col E. W. Strong by Grainger, Nov 7, 1962; AFXOPJ Book of Actions in SEA, 1961-64, p 25; *Jane's All the World's Aircraft, 1955-56*, ed Leonard Bridgeman (New York, n.d.), p 259; CINCPAC Rcrd, 3d SECDEF Conf. Feb 19, 1962; PACAF Ref Bk for Dec 61 SECDEF Conf, Tab A-5 and Action Tab A; msgs, CINCPAC to 13th AF, Dec 9, 1961, PACAF to 13th AF, Dec 13, 1961.

20. Talking Paper on USAF Ops in VN, atch 3, Folder Policy-Vietnam, Jan 1-31, 1964.

21. Moorman presentation to Congressional Committee, *ca.* Feb 63, I, 38; ltrs, Anthis to Maj Gen W. Martin, Sep 2, 1963, and Moorman to Anthis, *ca.* Feb 28, 1962; msgs, MACV to CINCPAC, Mar 12, 1962, and 13th AF to 2d ADVON, Mar 18, 1962; Rprt of CSAF's Visit to SVN, Apr 62, Ops Sec.

22. MACV Summary of Highlights, Feb 8, 1962-Feb 7, 1963, p 69; ltr, Lt Col Floyd K. Shafner, May 12, 1962.

23. 2d ADVON, Agenda and Info Bk for Mar 62 SECDEF Conf, Item 17; hist, 13th AF, 1962, pp 103-05.

24. Msgs, 2d ADVON to 13th AF, Mar 9, 1962, MACV to CINCPAC, Mar 12, 19, and 26, 1962.

25. Anthis presentation at May 62 SECDEF Conf; msgs, 2d ADVON to 13th AF, Mar 27, 1962, CINCPAC to JCS, Mar 30, 1962, and 2d AD to 13th AF, Nov 20, 1962.

26. Msgs, 2d ADVON to 13th AF, Mar 27, 1962, MACV to CINCPAC, Apr 9, 1962, and May 22, 1962, PACAF to CSAF, May 12, 1962, and CINCPAC to MACV, Aug 13, 1962; Hetherington rprt, Apr 25, 1962; hist, 315th TC Gp (Assault), 1962, p 27; rprt, Lt Col Howard P. Reaves, Aug 2, 1962.

27. *Ibid.*; Rprt of CSAF's Visit to SVN, Apr 62; PACAF Status Rprt, May 2 to 9, 1962; msg, CINCPAC to JCS, May 8, 1962.

28. Msg, MACV to CINCPAC, May 22, 1962.

29. JTF 116, AAR, Dec 8, 1962; msgs, 2d AD to 13th AF, Jul 28 and Nov 26, 1962, CINCPAC to JCS, May 25, 1962, to MACV, May 25, 1962; PACAF Summary of Actions, Gen Wheeler's Party, Jan 63.

30. One plane was lost without crew fatalities in a major accident on July 15. Hist, PACAF, Jan-Jun 62, III, May and June 62; hist, 315th TC Gp (Assault), 1962, pp 27-28; Reaves End of Tour Rprt, Aug 2, 1962.

31. Ltr, Moorman to Anthis, Sep 25, 1962; msgs, 13th AF to PACAF, May 26, 1962, PACAF to 13th AF, May 29, 1962, and AFCC JTF 116 to PACAF, May 29, 1962.

32. Ltrs, Moorman to CINCPAC, Jul 6, 1962, and to Anthis, Sep 25, 1962; PACAF SOs G-85 and G-92, Sep 19 and Oct 19, 1962; msgs, CINCPAC to MACV, Jul 18, 1962, MACV to CINCPAC, Aug 23, 1962.

33. PACAF Summary of Actions, Gen Wheeler's Party, Sec II, Tab C; ltrs, Anthis to Moorman, *ca.* Apr 16, 1962, and Bowers to Mann, *ca.* Jun 62 and Jul 25, 1962; Reaves End of Tour Rprt, Aug 2, 1962; JCS/2d ADVON Jt OPlan 62-2, Oct 17, 1962; Moorman presentation, *ca.* Feb 63, I, 38; msg, 2d AD to PACAF, Apr 5, 1962.

34. PACAF Summary of Actions, Gen Wheeler's Party, Sec II, Tab C.

35. Msgs, PACAF to 13th AF, Dec 9 and 13, 1961.

36. Doris Krudener, formerly of the Office of Air Force History, kindly supplied this documentation: Memos, JCS for McNamara, Nov 3, 1961, and William P. Bundy for Rusk and McNamara, Nov 14 and 30, 1961.

37. NSAM 115, Nov 30, 1961; Marvin E. Hintz, History of the Thirteenth Air Force, Jan 1-June 30, 1963, pp 75-76; msg, CHMAAGV to CINCPAC, Dec 23, 1961, in ISA files.

38. JCSM-2-62(U), Jan 2, 1962; msg, CINCPAC to CHMAAGVN, Dec 28, 1961; memo, SECDEF to the President, Feb 2, 1962; and see msg, CHMAAGV to CINCPAC Jan 17, 1962; and PACAF Ref Bk for Jan 62 SECDEF Conf, Tab 16A.

39. Msg, SECSTATE to AmEmb Saigon, Jan 4, 1962; and msg, CHMAAGV to CINCPAC, Jan 12, 1962.

40. Capt George T. Adams, *TAC Aerial Spray Flight Operations in Southeast Asia, 1961-1964* (TAC/SASF, n.d.), p 8.

41. Hist, PACAF, Jan-Jun 62, III, Apr 62; PACAF Ref Bk for Jan 62 SECDEF Conf, Tab 3, TP-1, and for Mar 62 SECDEF Conf, Items 3 and 4; Chief, AF Sec, MAAGV, Agenda Bk for Feb 62 SECDEF Conf, Item 3(1); CINCPAC Rcrd, 3d SECDEF Conf, Feb 19, 1962, Item 3, and 4th SECDEF Conf, Mar 21, 1962, Item 1; msg, PACAF to CSAF, Feb 20, 1962; Moorman memo, Feb 23, 1962. In April, when Tactical Air Command moved two spray planes to the Middle East to work against locust infestations and to save food crops, it added two standard C-123s to the Mule Train airlift detachment.

42. 3d ADVON Agenda Bk for SECDEF May 62 Conf, Item 3; CINCPAC Rcrd, 4th SECDEF Conf, Mar 21, 1962, Item 1; hist, PACAF, Jan-Jun 62, III, Apr 62.

43. MACV Rcrd, 4th SECDEF Conf, May 11, 1962, Item 12.
44. See CINCPAC Rcrd, 6th SECDEF Conf, Jul 23, 1962, Item 1.
45. Memo, Col William P. Brooks, Jr., for Harkins, Aug 2, 1962.
46. MACV Summary of Highlights, Feb 8, 1962-Feb 7, 1963, pp 59-61; msgs, CINCPAC to JCS, Aug 21, 1962, AmEmb Saigon to SEC-STATE, Sep 26, 1962.
47. CINCPAC Summary of Actions taken at 7th SECDEF Conf, Oct 8, 1962, paras 8 and 9; MACV Summary of Highlights, pp 59-61, 210; msg, AmEmb to SECSTATE, Oct 9, 1963.
48. *Ibid.*; hist, Dir/Plans, USAF, Jan-Jun 63, pp 237-38; and Hilsman, *To Move a Nation*, pp 441-44.

Chapter XI

Air Policy: Too Cautious?

1. Quoted in Henry F. Graff, *The Tuesday Cabinet: Deliberations and Decision on Peace and War under Lyndon B. Johnson* (Englewood Cliffs, 1970), p 35.
2. Msg, PACAF to CSAF, Dec 17, 1961; CINCPAC Rcrd, SECDEF Conf, Dec 16, 1961, Item 8-1.
3. *Ibid.*
4. Msgs, 13th AF to PACAF, Dec 28, 1961, CSAF to PACAF, Mar 23, 1963, and JCS to CINCPAC, Dec 26, 1961; PACAF Ref Bk for Feb 62 SECDEF Conf, I-B; LeMay intvw by Belden, Mar 29, 1972; intvw with Anthis by Gausche and Grainger, Aug 30, 1963.
5. Memo, Dir/Plans, USAF, for CSAF, Mar 1, 1962; JCS 2343/85, Feb 23, 1962; Report of CSAF's Visit to SVN, Apr 62, p 57.
6. Rowley, *USAF FAC Operations*, p 19.
7. PACAF, SECDEF Bk for Jan Mtg, Jan 15, 1962, Tab 3-B; msg, CINCPAC to PACAF, Feb 4, 1962.
8. Msg, PACAF to 2d ADVON, Feb 12, 1962.
9. Intvw, Maj Thomas J. Hickam with Capt Edwin J. Rhein, Jr., Tan Son Nhut, Jan 3, 1963; Martin and Clever, App 2, COIN intvws, Tab G; rcrd, 3d SECDEF Conf, Feb 19, 1962, pp 4-5; End of Tour Reports, Lt Col M. M. Doyle, John P. Gilbert, Feb 62-Aug 63.
10. Draft presentation, Anthis for Mar 62 SECDEF Conf; hist, 2d ADVON, Nov 61-Oct 62.
11. *Ibid.*
12. Lessons Learned 4, U.S. Army Sec, MAAG, Apr 11, 1962.
13. Futrell "Chron"; draft presentation, Anthis for Mar 62 SECDEF Conf, in Hist, 2d ADVON, Nov 61-Oct 62.
14. Rcrd, 3d SECDEF Conf, Feb 19, 1962, pp 1-6.
15. Hist, 2d ADVON, Nov 61-Oct 62, p 9; intvw, Maj Dean S. Gausche and Grainger with Anthis, Aug 30, 1963; Martin and Clever, App 2, COIN Intvws, Tab U; intvws, Grainger with Doyle and Lt Col Charles E. Trumbo, Jr., Jul 13, 1963, in Hist, 2d ADVON; Van Staaveren, *USAF Plans and Policies in South Vietnam, 1961-1963*, p 25; hist, SAWC, Apr-Dec 62, p 167.
16. Msg, Chief MAAG to CINCPAC, Dec 23, 1961.
17. Memo, Landsdale to Col David C. Jolly, Dec 27, 1961, Binder 1257-61, 66A-3410, box 37.
18. Memo, Maj Gen C H. Childre, ADCS/Plans & Programs, USAF, Dec 28, 1961, Binder Vietnam 1257-61, 66A-3410, box 37.
19. Van Staaveren, *USAF Plans and Policies in South Vietnam, 1961-1963*, p 26; hist, SAWC, Apr-Dec 62, p 167; *New York Times*, Feb 15, 1962; DAF-IR-1521904; msgs, 2d ADVON to PACAF, Jan 30 and Feb 24, 1962; Gleason paper, *ca.* Mar 1, 1962; CINCPAC Rcrd, 3d SECDEF Conf, Feb 19, 1962, Item 3; PACAF Ref Bk for Feb 62 SECDEF Conf, Tab 3C.
20. CINCPAC Rcrd, 3d SECDEF Conf, Feb 19, 1962, pp 3-22; msg, CINCPAC to MACV, Mar 2, 1963.
21. Msg, 2d ADVON to 13th AF, Mar 13, 1962.
22. Hist, 2d ADVON, Nov 61-Oct 62, p 184.
23. Ltr, Maj Gen W. K. Martin to SAF, Dec 11, 1964, Binder Vietnam 191-64, 68A-4994, box 8; hist, 2d ADVON, Nov 61-Oct 62, p 3; Gen Frank S. Besson, Jr., *Logistic Support in the Vietnam Era*, Vols I-III (Washington, 1970), p 265.
24. Intvw, Grainger with Maj William C. Johnson and Capt Ernest C. Cutler, Jr., Feb 7, 1963.
25. Msg, Chief MAAG to PACAF, Nov 18, 1961; hist, 2d ADVON Nov 61-Oct 62.
26. Hist, 2d ADVON, Nov 61-Oct 62, pp 52, 55; von Luttichau MS, CMH, pp viii, 56-57.
27. Rprt, Maj Gen Travis M. Hetherington, Staff Visits, Apr 25, 1962; hist, 2d ADVON, Nov 61-Oct 62; intvws, Maj Thomas J. Hickam with

TSgt Harry M. Nonamaker, Dec 11, 1962, with Capt Edwin J. Rhein, Jr., Jan 3, 1963, with Chaplain Squires, Jan 16, 1963, and with CWO William Weakley, Jan 10, 1963; Martin and Clever, App 2, COIN Intvws, Tabs F, G, and H.

28. Intvw, Maj Thomas J. Hickam with Capt (Chap) Donal M. Squires, Jan 16, 1963; Martin and Clever, App 2, COIN Intvws, Tab I; hist, 2d ADVON, Nov 61-Oct 62, pp 67-70; End of Tour Reports, Lt Col Kenneth M. Keyte, Apr 20, 1963, and Capt Forrest P. Meek, Apr 9, 1963.

29. Intvw, Hickam with Auten, Feb 15, 1963; ibid., Tab L; hist, 2d ADVON, pp 67-70.

30. Report of CSAF's Visit to SVN, Apr 62, p 11.

31. Maj Gen Spurgeon Noel, *Medical Support of the U.S. Army in Vietnam, 1965-70* (Dept of the Army, Wash D.C., 1973), pp 5 and 9.

32. Intvw, Hickam and Grainger with CWO A C. Liberator, Nov 20, 1962; Martin and Clever, App 2, Tab A.

33. Hist, 2d ADVON, pp 182-83.

Chapter XII

Farm Gate and the Vietnamese Air Force

1. Chief, AF Sec, MAAGV, Agenda Bk for Feb 62 SECDEF Conf, Item 5C; Gleason paper, *ca.* Mar 1, 1962; CINCPAC Rcrd, 4th SECDEF Conf, Item 5.

2. PACAF Ref Bk for Jan 62 SECDEF Conf, Tab 3, TP-1; Proj Corona Harvest Oral Hist intvw with King, pp 52-53; Futrell, personal conversations with Gleason and Dougherty.

3. DAF-IR-1521904; hist, 2d AD, I, xiv; CINCPAC Rcrd, 3d SECDEF Conf, Feb 19, 1962, Item 3; Gleason paper, *ca.* Mar 1, 1962.

4. Hist, 2d ADVON, p 144; ltrs, Anthis to Moorman, Mar 28, 1963, Det 2A to 2d ADVON, Jun 5, 1962.

5. Rprt, Cairney and Evans, May 4, 1962; Gleason End of Tour Report.

6. PACAF Ref Bk for Jan 62 SECDEF Conf, Tabs 2 nd 3; Palmer briefing in Hist, 5th AF, Jan-Jun 62, II, Doc 144.

7. CINCPAC Rcrd, 3d SECDEF Conf, Feb 19, 1962, Item 2.

8. Anthis briefing, Mar 62 SECDEF Conf, in Hist, 2d AD, II, Doc 206; msgs, PACAF to 13th AF, Mar 15, 1962, to CSAF, Mar 17, 1962, and to CSAF, Feb 20, 1962; Report of CSAF's Visit to SVN, Apr 62, pt 2; ltr, Moorman to Anthis, *ca.* Feb 28, 1962; CINCPAC Rcrd, 3d SECDEF Conf, Feb 19, 1962.

9. Msgs, MACV to CINCPAC, Feb 27, 1962, 2d ADVON to PACAF, Mar 17, 1962, and to MACV, Aug 22, 1962, AmEmb Saigon to SECSTATE, Mar 3, 1962; Martin and Clever, III, 60-63; Moorman presentation, *ca.* Feb 62, pt 1, p 30.

10. MACV hist monograph, *Military Assistance to the Republic of South Vietnam, 1960-1963*, p 11.

11. Msg, 2d ADVON to PACAF, Mar 21, 1962; msg, USAIRA Saigon to CSAF, Mar 21, 1962.

12. Msgs, AmEmb Saigon to SECSTATE, Mar 28, 1962, PACAF to 13th AF, Mar 22, 1962, JCS to CINCPAC, Mar 27, 1962; hist, 13th AF, 1962, I, 81-83; MR, Maj Gen John M. Reynolds, Mar 22, 1962.

13. Report of CSAF's Visit to SVN, Apr 62, Item 6.

14. Hist, PACAF, Jan-Jun 62, III; Monthly Hist Rprts, PFOCO, Mar and May 62; hist, PACAF, Jul-Dec 62, II; hist, PFODC, Jul 62; hist, 13th AF, 1962, I, 81-83; hist, 509th FISq, Jan-Jun 62, pp 166-67.

15. Msg, MACV to AmEmb Laos, Aug 22, 1962; Proj Corona Harvest Oral Hist intvw with Anthis, pp 129-31; ltrs, Harkins to O'Donnell and Felt, Mar 22, 1963.

16. Msgs, 13th AF to PACAF, Mar 10, 1962, MACV to CINCPAC, Mar 24, 1962, 2d ADVON to 13th AF, Apr 12, 1962; CINCPAC Rcrd, 4th SECDEF Conf, Mar 21, 1962, Item 5.

17. Msgs, 2d ADVON to 13th AF, Apr 21, 1962, and PACAF to CINCPAC, May 8, 1962; Report of CSAF's Visit to SVN, Apr 62, paras 4 and 7; 2d ADVON Bk for May 62 SECDEF Conf, Item 1A; Mueller to 2CCR, Jun 5, 1962.

18. Msg, 2d ADVON to PACAF, Jul 17, 1962.

19. Ltr, Anthis to Pritchard, Oct 20, 1962.

20. PACAF Ref Bk for Jul 62 SECDEF Conf, Tab 1; CINCPAC Rcrd, 6th SECDEF Conf, Jul 23, 1962, Item 2.

21. Msg, 13th AF to PACAF, Aug 6, 1962; ltrs, Anderson to Bowers, Jul 19, 1962, Anthis to Col Nguyen Xuan Vinh, Aug 8, 1962, and Anthis to Nguyen Dinh Thuan, Aug 11, 1962; hist, Asst for Mutual Security, USAF, Jan-Jun 62, p 57; Chief, AF Sec, MAAGV, Agenda Bk for Feb 62 SECDEF Conf, Item 5C; PACAF Summary of Actions, Gen Wheeler's Party, Sec I, Tab A. See also, PACAF Ref Bk for Oct 8,

1962, SECDEF Conf, Tab A3; ltr, Harkins to Moorman, Oct 1, 1962; CINCPAC Summary of Decisions Taken at Seventh SECDEF Conf, Oct 8, 1962, Item 6; msg, PACAF to TAC, Oct 13, 1962; Long rprt, Oct 18, 1962.

22. Msg, 13th AF to PACAF, Aug 6, 1962; hist, PACAF, Jul-Dec 62, III, Aug 13, 1962.

23. Msg, PACAF to CSAF, Sep 29, 1962; ltr, Pritchard to Anthis, Oct 1, 1962.

24. 1st and 2d Fighter Squadrons became the 514th and 516th; 1st, 2d, and 3d Liaison became the 110th, 112th and 114th; 1st and 2d Helicopter became the 211th and 213th; 1st and 2d Transport became the 413th and 415th; the Special Air Mission became the 312th Squadron; tactical reconnaissance elements formed the 716th Squadron; the 12th, 23d, 30th, and 41st Air Base Squadrons operated at Nha Trang, Bien Hoa, Tan Son Nhut, and Da Nang, respectively. Msg, CHMAAGV to CINCPAC, Sep 19, 1962.

25. Msg, DA to USARPAC, Aug 16, 1962.

26. Msgs, CSAF to PACAF, Oct 6, 1962, PACAF to CINCPAC, Oct 7, 1962; CINCPAC Summary of Decisions Taken at 7th SECDEF Conf, Oct 8, 1962, Item 6.

27. Msgs, PACAF to TAC, Oct 12 and 13, 1962; ltrs, Anthis to Pritchard, Oct 20, 1962, and Moorman to Anthis, Oct 23, 1962.

28. Msg, 2d AD to PACAF and 13th AF, Oct 22, 1962.

29. Msgs, MACV to CINCPAC, Nov 7, 1962, and CINCPAC to JCS, Nov 9, 1962.

30. Msgs, 2d ADVON to 13th AF, Mar 9, 1962, CINCPAC to ADMINO, CINCPAC, Oct 22, 1962, 2d AD to PACAF, Jan 24, 1963; Moorman presentation, ca. Feb 63, I, Question 11; PACAF Summary of Actions, Gen Wheeler's Party, Sec I, Tab C; msg, PACAF to CSAF, Feb 14, 1963.

31. Hilsman, *To Move a Nation*, pp 453-67.

32. AFXOPJ Book of Actions in SEA, 1961-1964, Item III F; msg, CSAF to PACAF, Dec 12, 1963.

Chapter XIII

Air Operations, 1962: Interdiction, Strikes, and Reconnaissance

1. Anthis presentation at Mar 62 SECDEF Conf, in Hist, 2d AD, II, Docs 200, 203, and 205; CINCPAC Rcrd, SECDEF Conf, Dec 16, 1961, Item 2.

2. Chief, AF Sec, MAAGV, Agenda Bk for Feb 62 SECDEF Conf; Moorman presentation to Congressional Committee, ca. Feb 63, I, pp 1-11, MACV Summary of Highlights, Feb 8, 1962-Feb 7, 1963, pp 14, and 27-30; PACAF Ref Bk for Dec 61 SECDEF Conf, Action Tab F.

3. PACAF Ref Bk for Jul 62 SECDEF Conf, Tabs 1A, 1C, and 5; msg, MACV to CINCPAC, May 1, 1962; ltrs, Anthis to Brig Gen H. D. Aynesworth, Oct 28, 1963, and to Gen Jacob E. Smart, Nov 25, 1963, and Col Harry O. Patterson to CINCPAC, Jun 62; rprt, Capt Charles H. Tardiff, Aug 4, 1962.

4. Report of CSAF's Visit to SVN, Apr 62, Intel Sec; MACV, Rcrd, 5th SECDEF Conf, May 11, 1962, Item 8.

5. Chief, AF Sec, MAAGV, Agenda Bk for Feb 62 SECDEF Conf, Item 5; PACAF Ref Bk for Feb 62 SECDEF Conf, Tab 5, TP-1; CINCPAC Rcrd, 3d SECDEF Conf, Feb 19, 1962, Item 5.

6. PACAF Ref Bk for Feb 62 SECDEF Conf pt I-B and Tab C; CINCPAC Rcrd, 3d SECDEF Conf, Feb 19, 1962, Item 5; msgs, AmEmb Phnom Penh to OSD, Jan 22, 1962, SECSTATE to AmEmb Saigon, Jan 24, 1962, and AmEmb Saigon to CINCPAC, Jan 26, 1962.

7. CINCPAC Rcrd, 3d SECDEF Conf, Feb 19, 1962, Item 3; msg, USAIRA, Bangkok, to PACAF, Jan 31, 1962; PACAF Ref Bk for Feb 62 SECDEF Conf, Item 5.

8. Msg, CINCPAC to CHMAAGV, Feb 4, 1962.

9. CINCPAC Rcrd, 3d SECDEF Conf, Feb 19, 1962, Items 2, 3, 4, 5; Moorman memo, Feb 23, 1962; PACAF Ref Bk for Mar 62 SECDEF Conf, Items 3 and 5; ltr, Maj Gen Richard G. Weede, Feb 27, 1962; msgs, JCS to CINCPAC, Mar 12, 1962, PACAF to CSAF, Feb 20, 1962.

10. Anthis briefing, Mar 62 SECDEF Conf, in Hist, 2d AD, II, Doc 205.

11. Msg, 13th AF to PACAF, Mar 4, 1962; PACAF Ref Bk for Mar 62 SECDEF Conf, Items 3 and 5.

12. PACAF Ref Bk for Mar 62 SECDEF Conf, Item 7; CINCPAC Rcrd, 4th SECDEF Conf, Mar 21, 1962, Item 5; Hilsman, *To Move a Nation*, pp 441-44.

13. Easley End of Tour Report, ca. Aug 5, 1962.

14. Ltr, Anthis to Pritchard, Dec 20, 1962.

15. The direction finder had been designed by

General LeMay in the basement of his quarters in Washington. LeMay was personally interested in electronics and he hoped that various air navigation aids, such as omnibearing radio range indicators, would give instant and unambiguous bearings on radio stations.

16. PACAF Ref Bks for Jan, Mar, and Jul 62 SECDEF Confs; CINCPAC Rcrd, 4th SECDEF Conf, Mar 21, 1962, Item 4A; hist, 6091st Recon Sq, Jan-Jun 63, p 1.

17. Hist, 2d AD, I, 157; msg, MACV to PACAF, May 28, 1963; PACAF Ref Bk for May 63 SECDEF Conf, Agenda Item 3, Tab 3; CINCPAC Rcrd, 8th SECDEF Conf, May 6, 1963, Item 3; 2CCR, Air Interdiction and Ground Support, ca. Apr 25, 1963, in Martin and Clever, V, Tab A, 97.

18. PACAF Ref Bk for May 63 SECDEF Conf, Agenda Item 3, Tab E.

19. Bernard B. Fall, *The Two Vietnams: A Political and Military Analysis*, 2d ed (New York, 1963), pp 355-56; see msgs, 2d ADVON to MACV, May 30 and Jun 14, 1964.

20. Report of CSAF's Visit to SVN, Apr 62, Intel Sec; MACV Rcrd, 5th SECDEF Conf, May 11, 1962, Items 1 and 8; 2d ADVON Agenda Book for May 62 SECDEF Conf, Item 1-A; hist, PACAF, Jan-Jun 62, I, pt 2, ch 3, citing PACOM Wkly Intel Digest, May 18, 1962; CINCPAC Rcrd, 6th SECDEF Conf, Jul 23, 1962; Item 5; msgs, CINCPAC to MACV, Sep 12, 1962, to JCS, Oct 22, 1962.

21. Msgs, MACV to PACAF, Jun 11, 1962, CINCPAC to MACV, Jul 9, 1962, and Sep 12, 1962, and to JCS, Jul 13, 1962.

22. Ltrs, Anthis to Thuan, Aug 11, 1962, Moorman to Harkins, Sep 3, 1962; and msg, CINCPAC to AIG-929, Nov 29, 1962.

23. Msg, CINCPAC to MACV, Sep 12, 1962.

24. Ltr, Harkins to Moorman, Oct 1, 1962; rprt, Maj Andrew J. Chapman to Dep Dir, III ASOC, Nov 16, 1962; msgs, CINCPAC to JCS, Oct 22, 1962, CINCPAC to AIG-929, Nov 29, 1962, and 2d AD to PACAF, Dec 20, 1962.

25. US Dept of State, *American Foreign Policy: Current Documents, 1962*, pp 1002-04; msgs, AmEmb Saigon to SECSTATE, Nov 21, 1962, CINCPAC to JCS, Oct 22, 1962; PACAF Ref Bk for SECDEF Conf, Oct 8, 1962, Tab J; Report of Visit by JCS Team to SVN, Jan 63, pt IV, para 8.

26. Msgs, CINCPAC to JCS, Oct 22, 1962, AmEmb Saigon to SECSTATE, Nov 21, 1962; MACV Summary of Highlights, Feb 8, 1962-Feb 7, 1963, p 40; memo, Lt Gen Le Van Ty, Limitation of Air and Artillery Supports along Vietnam Republic Border Corridor, Nov 15, 1962.

27. Msgs, SECSTATE to AmEmb Saigon, Dec 8, 1962, CINCPAC to AIG-929, Dec 16, 1962.

28. Msgs, CINCPAC to JCS, Nov 11, 1962, SECSTATE to AmEmb Saigon, Dec 8, 1962, and AmEmb to SECSTATE, Dec 15, 1962; ltr, Anthis to Pritchard, Dec 20, 1962.

29. PACAF Ref Bk for Mar 62 SECDEF Conf, Item 3; Anthis briefing at the Mar 62 SECDEF Conf, in Hist, 2d AD, Doc 203; Easley End of Tour Report, ca. Aug 5, 1962; 13th AF Final Rprt Analysis Directive Program No. 63-3, Apr 30, 1963, pp 39-43; msg, 13th AF to PACAF, Mar 8, 1962; see ltr, Moorman to Anthis, ca. Feb 28, 1962.

30. Capts Thomas N. Cairney and Douglas K. Evans rprt, Feb 14, 1962; Gleason paper, ca. Mar 1, 1962; msg, 2d ADVON to PACAF, Jul 17, 1962.

31. Cairney and Evans rprt, May 4, 1962; msgs, MACV to CINCPAC, May 16, 1962, 2d ADVON JOC to I ASOC and II ASOC, Jun 4, 1962.

32. Hetherington rprt, Apr 25, 1962; ltr, Easley to 2 ODC, ca. Jul 1, 1962; rprt, Cairney and Evans to Dep Dir, JOC, May 4, 1962; Easley End of Tour Report, ca. Aug 5, 1962.

33. Msgs, 13th AF to PACAF, Mar 8, 1962, MACV to CHMAAGV, Apr 12, 1962, and 2d ADVON to 13th AF, Apr 21 and 25, 1962; PACAF Ref Bk for Mar 62 SECDEF Conf, Item 3.

34. Msgs, MACV to CINCPAC, May 16, 1962, 2d ADVON to 13th AF, Mar 9, 1962; ltr, Easley to 2 ODC, ca. Jul 1, 1962.

35. Cairney and Evans rprt, May 4, 1962; msgs, PACAF to CSAF, Jul 17, 1962, 2d ADVON to 13th AF, Jul 18, 1962, to PACAF, Nov 7, 1962, and CINCPAC to MACV, Aug 3, 1962.

36. Cairney and Evans rprt, May 4, 1962; ltr, Lt Col William H. Lewis to 2 CCR, Mar 5, 1962; Gleason paper, ca. Mar 1, 1962; hist, 2d AD, I, 110; ltr, Anthis to Maj Carl G. Schneider, Sep 26, 1962.

37. MACV Summary of Highlights, Feb 8, 1962-Feb 7, 1963, pp 133-34; ltrs, Col John C. Haygood to C/S, 13th AF, Jun 10, 1962, Lt Col Miles M. Doyle to 2 CCR, Oct 11, 1962; msgs, PACAF to CSAF, May 9, 1962, 2d ADVON to PACAF, Feb 28, 1962, and 2d AD to PACAF, Nov 12, 1962; Gleason paper, ca. Mar 1, 1962; PACAF Ref Bk for Mar 62 SECDEF Conf, Tab 8. See also PFLPL, Counterinsurgency Lessons Learned, Sep 12, 1962; rprt, Col Winston F. Anderson, Jan 14, 1963; ltr, Anthis to Moorman, ca. Apr 16, 1963; 13th AF Final Report, Apr 30, 1963, pp 22-23.

38. Ltrs, Riha to Anderson, Nov 16, 1962, Moorman to Henderson, Jul 3, 1963, with incl, Jul 2, 1963; Report of Visit by Brig Gen Gilbert L. Pritchard, Jul 9-27, 1962, and Aug 3, 1962;

rprts, Maj Hal G. Bowers, Jan 9, 1963, and Capt Bryant C. Ruhman, Sep 4, 1962; 2d ADVON/AF Sec, MAAG, MAAG Symposium, Aug 9, 1962.

39. MACV Army Sec, Lessons Learned 1 and 6, Mar 30 and Apr 11, 1962; msgs, MACV to CINCPAC, Jun 1 and Jul 9, 1962, CINCPAC to JCS, Jul 9, 1962, and Aug 11, 1962, 2d AD to 13th AF, Dec 21, 1962, PACAF to 13th AF, Jul 30, 1962, JCS to MACV, Aug 3, 1962, to CINCPAC, Jul 27, 1962; CINCPAC Rcrd, 6th SECDEF Conf, Jul 23, 1962, Item 1. The Marine helicopters wished to be based at Da Nang, but because the U.S. Army had a company there, they went to the Soc Trang airfield in the delta. Later, they traded stations with an Army company, because they were more effective in mountainous terrain. Maj John J. Cahill and Jack Shulimson, Draft, "History of U.S. Marine Corps Operations in Vietnam, Jan-Jun 65," pp 14-16, and 76-81.

40. Mueller rprt, Aug 4, 1962; msg, CINCPAC to JCS, Aug 11, 1962.

41. Msgs, 2d ADVON to PACAF, Sep 16, 1962, and CINCPAC to MACV, Jul 28 and Aug 3, 1962; MR, Col S. H. Nigre, Jan 9, 1963.

42. Hist, 2d AD, pp 149-50; Martin and Clever, V, 52-53; Fall, *Two Viet-Nams*, pp 378-79; msg, CINCPAC to MACV, Sep 12, 1962.

43. PACAF Ref Bk for Jul 62 SECDEF Conf, Tab 1.

44. *Ibid.*; 2d AD, Ops Analysis Paper 3, Oct 15, 1962; msgs, MACV to CINCPAC, Jul 31 and Aug 27, 1962, CINCPAC to JCS, Aug 28, 1962.

45. Msg, CINCPAC to JCS, Aug 11, 1962; rprt, Maj Eugene R. McCutchan, Aug 24, 1962.

46. Ltr, Harkins to Moorman, Oct 1, 1962; hist, 2d ADVON, Nov 15, 1961-Oct 8, 1962, p 150; Martin and Clever, V, 54; End of Tour Report, Capt Edwin J. Rhein, Jr., Dec 28, 1962; msg, 2d AD to PACAF, Jan 6, 1963; 2d AD Ops Analysis Paper 3, p 17.

47. Rprt, Lt Col Byron R. Kalin, Sep 4, 1962; observations, Capt Bryant C. Ruhman, Sep 4, 1962; msgs, 2d ADVON to PACAF, Sep 22, 1962, and MACV to CINCPAC, Sep 14, 1962.

48. Ruhman observations; Capt Kenneth H. Wells, Sep 14, 1962; msgs, CINCPAC to MACV, Sep 5, 1962, and MACV to CINCPAC, Sep 14, 1962.

49. Rprt, Maj William J. Kuntz, Sep 30, 1962; msg, 2d AD to 13th AF, Dec 21, 1962.

50. Msgs, 2d AD to PACAF, Oct 31, 1962, and to CSAF, Dec 15, 1962; Burgin rprt, Nov 15, 1962; Anderson to PACAF, Jan 14, 1963; hist, SAWC, Apr 27-Dec 31, 1962, pp 188, 197.

51. MR, Anthis, Oct 19, 1962; ltr, O'Donnell to Harkins, Mar 8, 1963

52. PACAF Ref Bk for Jul 62 SECDEF Conf, Tabs 1A, 1C, and 5; ltr, Patterson to CINCPAC, Jun 62. Visiting Saigon in July, Gen. Walter C. Sweeney, Jr., Tactical Air Command commander, urged General Anthis to establish photo cells at Pleiku and Da Nang at once in order to speed the delivery of data to I and II Corps. Msg, 2d ADVON to PACAF, Jul 17, 1962.

53. CINCPAC Rcrd, 6th SECDEF Conf, Jul 23, 1962, Item 1; msgs, MACV to CINCPAC, Aug 8, 1962, and CINCPAC to JCS, Aug 8, 1962; PACAF Ref Bk for Oct 62 SECDEF Conf, Tab H.

54. Msg, CINCPAC to JCS, Sep 8, 1962; rprt, Col J. L. Asbury, Jr., Nov 22, 1963; hist, 2 ODC, Jan-Jun 64, in Hist, 2d AD, Jan-Jun 64, IX, Doc 9; Oakah L. Jones, *Organization, Mission and Growth of the Vietnamese Air Force, 1949-1968*, p 50; hist, PACAF, Jul-Dec 62, II, and Jan-Jun 63, II; hists, PFIDC, Sep 62, Apr 63; hist, 13th AF, Jan-Jun 63, I, xiv.

55. Msgs, CINCPAC to JCS, Sep 8, 1962, 2d AD to PACAF, Sep 14, 1962, and Nov 14, 1962, and to 13th AF, Nov 28, 1962; ltr, Harkins to Moorman, Oct 1, 1962; PACAF Summary of Actions, Gen Wheeler's Party, Sec II, Tab B.

56. Two other RB-26s went at the same time to Thailand. PACAF Ref Bks for Jan and Mar SECDEF Confs; msg, MACV to CINCPAC, May 1, 1962.

57. Msgs, 2d AD to PACAF, Nov 14, 1962, and Jul 10, 1963; PFLPL, Sep 12, 1963.

58. Ltr, Felt to MACV, Sep 1, 1962; MACV Summary of Highlights, pp 189, 213; msgs, 2d AD to CSAF, Nov 30, 1962, and MACV to CINCPAC, Apr 29, 1963; memo, Anderson for Anthis, Feb 23, 1963.

59. Msgs, 2d AD to PACAF, Sep 15, 1962, and Jun 26, 1963, and to 13th AF, Sep 26, 1962; ltrs, Anthis to Pritchard, Aug 4, 1962, and to Milton, Aug 9, 1962; PACAF Summary of Actions, Gen Wheeler's Party, pt II, Tab II; memos, Col Harvey W. Brown for Rowland, Apr 19 and 22, 1963.

60. PACAF Summary of Actions, Gen Wheeler's Party, Sec I, pt III, Tab A; msgs, 2d AD to PACAF, Dec 23, 1962, MACV to CINCPAC, Apr 29, 1963.

61. Memo, Dir/Plans, USAF, for DCS/Plans and Ops, USAF, Dec 17, 1962.

62. Ltrs, McElroy to Anthis, May 6, 1962, and Anthis to McElroy, May 22, 1962.

63. App C, RAAF ASU 18/3/Air (28), Jun 14, 1962.

64. Ltr, Anthis to Nguyen Cao Ky, Aug 11, 1962.

65. Msg, CINCPAC to DIA, Mar 13, 1963; PACAF Ref Bk for SECDEF Conf, Oct 8, 1962, Tab K-1, and for May 63 SECDEF Conf,

Agenda Item 3, Tab E; Bernard Fall, "Talk with Ho Chi Minh," *The New Republic*, Oct 12, 1963, and in Fall, *Ho Chi Minh on Revolution*, pp 320-24.

66. Msgs, CINCPAC to ADMINO, CINCPAC, Oct 22, 1962, and to JCS, Oct 22, 1962; CINCPAC Rcrd, 8th SECDEF Conf, May 6, 1963, Item 1B.

Chapter XIV

Ap Bac and Related Matters

1. CINCPAC Rcrd, 8th SECDEF Conf, May 6, 1962, pp 2-a/b-3.
2. PACAF Ref Bk for May 63 SECDEF Conf, Item 1; MACV Summary of Highlights, Feb 8, 1962-Feb 7, 1963, p 95.
3. Msg, JCS to SECDEF, Aug 13, 1962; rprt, J-5 to JCS, Aug 7, 1962.
4. *Ibid.*; memo, Review of USAF Actions and Progress since May 1, Ref Bk for July 62 SECDEF Mtg.
5. Ltr, O'Donnell to LeMay, Jul 28, 1962.
6. CINCPAC Rcrd, 6th SECDEF Conf, p 2-2.
7. Memo, JCS for SECDEF, Mar 7, 1963; memo and tabs, Lt Col Franklin Rose, Jr., Dir/Plans, USAF, to CSAF, Jan 28, 1963; MACV National Campaign Plan for SVN, Dec 15, 1962.
8. Msg, CINCPAC to DIA, Mar 13, 1963.
9. PACAF Ref Bk for May 63 SECDEF Conf, Item 1; Report of Visit by JCS Team to SVN, Jan 63, Sec III; MR, Col E. H. Nigro, Jan 9, 1963; intvw with Lt Col Charles E. Trumbe, Jr., by Grainger, Jul 13, 1963; msg, 2d AD to PACAF, Nov 5, 1962.
10. Msgs, USARMA to DA, Nov 26, 1962, 2d AD to PACAF, Oct 18, 1962; ltr, Col Winston P. Anderson to Dir/Mat, 2d AD, Jan 15, 1963.
11. Rprts, Bowers to Dep/Dir, JOC, Jan 9 and Feb 1, 1963, and Lt Col Donald K. Reamy, Feb 8, 1963.
12. Msg, 2d AD to PACAF, Feb 6, 1963; memo, Anderson for Anthis, Feb 23, 1963; ltr, Maj James C. Dunn to 13th AF, Jan 21, 1963.
13. Ltrs, Moorman to Harkins, Sep 3, 1962, and Rowland to Maj Gen Glen W. Martin, Mar 14, 1963, 2d AD to PACAF, Oct 22, 1962, and Jan 3, 1963.
14. Msgs, 2d AD to 13th AF, Oct 22, 1962, Dec 10, 1962, and Jan 10, 1963, and PACAF to 13th AF, Dec 8, 1962; hist, 13th AF, 1962, I, 107-08.
15. Memo, Anderson for Anthis, Feb 23, 1963; msgs, 2d AD to PACAF, Oct 22, 1962, Jan 8, 1963, and to 13th AF, Dec 10, 1962, and Jan 10, 1963, and CINCPAC to JCS, Nov 9, 1962.
16. Msgs, 2d AD to PACAF, Oct 22, 1962, Jan 27, 1963, and MACV to CINCPAC, Dec 2, 1962; MACV Summary of Highlights, p 66; PACAF Summary of Actions, Gen Wheeler's Party, pt II, Tab D; Air Staff Observations, South Vietnam, Jan 16-30, 1963, pp 9-1.
17. Msgs, 2d AD to PACAF, Sep 14 and 30, Oct 30 and 31, Nov 1, and Dec 23, 1962, Jan 27, 1963, and to CSAF, Sep 30, 1962; MACV to CINCPAC, Oct 25, Nov 17 and 19, 1962; PACAF Summary of Actions, Gen Wheeler's Party, Sec II, Tabs A and 10; msg, Maj Gen John W. Carpenter III to Burchinal, Jan 23, 1963.
18. Rprt, Capt Lester G. Frazier, n.d.; Nigro memo of Felt Visit with Diem, Jan 9, 1963; msgs, CINCPAC to JCS, Oct 22, 1962, and 2d AD to 13th AF, Nov 22, 1962; ltr, Bowers to Dep/Dir, JOC, Dec 11, 1962.
19. Bowers rprts, Dec 28, 1962, and Jan 10, 1963; Maj Eugene R. McCutchan rprt, Jan 15, 1963; Nigro memo, Jan 9, 1963; msg, 2d AD to PACAF, Mar 5, 1963.
20. Rprt, Maj Herbert L. Prevost, Jan 15, 1963; Report of Summary Briefing Given by Lt Col John P. Vann, Jan 6, 1963; Halberstam, *Making of a Quagmire*, p 146; Burchett, *Vietnam*, pp 193-94; JOC Briefing Summary, Jan 3, 1963; msgs, 2d AD to PACAF, Jan 3 and 7, Apr 6, 1963, and to 13th AF, Jan 4, 1963.
21. Msg, 2d AD to CSAF, Jan 18, 1963.
22. MR, Col S. N. Nigro, Jan 9, 1963; msgs, 2d AD to 13th AF, Jan 10 and 11, 1963, and CINCPAC to MACV, Jan 4, 1963.
23. Ltrs, Anthis to MACV, Jan 16, 1963, Anderson to Dir/Mat, 2d AD, Jan 15, 1963; intvw with Trumbo by Grainger, Jul 13, 1963; PACAF Ref Bk for May 63 SECDEF Conf, Agenda Item 1.
24. Rprts, Lt Col Donald K. Roamy, May 8, 1963, Maj William J. Kuntz, Feb 10, 1963, Lt Col Bill A. Montgomery to 2d AD, Aug 63, Oct 63, and Nov 63, and Lt Col Charles J. Chennault to 2d AD, Nov 13, 1963; End of Tour Report, Col Benjamin S. Preston, Jul 64; ltr, Capt B. L. Ruhman to Chief ALO/FAC Sec, 2d AD, Jul 2, 1963.
25. Ltr, Anthis to Smart, Nov 25, 1963.

26. Ltrs, Anthis to Gen Jacob E. Smart, Nov 25, 1963, and O'Donnell to Harkins, Mar 8, 1963; msg, CINCPAC to JCS, Feb 16, 1963.
27. Msg, CSAF to PACAF, Jan 9, 1963; ltr, Anthis to JCS, n.d.; Anthis notes on matters to be taken up with Gen LeMay, *ca.* Mar 63.
28. Ltrs, Harkins to O'Donnell and Felt, Mar 22, 1963.
29. Ltrs, Felt to Harkins, May 20, 1963, and to O'Donnell, May 24, 1963.
30. Ltrs, Harkins to Felt, Jun 21, 1963, Anthis to Martin, Sep 2, 1963; MACV Directive 44, Jul 8, 1963; intvw with Henderson by CHECO, Dec 20, 1963; msg, 2d AD to 13th AF, Feb 6, 1964.
31. Hilsman, *To Move a Nation*, pp 453-67.
32. Memo, Col W.V. McBride, Dir/Plans, USAF, to CSAF, Jan 5, 1963.
33. Report of Visit by JCS Team to SVN, Jan 63. The USAF contingent consisted of Lt. Gen. David A. Bruchinal, Lt. Gen. G.P. Disosway, Maj Gen William W. Momyer, Col Robert M. Levy, and Lt Col Harry M. Chapman.
34. Report of Visit by JCS Team to SVN, Jan 63, pt III.
35. *Ibid.*; see also msgs, 2d AD to PACAF, Jun 27, 1963, MACV to CINCPAC, Nov 17, 1962, CINCPAC to MACV, Nov 19, 1962, and PACAF to CSAF, Apr 16, 1963.
36. Report of Visit by JCS Team, Jan 63, Sec IV; msgs, JCS to CINCPAC, Feb 17, 1963, and CINCPAC to MACV, Feb 17, 1963; ltr, Moorman to Anthis, Feb 11, 1963.
37. Msgs, 2d AD to PACAF, Jan 24 and 27, 1963, PACAF to CSAF, Feb 14, 1963, SECSTATE to AmEmb Saigon, Feb 15, 1963; Report of Visit by JCS Team, Jan 63, pt IV.
38. Msgs, CINCPAC to MACV, Mar 2, 1963, and PACAF to 2d AD, Mar 2, 1963.
39. Report of Visit by JCS Team to SVN, Jan 63, Sec II, paras 2 and 2a, and Sec V, para 1a.
40. Air Staff Observations, South Vietnam, Jan 16-30, 1963.
41. Msg, MACV to DIA, Mar 12, 1963; Hearings before the Committee on Armed Services, US Senate, *Military Procurement Authorization, Fiscal Year 1964*, 88th Cong, 1st sess (Washington, 1963), pp 549-53; Martin and Clever, II, 8-10.
42. Burchett, *Vietnam*, pp 85-99.
43. *Ibid.*; intvw with Lt Col Charles E. Trumbe by Grainger, Jul 13, 1963; msg, CINCPAC to DIA, Mar 13, 1963; and PACAF Ref Bk for May 63 SECDEF Conf, Agenda Item 1.
44. MR, Col E. H. Nigro, Jan 9, 1963; *Public Papers of the Presidents: John F. Kennedy, 1963* (Washington, 1964), p 11; Report of Visit by JCS Team to SVN, Sec IV, para 7.
45. Msg, CINCPAC to MACV, Nov 9, 1962; CINCPAC Rcrd, 8th SECDEF Conf, May 6, 1963, Items 1b and 4; House of Representatives, *Viet-Nam and Southeast Asia*, 88th Cong, 1st sess (Washington, 1963), p 8; ltr, O'Donnell to Harkins, Mar 8, 1963; and PACAF Ref Bk for May 63 SECDEF Conf, Agenda Item 4.
46. MR, Conf with Ngo Dinh Nhu on Apr 12, 1963, Intel Rprts 63 and 69A-702, box 1/15; PACAF Ref Bk for May 63 SECDEF Conf, Agenda Item 4; msg, SECSTATE to AmEmb Saigon, May 13, 1963; House of Representatives, *Foreign Operations Appropriations*, 88th Cong, 1st sess (Washington, 1963), pt 2, pp 89-91.
47. *Ibid.*, pp 94-95; msg, CINCPAC to JCS, Apr 4, 1963; CINCPAC Rcrd, 8th SECDEF Conf, May 6, 1963, Items 1 and 1b; and PACAF Ref Bk for May 63 SECDEF Conf, Agenda Item 1.
48. *DOD Pentagon Papers*, Bk 3: IV.B.4., 11-12, Sec IV.B.5.,4; msgs, Dir/Plans, USAF, to PACAF, Apr 30, 1963, and to TAC, May 20, 1962; CINCPAC Rcrd, 8th SECDEF Conf, May 6, 1963, Items 2 and 4.
49. Hist, PACAF, Jan-Jun 63, II, Jun 63; Manpower Review and Analysis of 13th AF Activities, Jun 28, 1963; End of Tour Report, Lt Col James C. Dunn, Jul 22, 1963; hist, PACAF, Jul-Dec 63, I, pt 2, Oct 63; *DOD Pentagon Papers*, Bk 3: IV.B.4., 12-13, 15-16.
50. PACAF Ref Bk for Nov 63 SECDEF Conf, Tab 4C; intvw with Trumbo by Grainger, Jul 13, 1963.
51. Msg, MACV to JCS, Jun 13, 1963.

Chapter XV

Air Operations, 1963

1. Three C-123s were detached to Thailand. PACAF Ref Bk for May 63 SECDEF Conf, Agenda Item 1; msg, CINCPAC to MACV, Jun 24, 1963; hist, 315 TC Gp, Jan-Jun 63, p 15.
2. Msgs, USARPAC to CINCPAC, Apr 19, 1963, CINCPAC to USARPAC, May 1, 1963, and to MACV, Jan 24 and Jul 21, 1963, and 2d AD to PACAF, Jul 9, 1963; ltr, Anthis to

Martin, Sep 2, 1963; intvw with Kennedy by Gausche, Feb 4, 1964.

3. *Ibid.*; ltr, Anthis to Smart, Nov 25, 1963; msgs, 2d AD to 13th AF, Feb 25, 1963, and 315th AD to PACAF, Feb 25, 1963.

4. Hist, 315th TC Gp, Jan-Jun 63, pp 15, 19, 35; ltr, Maj Gen R.G. Weede to 2d AD, Apr 18, 1963; hist, PACAF, Jan-Jun 63, II, Jun 63.

5. Hist, 315th TC Gp, Jan-Jun 63, p 24; ltrs, Capt Louis W. Gaylor to USAFS(P)V, Jun 16, 1963, Anthis to Martin, Sep 2, 1963, and to 315th Gp, May 11, 1963; ACTIV, Final Rprt, p 9.

6. Hist, 13th AF, Jul-Dec 63, I, 17; intvw with Kennedy by Gausche, Feb 4, 1964; ltr, Anthis to Smart, Nov 25, 1963.

7. Msgs, 2d AD to PACAF, Mar 22, 1963, Sep 29, 1963, and Oct 5, 1963, MACV to CINCPAC, Oct 3, 1963, PACAF to 2d AD, Oct 30, 1963, CINCPAC to CSAF, Mar 15 and May 11, 1963; Hearings before the Committee on Appropriations, US Senate, *Foreign Assistance and Related Agencies Appropriations for 1965*, 88th Cong, 2d sess (Washington, 1964), pp 160-61; Hist Data Rcrd, 34th TG, Jul-Dec 63, p 1 and atch 3; hist, 13th AF, Jul-Dec 63, I, 116; hist, Asst for Mutual Security, USAF, Jul-Dec 63, pp 53-54; memo with atch, Col Roger E. Phelan, Dir/Plans, USAF, to Asst VCS, USAF, Aug 13, 1963; ltr, Carpenter to Moorman, Apr 1, 1963.

8. Hist, PACAF, Jul-Dec 62, II, Dec 62; hist, 13th AF, 1962, I, 107-08; msg, AF Sec, MAAGV, to PACAF, Aug 12, 1963; PACAF Counterinsurgency Lessons Learned, Sep 12, 1963.

9. Hist, PACAF, Jan-Jun 63, II, Jan 63; Van Staaveren, p 33; msgs, PACAF to 13th AF, Mar 1, 1963, 5th AF to 41st AD, Mar 27, 1963, 2d AD to 13th AF, Jan 10, 1963, MACV to CINCPAC, Mar 15, 1963; hist, 5th AF, 1963, I, 59; PACAF Summary of Actions, Gen Wheeler's Party, Sec I, Tab F; hist, PACAF, Jan-Jun 63, II, Mar 2, 1963.

10. Hist, PACAF, Jul-Dec 62, II, Nov 62; Report of Visit by JCS Team to SVN, Jan 63, Sec II, para 2c(5)(b); ltr, Anthis to Milton, Jan 11, 1963.

11. Msgs, 1st Air Commando Gp to AFLC Ln Ofc, Jul 1, 1963, 2d AD to PACAF, Aug 25 and Sep 21, 1963, MACV to CINCPAC, Mar 15, 1963, 5th AF to 41st AD, Mar 27, 1963, 13th AF to PACAF, Apr 12, 1963, 13th AF to 2d AD, May 6, 1963, 2d AD to 13th AF, Jun 27, 1963, and PACAF to 2d AD, Sep 13, 1963; hists, PACAF, Jan-Jun 63, II, Feb 24-Mar 2, 1963, III, Jun 63, and Jul-Dec 63, III, Jul 63; ltr, Henderson to Moorman, Jul 25, 1963; End of Tour Reports, Capt Harry G. Rudolph, *ca.* Oct 63, and Capt Joseph E. Simanonok, Oct 15,

1963; hist, 6091st Recon Sq, Jul-Dec 63, pp 11-15; PACAF Counterinsurgency Lessons Learned, Sep 12, 1963.

12. CINCPAC Rcrd, 8th SECDEF Conf, May 6, 1963, Item 3; ltr, Rose to MACV J-5, Oct 23, 1963; PACAF Ref Bk for May 63 SECDEF Conf, Agenda Item 4; msg, MACV to CINCPAC, Apr 29, 1963; intvw with Kennedy by Gausche, Feb 4, 1964.

13. Ltrs, Anthis to Brig Gen H. D. Aynesworth, Oct 28, 1963, and to Smart, Nov 25, 1963; Mellish rprts, Dec 9, 1963, and Jan 15, 1964; Col Harvey E. Henderson End of Tour Report, Feb 5, 1964; PACAF Ref Bk for May 63 SECDEF Conf, Agenda Item 4; Ops Analysis Ofc, 2d AD, Counterinsurgency Lessons Learned, Jan-Jun 64, Jun 4, 1964.

14. Rprt, Brig Gen Virgil L. Zoller to CSAF, Jul 5, 1962; see also Proj Corona Harvest Oral Hist Intvw 83 with Col William M. Martin, *ca.* Jan 30, 1971; PACAF Ref Bk for SECDEF Conf, May 13, 1964, Fact Sheet 6; MACV Summary of Highlights, p 135.

15. Msg, 2d AD to PACAF, Jul 10, 1963.

16. PACAF Summary of Actions, Gen Wheeler's Party, pt 2, Tab 20; Lt Col Miles M. Doyle End of Tour Report, Feb 6, 1963; intvw with Maj William J. Johnson and Capt Ernest C. Cutler, Jr., by Grainger, Feb 7, 1963; Anthis file of items to be taken up with Gen LeMay, *ca.* Mar 63; msgs, 13th AF to PACAF, Aug 9, 1963.

17. Ltr, Anderson to Anthis, Apr 12, 1963; hist, PACAF, Jan-Jun 63, II, May 63; ltrs, Anthis to Brig Gen Joseph W. Stilwell and to Moorman, May 28, 1963; msg, 2d AD to PACAF, Jan 10, 1964.

18. Quoted in msg, PACAF to CSAF, Jan 1, 1963.

19. To conceal B-26s as strike aircraft, they were referred to as RB-26s, the reconnaissance configuration.

20. Msgs, CSAF to JCS, Feb 8, 1963, PACAF to CSAF, Feb 20, 1963, 2d AD to PACAF, Feb 18, 1963; hist, SAWC, Jan-Jun 63, p 166.

21. Msg, CSAF to PACAF, Mar 5, 1963; rprt, Col Frank R. Pancake, Mar 20, 1963.

22. Ltr, Anderson to Anthis, Apr 12, 1963; msgs, 313th AD to PACAF, Apr 27, 1963, and 13th AF to PACAF, Apr 27, 1963; hist, PACAF, Jan-Jun 63, II, Jun 63; Manpower Review and Analysis of 13th AF Activities, RVN, Jun 28, 1963; Henderson End of Tour Report, Feb 5, 1964; hist, 13th AF, Jul-Dec 63, I, 10-11.

23. Hist Data Rcrd, 1st ACS, Jul-Dec 63, incl 4; hists, SAWC, Jan-Jun 63, II, Item 74, and Jul-Dec 63, p 119; hist, 13th AF, Jan-Jun 63, p 72; msgs, CSAF to PACAF, Jun 17, 1963, and PACAF to CSAF, Apr 30, 1963.

24. Hist, 13th AF, Jan-Jun 63, pp 22-23; Futrell, "Chronology," for 1954-67; William C. Greenhalgh, Jr., "Reconnaissance in SEA," p. I-90; End of Tour Report, Col John C. Haygood, Feb 19, 1963; ltrs, Moorman to Anthis, Feb 11, 1963, and Apr 15, 1963, Anthis to Moorman, Mar 28, 1963; hist, SAWC, Jul-Dec 63, pp 6-8; msgs, CSAF to PACAF, May 29, 1963, and 2d AD to PACAF, Jan 10, 1964; Anderson End of Tour Report, Apr 5, 1963; PACAF Order 0-40, Jun 13, 1963; hists, 315th TC Gp (Assault), Jan-Jun 63, and Jul-Dec 63, p 1; hist, PACAF, Jul-Dec 63, III, 1-5.

25. Msg, 2d AD to 6220th ABSq, Jan 30, 1963.

26. Report of Visit by JCS Team to SVN, Jan 63, Sec IV, para 8; MACV Summary of Highlights, p 41.

27. Nigro Memo of Felt-Diem Meeting, Jan 9, 1963; intvw with MacKellar by Grainger, Aug 29, 1963; ltr, Anthis to Milton, Apr 18, 1963; rprt, Capt John Sercel, ca. Apr 8, 1963; and ltr, Stilwell to Anthis, Sep 9, 1963.

28. Msg, AmEmb Saigon to SECSTATE, Apr 10, 1963.

29. Msg, SECSTATE to AmEmb Saigon, Apr 12, 1963, and AmEmb Saigon to SECSTATE, Apr 25 and 30, 1963; PACAF Ref Bk for May 63 SECDEF Conf, Agenda Item 1; and CINCPAC Rcrd, 8th SECDEF Conf, May 6, 1963, Item 6.

30. CINCPAC Rcrd, 8th SECDEF Conf, May 6, 1963, Item 1; AFXOPJ Bk of Actions in SEA, 1961-64, Items VI-E, F, G.

31. Hearings before the Committee on Foreign Affairs, House of Representatives, *Foreign Assistance Act of 1963*, 88th Cong, 1st sess (Washington, 1963), pp 744-45.

32. CINCPAC Rcrd, 8th SECDEF Conf, May 6, 1963, Item 3; msg, CINCPAC to ADMINO, CINCPAC, Mar 27, 1963; PACOM Wkly Intel Digest, Jul 20, 1962.

33. Rprts, Capt Lester G. Frazier, Jan 11, Feb 20, and Mar 15, 1963.

34. Rprts, Maj James F. Yealey, Apr 2, 1963, and Capt Edward M. Robinson, ca. May 63; PACAF Ref Bk for May 63 SECDEF Conf, Agenda Item 1.

35. Rprts, Lt Col Charles S. Allen, Jun 4, 1963, Capt Louis A. Klenkel, Apr 30-May 8, 1963, and Jun 3, 1963; CINCPAC Rcrd of Special SECDEF-SECSTATE Conf, Nov 20, 1963, Item A4; End of Tour Rprt, Maj Walter S. Bruce, ca. Jun 64.

36. Hist, 2d AD, Jan-Jul 64, IV, 13-14; 2d AD Regulation 55-5, Jan 22, 1963; msg, PACAF to CSAF, Apr 16, 1963; ltrs, Harkins to Anthis, May 13, 1963, Lt Col Charles S. Allen to 2d AD, May 15, 1963.

37. Mellish rprts, Oct 16, Nov 6, and Dec 9, 1963; msgs, 2d AD to PACAF, Jan 10, 1964, and III ASOC to 2d AD, Feb 5, 1964; marginal comments by Ross on Mellish rprt, Dec 9, 1963.

38. PACAF Ref Bk for May 63 SECDEF Conf, Agenda Item 3.

39. PACAF Counterinsurgency Lessons Learned, Sep 12, 1963; hist, 2d AD, Jan-Jun 64, VI, Doc 31; msg, 2d AD to 13th AF, Nov 15, 1963; Army Sec, MAAGV, Lessons Learned 37, Feb 10, 1964.

40. Martin and Clever, V, 67-69; msg, 2d AD to PACAF, Jul 10, 1963; Final Rprt, Operational Test and Evaluation, TACS in RVN, App M, p 11; ltr, Col Thomas M. Hergert to Hien, May 8, 1963; ltr, Hien to Rowland, May 9, 1963; PACAF Ref Bk for Nov 63 SECDEF Conf, Tab 2B.

41. Ltr, Capt B. L. Ruhman to 2d AD, Jul 2, 1963, and 1st Ind, Capt Fred W. Mayberry to Dep/Dir, AOC, n.d.; msg, CINCPAC to JCS, Jan 15, 1963; Cahill and Shulimson (draft), "History of US Marine Corps Operations in Vietnam, Jan-Jun 65," pp 16-17; msg, PACAF to CSAF, Jun 24, 1963; intvw with Ingalls by Gausche, Aug 21, 1963; ltr, Simmons to Gunderson, Nov 30, 1972; ltr, Capt Donald V. MacKellar to ALO/FAC Sec, 2d AD, ca. Jul 63; ltrs, Capt Ronald A. Johnson to ALO/FAC Sec, 2d AD, Jun 22-25, 1963, and Jul 2, 1963.

42. Ltr, Anderson to Anthis, Apr 12, 1963; rprt, Lt Col Henry C. Meir, to II ASOC, Jan 15, 1963, and 1st Ind, Lt Col James O. Cowee, n.d.

43. Rprt, Maj Magnus P. Johnson, Feb 4, 1963, and 1st Ind, Lt Col Charles S. Allen, Feb 11, 1963; ltr, MacKellar to ALO/FAC Sec, ca. Jul 63.

44. Rprts, Meier to II ASOC, Jan 15, 1963, and 1st Ind, Cowee to 2d AD, n.d., and Mar 2, 1963; rprt, Maj Magnus P. Johnson, to ALO II Corps, Feb 4, 1963, and 1st Ind, Lt Col Charles S. Allen, to 2d AD, Feb 11, 1963; rprts, Lt Col Charles S. Allen, Mar 15, 1963, and May 17, 1963; Van Staaveren, *Plans and Policies in South Vietnam, 1961-1963* (Ofc/AF Hist, 1965).

45. Rprt, Maj John G. Schmitt, Jun 13, 1963; Meier rprt, Jun 20, 1963.

46. Bruce End of Tour Report, ca. Jun 64; Hearings before a Subcommittee on Appropriations, House of Representatives, *Foreign Operations Appropriations for 1964*, 88th Cong, 1st sess (Washington, 1963), p 230; msg, 2d AD to 13th AF, Aug 21, 1963.

47. Mellish rprt, Oct 16, 1963.

48. CINCPAC Rcrd of Special SECDEF-SECSTATE Conf, Nov 20, 1963, Item A4; rprt, Maj William I. Burgin, Jan 10, 1963, and 2d Ind, Lt Col James O. Cowee, Feb 16, 1963; End of Tour Rprt, Maj Robert K. Butler, Jun 8, 1964; PACAF Ref Bk for May 63 SECDEF Conf, Agenda Item 1; Doyle End of Tour Report, Feb

6, 1963; msg, 2d AD to PACAF, Feb 15, 1963; hist, PACAF, Jul-Dec 63, I, pt 2, Nov 63; hist, PACAF, Jan-Jun 64, I, pt 2, Jan 64.

49. Rprt, Maj Clarence M. Van Meter, Jul 3, 1963; rprts, Lt Col Donald K. Reamy, Feb 28, 1963, Mar 8, 1963, and 1st Ind, Lt Col James O. Cowee, n.d.; rprt, Capt Bob W. Quinn, n.d., and 1st Ind, Cowee, Apr 8, 1963; MRs, Maj Stephen J. Carrig, Mar 28, 1963, Apr 1, 1963; rprt, Burgin, Apr 1, 1963, and 1st Ind, Cowee, Apr 8, 1963.

50. Rprt, Burgin, Apr 22, 1963, and 1st Ind, Cowee, n.d.; PACAF Ref Bk for May 63 SECDEF Conf, Agenda Item 1.

51. *Ibid.*; rprt, Burgin, Apr 21, 1963, and 1st Ind, Jun 6, 1963; rprt, Lt Thomas G. McInerney, Jun 22, 1963.

52. 1st Ind, rprt, Burgin, Apr 25, 1963; rprt, McInerney, Jun 22, 1963, and Cowee, 1st Ind. n.d.; rprt, Burgin, Jul 1, 1963.

53. Martin and Clever, V. 96-97; rprt, Capt Fred W. Maberry, Jul 5-6, 1963.

54. Doyle End of Tour Report, Feb 6, 1963; hist, 13th AF, Jul-Dec 63, III, Doc 79; Summary of Aircraft Lost and Damaged, 1963; msgs, 2d AD to PACAF, Jul 5 and Jul 10, 1963; ltrs, Martin to Anthis, Sep 17, 1963, and Anthis to Martin, Oct 9, 1963.

55. Anderson End of Tour Report, Apr 5, 1963; ltr, Maj Gen Robert R. Rowland to Maj Gen Robert N. Ginsburgh, Apr 72.

56. Hist, 2d AD, Jan-Jun 64, VI, Doc 31; PACAF Ref Bk for Nov 63 SECDEF Conf, Tab 28; ltr, Henderson to Moorman, Aug 1, 1963.

57. Msg, AmEmb, Vientiane, to SEC-STATE, Apr 26, 1963; PACAF Ref Bk for Nov 63 SECDEF Conf, Tab 2B; rprt, Mellish, *ca.* Aug 21, 1963; msg, USAIRA, Saigon, to DIA, Jul 18, 1963.

58. Msgs, JCS to CINCPAC, Nov 1, 1963, MACV to JCS, Jun 13, 1964, 2d AD to 13th AF, Aug 21, 1963.

59. Bruce End of Tour Report, *ca.* Jun 64; CINCPAC Rcrd of Special SECDEF-SECSTATE Mtg, Nov 20, 1963, Item A4; rprt, Maj Robert K. Butler, Oct 30, 1963; Butler End of Tour Report, Jun 8, 1964; Burchett, *Vietnam*, p 89.

60. Hearings before the Committee on Appropriations, US Senate, *Foreign Assistance and Related Agencies Appropriations for 1964*, 88th Cong, 1st sess (Washington, 1963), p 374; MR, Ross, Oct 7, 1963; Van Staaveren, *USAF Plans and Policies in South Vietnam, 1961-1963*, pp 73-74.

61. PACAF Ref Bk for Nov 63 SECDEF Conf, Tab 28; rprt, Capt Donald V. MacKellar, Oct 9, 1963; MR, Henderson, Oct 7, 1963; rprts, Maj John G. Schmitt, Jr., Sep 17, 1963, and Lt Col Bill A. Montgomery, *ca.* Aug 63.

62. End of Tour Report, Col Harold E. Walker, Aug 21, 1964; Debriefing of Walker, Sep 15, 1964; hist, 13th AF, Jul-Dec 63, III, Doc 79; rprt, Lt Col Garry Oskamp, Oct 1, 1963; ltr, Col R L. Gleason to Carl Berger, May 12, 1972.

63. Msg, 2d AD to 13th AF, Sep 2, 1963; ltr, Anthis to Maj Gen Sam Maddux, Jr., Oct 11, 1963; msg, PACAF to CSAF, Oct 9 1963.

64. Hist, 34th CAMRON, Jul 8-Dec 31, 1963; Henderson End of Tour Report, Feb 5, 1964; Capt Glenn E. Frick End of Tour Report, Jul 20, 1963; rprt, Mellish, Jan 15, 1964; End of Tour Reports, Capt Roy H. Lynn, Jr., Capt Thomas G. Cain, and Lt Wells T. Jackson, in Hist, SAWC, Jul-Dec 63, II, Doc 35.

65. Martin and Clever, IV, 62-64; Maj William I. Burgin End of Tour Report, Jul 11, 1963; rprts, McInerney, Jul 22, 1963, and Mellish, *ca.* Aug 21, 1963; MacKellar intvw by Grainger, Aug 29, 1963; Lt Col K. L. Collings rprt, Sep 15, 1963; Combat Ops, 19th TASS, Dec 31, 1962, in Hist, 13th AF, Jul-Dec 63, III, Doc 80; Mellish rprt, Oct 16, 1963; msg, 2d AD to PACAF, Oct 5, 1963; and Lt Col John J. Wilfong End of Tour Report, Jun 30, 1964.

66. Rprts, Mellish, Jan 15, 1964, and Maj. John G. Schmitt, Jr., Sep 2, 1963, and 1st Ind, Allen, Sep 12, 1963; memo, Ross for Anthis, Oct 10, 1963.

67. Van Meter, rprt, Jul 18, 1963, and 1st Ind, Cowee, n.d.; Maj Harold L. Johnson rprt, Sep 6, 1963, and 1st Ind, Allen, Sep 17, 1963; Schmitt rprt, Sep 18, 1963, and 1st Ind, Allen, Sep 28, 1963; Mellish rprt, *ca.* Sep 18, 1963.

68. Ltrs, Cowee to 7th Div ALO, Jul 8, 1963, and Mellish to Dep/Dir, III ASOC, Aug 20, 1963; Mellish rprt, Sep 16, 1963; msg, MACV to CINCPAC, May 18, 1963; PACAF Ref Bk for Nov 63 SECDEF Conf, Tab 2B; hist, 2d AD, Jan-Jun 64, VI, Doc 31; Quane rprt, Oct 19, 1963.

69. Msg, 13th AF to PACAF, Aug 12, 1963; PACAF Ref Bk for May 64 SECDEF Conf, II, Ops Fact Sheet 6; Lawrence J. Hickey, *Night Close Air Support in RVN, 1961-1966* (HQ PACAF, Proj CHECO, Mar 15, 1967), pp 5, 32; PACAF Ref Bk for Nov 63 SECDEF Conf, Tab 2B; msg, 2d AD to PACAF, Jan 10, 1964; intvw with Kennedy by Gausche, Feb 4, 1964; hist, msg, 2d AD, Jan-Jul 64, VI; msgs, 2d AD to PACAF, Nov 16, 1963, and PACAF to 5th AF, Oct 9, 1963.

70. Msg, 2d AD to 13th AF, Aug 21, 1963; Butler rprt, Oct 3, 1963; msg, 34 Tac Gp to 2d AD, Sep 13, 1963; Capt Thomas G. Cain, End of Tour Report, n.d., in Hist, SAWC, Jul-Dec 63, II, Doc 35.

71. Butler rprt, Oct 3, 1963; msg, 34th Tac Gp to 2d AD, Sep 13, 1963; Cain End of Tour

Notes to Pages 184-189

Report, n.d., in Hist, SAWC, Jul-Dec 63, II, Doc 35.
72. Collings rprt, Sep 15, 1963, and 1st Ind, Lt Col Milton R. Pierce, Sep 24, 1963; rprt, Capt Don O. Quane, Oct 23, 1963; Butler End of Tour Report, Jun 8, 1964.
73. Msgs, PACAF to 2d AD, Nov 19, 1963, to CINCPAC, Dec 1, 1963, and MACV to CINCPAC, Dec 24, 1963; hist, PACAF, Jan-Jun 64, III, hist rprt, Jan 64.
74. Butler rprt, Nov 26, 1963; ltrs, Pierce to Dep/Dir, AOC, Oct 19, and 21, 1963; Quane Notes, Oct 19-21, 1963.
75. McInerney rprt, Nov 27, 1963.
76. Msgs, MACV to JCS, Jun 13, 1964, and JCS to CINCPAC, Nov 1, 1963; Pierce, End of Tour Report, Jul 24, 1964.

CHAPTER XVI

Collapse of the Diem Government

1. CINCPAC Rcrd, 8th SECDEF Conf, May 6, 1963, Item MM 1b.
2. Martin and Clever, III, 64; Dennis J. Duncanson, *Government and Revolution in Vietnam* (New York, 1968), pp 327-33; Hearings before a Subcommittee of the Committee on Appropriations, House of Representatives, *Foreign Operations Appropriations for 1964*, 88th Cong, 1st sess (Washington, 1963), pt 3, pp 264-65.
3. DA Pamphlet 550-40, Area Handbook for Vietnam, Sep 62.
4. *Foreign Operations Appropriations for 1964*, pt 2, pp 14-17, and 89-91; *Public Papers of the Presidents: Kennedy, 1963*, p 421; msg, SECSTATE to AmEmb Saigon, May 13, 1963.
5. Martin and Clever, III, 65-70; msg, CINCPAC to MACV, Jun 5, 1963.
6. Msg, USAIRA Saigon to DIA, Jul 18, 1963.
7. Quoted in msg, PACAF to CSAF, Jul 23, 1963.
8. Schlesinger, *A Thousand Days*, p 988; Dept of State, *Bulletin*, Vol 56, 799.
9. Martin and Clever, III, 73-75; CQ Background, *China and US Far East Policy, 1945-57*, p 125.
10. Intvw with Anthis by Gausche and Grainger, Aug 30, 1963.
11. US Dept of State, *American Foreign Policy: Current Documents, 1963* (Washington, 1967), pp 862-66; *DOD Pentagon Papers*, IV.B.5., xiii; msg, SECSTATE to AmEmb Saigon, Aug 21, 1963; and see Hilsman, *To Move a Nation*, p 486.
12. Msgs, 2d AD to CINCPAC, Aug 21, 1963, and CINCPAC to JCS, Aug 21, 1963, and Aug 25, 1963.
13. According to General Taylor, the message was dispatched without concurrence by the Secretary of Defense or the Joint Chiefs of Staff, although Deputy Secretary of Defense Gilpatric and Taylor himself were informed of its contents. James C. Thompson, Jr., "How Could Vietnam Happen? An Autopsy," *Atlantic*, Apr 68, pp 50-51; Schlesinger, *A Thousand Days*, p 991; Hilsman, *To Move a Nation*, pp 483-88; Taylor, *Swords and Plowshares*, p 292; msg, State to Lodge, Aug 24, 1963, in *DOD Pentagon Papers*, Bk 12: 536-37.
14. John Mecklin, *Mission in Torment: An Intimate Account of the US Role in Vietnam* (Garden City, 1965), pp 193-95; Martin and Clever, III, 83; US Dept of State, *American Foreign Policy: Current Documents, 1963*, pp 862-66; msg CINCPAC to JCS, Aug 25, 1963.
15. Dept of State, *Bulletin*, Vol 56, 799; *Baltimore Sun*, Apr 4, 1968, p 4.
16. Hilsman, *To Move a Nation*, p 492.
17. Msgs, Lodge to Rusk, Aug 29, 1963, in *N.Y. Times, Pentagon Papers*, pp 197-98, State to Lodge and Harkins, Aug 29, 1963, in *DOD Pentagon Papers*, Bk 12: 538; Henry Cabot Lodge, *The Storm Has Many Eyes: A Personal Narrative* (New York, 1973), pp 208-13.
18. Msg, PACAF to CSAF, Aug 29, 1963.
19. US Dept of State, *American Foreign Policy: Current Documents, 1963*, pp 869-70; msg, PACAF to CSAF, Sep 8, 1963.
20. *Public Papers of the Presidents: Kennedy, 1963*, pp. 651-52.
21. Msg, CINCPAC to ADMINO CINCPAC, Oct 22, 1962; Martin and Clever, III, 127-28.
22. *Ibid.*, p 102; Buttinger, *Vietnam*, II, 186, 242; Mieczyslaw Maneli, *War of the Vanquished* (New York, 1971), pp 132-52.
23. US Dept of State, *American Foreign Policy: Current Documents, 1963*, pp 871-72, 882-83; Anthony T. Souscaren, *The Last of the Mandarins: Diem of Vietnam* (Pittsburgh, 1965), p 109.
24. Msg, PACAF to CSAF, Sep 8, 1963.
25. *Ibid.*; Mecklin, *Mission in Torment*, pp 222-23; Schlesinger, *A Thousand Days*,

313

p 995; Dept of State, *Bulletin*, Vol 56, 799. Kennedy on November 7 ended secret reports, and Lodge restored the country team concept.

26. Msg, 2d AD to PACAF, Mar 12, 1964; Martin and Clever, III, 80-81, 99-104; Halberstam, *Making of a Quagmire*, pp 252-53.

27. Halberstam, p 659; Schlesinger, *A Thousand Days*, pp 995-96; memo, McNamara and Taylor for the President, Oct 2, 1963, in *DOD Pentagon Papers*, Bk 12: 554-89; msgs, 2d AD to PACAF, Sep 29 and 30, 1963, and Oct 2, 1963, PACAF to 2d AD, Oct 9, 1963; ltrs, Frederick W. Flott to Harbin, Oct 2, 1963, Wade to CHMAAGV, Sep 30, 1963.

28. *Public Papers of the Presidents: Kennedy, 1963*, pp 759-60.

29. CINCPAC Comd Hist, 1963, p 280; US Dept of State, *American Foreign Policy: Current Documents, 1963*, pp 875, 877; CQ Background, *China and US Far East Policy, 1954-67*, p 129; Hearing before the Subcommittee on the Far East and the Pacific of the Committee on Foreign Affairs, House of Representatives, *United States Policy toward Asia*, 89th Cong, 2d sess (Washington, 1966), pt 1, pp 154-55, 157; Duncanson, *Government and Revolution in Vietnam*, pp 286-338.

30. Martin and Clever, III, 106-07, 109-10; Thompson, *Defeating Communist Insurgency*, p 42; Mecklin, *Mission in Torment*, pp 277-78; hist, 13th AF, Jul-Dec 63, I, 75; msg, PACAF to 5th AF, Aug 27, 1963; msg, JCS to CINCPAC, Oct 29, 1963; Shaplen, *Lost Revolution*, pp 188-212; Halberstam, *Making of a Quagmire*, pp 277-99.

31. *Ibid.*, pp 288-99; msgs, 2d AD to PACAF, Nov 28 and Dec 2, 1963; Martin and Clever, III, 110-18.

32. PACAF Ref Bk for Nov 63 SECDEF Conf, Tab 1A; hist, Dir/Plans, USAF, Jul-Dec 63, p 233; US Dept of State, *American Foreign Policy: Current Documents, 1963*, pp 879-80.

33. CINCPAC Record of Special SECDEF-SECSTATE Meeting, Nov 20, 1963, Item 1A; PACAF Ref Bk for Nov 63 SECDEF Conf, Tab 4A; msg, 2d AD to PACAF, Dec 3, 1963; Mellish rprt, Dec 9, 1963.

34. Martin and Clever, III, 118; PACAF Background Bk for SECDEF meeting of May 13, 1964, II, Ops Fact Sheet 6; hist, 2d AD, Jan-Jun 64, VI, Doc 31; CINCPAC Record of Special SECDEF-SECSTATE Meeting, Nov 20, 1963, Items A2 and B3.

35. *Public Papers of the Presidents: Kennedy, 1963*, p 846.

36. CINCPAC Record of Special SECDEF-SECSTATE Meeting, Nov 20, 1963, Items B3 and B4; Hearings before the Committee on Appropriations, US Senate, *Foreign Assistance and Related Agencies Appropriations for 1964*, 88th Cong, 1st sess (Washington, 1963), p 348; hist, 13th AF, Jul-Dec 63, I, 16 and 66.

CHAPTER XVII

Objectives Confirmed, Methods Expanded

1. PACAF Ref Bk for SECDEF Conf of May 13, 1964, II, Fact Sheet 4; hist, Dir/Plans, USAF, Jul-Dec 63, p 65; *New York Times, Pentagon Papers*, pp 232-33; *DOD Pentagon Papers*, Bk 3: IV.C.1.,4; Johnson, *Vantage Point*, p 45.

2. Msg, JCS to CINCPAC, Dec 6, 1963; Johnson, *Vantage Point*, p 45.

3. Msgs, 2d AD to PACAF, Dec 20 and 21, 1963; memo, McNamara for Johnson, Dec 21, 1963.

4. *Public Papers of the Presidents: Lyndon B. Johnson, 1963-64* (Washington, 1965), I, 106; PACAF Ref Bk for Mar 64 SECDEF Conf, Tab 8, for SECDEF Conference of May 13, 1964, pt II, Tab G; *Cong Rec*, May 9, 1968, p 12618; msg, 2d AD to PACAF, Mar 10, 1964.

5. CINCPAC Record of Special SECDEF-SECSTATE Meeting, Nov 20, 1963, Item 2A; Mellish rprt, Dec 9, 1963; rprt, Col Lawrence W. Brady, Dec 3, 1963; Halberstam, *Making of a Quagmire*, p 307.

6. McInerney rprt, Dec 11, 1963, 1st Ind., Butler, Dec 12, 1963, 2d Ind, Collings, n.d., 3d Ind, Pierce, Dec 22, 1963; msg, 2d AD to CSAF, Dec 1, 1963; 2d AF Ops Analysis Paper 4, Feb 11, 1964.

7. Capt Richard W. Von Hake, rprt, Dec 17, 1963.

8. Mellish rprt, Jan 15, 1964.

9. PACAF Ref Bk for Nov 63 SECDEF Conf, Talking Paper, Tab 2B.

10. Capt Kent C. Spears rprt, Jan 8, 1964; msgs, 2d AD to PACAF, Jan 4, 1964, CINCPAC to MACV, Jan 18, 1964; Martin and Clever, V, 99-102.

11. Mellish rprt, Jan 15, 1964.

12. Hearings before Subcommittees of the Committee on Appropriations, House of Representatives, *Supplemental Defense Appropria-*

tions for 1966, 89th Cong, 2d sess (Washington, 1966), p 62; msgs, 2d AD to PACAF, Dec 20 and 21, 1963; Shaplen, *Lost Revolution*, p 232; CINCPAC Record of Special SECDEF-SECSTATE Meeting, Item B3; see also memo, McNamara for the President, Mar 16, 1964, in *Gravel Pentagon Papers*, III, 502.

13. Marguerite Higgins, *Our Vietnam Nightmare* (New York, 1965), pp 153-54; DIA, Cold War (Counterinsurgency) Analysis, Republic of Vietnam, Dec 1, 1964, Sec D, pp 10-11; Hearings before the Subcommittee of the Committee on Appropriations, U.S. Senate, *Dept of Defense Appropriations for 1966*, 89th Cong, 1st sess (Washington, 1965), pt 2, p 764.

14. AFXOPJ Book of Actions in SEA, 1961-1964, Item VI-1; *Gravel Pentagon Papers*, III, 35-42.

15. Msgs, AmEmb Saigon to CINCPAC, Jan 30, 1964, MACV to CINCPAC, Jan 31, 1964; Hearings on *Military Posture . . .* before the Committee on Armed Services, House of Representatives, 88th Cong, 2d sess (Washington, 1964), pp 7120-21, and 154-56; *Public Papers of the Presidents: Johnson, 1963-64*, pp 256-60; *Gravel Pentagon Papers*, III, 38-39.

16. CJCS to Dir Jt Staff, Feb 5, 1964.

17. Msg, CSAF to Smart [Feb 64].

18. Capt Donald V. MacKellar rprt, Feb 10, 1964; Hearings before the Subcommittee to Investigate Problems Connected with Refugees and Escapees of the Committee on the Judiciary, US Senate, *Refugee Problems in South Vietnam and Laos*, 89th Cong, 1st sess (Washington, 1965), pp 294-95, and 298; 2d AD APEX CPSACT Rprt, Feb 6, 1964; Maj Gen Edward G. Lansdale, "Viet Nam: Do We Understand Revolution?" *Foreign Affairs*, Oct 64, pp 84-85.

19. CQ Background, *China and US Far East Policy, 1945-67* (Washington 1967), pp 134, 136; 2d AD Chronology, Jan-Dec 64.

20. Memo, McNamara for Taylor, Feb 21, 1964; see also msgs, PACAF to CSAF, Feb 21, 1964, and CSAF to Smart, n.d.

21. Hilsman, *To Move a Nation*, pp 527-34; *Public Papers of the Presidents: Johnson, 1963-64*, I, 304.

22. See msg, PACAF to CSAF, Feb 24, 1964.

23. Msgs, CINCPAC to JCS, Feb 8, 1964, and MACV to JCS, Jun 13, 1964; PACAF Ref Bk for SECDEF Conf of May 13, 1964, pt 1, Tab F.

24. Adm U. S. G. Sharp, CINCPAC, and Gen W.L. Westmoreland, COMUSMACV, *Report on the War in Vietnam (as of 30 Jun 1968)* (Washington, 1969).

25. Msg, 2d AD to PACAF, Mar 8, 1964.

26. *Gravel Pentagon Papers*, III, 43-45.

27. Msg, PACAF to CSAF, Feb 24, 1964.

28. AFXOPJ Book of Actions in SEA, 1961-64, Item IV; Hearings before a Subcommittee of the Committee on Appropriations, House of Representatives, *Foreign Operations Appropriations for 1965*, 88th Cong, 2d sess (Washington, 1964), pt 1, p 369; msg, JCS to SECDEF, Mar 2, 1964.

29. 2d AD Chronology, Jan-Jun 64; Sharp-Westmoreland, *Report*, p 92; Hearings before Subcommittee of the Committee on Appropriations, House of Representatives, *Supplemental Defense Appropriations for 1966*, 89th Cong, 2d sess (Washington, 1966), pp 64-65; msg, 2d AD to CSAF, May 12, 1964.

30. Msgs, 2d AD to 13th AF, Mar 3, 1964, and PACAF to 2d AD, Mar 13, 1964; Mellish rprt, Apr 15, 1964.

31. Taylor, *Swords and Plowshares*, p 310; msgs, 2d AD to CSAF, Mar 11, 1964, and PACAF to CSAF, Mar 12, 1964.

32. Msgs, 2d AD to PACAF, Mar 6, 8, and 10, 1964; PACAF Ref Bk for SECDEF Conf of Mar 12, 1964, Tab 2; memo, McNamara for Johnson, Mar 16, 1964.

33. Msgs, 2CCR-64-077C and 084B.

34. Memo, McNamara for Johnson, Mar 16, 1964.

35. AFXOPJ Book of Actions in SEA, 1961-64, Item IV-1; PACAF Ref Bk for SECDEF Conf of May 13, 1964, pt 1; *Public Papers of the Presidents: Johnson, 1963-64*, I, 387-88; Johnson, *Vantage Point*, pp 66-67; msg, CSAF to JCS, Mar 14, 1964; *Gravel Pentagon Papers*, III, 499-510.

36. Msg, JCS to SECDEF, Mar 17, 1964.

37. Hearings before the Committee on Foreign Relations, US Senate, *Foreign Assistance*, 1964, 88th Cong, 2d sess (Washington, 1964), pp 541-64; msg, MACV to 2d AD, Mar 27, 1964; msg, JCS to CINCPAC, May 12, 1964; msgs, MACV to 2d AD, Oct 29, 1964, and to 2d AD, Nov 20, 1964.

38. Msg, 2d AD to CSAF, Apr 17, 1964; PACAF Ref Bk for SECDEF Conf of May 13, 1964, Plans Fact Sheet 12; AFXOPJ Book of Actions in SEA, 1961-64, Item IV-M; msg, State to AmEmb Saigon, Apr 28, 1964; *Public Papers of the Presidents: Lyndon B. Johnson, 1966* (Washington, 1967), II, 760-63.

39. Cong Rec, May 9, 1968, p 12618; CQ Background, *China and Far East Policy, 1945-67*, p 139.

40. Hist, PACAF, Jan-Jun 64, I, pt 2, 66-67.

41. PACAF Ref Bk for SECDEF Conf of May 13, 1964, pt 1, Tab C; Butler to ALO IV Corps rprt, May 27, 1964; Sharp-Westmoreland, *Report*, p 93; msgs, 2d AD to CSAF May 12 and 13, 1964; *New York Times, Pentagon Papers*, p 246.

42. Memo, CJCS to SECDEF, subj: Alterna-

tive Courses of Action, Apr 14, 1964; Joseph C. Goulden, *Truth is the First Casualty: The Gulf of Tonkin Affair—Illusion and Reality* (Chicago, 1969), pp 87-91.

43. Hist, PACAF, Jan-Jun 64, I, pt 2; hist, Dir/Plans, USAF, Apr 64.

44. Lodge, Verbatim Rcrd of Conf, Saigon, May 12, 1964, p 19; PACAF Ref Bk for SECDEF Conf of May 13, 1964, pt II, Tab G; *New York Times, Pentagon Papers*, p 246.

45. *Ibid.*, pp 245-49; msg, JCS to CINCPAC, May 21, 1964.

46. *New York Times, Pentagon Papers*, pp 249-50.

47. *Ibid.*, p 250; Jules Davids, ed. *Documents on American Foreign Relations, 1964*, pp 232-29.

48. AFXOPJ Book of Actions in SEA, 1961-64, Item IV-O; CM-451-64, Jun 5, 1964.

49. *New York Times, Pentagon Papers*, pp 250-51 (*Gravel Edition*, III, 174-77).

50. *New York Times, Pentagon Papers*, p 256 (*Gravel Edition*, III, 182); Johnson, *Vantage Point*, p 67.

51. Msg, JCS to CINCPAC, Jul 2 and 9, 1964; hist, PACAF, Jul-64-Jun 65, II, Nov 64; AFXOPJ Book of Actions in SEA, 1961-64, Item IV-O.

52. Hist, PACAF, Jan-Jun 64, I, pt 2, 171-72; *New York Times, Pentagon Papers*, p 247.

CHAPTER XVIII

The War in Vietnam, 1964

1. Msg, 2d AD to PACAF, Jan 27, 1963; Sharp-Westmoreland *Report*, p 104.

2. Hist, PACAF, Jul 64-Jun 65, I, pt 2, 46-55; hist, Dir/Plans, USAF, Jul-Dec 63, p 233; ltr, Smart to Taylor, Apr 8, 1964.

3. Msgs, JCS to CINCPAC, Feb 15, 1964, PACAF to 13th AF, Mar 6, 1964, to CSAF, Mar 21, 1964, and CINCPAC to JCS, Mar, 22, 1964.

4. Ltrs, Smart to Taylor, Apr 8, 1964, Taylor to Smart, n.d.; msg, CINCPAC to JCS, Mar 22, 1964; hist, PACAF, Jan-Jun 64, I, pt 2, Apr 64.

5. Hearings before the Committee on Appropriations, US Senate, *Foreign Assistance and Related Agencies Appropriations for 1964*, 88th Cong, 2d sess (Washington, 1964), pp 206-07; msg, 2d AD to CSAF, Apr 17, 1964.

6. Talking Paper on USAF Ops in VN, Jan 1-31, 1964.

7. Msgs, 2d AD to CSAF, Apr 17, 1964, to PACAF, Mar 24, 1964, and to 5th AF, Apr 29, 1964.

8. Msg, 2d AD to PACAF, Apr 20 and 23, 1964.

9. Msg, 2d AD to PACAF, May 7, 1964; PACAF Ref Bk for SECDEF Conf of May 13, 1964, Plans Fact Sheet 8; hist, PACAF, Jan-Jun 64, I, pt 2, May 64.

10. *Ibid.*; PACAF Ref Bk for SECDEF Conf of May 13, 1964, Talking Paper 4.

11. Hist, PACAF, Jul 64-Jun 65, I, pt 2, 46-55.

12. AFXOPJ Book of Actions in SEA, Item VII-C; msgs, CSAF to PACAF, Jun 17 and 19, 1964, and MACV to JCS, Jun 19, 1964; hist, PACAF, Jul 64-Jun 65, I, pt 2, 46-55.

13. End of Tour Reports, Lt Col Bill A. Montgomery, Jun 27, 1964, Col Robert J. Loughry, Jul 22, 1964, Pierce, Jul 22 and 24, 1964, and Walker, Aug 21, 1964; msg, 2d AD to PACAF, Jan 28, 1965.

14. Ltr, Moore to Baron, Jan 18, 1965.

15. Dir/Plans, USAF, Debriefing Rprt of Col David T. Fleming, Aug 9, 1965.

16. Ltr, Col W. D. Ritchie to 2d AD, Oct 2, 1964.

17. Msg, PACAF to 2d AD, Jan 23, 1965.

18. 2d AD, Ops Analysis Div, Tech Memo 4, Jul 1, 1965.

19. Hist, MACV, 1965, p 95; MACV Dir 95-11, Jun 21, 1966; 7th AF Pamphlet 55-1, Mar 20, 1968, pp 25-26.

20. Hist, PACAF, Jul-Dec 63, I, pt 2, Dec 63; msgs, 2d AD to PACAF, Dec 3 and 9, 1963; ltr, Brig Gen Milton B. Adams to CHMAAGV, Dec 8, 1963; msg, PACAF to MACV, Dec 13, 1963; msg, PACAF to 13th AF and 2d AD, Dec 11, 1963.

21. The 41st Tactical Wing was established at Da Nang, the 516th Fighter Wing moved from Nha Trang to Da Nang, and the 62d Tactical Wing was organized at Pleiku.

22. Msgs, 2d AD to PACAF, Apr 20 and May 4, 1964, PACAF to 2d AD, Apr 18, 1964, to CSAF, Jun 3, 1964; Proj Corona Harvest Orai Hist intvw 241 with Lt Gen Joseph H. Moore, Nov 22, 1969, pp 2-3, and 29.

23. Lt Col Bill A. Montgomery rprt, Mar 12, 1964; ltr, Maj Gen J. H. Moore to Ky, Apr 3, 1964; msg, PACAF to CSAF, Jun 3, 1964.

24. Msg, 2d AD to PACAF, Apr 20 and May 2, 1964.

25. Montgomery rprt, Apr 16, 1964.
26. Ltr, Anthis to Smart, Nov 25, 1963; PACAF Ref Bk for Nov 63 SECDEF Conf, Tab 2A.
27. Ltr, Ross to MACV J-5, Oct 23, 1963; PACAF Ref Bk for Nov 63 SECDEF Conf, Tab 2A; msg, PACAF to CSAF, Nov 9, 1963; hist, PACAF, Jan-Jun 64, I, pt 2, Jan 64.
28. Msgs, 2d AD to PACAF, Jan 10 and Feb 21, 1964; 2d AD Ops Analysis Paper 4, Feb 11, 1964; hist, 2d AD, Jan-Jun 64, II, 28.
29. Hist, PACAF, Jan-Jun 64, I, pt 2, Jan 64; msg, 2d AD to 13th AF, Jan 23, 1964.
30. Msgs, 2d AD to PACAF, Feb 18, 1964, CINCPAC to JCS, Feb 21, 1964, MACV to JCS, Feb 22, 1964; AFXOPJ Book of Actions in SEA, 1961-64, Item III-K.
31. Msgs, 2d AD to PACAF, Mar 8 and 10, 1964; hist, PACAF, Jan-Jun 64, III, Mar 64.
32. Ltr, Smart to Taylor, Apr 8, 1964; PACAF Ref Bk for SECDEF Conf of Mar 12, 1964, Tab 1B; AFXOPJ Book of Actions in SEA, 1961-64, Item III-K.
33. Msg, 2d AD to PACAF, Mar 1, 1964; Preston End of Tour Report, Jul 64; hist, 2d AD, Jan-Jun 64, IX, Doc 12.
34. Hist, 2d AD, Jan-Jun 64, II, 31; msg, PACAF to CINCPAC, Mar 28, 1964.
35. 2d AD Chronology, Jan-Dec 64; hist, 2d AD, Jan-Jun 64, VI, Doc 21.
36. Msgs, 2d AD to PACAF, Mar 18, 1964, PACAF to CINCPAC, Mar 28, 1964, and CINCPAC to JCS, Apr 1, 1964.
37. Preston End of Tour Report, Jul 64; msgs, 2d AD to CSAF, Mar 25, 1964, and Apr 1, 1964; trip rprt, Justin MacDonald and Howard Anderson, McClellan AFB, Calif., Apr 10, 1964; ltr, Moore to LeMay, Apr 7, 1964; hist, PACAF, Jan-Jun 64, III, Apr 64; msg, 2d AD to 13th AF, Apr 24, 1964.
38. Msg, 2d AD to PACAF, Apr 12, 1964; Mellish rprt, Jan 15, 1964; ltr, Moore to MACV, Oct 22, 1964.
39. Capt Don O. Quane rprt, Jan 29, 1964.
40. Lt Olin B. Gundiff rprt, Jan 28, 1964.
41. 1st Ind to Gundiff rprt, ca. Jan 28, 1964; and Butler rprt, Jan 16, 1964.
42. Mellish rprts, Jan 15 and Mar 15, 1964; 2d AD Chronology, Jan-Dec 64, and Jan 16, 1964; Lt Anthony J. Zilinsky Report of Staff Visit, Mar 10, 1964.
43. Mellish rprt, Apr 15, 1964.
44. Quane rprt, Jan 30, 1964; Maj Earl D. Jameson rprt, Mar 10, 1964, 1st Ind, Mellish, Mar 13, 1964, 2d Ind, Lt Col Albert H. Holman, Mar 19, 1964; Mellish rprt, Apr 15, 1964; Mellish ltr, Mar 18, 1964, 1st Ind, Capt William M. Leimkuehler, Apr 1, 1964, and atchd memo, n.d.
45. Mellish rprt, Apr 15, 1964.
46. Butler End of Tour Report, Jun 8, 1964.

47. Quane rprt, Apr 14, 1964, 2d Ind, Osburne, Apr 22, 1964; Maj Alan G. Nelson rprt, May 4, 1964.
48. Butler rprt, May 27, 1964, 2d Ind, Lt Col Milton R. Pierce, May 30, 1964.
49. Msgs, PACAF to 2d AD, Apr 14, 1964, 2d AD to PACAF, Apr 15, 1964, MACV to CINCPAC, Feb 17, 1964; hist, 2d AD, Jan-Jun 64, I, 70-71.
50. Msgs, 2d AD to 13th AF, Mar 3, 1964, to ASOCs, Mar 21, 1964, to PACAF, Mar 18, 1964, and Apr 20, 1964.
51. Msgs, 2d AD to 13th AF, Jan 21, 1964, and Feb 6, 1964.
52. Msg, 2d AD to 13th AF, May 15, 1964.
53. Msgs, 2d AD to 13th AF, Feb 6, 1964, to PACAF, Apr 20, 1964.
54. Msg, 2d AD to 13th AF, Apr 12, 1964.
55. Msgs, 2d AD to 13th AF, Mar 2, 1964, to CSAF, Apr 15, 1964, to PACAF, Apr 20, 1964, and PACAF to 13 AF, May 8, 1964.
56. Msgs, 2d AD to PACAF, Apr 15, 1964, and to CSAF, Apr 17, 1964; ltr, Harkins to Maj Gen Tran Thien Khiem, Apr 17, 1964; PACAF Ref Bk for May 13, 1964, SECDEF Conf, Plans Fact Sheet 3; and AFXOPJ Book of Actions in SEA, 1961-64, Item III-N.
57. Ltr, Moore to LeMay, Apr 7, 1964; msgs, 2d AD to CSAF, Apr 12, 1964, PACAF to 2d AD, May 6, 1964, and CSAF to PACAF, Apr 30, 1964.
58. Memo, Sandborn for Moore, May 7, 1964.
59. Msgs, PACAF to CINCPAC, Apr 27, 1964, CSAF to PACAF, Apr 30, 1964, 13th AF to PACAF, May 8, 1964, and 2d AD to PACAF, May 8, 1964.
60. Memo, Rowland for Ginsburgh, Apr 2, 1972.
61. PACAF Ref Bk for SECDEF Conf of Mar 12, 1964, Tab 9; ltr, Rowland to Ginsburgh, Apr 72.
62. Msgs, 2d AD to 13th AF, Apr 24, 1964, and PACAF to CSAF, May 6, 1964.
63. AFXOPJ Book of Actions in SEA, 1961-64, Item III-M; msgs, CSAF to PACAF, Apr 30, 1964, PACAF to 2d AD, May 6, 1964, to CINCPAC, May 4, 1964, and CINCPAC to JCS, May 8, 1964.
64. Msgs, 2d AD to PACAF, May 11, 1964, to CSAF, May 13, 1964.
65. Msg, CSAF to PACAF, May 16, 1964; Hearings before the Committee on Appropriations, US Senate, *Foreign Assistance and Related Agencies Appropriations for 1965*, 88th Cong, 2d sess (Washington, 1964), p 181.
66. Msg JCS to CINCPAC, May 20, 1964.
67. Hist, 2d AD, Jan-Jun 64, I, 48-52; PACAF Ref Bk for SECDEF Conference of May 13, 1964, Item 6A; Maj Walter S. Bruce

End of Tour Report, *ca.* Jun 64; Sharp-Westmoreland, *Report,* p 90.

68. Montgomery Rprt, Jun 8, 1964; msg, 2d AD to PACAF, Jun 1, 1964.

69. Hist, 2d AD, Jan-Jun 64, IX, Doc 12; ltr, Moore to MACV, Jun 2, 1964.

70. Msgs, 2d AD to PACAF, Jun 64, to PACAF, Jun 4, 1964.

71. Msgs, 2d AD to PACAF, Jun 1 and 7, 1964, to CINCPAC and CINCPACFLT, Jun 3, 1964.

72. Msg, CINCPAC to JCS, Jun 17, 1964; AFXOPJ Book of Actions in SEA, 1961-64, Item VII G.

73. Preston End of Tour Report, Jul 64; msg, 2d AD to PACAF, Jun 4, 1964; ltr, Moore to MACV, Jun 2, 1964; intvw with Col William E. Bethea, Jan 65, in Hist, 2d AD, Jul-Dec 65, V. Doc 5; hist, PACAF, Jan-Jun 64, III, PFMSS Wkly Activity Rprt, Jun 26-Jul 3, 1964; rprt, Moore to MACV, Aug 3, 1964.

74. Ltr, Moore to MACV, Oct 22, 1964.

75. Msgs, 2d AD to CSAF, Apr 17, 1964, to PACAF, Apr 20, 1964, and May 18, 1964.

76. Ops Analysis Office, 2d AD, Counterinsurgency Lessons Learned, Jul 4, 1964; Lt Col Albert H. Holman rprt, Jun 8, 1964; and ltr, MSgt Clarence M. Hall to AOC, *ca.* Jul 1, 1964.

77. Hist Data, 2d AOC, Jul-Dec 64, in Hist, 2d AD, Jul-Dec 64, V, Doc 11; ltr, Moore to Col Oakley W. Baron, Jan 18, 1964.

78. Mellish rprt, May 15, 1964.

79. *Ibid.;* ltrs, Rowland to Ky, Oct 26, 1964, Hall to Dep/Dir OAC, *ca.* Jul 11, 1964; Maj Carlos O. Beasley Report, May 5, 1964; Butler rprt, Jun 4, 1964.

80. Mellish rprt, May 15, 1964; Montgomery End of Tour Report, Jan 27, 1964; Pierce End of Tour Report, Jul 24, 1964; hist, PACAF, Jan-Jun 64, I, pt 2, Hist Rprt, Dir/Policy, Jun 64.

81. Rprt, Moore to MACV, Aug 3, 1964.

82. Ltr, Moore to Brig Gen W. E. DePuy, Jul 17, 1964; Sharp-Westmoreland, *Report,* p 93.

83. Pierce End of Tour Report, Jul 24, 1964; hist, 2d AD, Jul-Dec 64, II, 58-60.

84. Capt Franklin D. Peschel rprt, Jul 29, 1964, 1st Ind, Maj Earl D. Jameson, Aug 1, 1964; hist, 2d AD, Jul-Dec 64, II, 61-64; ltr, Lt Col John P. O'Regan to Dep/Dir, III ASOC, Aug 21, 1964.

85. Ops Analysis Ofc, 2d AD, Counterinsurgency Lessons Learned, Jul 4, 1964.

86. Msgs, MACV to CINCPAC, Jul 16, 1964, CINCPAC to JCS, Jul 20, 1964, and MACV to CINCPAC, Jul 28, 1964.

87. Maj Alan G. Nelson rprt, May 4, 1964.

88. Msg, MACV to CINCPAC, Jul 16, 1964.

89. Msg, MACV to OASD/PA, Aug 20, 1964; 2d AD Operating Instructions 1, Aug 1, 1964; ltr, Col W. D. Ritchie to 2d AD, Oct 2, 1964; MACV Directive 95-4, Sep 7, 1964.

90. Ritchie rprt, Oct 2, 1964; hist, TAC, 1964, I, 294; msgs, PACAF to CINCPAC, Sep 5, 1964, CSAF to PACAF, Sep 7, 1964; Ops Analysis Div, 2d AD, Tech Memo 4, Jun 1, 1965.

91. Msg, 2d AD to CSAF, Sep 21, 1964; ltr, Moore to Baron, Jan 18, 1964; and Brooks End of Tour Report, Jan 9, 1964.

CHAPTER XIX

The Gulf of Tonkin Incident

1. Hist, PACAF, Jan-Jun 64, I, pt 2, Jan-Mar; Goulden, *Truth,* pp 33, 92-95.

2. Hist, SAC, Jul-Dec 64, III, 122-23.

3. *Ibid.,* pp 124-25; msg, CINCPACFLT to CINCPAC, Jul 24, 1964; hist, 41st Air Div, Jul-Dec 64, pp 66-70.

4. Msg, 13th AF to ATF, Oct 10, 1964; AFXOPJ Book of Actions in SEA, Item IV-Q.

5. Msgs, JCS to CINCPAC, Jul 2, 1964, and 2d AD to PACAF, Mar 23, 1964; ltr, Johnson to Taylor, Jul 2, 1964, quoted in msg, CINCPAC to PACAF, Jul 3, 1964; see Taylor, *Swords and Plowshares,* p 316.

6. Maxwell Taylor, "The Case for Continued Bombing of the North," *Washington Star,* Oct 22, 1967; see also Taylor, *Swords and Plowshares,* pp 315-17.

7. Msgs, MACV to CINCPAC, Jul 16, 1964, and CINCPAC to JCS, Jul 20, 1964; *DOD Pentagon Papers,* Bk 3: IV.B.3., 43-54.

8. Goulden, *Truth,* p 32; CQ Background, *China and U.S. Far East Policy, 1945-1967,* p 142.

9. Msgs, MACV to CINCPAC, Jul 17 and Aug 16, 1964.

10. Hist, PACAF, Jan-Jun 64, I, pt 2, Jan-Mar; Goulden, *Truth,* pp 92-95.

11. *New York Times, Pentagon Papers,* pp 258, 288-89.

12. Goulden, *Truth,* pp 86, 127-28.

13. The question of the covert activities and the South Vietnamese patrol-boat raids as provocation for the attacks on the *Maddox* can be followed in: Hearings before the Senate Com-

mittee on Foreign Relations, *The Gulf of Tonkin, The 1964 Incidents, Feb 20, 1968,* and pt II, *Dec 16, 1968,* 90th Cong, 2d sess (Washington, 1968); Goulden, *Truth;* John Galloway, *The Gulf of Tonkin Resolution* (Rutherford, N.J., 1970); Eugene G. Windchy, *Tonkin Gulf* (New York, 1971); and Anthony Austin, *The President's War* (New York, 1971).

14. Msg, CINCPAC to JCS, Aug 5, 1964.

15. AFXOPJ Book of Actions in SEA, Item III-P; msg, JCS to CINCPAC, Aug 5, 1964; Hist Data, Plans and Rqmts Div, 2d AD, Jul-Dec 64; hist, TAC, Jul-Dec 64, IV, Doc 4; hist, 405th Ftr Wg, Jul-Dec 64, II, Docs, 2, 3, and 4; hist, 41st Air Div, Jul-Dec 64, pp 55-58; hist, 401st TFWg, Jul-Dec 64, pp 33-34; hist, 27th Ftr Wg, Jul-Dec 64, App I; hist, 313th Air Div, Jul 64-Jun 65, p 302; hist, SAC, Jul-Dec 64, p 131. The Thai government approved the movement of additional USAF forces into Thailand but was reluctant to have combat sorties flown from the country. The Thais finally agreed to the latter if they were absolutely necessary and if their bases were not publicly revealed. Msg, DEPCOMUSMACTHAI, to CINCPAC, Aug 7, 1964.

16. Telecon 1, 2d AD to 13th AF, Aug 7, 1964.

17. Msg, MACV to CINCPAC, Aug 6, 1964.

18. *New York Times, Pentagon Papers,* pp 268-69; msgs, PACAF to CINCPAC, Aug 8, 1964, and 2d AD to multiple addressees, Aug 7, 1964; Sharp-Westmoreland, *Report,* p 13.

19. Msg, PACAF to CINCPAC, Aug 8, 1964.

20. Msgs, MACV to CINCPAC, Aug 7, 1964, and CINCPAC to MACV, Aug 8, 1964.

21. Msg, AmEmb Saigon to SECSTATE, Aug 9, 1964, in *New York Times, Pentagon Papers,* pp 346-48; excerpts from Summary of Taylor's Mission Rprt from Saigon, Aug 10, 1964, in *ibid.,* pp 291-94.

22. Sharp-Westmoreland, *Report,* pp 11-13; Hearings before the Committee on Foreign Relations, US Senate, *The Gulf of Tonkin, the 1964 Incidents,* 90th Cong, 2d sess, *passim;* Goulden, *Truth,* pp 76-81, 122-57; Davids, ed, *Documents on American Foreign Relations, 1964,* pp 216-17; Johnson, *Vantage Point,* pp 112-19.

23. Bundy Memo on Actions Available to the U.S. after Tonkin, in *New York Times, Pentagon Papers,* pp 294-98; AFXOPJ Book of Actions in SEA, Item IV-T.

24. Msg, CINCPAC to JCS, Aug 17, 1964, in *New York Times, Pentagon Papers,* pp 298-300.

25. Msg, U.S. Mission Saigon to State, Aug 18, 1964, in *ibid.,* pp 349-52.

26. Hist Data, Plans and Rqmts Div, 2d AD, Jul-Dec 64; msgs, 2d AD to PACAF, Aug 25, 1964, and 2d AD to 13th AF, Oct 28, 1964.

27. AFXOPJ Book of Actions in SEA, Item IV-X.

28. DIA, Cold War (Counterinsurgency) Analysis, Dec 1, 1964; Sharp-Westmoreland, *Report,* p 94; 2d AD Chronology, Jan-Dec 64.

29. JCS Memo for SECDEF, Aug 26, 1964, in *New York Times, Pentagon Papers,* pp 354-55.

30. AFXOPJ Book of Actions in SEA, Item IV-X.

31. Memo, Bundy for President Johnson, Sep 8, 1964, in *New York Times, Pentagon Papers,* pp 357-59.

32. AFXOPJ Book of Actions in SEA, Item IV-T; Johnson *Vantage Point,* p 120.

33. NSAM 314, Sep 10, 1964, in *New York Times, Pentagon Papers,* pp 359-60.

34. DIA, Cold War Analysis, Dec 1, 1964; Sharp-Westmoreland, *Report,* pp 90, 94-95; 2d AD Chronology, Jan-Dec 64; AFXOPJ Book of Actions in SEA, Item IV-V.

35. CINCPAC Comd Hist, 1967, II, 962; Goulden, *Truth,* pp 159-60; Briefing by Chief, PACAF Assistance Team, Sep 64, in Hist, 2d AD, Jan-Jun 64, VI, Doc 3; Hist Data, Plans & Rqmts Div, 2d AD, Jul-Dec 64; ltr, 20th PR to PACAF, Jan 1, 1965.

CHAPTER XX

Diffusion of Air Assets

1. Ltr, Moore to Ferguson, Mar 16, 1965.

2. AFXOPJ Book of Actions in SEA, Item III-C. Because forty air liaison officer and forward air controller teams would take all of STRICOM resources, only twenty were sent. Memo, SECDEF to JCS, Aug 7, 1964; DJSM-1349-64 to ADS/ISA, Aug 5, 1964.

3. Hist Data, 2d AD Ops Services Div, Jul-Dec 64; hist, PACAF, Jul 64-Jun 65, III, Hist Rprt, DPO, Jul-Dec 64; hist, TAC, 1965, p 627.

4. Msgs, JCS to CINCPAC, Aug 11, 1964, MACV to CINCPAC, Aug 19, 1964, PACAF to CINCPAC, Sep 5, 1964, CSAF to PACAF, Sep 7, 1964, 2d AD to CSAF, Sep 21, 1964;

Brooks End of Tour Report, Jan 9, 1965.

5. Hist, 2d AD, Jul-Dec 64, II, 5.

6. Msgs, MACV to CINCPAC, Feb 21, 1965, and PACAF to 5th AF, Apr 12, 1965.

7. CHECO intvw with Lt Col Garth Reynolds, Jan 65; rprt, 2 CCR to MACV, Sep 2, 1964. From July through September 1964, 3,553 requests for air support were received, of which 2,403 were honored; 918 were refused because of a lack of aircraft. Ltr, Moore to MACV, Oct 22, 1964.

8. Ltr, Lt Col Clarence R. Osbourne, Jr., to I CALO, Sep 3, 1964.

9. The 34th Group then discontinued the use of napalm on night support missions. Reynolds intvw, Jan 65; Hickey, *Night Close Air Support in RVN, 1961-1966*, p 34.

10. USAF advisors assigned to Vietnamese squadrons had never been prohibited from flying single-seater A-1Hs in strike formations, but Taylor first learned about this practice late in October. Thinking that high-ranking officials in Washington were unaware of this, he informed McNamara and General Wheeler, who saw no reason to change the situation. Rprt, 2 CCR to MACV, Sep 2, 1964; msgs, PACAF to CSAF, Sep 4, 1964, to CINCPAC, Sep 5, 1964, CSAF to PACAF, Sep 6, Oct 1, and Oct 17, 1964, and CINCPAC to JCS, Sep 25, 1964; and AFXOPJ Book of Actions in SEA, Item VIII-G.

11. Rprts, 2 CCR to MACV, Nov 3, 1964, Jan 4 and Dec 2, 1965; msg, 34th Tac Gp to 2d AD, Nov 11, 1964; Bethea intvw, Jan 65; MACV Monthly Eval Rprt, Dec 64, Annex B, p 22; Bailey End of Tour Report, Mar 20, 1965; Lt Col William R. Eichelberger End of Tour Report, *ca.* May 9, 1965; hist, 2d AD, Jul-Dec 64, II, 44-45; ltr, Rowland to Ginsburgh, Apr 72.

12. Hists, PACAF, Jan-Jun 64, I, pt 2, Jun 64, and Jul 64-Jun 65, III, Jul 64; Bethea intvw, Jan 65; msg, PACAF to 2d AD, Jun 10, 1964; Wilfong End of Tour Report, Jan 30, 1964.

13. Msgs, MACV to CINCPAC, Aug 11, 1964, and CSAF to PACAF, Aug 29, 1964; AFXOPJ Book of Actions in SEA, Item III-R.

14. Hist PACAF, Jul 64-Jun 65, III, Oct 64.

15. Bethea intvw, Jan 65; Oxburne to I CALO, Sep 3, 1964; Miller End of Tour Report, Feb 7, 1965; and ltr, Janssen to Woodyard, Oct 29, 1964.

16. Lt Clare C. Eaton rprt, n.d.

17. William B. Graham and Amron H. Katz, *SIAT: Single Integrated Attack Team, A Concept for Offensive Military Operations in South Vietnam* (The RAND Corp, 1965); ltr, Col William Burke to 2d AD, Oct 29, 1964; msgs, CSAF to 2d AD, Nov 20, 1964, 2d AD to 13th AD and 13th AF, Dec 3, 1964, MACV to CINCPAC, Feb 21, 1965; hist, PACAF, Jul 64-Jun 65, III, Oct 64.

18. Ltr, Moore to Baron, Jan 18, 1965; Hist Data, 2d AOC, Jul-Dec 64; ltr, Rowland to Ky, Oct 27, 1964; memo, Stilwell for C/S, RVNAF, n.d.; and ltr, Moore to Pritchard, Apr 27, 1965.

19. AFXOPJ Book of Actions in SEA, Item VII-G; msg, CSAF to PACAF, Feb 10, 1965.

20. Bethea intvw, Jan 65; hist, PACAF, Jul 64-Jun 65, III, Feb 65; rprt, 2 CCR to MACV J-3, Feb 5, 1965; Guthrie End of Tour Report, *ca.* Aug 65; Bailey End of Tour Report, Mar 20, 1965; Eichelberger End of Tour Report, *ca.* May 9, 1965; 2d AD Ops Analysis Div, Tech Memo 4, Jun 1, 1965.

21. Hist Data, 2d AD Ops Services Div, Jul-Dec 64; ltr, Maj Gen A. J. Kinney to Moore, Sep 2, 1964.

22. Hickey, *Night Close Air Support*, p 34; 2d AD Ops Analysis Office, Counterinsurgency Lessons Learned, Jan 18, 1964; PACAF Assistance Team Briefing, Sep 64.

23. Ltr, Kenny to Moore, Sep 2, 1964; Hist Data, 2d AD Ops Services Div, Jul-Dec 64; Capt Joseph Yarrish End of Tour Report, Mar 1, 1965.

24. An XM-70 pod for launching 40-mm grenades from A-1s as an antipersonnel weapon had a feed system that frequently malfunctioned. The old 2.75-inch aerial rocket, previously little used because it buried itself in the ground before exploding, received another warhead and an XM-427 super-quick graze-action fuze. A new "Westo" mix of napalm incendijel proved stable in storage, and stabilizing fins added to napalm tanks allowed delivery in a dive-bomb mode. But the fire pattern was small and left a long-burning incendiary puddle in the impact crater. The best napalm employment continued to be the low-level splash attack. Variable-time radar proximity-fuzed general purpose bombs failed to have good antipersonnel effect, and the 2d Air Division fell back on the "daisy-cutter" technique, whereby nose-fuze extenders attached to bombs produced a waist-high explosion. Yarrish End of Tour Report, Mar 1, 1965; address of Gen Moore at PACAF Commanders Conf, Feb 22-25, 1965.

25. Kenneth Sams, *First Test and Combat Use of AC-47* (HQ PACAF, Proj CHECO, Dec 8, 1965); ltr, Ferguson to Moore, Nov 12, 1964; msg, MACV to CSAF, Dec 29, 1964; Hearing before the committee on Armed Services, House of Representatives, *Fiscal Year 1966 Supplemental Authorization for Vietnam*, 89th Cong, 2d sess (Washington, 1966), pp 5125 and 5160; USAF Spec Ops Force, Proj Corona Harvest rprt, Jan 1, 1965-Mar 31, 1968, chap 3, pp 1-3.

26. Msg, 2d AD to CSAF, Mar 15, 1965; hist, TAC, 1965, I, 298-99.

27. Rprt, Asbury to PFODC, Nov 22, 1963;

Lt Col Paul W. Rainowski End of Tour Report, Sep 23, 1964.

28. Ltr, Ross to MACV J-5, Oct 23, 1963; msg, 2d AD to PACAF, Jan 10, 1964; Quane rprt, Jan 30, 1964.

29. PACAF Ref Bk for SECDEF Conf of Mar 12, 1964, Tab 8; hist, PACAF, Jan-Jun 64, III, Mar 64; msg, MACV to CINCPAC, Jan 4, 1965.

30. Hist, 2 ODC, Jan-Jun 64; ltr, Rowland to Ginsburgh, Apr 62; msg, 2d AD to PACAF, Jun 1, 1964.

31. Film processed at Tan Son Nhut was flown immediately to Clark Air Base, where the Armed Forces Courier Service picked it up and delivered it to Washington, usually within thirty-four hours after a photo mission. Other copies went to Udorn for the U.S. Air Attache in Vientiane, who received them within twenty-four hours. In July, two B-57s were assigned to the 2d Air Division as photo couriers. Msg, 2d AD to PACAF, May 22, 1964; Hist Data, 2 ODC, Jul/Dec 64; hist, PACAF, Jan-Jun 64, III, May 64; ltr, Col Allison C. Brooks to MACV J-2, Jul 25, 1964.

32. Three RT-28s were flown to Udorn, where Thai pilots used them to photograph the results of T-28 strikes in Laos. Since the U.S. air attaché in Vientiane wanted this photography within twelve hours, PACAF established a photo processing cell at Udorn. Hist, PACAF, Jan-Jun 64, I, pt 2, 186-87.

33. Hists, 2 ODC, Jan-Jun 64, AFAG, VNAF, Jan 65.

34. Msgs, JCS to CINCPAC, May 25, 1964, 2d AD to PACAF, Jun 7, 1964, PACAF to 13th AF, Aug 29, 1964, and to CSAF, Oct 11, 1964.

35. Msg, CINCPAC to PACAF, Mar 16, 1965.

36. Ltr, 2d AD to PACAF, Jan 1, 1965; msg, 2d AD to CSAF, Nov 13, 1964; rprt, 2 CCR to MACV J-3, Jan 4, 1965.

37. Col Alfred F. Hurley, *The EC-47 in Southeast Asia, May 1966-June 1968* (HQ PACAF, Proj CHECO, Sep 20, 1968), pp 4-5.

38. Msgs, 2d AD to PACAF, Jun 1, 1964, to CSAF, Sep 10, 1964, CSAF to 2d AD, n.d., and PACAF to CSAF, Oct 11, 1964.

39. Hist, 2 ODC, Jul-Dec 64; rprt, 2 CCR to MACV, Nov 3, 1964.

40. Hist, 2 ODC, Jul-Dec 64; rprt, 2 CCR to MACV, Jan 4, 1964; hist, Dir/Intel, 2d AD Jul-Dec 64.

41. Ops Analysis Ofc, 2d AD, Counterinsurgency Lessons Learned, Jan 18, 1965; Ops Analysis, TAC, draft, Planning and Control of the Air-Ground Operations in South Vietnam by Thomas W. Wasilewsky, Apr 65; ltr, Col Lauren L. Shaw, Jr., to 2d AD, Sep 4, 1965; MACV Monthly Eval Rprt, Jan 65, Annex B, pp 19,

21-22; msg, MACV to 2d AD, Mar 4, 1965

42. Msg, CSAF to PACAF, Mar 19, 1965; ltr, Col Edwin J. Witzenburger to MACV J-3, Feb 8, 1965.

43. 2d AD, Ops Analysis Div, Tech Memo 4, Jun 1, 1965; ltr, Col James P. Hagerstrom to 2d AD, Sep 26, 1965.

44. Msgs, CSAF to PACAF, Mar 19, 1965, and MACV to 2d AD, Mar 4, 1965; MACV Directive 95-11, Jun 21, 1966.

45. Hist, 2d AD, Jan-Jun 64, I, 102-3; Montgomery End of Tour Report, Jun 27, 1964.

46. Hist, 2d AD, Jan-Jun 64, I, 97-98, 104. Of the remaining thirteen Caribous of the U.S. Army's 61st Aviation Company, four were assigned to the 145th Aviation Battalion in III Corps, three to the I Corps Aviation Detachment, three to the 52d Aviation Battalion in the II Corps, three to the Delta Aviation Battalion in IV Corps, and one to Bangkok.

47. Dir/Plans, USAF, Debriefing Rprt of Fleming, Aug 9, 1965; 2d AD, Debriefing Rprt of Col Robert J. Jones, ca. Apr 10, 1965; Ops Analysis Ofc, 2d AD, Counterinsurgency Lessons Learned, Jan 18, 1965.

48. Hist, Dir/Materiel, 2d AD, Jan-Jun 64; msg, MACV to CINCPAC, Jul 17, 1964; hist, 2d AD, Jan-Jun 64, I, 104-05, and II, 51; B. A. Whitaker and L. E. Patterson, *Assault Airlift Operations, Jan 1961-Jun 1966* (HQ PACAF, Proj CHECO, Feb 23, 1967), pp 32, 40; rprt, 2 CCR to MACV, Sep 2, 1964; rprt, 2 CCR to MACV J-3, Jan 4, 1965; 2d AD Monthly Summary of Aviation Activities, Jan 10, 1965.

49. 2d AD Stat Rprt of Combat Support Missions, Jan-Jun 64, in Hist, 2d AD, Jan-Jun 64, VI, Docs 11-13.

50. Intvw with Kennedy by Gausche, Feb 4, 1964; Ops Analysis Ofc, 2d AD Counterinsurgency Lessons Learned, Jul 4, 1964; Lt Col Victor N. Curtis, End-of Tour Report, ca. Jan 65; Maj Leonard G. Hillebrandt End of Tour Report, Mar 31, 1965.

51. Fleming Debriefing Rprt, Aug 9, 1965; hist, 315th TC Gp (Assault), Jul-Dec 64; Hist Data, 2d AD Ops Services Div, Jul-Dec 64; rprt, 2 CCR to MACV, Nov 3, 1964; and Curtis End of Tour rprt, ca. Jan 25, 1965.

52. Whitaker and Patterson, *Assault Airlift Operations*, pp 32, 40; msgs, MACV to CINCPAC, Jul 16 and 17, 1964; AFXOPJ Book of Actions in SEA, Item III-C.

53. Hist, Dir/Plans, USAF, Jan-Jun 63, pp 237-38; msg, AmEmb Saigon to SECSTATE, Oct 9, 1963; Charles V. Coolins, *Herbicide Operations in Southeast Asia, July 1961-June 1967* (HQ PACAF, Proj CHECO, Oct 11, 1967), pp 1-7, 70.

54. Msg, AmEmb, Saigon to SECDTATE, Oct 9, 1963; rprt, Moore to MACV, Jun 2, 1964;

rprt, Montgomery to 2d AD, Jun 8, 1964; msg, 2d AD to PACAF, Jun 18, 1964; Collins, *Herbicide Operations in SEA*, pp 7-9.

55. Hist Data, 2d AD Ops Services Div, Jul-Dec 64; rprt, Moore to MACV, Oct 22, 1964; rprt, 2d AD to MACV, Nov 3 and Dec 2, 1964, and Jan 4, 1965; Collins, *Herbicide Operations in SEA*, pp 9-15.

56. Msg, 2d ADVON to PACAF, Jan 30, 1962; Gleason paper, *ca*. Mar 1, 1962; PACAF Ref Bk for Mar 62 SECDEF Conf, Tab 8; intvw with Col R.L. Gleason, May 12, 1972.

57. CINCPAC Rcrd, 3d SECDEF Conf, Feb 19, 1962, Item 3; msgs, JCS to CINCPAC, Mar 12, 1962, and CSAF to PACAF, Apr 20, 1963.

58. General Moorman presentation before Congressional Committee, I, *ca*. Feb 63; MACV Summary of Highlights, Feb 8, 1962-Feb 7, 1963, p 53.

59. Msg, CSAF to PACAF, Apr 20, 1963; ltr, Anderson to Anthis, Apr 12, 1963; MACV Summary of Highlights, Feb 8, 1962-Feb 7, 1963.

60. Ltr, Anderson to Anthis, Apr 12, 1963; ltr, Doyle to 2d AD, Oct 11, 1962; Maj John P. Anderson to D/AFTU-Vietnam, Aug 21, 1963,
and Ross to MACV, Nov 3, 1963.

61. Msgs, MACV to CINCPAC, Mar 11, 1963, CINCPAC to ADMINO, CINCPAC, Oct 22, 1962; CINCPAC Rcrd, 8th SECDEF Conf, May 6, 1963, Item 1; msgs, CINCPAC to MACV, May 11, 1963, and CSAF to PACAF, May 13, 1963.

62. Lt Col Ray A. Robinson, Jr., End of Tour Report, Apr 10, 1965.

63. Ltr, Ross to MACV, Nov 3, 1963.

64. *DOD Pentagon Papers*, Bk 3: IV.C.1., p 39; msg, SECSTATE to AmEmb Saigon, Apr 28, 1964.

65. USAF Spec Ops Force, Proj Corona Harvest, Apr 1, 1968-Dec 31, 1969, Sec 2, pp 25-26; rprt, Moore to MACV, Oct 22, 1964; Robinson End of Tour Report, Apr 10, 1965.

66. Ltr, Moore to MACV, Oct 2, 1964; USAF Spec Ops Force, Proj Corona Harvest, Apr 1, 1968-Dec 31, 1969, Sec 2, pp 25-26; and Robinson End of Tour Report, Apr 10, 1965.

67. Rprts, 2 CCR to MACV J-3, Dec 2, 1964, and Jan 4, 1965; Reynolds intvw, Jan 65, and Bethea intvw, Jan 65, both in Hist, 2d AD, Jul-Dec 64, V, Docs 5 and 8; Capt Earl E. Tighe End of Tour Report, Apr 15, 1965.

CHAPTER XXI

End of the Advisory Phase

1. Msg, 13th AF to MACV, Oct 7, 1964; ltr, Moore to Baron, Jan 18, 1965; and Guthrie End of Tour Report, *ca*. Aug 65.

2. Kenneth Sams, *Historical Background to Viegcong Mortar Attack on Bien Hoa* (HQ PACAF, Proj CHECO, Nov 9, 1964); Hit Rprt, PFOOP, Aug 64; Moore address at PACAF Commander's Conf, Feb 22-25, 1965; hist, PACAF, Jul 64-Jun 65, II, pt 2.

3. *Ibid*., Hist Rprt, PFOOP, Aug 64, III, and Sep 64; AFXOPJ Book of Actions in SEA, 1961-1964, Items IV-X, IV-V, and IV-Y; *New York Times, Pentagon Papers*, pp 320-22; Johnson, *Vantage Point*, p 119, LeMay intvw, May 29, 1972.

4. Hist, 2d AD, Jul-Dec 64, II, 94.

5. Sharp-Westmoreland, *Report*, p 95; rprt, Edwards to 2d AD Hist Ofc, *ca*. Jan 65; Guthrie End of Tour Report, *ca*. Aug 65.

6. "The Lowdown from the Top U.S. Command in Saigon," *Life*, Nov 27, 1961, pp 46, 51-53; AFXOPJ Book of Actions in SEA, 1961-1964, Item IV-Y.

7. *Ibid*.; *New York Times, Pentagon Papers*, pp 324-25.

8. AFXOPJ Book of Actions in SEA, 1961-1964, Items IV-Y and IV-Z.

9. Msg, MACV to 2d AD, Dec 19, 1964; *New York Times, Pentagon Papers*, p 335.

10. *Ibid*., pp 335-36; AFXOPJ Book of Actions in SEA, 1961-1964, Item IV-2; msgs, JCS to CINCPAC, Dec 19, 1964, and CINCPAC to MACV, Jan 9, 1965; Brooks End of Tour Report, Jan 9, 1965.

11. Msgs, 2d AD to 23d ABGp, Dec 24, 1964, and to 80th TFS, Dec 25, 1964, CSAF to PACAF, Dec 24, 1964; hists, 19th TFW, Jul-Dec 64, p 40, Jan-Jun 65, p3; Robert T. Helmka and Beverly Hale, *USAF Operations from Thailand, 1964-1965* (HQ PACAF, Proj CHECO, Aug 10, 1966), pp 81-82; AFXOPLC, Analysis of Southeast Asia Air Operations, I, Sec 2.

12. Msgs, Det 2, 18th TFW, to 2d AD, Jan 18, 1965, 2d AD to PACAF, Jan 17, 1965, 13th AF to PACAF, Jan 27, 1965, and 2d AD to CSAF, Mar 15, 1965; Helmka and Hale, *USAF Operations from Thailand*, pp 61-65, 123.

13. *Ibid*., p 91; *Public Papers of the Presi-*

dents: Lyndon B. Johnson, 1965 (Washington, 1966), I, 57; *New York Times, Pentagon Papers,* p 339.

14. Msgs, ADMINO, CINCPAC, to CINC-PAC, Feb 27, 1965, AmEmb Vientiane to SEC-STATE, Jan 18, 1965, to CINCPAC, Mar 1, 1965, and 13th AF to CINCPAC, Jan 30, 1965; AFXOPLC, Analysis of Southeast Asia Air Operations, I, Sec 2.

15. Msgs, CINCPAC to JCS, Jan 21, 1965, PACAF to 13th AF, Jan 23, 1965, AmEmb Vientiane to SECSTATE, Mar 6, 1965, USAIRA Vientiane to CSAF, Jan 24, 1965, JCS to CINCPAC, Jan 26, 1965, AmEmb Vientiane to CINCPAC, Jan 27, 1965, OASD/ISA to AmEmb Vientiane, Feb 3, 1965, 13th AF to PACAF, Feb 6, 1965, AFXOPLC, Analysis of Southeast Asia Air Operations, I, Sec 2, p 8-9; Helmka and Hale, *USAF Operations from Thailand, 1964-1965,* pp 19, 71, 84.

16. Msg, MACV to 2d AD, Dec 28, 1964; *New York Times, Pentagon Papers,* pp 336-37; Thompson, *Defeating Communist Insurgency,* pp 43, 166-67; James C. Thompson, Jr., "How Could Vietnam Happen?", p 51.

17. Sandborn, End of Tour Report, Dec 8, 1961; Thompson, *Defeating Communist Insurgency,* pp 106-08.

18. Hist, 2d AD, Jul-Dec 64, II, 99; ltrs, Moore to Ky, Dec 29, 1964, and Rowland to Ginsburgh, Apr 72.

19. Hist, 2d AD, Jul-Dec 64, II, 109-12; rprt, Capt Stanton R. Musser, Dec 14, 1964.

20. Ltr, Moore to Baron, Jan 18, 1965; rprt, 2 CCR to MACV J-3, Jan 4, 1965; Sams, *First Test and Combat Use of AC-47,* p 5.

21. Woodyard rprt; Kenneth Sames, The Battle of Binh Gia, 27 Dec 64 - 1 Jan 65 (HQ PACAF, Proj CHECO, Dec 27, 1965), p 2.

22. *Ibid.,* pp 2-6.

23. Woodyard rprt; hist, 2d AD, Jan-Jun 65, II, 12 and 15.

24. *Ibid.,* p 15.

25. Sams, *The Battle of Binh Gia,* pp 6-8.

26. *New York Times, Pentagon Papers,* pp 337-40.

27. Hist, 2d AD, Jan-Jun 65, II, 8 and 11; ltrs, Everding to Hiller, Jan 8, 1965, Rowland to Ginsburgh, Apr 72; Brig Gen A.W. Schinz Debriefing Report, Oct 22, 1966.

28. Msg, PACAF to CSAF, Jan 6, 1965.

29. Hist, PACAF, Jul 64-Jun 65, III, Jan 65; msgs, PACAF to 13th AF, Jan 23, 1965, and to 5th AF, Apr 12, 1965.

30. Sharp-Westmoreland, *Report,* p 107; memo, Edumunds for Moore, Jan 18, 1965; PACAF Activity Input to Proj Corona Harvest on *In-Country Strike Operations in Southeast Asia, 1 Jan 65 - 31 Mar 68,* V, pt 1, 1965, 15-18; and msgs, PACAF to 13th AF, Jan 23, 1965, and 2d AD to PACAF, Jan 28, 1965.

31. AFXOPJ Book of Actions in SEA, 1961-1964, Item V-1; msgs, MACV to CINCPAC, Jan 2, 1965, PACAF to 13th AF, Jan 23, 1965, CSAF to PACAF, Jan 29, 1965, and 13th AF to 2d AD, Feb 15, 1965.

32. Msg, 2d AD to PACAF, Jan 28, 1965.

33. Ltr, Col H.L. Price to 2d AD, Jan 2, 1965; MACV Immediate Release, Jan 65.

34. MACV, Monthly Evaluation Rprt, Jan 65, Annex B, Air Force, p 19.

35. Hist, 2d AD, Jan-Jun 65, II, 16-17, 22.

36. Msgs, JCS to CINCPAC, Jan 27 and Feb 4, 1964; hist, 2d AD, Jan-Jun 65, II, 29; Robinson End of Tour Report, Apr 10, 1965; MR, Woodyard, Mar 1, 1965.

37. *New York Times, Pentagon Papers,* p 337; Ball, *Discipline of Power,* pp 317-18; Taylor, "The Case for Continued Bombing."

38. Sharp-Westmoreland, *Report,* p 107; hist, 2d AD, Jan-Jun 65, II, 8.

39. Stebbins, *Documents on American Foreign Relations, 1966,* p 129; Cooper, *Lost Crusade,* pp 255-62; Donald S. Zagoria, *Vietnam Triangle* (New York, 1967), p 151; Johnson, *Vantage Point,* pp 122-24.

40. Rprt of Investigation, Pleiku Incident, by Board of Officers to Investigate Incident at MACV Compound and Camp Holloway, Pleiku, RVN, Maj Gen Milton B. Adams, USAF, President, Feb 16, 1965.

41. Sharp-Westmoreland, *Report,* pp 14-15; hist, 2d AD, Jan-Jun 65, pp 22-26.

42. Hist, PACAF, Jul 1, 1964-Jun 30, 1965, I, pt 2, 96; hist, SAC, Jan-Jun 65, II, 238-239; msg, PACAF to 13th AF and 5th AF, Feb 65.

43. Hist, 2d AD, Jan-Jun 65, II, 26-28; Bethea intvw, Jun 6, 1965; Guthrie End of Tour Report, ca. Aug 65.

44. Hist, 2d AD, Jan-Jun 65, II, 31-33.

45. Sharp-Westmoreland, *Report,* pp 107-108; hist, 2d AD, Jan-Jun 65, II, 34-35; ltr, Mataxis to 2d AD, Feb 28, 1965; msg, MACV to CINCPAC, Feb 21, 1965.

46. MACV, Monthly Evaluation Rprt, Mar 65, Annex B, p 23.

47. Msgs, PACAF to 2d AD, Mar 2, 1965, CSAF to PACAF, Mar 6, 1965, CS to CINCPAC, Mar 9, 1965, and ADMINO, CINCPAC, to MACV, Mar 10, 1965.

GLOSSARY

A-1E Skyraider	Prop-driven, single-engine, land- or carrier-based multipurpose aircraft, developed to permit greater versatility as an attack bomber or utility aircraft. Two crew. Formerly designated AD-5.
A-1H Skyraider	Prop-driven, single-engine, land- or carrier-based multipurpose aircraft. Carrying heavy stores on its centerline rack, this plane is especially equipped for low-level attack bombing. A single-seater, like all Skyraiders other than the AD-5 series. Formerly designated AD-6.
AC-47	The C-47 transport converted into a gunship by adding the General Electric SUU-11A minigun. The AC-47 had several nicknames: Puff the Magic Dragon, Dragon Ship, and Spooky.
AD-4 Skyraider	Prop-driven, single-engine, land- or carrier-based aircraft used for dive-bombing, tactical support, and other combat missions. One crew.
AD-5 aircraft	See A-1E Skyraider.
AD-5Q aircraft	See EA-1F Skyraider.
AD-6 aircraft	See A-1H Skyraider.
AA	antiaircraft
AAGS	Army Air-Ground System (US)
AAOS	Army Air Operations Section, MACV J-3
AAR	air-to-air refueling
AB	air base
ABAT	air base advisory team
ABGp	air base group
Able Mable	United States Air Force photographic reconnaissance detachment at Don Muang Royal Thai Air Force Base (1961-62) then at Tan Son Nhut Air Base.
ABSq	air base squadron
ACP	airlift command post; airborne command post.
ACS	air commando squadron
ACS/	Assistant Chief of Staff for
ACTIV	Army Concept Team in Vietnam (US)
AD	air division
ADCS/	Assistant Deputy Chief of Staff for
ADMINO	administrative office
ADVON	advanced echelon
ADWg	air depot wing
AF	Air Force

THE ADVISORY YEARS

AFAG	Air Force Advisory Group
AFB	Air Force Base
AFCC	Air Force component commander
AFCHO	Office of Air Force History, United States Air Force
AFF	Army Field Forces, South Vietnam
AFLC	Air Force Logistics Command
AF Sec, MAAGV	Air Force Section, Military Assistance Advisory Group, Vietnam
AFTU-V	Air Force Test Unit — Vietnam (US)
AFXOD	Director of Doctrine, Concepts, and Objectives, United States Air Force
AFXOP	Director of Operations, United States Air Force
AFXOPI	Special Air Warfare Division, Deputy for Tactical/Transport Forces, Directorate of Operations, United States Air Force
AFXOPJ	Assistant Director for Joint Matters, Directorate of Operations, United States Air Force
AFXOPLC	Tactical Division, Deputy for Tactical/Transport Forces, Directorate of Operations, United States Air Force
AFXPD	Director of Plans, United States Air Force
Agile	Remote area counterinsurgency research and development by Advanced Research Projects Agency.
AGM	air-to-ground missile
AGOS	Air-Ground Operations School (USAF)
AID	Agency for International Development (US)
AIG	address indicating group
AIRA	air attaché
Air Link	Southeast Asia Treaty Organization air exercise in Thailand (1957).
Air Progress	Southeast Asia Treaty Organization air maneuver in Thailand (1959).
ALCC	airlift control center
ALO	air liaison officer
ALPIT	Authorized Low Priority Interdiction Target
Amb	Ambassador
AMC	Air Materiel Command
AmEmb	American Embassy
AMFPA	Air Materiel Force Pacific Area (USAF)
AOC	air operations center
app	appendix
ARDF	airborne radio direction finding

ARMA	Army attaché
ARPA	Advanced Research Projects Agency. A separately organized research and development agency of the Department of Defense under the direction and supervision of the Director of Defense Research and Engineering.
ARPAC	Army Forces, Pacific (US)
ARVN	Army of the Republic of Vietnam
ASD/ISA	Assistant Secretary of Defense for International Security Affairs
ASI	Aerospace Studies Institute (USAF)
ASOC	air support operations center
Associated States in Indochina	Vietnam, Laos, and Cambodia
asst	assistant
A-Staff	Air Staff. Formerly used in numerical combinations as with J-Staff, which see.
ASU	aeromedical staging unit
atch	attachment
atchd	attached
ATF	air task force
ATF-13(P)	13th Air Task Force (Provisional) (USAF)
ATGp	air transport group
ATSq	air transport squadron
AVCO	aviation company (USA)
B-26 Invader	A three-place, midwing, all-metal monoplane, light-bombardment aircraft with tricycle landing gear. Powered by two prop-driven engines. Three crew.
B-47 Stratojet	A swept, high-wing, multi-engine jet aircraft with swept tail surfaces and tandem landing gear. Four engines are paired in pods below and forward of the wings. Other two engines are in individual pods at wing tips. Three crew.
B-57 Canberra	A wide-short, midwing, twin-jet bomber aircraft with retractable tricycle landing gear. Two crew.
B-58 Hustler	Long-range, high-altitude, high-speed aircraft. Wing is full cantilever midwing modified delta design. Powered by four turbojet engines equipped with afterburners. Engines mounted in individual nacelles, two per wing, mounted on pylons beneath each wing.
Bristol Type 170	Prop-driven, twin-engine, cantilever high-wing monoplane designed as a freight or passenger transport. Used in Southeast Asia by the Royal New Zealand Air Force.
British Supermarine I Sea Otter	An amphibious aircraft used by the British during World War II for reconnaissance and general naval duties, including air/sea rescue. The French Navy employed this aircraft in Indochina.

THE ADVISORY YEARS

Back Porch	United States troposcatter communications system in South Vietnam.
Bali Hai	Movement of French military personnel by air from Europe to Vietnam (1954).
Barn Door	Establishment of tactical air control system in South Vietnam (1962). Barn Door II extended the system to Thailand.
Barrel Roll	United States air interdiction in eastern Laos (1964) and later limited to air activity in northern Laos.
BDA	bomb damage assessment
Bell Tone	United States Air Force air defense detachment at Don Muang Royal Thai Air Force Base.
Bent Bow	Rapid delivery airdrop system.
Big Safari	Air Force Logistics Command technical rework of infrared equipment (1963).
Binh Lam Special Zone	Republic of Vietnam Armed Forces special tactical zone in the provinces of Binh Thuan and Lam Dong (1964).
bk	book
Black Watch	RB-26 photographic activity in Laos that was transferred to Vietnam (1962).
Booster Shot	Pacific Air Forces air-delivered village aid project in Laos (1958).
Box Top	United States Air Force intelligence operations over the Gulf of Tonkin (1964).
Brave Bull	An especially modified C-97 employed for reconnaissance in Southeast Asia during 1963.
C-45 Expeditor	Light, low-wing, prop-driven, twin-engine cargo aircraft of all-metal construction. Two crew, four passengers.
C-47 Skytrain	Prop-driven, twin-engine, low-wing monoplane with retractable landing gear, utilized as a cargo, ambulance, or troop transport. Two crew, twenty-four passengers.
C-54 Skymaster	Prop-driven, four-engine, low-wing monoplane with retractable tricycle landing gear. A long-range cargo, troop, or personal transport. Six crew.
C-119 Flying Boxcar	A twin-boom, high-wing, land monoplane of all-metal construction having a conventional tricycle gear with a steerable nose gear. Its two reciprocating engines have constant-speed, four-blade, reversible-pitch propellers. Five crew, forty-two troops.
C-123 Provider	Prop-driven, two-engine, high-wing monoplane. Used to transport combat and other equipment for airborne assault troops, the resupply by air of advanced combat positions, evacuation of wounded, and air transportation of paratroops to the drop zone. Two crew, sixty troops, or fifty litters plus four attendants. Also served as a forward air control/flareship. (The C-123K features two pod-mounted turbojets in addition to its piston engines.)
C-124 Globemaster	A low-wing monoplane powered by four reciprocating engines. Has clamshell cargo doors in front fuselage and loading elevator in center fuselage

	capable of transporting heavy ground-force and ordnance equipment in the main cabin. Five crew, two hundred troops or 127 litters plus twenty-five ambulatory patients.
C-130 Hercules	A high-wing, all-metal construction, medium-range, land-based monoplane, for rapid transportation of personnel, cargo, or paratroops. Powered by four turboprop engines. Four crew, ninety-two troops or sixty-four paratroops, or seventy litters plus six attendants.
CH-21 Workhorse	All-metal, semi-monocoque-constructed helicopter for transport and cargo operations. Crew compartment in nose, side-by-side seating. Has three-blade, all-metal rotors arranged in tandem and turning in opposite directions. Tricycle-type landing gear. Two crew, sixteen passengers. Formerly designated H-21.
CH-34 Choctaw	Sikorsky Model S-58 helicopter equipped with a four-blade, main rotor and a tail rotor. Has two-wheel main landing gear and small tail wheel. Two crew, eighteen passengers. Formerly designated H-34.
CV-2B Caribou	Prop-driven, twin-engine transport with load-carrying capacity comparable to that of the C-47. Has short-takeoff-and-landing capability. Crew of two and thirty-two passengers.
C/	Chairman or Chief of
CALO	corps air liaison officer
CAMRON	consolidated aircraft maintenance squadron (USAF)
Candy Machine	United States Air Force F-102 interceptor air defense teams in Vietnam. Superseded Water Glass.
CAP	combat air patrol
CAS	close air support
CASF	composite air strike force
CAT	Civil Air Transport Corporation
CATO	Combat Arms Training and Organization Division, United States Military Assistance Advisory Group, Saigon
Cat Paw	Provisional United States Air Force C-119 maintenance detachment in Vietnam (1954).
CBU	cluster bomb unit
CC	combat cargo
CCTG	combat crew training group
CCTS	combat crew training school; combat crew training squadron
CDNI	Committee for the Defense of National Interests, or Lao conservative political party.
CDTC	Combat Development and Test Center
C-E	communications-electronics
CHECO	Contemporary Historical Evaluation of Counterinsurgency Operations (1962); Contemporary Historical Evaluation of Combat Operations (1965); Contemporary Historical Examination of Current Operations (1970)

THE ADVISORY YEARS

Chien Thang	"The Victorious." Government of Vietnam military campaign plan officially issued in February 1965.
Chieu Hoi	"Open Arms." Government of Vietnam cause designed to persuade Viet Cong to rally to the government cause.
CHMAAGV	Chief, Military Assistance Advisory Group, Vietnam
chron	chronology
CI	counterintelligence
CIA	Central Intelligence Agency (US)
CIDG	Civilian Irregular Defense Group (RVN)
CINCARPAC	Commander in Chief, Army Forces Pacific
CINCFE	Commander in Chief, Far East
CINCPAC	Commander in Chief, Pacific Command
CINCPACAF	Commander in Chief, Pacific Air Forces
CINCPACFLT	Commander in Chief, Pacific Fleet
CINCUNC/FEC	Commander in Chief, United Nations Command/United States Far East Command (1950-1956)
CINCUSAFE	Commander in Chief, United States Air Forces in Europe
Civil Guard	See RF, Regional Forces.
CJCS	The Chairman, Joint Chiefs of Staff
CJTF	Commander, Joint Task Force
CM	Memorandum (The Chairman, Joint Chiefs of Staff)
CMH	Chief of Military History, United States Army
CNO	Chief of Naval Operations (US)
COC	combat operations center
COIN	counterinsurgency
Cold War	A hostile encounter between nations or groups of nations that stops short of actual armed conflict. It uses the weapons of politics, diplomacy, economics, espionage, police action, and propaganda to gain advantage.
comd	command
comdr	commander
COMFEAF	Commander, Far East Air Forces
COMPAF	Commander, Pacific Air Force
COMSEADEFCOM	Commander, Southeast Asia Defense Command (US)
COMUSMACTHAI	Commander, United States Military Assistance Command, Thailand
COMUSMACV	Commander, United States Military Assistance Command, Vietnam
Condor	French military thrust out of Laos toward Dien Bien Phu (1954).

conf	conference
Cong	Congress of the United States
Cong Rec	Congressional Record
Corona Harvest	United States Air Force evaluation of air operations in Southeast Asia.
COSVN	Central Office for South Vietnam (Viet Cong Headquarters)
counterinsurgency	Those military, paramilitary, political, economic, psychological, and civic actions taken by a government to defeat subversive insurgency.
CQ	Congressional Quarterly
CRC	control and reporting center
CRP	control and reporting post
C/S	Chief of Staff
CSAF	Chief of Staff, United States Air Force
CSAFM	Chief of Staff Air Force Memorandum
CTZ	corps tactical zone (RVNAF)
curr	current
DA	Department of the Army (US)
DABIN	Data Base Inventory
DAF	Department of the Air Force (US)
D/AFTU-V	Director of Air Force Test Unit — Vietnam
Dep/	Deputy for
DCS/	Deputy Chief of Staff for
DCS/S&L	Deputy Chief of Staff, Systems and Logistics, United States Air Force
DEPCINCUSARPAC	Deputy Commander in Chief, United States Army, Pacific
DEPCOMUSMAC-THAI	Deputy Commander, United States Military Assistance Command, Thailand
dept	department
De Soto	United States offshore intelligence collection.
DIA	Defense Intelligence Agency (US)
Dir/	Director of
dir	director; directorate; directive
direction finding	Procedure for obtaining bearings of radio frequency emitters with the use of a highly directional antenna and a display unit on an intercept receiver of ancillary equipment.
Dirty Thirty	United States Air Force C-47 transport pilots attached to the Vietnamese Air Force (1962-63). An unofficial nickname.

THE ADVISORY YEARS

div	division
DJSM	Director Joint Staff Memorandum
DMZ	demilitarized zone
doc	document
DOD	Department of Defense (US)
doppler radar	A radar system that differentiates between fixed and moving targets by detecting the apparent change in frequency of the reflected wave due to motion of target or the observer.
Duke's Mixture	Provisional United States Air Force aircraft maintenance detachment in Vietnam (1954). Formerly "Project Revere."
DZ	drop zone
EA-1F Skyraider	Similar to A-1E except that it is equipped for countermeasures. Four crew. Formerly designated AD-5Q.
EC-47 Skytrain	A C-47 that has electronic countermeasures capability or electronic devices to permit employment as an early warning radar station. Three crew.
Eagle Flight	A tactic for helicopter employment.
ECA	Economic Cooperation Administration (US)
EDC	European Defense Community
Elda	Nickname for Mk-44 bomb (1965). Formerly "Hail" and "Lazy Dog."
ELINT	electronic intelligence
est	estimate
eval	evaluation
F-4U Corsair	Prop-driven, single-engine, Navy fighter used in various models both during and since World War II.
F-5 Freedom Fighter	An all-metal, midwing, twin-engine, single-place, jet fighter. Has tricycle landing gear and steerable nose wheel. Nose is fitted with two M-39 20-mm cannon. Can carry sixty-two hundred pounds of ordnance. Has a range of four hundred miles and a speed of about nine hundred miles per hour.
F-6F Hellcat	A World War II, prop-driven, single-engine, Navy fighter.
F-8F Bearcat	A prop-driven, single-engine, Navy fighter.
F-63 Kingcobra	Prop-driven, single-engine, low-wing fighter. Developed during World War II chiefly for ground-attack work. One crew.
F-86 Sabre	All-metal, single-engine, low-wing, all-weather, jet fighter interceptor with swept-back wings and tail. Has tricycle landing gear and nose radar. One crew.
F-100 Super Sabre	Supersonic, single-engine, turbojet-powered, tactical and air superiority fighter. Has a low, thin, swept wing and nose air intake. Employs air

	brake and drag chute. Can provide close support for ground forces and be refueled in flight. One crew.
F-101 Voodoo	Single-place, twin-engine, swept midwing jet aircraft designed as an escort and penetration fighter. Has a swept one-piece horizontal stabilizer set high on its fin tricycle-type landing gear.
F-102 Delta Dagger	Single-engine, supersonic, all-weather, delta-wing, jet interceptor used in air defense. Has tricycle landing gear, speed brakes, and drag chute. One crew.
F-105 Thunderchief	A supersonic, single-engine, turbojet-powered, all-weather, tactical fighter. Capable of close support for ground forces. Its range can be extended by inflight refueling. One crew.
FAC	forward air control; forward air controller
FAG	forward air guide
FAR	Forces Armées du Royaume, or Royal Lao Army
Farm Gate	Detachment 2, 4400th Combat Crew Training Squadron, and subsequently United States Air Force air commando activity at Bien Hoa Air Base, Vietnam.
FEAF	Far East Air Forces (USAF) (1944-56)
FEALOGFOR	Far East Air Logistics Force (USAF)
FEC	Far East Command (US)
FIC	French Indochina
Field Goal	United States Air Force RT-33 photo jet reconnaissance in Laos (1961).
Fire Brigade	United States Air Force-Vietnamese Air Force air transport rapid alert capability for Army of the Republic of Vietnam airborne employment.
Firm Link	Southeast Asia Treaty Organization maneuvers in Thailand (1956).
FISq	fighter interceptor squadron
Flaming Dart	United States-Vietnamese Air Force air reprisal strikes against North Vietnam (February 1965).
FM	frequency modulation
fragmentary operations order	The daily supplement to standard operations orders governing the conduct of the air war in Southeast Asia. It contained mission number and function, type of ordnance, time on target, and other instructions.
FTD	field training detachment
ftr	fighter
FY	fiscal year
G	The measure or value of the gravitational pull of the earth or of a force required to accelerate or decelerate any freely movable body at the rate of about 32.16 feet-per-second. To pull "three Gs" means to be subjected to a G-force of three Gs.

THE ADVISORY YEARS

GCA	ground controlled approach
GHQ	general headquarters
GLO	ground liaison officer
GP	general purpose (bombs or forces)
gp	group
GPO	Government Printing Office (US)
Green Python	United States Air Force reconnaissance operations at Udorn Royal Thai Air Force Base, Thailand.
Green Turnip	Loan of United States Air Force C-47s to the French (1954).
G-Staff	Army staff; used in numerical combinations with J-Staff, which see.
GVN	Government of Vietnam
H-19 helicopter	See UH-19 Chickasaw.
H-21 helicopter	See CH-21 Workhorse.
H-34 helicopter	See CH-34 Choctaw.
H-43 helicopter	See HH-43.
HC-47 Skytrain	The C-47 transport especially equipped for search and rescue missions, and with twice the normal fuel load, a stronger landing gear, and jet-assisted takeoff. Three crew. Formerly designated SC-47.
HH-43	A twin rotor, single-engine helicopter designed for crash-rescue operations. Semi-monocoque-constructed fuselage. Rotors are intermeshing, counter-rotating rotors, each with two blades, mounted side-by-side. Has non-retractable, four-wheel type, landing gear. Two crew, three passengers. Formerly designated H-43.
HU-1 helicopter	See UH-1A Iroquois and UH-1B Iroquois.
HU-1A helicopter	See UH-1A Iroquois.
HU-1B helicopter	See UH-1B Iroquois.
HU-16 Albatross	Prop-driven, twin-engine, high-wing, amphibious aircraft with all-metal hull and fixed wing floats. For search and rescue missions. Four crew, ten passengers.
Hail	Initial nickname for Mk-44 bomb.
Hawk Eye	Experimental airborne radio direction finding C-47 (later EC-47) activity in Southeast Asia.
HF/DF	high frequency/direction finder
Hilo Hattie	An especially equipped United States Air Force C-54 reconnaissance aircraft employed in Vietnam (1962-63).
hist	history; historical
HMM	medium helicopter squadron (USMC)
Hoi Chanh	A Viet Cong returnee under the Chieu Hoi program.

Hop Tac	Sequential concentric military operations to safeguard Saigon under the Chien Thang plan.
HQ	headquarters
ICA	International Cooperation Administration (US)
ICC	International Control Commission
identification, friend or foe	A system using electronic transmissions to which equipment carried by friendly forces automatically responds, for example, by emitting impulses, thereby distinguishing themselves from enemy forces.
incl	inclosure
ind	indorsement
instr	instructor
intel	intelligence
in trail	Aircraft directly behind one another.
intvw	interview
IPIR	initial photographic interpretation report
IR	intelligence report; infrared
IRAN	inspection and repair as necessary
Iron Age	Overall program for United States Air Force materiel support of the French in Indochina (1953-54).
ISA	International Security Affairs (US)
JU-52	Prop-driven, three-engine, low-wing, transport monoplane built in Germany by Junkers.
JAAB	Joint Airlift Allocations Board (MACV)
JAGOS	Joint Air-Ground Operations System (MACV)
JAMMAT	Joint Military Mission for Aid to Turkey (US)
JAOC	joint air operations center
JATO	jet-assisted takeoff
JCS	Joint Chiefs of Staff
JCSM	Joint Chiefs of Staff Memorandum
JGS	Joint General Staff (RVNAF)
JOC	joint operations center
JOEG-V	Joint Operational Evaluation Group, Vietnam (MACV)
JRATA	Joint Research and Test Activity (MACV)
J-Staff	Joint Staff. Used in numerical combinations as J-1 (Personnel), J-2 (Intelligence), J-3 (Operations), J-4 (Logistics), J-5 (Plans), J-6 (Communications and Electronics).

THE ADVISORY YEARS

jt	joint
JTD	joint table of distribution
JTF	joint task force
Jungle Jim	The 4400th Combat Crew Training Squadron and subsequent United States Air Force air commando activity at Eglin Air Force Base, Florida.
JUSMAG	Joint United States Military Advisory Group
JUSMAP	Joint United States Military Advisory and Planning Group
KB-50 Superfortress	Tactical aerial tanker powered by four reciprocating engines and two turbojet engines. Capable of simultaneous aerial refueling of three fighter-type aircraft by the probe and drogue method. Six crew.
KC-135 Stratotanker	Long-range, high-performance tanker powered by four turbojet engines. Has a flying boom for aerial refueling. Performs high-speed, high-altitude refueling of bombers and fighters. Can be used as a cargo and/or troop transport, carrying up to eighty troops. Four crew.
KBA	killed by air
KIA	killed in action
kilometer	Equals 3,280.8 feet, about two-thirds (.62) of a mile.
L-18	Prop-driven, single-engine, braced high-wing, light monoplane. Enclosed cabin seats two in tandem. Has dual controls.
L-19 aircraft	See O-1 Bird Dog.
L-20 aircraft	See U-6 Beaver.
L-26 aircraft	See U-9 Aero Commander.
L-28 aircraft	See UH-10 Helio Super Courier.
landline system	Telephone or telegraph communication by wire over, on, or under the ground.
Lazy Dog	Nickname for Mk-44 bomb, earlier called "Hail" and later "Elda."
Leaping Lena	United States and Republic of Vietnam Armed Forces long-range reconnaissance interdiction teams.
ln	liaison
LOC	line of communications
LOP	line of position
LORAN	Long-range electronic navigation system that uses a time divergence of pulse-type transmissions from two or more fixed stations. Also called long-range navigation.
LPR	Laotian People's Rally, or neutralist political party.
ltr	letter

Lucky Dragon	High-altitude aerial reconnaissance flown by Strategic Air Command U-2 aircraft (1964). Later called "Trojan Horse."
LZ	landing zone
Marcel Dassault M.D. 315 Flamant	French prop-driven, twin-engine, all-metal, light military transport and liaison monoplane.
MIG-15	Single-engine, turbojet, Russian fighter aircraft, designed and developed by Mikoyan-Gurevich. One crew.
MIG-17	Single-engine, turbojet, Russian fighter aircraft that by 1953-54 began replacing the MIG-15 in the Soviet Air and Naval Service.
MK-IX Spitfire	British prop-driven, single-engine, low-wing fighter developed by Supermarine. One crew. The speed, rate of climb, superior maneuverability, and great firepower of the Spitfire made it one of the greatest combat aircraft ever built.
Morane-500 Cricket	Prop-driven, single-engine, high-wing, liaison aircraft. Built by Morane Saulnier, it is the French version of the German Fieseler Fl-156 Storch communications monoplane. Two crew.
MAAG	Military Assistance Advisory Group
MAAGV	Military Assistance Advisory Group, Vietnam
MACSOG	Military Assistance Command, Studies and Observations Group
MACTHAI	Military Assistance Command, Thailand
MACV	Military Assistance Command, Vietnam
MAG	Military Advisory Group
Mail Pouch	RT-33 photo courier service from Don Muang Royal Thai Air Force Base, Thailand (1961-62).
M&O	manpower and organization
MAP	Military Assistance Program
Market	Project for the loan of United States Air Force B-26s to the French in Vietnam (1954).
Market Time	United States Navy patrols off South Vietnamese coasts.
mat	materiel
MATS	Military Air Transport Service (USAF)
MDAP	Mutual Defense Assistance Program
memo	memorandum
meter	Equals 39.37 inches.
MG	machinegun
MIG	A popular designation for certain Russian fighter aircraft designed and developed by Mikoyan and Gurevich.
Millpond	United States covert assistance actions in Laos (1961).

THE ADVISORY YEARS

MONEVAL	monthly evaluation
Montagnards	Primitive mountain tribesmen (numbering about eight hundred thousand) who had a history of antipathy toward the Vietnamese. They were not absorbed into the mainstream of Vietnamese life.
MR	memorandum for record; military region
MRC	Military Revolutionary Council (GVN)
MS	manuscript
msg	message
MSTS	Military Sea Transport Service
Mule Train	Nickname of initial United States Air Force C-123 detachment in Vietnam.
NAMAP	Northern Air Material Area Pacific (USAF)
NATO	North Atlantic Treaty Organization
NCOIC	noncommissioned officer-in-charge
NCP	National Campaign Plan
n.d.	no date
NFLSVN	National Front for the Liberation of South Vietnam (Viet Cong political arm). Also sometimes abbreviated NFL or NLF.
NIA	National Intelligence Agency, South Vietnam
NIE	national intelligence estimate (US)
Night Owl	Night delivery of ordnance by F-4 aircraft under illumination of their own flares.
NISC	National Internal Security Council, South Vietnam
NLHS	Neo Lao Hak Sat (Pathet Lao)
Nomad	An armed T-28A trainer aircraft configured for the Mutual Defense Assistance Program.
NORM	not operationally ready — maintenance
NORS	not operationally ready — supply
n.p.	no place; no publisher
NSAM	National Security Action Memorandum
NSC	National Security Council (US)
NVA	North Vietnamese Army
O-1 Bird Dog	Single-engine, two-place tandem, closed cabin, high-wing aircraft of conventional strut-braced, two-spar design. All metal and semi-monocoque fuselage with a fixed pitch McCauley propeller. Twenty-four volt electrical system. Two crew. Formerly designated L-19.
OV-1 Mohawk	Prop-driven, single-engine, surveillance (day and night) airplane with visual observation and photographic capabilities. Crew of two.
OASD/ISA	Office of the Assistant Secretary of Defense, International Security Affairs

OASD/PA	Office of the Assistant Secretary of Defense, Public Affairs
ofc	office
OICC	office in charge of construction
OJT	on-the-job training
One Buck	United States Tactical Air Command composite air strike force deployment to Southeast Asia in August 1964 in response to the Tonkin Gulf attack.
On Mark	Extensive modification of B-26K aircraft performed by the On Mark Engineering Company.
OPlan	Operation Plan
ops	operations
order of battle	The identification, strength, command structure, and disposition of the personnel, units, and equipment of any military forces.
OSD	Office of the Secretary of Defense
PB4T-2 Privateer	A four-engine bomber and reconnaissance monoplane, developed by Consolidated Vultee during World War II for the United States Navy.
PBY-5A Catalina	Prop-driven, twin-engine, all-metal, parasol-wing patrol-bomber flying boat. Has amphibian capability, with a retractable tricycle undercarriage in the hull.
PACAF	Pacific Air Forces (USAF)
PACFLT	Pacific Fleet (USN)
PACOM	Pacific Command (US)
PAF	Pacific Air Force (1954-1956) (USAF)
Pagoda	Call sign of the control and reporting post at Pleiku.
Panama	Call sign of the control and reporting post (later control and reporting center) at Da Nang Air Base.
Paper Sack	Suspension of Mutual Defense and Assistance Program deliveries to Indochina following the Geneva agreements of 1954.
Paris	Call sign of the control and reporting center at Tan Son Nhut Air Base.
Parrot's Beak	The tip of the Cambodian salient west of Saigon, South Vietnam.
Pathet Lao	Laotian communists.
Pathfinder	Two or more aircraft using lead aircraft's LORAN for navigation.
Patricia Lynn	RB-57E reconnaissance aircraft equipped with improved day-and-night cameras and infrared sensors.
PBT Special Tactical Zone	Republic of Vietnam Armed Forces special tactical zone in the provinces of Phuoc Long, Binh Long, and Phuoc Thanh (1962-63).
PDJ	Plaines des Jars (Plain of Jars). A military strategic area north-northeast of Vientiane in Laos.
PEO	programs evaluation office
PF	Popular Forces, or the former Vietnamese Self Defense Corps. Locally recruited South Vietnamese volunteers, organized into squads and platoons, and used chiefly as security forces in villages and hamlets.

THE ADVISORY YEARS

PFDOP	Deputy Chief of Staff, Plans and Operations, Pacific Air Forces
PFIDC	Director of Intelligence, Pacific Air Forces
PFLPL	Plans Division, Directorate of Plans, Pacific Air Forces
PFMLP	Assistant for Logistical Plans, Directorate of Materiel, Pacific Air Forces
PFMSS	Supply and Services Division, Directorate of Materiel, Pacific Air Forces
PFOCO	Combat Operations, Assistant Chief of Staff Operations, Pacific Air Forces
PFODC	Assistant Chief of Staff Operations, Pacific Air Forces
PFOOP	Operations Plans Division, Directorate of Operations, Pacific Air Forces
Phyllis Ann	EC-47 airborne radio direction finding aircraft and project. Followed experimental "Hawk Eye."
Pierce Arrow	United States Navy retaliatory air strikes against North Vietnam, August 5, 1964.
Pipe Stem	United States Air Force photographic reconnaissance detachment at Tan Son Nhut Air Base (1961-62).
POL	petroleum, oil, and lubricants
POW	prisoner of war
PPC	Photographic processing cell. A facility, generally mobile, equipped for the processing, printing, and interpretation of reconnaissance sensor products and other production normally related to the reconnaissance intelligence function.
pres	president
proj	project
PRP	People's Revolutionary Party (southern branch of the North Vietnamese communist (Lao Dong) party).
PSP	pierced steel planking
pt	part
Queen Bee	United States Air Force communications reconnaissance missions over the Gulf of Tonkin (1964).
R-4D	United States Navy transport similar to the Air Force C-47.
RB-26 Invader	The B-26 modified for reconnaissance missions by changes in nose and installed equipment. Three crew.
RB-47 Stratojet	The B-47 modified and equipped for photographic reconnaissance missions. Three crew.
RB-57 Canberra	The B-57 modified for photo reconnaissance. Two crew.
RC-47 Skytrain	The C-47 transport with equipment permanently installed for photo-reconnaissance and/or electronic reconnaissance missions. Three crew.
RF-101 Voodoo	Day or night photographic reconnaissance version of the F-101.
RT-28 Trojan	The T-28 configured for photo reconnaissance. Two crew.
RT-33 Shooting Star	Reconnaissance version of the T-33. Two crew.
RAAF	Royal Australian Air Force

rad	radio
Ranch Hand	Nickname of United States Air Force C-123 aerial spray detachment deployed to Vietnam in 1961-62 and applied to later defoliation and herbicide activity.
RAND	Research and Development (The RAND Corporation, Santa Monica, California).
R&D	research and development
rcrd	record
recon	reconnaissance
ref	reference
Revere	Provisional United States Air Force aircraft maintenance detachment in Vietnam (1954). Later called "Duke's Mixture."
RF	Regional Forces (the former Vietnamese Civil Guard). These were local South Vietnamese defense forces, recruited and used within one of the administrative regions into which the country was divided.
RKG	Royal Khmer (Cambodian) Government
RLAF	Royal Laotian Air Force
Rolling Thunder	Sustained United States air strikes against North Vietnam (March 1965-October 1968).
rprt	report
rqmt	requirement
RTAF	Royal Thai Air Force
RTAFB	Royal Thai Air Force Base
RVN	Republic of Vietnam
RVNAF	Republic of Vietnam Armed Forces
SC-47 aircraft	See HC-47 Skytrain.
SA	Secretary of the Army
SAC	Strategic Air Command (USAF)
SACSA	Special Assistant to the Director, JCS Joint Staff, for Counterinsurgency and Special Activities
Saddle Soap	Loan of B-26 aircraft to the French by the United States Air Force (1954).
SAF	Secretary of the Air Force
SAMAP	Southern Air Materiel Area Pacific (USAF)
SAMSq	special air mission squadron
SAR	search and rescue
SASF	special aerial spray flight
SAW	special air warfare
Saw Buck	United States Tactical Air Command composite air strike force deployments to Southeast Asia in mid-1962 and afterward. Also the nickname of the United States Air Force C-123 detachment deployed to Vietnam in mid-1962.

THE ADVISORY YEARS

SAWC	Special Air Warfare Center (USAF)
SCAR	strike control and reconnaissance
SCAT	selected counterinsurgency air target
scramble	To take off as quickly as possible (usually followed by course and altitude instructions).
SDC	Self Defense Corps (RVN)
SEA	Southeast Asia
SEAAS	Southeast Asia Airlift System
SEACOORD	Southeast Asia Coordinating Committee for US Missions
Sea Dog	Project for the loan of United States Air Force C-47s to the French (1953).
Sea Swallow	Government of Vietnam clear-and-hold operation in Phu Yen Province (1962).
SEATO	Southeast Asia Treaty Organization
sec	section
SECDEF	Secretary of Defense (US)
2 CCR	Commander, 2d Advanced Echelon; Commander, 2d Air Division
2 ODC	Director of Current Operations, 2d Advanced Echelon; Director of Current Operations, 2d Air Division
SECSTATE	Secretary of State (US)
secy	secretary
sess	session
SHAPE	Supreme Headquarters Allied Powers Europe
shoran bombing	Bombing done after positioning the aircraft to the bomb-release point by radar adapted to the purpose.
Short Count	Air surveillance flights over South Vietnamese coastal waters flown by Farm Gate (1961-62).
Shufly	Nickname for United States Marine Corps helicopter squadron and detachment in Vietnam.
SIAT	single integrated attack team
SLAR	Side-looking airborne radar. Views at right angles to the axis of the vehicle, which produces a presentation of terrain or moving targets.
SLAT	Special Logistics Actions, Thailand
SM	staff memorandum
SNIE	special national intelligence estimate
SO	special order
Special Forces	Military personnel with cross-training in basic and specialized military skills. They were organized into small multiple-purpose detachments with the mission to train, organize, supply, direct, and control indigenous forces in guerrilla warfare and counterinsurgency operations, and to conduct unconventional warfare operations.
sq	squadron
SSB	single sideband
stf	staff

STRICOM	Strike Command (US)
subj	subject
sum	summary
Sunrise	"Binh Minh." Highly publicized Government of Vietnam clear-and-hold operation in Binh Duong Province (1962).
SVN	South Vietnam
Sweet Sue	Experimental RB-26L night reconnaissance aircraft equipped with early infrared sensors.
Swing Back	Spare parts support for F-8F aircraft through cannibalization.
Swivel Chair	Project for the loan of United States Air Force C-119s to the French and associated USAF maintenance support (1953).
T-6 Texan	Prop-driven, single-engine, two-seat, low-wing, trainer airplane.
T-28 Trojan	Prop-driven, single-engine, low-wing, all-metal monoplane with retractable tricycle landing gear with steerable nose wheel. For primary pilot training. Two crew. The T-28D version is an attack plane, capable of carrying a variety of ordnance on counterinsurgency missions.
T-33 Shooting Star	Single-engine, all-metal, full-cantilever low wing, two-seat, high-performance jet aircraft. Designed for training of flight personnel. Incorporates laminar-flow wing sections, dive flaps, pressurized and heated cockpit. Has hydraulically operated tricycle landing gear. Two crew.
T-37	All metal, jet-powered, two-place, full-cantilever, low-wing monoplane primary trainer employing a retractable tricycle landing gear. Is completely equipped with flight instruments. Features side-by-side seating. Nose gear is equipped with power steering. Two crew.
TF-102 Delta Dagger	Similar to F-102 except that it is a two-place, side-by-side trainer version for combat use. Two crew.
tac	tactical
TAC	Tactical Air Command (USAF)
TACC	tactical air control center
TACOP	tactical operation
TACP	tactical air control party
TACS	tactical air control system
TADC	tactical air direction center
TAIWANDEFCOM	Taiwan Defense Command (US)
TARC	tactical air reconnaissance center (USAF)
TASE	tactical air support element (MACV)
TAWC	Tactical Air Warfare Center (USAF)
TC	troop carrier
TDY	temporary duty
tech	technical
TERM	Temporary Equipment Recovery Mission
TF	task force

THE ADVISORY YEARS

TFS	tactical fighter squadron
TFW	tactical fighter wing
TMC	transport movement control
TO&E	table of organization and equipment
TOC	tactical operations center
Toy Tiger	Night photographic modification of RF-101 aircraft.
TRAC	Targets Research and Analysis Center (MACV)
Triangle	Military operation by Royal Lao Army in north-central Laos (July 1964).
TRIM	Training Relations and Instruction Mission
Trojan Horse	High-altitude aerial reconnaissance flown by SAC U-2 aircraft. Formerly "Lucky Dragon."
TSG	tactical support group
Turnaround	The length of time between arriving at a point and departing from that point. It is used in this sense for the turnaround of shipping in ports, and for aircraft refueling and rearming.
U-1 Otter	Prop-driven, single-engine, short-range, high-wing, light, utility aircraft. Can operate on wheels, wheel-skis, or floats. Has throw-over control column, dual rudder controls, tailwheel powered steering, and double-slotted wing flaps. Two crew, eight passengers.
U-2	Single-seat, single-engine jet aircraft. Has long, wide, straight wings to give it a glider-like characteristic and increase its load capacity to accommodate data-collection instruments, as well as the ability to operate above seventy thousand feet. Used for high-altitude reconnaissance and weather sampling.
U-3	Prop-driven, twin-engine, low-wing monoplane with a tricycle landing gear. Used for administrative and light-cargo purposes. Two crew, three passengers.
U-6 Beaver	Single-engine, high-wing, all-metal monoplane. Has fixed landing gear, throw-over controls, and dual rudder controls. For general utility missions. One crew, five passengers. Formerly designated L-20.
U-9 Aero Commander	Prop-driven, twin-engine, light, high-wing, cantilever monoplane with tricycle landing gear. For administrative missions. One crew, five passengers. Formerly designated L-26.
U-10 Helio Super Courier	Prop-driven, single-engine, light, short-takeoff-and-landing aircraft used for general utility missions. Two crew, two passengers. Formerly designated L-28.
U-17	Prop-driven, single-engine, high-wing, all-metal, six-place, utility aircraft with conventional fixed landing gear and tail-wheel. Adaptable for various missions such as personnel, cargo, and ambulance operation.
UH-1 helicopter	See UH-1A Iroquois and UH-1B Iroquois.
UH-1A Iroquois	Used for transporting personnel and supplies. Has two-blade, helicopter shaft driven by a gas turbine engine. Torque counteracted by a two-blade, tail rotor mounted on a tail boom. Has skid-type landing gear. Provisions for dual controls and internal ferry tank. One crew, five passengers. Formerly designated HU-1A.
UH-1B Iroquois	Used to transport personnel and supplies and as a gunship. Similar to UH-1A except for engine and wider rotor blade, copilot controls, provi-

	sions for armament, and capability to carry three litters. Two crew, seven passengers. Formerly designated HU-1B.
UH-19 Chickasaw	All-metal, semi-monocoque fuselage helicopter. Has one all-metal, three-blade, main rotor and an all-metal two-blade, antitorque, tail rotor. Engine mounted in nose, quadricycle landing gear, side-by-side seating, external cargo sling, dual controls. Used for general utility operations. Two crew, ten passengers. Formerly designated H-19.
UH-34 Seahorse	Similar to CH-34 Choctaw. Utility version. Two crew, twelve passengers.
UHF	ultra high frequency
UN	United Nations
UNC	United Nations Command
US	United States (of America)
USA	United States Army
USAF	United States Air Force
USAIRA	United States air attaché
USAmb	United States Ambassador
USARMA	United States Army attaché
USARPAC	United States Army, Pacific
USASF(P)V	United States Army Special Forces, Vietnam (Provisional)
USAWC	United States Army War College
USMC	United States Marine Corps
USN	United States Navy
USOM	United States Operations Mission
Vayabut	Southeast Asia Treaty Organization exercise in Thailand (1958)
VC	Viet Cong
VCS	Vice Chief of Staff
VHF	very high frequency
Viet Cong	Vietnamese communists, usually South Vietnamese communists.
Viet Minh	Initial description of Vietnamese communists. Was later used to indicate ethnic North Vietnamese forces who entered Laos prior to regular North Vietnamese Army troops.
VIP	very important person
VN	Vietnam
VNAF	Vietnamese Air Force
VOA	Voice of America
vol	volume
Vulture	Proposed United States Air Force bombing operation in relief of Dien Bien Phu (1954).
Water Glass	United States Air Force F-102 rotational air defense deployments to Tan Son Nhut (1962-63). Superseded by "Candy Machine."

THE ADVISORY YEARS

Water Pump — Detachment 6, 1st Air commando Wing (USAF), deployed to Thailand in 1964 and applied to subsequent special air warfare activity at Udorn Royal Thai Air Force Base.

wg — wing

WIA — wounded in action

Wounded Warrior — United States Air Force aeromedical evacuation of French repatriated sick and wounded military personnel from Vietnam to Europe (1954).

Wring Out — United States Air Force project to reach authorized strength of 137 wings with existing personnel (1956).

Yankee Team — United States tactical air reconnaissance missions in Laos.

Z — Zulu Time (Greenwich Mean Time)

Bibliographic Note

For the purposes of both history and self-evaluation, the United States Air Force began in 1962 an extensive effort to identify and collect documents on its role in the conflict in Southeast Asia. At the same time, the Air Force expanded its normal historical program. It also established a new activity named Project Contemporary Historical Evaluation of Counterinsurgency Operations, later called Contemporary Historical Evaluation of Combat Operations (CHECO). During the next several years, USAF commands and agencies involved in the war searched their records and selected papers pertinent for historical research. Records of USAF staff agencies in the Washington National Records Center at Suitland, Maryland, and of the Commander in Chief, Pacific Command (CINCPAC) in the Federal Records Center at the Naval Supply Depot, Mechanicsburg, Pennsylvania, were screened for data on the air war.

All these sources, together with others, were indexed into the computer-processed Data Base Inventory (DABIN) System at the Aerospace Studies Institute, Air University, Maxwell Air Force Base, Alabama. Maintained by the Technical Systems Branch of the Albert F. Simpson Historical Research Center at Maxwell AFB, DABIN identifies source materials ranging from multivolume studies to single-page messages, including title, issuing agency or author, date, general subject, and significant key words in titles. It reveals the location of sources by repository and finding numbers in the collections noted above as well as those in the Reference Division of the Historical Research Center and the Air University Library. A query to DABIN by an authorized researcher can obtain the listings of sources and, more specifically, the locations of the items referenced in the footnotes of this volume of history.

GOVERNMENTAL SOURCES

Books and Documents

DEPARTMENT OF DEFENSE

The records kept by the United States Air Force and its subordinate commands and agencies are the major source materials for this volume. At the Washington level, the holdings of the Deputy Chief of Staff, Plans and Operations, are the most useful collection of high-level Air Force policy and planning papers. The semiannual histories of the Directorate of Plans and of the Assistant for Mutual Security give succinct information on policy formulation. The study cited in this history as AFXOPJ Book of Actions in Southeast Asia, 1961-64, July 21, 1967, was prepared in the Directorate of Operations. It summarizes recommendations of the USAF Chief of Staff with respect to the conflict. Special studies prepared by the Office of Air Force History also give perspective on policy matters, and the following are particularly useful:

THE ADVISORY YEARS

Hildreth, Charles H. *USAF Counterinsurgency Doctrines and Capabilities, 1961-1962.* February 1964.
_____. *USAF Special Air Warfare Doctrines, 1963.* August 1964.
Lemmer, George F. *The Laos Crisis of 1959.* May 1961.
Van Staaveren, Jacob. *Air Operations in the Taiwan Crisis of 1958.* November 1962.
_____. *USAF Plans and Policies in South Vietnam, 1961-1963.* June 1965.
_____. *USAF Plans and Policies in South Vietnam and Laos, 1964,* December 1965.
_____. *USAF Plans and Policies in Southeast Asia, 1965.* October 1966.

The officially published *United States-Vietnam Relations, 1945-1967: Study Prepared by the Department of Defense* (Washington: Government Printing Office, 1971) and *The Pentagon Papers*, published in various editions, also provide essential information on high-level policy decisions. The Historical Office of the Joint Chiefs of Staff kindly screened and made available from its files selected documents pertaining to this volume.

Military command histories and their supporting documents have been useful sources. The annual CINCPAC Command Histories are of high quality, and annual MACV Command Histories are available for 1964 and 1965. A special historical study prepared by the Directorate of Historical Services, Far East Air Forces (FEAF), *FEAF Support of the French Indo-China Operations, 1 July 1952-30 September 1954*, contains details on the beginnings of USAF activities in Southeast Asia. After 1956, Pacific Air Forces (PACAF) histories (semiannual, except for a one-year coverage from July 1964 to June 1965) give information on Southeast Asia, as do reports and diaries of PACAF staff agencies. Thirteenth Air Force histories offer progressively less detail as the war progressed. A perfunctory History of the Second Advanced Echelon, Thirteenth Air Force, July 1, 1961-December 31, 1961, contains little of value for research. But a History of the 2d ADVON, November 15, 1961-October 8, 1962 (prepared by Joseph W. Grainger and TSgt George P. Day and issued on November 12, 1963) is an excellent narrative with supporting documents. No narrative history of the 2d Air Division in 1963 exists, but supporting documents for such a history afford a good coverage of the period. Excellent semiannual 2d Air Division histories were completed from January 1964 under the direction of Kenneth Sams, 2d Air Division historian and director of CHECO in Saigon.

Valuable operations information is contained in the following studies:

Anthony, Maj Victor B., USAF. *The Air Force in Southeast Asia: Tactics and Techniques of Night Operations, 1961-1970.* Washington: Office of Air Force History, March 1973.
Bowers, Col Ray L., USAF. "The Air Force in Southeast Asia: Tactical Airlift." Washington: Office of Air Force History, draft manuscript, 1971.
Cahill, Maj John J., USMC, and Shulimson, Jack. "History of U.S. Marine Corps Operations in Vietnam, January-June 1965." Washington: Historical Branch, G-3 Division, United States Marine Corps, draft manuscript, 1968.
Komer, Robert W. *The Malayan Emergency in Retrospect: Organization of a Successful Counterinsurgency Effort.* R-957-ARPA. Santa Monica: The RAND Corporation, February 1972.
Lewis, Thomas T. "The U.S. Military View of the Vietnamese War in 1963: Realistic Optimism or Bureaucratic Distortion." Master's Thesis, George Washington University School of Government and Business Administration, September 1972.
Rowley, Maj Ralph A., USAF. *USAF FAC Operations in Southeast Asia, 1961-1965.* Washington: Office of Air Force History, January 1972.
von Luttichau, Charles P. "The U.S. Army Role in the Conflict in Vietnam." Washington: Center of Military History, United States Army, draft manuscript, n.d.

Project CHECO, established in October 1962, was designed to give PACAF an immediate reporting capability on airpower operations. In 1968, CHECO was additionally charged to microfilm documents for incorporation in DABIN at the Air University. A few microfilmed documents trace back to the period of this history, but the major importance of CHECO as a source to this history of the pre-1965 period lies in the following studies, most of which are often accompanied by voluminous supporting documents:

Anderson, Capt B. Conn, USAF. *USAF Search and Rescue in Southeast Asia, 1961-1966.* October 24, 1966.
Bear, James T. *RAAF in SEA, 1965-1970.* September 30, 1970.
Coffin, Lt Col Monty D., USAF, and Merrell, Maj Ronald D., USAF. *The Royal Thai Air Force.* September 3, 1971.
Collins, Capt Charles V., USAF. *Herbicide Operations in Southeast Asia, July 1961-June 1967.* October 11, 1967.
Helmka, MSgt Robert T., USAF, and Hale, TSgt Beverly, USAF. *USAF Operations from Thailand, 1964-1965.* August 10, 1966.
Hickey, Lawrence J. *Night Close Air Support in RVN, 1961-1965.* March 15, 1967.
Hurley, Col Alfred F., USAF. *The EC-47 in Southeast Asia, May 1966-June 1968.* September 20, 1968.
Jones, Maj Oakah L., Jr., USAF. *Organization, Mission and Growth of the Vietnamese Air Force, 1949-1968.* October 8, 1968.
MacDonough, Lt Col Robert A., USAF, and Porter, Melvin F. *Air Traffic Control in SEA, 1955-1969.* February 14, 1969.
McNaughton, Lt Robert L., USAF. *Yankee Team, May 1964-June 1965.* March 8, 1966.
Martin, Lt Col Donald F., USAF, and Clever, Carl O. *CHECO Southeast Asia Report, October 1961-December 1963.* May 1964.
Melyan, Wesley R.C. *The War in Vietnam, 1965.* January 25, 1967.
Paterson, L.E. *Evolution of the Rules of Engagement for Southeast Asia, 1960-1965.* September 30, 1966.
Porter, Melvin. *Tactical Control Squadron Operations in SEASIA, 1962-1969.* October 15, 1969.
Pratt, Maj John C., USAF. *Royal Laotian Air Force, 1954-1970.* September 15, 1970.
Sams, Kenneth. *The Battle of Binh Gia, 27 December 1964-1 January 1965.* July 1, 1965.
―――――. *Command and Control, 1965.* December 15, 1966.
―――――. *Escalation of the War in Southeast Asia, July-December 1964.* ca. December 1965.
―――――. *Final Test and Combat Use of the AC-47.* December 8, 1965.
―――――. *Historical Background to Vietcong Mortar Attack on Bien Hoa.* November 9, 1964.
Sams, Kenneth, and Alton, Lt Col Bert B., USAF. *USAF Support of Special Forces in SEA, November 1961-February 1969.* March 10, 1969.
Smith, Capt Mark E., USAF. *USAF Reconnaissance in Southeast Asia, 1961-1966.* October 25, 1966.
Thompson, Maj A.W., USAF. *Strike Control and Reconnaissance in SEA, 1962-1968.* January 22, 1969.
Vallentiny, Capt Edward, USAF. *VNAF FAC Operations in SVN, September 1961-July 1968.* January 28, 1969.
Vining, Capt Robert L., USAF. *Air Operations in the Delta, 1962-1967.* December 8, 1967.
Whitaker, Lt Col B.A., USAF, and Paterson, L.E. *Assault Airlift Operations, January 1961-June 1966.* February 23, 1967.

The USAF Southeast Asia End of Tour Report Program was established in 1962 in response to a requirement by the Joint Chiefs of Staff for all the armed services to provide observations from all senior officers completing a tour of duty in an area threatened by insurgency. After the number of officers in Southeast Asia grew to sizable proportions, the Joint Chiefs relaxed the requirement. However, the Air Force continued the End of Tour Reports as an internal program initially under PACAF and later the Office of Air Force History. The

THE ADVISORY YEARS

observations in these reports frequently supply insights not captured by formal reporting systems.

The Southeast Asia Oral History Program was started in 1967 to plan, conduct, and process tape-recorded interviews with knowledgeable persons and to record their experiences, observations, and recommendations. These oral interviews are especially worthwhile in filling informational gaps in written sources. The Office of Air Force History has continued the oral history program and has expanded it to encompass USAF activities well beyond Southeast Asia.

The Reference Division of the Albert F. Simpson Historical Research Center maintains guides to End of Tour Reports and oral histories. Some of the latter are privileged and unavailable to researchers until a future time.

Other Department of Defense studies consulted include:

Climatology of Southeast Asia. Maxwell Air Force Base, Ala.: Project Corona Harvest, August 1968.
Communist Policy Towards Southeast Asia, 1954-1969: A Chronological Compendium. Prepared by Battelle Memorial Institute, Columbus, Ohio. Maxwell Air Force Base, Ala.: Project Corona Harvest, October 1, 1970.
The Employment of Airpower in the Greek Guerrilla War. Maxwell Air Force Base, Ala.: Aerospace Studies Institute, 1964.
Farmer, J., and Strumwasser, M. J. *The Evolution of the Airborne Forward Air Controller: An Analysis of Mosquito Operations in Korea.* RM-5430-PR. Santa Monica: The RAND Corporation, October 1967.
Futrell, Robert F. *The United States Air Force in Korea, 1950-1953.* New York: Duell, Sloan and Pearce, 1961.
―――. *United States Policy Toward Southeast Asia, 1943-1968: A Chronological Compendium.* Maxwell Air Force Base, Ala.: Project Corona Harvest, 1968.
―――. *A Chronology of Significant Airpower Events in Southeast Asia, 1950-1968.* Maxwell Air Force Base, Ala.: Aerospace Studies Institute, 1969.
―――. *Ideas, Concepts, Doctrine: A History of Basic Thinking in the United States Air Force, 1907-1964.* 2 vols. Maxwell Air Force Base, Ala.: Aerospace Studies Institute, 1971.
Goure, Leon. *Some Impressions of the Effects of Military Operations on Viet Cong Behavior.* RM-4517-ISA. Santa Monica: The RAND Corporation, March 1965.
Graham, William B., and Katz, Amron H. *SIAT: Single Integrated Attack Team: A Concept for Offensive Military Operations in South Vietnam.* RM-4400-PR (Part II). Santa Monica: The RAND Corporation, November 17, 1964.
Physical and Cultural Environment of Southeast Asia. Maxwell Air Force Base, Ala.: Project Corona Harvest, November 1, 1968.
Sharp, Adm U.S.G., USN, and Westmoreland, Gen W.C., USA. *Report on the War in Vietnam (As of 30 June 1968).* Washington: Government Printing Office, 1969.
Vigneras, Marcel. *Rearming the French.* [*United States Army in World War II: Special Studies*]. Washington: Office of the Chief of Military History, Department of the Army, 1957.

Congress

Senate. Report of Senator Mike Mansfield on a Study Mission to the Associated States of Indochina, October 27, 1953. *Indochina.* 83d Cong, 1st sess. Washington: Government Printing Office, 1953.
House. Hearings before the Committee on Foreign Affairs. *The Mutual Security Act of 1954.* 83d Cong, 2d sess. Washington: Government Printing Office, 1954.
Senate. Compilation of Studies and Surveys Prepared Under the Direction of the Special Committee to Study the Foreign Aid Program. *Foreign Aid Program.* Senate Document 52. 85th Cong, 1st sess. Washington: Government Printing Office, 1957.
House. Hearings before the Subcommittee on the Far East and the Pacific of the Committee on Foreign Affairs. *Mutual Security Program in Laos.* 85th Cong, 2d sess. Washington: Government Printing Office, 1958.

Senate. Hearings before the Subcommittee on State Department Organization and Public Affairs of the Committee on Foreign Relations. *Situation in Vietnam.* 86th Cong, 1st sess. Washington: Government Printing Office, 1959.

House. Seventh Report by the Committee on Government Operations, June 15 1959. *U.S. Aid Operations in Laos.* House Report 546. 86th Cong. 1st sess. Washington: Government Printing Office, 1959.

Senate. Hearings before the Subcommittee to Investigate the Administration of the Internal Security Act and Internal Security Laws of the Committee on the Judiciary. *Analysis of the Khrushchev Speech of January 6, 1961.* 87th Cong, 1st sess. Washington: Government Printing Office, 1961.

Senate. A Study Submitted by the Subcommittee on National Security Staffing and Operations. *The Ambassador and the Problem of Coordination.* Senate Document 36. 88th Cong. 1st sess. Washington: Government Printing Office, 1963.

Senate. Report of Senator Mike Mansfield . . . to the Committee on Foreign Relations. *Vietnam and Southeast Asia.* 88th Cong, 1st sess. Washington: Government Printing Office, 1963.

House. Hearing before the Special Subcommittee on Tactical Air Support of the Committee on Armed Services. *Close Air Support.* 89th Cong, 1st sess. Washington: Government Printing Office, 1966.

Senate. Hearings before the Subcommittee to Investigate Problems Connected with Refugees and Escapees of the Committee on the Judiciary. *Refugee Problems in South Vietnam and Laos.* 89th Cong, 1st sess. Washington: Government Printing Office, 1965.

House. Hearing before the Committee on Armed Services. *Fiscal Year 1966 Supplemental Authorization for Vietnam.* 89th Cong, 2d sess. Washington: Government Printing Office, 1966.

Senate. Hearings before the Committee on Foreign Relations . . . on S. 2793. *Supplemental Foreign Assistance Fiscal Year 1966—Vietnam.* 89th Cong, 2d sess. Washington: Government Printing Office, 1966.

House. Hearings before the Subcommittee on the Far East and the Pacific of the Committee on Foreign Affairs. *United States Policy Toward Asia.* 89th Cong, 2d sess. Washington: Government Printing Office, 1966.

Senate. Committee on Foreign Relations. *Background Information Relating to Southeast Asia and Vietnam.* 90th Cong, 1st sess. 3d revised edition. Washington: Government Printing Office, 1967.

Senate. Hearings before the Committee on Foreign Relations. *Submission of the Vietnam Conflict to the United Nations.* 90th Cong, 1st sess. Washington: Government Printing Office, 1967.

Senate. Hearing before the Committee on Foreign Relations . . . on February 20, 1968. *The Gulf of Tonkin, The 1964 Incidents.* Parts 1 and 2. 90th Cong, 2d sess. Washington: Government Printing Office, 1968.

"Working Paper on the North Vietnamese Role in the War in South Vietnam." *Congressional Record,* May 9, 1968, pp 12614-12620.

Senate. Hearings before the Subcommittee on United States Security Agreements and Commitments Abroad of the Committee on Foreign Relations. *United States Security Agreements and Commitments Abroad. Kingdom of Laos.* Part 2. 91st Cong, 1st sess. Washington: Government Printing Office, 1970.

Presidential Papers

The Public Papers and Addresses of Franklin D. Roosevelt: Victory and the Threshold of Peace. New York: Harper and Brothers, 1950.

Public Papers of the Presidents of the United States: Harry S. Truman, 1950. Washington: Government Printing Office, 1965.

Public Papers of the Presidents of the United States: Harry S. Truman, 1951. Washington: Government Printing Office, 1965.

Public Papers of the Presidents of the United States: Dwight D. Eisenhower, 1954. Washington: Government Printing Office, 1960.

Public Papers of the Presidents of the United States: Dwight D. Eisenhower, 1955. Washington: Government Printing Office, 1959.

Public Papers of the Presidents of the United States: Dwight D. Eisenhower, 1957. Washington: Government Printing Office, 1958.

Public Papers of the Presidents of the United States: Dwight D. Eisenhower, 1958. Washington: Government Printing Office, 1959.

Public Papers of the Presidents of the United States: Dwight D. Eisenhower, 1960-61. Washington: Government Printing Office, 1961.

THE ADVISORY YEARS

Public Papers of the Presidents of the United States: John F. Kennedy, 1961. Washington: Government Printing Office, 1962.
Public Papers of the Presidents of the United States: John F. Kennedy, 1962. Washington: Government Printing Office, 1963.
Public Papers of the Presidents of the United States: John F. Kennedy, 1963. Washington: Government Printing Office, 1964.
Public Papers of the Presidents of the United States: Lyndon B. Johnson, 1963-64. Washington: Government Printing Office, 1965.
Public Papers of the Presidents of the United States: Lyndon B. Johnson, 1965. Washington: Government Printing Office, 1966.
Public Papers of the Presidents of the United States: Lyndon B. Johnson, 1966. Washington: Government Printing Office, 1967.

DEPARTMENT OF STATE

American Foreign Policy, 1950-1955. Washington: Government Printing Office, 1957.
American Foreign Policy: Current Documents, 1956. Washington: Government Printing Office, 1959.
American Foreign Policy: Current Documents, 1957. Washington: Government Printing Office, 1961.
American Foreign Policy: Current Documents, 1958. Washington: Government Printing Office, 1962.
American Foreign Policy: Current Documents, 1959. Washington: Government Printing Office, 1963.
American Foreign Policy: Current Documents, 1962. Washington: Government Printing Office, 1966.
American Foreign Policy: Current Documents, 1963. Washington: Government Printing Office, 1967.
The Conferences at Malta and Yalta, 1945. Washington: Government Printing Office, 1955.
A Threat to the Peace: North Viet-Nam's Effort to Conquer South Viet-Nam. Washington: Government Printing Office, 1961.

Articles

Bundy, William P. "The Path to Viet-Nam: A Lesson in Involvement." US Department of State *Bulletin* 57, September 4, 1967, pp 275-287.
Durbrow, Ambassador Elbridge. "Hanoi's Intensified Aggression—1959." Air War College *Supplement*, November 1967, pp 7-8.
Kennedy, Col Thomas B., USAF. "Airlift in Southeast Asia." *Air University Review* 16 (January-February 1965), 72-82.
Knox, Capt Thomas R., USAF. "Waterpump, 1964-1965." *Aerospace Commentary* 2 (Spring, 1970), 51-59.
Milton, Maj Gen Theodore R., USAF. "Air Power: Equalizer in Southeast Asia." *Air University Review* 15 (November-December 1963), 2-8.
Secord, Mack D. "The Viet Nam Air Force." *Air University Review* 15 (November-December 1963), 60-67.
Smith, Gen Frederic H., Jr., USAF. "Nuclear Weapons and Limited War." *Air University Quarterly Review* 12 (Spring, 1960), 3-27.
Sunderman, Lt Col James F., USAF. "Air Operations in Viet Nam: Night Flare Strike." *Air University Review* 15 (September-October 1964), 82-91.

NON-GOVERNMENTAL SOURCES

Books

Acheson, Dean. *Present at the Creation: My Years in the State Department.* New York: W. W. Norton and Company, 1969.
Austin, Anthony. *The President's War.* New York: J. B. Lippincott, 1971.

Ball, George W. *The Discipline of Power: Essentials of a Modern World Structure*. Boston: Little, Brown and Company, 1968.

Bates, Victor. *Vietnam, A Diplomatic Tragedy: The Origins of the United States Involvement*. Dobbs Ferry, N.Y.: Oceana Publications, 1965.

Beal, John Robinson. *John Foster Dulles, 1888-1959*. New York: Harper and Brothers, 1959.

Bouscaren, Anthony Trawick. *The Last of the Mandarins: Diem of Vietnam*. Pittsburgh: Duquesne University Press, 1965.

Burchett, Wilfred G. *Vietnam: Inside Story of the Guerrilla War*. New York: International Publishers, 1965.

Buttinger, Joseph. *Vietnam: A Dragon Embattled*. 2 vols. New York: Frederick A. Praeger, 1967.

Champassak, Sisouk Na. *Storm Over Laos: A Contemporary History*. New York: Frederick A. Praeger, 1961.

Cole, Allan B., ed. *Conflict in Indo-China & International Repercussions: A Documentary History, 1945-1955*. Ithaca: Cornell University Press, 1956.

Cooper, Chester L. *The Lost Crusade: America in Vietnam*. New York: Dodd, Mead and Company, 1970.

CQ Background. *China and U.S. Far East Policy, 1945-1967*. Washington: Congressional Quarterly Service, 1967.

Curl, Peter V., ed. *Documents on American Foreign Relations, 1954*. New York: Council on Foreign Relations, 1955.

Davids, Jules, ed. *Documents on American Foreign Relations, 1964*. New York: Council on Foreign Relations, 1964.

de Gaulle, Charles. *The War Memoirs of Charles de Gaulle*. Vol 3: *Salvation, 1944-1946*. New York: Simon and Shuster, 1960.

Dommen, Arthur J. *Conflict in Laos: The Politics of Neutralization*. New York: Frederick A. Praeger, 1964.

Duncanson, Dennis J. *Government and Revolution in Vietnam*. New York: Oxford University Press, 1968.

Eden, Anthony. *The Memoirs of Anthony Eden: Full Circle*. Boston: Houghton Mifflin Company, 1960.

Eisenhower, Dwight D. *The White House Years: Mandate for Change, 1953-1956*. Garden City, N.Y.: Doubleday and Company, 1963.

_____. *The White House Years: Waging Peace, 1956-1961*. Garden City, N.Y.: Doubleday and Company, 1965.

Fall, Bernard B. *Hell in a Very Small Place: The Siege of Dien Bien Phu*. Philadelphia: J. B. Lippincott Company, 1967.

_____. *Ho Chi Minh on Revolution*. New York: Frederick A. Praeger, 1967.

_____. *Street Without Joy: Insurgency in Indochina, 1946-1963*. 3d revised edition. Harrisburg: The Stackpole Company, 1963.

_____. *The Two Viet-Nams: A Political and Military Analysis*. 2d Edition. New York: Frederick A. Praeger, 1963.

Galloway, John. *The Gulf of Tonkin Resolution*. Rutherford, N.J.: Farleigh Dickinson University Press, 1970.

Gould-Adams, Richard. *The Time of Power: A Reappraisal of John Foster Dulles*. London: Weidenfeld and Nicholson, 1962.

Goulden, Joseph C. *Truth is the First Casualty: The Gulf of Tonkin Affair—Illusion and Reality*. Chicago: Rand McNally, 1969.

Graff, Henry F. *The Tuesday Cabinet: Deliberation and Decision on Peace and War under Lyndon B. Johnson*. Englewood Cliffs, N.J.: Prentice-Hall, 1970.

Halberstam, David. *The Making of a Quagmire*. New York: Random House, 1965.

Halpern, Joel M. *Government, Politics, and Social Structure in Laos: A Study of Tradition and Innovation*. Yale University Southeast Asia Series, No. 4. New Haven: Yale University Press, 1964.

Hemmer, Ellen. *The Struggle for Indochina*. Stanford, Calif.: Stanford University Press, 1954.

Higgins, Marguerite. *Our Vietnam Nightmare*. New York: Harper and Row, 1965.

Hilsman, Roger. *To Move a Nation: The Politics of Foreign Policy in the Administration of John F. Kennedy*. Garden City, N.Y.: Doubleday and Company, 1967.

Hull, Cordell. *The Memoirs of Cordell Hull*. New York: The Macmillan Company, 1948.

Johnson, Lyndon B. *The Vantage Point: Perspectives of the Presidency, 1963-1969*. New York: Holt, Rinehart and Winston, 1971.

Khrushchev in New York. New York: Crosscurrents Press, [1960].
Khrushchev, Nikita S. *Khrushchev Remembers.* Translated and edited by Strobe Talbott. Boston: Little, Brown and Company, 1970.
Lacoutre, Jean, and Devillers, Philippe. *La Fin d'Une Guerre, Indochine 1954.* Paris: Editions due Seuil, 1960.
Lansdale, Edward Geary. *In the Midst of Wars: An American's Mission to Southeast Asia.* New York: Harper and Row, 1972.
Lederer, W.J. *A Nation of Sheep.* New York: W.W. Norton and Company, 1961.
Lodge, Henry Cabot. *The Storm Has Many Eyes: A Personal Narrative.* New York: W.W. Norton and Company, 1973.
Mecklin, John. *Mission in Torment: An Intimate Account of the US Role in Vietnam.* Garden City, N.Y.: Doubleday and Company, 1965.
Navarre, Henri. *Agonie de L'Indochine, 1953-1954.* Paris: Librairie Plon, 1956.
O'Ballance, Edgar. *The Indo-China War, 1945-1954: A Study of Guerrilla Warfare.* London: Faber and Faber, 1964.
Pike, Douglas. *Viet Cong: The Organization and Techniques of the National Liberation Front of South Vietnam.* Cambridge: The Massachusetts Institute of Technology Press, 1966.
————. *War, Peace, and the Viet Cong.* Cambridge: The Massachusetts Institute of Technology Press, 1969.
Randle, Robert F. *Geneva 1954: The Settlement of the Indochinese War.* Princeton: Princeton University Press, 1969.
Raskin, Marcus G., and Fall, Bernard B., eds. *The Viet-Nam Reader.* New York: Random House, 1965.
Ridgway, Gen Matthew B. USA. *Soldier.* New York: Harper and Brothers, 1956.
Roy, Jules. *The Battle of Dienbienphu.* New York: Harper and Row, 1965.
Schlesinger, Arthur F., Jr. *A Thousand Days: John F. Kennedy in the White House.* Boston: Houghton Mifflin Company, 1965.
Scigliano, Robert. *South Vietnam: Nation Under Stress.* Boston: Houghton Mifflin Company, 1964.
Shaplen, Robert. *The Lost Revolution.* New York: Harper and Row, 1965.
Sorenson, Theodore C. *Kennedy.* New York: Harper and Row, 1965.
Stebbins, Richard P., ed. *Documents on American Foreign Relations, 1961.* New York: Council on Foreign Relations, 1962.
————., ed. *Documents on American Foreign Relations, 1963.* New York: Council on Foreign Relations, 1964.
————., ed. *Documents on American Foreign Relations, 1966.* New York: Council on Foreign Relations, 1966.
Taylor, John W.R., ed. *Combat Aircraft of the World.* New York: G.P. Putnam's Sons, 1969.
Taylor, Maxwell D. *Swords and Plowshares.* New York: W.W. Norton and Company, 1972.
Thompson, Robert. *Defeating Communist Insurgency: The Lessons of Malaya and Vietnam.* New York: Frederick A. Praeger, 1966.
Toye, Hugh. *Laos, Buffer State or Battleground.* London: Oxford University Press, 1968.
Truman, Harry S. *Memoirs: Years of Trial and Hope.* Garden City, N.Y.: Doubleday and Company, 1956.
Vandenbosch, Amry, and Butwell, Richard A. *Southeast Asia Among the World Powers.* Lexington: University of Kentucky Press, 1957.
Warner, Denis. *The Last Confucian.* New York: The Macmillan Company, 1963.
Windchy, Eugene C. *Tonkin Gulf.* New York: Doubleday and Company, 1971.
Zagoria, Donald S. *Vietnam Triangle.* New York: Pegasus, 1967.
Zinner, Paul E., ed. *Documents on American Foreign Relations, 1956.* New York: Council on Foreign Relations, 1957.
————., ed. *Documents on American Foreign Relations, 1959.* New York: Council on Foreign Relations, 1960.

Articles

Alsop, Stewart. "Kennedy's Grand Strategy." *The Saturday Evening Post,* March 31, 1962, pp 11-16.
Bowers, Ray L. "Americans in the Vietnamese Air Force: 'The Dirty Thirty.'" *Aerospace Historian,* September 1972, pp 125-131.
Bullitt, William C. "The Saddest War." *Life,* December 29, 1947, pp 64-69.

Chassin, Gen G.J.M., French Air Force. "Lessons of the War in Indochina" *Interavia* 7 (1952), 670-75.

Collins, Gen J. Lawton, USA. "What We're Doing in Indochina." Interview. *U.S. News & World Report*, March 4, 1955, pp 82-88.

Fall, Bernard B. "Talk with Ho Chi Minh." *The New Republic*, October 12, 1963, pp 19-22.

Ford, Corey. "The Flying Tigers Carry On." *Saturday Evening Post*, February 5, 1955, pp 24-25ff, and February 12, 1955, pp 30ff.

Graff, Henry F. "Teach-In on Vietnam by . . . The President, the Secretary of State, the Secretary of Defense and the Under Secretary of State." *New York Times Magazine*, March 20, 1966, pp 25, 128-133.

Kuter, Gen L.S., USAF, CINCPACAF. "The Pacific Air Forces." *Air Force*, October 1957, pp 63-66, 69-70.

Lansdale, Maj Gen Edward G., USAF. "Viet Nam: Do We Understand Revolution?" *Foreign Affairs*, October 1964, pp 75-86.

"The Lowdown from the Top U.S. Command in Saigon." *Life*, November 27, 1964, pp 46, 51-53.

McNamara, Robert S. "The Communist Design for World Conquest, Some Shift in our Military Thinking Required." *Vital Speeches of the Day*, March 1, 1962, pp 296-99.

Nixon, Richard M. "Cuba, Castro and John F. Kennedy." *Reader's Digest*, November 1964, pp 283-300.

Rose, Jerry A. "Our Undeclared War in Vietnam." *Reporter*, May 10, 1962, pp 30-32.

Taylor, Maxwell. "The Case for Continued Bombing of the North." *Washington Star*, October 22, 1967, p E2.

Thompson, James C., Jr. "How Could Vietnam Happen? An Autopsy." *Atlantic*, April 1968, pp 47-53.

Waddell, L.S. "Phase Out for Charlie-One-One-Nine." *Pegasus*, October 1955, pp 1-6.

Weyland, Gen Otto P., USAF. "Can Air Power Win 'Little Wars'?" Interview. *U.S. News & World Report*, July 23, 1954, pp 54-61.

Williams, Lt Gen Samuel T., USA, Ret. "Why the US is Losing in Vietnam—An Inside Story." Interview. *U.S. News & World Report*, November 9, 1964, pp 62-72.

Index*

A Luoi Valley: 248
A Shau Valley: 175, 248
Able Mable: 147-148, 171, 229, 241-243
Acheson, Dean: 11
Adams, Milton B.: 207
Advanced Echelon (ADVON), 2d: 95-102, 108, 110-113, 122, 124, 138
Advanced Research Projects Agency: 73, 112, 116
Advisors
    assessment of accomplishments: 267-268
    civilian: 204
    in combat role: 105, 218-219
    French, with MAAG: 39
    details from MAAG: 40, 75
    number, expansion and reduction: 97, 151, 162, 166-167, 171, 192, 195, 216, 268
    range of operations: 151, 162, 216
Aerial Port Squadrons
    8th: 111, 167
    6493d: 111
Aerial Resupply Unit, 8081st: 16
Agency for International Development: 144
Air America: 257
Air Asia: 181
Air Base Group, 23d: 171
Air Base Squadrons
    33d: 171
    34th: 171
    6220th: 101
    6221st: 101
    6222d: 101, 171
    6223d: 101
Air bases. *See* Airfields
Air Commando Squadrons
    1st: 171, 181, 200-201, 212-214, 218-220, 238, 246, 251
    19th: 236
Air Defense, RVN Air Force: 128, 131
Air Depot Wing, 24th: 11, 15
Air Divisions
    2d: 101, 112, 141, 146, 153, 160, 171-172, 175, 178, 182, 207-208, 210-211, 216-217, 219, 225, 230, 232, 235, 241, 244-246, 250-253, 264
    315th: 16, 31, 41, 45, 81, 106, 108, 111, 171, 247
    322d: 22
Air drops. *See* Airborne operations; Airlifts of troops and supplies
Air Forces
    Far East: 10-11, 15-17, 23, 41-42
    Fifth: 41, 43-45, 74-75, 131
    Pacific: 41, 43-44, 47-48, 81, 83, 95, 101, 106, 112, 120, 217, 229, 232, 236, 241, 244, 250, 253 263-264, 266
    Thirteenth: 41-42, 45, 47, 81, 83, 95, 101, 106, 108, 120, 124, 131, 133, 147, 232
Air-ground liaison: 106, 128, 131, 140, 143, 159, 168, 178, 182, 196, 215-216, 239, 244
Air-ground operations. *See* Tactical air support
Air-Ground Operations School: 178, 240

*Numerals in italic indicate an illustration of the subject mentioned

Air Materiel Command: 42
Air Materiel Force Pacific Area: 42
Air National Guard: 65
Air operations
    air-ground liaison: 106, 128, 131, 140, 143, 159, 168, 178, 182, 196, 215-216, 239, 244
    air strike missions: 120-122, 128, 136-139, 172-174, 178, 183-184, 191, 196-197, 199, 212, 214-216, 220-221, 224, 245, 254, 257-267
    artillery fire direction: 37
    bombing missions: 25-26, 120, 139, 156, 158, 172, 264
    communications intercept missions: 228
    communications systems and equipment: 55, 81, 106-107, 142-144, 146, 159-160, 172, 175, 177-178, 221, 247
    composite strike force in: 46, 247
    convoy support missions: 174, 178
    coordination and control: 42-44, 55-56, 74-75, 82-83, 95-96, 105-106, 124, 136, 159, 175, 211, 214-215, 217, 225, 227, 260-261
    crop-destruction missions: 219, 247-250
    damage assessments: 174, 199, 212
    defoliation missions: 73, 112-113, 117, 247-250, 264
    effect on pacification: 236-238
    effectiveness, studies on: 25, 134, 157, 213
    electronic intelligence missions: 235
    escort missions: 25, 133, 145
    forward air controllers in: 106-107, 121, 128, 136, 138-140, 142-144, 151, 168, 172-176, *180*, 181-182, 184, 197, 199, 214-215, 221, 224, 236, 267
    hamlet defense, support of: 174
    helicopter missions, escort of: 144, 146, 157-158, 174, 176, 197, 267
    identification, friend or foe: 131
    infrared reconnaissance missions: 138, 148, 168-169, 243-245, 266
    intelligence collection and transmission in: 138
    joint operation, first: 128
    joint operations center in: 83, 106, 128, 142, 211
    language barrier in: 221
    logistics centralization: 42
    mixed crews in combat: 220, 267
    mobile combat reporting post: 74, 82
    napalm strikes: 10, 19, 121, 128, 141, 146, 156, 158, 179, 238, 260
    night missions: 96, 127-127, 132, 168, 174-175, 182-173, 214, 224, 244, 247, 259-260
    operations center in: 142
    photographic reconnaissance missions: 74-75, 127, 135, 138, 147-148, 168, 241-243
    psychological warfare missions: 122, 219, 251-252
    reconnaissance missions: 25, 37, 82, 128-129, 139, 143, 147-148, 169, 171, 174, 182, 196, 227, 239-241, 243-244, 256-259, 268
    restrictions on: 133, 141, 159, 172, 224
    results, assessment of: 134
    rocket assault missions: 158, *130*, 158, *237*
    roles and missions in: 49
    search-and-rescue missions: 50, 170, 183
    tactical air support missions. *See* Tactical air support missions
    target acquisition and designation: 55, 136, 138-139, 140, 143, 146, 156, 196, 245
    traffic control in: 131
    warning system: 129

Air refueling Squadron, 421st: 229
Air Rescue missions. *See* Search-and-rescue missions
Air Rescue Service (Pacific): 45
Air Rescue Squadron, 31st: 45
Air Training Command: 154
Air warning system: 129
Airborne operations
    American: 120, 167
    French: 16-18, *20*, 26
    Republic of Vietnam: 112, 156-159, *164*, *180*, 196, 228, 246
Aircraft
    armament loads: 128, 132, 240, 256-257
    casualties evacuation by: 31, 122, 219, 260, 267
    combat readiness and faults: 181, 212-214, 218, 20, 238, 243, 246
    corps, assignment to: 211
    jet-assisted takeoff: 79
    losses: 116, 146, 158, 178, 181, 183-184, 213, 220, 229-230, 238, 246-247, 250, 253, 257, 260, 265-266. *See also* Helicopter losses
    maintenance and repair: 50-52, 55, 125, 181
    modifications in: 79-80
    obsolete models: 54-55
    spare-parts stocks: 50
    types. *See* Aircraft types
Aircraft types
    A-1: *77*, 153, 174-176, 179, 181-184, 196-197, 199, 212-214, *222*, 224-225, 238-240, 243, 253-254, 257, 259-261, 263-264, 266-268
    AC-47: 241, *242*, 260-261, 266
    AD-4: 55
    AD-5: 131, 169
    AD-6: 55, 67, 75, 82, 84, 121, 127-129, 132, 137, 139, 142-143, 145-146, 156-158, 178
    B-26: 7, *9*, 10, 17-18, 24, 31, *77*, 79-80, 121, 127-129, *130*, 131, 133-134, 136-137, 139, 145-146, 151, 154, 156-158, 171, 174-176, 178, 181, 183-184, 196-197, 199, 212-214, 217, *242*
    B-29: 22-23, 25-26, 29
    B-52: 263
    B-57: 69, 212-213, 217, 229, *237*, 238, 245, 253, *262*, 263, 267
    Bristol Type 170: 246
    C-45: 50, 147
    C-47: 6n, *8*, 10-11, 16-17, 19, 24, 26, 31, 49-50, 55, 67, 73 *77*, 79, 82, 96, 108, 112, 123, 128, 131-135, 147, 153, 156, 167, 171-172, 174-175, 181-183, 196, 214, 220, 224, 240-241, 244, 246-247, *249*, 251, 260-261, 267
    C-54: 138
    C-119: *8*, 15-17, 19, 22, 25-26, 31
    C-123: 93, 108, *109*, 110-113, *114-115*, 116, 119-120, 141, 146, 152, 154-156, 167, 180, 182-183, 196, 224, 236, 245, 247-250, 257, 261, 264, 268
    C-124: *20*, 22, 31
    C-130: 58, 81, 228, 230
    CH-34: *222*
    CV-2: 107, 110-112, 146, 154-155, 167, 215, 236, *238*, 246-247, 265
    Dassault M.D.-315 Flamant: 10, 36
    EA-1: 169-170
    EC-47: 244
    F-4: 257
    F-4U: 24
    F-5: 153

F-6F: 7, 24, 26
F-8F: 7, *8-9*, 10, 19, 24, 49-50, 52, 54
F-63: 6n, 7
F-86: 75
F-100: 229-230, 237, *238*, 256-257, 267-268
F-101: 229
F-102: 69, *130*, 131, 141, 169-170, 229, 268
F-205: 229-230, 256-257, 268
FB-26: 241
H-19: 19, 24, 50, *51*, 55, 67, 154, 168
H-21: 107, 128, 144-145, 158-159, 178, 184, 196
H-34: 55, 107, 116-117, 120, 145, 175, 219, 251
H-43: 253
HU-1: 157
JU-52: 6n
KB-50: 229
KC-135: 230
L-18: 107
L-19: 50, *51*, 55, 67, 75, 107, 112, 121, 127-128, 132, 135, 138, 140, 143-145, 153, 158, 168, 174, 176-177, 181-182, 196-197, 215, 219, 224, 250, 260
L-20: 24, 107, 138, 155, 219
L-26: 50
L-28: 81, 144, 151, 155, 168, 250
MIG-15: 230
MIG-17: 230
MK-IX Spitfire: 6n, 7
Morane-500 Cricket: 9, 10, 18-19, 36
N-156: 153
O-1: 167-168, *180*, 182, 199, 215, 224, 239-240, 259-260, 263, 266, 268
OV-1: 148, 155, 169-170, 174-175, 215, 243-245
PB4Y: 19, 24
PBY-5A: 6n
R-4: 112
RB-26: 7, 17, 129, 148, 154, 168-169, 171, 213, 241, 243
RB-47: 235
RB-57: 168-169, 241, 244-245, 268
RC-47: 147, 212, 243
RF-101: 74-75, *77*, 135, 147-148, 154, 168, 229, 241, 245, 256-257, 268
RT-28: 147, 153, 212, 243
RT-33: 54, 74-75, 147, 153, 168
SC-47: 79, 96, 121-122, 127, 129, 136, 250
Supermarine-1: 6n
T-6: 58
T-28: 50, 75, *77*, 79, 82, 84, 93, 96, 120-121, 127-129, *130*, 131-134, 136, 139, 142, 144, 146-147, 153-154, 156-158, *164*, 171-172, 174, 176-179, 181, 183-184, 196-197, 199, 212-215, 217, 219-221, 256, 268
T-33: 54
T-37: 58
TF-102: 131
U-1: 110, 154, 167, 215
U-2: 195, 227, 243
U-3: 169
U-6: 251
U-10: 144, 146, 171, 250-251
U-17: 239-240, 251

UH-1: 107, 144, 147, 155, 157-158, *164*, 167, 175, 178, 183, 196-197, 214-215, 236, 260, 265, 267
UH-34: 144
Airfields
    air strikes against: 173
    conditions at: 55, 123-124, 132, 177, 183, 215, 263
    construction and repair: 39, 52, 81, 151, 177, 184, 217, 238, 263
    defense of: 82, 264
    security measures at: 170, 253, 264
    suitability survey: 110
    tenant status of USAF: 123
    Viet Cong attacks on: 253
Airlifts of troops and supplies: 8, 16, 19, *20-21*, 24-27, *33*, 50, 55, 58, 73-74, 106, 108, 110-112, 121-122, 128, *130*, 144-146, 154-156, 171, 178, 182-184, 196, 204-205, 214, 219, 245-247, 254-255, 260-261, 266
Airmen, personal hardships of: 124
Ambush operations by Viet Cong: 53, 112-113, 145, 174, 179, 196-197, 224, 259-260
An Khe: 176, 267
An Lao: 259
An Xuyen Province: 178, 196, 214
Andersen Air Force Base: 230
Anderson, Winston P.: 250
Annam: 4-5
Anthis, Rollen H.: 99
    and air operations coordination and control: 106, 136, 142-144, 147-149, 153, 155, 159-161, 171
    and airborne operations: 112
    and aircraft overuse: 181, 212
    and aircraft strength expansion: 133-134, 154
    and airlift operations: 111-112
    appointed special assistant for counterinsurgency: 227
    on Army concept of aircraft use: 160
    on combat role for Air Force: 123
    commands ADVON: 95-96
    commands MACV air components: 97-98
    commands 2d Air Division: 101
    and communications systems: 160, 178
    on defensive measures: 178
    Diem and Nhu, assessment of: 187
    and escort missions: 145
    Harkins, relations with: 101-102
    and helicopter missions escorts: 159
    on intensifying operations: 192
    on interdiction missions: 135
    and MACV command authority: 98
    and mixed crews in combat: 131
    and pilots training: 132, 152
    and radio homing: 168
    and reconnaissance operations: 171
    on roles and missions: 148
    and self-sustaining RVN Air Force: 134
    sonic boom, use of: 141
    and sorties by RVN Air Force: 132
    and tactical air strikes: 120, 136-139, 171-172
    and tactical target designations: 140-141
    and training programs: 127

Antiaircraft operations and systems
  Viet Cong: 283-285
  Viet Minh: 17-19, 25-26, 212
Ap Bac: 157-160, 163, 177, 264
Armed Forces Council, RVN: 267
Armor operations: 261
Armorers. *See* Technicians
Arromanches (French carrier): 18, 24
Artillery fire support, Viet Minh: 18
Assissinations by Viet Cong: 52, 67, 72
Atomic weapons. *See* Nuclear weapons
Atrocities by Viet Cong: 52, 67, 72
Australia: 35

Ba Thu: 136
Ba Xuyen Province: 103
Bac Lieu: 183, 202
Ball, George W.: 100, 187-188
Ban Boung Bau road bridge: 257
Ban Ken bridge: 257
Ban Me Thuot: 53, 122, 148, 151, 169, 177, 179, 182
Ban Tang Vai: 259
Bao Dai: 3, 5, 7, 10-11, 34
BARREL ROLL Operation: 256
Bartley, John P.: 170
Bay of Pigs incident: 63, 68
Ben Cat: 145, 197, 224, 254
Ben Cau: 199
Ben Suc: 255
Ben Tuong: 182
Berlin blockade: 5
Bethea, William E.: 221, *222*
Bidault, Georges: 26
Bien Hoa Airfield: 50, 52, 55, 81, 83, 96, 104, 113, 116, 124, 127, 129, *130*, 136, 145, 148, 151, 157, 168, 171, 175, 181-182, 184, 195, 197, 211-220, 229, 233, 235, 238-239, 243, 250, 253-254, 260-261, *262*, 267-268, 271-272
Bien Hoa Province: 75, 200
Binh Dinh Province: 37, 255
Binh Duong Province: 104, 200, 224
Binh Gia: 260, 263
Binh Hung: *109*
Binh Long Province: 156, 197
Binh Thuy (formerly Can Tho): 238-239
Binh Xuyen (religious group): 37
Black Watch: 171
Blanchard, William H.: 217-218
Boat bases, air strikes against: 230
Boi Loi woods: 264
Bomb loads and types: 128, 181, 197, 212, 230, 240, 257
Bombardment Squadrons, 8th and 13th: 229
Bombardment Wing, 3d: 212
Bombing missions. *See* Air operations
Bonin Islands: 44
Bowers, Charles J.: 142

Bridges, air strikes against: 173
Brink, Francis G.: 7
Brink Hotel incident: 261, *262*
Brohon, Raymond: 22
Brooks, Allison, C.: 225
Buddhists, demonstrations by: 185-186, 190, 233, 265
Buen Enao: 66
Bundy, McGeorge: 192, 265-266
Bundy, William P.: 205, 232, 254-255, 265
Bunker systems, Viet Cong: 173

C. Turner Joy, USS: 229
Ca Mau Peninsula: 116, 182-183, 196, 204, 248
Cai Nuoc: 183
Cai Nuoc River: 196
Caldara, Joseph D. C.: 25
Cambodia
    American recognition of: 5
    bombing operations in and near: 120-121, 156-157
    border violations charged by: 136, 141, 199
    breaks relations with RVN: 188, 197
    breaks relations with United States: 198
    French patrol of: 3
    Japanese occupation of: 3
    military assistance to: 16
    neutral status sought by: 140
    as sanctuary: 163, 197, 202
    relations with RVN: 140
    supply organization for: 42
Cameron, William W.: *164*
Camouflage, use of
    by Viet Cong: 127-128
    by Viet Minh: 19
Camp Courtney: 64
Camp Holloway: 265
Can Tho (later Binh Thuy) Airfield: 153, 167, 171, 177, 179, 182, 184, 202, 211, 215, 217-218, 220, 238, 272
Cao Dai (religious group): 37
Cap Saint Jacques Airfield. *See* Vung Tau Airfield
Cap Varella: 266
Capital Military District, RVN: 153
Card, USS: 168, 204
Carpenter, John W., III: 168
Carrier aircraft, strikes by: 22, 173
Castro, Fidel: 58
Casualties
    from air power, estimates of: 134, 157, 213
    American: 116, 122, 145, 158, 178-179, 184, 199, 204, 213, 218, 224, 250, 253, 261, 265-266
    attitude toward figures: 34
    Australian: 224
    civilians: 120, 139, 158, 183, 204
    evacuation by airlift: 31, 122, 219, 260, 267
    first in USAF: 116
    French: 30-31

Navy, evacuation by: 31
Republic of Vietnam: 145, 156-158, 177, 179, 184, 191, 196-197, 199, 213-214, 224, 250, 253, 259, 261, 266
Viet Cong: 121-122, 128, 137, 139, 145, 156-158, 172-174, 177-178, 183-184, 191-192, 196, 199, 204, 213-214, 254, 259-260, 264, 266-267
Viet Minh: 22
Cat Bi Airfield: 15-16, 18-19, 26, 31
Central Highlands: 30, 53, 103, 267
Central Intelligence Agency: 47, 63, 69, 155, 190-191, 198, 250
Central Office for South Vietnam (VC): 157
Central Target Analysis and Research Center: 245
Ceylon: 20
Cha La: 196
Chassin, G. J. M.: 34
Chemical agents
　tests of: 73
　use charged: 113-114
Chemical plants, air strikes against: 173
Chiang Kai-shek: 4, 188
China, Nationalist: 5
China, People's Republic of
　on Air Force combat role: 100
　India, incursions into: 53
　intervention, threat of: 23, 55, 65-65, 68-69, 141, 203, 253
　military assistance by: 6, 16, 18, 34, 198-199
　nationals, evacuation of: 31
　Taylor mission, reaction to: 85
China Theater extended: 4
Chou En-lai: 30, 85
Chuong Thien Province: 215, 224
Churchill, Winston: 23, 30
Civil affairs: 54
Civil Air Transport: 15, 26, 31
Civil Guard, RVN: 37, 39, 54, 65-66, 67, 71-73, 184-185, 191
Civilian Irregular Defense Group, RVN: 69, 82, 155, 172, 267
Civilians
　casualties: 120, 139, 158, 183, 204
　evacuation of: 31, 188, 200, 266
Clark Air Base: 11, 16-17, 25, 31, 42, 45, 58, 75, 81, 107-108, 111, 113, 124-125, 131, 213, 229-230, 247, 253
Cluster bombs: 230, 240, 257
Cochin China: 5
Collins, J. Lawton: 38
　and air support for RVN: 49
　and armed forces strength estimates: 37, 39
　and army loyalty, investigation by: 37
Combat Application Group, 1st: 240-241
Combat Cargo Group, 6492d: 111
Combat Crew Training Squadron, 4400th: 79-84
Commander in Chief, Pacific. *See* Felt, Harry D.; Sharp, Ulysses S. Grant; Stump, Felix B.; Pacific Command
Commander, United States Forces, Vietnam: 69
Communications intercept missions: 228

Communications systems, equipment and operations: 55, 81, 106-107, 121, 142-144, 146, 159-160, 172, 177-178, 221, 247
Composite Air Strike Force: 46, 247
Composite Reconnaissance Unit, 363d: 230
Congress
    and American commitment: 23
    military assistance, amendment to: 190
    and reserve units call-up: 65
Consolidated Aircraft Maintenance Squadrons (CAMRON)
    23d: 171
    33d: 171, 181
    34th: 171
    41st: 220
Constellation, USS: 230
Convoys. *See* Motor convoys
Core, USNS: *115*
Corps Tactical Zones
    I: 106, 140, 142, 145-146, 159, 161, 174, 190, 200, 211-214, 267
    II: 106, 121, 129, 137, 140, 142, 173, 175, 177, 190, 200, 211, 219, 240, 253, 265-266
    III: 106, 129, 142, 145, 156-157, 175, 177, 179, 182, 190, 197, 199-200, 213-217, 243, 245, 248, 253, 263
    IV: 153, 157-159, 172, 175, 177, 179, 182-183, 191, 200, 215, 235, 243, 253, 263
Counterinsurgency
    policy of differentiating: 224
    RVN concept of: 39, 54, 103
Crew chiefs. *See* Technicians
Crop-destruction missions: 219, 247-250
Cua Ron: 229
Cubi Point, Philippines: 131
Curtis, Victor N.: 247
Czechoslovakia: 5

Da Lat: 96, 122, 248, 250
Da Nang Air Base: 4, 7, 17, 22, 24, 31, 49, 52, 68, 74, 83, 101, 106-108, *109*, 110-111, 127, 129, 132, 136, 142, 145-147, 159, 167, 169, 171, 174-176, 179, 198, 211, 219-220, 228-230, 233, 235, *237*, 238, 246, 248, 254, 256-257, 259, 266, 268, 272-274
Dak Ket: 139
Dam Doi: 183
Dau Tieng: 197
Decker, George H.: 64, 133
Defense, Department of (see also McNamara, Robert S.; Wilson, Charles E.)
    cold-war defense, responsibility for: 63
    in command structure: 65
    military assistance programs, role in: 7, 47
    Reorganization Act (1958): 46
Defense Intelligence Agency: 186
Defoliation project: 73, 112-113, 117, 247-250, 265
De Gaulle, Charles: 58, 188-189
Delmore, Fred J.: 116
Demilitarized zone established: 30
Democratic Republic of Vietnam. *See* North Vietnam
Demolitions operations by Viet Cong: 181, 204, 261, 265
DePuy, William E.: 208, 263
Deserters from Viet Cong: 173

Diem, Ngo Dinh: *38*
    advisors criticized by: 165
    and air operations and units, control of: 94, 106-107, 129
    and air units commitment: 73
    and American troops commitment: 70, 80, 85
    and armed forces expansion: 49, 54, 71-72, 75
    and armed forces reorganization: 153
    assassinated: 191
    and bombing operations: 104, 120, 140
    on Cambodia as sanctuary: 140, 156
    Central Intelligence Organization formed by: 67-68, 75
    charges invasion by North: 56, 103
    and Civil Guard improvement: 75
    and clear-and-hold operations: 104, 119
    command structure fixed by: 68
    conspiracies against: 36, 75, 186, 190-191
    and counterinsurgency operations: 54, 68, 71, 103-104
    defense treaty with U.S. sought by: 73
    and defoliation project: 112-113, 116-117
    on economic assistance: 165
    elected President: 34, 67
    fiscal reforms, promised by: 67
    and government reforms: 36, 67, 103
    infiltration, alarm over: 72-73
    intelligence activities control by: 53, 71
    jets requested by: 54, 129
    Kennedy program, reaction to: 93-94
    and MAAG expansion: 71, 73
    and MACV activation: 97
    martial law declared by: 187
    and military command formation: 67-68, 70, 103-104
    military operations, control by: 50, 53-56, 71, 105, 152
    and national campaign plan: 152
    and National Internal Security Council: 68, 75
    and navy, formation of: 67
    optimism of: 149
    plebiscite protested by: 39-40
    and political disturbances: 185-189
    popular support lacking: 71
    ranger units activated by: 75
    relations with United States: 58, 165, 185-187
    religious affiliation: 185
    resettlement project: 53, 103
    residence attacked: 129, 163, *164*, 191, *192*
    security agency formed by: 68
    strategic hamlets plan: 104, 153, 173, 183, *223*
    and supply routes, interdiction of: 104
    on tactical air support: 120, 145
    and tactical zones organization: 68
    Taylor evaluation of: 86
    threats to government, complaints about: 85
    and training programs: 40, 49-50, 65
    unification, opposition to: 52
    Viet Cong elimination, estimates for: 153

Dien Bien Phu: 8, 9, 16-19, 22, 25-26, 29, 205
Dillon, C. Douglas: 22
Direction finders: 138, 168
Do Son Airfield: 17, 31
Do Xa War Zone: 139, 173, 176
Dohs, use by patrols: 73
Don, Tran Van: 186-187, 190-191
Don Muang Airport: 75, 81, 135, 228, 268, 279-280
Dong Hoi: 173, 266
Dong Nai River: 196
Dougherty, William E.: 128
Doyle, Miles M.: 146
Dulles, John Foster: *33*
    and American commitment: 23, 25-26
    on Communist threat: 52
    and Geneva Accords: 18
    and military assistance program: 15, 19
    and military forces of RVN, concern for: 35-36
    plebiscite protested by: 39
Dunning, John A.: 97
Durbrow, Elbridge
    on armed forces strength: 49, 54
    and government reforms: 67
    and intelligence organizations: 54
    relations with Diem:

Eden, Anthony: 22, 26
Edmunds, Alan C.: 263
Edwards, USS: 235
Eglin Air Force Base: 79, 212, 240
Eighth Army: 44
Eisenhower, Dwight D.: 11, *22*
    and air uits commitment: 17
    ambassadors role strengthened by: 65
    and American commitment: 17, 19, 23-24
    and armed forces strength: 49
    armistice proposals by: 30
    and Chinese intervention: 29
    and defense of RVN: 43
    and Dien Bien Phu defense: 18
    government stability, concern for: 36
    and independence movement, policy on: 15, 23
    and Laos, intervention in: 58-59
    and military assistance programs: 15, 17-22, 34
    and requisites for French success: 15
    support of RVN: 35
    and training programs: 36
Electricians. *See* Technicians
Electronic intelligence missions: 235
Ely, Paul H. R.: 18-19, *21*, 22, 29, 36
England. *See* United Kingdom
Equipment losses. *See* Materiel losses
Escort missions: 25, 133, 145

Far East Air Logistics Force: 16-17, 41
Far East command: 41, 43
Farm Gate: 78-84, 95-96, 100-101, 107, 113, 120-124, 127-134, 136-140, 144-146, 148, 151, 155, 157-159, 168, 170-172, 174, 181, 183, 200, 212, 214, 219, 248, 250
Felt, Harry D.: 87
    and advisors in combat role: 219
    and advisors force reduction: 165
    and ADVON operations: 95-96, 100
    and air commando units: 81-82, 86, 95
    and air-ground liaison: 136-137, 170
    and air operations coordination and control: 83, 95, 155-156, 160-161
    and air operations, restrictions on: 172
    and air strikes against North: 201, 206
    and air units commitment: 69
    and aircraft armament: 162
    and aircraft for Army: 110-111
    and aircraft for RVN: 54, 75, 86, 131, 213
    and aircraft strength expansion: 134, 138
    and airfields construction: 86, 184
    and airlift operations: 108, 111
    and Ap Bac disaster: 159
    and armed forces expansion: 54
    and Cambodia, incursions into: 204
    and Chinese pilots for RVN Air Force: 133-134
    and clear-and-hold operations: 104
    and combat role for U.S. Air Force: 123
    in command structure: 46
    and commander for U.S. forces: 94
    and commanders' lack of initiative: 86
    and counterinsurgency operations: 54, 170
    and covert actions against North: 195
    and defoliation project: 116
    Diem reassured on U.S. support: 149
    on firepower of airplane vs. helicopter: 197
    on forward air controllers: 170
    Harkins, evaluation of: 102
    and Harkins' command authority: 98
    and Harkins' relations with Anthis: 101-102
    heads Pacific Command:
    and helicopter missions, escort for: 143-144, 159
    and initiative against Viet Cong: 139-140
    and intelligence collection and transmission: 138
    on intensifying operations against North: 192, 204
    and interdiction missions: 135
    and jets for RVN Air Force: 147-148, 168
    joint task force concept: 46-47
    and Kennedy program: 71
    and Laos, incursions into: 58, 204
    on MAAG reorganization and expansion: 69, 73
    on MACV organization and staff: 97-98, 207-208
    and Marine Corps commitment: 188
    and military assistance programs: 47
    and military operations, control of: 56
    and mixed crews and air combat: 83, 123

  and mobile combat reporting post: 74
  and napalm strikes: 141
  and national campaign plan: 152, 170
  and pilots training program: 82, 220
  on political disturbances: 186
  on province chiefs' meddling: 86
  and reconnaissance missions: 83, 86
  retires: 210
  on supplies pre-positioned: 86
  and supply routes, air interdiction of: 83
  and tactical air strikes: 120, 139, 173
  and target acquisitions: 140-141
  and targets in North: 173
  training programs: 82
  and troop units commitment: 69, 71, 86, 89
  and U-2 flights: 195
  and unified command for Vietnam: 94
  Weede, evaluation of: 102
Field Hospital, 8th: 125
Fighter Commando Squadron, 602d: 238, 267
Fighter Interceptor Squadron, 509th: 131, 229
Fighter Squadron, 16th: 229
Finned ammunition: 24-25, 240, 261, 266
FLAMING DART I and II Operations: 266
Flares, use of: 182-183
Fleming, David T.: 246
Fleury, R.L.: *130*
Flight Service Center and Network: 160, 170
Floods, effect on operations: 74, 255
Food service, deficiencies in: 124-125
Foreign Legion: *20*
Forrestal, Michael V.: 134, 161, 187
Fortified hamlets plan. *See* Strategic hamlets plan
Forward air controllers: 106-107, 121, 128, 136, 138-140, 142-144, 151, 168, 172-176, *180*, 181-182,
     184, 197, 199, 214-215, 221, 224, 236, 267
France
  advisors with MAAG: 39
  air operations by: 23-25, 34
  aircraft deliveries to: 6-7, *8-9*, 10-11, 15-17, 22-24
  aircraft losses: 18-19, 26-27
  aircraft recovered from: 31, 50
  aircraft strength: 5-6, 25
  airfield construction and repair: 52
  ammunition deliveries to: 24-25
  casualties: 30-31
  finned missiles, use by: 24-25
  flight crews, lack of: 23
  Foreign Legion: *20*
  government, aid in stabilizing: 35
  independence, agreement on: 16
  manpower strength: 10, 15, 17, 34
  materiel losses: 19
  military assistance to: 5-7, 16
  Mobile Group 100: 30

sorties, number of: 7, 19
and Southeast Asia Defense Treaty: 35
supply requirements: 19
supply system and operations: 10
support of war declines: 11
training programs: 36, 49-50
and Vietnam partitioning: 30
Vietnamese, alienation of: 17, 23-24, 34
Vietnamese, desertions from: 29
withdrawal to south: 29-30
withdrawal from Vietnam: 39-40, 50
Freeman, Edmund F.: 7
Fuel supplies: 124
Fulbright, J. William: 68

Galbraith, John K.: 94
Gatling gun (minigun): 240-241, *242*
Gavin, James M.: 19, 24
Geneva Accords: 18, 23, 26-27, 30-31, 35, 52, 54, 64-65, 74-75, 123, 147, 172, 206, 257
Gia Dinh Province: 200
Gia Lam Airfield: 15, 18
Gilpatric, Roswell L.: 68, 70-71
Gleason, Robert L.: 128, 136
Gouré, Leon: 236
Graham, William B.: 239
Great Britain. *See* United Kingdom
Greece, civil war in: 5
Greene, Wallace M., Jr.: 204, 234, 254
Ground crews. *See* Technicians
Groups support. *See* Tactical air support
Guam, supply organization for: 42
Guerrilla operations
    by Viet Cong: 53, 56, 103, 116, 120, 145, 181, 191, 196-197, 199, 259
    by Viet Minh: 3-5, 10, 18
Gulf of Tonkin crisis: 229, 234-235, 239, 243, 247

Hail (Lazy Dog) missiles: 24, 26
Hainan Island: 24, 230
Haiphong: 4, 8
    air strikes against: 173, 254
    operations at: 5, 16-18, 29
Halberstam, David: 163
Hamlet defense, support of: 174
Hanoi
    air strikes against: 254, 256
    aircraft strength in: 25
    operations at: 5, 16, 18, 29
    Viet Minh control of: 3-4
Hanoi Delta: 24
Hao Cain: 66
Harkins, Paul D.: *87, 164*
    and ADVON reorganization: 100
    and air operations coordination and control: 131, 144, 155, 160-161, 167, 169
    and air operations, restrictions on: 172, 203

and Air Force representation at MACV: 101-102, 162
and aircraft for Army: 110-111, 148, 181
and aircraft for RVN: 172, 213
and aircraft strength expansion: 131, 133-134, 155
and airlift operations: 110-112, 155-156
and American phase-out: 132, 151
and Ap Bac disaster: 159
and Army control of Marine Corps aviation: 161
and assistance withdrawal threat: 188
and authority as MACV commander: 97-98
and Cambodia border violations: 203
and clear-and-hold operations: 200
and command of RVN forces: 207
commands MAC Thailand: 100
commands MAC Vietnam: 97
and defoliation project: 116-117
and Diem-Nhus crisis: 188, 191
and helicopter missions, escort of: 142-144, 159
and helicopter units, control of: 98
on initiative against Viet Cong: 140, 163, 166
on intensifying operations: 192, 205
and jets for RVN Air Force: 147-148
Khanh, assessment of: 198
and MACV staff structure: 98, 207
military situation, report on: 179
and napalm strikes: 141
and national campaign plan: 152-153
and political disturbances: 185-186
and radar operations: 170
retires: 210
and tactical air strikes: 137, 139
and tactical air support: 145, 160
Viet Cong elimination, estimate for: 151, 153
and Vietnamization of conflict: 151-152
Harriman, W. Averell: 66, 209
on bombing operations: 104, 201
on Diem support: 188
and government reforms: 67
and political disturbances: 187
and troop units commitment: 83
Harris, Hunter, Jr.
and air operations coordination and control: 227
and air strikes against North: 230-232
and Laos, incursions into: 259
and low-altitude reconnaissance: 243
Hau Nghia Province: 200
Haven, USS: 31
Heat detecting devices: 243
Heath, Donald R.: 6-7, 10, 24, 36
Helicopters
airplane escort of: 144, 146, 157-158, 174, 176, 197, 267
in airlifts: 144-146, 154-156, 178, 182-184, 196, 214, 254-255, 260-261
armament loads: 146-147
Army concept of use: 146-147

casualties evacuation by: 267
   control by Army: 144
   in gunship role: 157-168, 177, 197, 199, 215, 225
   losses: 158, 184, 196, 214
   Marine Corps operations: 175
   tactical strikes by: 121, 144
   transfer to RVN Air Force: 133
   types. *See* Aircraft types
Henderson, Harvey E.: 179, 197, 241
Hergert, Thomas M.: 218
Hewitt, Albert G.: 17, 34
Hickam Air Force Base: 41, 44, *114*, 195, 230
Hicks, Robert W.: 17
High National Council, RVN: 235
Highways (numbered). *See* Routes
Hilsman, Roger
   on air power lethality results: 134
   on bombing operations: 104, 201
   on border control operations: 173
   criticizes air and military operations: 161
   and political disturbances: 187
   on tactical air strikes: 138
Ho Chi Minh
   Diem praised by: 149
   and Dien Bien Phu: 18, 27
   and independence movement: 3-5, 30
   intensified operations, reaction to: 204, 230
   plebiscite, demand for: 39
   support by China and Soviet: 5
   Taylor mission, reaction to: 85
   unification, plans for: 35
Ho Chi Minh Trail: 72
Hoa Hao (religious group): 37, 202
Holden, Paul: 26
Hon Me Island: 228
Hon Ngu Island: 228
Honolulu conferences: 119, 123, 138, 147, 151-152, 166, 172, 185, 192, 202, 205-206, 213. *See also* Saigon, conferences at
Hue: 3, 151, 185-187, 202
Hung Nhon: 137
Hurlburt Air Force Base: 79, 81
Hutchinson, Donald R.: 47

Identification, friend or foe: 131
Indochina *(see also each area by later name)*
   allied cooperation in: 4
   American policy toward: 3-5
   Chinese policy in: 4
   French control of: 3-5
   geographical features: 3
   independence movement: 3-4
   Japanese occupation: 3
Infrared devices: 138, 148, 168-169, 243-245, 266
Inman, Harold: *242*

372

Intelligence collection and reports: 18, 54, 85, 135, 137-138, 152, 157, 163, 169, 179, 199, 227-228, 235, 243, 245, 250, 261
Inter-Ministry Committee for Strategic Hamlets, RVN: 104
International Control Commission: 30, 40, 50, 53, 85, 100, 162, 189, 230
International Cooperation Administration: 52
Interzone V: 139, 173

Jablonsky, Harvey Jr.: 137-138
Japan, supply organization in: 42
Johnson, Harold K.: 204
Johnson, Lyndon B.: 209
    and advisors, reduction in force: 195, 204
    and air strikes against North: 229, 253-254, 256, 265-266
    and aircraft for RVN: 213, 229
    becomes President: 192
    and bilaterial consultation agreement: 230
    Congress supports military operations: 232
    and covert actions against North: 195, 227, 234
    Diem, conference with: 70
    and government, stability for: 256
    and Gulf of Tonkin incident: 229
    on intensifying operations: 195, 198-199, 203
    and jets for RVN Air Force: 238
    Khanh, relations with: 198
    and Laos, incursions into: 195, 234
    and MACV, officers assigned to: 195
    and military assistance programs: 70
    and patrols by Navy: 229, 234
    policy of Vietnam: 195
    and provisional government: 195
    and psychological warfare missions: 251
    on support for U.S.-RVN units: 203
    and Taylor authority: 227
    and U-2 flights: 195
    on Viet Cong control by North: 195
    and Vietnamization of conflict: 195
Johnson, U. Alexis: 261
Joint Airlift Allocation Board: 246
Joint Chiefs of Staff
    and advisors in combat role: 105, 219
    and air base defense: 254
    and air commando units: 80, 83
    and Air Force expansion: 41
    and air operations coordination and control: 216
    and air strikes against North: 205-206, 234-235, 253-254
    and aircraft for RVN Air Force: 75, 111, 167-168, 212, 229, 238
    and aircraft strength expansion: 134, 218, 220, 229, 238, 266
    and American aircraft in combat: 267
    and Cambodia border violations: 141, 203
    and China, pre-emptive strikes against: 29
    and clear-and-hold operations: 20
    cold-war defense, responsibility for: 63
    and combat role for U.S. Air Force: 131
    and command structure: 43, 65

and communications systems and equipment: 107
and counterinsurgency operations: 54
and defense of RVN: 43
and defoliation project: 112, 247
on Diem crisis, security during: 191
government, concern for stability: 35-36
and helicopters combat role: 162
on intensifying operations against North: 198-199, 201, 203-205
and jets for RVN Air Force: 200, 238, 264, 266
and Laos, incursions into: 64, 204-205, 254
and Laos as infiltration route: 64
and MACV commander authority: 97
and MACV staff structure: 207, 210
and military assistance programs: 6, 35-36
military situation, report on: 179
and mixed crews in combat: 82-83, 144, 238
and national campaign plan: 152
and psychological warfare missions: 250
and RVN armed forces strength: 36, 39, 71-72
and Special Forces assignment: 228
and supply routes, air interdiction of: 80
on supportr for U.S.-RVN units: 203
and targets in North: 172-173, 233-234
Taylor report, reaction to: 88
and training programs and proposals: 36, 69, 72, 220
and troop units commitment: 69, 71, 88, 198, 254
on unified command for Vietnam: 94
Joint Frequency Coordinating Board: 178
Joint General Staff, RVN
    and air operations coordination and control: 55, 172, 221
    air operations, restrictions on: 141, 159, 172, 221
    and airborne operations: 112, 158
    and aircraft assignments: 107
    and airlift operations: 246
    Army domination of: 50
    bombload restrictions by: 129
    intelligence collection and transmission: 138
    intensifies operations: 166
    and jets in strike role: 265
    and political crises: 56, 187
    recognized by provisional government: 191
    and tactical air strikes: 139
Joint military mission, U.S.: 15
Joint operations center: 83, 106, 128, 142, 211
Joint Operations Evaluation Group, RVN: 159
Joint Strategic Survey Council: 90
Joint Task Force 116: 46-47, 58, 64, 94
Jungle Jim units: 79-84, 100

Kadena Air Base: 229-230, 243, 257
Kalin, Byron R.: 146
Katz, Aaron H.: 239
Kennedy, John F.
    activates MAAG Laos: 64

    aggression blunted, belief in: 163
    and air units commitment: 77, 79, 170
    and aircraft deliveries to RVN: 89
    assassinated: 192
    and assistance withdrawal threat: 189-190
    ambassadors, role strengthened by: 65-66
    civic action program: 68
    and cold-war defense, responsibility for: 63
    on combat developments and test center: 68
    counterinsurgency plans: 63, 65, 73, 105
    and Cuba crisis: 64
    and defoliation project: 112-113, 117, 247
    on Diem-Nhu's replacement: 188-190
    economic development program: 68, 71-72
    and government reforms: 67, 89
    on guerrilla warfare, danger from: 63
    on Harkins as MACV commander: 97
    on intensifying operations: 192
    and Laos, intervention in: 59, 63-65
    MAAG expansion: 68, 94
    and military assistance programs: 70, 89, 105
    nuclear tests resumed by: 65
    policy on Vietnam: 68, 71, 190, 192
    and radar facilities: 68
    reserve units, call-up by: 65
    and RVN armed forces expansion: 65, 69, 72
    RVN government, aid to: 77
    Special Forces commitment: 69, 73, 80
    Special Group (Counterinsurgency) formed by: 105
    Taylor mission to RVN government: 77, 84-91
    training programs expanded by: 65
    troop units commitment by: 68, 89, 91, 100, 119
    and Viet Cong atrocities: 67
    and Vietnamization of conflict: 133-134, 185
Khanh, Nguyen
    and air strikes against North: 204, 230
    and bilaterial consultation agreement: 230
    chief of state, proposal for: 235
    civil government overthrown by: 259
    and clear-and-hold operations: 200
    command structure reorganized by: 201, 235, 239-240
    fall of predicted: 265
    forms government: 198
    government of, instability: 232-233
    on intensifying operations against North: 202, 228
    leads attacks: 254-255, 261
    and National Pacification Plan: 200
    proclaimed acting premier: 234
    proclaimed President: 233
    resignation considered by: 228
    resigns: 233, 267
    and Special Forces expansion: 204
    and standard of living, enhancing: 200
    support by United States: 202

and war declaration against North: 204
Khrushchev, Nikita S.
    and Laos, cease-fire in: 65, 71
    on national liberation wars: 55-56, 63, 71
    and West Berlin, threat to: 58
Kidnappings by Viet Cong: 52
Kien Giang Province: 178
Kien Hoa Province: 178, 214
Kien Long: 204, 215
Kien Phong Province: 53
Kim, Le Van: 190
King, Benjamin H.: 79, 81-82, 96, 127-128
Kontum: 53, 56, 122
Kontum Province: 173, 263
Korat Air Base, Thailand: 229-230, 256, 280
Kosygin, Aleksei N.: 265
Krulak, Victor H.: 189
Kuter, Laurence S.: *45*
    and air units, control of: 43-44
    on command structure: 43-44
    and local air forces, relations with: 42, 45
    and logistics, control of: 42
    and military assistance programs: 47
    mobile strike force concept: 45-46
Ky, Nguyen Cao: *222*
    and air operations coordination and control: 211-212
    commands air force: 211
    and corps, assignment of aircraft to: 211
    and intensification of operations: 228
    leads Zone D assault: 254
    and paradrops into North: 228
    personal anti-coup aircraft: 263, 267
    teamwork, appeal for: 110
Kyes, Roger M.: 23

Lackland Air Force Base: 79
Langley Air Force Base: 112
Language barrier: 221
Laniel, Joseph: 22
Lansdale, Edward G.: 122, 199
Lao Dong Party: 52, 56, 58, 103
Laos
    aircraft deliveries to: 58
    American recognition: 5
    French control of: 3
    incursions into: 58-59, 64
    Japanese occupation: 3
    military assistance to: 16
    operations in: 15, 17, 53, 58, 63, 148
    photographic reconnaissance over: 74-75, 243
    as sanctuary and infiltration route: 56, 58, 67, 72-73, 163, 204, 227
    supply organization for: 42
Larson Air Force Base: 22
Lassman, B. D.: *180*

Lattre de Tassigny, Jean de: 10
Lazy Dog finned ammunition: 24-25, 240, 261, 266
Leaflet drops: 37, 122, 196, *249*, 250
LeMay, Curtis E.: *87*
    and ADVON reorganization: 100
    and air-base defense: 264
    and air commando units: 79-84, 100
    and Air Force representation on MACV: 101
    and air operations policy: 119, 201
    and air strikes against North: 201, 204-205, 254
    and air units commitment: 90
    and aircraft for Army: 110, 244
    and aircraft for RVN Air Force: 168
    and aircraft underuse: 125
    and airlift operations: 245
    and armed C-47 evaluation: 241
    and combat role for U.S. Air Force: 132
    criticizes air and military operations: 161
    on Farm Gate declassification: 170-171
    and helicopters as gunships: 225, 236
    on intensifying operations against North: 203
    and joint operations center: 142
    and Laos, incursions into: 64-65, 227, 257
    and MACV staff structure: 97-98, 210
    and mixed crews in combat: 132
    and options for action against North: 234
    and RVN Air Force combat effectiveness: 131-132
    strategic plans, disagreement with: 152
    and troop units commitment: 90
    on Vietnam policy: 91
Lemnitzer, Lyman L.: *66*
    and air commando missions: 83
    and clear-and-hold operations: 119
    and command structure: 44
    and government reforms: 67
    on mixed crews in combat: 84
    on troop units commitment: 69
Lenin, Nikolai: 55
Lloyd, Robert M.: 17
Lodge, Henry Cabot
    and air power, RVN failure to use: 197
    and air strikes against North: 206
    and assistance withdrawal threat: 188-189
    becomes ambassador: 186
    and conspiracies against Diem: 186
    on Diem-Nhu replacement: 188-190
    on intensifying operations against North: 202-205
    Khanh, assessment of: 198
    on motivating Vietnamese: 192
    and political disturbances: 187-188
    and political reforms: 191
    resigns: 210
Logistical operations and systems. *See* Supply operations and systems
Long An Province: 198, 200

Long My: 260
Loudspeaker, use of: 122, *249*, 250-251

Ma Da River: 173
MacArthur, Douglas: 64
Maddox, USS: 228-229, 232
Maddux, Sam, Jr.: 211, 216-217
Mail service: 125
Maintenance crews. *See* Technicians
Maintenance and repair: 10, 50-52, 55, 125, 181
Makins, Roger M.: 23
Mang Yang Pass: 267
Manila: 35, 203
Mansfield, Mike: 165
Mao Tse-tung: 4
Mariana Islands, in command structure: 44
Marseille, airlift from: 22
Marshall, Carl W.: 112
Mataxis, Theodore C.: 267
Materiel Group, 6410th: 41
Materiel losses
    by France: 19
    by RVN forces: 192
    by Viet Cong: 178, 219
Mathison, Richard A.: *77*
McCarty, Chester E.: 15
McClintock, Robert: 25
McCone, John A.: 192, 203, 265
McConnell, John P.: 241
McDonald, David L.: 204
McElroy, Stephen D.: 149
McGarr, Lionel C.
    and air commando mission: 83
    aircraft assignment by: 107
    and bombing operations: 104
    commands U.S. Forces, Vietnam: 95
    on crisis in Vietnam: 91
    heads MAAG: 54
    and military operations, control of: 56
    and RVN Army expansion: 54
    and tactical air control system: 107
McGovern, James B.: 27
McKee, William F.: 47
McKinney, Claude G., Jr.: 81
McNamara, Robert S.: 66
    and advisors, number of: 93, 166, 190
    and air commando training mission: 83, 219
    and air operations coordination and control: 155-156
    and air strikes against North: 173, 205-206, 234, 253-254
    and aircraft for RVN Air Force: 75, 91, 93, 131, 167, 202, 212-213, 239-240
    and aircraft strength expansion: 134, 218, 236, 240
    and airlift operations: 110, 119
    and American phase-out: 132-133, 151
    on American combat role: 162

    on Army mission in Vietnam: 119
    assistance withdrawal threat: 189-190
    and B-57 for contingency use: 218
    centralizes decision-making: 123
    and China, intervention by: 234
    and Chinese pilots for RVN Air Force: 133
    and clear-and-hold operations: 104, 119
    and Combat Developments and Test Center: 73
    on combat role for U.S. Air Force: 123
    and communications systems and equipment: 107
    comprehensive measures for RVN aid: 93
    conferences with commanders. *See* Honolulu conferences; Saigon, conferences at
    and counterinsurgency forces, expanding: 63, 80
    and counterinsurgency plans: 80, 82
    and defoliation project: 112-113, 116-117
    on Diem-Nhu replacement: 190
    on flares, use in air strikes: 137
    ground war, stress on: 259
    and Gulf of Tonkin incident: 229
    and helicopter deliveries to RVN Air Force: 144
    hostilities end, predictions of: 122, 151, 190
    on intensifying operations: 192, 202
    and jets for RVN Air Force: 147
    and Laos, incursions into: 195, 256
    and Laos, intervention in: 64
    and MACV organization and staff: 97, 171, 207-208, 210
    and materiel transfer to RVN: 166
    and military assistance programs: 105, 151, 192
    and mining operations: 202
    missions to Vietnam: 190, 195, 202
    and mixed crews in combat: 82-83, 131, 218, 238
    monitors aid program: 93
    and negotiations to secure peace: 265
    and nuclear tests, resumption of: 65
    and options on action against North: 203, 234
    and pilots shift to airlifts: 110
    on political conditions in RVN: 179
    and political disorders: 185
    on priorities for RVN: 72
    on provisional government: 192, 195
    and psychological warfare missions: 123, 250
    and radio use in air warnings: 137
    on roles and missions: 102
    and supply routes, air interdiction of: 80
    on tactical air control systems: 93, 106
    and tactical air control: 121, 138, 217
    Taylor report, reaction to: 88
    and training programs: 133, 220, 243
    and troop units commitment: 69, 88-89, 91
    and U-2 flights: 195
    and unified command for Vietnam: 94
    and Viet Cong elimination, estimates for: 151
    and Vietnamization of conflict: 133, 137, 151-152, 166, 218, 220
McNaughton, John T.: 255

Medical Air Evacuation Group, 6481st: 31
Medical services: 31, 122, 125, 219, 260, 267
Meier, Henry C.: 176
Mekong Delta, operations in: 34, 37, 49, 72, 74, 153, 157, 177, 179, 183, 204, 217, 221
Mellish, David S.: 174, 215
Mendenhall, Joseph A.: 189
Mendes-France, Pierre: 30, *33*
Military Air Transport Service: 31, 81
Military assistance advisory groups
    Air Force — Army representation on: 47, 49
    local air forces, developing: 48
    military assistance, role in: 47-48
Military Assistance Program
    annual allotments: 151
    priorities in: 7
Military Revolutionary Council, RVN: 191, 233
Military Sea Transport Service: 31
Milton, Theodore R.: 54, 111
Minh, Duong Van: 186, 190-191, 195, 198, 233-234
Minh, Tran Van: 267
Minh, Tri Pham: 77
Minigun. *See* Gatling gun
Mining operations by Viet Cong: 183
Misawa Air Base: 229
Missile assaults: 230, 257
Mobile combat reporting post: 74, 82
Mobile Communications Group, 1st: 107
Mobile Group 100: 30
Molotov, Vyacheslav M.: 30
Monroe Doctrine: 58
Montagnards: 73, 116-117, 173, 179
Moody Air Force Base: *130*
Moore, Joseph H.: *209*
    and advisors grades: 216
    and air base defense: 253
    and air escort missions: 225
    and air-ground liaison: 216
    and air operations coordination and control: 211, 216, 225
    and aircraft strength expansion: 217, 238
    commands 2d Air Division: 208
    and helicopters as gunships: 236
    and helicopters, removal from air bases: 264
    and infrared reconnaissance: 244
    and jets, use of: 264
    and joint air operations center: 221
    Joint General Staff, liaison with: 217
    and Laos, incursions into: 257
    and liaison and strike aircraft shortage: 238
    and MACV staff structure: 208
    and mixed crews in combat: 218, 264
    and RVN Air Force organization: 211
    and tactical air support controls: 216-217
    and tactical air support missions: 217

Moorman, Thomas S.
    and ADVON reorganization: 98-100
    and airlift operations: 245
    and defoliation project: 116
    heads mobile strike force: 45
    and self-sustaining RVN Air Force: 134
Morale status
    American: 82, 122, 181, 214
    RVN Air Force: 181, 217
    RVN armed forces: 232
    Viet Cong: 173
Morse, Wayne L.: 257
Mortar assaults, by Viet Cong: 179, 183, 253, 265
Morton, USS: 235
Motor convoys
    support missions for: 174, 178
    Viet Cong attacks on: 197
Mountbatten, Louis: 4
Mueller, Eugene H., Jr.: 144
Mule Train: 108, *109*, 110-112, 116, 152, 156, 170-171
Mutual Defense Assistance Act (1949): 5-6
Mutual Defense Assistance Agreement (1950): 7, 17, 48-49
My Tho: 157

Naha Air Base: 229
Nam Dong: 224
Napalm strikes: 10, 19, 121, 128, 141, 146, 156, 158, 179, 238, 260
Nape road bridges: 256
Narr, Wilfred G.: *130*
Nash, Frank C.: 17
National Intelligence Agency, RVN: 68, 85
National Liberation Front (Viet Cong): 58, 149, 156, 163, 189, 255
National Security Council
    and air strikes against North: 233, 254-255
    and Communist expansion, threat of: 35
    and defense of Vietnam: 43
    and Diem support: 188
    on intensifying operations against North: 203, 205, 233, 255
    and Laos, incursions into: 233, 255-256
    and military assistance program: 6
    military operations, proposals for: 232-233
    and naval patrols resumption: 233, 255
    and RVN armed forces expansion: 69
    and training programs: 36, 233
    on troop units commitment: 83, 89
Navarre, Henri Eugene: 15-18, 22-23, 25-26
Navigation systems: 243
Nehru, Jawaharlal: 22
New York Times: 100, 163
New Zealand: 35. *See also* Royal New Zealand Air Force
Newman, Ralph A.: 140
Ngai Giao: 260
Ngo Dinh Diem. *See* Diem, Ngo Dinh
Ngo Dinh Nhu. *See* Nhu, Ngo Dinh

Nha Trang Airfield: 10-11, 15, 36, 50, 96, 101, 107, 125, 127, 132, 142, 148, 151, 154-155, 168, 171, 176-177, 181, 185, 211, 239, 246-247, 263, 274-275
Nhu, Madame Ngo Dinh: 163-186
Nhu, Ngo Dinh: 34, 56, 58, 104, 129, 139, 165, 185-191. *See also* Diem, Ngo Dinh
Night operations
    by RVN forces: 96, 127-128, 132, 168, 174-175, 182-183, 214, 224, 244, 247, 259-260
    by Viet Cong: 253, 260
    by Viet Minh: 22
Night-vision devices: 148
Nixon, Richard M.: *33*
Nolting, Frederick E.: *87*
    and ADVON operations: 95-96, 101
    and air commando units: 81-82
    and air operations, restrictions on: 172
    and aircraft deliveries to RVN air force: 75, 131
    and American combat role: 170
    and Cambodia border violations: 141
    and defense treaty with United States: 73
    and defoliation project: 113, 116-117
    Diem reassured on U.S. support: 149
    on Diem reply to Kennedy program: 94
    on Diem support: 188
    and jets for RVN Air Force: 129
    and Kennedy comprehensive plan: 71
    and napalm strikes: 141
    on relations with RVN: 166, 185
    and tactical air control: 83
    and tactical air strikes: 129, 137-139
North American Aviation, Inc.: 214
North Atlantic Treaty Organization: 5
North Vietnam (*see also* Ho Chi Minh)
    aggression by affirmed: 100
    air strikes against: 230
    aircraft strength: 230
    airlifts of troops and supplies: 128-129
    Communist control of: 34
    Diem overthrow exploited by: 191
    independence proclaimed: 4
    invades South: 53
    migration to South: 31, 34
    navy, assaults by: 229, 232
    Nhu contact with: 189
    number in South: 198
    peace negotiations rejected by: 206
    population: 34
    recognition by China and Soviet: 5
    regular forces move to South: 204, 227
    supply system and operations: 195, 198
    Taylor mission, reaction to: 85
    on USAF combat role: 100, 162
    and Viet Cong expansion: 163
Northern Air Materiel Area Pacific: 42
Nuclear weapons
    considerations on use: 29, 64-65

    in test exercise: 46

Observers training programs: 10
O'Daniel, John W.
    and French advisors: 39
    and French plans: 15
    and Dien Bien Phu defense: 18, 25
    heads MAAG: 19
    and training programs: 36
Oden, Delk M.: 225
O'Donnell, Emmett: 87
    and Air Force representation at MACV: 101
    and air commando units: 82-83
    and air operations coordination and control: 129, 160
    and air operations, restrictions on: 172
    on air operations policy: 119
    and aircraft strength expansion: 133
    airlifts, control of: 108
    and bombing strikes: 104
    commands Pacific Air Forces: 47
    and defoliation project: 113, 116
    and Laos, intervention in: 65
    and military assistance programs: 48
    on RVN Air Force deficiencies: 69
    strategic plans, disagreement with: 152
    and tactical air control: 106, 160
    and tactical air strikes: 135, 137
Office of the Special Assistant for Counterinsurgency and Special Activities: 227
Office of Strategic Services: 3
Oil-spot concept. *See* Clear-and-hold operations
Oil storage plans, strike against: 173, 229, 230, 254, 256
Okinawa, supply organization in: 42
Olson, Arvid E.: 10
On Mark Engineering Company: 181, 212
O'Neill, James E.: 170
Osborne, Clarence R., Jr.: 215
Overseas Press Club: 22

Pacific Command (*see also* Felt, Harry D.; Sharp, Ulysses S. Grant; Stump, Felix B.)
    in command structure: 41, 43-44, 46, 65
        territorial area: 46
Pacific Fleet: 44, 219, 229, 232
Pacification, effect of air operations on: 236-238
Page Communications Engineers, Inc.: 107
Pakistan: 35
Paramilitary units: 67-68, 152, 157, 225. *See also* Civil Guard; Civilian Irregular Defense Groups;
            Montagnards; Popular Forces; Regional Forces; Self-Defense Corps
Paratroopers. *See* Airborne operations
Paris, airlift from: 22
Parrot's Beak: 136
Partridge, Earle E.
    and air operations conduct: 29
    and American commitment: 29
    begins USAF withdrawal: 31

in command structure: 41
　　　logistics, control by: 42
　　　and military assistance program: 24-25, 31
Passman, Otto E.: 185
Pathet Lao: 63, 204, 268
Patricia Lynn: 171
Patrols
　　　ground: 179
　　　naval: 227-229, 234-235, 266
Pay service: 125
People's Revolutionary Party (North Vietnam): 103
Personnel carriers: 157-158, 260
Petroleum, oil, lubricants (POL). *See* Fuel supplies
Phan Thiet: 215
Philippine Air Lines: 31
Philippines
　　　in command structure: 44
　　　nationals, evacuation of: 31
　　　and Southeast Asia Defense Treaty: 35
　　　supply organization in: 42
Phnom Penh: 129, 163
Pho Sinh: 182
Photographic reconniassance missions: 74-75, 127, 135, 138, 147-148, 168, 241-243
Phu Quoc Island: 141
Phu Yen Province: 116-117, 236
Phuc Yen: 230, 235, 254
Phuoc Long Province: 117, 145, 156
Phuoc Thanh Province: 75, 156, 174, 250
Phuoc Tuy Province: 200, 215, 245, 261, 266-267
Phuoc Vinh: 72
Pilots
　　　civilian. *See* Civil Air Transport
　　　friction with Vietnamese: 110
　　　training programs. *See* Training programs
Plain of Jars: 204-205, 233
Plain of Reeds: 53, 157
Pleiku: 30, 53, 56, 83, 106-107, 122, 127, 129, 132-133, 136, 142, 147, 151, 169, 171, 174-176,
　　　211, 263, 265-266, 275
Pleiku Province: 263
Pleven, René: 18
Poland: 25
Polei Kleng: 122
Polei Krong: 122
Pope Air Force Base: 108, 111-112
Popular Forces, RVN: 177, 215, 225
Porter, Daniel B., Jr.: 158
Porter, John M.: 220
Potsdam Conference (1945): 4
Power plants, strikes against: 173
Press reports, effect of: 163, 170, 185-186, 257
Preston, Benjamin S., Jr.: 213-214, 220
Prevost, Herbert L.: 157-158
Prisoners of war
　　　interrogating and processing: 135

384

Viet Cong: *109*, 121, 128, 156, 158, 178
Pritchard, Gilbert L.: 133
Propaganda compaigns by Viet Cong: 113-114, 117, 137-138
Prouty, Robert V.: 24
Psychological warfare missions: 37, 54, 122, 219, 251-252

Quang Duc Province: 247
Quang Ngai: *109*, 145-146, 175-176, 219
Quang Ngai Province: 37, 173, 177, 179, 255
Quang Tin Province: 173
Quang Tri: 185
Quartermaster Airborne Supply and Packaging Company, 8081st: 26
Quarters, conditions in: 124-125
Qui Nhon: 151, 167, 170, 175-176, 266

Rach Gia: 178
Radar systems and operations: 25, 68, 74, 121, 129, 131, 136, 148, 169-170, 244
Radford, Arthur W.: 19-20, *21*, 22-23, 26
Radio communications. *See* Communications systems and equipment
Radio direction finding: 138, 157, 168, 243
Radio Research Unit, 3d: 244
Ranch Hand: 112-117, 247-250, 264
RAND Corporation, studies by: 236, 239
Ranger Units, RVN: 53, 55, 73, 145-146, 156-158, 173, 177, 197, 221, 260
Reconnaissance missions: 25, 37, 82, 128-129, 139, 143, 147-148, 169, 171, 174, 182, 196, 227, 239-241, 243-244, 256-259, 268
Reconnaissance Squadron, 6091st: 168, 228
Reconnaissance Technical Squadron, 13th: 147, 241, 243-245
Red River and Delta: 19, 29, 31, 34
Refueling operations: 22, 230
Region 5, Viet Cong: 174
Regional Forces, RVN: 67, 228
Religious groups, demonstrations by: 37, 185-186, 190, 233, 265
Republic of Korea
    supply organization in: 42
    war in: 6, 16, 27
Republic of Vietnam (RVN). (*See also* Diem, Ngo Dinh)
    American troop strength in: 151
    border defenses: 172
    Cambodia, relations with: 140
    economy, plans for improving: 54
    elections in: 31, 67
    financial procedures, improving: 54
    government stability, concern over: 35-36
    independence proclaimed: 39
    infiltration by North: 40, 52-54, 56, 58, 72-73, 103
    materiel delivered to, value of: 151
    migration from North: 31, 34
    military staff inaction, effects of: 235
    political disturbances in: 37, 52, 54, 56, 58, 185-191, 233
    population: 34
    provincial organization: 57
    provisional government recognized: 191
    terrain features: 73

warfare begins in: 53
Republic of Vietnam Air Force (RVNAF). *See also* Republic of Vietnam armed forces
    air crews, combat effectiveness: 176-177
    air defense by: 128, 131
    airborne operations. *See* Airborne operations
    and aircraft assignment and control: 107-108, 142
    aircraft deliveries to: 49-50, 52, 54-55, 75, 127, 132-133, 151, 153-154, 179, 238-239, 243, 251, 263, 267-268
    airlifts of troops and supplies. *See* Airlifts of troops and supplies
    combat effectiveness: 67, 75
    command positions, Army officers in: 50
    equipment shortages: 179, 239
    ground crews effectiveness: 132
    morale status: 181, 217
    organization and strength: 37-39, 49, 75, 153, 207
    organizational unity: 133
    pilots, combat effectiveness of: 50, 54, 127, 131-132
    relations with U.S. Air Force: 42
    resources parceling by: 211
    scramble time: 132, 175, 182, 215
    sorties, number flown: 55, 67, 131-133, 149, 174-175, 197, 214-217, 219-221, 238, 243, 264
    squadrons renumbered: 133
    surprise applied by: 219
    Taylor Report on: 86
    training programs: 10, 36, 50, 79-84, 125, 127-128, 131, 134, 147, 151-152, 154, 168, 179, 219, 221, 239, 243, 251
    units activated: 50
        62d Tactical Wing: 263
        1st Air Transport Group: 50, 55, 108, 131
        1st Liaison Group: 10, 36
        43d Transport Group: 243
        1st Air Transport Squadron: 50
        1st Fighter Squadron: 50, 54-55, 127, 129, 132
        1st Helicopter Squadron: 50, 55
        1st Liaison Squadron: 50, 127
        1st Radar Squadron: 74
        2d Air Transport Squadron: 50
        2d Fighter Squadron: 127, 131-132
        2d Liaison Squadron: 50, 127
        3d Liaison Squadron: 127
        110th Liaison Squadron: 176
        112th Liaison Squadron: 177, 215
        116th Liaison Squadron: 239
        122d Liaison Squadron: 177
        312th Special Mission Squadron: 10
        514th Fighter Squadron: 175, 179, 213-215
        516th Fighter Squadron: 179, 219-220, 224, 238, 259, 263
        518th Fighter Squadron: 212-213
        520th Fighter Squadron: 220, 238
        716th Composite Reconnaissance Squadron: 147, 212, 218-219, 241-243
Republic of Vietnam armed forces
    casualties: 145, 156-158, 177, 179, 184, 191, 196-197, 199, 213-214, 224, 250, 253, 259, 261, 266
    civil affairs, neglect of: 54
    Civil Guard: 37, 39, 54, 65-66, 67, 71-73, 184-185, 191

Civilian Irregular Defense Groups: 69, 82, 155, 172, 267
Combat Developments and Test Center: 73
commands, discontent in: 201
counterinsurgency operations: 39, 54, 103
desertions from: 36, 201
discontent over Diem policies: 58
intelligence collection & dissemination: 54
joint operations center: 211
Montagnards: 73, 116-117, 173, 179
materiel losses: 192
morale status: 232
offensive actions, number of: 166
organization and strength: 36, 40, 65, 152-153
paramilitary units: 67-68, 152, 157, 225
Popular Forces: 177, 215, 228
psychological warfare campaigns: 37, 54
Regional Forces: 67, 228
security systems: 56, 124
Self-Defense Corps: 37, 39, 66, 67, 71-72, 191
supply operations and systems: 50, 52, 124
women in: 66
Republic of Vietnam Army (*see also* Republic of Vietnam armed forces)
airborne operations. *See* Airborne operations
airborne units: 261
airfield defense by: 82
armor operations: 261
artillery fire support: 37, 157, 199, 214
combat effectiveness: 67, 163
command structure, defects in: 75
communications systems and equipment: 121
defoliation project: 117
guerrillas, training to fight: 54
operations, number of: 179, 196
organization and strength: 49, 54, 67-68
ranger units: 53, 55, 73, 145-146, 156-158, 173, 177, 197, 221, 260
search-and-clear missions: 214, 219
search-and-destroy missions: 104, 128
security, diversion to: 67
Special Forces units: 145-146, 175, 187, 191, 239
training programs: 36, 39, 53, 67, 73
1st Division: 175
2d Division: 175, 183
5th Division: 140, 156, 177, 197, 214-215
7th Division: 157-158, 177-178, 196, 214-215
9th Division: 176
21st Division: 177-178, 183-184, 196, 214-215
23d Division: 148, 177, 182
25th Division: 176
14th Regiment: 239
40th Regiment: 266
Republic of Vietnam Marine Corps: 173-174, 183, 260-261
Republic of Vietnam Navy
assaults by: 141, 228-229
organization and equipment: 68

patrols by: 228
Richardson, John H.: 165, 189
Ridgway, Matthew B.: 19, 24
Road construction and repair by Viet Cong: 257
Roadblock construction by Viet Cong: 183
Roberts, C. A.: 87
Rocket assault missions: 128, *130*, 158, *237*
Roles and missions defined: 46
ROLLING THUNDER Operation: 266
Roosevelt, Franklin D.: 3
Ross, Donald H.: 174
Rostow, Walt W.: 85-86, 89, 201
Route 7: 257
Route 8: 256-257
Route 12: 257
Route 15: 113
Route 19: 30, 266-267
Route 23: 257, 259
Route 121: 257
Rowan, Carl T.: 251
Rowe, Leonard A.: *242*
Rowland, Robert R.: 98, 153-154
Royal Australian Air Force: 149, 236, *237*, 246
Royal New Zealand Air Force: 246
Ruddell, George I.: 213
Rung Sat: 37
Rusk, Dean: 66
    and air operations, restrictions on: 172
    and air strikes against North: 254
    and aircraft deliveries to RVN Air Force: 75
    and aircraft strength expansion: 134
    on Americans combat role: 162, 170
    and assistance withdrawal threat: 188-190
    and Cambodia border violations: 136, 141, 203
    on commander for U.S. forces: 94
    and defoliation project: 112-113, 116-117
    on information on combat, releasing: 162
    on intensifying operations: 192, 203-204
    and jets for RVN Air Force: 147, 168
    Khanh government supported by: 235
    and Laos, incursions into: 58, 65, 256
    and MACV organization: 97
    on military assistance increase: 192
    and napalm strikes: 141
    and options for action against North: 234
    and political disturbances: 187-188
    on RVN neutralization: 71
    and troop units commitment: 83, 89
Russia. *See* Soviet Union
Ryukyu Islands in command structure: 44

Saigon: 10, 31, *115*, 202
    as Capital Military District: 153
    in communications system: 107

    conference at: 119, 212. *See also* Honolulu conferences
    operations in and around: 49, 56, 103-104, 145, 177, 196, 248, 255, 261, 266
    political disturbances in: 185-187, *192*, 266-267
    as special tactical zone: 68
    troop unit arrivals in: 17
    Viet Minh control of: 3-4
Saigon River: 204
Saipan, USS: 24
Salan, Raoul: 10
Sandborn, Richard T.: 217
Sanders, William B.: 24-25
Schell, D.F.: *180*
Scobel, Uwe-Thorsten: 199
Seaborn, James B.: 206
Sealift of troops: 154
Search-and-clear missions: 214, 219
Search-and-destroy missions: 104, 128
Search-and-rescue missions: 50, 170, 183
Security measures: 17
Self-Defense Corps, RVN: 37, 39, 66, 67, 71-72, 191
Sercel, John: 172
Seven Mountains: 172, 178
Seventh Fleet: 22, 259, 266
Shank, Edwin G., Jr.: 213, 218
Sharp, Ulysses S. Grant: *209*
    and air base defense: 233
    and air operations coordination and control: 232
    and air strikes against North: 229, 232, 235, 253
    and aircraft assignment and replacement: 212
    appointed CINCPAC: 210
    and covert operations against North: 233
    and Laos, incursions into: 233, 256, 259
    and low-altitude reconnaissance: 243
    and MACV staff structure: 210
    and naval patrols: 233
    and troop units commitment: 233
    and troop units strength, expanding: 228
Shaughnessy, John F., Jr.: 170
Shaw Air Force Base: 74
Shofner, Floyd D.: 108
Side-firing system: 240
Sides, J. H.: 87
Sihanouk, Norodom: 140-141, 199
Slavich, Ivan L.: *164*
Smart, Jacob E.: *209*
    and advisors in combat role: 219
    and aircraft assignment and replacement: 213
    and B-57 for contingency use: 218
    Chiang, conference with: 188
    and corps, assignment of aircraft to: 211
    and Diem crisis: 189
    and Hail finned missile: 208
    at Honolulu conference: 192
    and MACV staff structure: 207-208, 210

on tactical air support missions: 213
Smith, Frederic H., Jr.: 46
Smith, Sory: 41-43
Smith, Walter B.: 31
Smoke bombs and markers: 128, 174, 224, 247
Soc Trang Airfield: 133, 171, 177, 183-184, 213, 215, 260
South Korea. *See* Republic of Korea
South Vietnam. *See* Republic of Vietnam
Southeast Asia Airlift System: 111-112, 156, 167, 236, 246
Southeast Asia Command: 4
Southeast Asia Defense Treaty (1954-55): 35
Southeast Asia Treaty Organization: 35, 58, 203
Southern Air Materiel Area Pacific: 42, 50
Soviet Union
　　　armistice proposals: 30
　　　and Geneva Accords: 31, 205
　　　intervention, threat of: 203
　　　and Laos, cease-fire in: 64
　　　military assistance by: 17-18, 103, 128, 199
　　　nuclear explosions by: 65
　　　Taylor mission, reaction to: 85
　　　and Viet Cong expansion: 163
　　　West Berlin, threats to: 65
Spare parts: 50
Spears, Ken C., Jr.: 197
Special Aerial Spray Flight: 112
Special Air Warfare Center: 240
Special Assistant to the Director for Counterinsurgency and Special Activities: 105
Special Forces
　　　American: 53, 73, 82, 155-156, 172-173, 179, 224, 246-247
　　　Republic of Vietnam: 145-146, 175, 187, 191, 239
Staley, Eugene: 71-72
State, Department of. *See* Acheson, Dean; Rusk, Dean
Stead Air Force Base: 79
Steel plants, strikes against: 173
Sternberg, Ben: 207
Stilwell, Richard G.: 208
Strategic Air Command: 195, 227, 230, 264
Strike Command: 160, 229
Students, demonstrations by: 233
Stump, Felix B.
　　　and air units, control of: 44
　　　and American commitment: 29
　　　and command structure: 41-44
　　　and defense of RVN: 43
　　　and military assistance programs: 41-42
　　　and mobile forces, reliance on: 46
Sullivan, William H.: 199, 204
Supply operations and systems
　　　Air Force organization for: 42, 45, 47-48, 108
　　　Air Force withdrawal from: 31
　　　air units, commitment of: 17
　　　aircraft, use in. *See* Airlifts of troops and supplies
　　　American: 15, 24

    centralization of: 42
    French: 10
    in Laos: 195
    losses in. *See* Materiel losses
    North Vietnamese: 195, 198
    reserve stocks, lack of: 124
    Republic of Vietnam: 50, 52, 124
    surface vessels in: 24, 124
    suspension of: 31
    Viet Cong: 72, 117, 227, 266
    Viet Minh: 18
Support Group, 6499th: 138
Sweeney, Walter C., Jr.: 133
Sweet Sue: 171

Tachikawa Air Base: 81, 246
Tactical Air Command: 46, 79, 217, 229, 240-241, 247-248
Tactical Air Reconnaissance Center: 241
Tactical air support: 18-19, 26, 82, 120, 141-142, 145, 146-158, 172, 174-178, 182, 184, 196, 211-212, 214-216, 221, 224-225, 236, 239-240, 261, 264, 267
Tactical Air Support Squadron, 19th: 168, 171, 181-182, 212, 217, 224, 239-240
Tactical Control Groups
    5th: 106
    507th: 74
Tactical Fighter Squadrons
    36th: 229
    44th: 257
    67th: 257
    80th: 256
    428th: 257
    522d: 229
    613th: 267
    614th: 229
    615th: 229
Tactical Fighter Wing, 405th: 129-131, 229, 267
Tactical Groups
    33d: 171, 241
    34th: 171, 212-213, 220-221, 238-239, 241
Tactical Reconnaissance Squadron, 15th: 74
Tactical Support Groups
    6009th: 81
    6010th: 81, 101
Tactical Wing, 41st: 212
Taiwan: 15, 42
Takhli Air Base, Thailand: 229, 253, 268, 280
Tam Ky: 259
Tan Hiep Airfield: 158
Tan Son Nhut Airfield: 10, 50, *51*, 52, 69, 74-75, 81, 83, *87*, 95, 101, 106, 108, 110, 113, 121, 123, 129, *130*, 131, 135-136, 142, 147-148, 151, 154, 158, 160, 167-171, 177, 183, 197, *222*, 229-230, 233, 236, *237*, *242*, 245-246, 251, 254, 261, 263, 267-268, 275-278
Tank losses, RVN Army: 224
Target acquisition and designation: 55, 136, 138-139, 140, 143, 146, 156, 196, 245
Tay Ninh: 156, 197

Tay Ninh Province: 37, 157, 174, 177, 214
Taylor, Maxwell, D: *87*
    and advisors, number of: 190
    and advisors in combat role: 219
    and air strikes against North: 205-206, 233, 253-255, 261, 266
    and aircraft strength expansion: 218, 263
    appointed ambassador: 210, 227
    authority in military affairs: 227
    and covert actions against North: 233, 255
    and crop-destruction project: 248
    and Diem-Nhu replacement: 190
    and government, stability for: 228, 255-256, 259
    and helicopters as gunships: 219
    hostilities end, prediction of: 190
    and infiltration routes interdiction: 255
    on intensifying operations against North: 192, 198, 204, 228
    and jets for RVN Air Force: 264-265
    Khanh government, assessment of: 227, 232
    and Laos, incursions into: 233, 255-256
    and MACV staff structure: 208, 210
    and mixed crews in combat: 238
    and naval patrols resumption: 233
    missions to RVN: 77, 84-89, 190, 202
    and options for action against North: 233
    on political conditions in RVN: 179
    and reconnaissance missions over North: 233
    Special Group (Counterinsurgency) headed by: 105
Tchepone: 74, 205, 257
Technicians
    commitment to Vietnam: 15, 17
    French lack of: 34
    training programs: 10
Temporary Equipment Recovery Mission: 53
Terrain, effect on operations: 26, 157, 169, 177, 221, 261
Terry, Ronald W.: 241
Thailand
    air strikes from: 173
    aircraft strength in: 268
    Diem crisis, reaction to: 188
    mobile strike force test: 46
    and Southeast Asia Defense Treaty: 35
    supply organization for: 42
    threats to: 15
Thanh Phu District: 214
Thant, U: 188-189
Thompson, Robert G. K.: 91, 103-104, 165
Throckmorton, John L.: 210
Thua Thien Province: 117
Ticonderoga, USS: 229-230, *232*
Timmes, Charles J.: 97, 137
Tonkin: 4-6, 11, 15-17
Tourane. *See* Da Nang
Traffic control: 131

Transport Squadrons, Provisional
    1st: 110, 112
    2d: 111
Trapnell, Thomas J. H.: 10, 16
Tribal Area Development Program: 69
Troop Carrier Group: 171, 236, 246, 248
Troop Carrier Squadrons
    309th: 171
    310th: 171, 247
    311th: 171
    346th: 108
    773d: 58
    776th: 108
    777th: 111, 167
Troop Carrier Wings
    62d: 22
    314th: 230
    463d: 230
    464th: 112
    483d: 16
    516th: 230
Truehart, William C.: 186
Truman, Harry S.: 6
Trung Lap: 221
Tuan Giao: 25
Tunis, airlift from: 22
Tuy Hoa: 151
Twining, Nathan F.: 38
    and Air Force expansion: 41
    French air operations, evaluation by: 34
    and military assistance program: 23
    and organizational pattern, RVN Air Force: 37-39
Tyrell, Robert L. F.: 186

Ubon, Thailand: 107, 169
Udorn Air Base, Thailand: 268, 280-281
United Kingdom
    and intervention in Indochina: 23, 26
    and Laos, cease-fire in: 64
    and Southeast Asia Defense Treaty: 35
    and Soviet strength: 3
United Nations
    and Cambodia border violations: 205
    and Diem crisis: 189
United Natios Command, in command structure: 41, 44
United Press International: 123
United States
    and Geneva Accords: 31
    nationals, evacuation of: 31, 188, 200, 266
    and NATO formation: 5
    Pacific command structure: 41
    public dissent against war: 190
    and Southeast Asia Defense Treaty: 35
    Southeast Asia security, policy on: 35

war materiel, embargo on: 5
United States Air Force
    advisors. *See* Advisors
    and air units commitment: 70, 74
    airborne operations. *See* Airborne operations
    aircraft for Army needs: 110
    aircraft deliveries to RVN Air Force: 131, 133, 148, 167-168, 171-172, 208, 212-213, 219, 229-230, 238, 250, 268
    airlifts by. *See* Airlifts of troops and supplies
    Army, rivalry with: 148
    combat role situation: 100-101, 138-139
    counterinsurgency units: 79-84
    first units committed: 11
    expansion program: 42
    MACV staff, representation on: 97, 207-208, 210-211
    morale status: 82, 122, 181, 214
    personnel strength. *See* Advisors
    policy direction, role in: 207
    relations with RVN: 42
    sorties, number flown: 108, 135, 144, 148, 167, 174, 181, 184, 191, 238, 251, 264
    Taylor report, reaction to: 90
    tenant status at airfields: 123
    on troop units commitment: 68
    turnaround time rates: 181
    unit reorganization: 171
    weapons development by: 240-241
    on Wheeler assessment: 162-163
United States Air Force Council: 37-38
United States Air Force Pacific: 43-44
United States Air Force Reserve: 65, 236
United States Army
    and air base defense: 264
    Air Force, rivalry with: 148
    and air operations coordination and control: 143
    aircraft assignments: 215
    aircraft losses: 246, 260, 265-266
    aircraft strength: 148
    communications systems: 221
    defoliation and crop-destruction projects: 248
    helicopters, concept on use: 146-147
    helicopters, control of: 144
    helicopters in gunship role: 157-158, 177, 197, 199, 215, 225
    and loudspeaker missions: 251
    photographic reconnaissance by: 148
    reconnaissance missions: 182
    sorties, number flown: 215
    Special Forces units: 53, 73, 82, 155-156, 172-173, 179, 224, 246-247
    in tactical air strikes: 121
    tactical air support, concept of: 160, 167
    troop strength in Vietnam: 151
    and troop units commitment: 70
    52d Aviation Battalion: 265
    1st Aviation Company: 111, 167
    18th Fixed Wing Aviation Company: 110

    61st Aviation Company: 167
    73d Aviation Company: 181
    93d Helicopter Company: 157
    23d Special Air Warfare Detachment: 148
United States Army, Pacific: 43-44, 95, 98
United States Army Security Agency: 138
United States Army Support Command, Saigon: 251
United States Army Support Command, Vietnam: 225
United States Army Support Group, Vietnam: 98
United States Forces, Japan: 44
United States Forces, Korea: 44
United States Forces, Vietnam: 94
United States Marine Corps
    and air base defense: 264
    and air operations coordination and control: 225
    helicopter deliveries to RVN Air Force: 144
    helicopter operations by: 175
    HMM-162 Helicopter Squadron: 175
    troop strength in Vietnam: 151
    troop units commitment: 266
United States Military Assistance Advisory Group, Indochina (see also Harkins, Paul D.; McGarr, Lionel C.): *38*
    activation and mission: 7
    Air Force representation on: 42, 95, 208
    air patrols proposed by: 73
    and aircraft for RVN Air Force: 55
    and airlifts, control of: 108
    arrivals: 6-7
    in command structure: 41-42
    and counterinsurgency operations: 54
    defoliation project: 112-117
    functions shifted to MACV: 97-98
    inactivated: 208
    MACV, relationship with: 207
    military assistance programs, role in: 47
    organization and strength: 16, 36, 40, 53, 68, 71, 93, 96
    and photographic jets for RVN Air Force: 147
    training programs: 36-37, 39, 54
United States Military Assistance Command, Laos: 64
United States Military Assistance Command, Vietnam (MACV). *See also* Harkins, Paul D.; Westmoreland, William C.
    activated: 98
    Air Force representation: 97, 207-208, 210-211
    deputy commander authorized: 207
    Geneva Accords violation affirmed: 100
    MAAG, relationship with: 207
    organization and staff structure: 97-102, 208, 210
    personnel strength: 97, 167, 171
United States Navy
    and air base defense: 264
    air operations by: 22, 173, 230, 257-259
    aircraft deliveries to RVN Air Force: 75, 131
    aircraft losses: 230
    Amphibious Group One: 31

escort missions: 25
patrol operations: 227-229, 234-235, 266
personnel strength in Vietnam: 151
pilot training program: 219
VA-152 Squadron: 219-220
United States Navy, Pacific: 43, 48
United States Taiwan Defense command: 44, 97

Vann, John P.: 157-158
Vienna Conference (1961): 64, 71
Viet Cong
  air defense operations: 283-285
  airfields, attacks on: 253
  ambush operations: 53, 112-113, 145, 174, 179, 196-197, 224, 259-260
  assassinations by: 52, 67, 72
  bunker systems: 173
  camouflage use: 127-128
  casualties: 121-122, 128, 137, 139, 145, 156-158, 172-174, 177-178, 183-184, 191-192, 196, 199, 204, 213-214, 254, 259-260, 264, 266-267
  cover and concealment, use of: 135, 266
  demolition by: 181, 204, 261, 265
  desertions from: 173
  geurrilla operations: 53, 56, 103, 116, 120, 145, 181, 191, 196-197, 199, 259
  infiltration into South: 35
  influence and control extended: 201-202
  intensification of attacks: 72, 129, 131, 179, 183-184, 191, 224, 253, 259-260
  kidnappings by: 52
  materiel losses: 178, 219
  Nhu contact with: 189
  mining operations: 183
  morale status: 173
  mortar assaults: 179, 183, 253, 265
  motor convoys, attacks on: 197
  night operations: 253, 260
  organization and strength, estimates of: 53, 64, 67, 72, 85, 139, 163
  paramilitary units: 139
  prisoners of war lost: 109, 121, 128, 156, 158, 178
  propaganda campaigns: 113-114, 117, 137-138
  road construction and repair: 257
  roadblocks, use by: 183
  ruses by: 56, 137
  supply operations and systems: 72, 117, 227, 266
  tactics: 163, 184
  war aims, identification of: 85
  9th Division: 266
  48th Regiment: 260
Viet Minh: 3-4
  aggression by, threat of: 35
  air defense operations and systems: 17-19, 25-26, 212
  artillery fire support: 18
  camouflage use: 19
  casualties: 22
  guerrilla operations: 3-5, 10, 18
  night operations: 22

supply operations and systems: 18
withdrawal to North: 30
Vietnam, State of
    air force activation and strength: 10, 36
    aircraft deliveries to: 10, 16
    American recognition of: 5
    armed forces effectiveness: 36
    armed forces expansion: 10
    armistice supervision: 30-31
    demarcation line agreed on: 30
    elections scheduled: 30
    refugees, evacuation by aircraft: 31, *32*
    withdrawals by U.S. Air Force: 31
Vietnam Coordinating Committee: 199, 204
Vinh: 173, 205, 228-230
Vinh Binh: 121
Vinh Binh Province: 239, 266
Vinh, Kuan: *209*
Voice of America: 187
Von Hake, Richard W.: 196
Vung Ro Bay: 266
Vung Tau Airfield: 50, 52, 110, 113, 261

War Zone C: 136, 177, 244
War Zone D: 112-113, 128, 139-141, 145, 156, 173, 177, 197, 244, 248-250, 254-255, 264
War Zone X: 140
Warning systems: 129
Weapons losses. *See* Materiel losses
Weather, effect on operations: 25-26, 139, 144, 146, 156, 169, 175, 229, 266
Weede, Richard G.: 97, 112, 153, 208
Wells, Joseph B.: 7
Westmoreland, William C.: *222*
    on adivors in combat role: 219
    and advisors grades: 216
    and air escort missions: 225
    and air-ground liaison: 216
    and air operations coordination and control: 225
    and air strikes against North: 230, 261, 266
    and aircraft strength expansion: 211-212, 220, 236, 238, 240
    and aircraft strength reduction: 239
    appointed MACV commander: 210
    appointed MACV deputy commander: 207-208
    Army air doctrine, adherence to: 236, 245, 264
    commands Army components: 210
    and helicopters on alert: 225
    and helicopters as gunships: 236, 263
    and infrared reconnaissance: 244
    on intensifying actions against North: 205, 263
    and jets in combat role: 265-267
    and joint air operations center: 221
    Joint General Staff, advisor to: 217
    and markings for U.S. aircraft: 267
    and mixed crews in combat: 220, 267
    and Moore as combined air commander: 232

       and pilot training program: 220
       and Special Forces units: 225
       and supply operations: 236
       and tactical air support: 236, 264
       on target acquisition: 263
       and troop units strength, expanding: 228
       Viet Cong success, concern over: 224
Weyland, Otto.P.: 17, 19
Wheeler, Earle G.: *164*
       and air operations coordination and control: 208
       and aircraft strength expansion: 218
       on intensifying operations against North: 203
       and MACV staff structure: 210
       and options for actions against North: 234
       and tactical air control: 217
       Vietnam situation, assessment of: 161-163
White, Thomas D.: 19, *45*, 47-48
White phosphorus bombs: 212
Wilfong, John J.: 182
Williams, Samuel T.: 39-40, 49
Wilson, Charles E.: 16-17, 31, 41-44
Wilson, H. R.: *130*
Women in RVN forces: *66*

Xang Cut: 224

Yokota Air Base: 213, 229
York, Robert H.: 196

Zuckert, Eugene, M.: 80, *99*

www.ingramcontent.com/pod-product-compliance
Lightning Source LLC
Chambersburg PA
CBHW060229240426

43671CB00016B/2891